# DREAMGIRL

*My Life as a Supreme*

Dedicated
to
my mom, Johnnie Mae Wilson, whose eyes have always shown love,
to
my aunt and uncle, I. V. and John L. Pippin,
and to the memory of
Florence "Blondie" Ballard

*There is one person who must be thanked apart from all the rest, the person who is responsible for pulling this book together and making it happen. Thank you, Patty Romanowski.*

# ACKNOWLEDGMENTS

I am grateful to God for giving me the opportunity to live the life of a Supreme. This story has all the elements of a classic opera, the comedy, the tragedy, and finally the will to survive. And like all good theater the stage must be shared with a multitude of co-stars, supporting cast, and bit players. I must sing their praises.

Once the Primettes came into being, Milton Jenkins did everything in his power to make our dreams come true; I am only sorry he didn't reap the benefits of his initial hard work. Jesse Greer, Richard Morris, and John O'Den are among the many who saw the same bright potential and tried to help us achieve our goals.

Thoughout those early days we had the support of the Primes, including Eddie Kendricks, Kel Osborne, and the late Paul Williams.

Berry Gordy, Jr., orchestrated and directed the whole fairy-tale. I would have no story to tell if it were not for Berry making us his "girls."

My deepest gratitude must go to John L. Pippin, my aunt I.V., my cousin Josephine, and Jackie Burkes for traveling down Memory Lane with me to the days when I was just little Mae-Mae in a starched dress and pigtails.

Florence Ballard's sisters, Barbara, Pat, and Maxine were invaluable in helping me piece together Florence's life after the Supremes.

There are too many members of the Motown family to name in this small space. But I want to especially mention Janie "Money" Bradford, who spent hours laughing and reminding me of the "good old days," and Thomas "Beans" Bowles, Choker Campbell, Joe Hunter, and Teddy Harris, who helped me reminisce about the Motown days. And, of course, we must also remember the likes of James Jamerson, Benny "Papa Zita" Benjamin, and Hank Cosby, just a few of the musicians who provided the sound that inspired so many voices to sing their hearts out.

Brian and Eddie Holland and Lamont Dozier's music gave the

Supremes the perfect vehicles to ride. I thank you, gentlemen. Among our early songwriter/producers were also Freddy Gorman and Smokey Robinson.

The Temptations have always been some of my staunchest allies, especially Melvin Franklin (who always believed in me) and Richard Street. And let's not forget Joe Billingslea of the Contours, Bobby Rogers of the Miracles, Gladys Horton of the Marvelettes, Rosalind Ashford of the Vandellas, Clarence Paul, Joe Shaffner, Kim Weston, who continues to encourage the young voices of Detroit to sing out, Cholly Atkins, who made the moves possible, and his beautiful wife, Maye "Mom" Atkins, Esther Edwards who tried to lead us down the straight and narrow path of life, Maurice King and Gil Askey for their musical support and guidance, Nate McAlpine, Norris Patterson, Eddie Bisco, Winnie Brown, Shelly Berger, Don Foster, Weldon McDougle, and Sylvia Moy, just to name a few of the people who laughed, cried, and relived our past.

Dick Clark helped to launch the Supremes and he continues to be one of Motown's greatest supporters and admirers. I also would like to thank so many of the other artists on the Dick Clark tour who shared their memories of those crazy tours with me, especially singer Mike Clifford.

Mark Bego was the first to help me try to compile my memoirs and I thank him for setting me on the right path. Bart Andrews and Sherry Robb of Andrews and Robb Agency were the first to set the wheel in motion so that this book could become a reality.

Because of the grace of God, the Supremes have touched many lives, so it is with great passion that I thank our many fans, who have shared our dream and made it a reality. Without the help of the fans, this manuscript could never have come into being. The clippings, photos, and stories they provided were an invaluable part of its creation. I must thank Carl Feuerbacher, president of the Supremes fan club, who at his own expense has continued to publish the monthly newsletter and gather materials and information for *Dreamgirl*, and also Tom and Barbara Ingrassia and the many fans who helped. His help and continued support is worth more than words can ever express. Allen Poe, my godson and personal assistant, gave me a supporting hand throughout the writing of this book and I shall not forget it.

I must also thank my New York research team, Jim Lopes, and— again—Mark Bego, John Christe, Edmund Grier, Tony Turner, and

# Acknowledgments

Mark Case, my Los Angeles research team, David Horii and John Wyman, my Detroit research team, Martha Harris and Alice Fletcher, and my European research team.

To my attorney, Robert P. Kragulac, Esq.: Thanks for keeping me afloat and my corporation together.

Esther Gilmore's busy fingers transferred hours of chatter into legible transcripts. Constance Pappas Hillman gave me access to her library and Brother Prince was a patron when I needed him. Each of these people is an integral part of the book.

A thank-you to Ahrgus Juilliard, who sat and worked with me for a year and a half, pulling my diaries, scrapbooks, transcripts, and thoughts together for this book. Thanks, girl.

And a special thank-you to Pedro Ferrer, my ex-hubby, for telling me to get started on writing this book.

None of this could have been possible without my main sister, Hazel Bethke Kragulac, who since 1972 has been much more than my secretary, friend, and Executive Assistant.

But most of all I give my sincerest gratitude to Bob Miller, my editor, who has encouraged and supported me for the past few years as I labored through this manuscript. Bob never lost sight of our ultimate goal and he never lost faith that we'd achieve it.

God bless you all.

Mary Wilson
Los Angeles, California
1986

Since the Supremes' last official farewell concert in 1976 at London's Drury Lane Theater, with Scherrie Payne and Susaye Green, I have pursued a solo career. It was strange at first. I had sung almost all my life, but after Berry Gordy had designated Diane Ross as the sole lead vocalist of the original Supremes, I assumed my position in the background, knowing that my turn would come again.

When it finally did, fourteen years later, I was scared to death but exhilarated. I took my show on the road from 1977 to 1979, touring the world and working only occasionally in the United States. It's amazing how many performers will stay in the States and suffer at the hands of a fickle record industry while all over the world there are hundreds of thousands of fans dying to see them and buy their records. I went to those far-off, exotic places and started over again. I met some wonderful people over there, but each time I'd come home I would inevitably run into someone who would ask, "Are you still singing?" Worse yet, many people assumed I was broke, probably living in some tawdry apartment, wearing a frayed, ancient floor-length sequined gown, looking through old scrapbooks of my Motown days, like some sort of pop-music Miss Havisham with a wedding cake made of gold records.

In fact, throughout the seventies, I not only reestablished my own career but got married, had three children, and continued traveling, working anywhere between nine and eleven months a year. I also began studying acting and singing with several teachers, and have spent twelve years with my voice teacher, Guiseppe Belestrieri.

In 1979 I recorded my first solo album, *Mary Wilson* (Motown), from which was released the single "Red Hot." I felt ready to return to the States and make my American solo debut. I was booked into the New York, New York club in Manhattan, and the audience included friends from the music business as well as fans, the rich and the famous. The critics didn't think I was so hot, but the kindest among them at least gave me credit for having courage. This disappointment sent me back to Europe, where I vowed I'd learn to sing lead again. It had taken ten years of singing "oohs" and "aahs" in the background for me to lose my confidence; it would take me some time to get it back.

That year Motown released me from my contract after I recorded four contemporary pop tunes in London. The release marked the close of a huge chapter in my life. I'd been with Motown for twenty years, and in that time I'd seen almost every dream I could imagine as a young girl come true. But now I was on my own.

I decided to write my memoirs, and had just started contacting all my old friends, relatives, and colleagues when a friend suggested I see a new Broadway musical called *Dreamgirls*. By the second act I was crying because while many of the incidents depicted in the play could have happened to any of a number of female singing groups, I knew in my heart that this story rang far truer than the producers could have imagined. There were bits and pieces of my life—and the lives of my two best friends—up there. I was awed at the powerful influence of the Supremes legacy. And I was more determined than ever that the real story be told.

I have no desire to expose or indict anyone. I want to tell the true story behind the rise and fall of the greatest female pop group of all time—a real-life Cinderella story and a tragedy deeper than anyone ever knew: my life as a Supreme.

# PROLOGUE

It had now been nearly five hours since the taping of Motown's twenty-fifth-anniversary special, "Motown 25," began. At the rate things were going, I could see this was going to last until midnight, but I didn't mind. I was happy to be back among my friends: the Four Tops, the Temptations, Marvin Gaye, Stevie Wonder, Martha Reeves, Smokey Robinson—people I'd worked with for years at Motown. I was also proud, knowing that within just moments, I would be standing onstage with my friends Diane Ross and Cindy Birdsong for our first reunion in over thirteen years. I just tried to relish every second. Next on the show were DeBarge, High Inergy, and a clip of Rick James, followed by Smokey Robinson and Linda Ronstadt's duets on "Ooo Baby Baby" and "The Tracks of My Tears." The segment ended on two lighter notes—a film of Motown staffers, many of whom had been with the company from the start, singing the company song Smokey wrote years ago (with lines like, "We're a swinging company . . .") and Richard Pryor's comic medieval fable about the young warrior Berry's quest for gold records in the kingdom of Hitsville. We were "three fair maidens from the Projects of Brewster." How far from that I was now, but, thinking minutes ahead to the reunion, I knew that I was going home.

Adam Ant started singing his version of the Supremes' first number-one hit, "Where Did Our Love Go." I was as surprised as everyone else backstage to see him doing our song. "Why is *he* doing that?" people asked over and over. Ant was typical of the British New Wave rockers, with his makeup, chains, feathers, and earrings. Our eyes were glued to the monitor when suddenly we heard the audience screaming. Ant grinned until he saw what the commotion was all about. The camera cut to stage right, and we saw Diane in a short black satin skirt and silver-beaded jacket moving toward Ant, doing a bump and grind. For a second, Ant was caught off guard, but he

*1*

moved toward her and danced along with her as much as he could before she disappeared again.

People in the room were mortified.

"I can't believe Diane would do that!"

"The Supremes were always so classy, why would she act like that?"

"How could she just jump up there while someone else was performing?"

The wings were filling with people, all trying to get the best view of the reunion. There were some more clips of us, including our last appearance with Diane on Ed Sullivan's show on December 14, 1969. Diane was walking up the aisle, toward the stage. Once she got onstage, she took the white fox stole she'd flung over her shoulder and tossed it to the floor as the crowd gave her a standing ovation. The applause got louder, and I was surrounded by Nick Ashford, Valerie Simpson, Richard Pryor, Martha Reeves, and some of my friends from the Temptations. Suddenly I heard Diane reciting the first lines to Nick and Valerie's "Ain't No Mountain High Enough":

"If you need me, call me . . ."

Knowing Diane as they did, my friends backstage were encouraging me to do something when I got out there:

"Step on that fur, Mary!" Richard Pryor urged me, half-teasing.

"Kick it!" shouted a female voice.

I knew where they were coming from, and I had a little laugh over it, but I was soon swept up in the moment. Suddenly, everyone got quiet and Diane began speaking. She said she would be there forever if she started to talk about her life with Motown. Then she said a strange thing:

"But Berry had always felt that he's never been appreciated . . ."

When the camera picked out Berry Gordy, Motown's founder and president, it seemed to me, from the look on his face, that he was puzzled by her remarks. Then Diane said, "It's not about the people who leave Motown"—of which Diane was one—"but it's about the people who come back, and tonight everybody came back." At that moment I thought of all the people, like my dear friend Florence Ballard, who couldn't come back. Diane's words prompted a standing ovation, and she gave Berry the high sign. He responded in kind, then turned his palms upward, as if to say, "I let you go."

The applause died down as the opening notes of "Someday We'll Be Together" filled the room. "Mary, Cindy," Diane said as she looked to the wings. Cindy entered from stage right to more applause. After Cindy reached Diane's side, I sauntered out from stage left, doing my slowest Detroit strut, just like we used to do in the Projects. The crowd roared. When Diane looked at me, she stopped singing. She hadn't reached the bridge of the song, so I couldn't understand why she stopped. Thinking that perhaps she'd temporarily forgotten the words, I picked up the lead, certain that Diane would come back in on the next line and everything would be fine. After a few seconds, Diane introduced us again.

"This is Cindy Birdsong," and *"That's* Mary Wilson," she said, pointing at me. There was more applause, and then Diane started moving toward the edge of the stage. Before the show, I'd told Cindy to follow my every move. We'd had no rehearsal and there was no telling what could happen. When Diane took a couple of steps forward, we took a couple of steps forward. Diane moved up again, and we moved up again, all the while singing, "Someday—we'll be together . . ." But on the third surge forward, Diane suddenly turned and pushed me. The audience gasped. In a flash I saw something in her eyes that told me she knew she'd crossed the line. Of course, this was later cut from the tape. When Diane saw that I would ignore her behavior, she hung back, so that on the tape you see me and Cindy standing in front of her. Within seconds Smokey was onstage, and we weren't even halfway through the song. Many observers would correctly guess that he had been sent out on a rescue mission.

Before we knew it, other performers were filling the stage. There was Harvey Fuqua and the Tempts. Melvin Franklin of the Tempts came over to hug me. Then Michael Jackson came on, almost tripping over Miracles guitarist Marvin Tarplin in his rush to get to Diane. Richard Street and Marvin Gaye were onstage hugging me, followed by Dick Clark and the Commodores. I glanced over to see Martha Reeves and Stevie Wonder sharing a microphone, and I thought about how close we all were. Then I realized that Stevie wanted to have the microphone all to himself.

Before the next song, "Reach Out and Touch (Somebody's Hand)," started, Diane tried to take control of the stage, shouting, "Stand back! Everybody stand back!" I could tell she was angry, and she even tried to push people back, but there were too many of us, and we all pretty much ignored her.

The stage was getting crowded, and I was still singing. I stopped and beckoned the audience to stand. Diane made another short speech, a tribute to Berry. When she finished, I called up to Berry, "Berry, come on down!"

The next thing I knew, Diane forced my left hand down, pushing the microphone away from my mouth. Looking me right in the eyes, she said loudly, "It's been taken care of!" On the tape all you see of this episode is Diane turning around and calling out to Berry, "How long will it take you to get down here, Blackie [her nickname for him]? Well, come on."

Once Berry got onstage, Diane stood at the edge hopping up and down like a little girl, waiting for her turn to kiss him. He went to everyone, kissing or hugging each as was appropriate. He thanked Diane after he kissed her, and then he and Michael Jackson embraced. As he stood there with us, Diane was behind him, poking him in the head and pinching his rear end like she would when we were teens.

After Berry and Marvin embraced, Berry came to me. We hugged and kissed, then he whispered in my ear, "You finally learned how to sing, huh?" I held his hand and raised his arm into the air.

The next thing I knew, Diane ran to the back of the stage and climbed the orchestra platform, so that she was standing high above the rest of us. When the song ended, the producers asked us all to stay onstage so that a photographer from *Life* magazine could take our picture. In seconds, Diane had scurried down from her perch and pushed her way to the center of the stage. She grabbed for Stevie Wonder and kissed him. When the photo ran, sure enough, she was smack in the middle.

In the earlier days, Diane would do things like this, but never in public. We were best friends and I would ignore her antics. But tonight of all nights, why did it have to be this way? This was to be a joyous reunion. Even people whose parting with Motown had been less than amicable had returned with nothing in their hearts but love. Part of the Supremes' magic and appeal came from the fact that we were a fantasy, a dream come true. Our personal problems were kept under wraps. Over the years, I'd gotten a pretty good idea of how the public viewed the Supremes, Florence's dismissal, and Diane's leaving the group. And deep in my heart, I knew people were anxious to see a cat fight. That Diane had so foolishly given them that satisfaction hurt me deeply. Her actions seemed to say that the Supremes were unimportant, when in fact we both knew that the Supremes had changed our lives forever.

I returned to my dressing room hurt and angry. What a terrible way to end an evening, a career, a friendship. We had always been there for each other; Diane and I knew each other like books. She has done many things to hurt, humiliate, and upset me, but, strangely enough, I still love her and am proud of her.

Similarly, I will always hold Berry Gordy in the highest esteem, no matter what he does. As young performers, we brought him the raw materials of success, but he saw our potential and made it all work. Berry and I may have our differences, but the bottom line is that he, Diane, and I are inextricable parts of one another's lives.

These thoughts ran through my mind as four security guards escorted me across the street to the Pasadena Plaza Mall. The gala celebration was in full swing, and I was welcomed and comforted by my friends there. I felt the old camaraderie and love that brought me here. I didn't see Diane for the rest of the night.

And the historic Supremes reunion?

"Guests at Motown's twenty-fifth-anniversary bash are still buzzing about the finale. . . ."
*—Los Angeles Herald Examiner*

"Ross [did] some elbowing to get Wilson out of the spotlight."
*—People*

"Not once were they introduced as the Supremes, much to the audience's dismay."
*—US*

As always, the press had the last word, and the public knew everything —or at least they thought they did. But the Supremes' story was never that simple, and the whole truth has never been told.

Until now.

# CHAPTER 1

I was born on March 6, 1944, in Greenville, Mississippi, a small, quiet Southern town near the Mississippi Delta. It was, I've been told, a hot, humid day in March when my mother, Johnnie Mae Wilson, began her labor. Though she was thirty, she'd married only recently. I was her first child. She was so afraid of the pain that she told her mother that she didn't want to have me; it hurt too much. Though Grandmama knew that my mother's labor was unusually hard and going too slowly, she was exasperated. A college-educated woman who'd given birth to all seven of her children at home, my grandmother couldn't understand why Johnnie Mae didn't just get on with it.

My father, Sam Wilson, had left to work on the riverboat, and my grandmother awaited anxiously the midwife's arrival. Home births were common here, yet few women would even think of bearing a child without a midwife present. In rural areas like Greenville, where medical care was far away and too expensive for most people, the midwife's knowledge and experience could be a woman's only comfort. Today no midwife could be found.

When the midwife finally arrived hours later, the house was cleared. She and Grandmama tried everything. Though darkness had fallen and the night air was mercifully cool, both women worked up a sweat.

"This baby should have been here a long time ago," said the midwife. Grandmama could only shake her head when the midwife suggested that my mother be taken to the hospital; my father could not afford it. That settled, she and the midwife returned to coaxing and coercing my mother along. Before it was all over, Grandmama lost her motherly tact: "You fool! You can't let that baby stay inside of you! It's got to come out!"

A little past midnight, I was finally born. I now wonder if my first appearance in life was somehow indicative of the path my life would later take. Even at my birth, I was a fence-sitter.

Grandmama and the midwife cleaned the room and changed the linens. When they heard Daddy's footsteps coming up the stairs, they realized that no one had chosen a name for me. After they'd placed me in his trembling arms, they asked him for his suggestions.

"She's so cute," he said, smiling, "I would like to name her after one of my old girlfriends: Mary."

Few women would have stood for that, but my mother loved the name, so she wasn't worried about its inspiration.

That my life began so unremarkably makes what would happen to me years later all the more amazing. My parents were in many ways typical of their time and place. Greenville was an unusual Southern town where blacks, whites, and Asians lived together peacefully. My father, who was twenty years older than my mother, was a butcher; my mother did not work.

My mother was tall and slender, with skin the color of polished ebony and a deceptively shy manner. Seemingly soft and delicate, she always appeared frail, partly as a result of cultivated feminine charm, and partly due to a minor, chronic childhood illness that had led her mother and her siblings to be overprotective of her. Grandmama hovered over her. While the five younger children—Preston, Rufus, Monever, Margaret, and I.V. (a corruption of the name Ivory)—attended school regularly in Moorehead, Mississippi, Johnnie Mae was kept home. Grandmama surely meant well, but as a result my mother would be nearly illiterate for the rest of her life. Despite this, my mother always had a wisdom about people, and she had a love of life that I have inherited from her. Whenever anyone treated her badly, she would forgive them. She believed that people were basically good, that no matter what happened, anyone would eventually be redeemed.

Grandmama's parents were slaves, but she attended college shortly after the turn of the century and was an intelligent and progressive woman. She married four, maybe five, times; no one is really sure. Grandmama struggled to raise a well-mannered, hardworking, God-fearing family. They adhered to all the traditions of the region and local culture, attending the local Baptist church regularly. Summers would find the children out picking cotton to earn extra money. As the four daughters grew to womanhood, they longed to live in the city, where people said there were better jobs, nicer houses, and more men. My mother may have been the most eager of all to leave, but before she could pull up stakes, Sam Wilson came to town.

He was tall, fair, good-looking, and suave—a real charmer. He didn't talk much, so even though he was a friend of my Aunt Margaret's husband, no one could vouch for his background. Even years later, my mother's family would know very little about my father. He was from Louisiana—probably New Orleans. Most of his family were dead; he'd spent some time in jail—why was never clear.

Mother's family immediately distrusted Sam. It was obvious that he loved the fast life. Although he had a trade, he couldn't hold a job, had long been a drifter, and, worst of all, he was a compulsive gambler. To proud and religious people like my mother's kin, Sam Wilson was just plain weak. My mother was always the quietest and most reserved of her siblings, but when it came to Sam, nothing they said could change her mind. She loved him.

That my mother's family came to accept my father is more a testament to their warmth and generosity than to any drastic change in his attitude. The little bedroom with the four-poster mahogany bed where I was born, was the struggling couple's first home. Grandmama always had a full house and a big heart. She was the center of a loving family that, despite differences, would always unite against hard times and trouble.

After the whole family moved to Greenville, a town about ninety miles from the state capital of Jackson, they came to regard Moorehead as a real hick town. There were so many more opportunities in Greenville. But like all fathers, mine wanted to make a better life for us, so when I was about a year old we moved to Saint Louis, a town known for its loose women, hot music, and a scarcity of legitimate employment. My mother knew the score. She demanded that my father leave Saint Louis, and he did. Next, we moved to Chicago, where, while living on the tough South Side, my father managed to do fairly well. He was working regularly, but even when he was on his best behavior my mother worried. As the old blues song goes, "When the eagle flies on Friday"—in other words, when Daddy got his paycheck—unless my mother "caught it" as soon as he got home, it would surely have flown away, spent on gambling and good times, before Monday morning rolled around.

My father tried everything he could to be a good provider, but soon he was back to his old ways. Holding a steady job, from which he could earn a pittance at best, was just too slow for him. There was fast money—and lots of it, he believed—to be made gambling. He could only be happy living the fast life, and he made no bones about it. My mother worried constantly about me and my baby brother Roosevelt. She hadn't minded being the main breadwinner in the early days of their marriage; she knew her man didn't like to work, and she got by working in Greenville and Moorehead. But living in the big city, far from friends and family, was something else. Despite her misgivings, my mother had followed him to Chicago; now she was stranded. Her youngest sister I.V. and her husband John L. Pippin came to see what they could do to help.

I.V. was ten years younger than my mother. A petite woman, I.V. was fine-featured and beautiful, but had a will of iron. John L., at over six feet, towered above his wife, but there was no mistaking who was the boss, at least most of the time. John L. was a man of integrity and sound judgment. He was reasonable, patient, kind, and generous. Every woman in my mother's family considered him the ideal husband. The Pippins had just purchased a lovely home on the outskirts of Detroit, near Dearborn, for $7,100 on a GI loan. After two years of marriage they were childless. They felt their taking me back to live with them would relieve some of my mother's burden. She was frightened, down to her last few dollars, and still without a job. She promised reluctantly that she would consider it.

No matter how much my mother loved me, her life was beyond her control and periodically complicated by my father's unpredictable appearances and disappearances. Any money that my mother might have squirreled away in his absence, Sam Wilson would surely squander upon his return. She loved him, but she loved us too. I hardly remember my father at all from this period. My only image of him—in a handsome light-colored suit posed in front of a shiny convertible—comes from a treasured photo.

And so in 1948, when I was three years old, Aunt I.V. and Uncle John L. drove me back to the little house at 3800 Bassett Street in Detroit, and my mother returned to Mississippi, where she would live with Grandmama and baby Roosevelt for the next several years.

I was only three then, too young to know what was going on, much less understand it. In fact, within a few years I would forget my real parents altogether, and call I.V. and John L. "Mom" and "Daddy." What I remember now most from my first few weeks in my new home was the house itself. Though it was typical of thousands of development houses built to accommodate young GIs and their families, compared to the dark apartment I grew up in, it seemed like a mansion. The three-bedroom house was filled with heavy, dark furniture, and on each piece were perched several stiffly starched, elaborately crocheted doilies. I had my own bedroom, decorated in blue with frilly ruffled curtains and a satin bedspread. Being in an immaculate new house surrounded by trees and soft green lawns seemed wonderfully alien.

Like many cities then, Dearborn was all white. Blacks could work and shop there, but they couldn't live there. Our neighborhood, just outside Dearborn, was working class and middle class, but all black. Like most people in the area, Daddy worked in the auto industry, at Chrysler; Mom worked for Hudson's Dry Cleaners. They were almost affluent by most standards, and our house was full of wondrous things: a new Eureka vacuum cleaner, freezer chests, a beautiful radio that was as big as a refrigerator. We were the first family on the block to own a television, and every year Daddy bought a shiny new Chrysler for himself and a stylish Chevrolet for Mom.

To ensure that our family wanted for nothing, Daddy always held down two jobs, working at Chrysler and then moonlighting, doing things like running a small gas station, so he had little time for leisure. When he did have time to spare, he liked fixing up things around the house, or sitting in the dark-wood-paneled basement recreation room he'd built and listening to his collection of 78-rpm R&B records by Nat "King" Cole, Sarah Vaughan, Glenn Miller, Duke Ellington, Cab Calloway, LaVern Baker, Brook Benton, and Joe Williams. It was through listening to these wonderful records that I fell in love with music—everything from jazz to Doris Day. John L. also liked to give parties, so the basement had a wet bar and red upholstered barstools. I.V.'s job left her exhausted at the end of the day, too, but both believed that having a nice home and the means to provide for themselves and help others was worth all the effort.

I.V. was a stylish dresser whose expansive collection of different colors of fingernail polish and fashion magazines, such as *Vogue*, kept me occupied for hours. She wanted me to always look my best and spared no expense on my clothing. My dresses were always ruffled or pleated, crisply pressed and starched and always worn over drifts of dainty white petticoats. My favorites were the frilly multicolored nylon "party dresses" for special occasions. I wore little black patent-leather shoes and lace-trimmed anklets, and my long thick hair was neatly braided and adorned with ribbons and bows. As far back as I can remember, I felt like a miniature fashion plate.

Large parts of our neighborhood were still under development, and some areas were almost like the country. Passing fruit orchards on our way to and from school, my little friends and I would pick all the peaches and apples we could carry, along with bunches of wild grapes that seemed to grow everywhere. We could play across the highway at Pepper Creek. Though I was basically a very dainty little girl, I loved to make mud pies and catch snakes and toads—which I would bring home to unappreciative parents.

Any seemingly idyllic existence has its share of drawbacks, and mine was no different. I dreaded having my hair fixed, and the daily ritual of I.V. hurting me as she tried to comb through that wild, tangled mess and me crying my eyes out came to exemplify my relationship with her. Looking back I see in this daily trauma the beginnings of several personality traits, such as a fear of authority and a reluctance to speak out. Though the tiny voice deep inside me told me that I was strong, I also knew that I was powerless to change my situation. Like all children, I viewed my parents—and I thought John L. and I.V. were my parents—as perfect, and I lived for their love. Their approval meant everything to me; their anger could throw me into confusion and self-doubt.

I learned very early on to quietly please and pacify I.V. however I could. This was especially difficult at times because I.V. Pippin had little patience for anyone or anything, and becoming an "instant mother" certainly must have tried what little patience she did have to the limit. I.V. was a no-nonsense woman and an almost fanatical perfectionist. The house had to be immaculate, her clothes had to be the finest, and her family had to reflect the highest qualities at all times. Given all this she—and I—were very lucky that she'd married John L. A more wonderful father simply doesn't exist. When I.V. would lose her temper with me, he would intervene on my behalf. After an incident, he'd take me aside and say, "She doesn't have much patience, you know."

I admit that I often hated her for forcing me to do everything exactly right, or do it over, or finally get a spanking. Now I realize that she meant well but was basically incapable of being flexible. When things were running smoothly, she was warm and loving, though always strict. When she insisted that everything be done her way, it wasn't out of meanness, but because she wanted me to grow up to be the best that I could be. She feared that I may have inherited what she viewed as my mother's "faults," like her lack of desire for education. Though I felt the brunt of her anger many times, I know that the values I.V. taught me have stood by me throughout my life and have given me confidence and poise and the will to survive. I still work hard and strive for perfection, though perhaps not to I.V.'s extreme standards.

I was five years old before I had any extensive contact with whites. In 1949 I started kindergarten at the Boynton School. My school in southwest Detroit was integrated. Most of my teachers were white. My first teacher, Mrs. Shufeldt, encouraged me to join the school glee club. When we participated in a citywide choir competition at the Ford Auditorium, I felt like the luckiest six-year-old in town. I loved to sing, and would take as many singing classes as I could throughout school. Making other school trips showed me that there was a great big world out there beyond Bassett Street.

By the age of eight, and with just a couple years of I.V.'s training, I was mother's little helper. I.V. was trying to instill in me a sense of cleanliness and pride in housekeeping. She couldn't know then that my greatest ambition was to never have to do housework when I grew up. She outlined my responsibilities for me and didn't give an inch. Each and every piece of stylish furniture, every floor and window had to sparkle. If I made even the smallest mistake or failed to polish the tiniest crevice, she'd say, "Go get me the belt," and I tearfully obeyed. After several years I came to fear I.V. Why was she beating me? Once my fear of her looming over me was so strong that I forgot my ABCs.

"Now, I.V., you're being too rough on that girl," John L. would say calmly. "So just calm down and talk to her." I couldn't understand why he didn't just make her stop, but he didn't.

My fear was manifested in a bed-wetting problem that lasted until I was about nine years old. Of course the problem, which was created by the beatings in the first place, was only aggravated by the beatings I received for wetting the bed. Scared to death that I.V. would ever find my bed sheets soiled, I awoke earlier than the rest of the household. If my bed was wet, I would run down into the cold basement and wash the sheets and remake my bed before I.V. woke up.

Finally my parents sought medical advice. Though most parents probably would do this today, in the early fifties bed-wetting was regarded as primarily a discipline problem. The doctor, a kindly pediatrician, assured my parents that my bed-wetting was nothing out the ordinary. After a physical checkup showed nothing wrong, the doctor said, "Mrs. Pippin, most children do this when they are under stress."

"Stress?" sniffed I.V. "She's not under any stress!"

I knew differently, but what could I say? I felt like a common criminal. It was all the more confusing to me because John L. would try to reason with me instead of yelling or hitting. "Mae Mae," he'd say, calling me by my pet name, "why don't you get up at night and go to the bathroom?"

"I will, Daddy," I promised, my head bent in shame.

I.V. wasn't a child beater in the usual sense of the term. She was from the old Baptist school of "Spare the rod, spoil the child." She didn't spank me all that often, but since I was bad so rarely, I thought she could have reprimanded me verbally instead. If only she could see what was happening to me.

Thank God for daydreams. I could always escape by mooning away about my fabulous future as a movie star. I loved any kind of fantasy—fairy-tales, radio shows, and movies. Before we got the television, I would watch the radio while listening to *The Shadow* or *The Lone Ranger*. I loved horror movies, mysteries, adventures, like Erroll Flynn swashbucklers, and, of course, musicals. Even my friends noticed that when I was seeing, listening to, or talking about a show or a story or a dream, I would be transported. For those precious moments, it was all very real to me. I would sit around for hours, waiting at the front picture window for my mother's return, planning and dreaming and visualizing myself in these fantasies. John L. would be home, napping before leaving for his night job, so I was as good as alone.

I loved Christmas. Every year, Hudson's department store would be remade into a winter wonderland, complete with Santa Claus, reindeer, little gingerbread houses peopled with elves, and every Christmas decoration imaginable. Once I stepped into the store, I believed I was at the North Pole. Even when I was old enough to know better, I could still believe in my dream.

Christmas was especially important to our family. Our tree was always one of the prettiest on the block, and I would beg my parents to keep it up for the whole year. Many times John L. Pippin was Santa Claus to every child belonging to kin. If my Aunt Monever didn't have the money, she could always depend on the Pippins' generosity. One of my favorite Christmas gifts was a set of miniature walnut dining-room furniture and a beautiful porcelain tea set. John L. and I.V. didn't buy me the toy versions of these things, but expensive, smaller-scale reproductions of the real things they treasured.

One spring day after school, I came home and assumed my usual position, sitting in front of the large picture window in our dining room. Every day I would patiently wait there until it was time for me to set the table for dinner.

When I spotted a little girl who lived down the street, I suddenly felt lonely, and waved to her to join me in the house. For some reason, John L., who should have been home napping, was out so I had the house to myself.

We were playing house and I suggested we have a real tea party with my tea set. We raided the refrigerator, helping ourselves to a large, juicy slice of watermelon, a bottle of soda pop, and some home-made cookies. Then I got a brilliant idea: Why not make this the most elegant tea party ever? "Girl," I said, "let's dress up in some of my mama's clothes."

My friend looked at me wide-eyed. "Won't your mama be mad at us?"

"She won't even know. We'll just wear them for the tea party and then hang them back up."

It was no problem fitting into I.V.'s petite clothes; on our tiny bodies, the hems just grazed the ground. She was one of the smartest dressers around. Over the past few months she had been accumulating a fabulous new wardrobe of brightly colored dresses especially for the long-overdue second honeymoon she and John L. would be taking in New York City. Naturally, she didn't skimp on quality, and for months her new outfits were the main topic of conversation. *Vogue* was I.V.'s bible, and once she was convinced that New York was a city for hats, she bought a straw hat for each outfit.

In our quest for glamour, we of course put on the prettiest and best outfits first. With our invited guests—two dolls—we sat slurping the watermelon and sipping strawberry pop. Within minutes, our "gowns" were covered with sticky, bright pink stains, prompting the next great solution: change clothes. And so we happily proceeded through the entire closet, making sure to wear the matching gloves, shoes, hats, and bags, and to parade up and down the block so everyone could see.

As if started out of a dream, I realized that I.V. and John L. would be home any minute and the clothes were a disaster. If we just hung the clothes back in the closet as neatly as possible, no one would be the wiser. Or so we hoped. Although I knew that these clothes were filthy and that I would be found out, I went along with it.

As I hid down the street, I worried about what was happening at home. I.V. opened her closet, as she did every night, to admire her new wardrobe. Within seconds John L. was running up the stairs and to find I.V. screaming, "Somebody's robbed us! Somebody has come in and robbed us!" One look at the evidence and he was convinced but puzzled. Everything was filthy, but nothing was missing.

John L. hurried down to the basement, where he kept his expensive phonograph, a couple of freezers, and some other valuables. After checking everything, he was relieved to see that nothing had been taken. Finally they realized what must have happened. And it didn't take them too long to know who did it.

When John L. asked a neighbor if she'd seen me, she said no, but made sure to mention how cute I had looked strutting up and down the sidewalk. Then I heard the call—"Mae-Mae, get your butt in here!"—and I knew it was the voice of doom. I had never heard him sound so angry. He had never spanked me; he always told I.V. that spanking wasn't the way. I hoped he would remember that. But with one look, I could see that they both wanted to kill me. All John L. said was, "Get the belt, Mary."

He almost never called me Mary, which made it all the more frightening. Just the thought of this huge man whipping me made me weak. As I carried the belt to him, it felt like a chain of iron.

"I.V. has been planning this trip for a long time," he said through clenched teeth. "And now we can't go because she doesn't want to go, and I will hear about this trip for another year or maybe two. That's why I whipped your ass." With that, he left the house.

For the next couple of weeks my parents made me feel that I was the only person in the house. John L. was right: I.V. did refuse to go on the trip and carried on about it for the next year. I thought she was just being mean; the clothes could have been cleaned where she worked for little or nothing. But that wouldn't have satisfied her. What I didn't know until years later was that I.V. and John L. were having problems with their marriage. I was too young then to see John L. and I.V. as people. After all, they were very young, newly married instant parents. Then, though, all I could think of was the trouble I had caused. I meant no malice. Like most children—even the best children—I lived in the moment and saw no further than the fun I was having. Based on what I saw as my parent's anger over the incident, I concluded that I must have been terribly bad, and I vowed that I would never cause this kind of trouble again. From this I learned a lesson that stayed with me for the rest of my life: to maintain peace, no matter what the cost.

# CHAPTER 2

The summer of 1950 began like every summer I could remember, with me looking forward to the annual visit from my favorite aunt, Johnnie Mae. She was tall and pretty, and always especially nice, lavishing gifts of clothes and candy upon me, and smothering me with soft kisses and lingering hugs. I was instantly drawn to her. It felt so natural to me, so different from my own mom.

This year's visit was somehow different. Aunt Johnnie Mae stayed longer than usual this time, and there was tension in the house. I remember coming home and seeing them—Mom, Dad, and Johnnie Mae—huddled together around the dining-room table, talking in harsh, abrupt whispers.

One day, while I was outside playing, our neighbor Ruby Mae approached me. "I heard your mother is coming to live with you."

"What do you mean?" I asked, surprised. "I live with my mother already."

"No, child, I.V. ain't your mama. Johnnie Mae is."

"You're wrong," I said, summoning up all the courage a six-year-old could muster. "Johnnie Mae is my aunt, not my mother."

"No, no," Ruby Mae persisted. "Johnnie Mae is your mother."

Her words rang in my ears as I walked home, trying to convince myself that Ruby Mae was wrong. It was impossible. My real mother was I.V., and that was that. But no matter what I told myself, once I got home I began to look at my parents and Aunt Johnnie Mae differently.

A few days later, Johnnie Mae took me aside. She tried to explain to me as gently as she could that she was my real mother. Her voice and manner were so soft that the meaning of her words just didn't seem to penetrate. When I resisted what she had said and refused to believe it—which must have hurt her terribly—she didn't get angry, the way I knew I.V. would have. She tried only to comfort me, but nothing could help. My whole world had been turned upside down. I'd trusted these people, and they had lied to me.

Crying uncontrollably, I ran out of the house. I don't know how many times I walked up and down the block, crying my eyes out, convinced that all grown-ups were crazy.

By this time, Johnnie Mae had officially moved in with us. My younger brother Roosevelt and sister Cathy, or Cat, were still living in Greenville with Grandmama. Though in later years I could recall specific incidents from my childhood with my mother, I had forgotten her, my father, and baby Roosevelt. I still had not completely accepted Johnnie Mae as my mother, but I loved being around her because she made me feel safe.

A couple of months after she moved in, Johnnie Mae suddenly became ill. She was in a great deal of pain, sometimes so severe that she was unable to get around without help. I was too young then to know that she was suffering a miscarriage, but I did feel her great sadness. For a while our roles reversed, with me taking care of and comforting her. We were now closer than ever; she was really my mother.

One day I heard my mother fighting with John L. and I.V.

"I never said you could have Mary. I just said you could keep her until I was on my feet again."

"Johnnie Mae," John L. said, fuming, "you know we had an agreement that Mary was ours. You promised that she was ours."

"No, I didn't!"

"Yes, you did. You said—" John L. stopped when he spotted me on the other side of the room. "Mary," he said firmly, "go outside."

By this time John L. and I.V. had their own daughter, Pat, but that did not diminish their love for me. I know they tried to do what was best for me. Though I.V. was my mother's baby sister, she regarded Johnnie Mae as someone in need of constant protection. They didn't think my mother was in a good position financially; they worried about how she would take care of me. She took work living with an affluent white family and was home with us only on weekends. Up until then, John L. and I.V. were certain that I would be with them forever. To this day, Daddy (as I still call John L.) says that Mom promised them that they could keep me.

Despite all the anger and hurt, our family remained close. Eventually Roosevelt and Cat were brought up from Mississippi to live with my mother and me permanently. With their arrival, the quiet little house on Bassett Street became noisy and overcrowded. I so loved taking care of Pat that I ignored my two blood siblings, at least at the beginning. I turned up my nose at them; they seemed so country, and not as refined as I thought my other little friends were. I also loved Pat, who was like the most perfectly beautiful living doll. But soon enough I grew to love Roosevelt and Cat, too. They were rambunctious and cute, and, like our mother, open and happy.

As much as I loved my mother and the kids, I never wanted to leave the Pippins' home; it was *my* home. But seven people were too many. I knew we had to move. Still, I wondered if I'd done something to make the Pippins not love me anymore. I had always been a good girl; at least I had tried to be. My parents had given me everything I'd ever wanted, so I should have been perfect. But some people thought that was just my problem: maybe they gave me too much.

My mother took the three of us to live with her other sister, my Aunt Monever. We moved into Monever's row house in southwest Detroit. I.V. had helped Monever get a job working at Hudson's Dry Cleaners. Things seemed to be working out for us at last. Now the only children left with Grandmama and Big Daddy—Grandmama's latest husband—were Monever's two daughters, my older cousins Josephine, or Jo, and Christine.

My mother and aunts made plans for us to spend the summer of 1953 in Mississippi with my grandparents. This summer sojourn would become an annual event for the three sisters. Sometimes we'd all travel down by car, sometimes we'd take a train, and once everyone went on a Greyhound bus. There would be bags of food for all of us. John L.'s mother would bake pastries, fry up loads of chicken, and make us her specialty—fried apple pies.

We looked forward to this trip for weeks. I had gone almost every year for a couple of weeks with I.V., but this time would be different —I was going to spend the whole summer there. I would see my grandparents and finally get to know my real father, whom I barely remembered. Though certain kids would probably experience this as a trauma, I saw it as a great adventure.

While my mother struggled to keep us all together in Detroit, my father had returned to Mississippi. At age sixty, after years of roaming, he was trying to change his life. He began working steadily at a factory and was finally settling down when he lost his leg in an accident on the job. He could never work again. He moved in with Grandmama and Big Daddy, and they took care of him until he recovered from his operation. Though Sam Wilson had hardly been an ideal son-in-law, he was still my mother's husband, and her family was the only one he had.

Sam Wilson lived near my grandparents in a tiny house on Wilson Street. People there had named the street after him because his was the only house on it. Although he hadn't spent much time with his children over the years, we felt that he really did love us. He was so proud; he took us around and introduced us to all the shopkeepers in Greenville, treated us to ice cream cones, and gave us spending change.

Moving from the Pippins' house on Bassett Street did not separate me from John and I.V.; I would visit them on weekends and keep in touch with my good friends like Jackie Burkes. Jackie was my very best friend. We spent hours together, daydreaming, talking about boys, or sitting down in John L.'s basement, singing along to records such as LaVern Baker's "Jim Dandy," or Hank Ballard's "Annie Had a Baby." It would be years before I lived in a real house again and could enjoy the lush life of suburbia. We left Aunt Monever's and moved from one small apartment to another. Despite my mother's hard work, one day we found ourselves living on welfare. We had hit bottom.

Moving to the Brewster Projects in 1956 was a turning point in my life. It was a new complex of government-owned apartment buildings and older row houses on the east side of Detroit, within walking distance of downtown. There were about eight fourteen-story buildings grouped all together, each surrounded by patches of grass, and a brightly painted playground.

Many people would have considered a move into the Projects to be a step down. But for me, having already stepped down from a middle-class neighborhood to various apartments in the inner city, this was a step back up. I felt like I'd just moved into a Park Avenue skyscraper. The minute we kids finished helping cart our humble furnishings up to our second-floor apartment, we ran outside to explore the new world that was our home.

Hundreds of kids—from infants to young adults—lived in the Projects. It was quite crowded compared to suburbia, but I loved it; the more the merrier. The Projects were also a great school of life. You had to learn to get along with all kinds of people. I looked forward to every new day. I was not an A student, but I.V. had instilled in me the desire to learn and an equally strong fear of failure, so I did well enough. The social aspects of school were also very important to me. Only we kids could comprehend the significance of knowing and spreading the latest gossip, which our parents considered nonsense.

One negative aspect of living in Detroit then was the street gangs. If you were wise enough not to belong to a gang but unlucky enough to be cornered by one, you were in trouble. The vicious mob psychology sometimes scared otherwise good kids into joining gangs just for the protection. I never joined anything, not even clubs, but managed to ensure my own protection by being a gang leader's girlfriend. I was very young, and thought he was cute. Later I was befriended by a tough and unpopular girl, but only after she had beaten me up. After that, I was accepted by the other kids in the Projects. I didn't have an "attitude"; I was just open and friendly, and probably not very threatening.

I was in the fifth grade when they began busing us from the Projects to Algers Elementary School in 1956 to integrate the public schools. Among my new classmates was Carolyn Franklin, the daughter of the Reverend C. L. Franklin, whose New Bethel Baptist Church my family attended.

The New Bethel Baptist Church was probably the most famous church in Detroit. It was a huge, beautiful church, and the Reverend Franklin was certainly one of the most engaging speakers around. He would deliver his sermons, starting out speaking softly, then shouting dramatically before breaking out in song. Many women became quite excited during these presentations, and they would shout, "Preach, Reverend Franklin, preach!" As the tensions mounted, they'd be rocking back and forth in the pews, saying, "Yes, Jesus. Yes, Lord." There were several women in starched white nurses' uniforms, and they would go over to the most hysterical churchgoers and fan them. Roosevelt and I loved going to church. We would sit back and bet which of these middle-aged women was going to "get happy" first. As we watched the rocking get faster as the Reverend's sermon got more intense, we'd pick who we were betting on.

"Look! It's gonna be the woman in the pink! Look at her," I'd say.

"No," Roosevelt would reply, "the one in the red. See how fast she's going?"

Finally, it would just get to be too much, and several of the female worshipers would jump up, throw off their hats, toss away their purses, and scream. Once they'd calmed down, a nurse would accompany them back to their pews, and then it would start all over again.

Carolyn and her older sisters, Aretha and Erma, sang in the church's choir and often took solos. I remember being impressed by Aretha's piano playing as well. In Detroit, the Franklin girls were local celebrities. Unbeknownst to anyone in her family, Carolyn had formed her own singing group.

It had never occurred to me that I might want to be a singer. All of my fantasies revolved around becoming an actress; then maybe I'd sing too, but for now I sang just for pleasure. That all changed when I discovered the great new rock 'n' roll I heard played on DJ Frantic Ernie Durham's show on station WCHB. When I saw Frankie Lymon and the Teenagers—a very clean-cut young black quintet—singing on Ed Sullivan's television show one Sunday night, the die was cast. I wanted to sing, and I decided that getting into Carolyn's group would be the best way to start.

I made it a point to hang around Carolyn's area of the playground. She was a big wheel in the school, despite her petite size. She was always the center of attention, and her friends towered over her as she held court in the schoolyard. Although her tough attitude intimidated me, I finally got the courage to start a conversation with her. Having steered our chat to the subject of singing, I said nonchalantly, "I hear you guys have a group here. I'd like to maybe practice with you all, or join."

"You sing?" Carolyn asked, surprised.

"Oh yeah," I replied offhandedly. "I've been singing all my life, and I just decided that I want to join a group."

Carolyn just smiled. Hovering nearby was a very fair-skinned redhead named Alice. She was giving me the once-over and I could tell she hated me on sight. I knew Alice would make things difficult for me; still I met up with Carolyn every day, no matter who was around. Finally my audition was set.

When the big day arrived we were all standing on the school auditorium stage. I was thrilled to be there, but my stomach was in knots. If I passed, Carolyn would let me perform with them in the upcoming school talent show. We were going to sing a current hit, which Carolyn had chosen and for which she'd devised separate parts and harmonies. Even at the age of eleven or twelve, Carolyn showed promise as an arranger. Carolyn gave us the downbeat and we began singing a cappella. I had to concentrate so hard just to keep my knees from shaking and stay on my part. I was nervous enough, but then I realized that Alice was deliberately trying to drown me out. Before the song was over, Alice was shouting, "This girl can't sing! She messed up the harmony!"

"I did not! You're just starting trouble!"

"Girl, you can't sing!"

Before I knew it, I had shoved Alice halfway across the stage. She retaliated with even greater force, and the brawl was on. Out of the corner of my eye, I saw Carolyn staring in shocked dismay while the other girls tried to separate Alice and me.

I was not a fighter, but I would fight to be part of a group. I knew I had screwed up, but it was because of stage fright. I was sure that I would have passed my audition if Alice hadn't sabotaged it. In the end I had to admit that I had failed. Before this, I hadn't realized how much difference there was between singing solo or in a choir and singing in a doo-wop-style group.

At this time, these groups were all the rage, and every local street-corner was occupied by trios, quartets, and quintets of kids teaching themselves the intricate harmonies they picked up off current hit records by the Platters, the Drifters, the Coasters, the Cleftones, the Flamingos, Mickey & Sylvia, Elvis Presley, and others. We all loved Little Richard, Chuck Berry, and Sam Cooke, and my personal favorites included the McGuire Sisters, Doris Day, and Patti Page. By 1956 every major city's black ghetto housed hundreds of young singing hopefuls, the vast majority of whom, I thought, were living in the Brewster Projects. Very few of them would ever consider solo careers, and most were parts of vocal groups. Kids who played instruments were rare, and those who did were either playing with a church group or had their sights set on far more respectable occupations than entertaining.

Some groups used the roof for a stage, others used the hallways in the Projects buildings. Because of their smooth hard walls and echo, these spots were prized for their acoustics. The lucky kids had access to parent-free apartments, which served as rehearsal studios between the last school bell and dinner time.

Competition among members of rival groups and their fans could be fierce. They were competing for attention, competing for a choice space to sing in, competing for some kind of recognition in a place that didn't offer too much hope to any of them. You didn't need any formal training; all you needed was heart and the courage to take some chances and do something with whatever God gave you that would make your singing different or better. Friends, neighbors, and passersby made up a critical and vocal audience. If you didn't have a good sound, or if the group wasn't up to par, the audience and your rivals would ask you—in quite unflattering terms—to vacate the spot. The more cherished the spot—say, a building stairwell—the tougher it was to keep it.

Since Elvis Presley and other stars had made R&B and rock 'n' roll big business, more than a few struggling youngsters saw singing as a ticket out. Though the average person might automatically think of anyone living in public housing as being deprived, we barely knew the meaning of the word. Our parents constantly reminded us that we were far better off than they had been at our age, and the camaraderie and freedom we felt as kids contributed to making mine perhaps the first generation of black youths to believe their individual potential was unlimited. Sadly, some would learn differently, but at that moment the sky was the limit. And there were few other legitimate ways of making it as big as you could make it in music, if you were lucky.

The images of our idols inspired our young dreams. The success of outrageous rockers like Little Richard and Chuck Berry, smooth singers like Sam Cooke and Clyde McPhatter or sexy guys like Jackie Wilson gave us something to aspire to. And I loved the Shirelles. We were also relating to the original teen rebel, James Dean, and we wore leather jackets and blue jeans; a red bandana carefully hung from the back pocket completed the picture. For the guys, emulation of white teens required processing their hair, a tedious and unpleasant chore most were glad to give up when it went out of style. But back then the look was everything, especially since few could afford the ultimate accessory—a motorcycle.

Around this time, nightclubs were becoming more popular than ever. Many of our parents frequented these places nightly, and the entertainment and music offered in some of them is legendary. One of Detroit's most popular spots was the Flame Show Bar, which presented most of the current jazz greats and popular singers, such as Dinah Washington, Sam Cooke, Nat "King" Cole, and Sarah Vaughan. No matter where you went or what your age, music seemed to be everywhere in Detroit.

Over the next couple of years, I stayed with the school glee club, but it just wasn't enough. It was 1958, and in the seventh grade, at age fourteen, I felt quite grown-up. With my friends Betty and Olivia, I would go downtown to see the latest Alan Freed rock 'n' roll movie. We would leave our houses looking very innocent, then sneak on nylon stockings and heels. When we weren't at the movies, we were roller-skating or playing the machines in the arcade next to the Arcadia rink. I remember skating, timidly keeping to the rail, and watching Aretha Franklin whiz by. She didn't just skate: she bopped. In the arcade was a place where you could record an acetate of your voice. I made a record of me singing a song called "I'm Sorry."

This year, a new girl moved into our neighborhood. Her name was Diane Ross. Her building was sort of catty-corner from mine, but because she went to the junior high in her old neighborhood, I saw her only after school. She had a crush on one of my friends, Tommy Rogers, so she came into our circle through him. But our cliques included dozens of kids. You could know someone and maybe you went to see a movie with them every so often, but you wouldn't exactly be close friends. That was my relationship with Diane then. But even though I didn't know her well, I admired her enthusiasm about things.

One day in 1958 I impulsively signed up to sing in the talent show as a solo. After I realized what I'd done, I wondered where I'd got the nerve. I had no idea what song I would sing, though I was pretty sure it would be a rock 'n' roll song, or how—or even if—I could sing it a cappella. At the eleventh hour I was struck by inspiration. I would mime, or lip-synch, to the Teenagers' hit "I'm Not a Juvenile Delinquent," which I'd seen them perform in one of my favorite rock 'n' roll movies, Alan Freed's Rock! Rock! Rock!

As the moment of my debut neared, I peered down at the oversized leather jacket hanging from my small shoulders, wiped my sweaty palms on my tight stovepipe pants, and adjusted the red doorag wrapped around my head. In this outfit, which I'd borrowed from Roosevelt at the last minute, I came out of my normally shy self and projected the cocksure attitude of a neighborhood punk, even though the song I'd chosen to perform was about being well-mannered.

I heard my name announced and, as if in a trance, I strutted across the stage in an exaggerated swagger to the beat while I sang "live" to the record. Once I started, there was no stopping. A couple hundred kids were yelling and hooting for me. The spontaneous and enthusiastic applause at the finish made my heart soar.

I stayed and watched the rest of the show from the wings. One of the girls who went on after me was a neighbor, Florence Ballard. I would see her walking around the neighborhood and think that she was such a pretty girl, with her fair skin, auburn hair, long legs, and curvaceous figure. In those days, a large bustline was considered a prerequisite of female beauty, and compared to the rest of us, Flo looked like a movie star. Even without makeup, Flo's face was perfect, her big brown eyes perfectly balanced with her full, sensuous lips and valentine-pointed chin. Because her hair was relatively light, everyone called her "Blondie."

That night, her voice was magnificent as she sang a classical piece. It may have been "Ave Maria," a song I know she sang in school. When she finished, the audience applauded loudly. I felt very happy for her. We traded congratulations and hugged, jumping up and down, like teenage girls do. We started talking about how much we loved singing, and the words just poured out. We didn't even notice that the show had ended and we were the only ones left in the place.

As we walked home, we discussed every possible detail of our performances. We promised each other that if either of us were ever asked to join a singing group, she would call the other. After lingering outside my building for a while, we reluctantly said good-bye. There was a bond between us. We could not have known that it would last a lifetime.

# CHAPTER 3

Soon after our meeting at the talent show, Flo and I became good friends. Once offstage, I was still the same shy little girl, and Flo, as always, seemed streetwise and much older than her years. Flo seemed so sure and so confident, and I really admired her for that. About six months had passed since the talent show. I would see Flo around, and we would talk, but I had forgotten about the promises we had made to bring each other into a group.

The eighth of thirteen children born to Jesse and Lurlee Ballard, Flo was a true product of the Motor City. Her father, like so many blacks from the rural South, took the train north to Detroit in 1929. Her mother was a buxom young woman with fair skin and pretty eyes. She always wore her waist-length hair in a long braid down her back. Soon after she and Jesse got together, their first child was born. As a young man Jesse had dreamed of finding a job up North and leaving the South behind forever. He landed a job with Chevrolet, and Lurlee soon followed her husband to the big city. Being with him was the only way she would ever escape the stifling atmosphere of Rosetta, Mississippi, so she happily left to join her husband.

Most of the Ballard children grew up in what they referred to as the "big house" on MacDougal Street, which their parents had moved into in the early fifties. Though their house was not really far from where I grew up, our paths never crossed, and we did not meet until after the Ballards moved to the Projects following the birth of their last child.

The Brewster Projects were where the family shared some of its fondest memories. Because of their many children, the Ballards were assigned one of the attached row houses, a two-story affair with enough bedrooms so that they were a little crowded but not as cramped as many of the other families. There were few luxuries in the ghetto; even so, this move marked a major advancement over what the Ballard children might have had if their parents had remained down South.

The burden of Mr. Ballard's daily job and the constant worry that he might one day be unable to feed his family never diminished his positive attitude and warm disposition. His children saw that with the move to the Projects, their father seemed to relax. He spent hours on end singing and playing the guitar for his kids, and he taught Flo to sing. Flo would tease him, saying that someday he would be a star. Years later, his daughters would reminisce about their father. "He'd get to playing that old guitar, and he'd just go down to the ground," Flo would say. "Boy, Daddy could play," her sister Barbara would add.

Mrs. Ballard took pains to see that her children were safe and secure. There was real love and caring in that family, and their affection for one another went beyond what most people think of as "close." I envied Flo having so many brothers and sisters, especially the older ones. I longed to have a sibling mentor, someone to show me how to do my nails or to talk with about boys. Coming from a smaller and much quieter family, I was taken aback at first by how loud and boisterous the Ballard kids could be when they were all together. But before long I grew comfortable there, and in time the Ballards' house would seem like my second home.

Though they'd lived in Detroit for many years, the Ballards all retained a "country" attitude and lifestyle. One advantage of this was that no matter what happened, they all stuck together. Problems were not discussed outside the family, and if one of the Ballards was after you for something, you knew they all were. Family always came first. All the kids were close, no matter how many years' difference there was between their ages. Bertie, the eldest daughter, was twenty years older than Flo, and Flo had five younger brothers and sisters. I eventually learned all of their names: Bertie, Cornell, Jesse, Jr., Gilbert, Geraldine, Barbara, Maxine, Flo, Billy, Calvin, Pat, and the baby, Linda. One of Flo's younger brothers, Roy, had been killed at the age of three in a freak accident. That tragedy and Jesse Ballard Sr.'s death from cancer in 1959 reinforced Mrs. Ballard's conviction that her children must be shielded from danger at all costs.

I was in the eighth grade, going through my usual school routine one day in early 1959, when Flo ran up to me in the hallway. Between her gasps for breath, I could see she was grinning from ear to ear. She grabbed my arm and asked excitedly, "Mary, do you want to be in a singing group with me and two other girls—"

"Yes!" I replied before she even finished the question. It didn't occur to me to ask what the group was about, or who was in it, or anything. The only word I heard Flo say was "singing," and that was enough for me.

From what little I knew of Flo then, I could see how excited she was. Generally a low-key type, Flo was now pressing my arm so hard it almost hurt. We agreed to meet after school on the playground.

By the time the last bell sounded, I felt like I had survived the longest school day of my life. Once school ended, I rushed to our meeting place, but Flo wasn't there. Five and then ten minutes passed, and I began to wonder if Flo was going to show at all. Did Flo change her mind about me joining the group? Did something happen on her way over? Or did she just forget about me? I said a silent prayer that nothing had happened to change our plans. And I waited. When I finally realized that I was one of the last kids left in the schoolyard, I slowly headed for home.

I'd gotten only a few yards down the sidewalk when Flo ran up from behind, redfaced. She'd had to finish a few things in school; she apologized. Then the excitement returned to her voice as she filled me in with the details of her original proposition.

She had been approached by a member of a male vocal trio called the Primes and their manager, Milton Jenkins, about forming a "sister" group to perform with his clients. Two other girls had already been recruited. The Primes were a classic vocal group, but their repertoire extended beyond the teenage doo-wop tunes we liked and included sophisticated material such as that of the Mills Brothers. The three young men—Kel Osborn and Paul Williams, and a slender high tenor named Eddie Kendricks—had recently arrived in Detroit from their native Alabama. Though we would have a long and enduring relationship with members of the Primes for the rest of our career, at the time Milton Jenkins was the most important person. He would ultimately be responsible for our early success.

Like his clients, Milton also hailed from Alabama. One of thirteen children—many of whom had died in a tuberculosis epidemic years before—Milton grew up feeling responsible for his family. There was nothing for Milton in Birmingham, Alabama, and after years of streetwise hustling failed to yield satisfactory financial rewards, he decided to try his luck up North.

Upon his arrival in Detroit, Milton became part of the show-business crowd that hung out on Hastings Street, an area which boasted many of the city's hotter nightclubs, hotels, and restaurants. There was something seedy yet glamorous about the area; it was a place where things happened. Here were big spenders and gorgeous women, all living the easy life, or at least a life that seemed a lot easier than working in an auto factory. Milton moved into a residential hotel —actually a four-family house that had been converted into a single-room-occupancy hotel—across from the Flame Show Bar, and was only too happy to meet and rub elbows with the musicians and singers who passed through. Although he lacked artistic talent, he loved show business. As we would later learn, Milton was a man of contrasts.

Much of Milton's early success can be attributed to his enthusiasm and a real drive to make money—big money. When he met the Primes they were just one of many unknown groups around. Once he saw their show, he was convinced they had star potential. They were young, good-looking, and talented, and that, combined with his business savvy, could take them all to the top. He convinced them to let him develop them, and soon he was investing every extra cent he made into the Primes' new suits and stylish processed hairstyles, or processes. The Primes moved into Milton's apartment. Though Milton's formal education was limited, he always impressed people; he seemed worldly and easily commanded attention. He was obsessed with appearances, and insisted that everything about him and his act be first class, from his sharply tailored suits to his red 1957 Cadillac, in which he chauffeured the Primes to every gig they played. Years before it would seem feasible to most people, Milton Jenkins saw the music business as his ticket out of the inner city.

We never knew exactly where Milton's investment capital came from—he never had a nine-to-five job, and he never volunteered any information. Of course, to the streetwise, the answer was probably obvious. Because we were so young—Diane and I were fourteen, Flo was fifteen—we didn't really think too much about it. Milton was one of the most interesting people any of us had ever met.

Paul Williams was dating a girl named Betty McGlown, who he thought might be good in the group, and he also knew two other girls who liked to sing. It didn't take much for Paul to sell Milton on the idea of developing a sister group, a briefly popular gimmick. And Flo sold me. I knew this could be my dream come true, and with typical youthful optimism, I believed this might even be the chance of a lifetime.

I rushed home, bursting with excitement. "Mama! Mama! Can I

join this singing group? It's called the Primettes. Please?" I said it all in one quick breath and then looked at my mother pleadingly.

"The Primates?" she asked distractedly. She was concentrating on dinner and not paying much attention.

"No, Prim*ettes*. My friend Flo says the Primes are looking for a sister group, so she asked if I wanted to be in it with her. Please, Mama, please. And the man who is their manager says he will pay for all our outfits and everything. Flo says that he has a lot of money and he drives a big red Cadillac. And he's real nice. Flo says the Primes can really sing good, too. And—"

"What about your after-school chores?"

"Roosevelt and Cat can help out, can't they? Please, Mama, they're big enough now. Flo says—"

"And just who is Flo?"

Now, I thought, Mama will listen. I took a deep breath and re-peated everything as calmly as I could. After I told her all about Flo and her family I pleaded, "Please, Mama. Flo says the Primes are gonna be stars someday. Maybe we will, too. I know we've got a chance because my music teacher said—"

She didn't say anything else for a while, but I wasn't worried. Like any child, I could read my mother's face. She was thinking hard, but I sensed that she was pleased about the prospect. Rehearsing and performing in shows would keep me out of trouble and off the streets. I had my fingers crossed as I watched her. After what seemed like an eternity, she agreed. I was ecstatic.

The next day I was floating on a cloud. Flo promised that we'd meet the Primes and Milton Jenkins right after school. I don't remem-ber how we got there, but the next thing I knew we were standing in the lobby of his hotel. Though anyone else would have thought it shabby, I remember it as being very fancy. What was left of the plas-terwork inside revealed that at one time the house had been a very nice place; from the outside, it just looked dilapidated. To me, the east side was a place where the people seemed like peacocks, strutting about in flashy clothes, but with cultivated manners that set them apart from everyone else.

Up in Milton's room—a bachelor suite he shared with the Primes —I was one of four nervous young girls. There was me; Flo; Paul Williams' girlfriend, Betty McGlown, a tall, pretty, dark-skinned girl who seemed a little older; and a fourth girl, about my age, with large, luminous brown eyes—my new friend Diane Ross.

The Primes were in the middle of rehearsal. They were a lot more polished than I expected. Their voices harmonized so beautifully, the songs seemed to float through the air on velvet waves. Then I noticed Eddie Kendricks' clear, romantic falsetto, and from that moment on I was madly in love with him. In fact, this attraction was the beginning of a crush that, though unrequited, continues to this day.

When the Primes finished their tune, Milton looked the four of us over with a bemused smile. He seemed to like what he saw. Milton was tall, dark-skinned, and slender. He was always impeccably dressed in sharkskin or mohair suits. Milton's suits were tailor-made, in black or dark colors, and he wore a tie and matching handkerchief. He was always immaculately groomed, soft-spoken, and, from the day we met him, had his arm in a cast and a sling.

We were all pretty quiet; only Betty seemed a bit more relaxed, but that was probably because she was Paul's girlfriend. Flo and Betty looked like real women, while Diane and I, each weighing less than one hundred pounds, were waifs. After Flo replied "yes" for me to all of Milton's questions, I knew I was a Primette.

Then something almost magical happened. Milton asked us if we knew any songs, and Flo jumped right in and started singing "(Night Time Is) The Right Time," a Ray Charles hit. Without having had a minute of rehearsal, without having even discussed what we were going to sing, we all fell into our parts, and we sounded wonderful. It was like a miracle. Milton had the Primes critique our performances. Getting the Primes' nod of approval boosted our confidence. I was impressed and a bit intimidated working with new people who were much older and more experienced, even though at the time Eddie Kendricks wasn't more than eighteen.

Paul, Kel, and Eddie taught us some songs. None of us read music, so we had to learn everything by ear. Paul then decided that we should learn a new song, "The Twist." This also was a natural for Flo. Then Diane took the lead on the Drifters' hit "There Goes My Baby." Each time, we all found our parts and harmonized together beautifully.

Paul was a fabulous dancer, and elements of his style were later evident in all the Temptations' great moves. The steps and hand gestures Paul created were clever, sexy, and unique. Since he had already choreographed the Primes' onstage routines, he started working out similar moves for us. When our fancy new steps were combined with our new vocal arrangement for "Night Time"—Flo singing Charles's "call" parts and Diane providing the Raelettes' "responses," while Betty and I sang "night and day" over and over, we sounded like pros.

Milton was obviously pleased with the results. He had a self-satisfied attitude, as if every time he looked at us he saw a way to make his dreams come true.

Flo, Diane, and I whooped and sang all the way home. We talked about how Milton had promised that he would send us out shopping with one of his lady friends, and about what type of stage outfits we would like to wear. I was so grateful to Flo for keeping her word and getting me in.

As we reached the Projects, we could hear all the different groups singing, but it did not daunt our spirits one bit. We believed the Primettes would make it.

We started our daily rehearsals at Milton's the very next afternoon. Once it was clear that we would all be working together, Milton wanted to meet our parents and reassure them that everything was on the up and up. I waited anxiously in our apartment for Milton to arrive.

Living in the Projects was like living in a small town—everyone knew or wanted to know everyone else's business. When Milton and a couple of the fellows pulled up in that shiny red Cadillac, every window flew open. All the little kids playing in front of my building surrounded them. With their finely tailored suits and beautifully styled hair, Paul and Eddie looked like nobody these kids had ever seen before, at least not in this neighborhood. Some of the braver ones even followed them into the building to see what apartment they were going to visit. They might as well have been royalty.

Milton charmed my mother, and Paul's and Eddie's sincerity was the icing on the cake. The fellows explained their plans to make us a popular, complementary component of the Primes. Their praise of my singing made my mother proud. They agreed we would play only sock hops and local social-club engagements—no nightclubs or bars. Milton stressed that we would have to spend hours rehearsing, and asked my mother for permission for me to come to his hotel with Flo and Diane straight from school. When she agreed, everyone was pleased, but no one more than me.

My mother was relieved that I would have my free time occupied by something constructive. This would keep me off the streets, and she would know where to find me at all times. Before access to birth control or legal abortion, all parents worried that their daughters might end up as unwed teenage mothers. That was probably why all our parents agreed to let us become Primettes. If keeping our minds on singing would keep our eyes off the boys, that was good enough for them. Milton, keeping a promise he made to our parents, put his girlfriend in charge of us, and so we had a chaperone, of sorts. The thought that we might also one day become stars never entered our parents' minds, but it was all we thought about.

Once our daily rehearsals began in earnest, we all got to know each other better. Betty was a no-nonsense girl with a great sense of humor. She was older than we were by just a year or so, and because Flo was about six months older than Diane and me, Betty and Flo paired off. They made it clear to us that they were the bosses. Because Betty lived in a different neighborhood, we didn't see her as often as we saw one another, but we liked her a lot and kept in touch with her over the phone.

Just as there had been a strong, instantaneous affinity between me and Flo, Diane and I got along from the start, too. But somehow our relationship was different. Diane was born in Detroit exactly twenty days after me. Even though there was less than a month's difference in our ages, Diane and I were born under different signs. Diane's birth sign, Aries, is the symbol of the ram, an animal often depicted butting its way to the top of the mountain. Aries people are also considered natural leaders and very independent. She was always very energetic and talkative. I really admired her. In her I found a missing part of myself, a more aggressive side I could never express comfortably. Diane was a wonderful friend. I would be sitting around, doing nothing in particular, and Diane would come over to my house, grab my arm, and say, "Let's go!"

Diane was Fred and Ernestine Ross' second of six children and second daughter. The Rosses had moved to Detroit from Alabama, seeking a better life. Fred Ross worked at the American Brass Company. After he was secure in his job, he and Ernestine started their family. Proudly old-fashioned, he refused to let his wife work outside the home, so to make ends meet he always had a second job, working nights as a mechanic.

When I first visited Diane's house I noticed a major distinction between her family and most of those in our neighborhood: There was a father at home. I had been exposed to many more "traditional" families while I lived with John L. and I.V., but here in the Projects most families were headed by a single—divorced, widowed, or abandoned—mother, and things were never easy.

Diane's family was very close, but in a different way than Flo's.

Unlike many other families then, the Rosses didn't cling to the old idea that the family always came before the individual. Instead, they emphasized the importance of each child's personal achievements, and, education was considered crucial. Diane always had a streak of daring and independence. Though Fred Ross was strict, he encouraged his children to be self-determined and to work toward their goals.

Before long, Diane, Flo, and I were best of friends. Almost every day, I'd look out my window and see Diane, then I'd run outside and we'd do something. We were no longer just passing acquaintances. Later, she'd come running over to my house. As time passed, even Roosevelt and Cat would have best friends in both the Ross and Ballard families. Of course, we were obsessed by music, but we also talked about boys, and school, and all of our dreams.

We never could have guessed just how many of them would come true.

# CHAPTER 4

Even though we had been coming to Milton's for a few months, the area never ceased to fascinate us; we could watch the passersby for hours, hoping to catch a glimpse of a famous star going into the Flame. Once we saw Sam Cooke. It was on one such afternoon in late 1959 that we spotted Marvin Tarplin and his guitar.

"Can you play that guitar," I yelled down at him from the window, "or are you just carrying it?"

"I can play it," he said, looking up at us and smiling shyly.

"Well, come on up here, and let us hear you play," one of us replied flippantly. We all knew this kind of behavior—calling down to and inviting up a strange young man—would never be accepted at home. But we weren't at home.

Once we realized what we'd done and Marvin was on his way up, we began to giggle nervously, not certain this was the right thing. He seemed genuinely sweet; he was a tall, lanky, somewhat funny-looking kid. Marvin was always soft-spoken and just too nice. I recognized him from school.

Once Marvin was inside the suite we prevailed upon him to play every single song we requested. By this time we knew a lot of songs, and Marvin seemed familiar with all the latest hits. As he played, we sang along: twelve-bar blues, Hank Ballard tunes, "There Goes My Baby," and "(Night Time Is) The Right Time." The combination of our voices and his acoustic guitar added a whole new dimension to our sound, and without too much discussion. Marvin became the fifth Primette on the spot. He was thrilled.

Before we met Marvin, the Primes arranged our harmonies; for that reason alone, none of us ever had to learn to read music. We did everything by sound. Marvin read music, and so he could teach us any song. Having our own musician made us unique among the other local singing groups, because at the hops, they would have to lip-synch to the hit records, while we sang live. And we were very proud of Marvin. Once he became part of the group, he was as dedicated as we were and was with us every minute.

From the start, Flo took most of the leads, singing in her warm, gospel-tinged style. Her raw spirit was always the soul of the Primettes. It all seemed so easy for her. In the beginning a concerned Milton attended every rehearsal, making sure that we had everything we needed. The Primes continued to teach us songs and everything they knew about staging—how to stand, what to say, how to give and follow cues. Some days, Milton would pick us up at our houses and drive us to rehearsal in his Cadillac. The minute he pulled up, everyone on our block gathered around, wondering, I'm sure, just what we were doing. Though Milton seemed to have more than his share of beautiful, sexy girlfriends, we attributed his success with the ladies to his handsome face and irresistible charm. When it came to us, however, Milton was always a perfect gentleman, sometimes acting as if we were his daughters. "Look at those girls, those are my girls," he would say proudly to anyone around.

Several months later we had our first professional engagement, singing at a gigantic party in a hall for a large local union. Milton's well-dressed lady friend took us shopping for stage outfits. Milton wanted us to look sharp but innocent. We all looked forward to these shopping jaunts. Fortunately, her taste in clothes was not as brassy as we feared it might be, and we all agreed on the collegiate look that Frankie Lymon and the Teenagers had made so popular. We picked out white pleated skirts, white sweaters embossed with big letter Ps, white bobby sox, and white gym shoes.

The people attending were bigwigs, or at least fairly well to do, or so we thought, since none of them came from our neighborhood. Also on the bill with us was a young singer named Freda Payne. The union's membership was primarily black and middle- or upper-middle-class, a group we referred to as the "elites." Perhaps they were better educated, or their skin was lighter, or they had managed to banish any Southern accent or language from their speech. These blacks frowned upon other blacks whose appearance, manner of expression, or attitude diverged from the "white" standards the black middle class sought to emulate. In many ways these people, most of whom sent their children to the "better" schools, such as Cass Technical High School, could be as nasty to the blacks they thought were beneath them as any white bigot, and kids from the Projects were in that group.

They say that you never forget your first time at anything, and that's especially true of performing. I can remember this evening so vividly. Flo sang lead on "Night Time," Diane sang "There Goes My Baby," and I sang the ballads. We also did "The Twist." Everything came so naturally for me, and we all did well. Flo was as earthy and soulful as ever. Diane looked as excited as a young leopard, and Betty was her usual sparkling, confident self. We were great. And from the first sound of applause, I knew that my place was on the stage.

After our big splash, Milton tried to book us on any show willing to take us. We began to be popular around the Detroit area playing sock hops. These were dances organized by local disc jockeys, where they played records and presented young local acts, like us, who didn't yet have an extensive repertoire of original material. We did many of these shows with disc jockeys, including Ernie Durham, and later Bill Williams, Long, Tall, Lean, Lanky Larry Dean, and Robin Seymour. Our act usually consisted of our own renditions of the most popular tunes.

Milton was always there beside us. He took his job of manager very seriously, driving us to the gigs, protecting and guiding us. If we were ever paid for these performances, we never knew it. Besides, the money would have represented only a fraction of what Milton spent on us. Still, as time passed, we became increasingly curious about what we had come to think of as Milton's secret life.

We now felt we had arrived, and our top priority became making our group the best around. After all, weren't we the only group in the Projects with our own guitarist? Weren't we one of the few groups who wore stylish matching stage costumes? Couldn't we be considered some of the prettiest girls singing in the Brewster complex (or anywhere in town, for that matter)? And, we were proud to say, we had never had to sing on streetcorners; the Primettes played real dates, right from the beginning.

After my mother purchased a new sewing machine on credit, the four of us decided that we could make more original stage costumes than the ones Milton's girlfriends had been choosing for us, which now included things like shirtwaist dresses. I had learned the basics of sewing in my seventh-grade home economics class at Bishop, and Diane, whose mother had done some dressmaking, also knew how to sew. The few skirts and dresses I made were never completely finished, but they were wearable.

Diane and I went downtown shopping. We chose some wonderful

orange and yellow floral print material and a pattern for a short, sleeveless balloon dress, which went out at the waist like any full skirt, but then tapered at the knee. Diane and I spent many afternoons and evenings together pressing, cutting, marking, and pinning the material. Every day for weeks there would be scissors, cloth, pattern tissues, straight pins, and tape measures all over the floors at her house and mine.

I didn't do as much detailing on my dress as Diane had on hers, and later I had to go back and touch up a few crooked seams. Once on, though, our new dresses looked beautiful. These were our very first stage gowns and we felt very grown-up in them. We had our peau de soie pumps dyed orange to match. At last we looked—we thought—as sophisticated and worldly as we felt. These might have been designer creations from Paris for all we cared.

We were four teenage girls convinced we could become the best girl group Detroit had ever produced. We were obsessed with music. Deep down, we knew we could achieve our goal only through commitment, and though each of us was probably more serious about our careers than most of our singing peers, it was Flo's voice that put us over. Though unsure of herself in so many other ways, Flo knew she could sing, and she knew we could make it. Singing was Flo's ticket out, and so the Primettes became her life. Of course, none of us really knew how we were going to accomplish all this, but the details didn't matter then.

With practice, our stage presence became more exciting; with repetition even the most carefully planned movements, gestures, and lines began to look perfect and spontaneous. Once we had learned these basics and they became automatic, we felt more relaxed, and before long being onstage seemed like second nature.

We were still taking turns singing the lead on songs, and we were all good, but almost everyone who heard us agreed that Flo was the best. Her sound and style were very similar to Aretha Franklin's; she would attack each number with a passion that every audience responded to immediately. We were still singing other peoples' hits, but Flo was able to make any song she sang like her own. Diane's voice was higher, and she had gotten into the habit of singing through her nose, with her shoulders all drawn up. Still, on the right song, like "There Goes My Baby," or with the right part, like in "(Night Time Is) The Right Time," Diane was great. Betty's singing was very good, and we urged her to take more leads, but she never would. Because she was an alto, she thought her voice was too deep. She did, however, give the group a special charisma that audiences really warmed to. And for the most part, I stayed cool, projecting a calm, certain air, while my heart pounded a thousand beats a minute. Of the four of us, Diane changed the most once onstage. Her nervous habits, like biting her nails, disappeared and she seemed confident and at home. She also had a way of constantly moving onstage that caught the eye.

I think it's hard for people who haven't performed to understand how it feels to stand up before a crowd of strangers and really open your heart. It was very special to us, and looking back I can see how each of us contributed to keeping it together. After each show we would tell one another over and over again that we were a smash, and we would build one another up, downplaying our own insecurities and doubts. All that mattered was that we excel as a group. We really didn't see ourselves as four individuals. Perhaps we each knew that as individuals, without the others, we had no chance. As the Primettes, though, we had everything going for us. Or, as Flo would later say, "Honey, we is terrific."

When we weren't together, we were talking on the phone. We each seemed always to be talking with one of the others. All our conversations were about singing and the Primettes—where we were playing next, what we would wear, what we would sing, who might see us there, how we would get there, and so on. We would drive our parents crazy asking if we could go to one of the other girls' homes. Once, to do a show, we even lied to our parents, saying we were spending the night at one of the others' houses. Our being such good girls gave us a brazen confidence; we reasoned that since we had hardly ever lied to our parents before, we probably wouldn't get caught. Even boyfriends were on the back burner now.

We weren't the only group making a name. Several other groups we knew—like the Peppermints, and Otis Williams and the Distants —were getting around. Melvin Franklin and Richard Street were members of the Distants, and, like us, they were regulars on the sock-hop circuit, though we didn't meet them until the night we shared a bill at the Gold Coast, a popular local club. The other highlight of that evening was a fight that broke out on the dance floor. Fistfights were so common in many of the clubs we played, we came to view them as added entertainment.

Melvin came to see our group because he wanted to see Betty. For some reason, Betty didn't show up for this particular gig, but

Melvin stayed to catch our act. His cousin, Richard Street, knew Diane from their days at McMichaels Elementary School. There seemed to be an empathy between Melvin and me. Even then, he was very spiritual. He had one of the deepest, huskiest voices I had ever heard. I was just learning how to tell when a boy had a crush on me, but both he and Richard were very shy, so there was no way I could be sure. Soon Richard became infatuated with Diane. I doubt she even knew it; she seemed to have eyes for everyone but him.

Despite these romantic intrigues, the only subject we could all really open up about was singing. We knew we were on the right track, and we were always telling one another to stick to it, to persevere. Richard had been playing in nightclubs since he was thirteen, and because he seemed so experienced, we all assumed that he was older when in fact he was one of the youngest in our crowd. Knowing Melvin and Richard during this time helped me to see more objectively what we were all going through. We were still young, but performing, even in the best places, brought us into contact with parts of the real world most kids don't see. Most of us had come from the South, but some of us were raised with so little awareness of what that life was about that we might as well have been Detroit natives. Other young singers, like our friends from the Primes and Melvin, had trouble adjusting to life in Detroit.

We knew of prejudice that crossed racial lines, but few of us knew that there could be as much discrimination from within our own race as from outside it. Melvin learned about this other unspoken prejudice the first time he failed an audition for a group because he was "too dark." "I have big eyes," Melvin told me later, "and the group's leader, who was gay, showed no mercy. 'We don't want no black, bug-eyed boy over here with us.' They never gave me the chance to sing."

Without Richard's and his own mother's encouragement, Melvin might have given up. Instead he decided that he would one day be accepted in a great vocal group, and he knew that the only way he'd be accepted by the elites was to practice and practice and practice. And that's exactly what he and Richard did. Because Melvin was even shyer than his cousin, Richard had to coax him into talking to us.

Lately, it seemed that all our relationships were growing out of music, and a network of young singers and musicians was forming among our friends. Marv Tarplin, for example, had known Richard years before either of them knew us. Fate seemed to be bringing us all together, and, in my youthful idealism, I believed we would be in one anothers' lives forever.

*  *  *

As we got older, we came to view school as a mildly annoying necessity. On the positive side, it was a refuge from the group, which by now was taking up so much time and energy that we each felt an acute need for time alone. As enjoyable as performing was, we took it seriously and the realization of how great our responsibilities were could be overwhelming.

Just a few months after the Primettes were formed, in the spring of 1959, Flo, Diane, and I graduated from the eighth grade. I hadn't really thought much about what high school I would be attending until one of my teachers, Mr. Curley, suggested that I consider going to Commerce, where they taught business skills, instead of Northeastern. My mother had been saving up so I could go to college, and all I knew about choosing a career was that I didn't want to be a nurse; I was too emotional for that.

Diane chose to attend Cass Technical High School, her father's alma mater, where she studied dress design and costume illustration. Cass was considered one of the better high schools in the area, and was the choice of many "elites." Few kids from our neighborhood went there, so we thought of Cass as something of a snob school.

My first day at Commerce brought me the shock of my life: There were hardly any boys there! Almost all of the other girls there were white and very businesslike, and there weren't any kids around from my neighborhood. After getting my schedule, my locker, and my home-room assignment, I told my counselor that I'd made a serious mistake. I was offered the chance to go to Cass, but I wasn't interested. Although I was a good student, I rarely studied. I would never have failed anything, but I didn't want to do the extra schoolwork I knew I'd get if I went to Cass. Northeastern was further from my home, but I knew the kids there and—best of all—there would be boys. Though I dreamed of singing professionally, I knew I had to be prepared to take a regular job. Though Northeastern offered no special curriculum for business studies, I didn't care. I took many music classes, including some with Flo. I would probably go to college anyway, and I wanted very badly to be with my friends from the neighborhood and the Brewster Center, the community recreation facility.

Northeastern was considered a rough school. Though it was located in the Polish neighborhood, more than eighty percent of the students were black. I know it's not as common today, but back then the teachers in the inner-city schools strove to make sure the academic standards were high. Our instructors were exceptional, and the faculty was thoroughly integrated. The whites, most of whom were of Polish descent, made an extra effort to mix with the black kids. There were racial problems and incidents all over Detroit, but I was never aware of any trouble during my years at Northeastern. For that I credit the faculty, who socialized together without any regard to race and so set the tone for the whole school.

As I got older, I came to fully appreciate my hardworking teachers' dedication and how much it influenced me. We had an exceptional music department, headed by Mr. Silver, and each semester I took as many different music classes as I could. Both Flo and I were in the glee club, which we loved. However, once we started hanging around at Milton's, our instructor, Mrs. Breaux, got upset. Not only were we missing rehearsals but she felt that both of us should be studying opera. In fact, for one school program, Flo and I sang Handel's *Messiah*. I will always remember Mrs. Breaux for saying to us, "I don't know why you sing all that rock and roll stuff. It's not going to get you anywhere." Still, without the support and guidance of many of those instructors, I would never have even dreamed, much less achieved my later goals. Even when I took a class that I wasn't particularly suited for—like the time I took Latin, thinking it would help me when I traveled the world—I stuck with it. Though it is a dead language, I did benefit from knowing it later on.

When I wasn't thinking about singing, I was daydreaming about boys. Each of our mothers had decided that we were all too young at fifteen to "receive company." But when did that stop young love? It didn't stop me from having my first grown-up boyfriend, Arnett Webster, who was several years older than me and just out of the service. Before I met Arnett, it never occurred to me to want to bring boys over to my house. With Arnett, I soon realized that while I may have been a virgin, I wasn't just a kid anymore. We would sit, talk, and walk around, holding hands. It was very romantic, and Arnett was always a gentleman. In fact, Flo, Diane, Betty, and I seemed to attract only nice young men who treated us respectfully.

Though I'd taken my first tentative steps into the realm of sexuality, I still wasn't aware of all the changes in my body. That didn't mean, however, that certain fast-moving boys in my neighborhood weren't hip to all this. One of these young men was Jimmy Abner, a handsome tenor who sometimes sang with Melvin and Richard. Our mutual love of music brought us together, but it wasn't long before our romance took precedence over everything else. With Jimmy I learned what kissing was really all about.

Sometimes when we were making out, it was almost impossible to stop. I would discover my top off before I could pull away. It was difficult, but I forced myself to hold back. This went on for weeks, with Jimmy begging me to submit to my "true feelings." I really enjoyed all this heavy petting, as we used to call it, so finally I agreed to go all the way. When I told Jimmy that I would, I could sense his excitement, despite his great efforts to appear cool. Unlike many young girls at the time, I didn't bother pretending that I wanted to wait for marriage or that I was too good or too innocent.

The moment of truth came one night when Jimmy's parents were out of town and we had the house all to ourselves. I was eager but torn between knowing it was wrong to have sex (my mother would have murdered me if she found out) and feverishly wanting to surrender to my desires and not look like a coward in front of Jimmy.

When we got to Jimmy's, the house was dark, and I begged him not to turn on the lights. In the back of my mind, I almost convinced myself that if we did this forbidden thing in the dark, no one could know, or maybe I would not have to accept the fact that it was really happening. Sensing my unease, Jimmy slowly undressed me. There was no awkward fumbling, and before I knew it, Jimmy's strong body was on top of mine. Within seconds we were in the throes of passion. After what seemed like an eternity of foreplay, Jimmy gently spread my legs with one hand, and I could feel him trying to enter me. I screamed for him to stop, and he did, but continued to kiss me passionately. He tried again and again, but I stopped him each time. I forgot about how much I loved him and how long I'd waited for this and how good it felt. It just wasn't right. Where were the shooting stars I'd heard about? There was no magic here. Finally, I made him stop. I tearfully told him that I couldn't go on; it hurt too much. We broke up soon after.

With this embarrassing experience behind me, I felt I'd emerged from innocence. I wanted to share this with someone, but I knew it couldn't be Flo or Diane. Betty seemed the logical choice, since I suspected that because of her relationship with Paul, she probably knew a lot more about all this than I did. Ultimately, I told no one. It was just not my nature—or Diane's or Flo's or Betty's—to discuss such things. Our lives inside and outside of the Primettes were kept separate.

I would always go to Diane's house after I'd finished my chores and homework. My mother had agreed that I could join the Primettes, but she didn't let me off the hook from doing housework. I was the eldest, and a girl to boot, so the bulk of the responsibility for keeping the house in order was mine. My brother didn't have to do house-work because he was a boy, and Cat was still too young really to help.

I always looked forward to seeing Diane. We would go out to see a rock 'n' roll movie, go roller-skating, or just run around the neigh-borhood. Diane was always very intense about things. When she wanted to go, she wanted to go, and I enjoyed being caught up in her enthusiasm. Neither of us could afford to buy all the clothes we wanted—what teenage girl can?—so we shared. We wore the same sizes and liked the current style, wearing V-neck pullover sweaters over different-colored dickies.

One day I found Diane feeling really down. She was unusually quiet, and when I asked her what was bothering her, she said nothing. After I'd plied her with questions, she eventually admitted to me that some kids at Cass were making it hard for her to join one of the sororities, the Hexagons. It was a very "in" club, so their snubbing Diane just made her all the more determined to get in. Typically, she would jump right in to be at the center of attention, and while this usually worked with our crowd, the kids at Cass looked down on Diane because she was from the Projects. In order to get into the sorority, you had to belong to another school club, so Diane set her sights on that. Girls at that age tend to be catty, anyway, and for some reason that I didn't see, Diane was bringing out the worst in these girls. Diane never took a snub lightly, and she set out to change things.

She made an extra effort to participate in all the extracurricular activities, and made the swim team. Winning many local competitions for Cass proved to be a real turning point. She had finally found her niche, and the other students began to notice and appreciate her. I was happy for her, and I could see that she was back to her old, happy self. She was thrilled about being accepted by her fellow students, and anything that she loved—like swimming—consumed her.

Around this time, Flo started dating Jesse Greer, who, like most of the boys in our circle, was a gentleman. He was a handsome, intelligent, soft-spoken boy who also sang. Along with some former basketball buddies, he formed the Peppermints. At the time they met, Flo was attending Northeastern, and Jesse was in his last year at East-ern High. Jesse would share his dreams of stardom with Flo, and she was a good listener; she could be very reserved and quiet. He knew that she had a great voice, too. Flo would sometimes meet Jesse at

Carmen Murphy's House of Beauty after school and stay and watch his group rehearse, then Jesse would walk her home.

Jesse respected Flo, who was then only fifteen. After meeting her family, he became even more resolved in his conviction not to sleep with her, and so he took special care not to get carried away with Flo, he later told me.

After Jesse graduated from high school, he and Flo stopped dating. Flo told me that the reason she and Jesse had drifted apart was that he was "too nice" for her, but I never knew what she meant by that. Jesse was a few years older than Flo, and he seemed much more mature. And while Flo could seem much wiser, and certainly appeared to be older, in many ways she was not as mature as she seemed. Some people took Flo's silence as a mark of her maturity; in fact she was often quiet because she feared being ridiculed. Her family still held on to those country ways and made no pretense of being more sophisticated than they were. While Diane and I were encouraged by our families to work toward our goals, even if this entailed some risk, Flo was constantly reminded to be cautious and not to venture too far.

Though Jesse liked Flo, she would just close up around him; she didn't know what to do. Once they stopped dating, they became the best of friends, more like brother and sister. Sitting on her porch, the two of them would talk about everything, but especially music. By then the Peppermints were well known locally, having played the Flame Show Bar and the Twenty Grand Club. At the time, the only local act working those venues was the Four Tops. With the pressure off, Flo told Jesse all about her life and her feelings, and to him she revealed the fun part of her personality, an openness that she shared with very few and kept hidden from the rest of the world.

# CHAPTER 5

Any weekend that we weren't booked for a sock hop would find us attending a 25-cent house party. It was at these gatherings that we began testing our mettle by sipping cheap wine; the boys always kept a supply in the basement of whatever house the party was in. The guys and girls would gather downstairs and get down, drinking and making out.

For the most part, we never gave too much serious thought to anything. But in early 1960 things began to change. For one thing, Milton began to fade from our lives. At first he just missed a rehearsal every now and then, or maybe a show. But as time passed, Milton became harder to get in touch with, and sometimes he just disappeared. We later found out that Milton's arm, which he had injured in a serious car accident, had become gangrenous, and he was hospitalized. Things with the Primes had not been going smoothly, and they drifted away from Milton and broke up. But while their career had gone on ice, after less than a year of hard work, ours was just heating up. We had something great with Marvin, so we took it upon ourselves to run our own rehearsals at Betty's house.

We weren't about to let Milton's disappearance affect us, and we'd built up enough momentum under his aegis to keep us in jobs for the foreseeable future. Still, show business is a rough business, and Milton had protected us. There was no telling what might happen to us out on our own. Milton Jenkins saw potential in kids that sometimes even they didn't see. He gave us direction and taught us about discipline. Milton's departure signaled the beginning of some very rough times.

As the Primettes became established, we began to feel like we were leading a double life. On one hand, we were devoting everything to singing. On the other, Flo, Diane, and I still had two years of high school ahead. We were thrilled when people around town started recognizing us. The Primettes sang at one of Diane's school functions at Cass. She still had not been accepted by the Hexagons. Sometimes I would go with her to one of their parties. I never knew if she had actually been invited, but she took me along with her anyway, for backup, I think.

I have to give her credit for persistence. She was finally invited to join the sorority. This was what she'd been working for, and she would do anything they asked, even if it meant scrubbing a floor with a toothbrush. I knew that she wanted to be a Hexagon more than anything, and once she got in, she acted like she'd pulled a real coup and was justifiably proud. The sorority gave picnics and parties, which were a lot of fun.

Diane enjoyed being away at school. Cass was more like a college campus than a high school, and I suppose that had some appeal for Diane. But whereas I lived for the time after school to spend with the group, Diane didn't seem to mind being away from us.

I always enjoyed school; I found meeting other kids and making new friends exciting. I also liked learning new things, even though I wasn't a bookworm. I got good grades with little effort. Flo, on the other hand, really didn't like school very much. She was smart, but not really interested.

The only time I got to see Flo was at rehearsals. Luckily, Jesse Greer began rehearsing us at the Brewster Center. Jesse had been working for Mrs. Murphy, playing music at her fashion shows. Mrs. Murphy taught cosmetology, modeling, and hairstyling at her House of Beauty. Her school turned out the majority of Detroit's black models and beauticians. When Diane and my cousin Josephine took classes in cosmetology, I became their favorite guinea pig/model, and between the two of them my hair changed from one week to the next —from red to brown with blond streaks, to anything else.

Jesse's knowledge of and interest in music made him seem like a real professional to us. He tried to inspire us, and he encouraged me to take more leads; he also told Diane not to sing through her nose so much. Like many people, including me, Jesse believed that if Flo would sing more, she would really catch on, and that the Primettes could make it. At that time, I thought Flo had the best lead voice, then Diane, then me. Betty wasn't singing that many leads at the time; she really had no aspirations to be a singer and was more or less in the group for fun. But Jesse tried to convince me that I would have a stronger lead voice if I would just project more. He thought that I lacked confidence. Maybe I did. Ultimately, though, we split the leads evenly, with me taking all the ballads.

Jesse taught us the standards and classic ballads and how to sing harmony. The ballads were a real challenge for all of us. Songs like "Canadian Sunset" and "Moonlight in Vermont" were among our favorites. We always loved singing any song that called for complex three- or four-part harmonies. We spent hours at the Brewster Center learning the intricate harmonies of the Mills Brothers and the Four Freshmen. As far as the leads went, though, I could see that a rivalry over the singing was already brewing between Diane and Flo.

We felt almost lost without a manager, but we did the best we could. Around this time, I began to notice in Diane a different kind of aggressiveness. Diane was always one to do it by the book. Having studied fashion at Cass, she was certain that she knew everything, and no matter what someone else did, if it didn't follow the rules, Diane would comment on it. I had started wearing what were considered some pretty wild color combinations—pink with red, electric blue with kelly green. Today this style is in vogue, but back then the style was to wear more subtle colors. I wasn't wearing these colors just to be different—though it did look that way; I honestly thought I looked great. One day, I was wearing all blue and green, and Diane said, "Mary, what are you wearing? You know you can't wear that—those colors don't go together."

"Why not?" I replied. "I think they look fine."

"Well, because you can't. Those colors just don't go together." Then she would look at me like I was crazy. It was hard to be offended by her attitude; it was just the way Diane was.

The culmination of our dreams came when we took first place in the Detroit/Windsor Freedom Festival amateur talent contest in July 1960. The festival, an annual event held just across the river from Detroit in Windsor, Canada, was sponsored by radio stations on both sides of the border. The contest was open to all amateur performers, but to participate we needed our parents' permission. That seemed easy enough to get, but when Diane mentioned going there, her father refused to permit it. Diane's father put his foot down; she was not going to Windsor.

We went ahead with daily rehearsals anyway, convinced that we could get Mr. Ross to change his mind. Each of us approached him individually, and then we all spoke to him together, to plead on Diane's behalf, but Mr. Ross, who was usually fairly easygoing, was firm about this. "Diane," he would say, "what about your schooling? You're putting a lot of time into this singing group."

Actually, we probably weren't putting much more time into it than we had a year or so earlier, when we started. But the closer we got to graduation, the more our parents began to worry that we might be singing instead of going to college. Mr. Ross was trying to reason with her, but Diane would have none of it. She wasn't crying, but she was chewing her nails, and you could tell by the way she looked at her father that nothing was going to stop her from going. We took her father's disapproval very seriously. Sure, we had snuck out with boys and told the occasional white lie. But disobeying a parent was still considered the wrong thing to do. Somehow, Diane worked it all out, and we went to Windsor.

Living in Detroit with Canada just across the river, I had never thought of it as another country. Most of the other young performers who were going there, though, saw it as an international event. It was the most exciting and prestigious amateur competition in the area.

Having spent the previous weeks practicing, we felt ready for the big day. We were surprised at the wide range of acts on the bill. There were not only other doo-wop groups, but belly dancers and ventriloquists, including my high school friend Willie Tyler and his dummy Lester. I particularly remember a gay male dancer named Oscar Huckleby; he looked like the actor Geoffrey Holder.

Finally we were on. All I remember clearly was that we were introduced and went onstage. It was so thrilling to be standing up in front of several thousand people. Once we started singing we had no idea how strong our chances of winning were. We could see that the crowd—which included people of all ages and races—was up and moving and having the time of their lives while we were on. From where we stood, the audience seemed to be in a frenzy. I can't recall all the numbers we performed, but the songs that put us over were our old standby, "(Night Time Is) The Right Time," "The Twist," and "There Goes My Baby." On "Night Time," while Flo sang the deeper blues part, the audience looked amazed; then, when Diane took her high part, the whole place just went crazy.

After the show, we waited for the winners to be announced. I had my fingers crossed, but with all the other talented performers there, I wouldn't have been surprised if someone else had won. When we heard our names called out, we were screaming with joy. This was the highlight of our career thus far; we had really made it. Interestingly, unbeknownst to us, there were scouts in the audience, including some from Motown. Years later, some people would claim that Robert Batemen, one of Berry Gordy's early associates, had seen us there and told Berry about us. But we were never approached by anyone that day.

We were all flying higher than kites, and with our prize money— a whopping $15, the first money we'd ever earned performing—we set out for the carnival to celebrate.

After losing Milton, we each took a share of the responsibility for running the group. As secretary, it was my duty to collect and manage the money. We changed from our stage outfits and set out for the park. Every place we went, people we knew were congratulating us. We happily roamed around spending money on rides and snacks. After we'd each exhausted our personal funds, we decided to split up the prize money.

"Mary, where's the prize money?" Diane asked.

I reached into my pocket, but it was empty. I tried all my other pockets, but still nothing. I prided myself on being honest and responsible, and I knew I had put the money in my pocket. But it was gone. When I told the others that I must have lost it, Diane teased, "Are you sure you haven't been spending it on your rides and stuff, Mary?"

I didn't even try to defend myself. We traced our steps back to all the places we'd been that day, but to no avail. Though Diane's attitude was upsetting, I wasn't so much angry as I was hurt, and I quietly punished myself for being so careless.

Later that night, Marv said, "My friend Richard Morris said for me to tell you that you should come over to Motown."

"Well," I reasoned aloud, "we've got to make a record somewhere. If other groups can do it, I know we can too if we sound as good as we sounded today."

I made that statement with all the confidence in the world. All day long the five of us had been strutting and prancing around, acting very much like the stars we felt we were. It must have been that, having won this contest, we sensed that our days as amateurs were numbered. We had to go pro, and the only way to do that was to cut a record.

"Isn't Motown the record company that cheats its artists?" Flo asked suspiciously. We'd all heard the rumors about the up-and-coming company, and in our naïveté we assumed that all other small record labels were totally honest, and Motown was an aberration. For that reason alone, we initially dismissed the idea of going to Motown. We knew that once we got back home we'd have to make some serious decisions about where the Primettes were headed, but for tonight all we wanted was to revel in our success.

After a couple weeks back in Detroit, we realized that we knew nothing about the record business, and so, after much thought and discussion, we decided to approach Motown after all. It was the newest company and seemed most open to fresh young talent. Before Diane's family had moved to the Projects, they had lived in the same neighborhood as Smokey Robinson, and she knew his cousin, Sylvia. We knew that the Miracles had been working at Motown and had a hit with "Got a Job," an "answer" record to the Silhouettes' smash "Get a Job." Smokey had formed the group with some high school friends—Ronnie White, Peter Moore, and cousins Bobby and Sonny Rogers. Sonny had left the group and his sister Claudette had stepped in. They had been around just a brief time before Berry discovered them. In our eyes, the Miracles were big stars with important connections, so Diane talked to Sylvia, and Sylvia talked to Smokey. He said that we could audition for the Miracles first. If we were good, he might talk to Berry Gordy on our behalf.

We planned to meet the Miracles after school at the Rogerses' house, where they rehearsed in the living room. Many girls found Smokey very attractive, with his light reddish hair, fair skin, and beautiful gray-green eyes. We were dying to make a great impression, so we tried to dress as sharp as we could. We took special pains to warn Marvin to be on time. Our guitarist was our pride and joy, and we wanted to be sure everything would run smoothly. Because Diane knew Smokey, she did most of the talking and made the introductions. I also knew Bobby Rogers. He was a year ahead of me in school, so I didn't know him that well, but I had admired him from afar. He had a reputation for being a ladies' man, and with his beautiful smile, quick wit, and gorgeous processed hair, all the girls thought he was an absolute dreamboat.

It came time for us to show our stuff, and without hesitation Flo launched into the verse of "(Night Time Is) The Right Time," and we all fell into our parts. Next we did "There Goes My Baby," and finished up with "There's Something on Your Mind," one of the songs where I took the lead.

Smokey seemed to like us, and when he promised to introduce us at Motown, we were thrilled. Soon, however, it was evident that Smokey was even more interested in Marvin. Smokey was asking Marvin if he could play this song or that song, or this chord or that chord, and Marvin shyly complied with all of Smokey's requests. At the end, Smokey asked Marvin if he could go on a short trip with the Miracles.

"Well, you have to ask the girls," Marvin replied softly.

We all sort of said yes, thinking that it might be good for Marvin to go with Smokey on this one little trip. Little did we know that we had lost Marvin forever. Marvin's been with Smokey ever since then, and has co-written some of the Miracles' and some of Marvin Gaye's greatest hits.

A short time later, Richard Morris, a young writer and engineer at Hitsville whom Marvin Tarplin had told about us, agreed to see us. The appointment with Berry Gordy was set. We couldn't help thinking about all the rumors we had heard. We knew, though, that we had to make a record; it was our main concern. Our faith in ourselves would surely pull us through.

At this time, the Miracles were company pets. Not only were they recording steadily, but Smokey was writing songs with Berry and beginning to show promise as a producer. Being a small organization, Motown looked to everyone there to contribute in more than one area. The Miracles were young, enthusiastic, and hardworking— everything Berry respected. Also, Berry was Smokey's mentor. We had faith that we could carry the audition on our own, but having Smokey and the Miracles as friends and supporters convinced us we'd be in at Motown in no time.

Our audition for Mr. Gordy was set up for sometime in the late summer of 1960. We all met there after school. I remember the four of us walking toward the building and the impression it made on me. It was, in fact, a small nondescript two-story house that had been converted to a photography studio. But as we approached, the big letters on the front that read HITSVILLE U.S.A. seemed to loom over us. In the window was a poster that read "The Sound of Young America." Flo was her usual confident self, and I remember Betty taking long strides ahead of me. Diane and I just kept quiet, though in our silence we each worked hard at being charming. I just wanted to see and remember every little detail. Once we were there, all our doubts about Motown seemed to fade. This could really be it, and we knew it. No records, no career.

Once in the tiny, bare reception area, I was relieved to see a familiar face. Seated behind the front desk was Janie Bradford, whom we had met during our days with Milton Jenkins. We were surprised to see her there. She greeted us warmly and suggested we wait in the lobby, a small area to the left of her desk.

The time we spent waiting couldn't have been much longer than an hour, but it felt like a year. I must have memorized every inch of that room. There was the plate-glass display window and the only thing to sit on was a long, hard upholstered bench, like the ones you find in a doctor's office. Speaking in a whisper, Flo reiterated that we should not appear too eager, that Motown's reputation was none too good. Flo had a cocky attitude about this whole business; she thought that a company like Motown should consider itself lucky that groups as good as the Primettes would even be willing to record with them. I'd have liked to believe that one myself, but it just wasn't true. We would be the lucky ones. To lighten up the atmosphere, Betty kept on making little jokes, while Diane sat quietly, trying to appear sophisticated and worldly. I was silent except to giggle at a joke or answer with a brief remark. Our attempts at being cool were pretty successful, at least until Barrett Strong walked through the lobby. We knew his song "Money," but didn't recognize him until Janie told us who he was. In an instant we became as skittish as kittens.

We were finally shown into the studio and introduced to Richard Morris, Robert Bateman, talent scout and producer, and Berry Gordy. I was surprised to see that the big man everybody in Detroit was talking about was actually small, about five feet seven inches tall. He wasn't what you'd call handsome, but he exuded a certain confidence that hinted he could take care of himself. Berry was nice enough to us, but he seemed much more serious about things than other people I'd met in the music business. I sensed that his mind was clicking every moment, even when he was talking to us. And although he could make anyone feel at ease, if you were smart you knew that there was something going on behind his smile.

The audition began. Richard basically handled it; Berry would go in and out of the room. I remember thinking how small everything was. Once we were in position, Richard gave us the cue to start singing. Since the Miracles had absconded with Marvin, we had to sing our four songs a cappella: "There Goes My Baby," "Night Time," "The Twist," and "There's Something on Your Mind." Undaunted, we gave this private show our all, pulling out all the stops to make it great.

Though we were concentrating on our performance, we were

each trying to read all their faces. He listened very attentively and seemed most interested in our rendition of "There Goes My Baby," on which Diane sang lead. Not everyone cared for Diane's voice, which was sometimes shrill, but Berry seemed to like it.

At the end, Berry told us that he liked the song and us, but he was not offering us a recording contract. In a very serious tone, he said we should come back after we all had finished school. (The press has mythologized this little incident, making it sound like Berry gave us this advice because he felt that we shouldn't quit school, and that may have been at least partially true. But ultimately the real reason for Berry's initial refusal was business. The last thing Berry wanted at this early stage of his career was the responsibility for four female minors. And this gave Berry a good out, so he didn't have to even consider us again for the next year or so. As it happened, when we eventually did sign, three of us were still in school.)

We respectfully listened to Berry's pronouncement. If we had not been so young or so shy or so intimidated, we would have told him that we were good girls and to give us a chance. But he was an adult and we were just kids. Smiling sweetly, he dismissed us.

# CHAPTER 6

We didn't want to leave after the audition. The atmosphere at Hitsville was charged with excitement; everyone there seemed to believe that great things were going to happen. The fact that Berry Gordy did not sign us then only fueled our desire to be part of Motown—officially or otherwise. We were forced to make last-ditch efforts; without a record, our singing careers were as good as over. We simply would not take Berry's no for an answer. The day we auditioned and were refused, we just couldn't bring ourselves to get up and leave.

We returned to the reception area, feeling both numb and all wound up from singing. Janie was talking on the telephone, obviously too busy for us, so we just all sat down on the long bench and watched the parade passing through. The first afternoon there we met Eddie and Brian Holland, two short but very good-looking brothers. Eddie was very outgoing, intelligent, and opinionated. He had a head full of curls, half slicked back with grease to create the illusion that it was processed. Brian seemed very quiet, but he had a mischievous look that made you wonder just how quiet he really was.

We also met Norman Whitfield, a young producer, and two of Motown's biggest stars, Marv Johnson and Mary Wells. This was turning out to be our lucky day after all. We knew that this was where we belonged.

We agreed that it would be in our best interests to go to Hitsville each and every day after school. Even without a manager, we were rehearsing on our own at Betty's. We were convinced that someday Hitsville would have to give in and record us, and we wanted to be ready. Every day we would hitch rides with friends to West Grand Boulevard, and the four of us would meet outside the lobby.

Even while we worked our way up to the better clubs, we were still doing the hops. Because our audience was mostly made up of teenagers, we would rush to change from our "glamorous" stage outfits—or uniforms, as we called them—and put on our bobby sox, saddle shoes, and tight skirts, so that we could hang out with the other kids after the show. It was all so much fun. Still, nothing beat hanging out at Hitsville.

The building on West Grand Boulevard was a home away from home for many young singers and musicians then. The company was still serving hot family-style meals for everyone who happened to be around. Those of us who loved Motown remember fondly these times of special closeness and friendship. Things were still fairly casual then, and we were allowed to watch artists—including Mary Wells, Mabel John, Henry Lumpkin, Barrett Strong, Richard "Popcorn" Wiley, and the Rayber Voices—record. We tried to learn as much as we could, and in those days there were plenty of people to watch; young performers seemed to find their way there in droves. The negative rumors about Motown deterred very few; it was still one of the few places in Detroit a young musician or singer could make a buck or get the chance to really succeed.

We got to know Richard Morris, a tall young recording engineer and musician who had been working with Berry in different capacities for a couple of years. Richard had been the leader of a street gang called the Shakers, but he had cleaned up his act. He'd been friendly with us, and there had been some discussion that we might be used to cut some background vocals, but nothing was really happening for us. One day, after we'd been hanging around Hitsville for a couple of months, I began nagging him in a kidding manner.

"When are we going to make our own record, Richard?" I asked.

Diane piped in, "We need to get in the studio and make a recording for the Primettes." Flo and Betty both gave Richard meaningful glares. We were acting as if it were his fault that we hadn't been assigned a producer or cut a record—and we didn't even have a contract!

"After all," Diane reminded him, "you told Marvin Tarplin that we should come here in the first place. Can't you talk to the big man, or something? We're getting tired of sitting around here doing practically nothing."

Richard just laughed and shook his head. "I'll see what I can do." Richard voiced our grievances to Berry, but in the end Berry told Richard that our ages still "bothered" him and he just couldn't be involved with us now. "Well, man," Richard suggested, "let me work with them on the side when I finish my job here." Berry agreed to that.

Richard later gave us the news along with his assurances that he believed in the Primettes and that someday soon we would be making records. Over the next few months we worked with Richard, ceasing our daily visits to Hitsville. Richard helped us run our rehearsals, and we were confident that we would end up back on West Grand Boulevard eventually. This was just a temporary detour; we were well on our way.

With Richard and his friend Homer Davis in charge, the Primettes' bookings increased. Things were on the upswing again, and Richard was working hard to bring the Primettes to the attention of anyone in the industry who might help us. By this point, we needed his support and were grateful for anything he could do.

Because we rarely had time to change after school before rehearsal, we dressed as nicely as we could each morning. No doubt we were some of the sharpest-dressed girls at our schools. Though we weren't wearing our stage uniforms to class, we dressed so that our clothes blended in terms of color and style. None of us had a lot to spend on clothes, but by borrowing from one another, we did all right. Judging from the reactions of the young men whom we met at school or who made up our audiences before, during, and after rehearsals, our efforts were not in vain.

Working with Richard got us into some of the bigger places, like the Graystone Ballroom or the Twenty Grand, where we played on the same bill with such stars as the Falcons, whose big hit was "You're So Fine," and Wilson Pickett. We were working all over Detroit. Other acts on the bills were usually established recording artists like the Isley Brothers, Eddie Holland (who was still singing), Johnny Mathis, and Joe and Al (the Joe in the team was Johnny Bristol, who later co-wrote "Someday We'll Be Together"). The Primettes were the opening act, and our spot on the bill was obviously less prestigious, but we were sure that would change with time. The constant exposure to more experienced singers helped us polish our own act. There were hundreds of teenage singers like ourselves, dying to get a foot in the door. I recall Martha Reeves and her group, the Del-Phis, making the same rounds for jobs as we did. The competition was so keen that we were thankful to be able to work as often as we did and in such good places.

Richard had a very good rapport with our parents, earning their trust with his sincere manner. He took his responsibility for us very seriously. Richard was not always the easiest person to get along with, but because he worked so hard for us, he was easy to forgive. I began to hang out with him. I wanted to learn about everything that was going on and I felt uncomfortable always having to play the diplomat in group crises. Richard and I would have long talks about things in general, and he treated me like a younger sister.

I was flattered when he told me that I had "intelligence, wit, and softness." I also knew that he liked Betty and had the utmost respect for Flo. His problem was with Diane. Though he admired her and liked her, she did things that tried his patience. Once Richard became upset when I asked why he always got angry with Diane for being sick. After all, I reasoned, when someone's sick, they're sick. But Richard didn't buy that. He thought Diane's excuses were pretty flimsy and that it was just her personality.

He was very good about treating the four of us equally and showing no favoritism. He was also patient, no matter how late I was. Most important, he really believed in us.

But things were never calm for too long. Our problems now seemed to come from inside the group. Diane had stopped being a tomboy and was becoming a real lady. Still, her stubbornness about certain things was almost childlike. Often, when Diane would demand to sing a particular song, for example, Betty would step in and say something to her. Because Betty was a year or so older than Flo and I, she had more leverage with Diane. Even Richard came to depend on Betty to help with Diane.

Richard was no wimp, but once Diane set her mind to do something, no one could stop her. Richard had been around; he knew that some of the places we played weren't the nicest, and that men in the audience could be very aggressive. We were working some tough places—sometimes illegally—and Richard once had his shirt torn off by some guys who tried to get at us while we were onstage in Lansing, Michigan. Richard set down rules about how we were to behave at the shows. We were not to talk with or mingle with any of the audience; our only contact with the crowd was our performance. Aside from concerns about our safety, Richard also knew that an unattainable performer has a special mystique.

Diane regularly defied Richard, and once, at the Graystone Ballroom, she jumped out onto the floor and started dancing with a guy. When Richard tried to stop her, she said some unladylike things to him, pouted, and kept on dancing. Richard was about to grab Diane and drag her off the floor, but instead he called Betty over. Betty just walked out to Diane, talked to her for a few minutes, and Diane came back.

We looked to Betty to act as a big sister on behalf of Flo and me, to nip Diane's little displays in the bud. That worked until Betty began to lose interest in the Primettes; she had less time to dedicate to it and she had less invested in it. While those two facts may have made her less prone to start something with Diane, they also gave her an advantage in dealing with her. If for some reason Betty left, it wouldn't be the end of the world for her. She was still having fun with it, but that's all the Primettes meant to her.

I saw the group as something bigger and more important than any one of us. I was content to play on the team. Diane didn't feel that way about things, and her attitude was obvious to everyone we worked with, especially Richard. "I want to keep everyone even with each other," he once said. "That's why I wrote a song for you and a song for Diane." But Richard's efforts weren't enough to keep things in balance.

Looking back, I shouldn't have been surprised to see that, as our career grew, so did feelings of competitiveness, jealousy, and distrust. It upset me once in a while, but I became an expert at stifling my feelings if I thought expressing them would endanger the group. No doubt part of my reactions stemmed from my dealings with I.V. as a child. While I felt very strongly about what was right and what was wrong, my belief that things would work themselves out and my fear of being responsible for destroying our dreams usually won out. Instead of keeping a scorecard on who was doing what to whom, I focused all my energies on singing.

Like many young performers, I was so wrapped up in the music that I did not see what was happening on the business side. Perhaps we thought so little about that part of our careers because we never made any amount of money worth worrying about. Too late we would discover that we had been featured on a bill advertising a show with such performers as Jackie Wilson. We'd arrive to perform and when the promised star failed to appear, we would suffer the unhappy audience's wrath. As it turned out, the stars had never been contacted. It was simply advertising to draw a crowd.

I later worked after school at a record shop. Now that I was earning money, I spent more on clothes. I loved finally getting to wear nice stockings and spent hours just trying to get the seams to run in a sexy straight line up the back of my skinny legs. Skinny or not, I was determined to show them off to the best advantage.

Diane had a job working at Hudson's department store, so she was buying more clothes, too. To us, as teenage girls, wardrobe was everything. We would spend hours discussing the length of skirts, what colors and what fabrics were fashionable, and what accessories to wear with everything. Flo, Betty, and I consulted one another constantly about these issues and each of us kept abreast of what the others were planning to wear. Characteristically, after we'd all agreed how we'd dress, Diane would turn up at the last minute in something entirely different. With hindsight, one can see that Diane had a plan.

One day late that summer, Betty suddenly announced that she was leaving the Primettes; she was getting married. Since her house had become our favorite rehearsal site, we'd become closer, and we were disappointed and frightened by our "big sister" 's departure. Even though Betty was just a little over a year older, at our age that was a significant difference. I thought she loved the group as much as we did. She'd broken up with Paul Williams and found someone else. I guess having a marriage and a family was more important to her. We did everything we could to convince her to stay with us, but her mind was made up. We stayed in touch, and Flo and I attended her wedding that fall.

The most difficult part for us to accept was the prospect of finding a girl to take her place. The three of us had rehearsed together at times and knew we sounded fine as a trio, but in those days singing groups had a minimum of four members. For the Primettes to go on as a trio was unthinkable. And what would our harmonies sound like on all the songs we'd perfected with four parts? Deep inside, I think we knew we could handle the singing; subconsciously, though, Flo and I realized that, with Betty gone, it would be hard to hold Diane back.

Betty's announcement was quite a jolt for all of us, but nothing compared to what lay ahead. Sometime later that fall, we stopped hearing from Flo. She wouldn't show up for rehearsals, and she would not come to the phone when we called. Diane and I were confused. Finally Mrs. Ballard answered the phone one day and told us that Flo no longer wanted to sing with us. She offered no further explanation. Flo not wanting to sing? We just couldn't believe it. One minute we were a group on the rise—the next minute, it was just me and Diane.

We knew that Mrs. Ballard had never really approved of Flo singing so much. She wanted to see her daughter make something of herself, and a singer was not what she had in mind. Knowing this, we greeted Mrs. Ballard's explanation with some skepticism. It all seemed very unlike Flo. We were both upset, but all we could do was meet each other after school, put in a call to Flo, then spend the rest of the day talking about it. As the days wore on, Diane became upset with Flo for not calling, regardless of what had happened. Flo was our friend, and she knew we depended on her. Why was she acting this way?

We would talk about getting new members, but we knew that the group would not be as dynamic without Flo. Looking back now, I feel that had Diane not seen Flo's energy as one of our main assets, she would have been just as happy to replace her.

We continued to call Flo's house every single day, but she never came to the phone. With the passing weeks our apprehension turned to fear. Something had to be wrong with Flo; something terrible had happened. But if so, why hadn't she told us? We were her best friends. None of it made any sense. How could a group that was making so much headway, that had had such potential, just lose it like that? I was learning some of life's hardest lessons: not to depend on anyone, to accept all of life's surprises, no matter what, and, finally, that nothing is ever permanent. I couldn't accept all this. It wasn't fair.

Weeks passed without word from Flo. We'd call every few days or so and get the usual response—"She doesn't want to talk to you"—and go back to our daydreams. Somehow Diane and I would pull it all back together again, but the longer we went without rehearsing or performing, the further the possibility seemed to slip from our grasp.

Our prayers were answered when Flo finally called. She nonchalantly asked, "How's everything been going?" She sounded distant and very strange when she asked if the three of us could get together the next day. Diane was obviously relieved, but acted as if Flo really had a lot of nerve just to call us like that, so casually, as if nothing had happened. As far as Diane was concerned, Blondie had better come with a good excuse.

We arranged to meet. The appointed time came and went and still no Flo. As the minutes ticked by, I began to get scared. Something was very wrong.

The minute I laid eyes on Flo all my gravest fears were confirmed. She was like another person. There was a faraway look in her eyes that was frightening. Everything about her was different. There was no sign that she was happy to see us, her skin was incredibly pale, and she had circles under eyes so large and dark that she seemed to be wearing a mask. Usually a hip dresser, Flo looked unkempt, and her labored steps made it seem as if she were in a trance.

Everything about Flo seemed to be running in slow motion. She'd start to say something, utter a few words, then falter, as if she had forgotten what she wanted to say. She was never totally comfortable being intimate with anyone, and today she avoided making eye contact with either of us, just staring straight ahead at nothing.

After some small talk, Flo eased her way into telling us what had happened. Her calm recitation of the facts had the mesmerizing quality of a primitive story.

It had all started one night several weeks before at the Graystone Ballroom. It was one of Frantic Ernie Durham's sock hops, which were considered safe entertainment for teens, since no alcohol was served and the admission was only 50 cents. This night, Flo was going to the dance with her brother Billy; Flo wasn't dating that much, and Mrs. Ballard would never let any of her daughters go out alone. Sometime during the evening the two got separated, but even when it began to get late, Flo didn't worry. Most of the kids were leaving, so she just stood near the door, expecting to see Billy any moment.

Someone called out her name, and, thinking it was Billy, Flo ran out to a car waiting in a darkened area beside the ballroom. At first she didn't recognize the fellow, but as he pulled his car closer to the curb, she realized he was someone she'd met, either through one of her brothers or maybe Jesse. The important thing was that she knew him and he could give her a lift home.

Once inside the car, Flo sat quietly. He didn't seem interested in conversation, so Flo hummed along to the radio, thinking how fortunate she was not to have to take a bus alone. Suddenly she noticed that none of the streets was familiar; the driver was on Woodward, but headed in the opposite direction of her home. When she told him he was making a mistake, he just kept on driving without saying a word. It was then that Flo knew something was wrong.

A sickening feeling came over her as he pulled the car to an abrupt stop on a dark, empty street. When Flo asked him why they'd stopped, he told her he was going to have sex with her. Though her initial shock had given way to fear, Flo still tried to act tough, and she bravely demanded that he take her home immediately. But he wasn't listening.

At this point in the story, Flo stopped and couldn't start talking again. Tears welled up in her eyes, and some time passed before she could speak again. Diane and I tried to comfort her, but we were scared too. Nothing like this had ever happened to anyone we knew, at least not to our knowledge. Finally Flo mumbled something nearly unintelligible. The only word I could make out was "knife." I leaned closer to Flo and asked her to repeat it, and as I came nearer to her I knew what people meant when they said fear has a smell. Flo's fear was almost tangible. I could see her suffering, and her eyes reflected a gamut of emotions—fright, embarrassment, distrust. I was shocked to realize some of those feelings were directed at Diane and me.

Finally Flo's words erupted from her. As her tears fell, she told us about how before she knew it, the man had put the knife to her throat and forced her into the backseat. She vainly tried to fight him off, but he wouldn't be stopped. He ripped away her panties and began fondling and kissing her all over. Flo was a virgin; she didn't understand what he was trying to do. She was repulsed and scared for her life. When she pleaded with him to stop because she'd never had sex, he ignored her. All she could say to us was, "He hurt me."

Worse than the rape itself was his attitude. When he had finished with her, he acted as if nothing had happened. He was sure she was just lying—that she knew the score. When he dropped her off at her house, he said, "Why are you so upset? The way you walk around . . ." The next day Flo wouldn't even remember where she was or the ride home. His words, though, would be with her always.

"Why did he do it?" Flo repeated over and over again. "I trusted him. I thought he was my friend. Why did he do it?"

Neither Diane nor I nor anyone in the world could ever answer that. Finally knowing what had happened to our friend left us more confused than ever. The brutality Flo had suffered at the hands of someone she trusted was beyond our comprehension. Before this day, boys had been just cute and fun and sweet. We knew now the world was a darker, uglier place.

All women who are raped suffer, some in different ways than others. In Flo's case the betrayal of trust was the greatest shock. Despite her self-assured attitude, she was an innocent. From this day on, I'd see Flo's basic personality undergo a metamorphosis, from being reticent and shy with a sassy front to being skeptical, cynical, and afraid of everyone and everything. We could never have pictured Flo needing help. Her will had brought the Primettes together, and few people would ever try to mess with her. But all that had changed.

My heart was wrenched at the thought of Flo's suffering. My anger over the fact that someone could do this to my friend faded into a quiet fear as I realized that what happened to Flo could have happened to any one of us, including me. When I saw Flo's pain, I became angry with Mrs. Ballard for keeping Flo from us when she needed her friends so badly. I know that Mrs. Ballard was only protecting Flo, but now I began to think about how little anyone could protect anybody, no matter how hard they tried. After this incident, Mrs. Ballard would try to keep Flo further and further from the rest of the world. Her family's love for Flo would become a guarded fortress, with Flo sequestered inside and everyone outside considered a stranger, an enemy. From this day on, Flo would turn to them, not us, and their advice would color her every move.

Flo never mentioned the rape to us again, except when she had to go to the police station to pick her attacker out of a lineup, and later when she testified against him in court. Flo was one of the very few women who ever get to see their rapists convicted and sent to prison. We all tried to be as supportive as we could, but the ordeal of the trial extracted yet another toll from Flo.

There was no question that Flo needed psychiatric help, but, living in an area where acutely ill kids were lucky to see a family doctor, we didn't think in those terms. Her family's background and attitude toward such things was old-fashioned; Mrs. Ballard believed that a mother's love could cure anything. In the meantime, Flo kept having nightmares. Her self-esteem and self-image had been shattered; she became vulnerable in so many ways. Walking down the street with her, I'd catch her looking over her shoulder or off in the distance, checking out every man who even vaguely resembled the man who had raped her.

During the time we'd lost contact with Flo, she had also stopped going to school. Now she was trying to pick up the pieces, and getting back with the group was her first step back into the world. School came next. She soon became wholeheartedly involved with the Primettes again, and I believe this was therapeutic for her. On the outside, she started acting like the old Flo we knew. In our ignorance, we assumed that this meant everything would be all right. But her new belief that no one—not even friends—could be trusted would haunt her for the rest of her life.

Diane and I never discussed it again, not even between ourselves. I chalk that up to our youth. But even today most people still don't

know how to respond to rape. What Flo experienced was just a variation of what we now call date rape. Men read different messages in
women's mannerisms, dress, words. A rapist's favorite explanation is
that the victim "really wanted it," even if she screamed and tried to
fight. In Flo's case, her body and her attitude sent a message that told
this guy what he did was okay.

The man who raped Flo killed part of her that night. My friend
was never the same.

# CHAPTER 7

Both Diane and I told Jesse that we wished he and Flo were still going together. Flo's moodiness was beginning to worry us, and since Jesse was the only person outside the group or her family whom she told about the rape, we thought that if they were back together, Flo would be happy again. Meanwhile, whatever doubts Mrs. Ballard had about Flo's being in the group intensified. She thought it was a waste of time, and I now wonder if she would have let Flo go on at all if it weren't for Jesse. After the rape, Jesse had to promise Mrs. Ballard he would walk her home and make sure she got in early after our rehearsals at Brewster Center.

Jesse was probably the only other person who truly knew Flo well, and the change in her after the rape bothered him as much as it did us. "Flo changed after her attack," he once said. "She was a different person. She used to be a little mischievous, and had that haughty air. She was really happy. After that, there was no laughter, no fun left in her."

We were relieved to have Flo back and be a group again, but the weeks in limbo had destroyed our momentum. And we still hadn't replaced Betty. We had lost so much precious time; making a record took on new urgency. We got back to playing all the local places we could, including the Twenty Grand Club, *the* nightspot. Frantic Ernie Durham and the other sock-hop jocks were still hiring us, too. We loved it but began to feel we had sort of outgrown it, too.

Flo's disappearance hadn't dampened Richard Morris' enthusiasm for working with us, and so, that fall, his plan for us went into action. He arranged for us to begin recording for Robert West at the Flick and Contour studios. At the time, Flick and Contour were pretty hot. The group the Contours, for example, took their name from the label, and among the artists recording with West then were the Falcons.

Unlike Milton, Richard could not afford to support the Primettes financially. We made the best of our homemade costumes and followed our own instincts about hairstyles, makeup, and the fine points of staging. Still, Robert West liked us enough to record us. We were thrilled when he told us a new label would be created just for us—LuPine. Why that name was chosen, I'm not sure. Richard had two songs for us: "Tears of Sorrow," for which Richard had recorded the music tracks at Hitsville, and which Diane would sing lead on; and a rock ballad, "Pretty Baby," for me. Once we learned the songs, we started rehearsing day and night.

The morning of the session, Richard, Flo, Diane, a male singer named Alonzo, and two other female singers, Barbara Randolph and Betty Kendrick, met and took the same bus down Woodward Avenue to the Flick studios. Richard brought along Betty and Barbara because he was worried that without Betty McGlown, our vocals wouldn't sound full enough. Richard was so furious with me for being late that he told Flo she could sing lead on "my" song, "Pretty Baby," and she would have if I hadn't gotten to the studio within minutes of the others. Punctuality was never one of my strong points.

The "studio" was actually the drab little basement of a small house on Forest Street. It was a hot day, but each of us wore our nicest cotton blouses and skirts with stockings—and matching shoes and bags, of course. When we walked in Wilson Pickett was there rehearsing with the Falcons. He looked and acted pretty much the same as he does now; he was what we considered a real street guy. He had just been chosen to assume Joe Stubbs' (the Four Tops' Levi's brother) place as the group's lead singer. Wilson was only one of many up-and-coming young stars we crossed paths with in the early years.

Richard had assembled a great backing band for us that included Falcons keyboardist Willie Schofield, Charlie Gabrielle on sax and flute, a guitarist named Eugene Crew, bassist Charlie O., drummer Benny Benjamin, and Marvin Tarplin, the onetime Primette.

Alonzo was a dark-skinned guy with shiny processed hair and a high falsetto. He may have been one of Richard's other clients. Richard was no doubt trying to economize, and so, before our session, we all sang backup on Alonzo's record, and on Eddie Floyd's. Next we did the backup for our first recording, "Tears of Sorrow," and Diane sang lead. We all liked "Tears" but were convinced that "Pretty Baby" would be the hit. Both songs were typical of the girl-group records out then—self-pitying lyrics about the boy who got away. Because our voices aren't really separated as clearly as they would be on later records, you can really hear Flo on the backgrounds, her strong, soulful voice overpowering everything—even Diane's lead on "Tears." (Years later, HDH would have Flo stand as far as seventeen feet from the microphone, while I stood right in front of it; that's how strong her voice was.)

Even our first recording session had to have problems. Diane and Barbara were arguing. Barbara thought we should all follow Richard's instructions to the letter, while Diane wanted to sing it her way; she didn't want to follow the melody line as closely as Richard wanted her to. Flo and I had become almost immune to Diane's little outbursts, but you could see that people who didn't know her well took these things to heart. Flo and I were too excited to pay much attention. After the session Willie Schofield gave us a ride back to the Flick and Contour offices, and a secretary there made us a big lunch. We ate our sandwiches and happily daydreamed aloud about our new "hit."

"Girl, do you think they'll play it on the radio soon?" Flo asked no one in particular.

"Blondie, they'll be playing 'Pretty Baby' all over the country soon," Betty Kendrick replied.

"I sure hope so," Flo said quietly.

"I know 'Pretty Baby' will be a big hit. I can just feel it!" As always, I was the most optimistic one, and why not? It was about time things started going our way.

That was the last time we ever saw Barbara and Betty again. Both later married; Barbara is a minister, and still singing in Detroit.

For some reason, Richard wasn't happy with "Pretty Baby," though he never let on about it to us. As far as we were concerned, it was enough just to hear our voices. In the end, however, what any of us thought didn't make one bit of difference. A few weeks after the session, with our first records pressed and ready to ship, Robert West's distributor, B&H—an independent black distributor in Detroit—was targeted for a payola investigation. Without anyone's guilt or innocence proven, our record was as good as gone. The news hit us like a bolt of lightning. The records were eventually released—about twenty years later, in Japan, and some found their way to Great Britain.

Our morale was slipping, and the revived feelings of unity the recording inspired were crushed by dissension. The one thing Richard could do for us now was help us find Betty McGlown's replacement. Not having a fourth member was threatening our bookings.

I was still very close to John L. and I.V. Pippin. I had never forgotten the love and warmth they'd given me, and after I moved to the Projects, I continued to visit them and keep up my childhood friendship with Jackie Burkes.

Jackie was singing in a group in southwest Detroit, but I was so confident that the Primettes were on to something that I tried to woo her to join us. Once, when it seemed that Flo was never coming back, I'd given Jackie a big sell about the Primettes and even introduced her to Diane over the phone. From the beginning she and Diane didn't get along, and Jackie could never understand why.

One day that fall, I took Diane over to John L. and I.V.'s house, where Jackie was going to audition for us. After we'd run through a few songs, I said, "Diane, see how nice our blend is?"

Diane made it obvious that she was anything but impressed; Jackie was confused and disheartened. "Maybe she doesn't want me," she said.

"Don't pay any attention to her," I replied. "She's funny like that. When you get to know her, it'll be fine."

"Mary," Jackie insisted, "this chick just doesn't like me."

We sang a couple more songs, like Gladys Knight and the Pips' "Letter Full of Tears," and we were having fun, but there was a definite lack of warmth between my two good friends. Finally Jackie told me to forget it. She could see how things would be with Diane and she wasn't interested. I tried to convince her otherwise, but after getting the cold shoulder from Diane, Jackie would have been crazy to pursue it. We were desperate for another girl, but I knew deep in my heart that Jackie had made the right decision.

Word was still out that the Primettes needed a fourth member. Like me, Flo had studied music all through school. One of her teachers, knowing that Flo's group needed another singer, remembered that Barbara Martin sang with Richard Street. Since Flo knew Richard, the teacher told Flo about Barbara, then Flo told Richard Morris. None of us knew Barbara personally, but we all knew she was the tall, pretty girl who danced like a dream every weekend at the Graystone Ballroom. We didn't even know if she could sing all that well, but we were hoping.

For some reason, I was the only Primette with Richard when we met Barbara. We could hear right away that Barbara was not a great singer, but she had a wonderful attitude about the Primettes that was very appealing. When we all got together a few days later, we all got along very well.

Flo and Barbara seemed to have an instant rapport, and we all got along beautifully. No matter how anyone acted toward Barbara, she could just win them over. Diane's ego was still smarting from Betty's reprimands, and so Barbara's open personality was a great help. The tension in the group caused by Diane's conflict with Betty disappeared. We'd suffered so many disappointments in such a short time —we'd only been together now a couple months short of two years— we really appreciated having Barbara around. Barbara joining marked a turning point in the group relationships. Feeling like a whole group again, the four of us couldn't have been happier. We assumed our cheerful dispositions and kept building one another up: We were great, we were stars, we were the Primettes. I was just happy that we were back on the track. I crossed my fingers and prayed that Barbara would have the commitment to stick with us. The prospect of another change was unthinkable.

The situation with LuPine was out of our hands. Years later, I would learn that B&H's problems with the payola investigators were the product of racism; only black distributors had been harassed. I was still too young to fully comprehend the significance of this.

Only days after we'd discovered Barbara, our gigs petered out, and we didn't hear from Richard for a few days. We gave it little thought until Flo told us that Richard had been arrested for a parole violation. Not again, we thought. We'd heard of the triple whammy, but our bad luck was running in fives and sixes. We questioned Flo, but she knew no more about it than we did. What were we going to do now? we wondered aloud to one another. We knew the answer: Go back to Berry Gordy and Motown. The only question was, would they want us?

Berry Gordy hailed from a prominent, middle-class Detroit family. His parents, Berry and Bertha, had moved up from the South in 1922, but, unlike most blacks who came North during that era, Berry Gordy, Sr.—or Pops, as we all called him—was an experienced businessman, having run and managed his family's farm after his father's death. In an environment where whites controlled most black people's property, Pops had saved his family's assets by learning all he could about business and law. He believed in hard work, discipline, and education, and, after several tough years in Detroit, eventually established his own businesses, including a printing shop. The eight Gordy children —Esther, Gwen, Anna, Loucye, Robert, Fuller, George, and Berry— would find varying degrees of success in life. None of the others would realize a dream as grand as Berry's.

Ironically, as a young man, Berry seemed to show the least promise of all the Gordy offspring. By the mid-fifties, at age twenty-seven, Berry had been a prize-fighter, serviceman, jazz record-store owner, auto assembly-line worker, and husband. He had children to support and no desire to join his brothers working in the family business. Berry had worked hard, but so far had failed to find either his niche or the kind of money he wanted. While living in his sister Loucye's house following his separation from his first wife, Thelma, Berry was writing songs.

The Flame Show Bar was the Apollo Theater of Detroit, and every major black performer played there at least once. For black entertainers, the Flame Show Bar was as prestigious as the Latin Quarter, New York's Copacabana, or the Hollywood Palladium. Many of the old-time performers who played there had started in vaudeville and burlesque. A few black artists then were fortunate enough to work both circuits, but they were the exception. In the fifties, though, Sam Cooke, Sarah Vaughan, Della Reese, Brook Benton, B. B. King, and Bill Williams were regulars at the Flame, and Berry's sisters Anna and Gwen, who ran the photography concession there, introduced their brother to anyone who would listen to his songs.

Knowing Berry as I do, I'm not surprised that he made headway as quickly as he did. He was confident and determined. There were lots of young entrepreneurs like Berry around in the fifties, and we were fortunate to meet and work with some of them. Milton, Jesse, Richard—they all had the same idea. In those days, some of these men were looked upon as hustlers and, to some degree, I guess they were. The music business, though, was unlike any other hustle. Smooth talk went only so far; sooner or later you had to deliver the goods. Berry started looking at other business people and companies, analyzing the way they worked with the same discriminating eye for detail and judgment he applied to songwriting.

From the start, Berry was guided by the bottom line. While other young writers toiled in solitude, Berry sought out collaborators. He had exceptional instincts about melodies and knew what was commercial, and while he wasn't especially good at writing lyrics, he knew what kind of lyrics made for hits.

One of the first people Berry teamed up with was Billy Davis, an aspiring young musician who was dating his sister Gwen. Davis introduced Berry to the Reverend C. L. Franklin. Each of the reverend's daughters—Aretha, Erma, and Carolyn—was known around Detroit as a great singer, but Berry and Billy were interested only in Erma.

The Reverend Franklin told Berry that he should work with Aretha, but Berry didn't care for Aretha's singing style. Erma sang on some of the demonstration records, or demos, Billy and Berry made for publishing companies and record labels, in the hope that one of the songs might be recorded by an established act. Because demos aren't finished records and generally are never heard by the public, they can be very basic, maybe just someone singing to minimal accompaniment. There's no telling what Berry, Billy, and Erma's early demos sounded like, but Berry and Billy (who wrote under the name Tyran Carlo) spent a great deal of time crafting them. Often Berry had just scraped together enough money to cover the studio costs and the musicians' fees, so every detail had to be carefully planned beforehand and the demo cut in as little time as possible.

Berry was getting around and making contact with other young writers, singers, and musicians. Gradually, Loucye's basement became a hangout where songs were written and rehearsed. Any friend of a friend with the slightest bit of talent was welcome.

"It seems unusual," Janie Bradford recalls, "but at that particular time in Detroit there were no outlets like there are today. Berry was into what he was doing and wanted to bring in whoever he could to help him build it." At this point, Berry still hadn't defined what "it" was, but he was headed in the right direction.

In 1957 Berry Gordy met two young men who changed his life. Berry either was introduced to Jackie Wilson during one of the latter's engagements at the Flame, or knew him from their days as Golden Gloves boxers. At the time, Wilson was one of the hottest and sexiest singers around. Women were wild about him, and one look at any film of him shows why. Wilson had been solo for about a year, and was already known to fans, having replaced Clyde McPhatter four years earlier in Billy Ward and His Dominoes, but he still hadn't scored a hit. Berry, Billy, and Gwen started writing for Wilson, and Billy and Berry's "Reet Petite" was Jackie Wilson's first big pop success.

Janie Bradford was a fourteen-year-old poet when she met Berry shortly after the success of "Reet Petite." Though Berry was making a name for himself, Janie was naturally more impressed by the singer. She and Berry's first conversation ended with Janie telling Berry she could outwrite him any day, and Berry promising to take her up on her challenge. She gave him her phone number and then forgot all about it.

A few months later, Berry and a friend turned up on Janie's doorstep. When he had to remind her who he was, she was embarrassed and invited them in. She showed Berry her collection of poems, and she and Berry began working on songs together.

Berry and his collaborators kept Wilson in hits for almost two years, with "Lonely Teardrops," "To Be Loved," "I'll Be Satisfied," and "That's Why (I Love You So)," one of my favorites. Wilson's album *Lonely Teardrops*, which included two of Janie's compositions, went gold, and Berry's place in the music business seemed secure.

One summer afternoon Berry met the Miracles—then known as the Matadors—when they came to audition for Jackie Wilson's manager. Because of their four-boy, one-girl lineup, the manager thought they were too much like the Platters, so he passed. Berry got to talking with lead singer Smokey and soon learned that Smokey also wrote poems and song lyrics. Smokey would later admit that most of what he had written at that point wasn't even that good, but Berry saw something in his work worth developing. As he had done with Janie and would do later with others, Berry told Smokey his ideas on what made great lyrics. They had to be written in the first person, usually in the present tense, and they had to have some kind of clever gimmick in the use of the words.

Things seemed to be going Berry's way until Jackie Wilson's manager decided to move his offices from Chicago to New York. This, coupled with Berry's realization of just how little of a hit record's profits went to the writers, convinced him that he needed more control. He'd already started producing his demos and a few acts' records because that was the only way he could faithfully translate to vinyl the sounds he heard in his head. Still, no matter how good a song was, the odds were against it being a hit, unless a star recorded it. And Berry had no idea when or if he would ever hook up with someone as hot as Wilson again. Erma Franklin had dropped out of the music business, and the Miracles hadn't yet found the right song.

Along came Eddie Holland, a young singer Berry had met at the Graystone Ballroom, and who he thought sounded just like Jackie Wilson. In 1958 Berry released Eddie Holland's "You," his brother Brian's "Shock," and the Miracles' "Got a Job." He also met Raynoma Liles, who would become his second wife, business partner, and collaborator.

Soon Berry, Ray, and anyone else around them was working on songs. Thomas "Beans" Bowles, who would play a major role at Motown in years to come, recalled working with Berry back then. "Berry invited me over to his and Ray's two-room apartment. I was surprised they had a piano in a little place like that. They were rehearsing some stuff, and Joe Hunter was there, too. Ray wanted me to be in on the music thing."

Robert Bateman, a singer and talent scout, was acting as engineer. Like everybody around then, Bateman wore more than a couple hats, and was also a member of the Rayber Voices, a background vocals group that included Ray, Brian Holland, and others.

Late in 1958 Berry began recording Marv Johnson, another singing songwriter. Marv recalls, "I went around to Berry's house and took some of my material. One of the songs was 'Come to Me.' That was a song I had written, but I got a lot of help from him and his wife as far as producing was concerned, with chord changes and things. The song originally was mine, but by the time it came out, the writing credits were shared with Berry Gordy."

Marv Johnson's "Come to Me" was Berry's first big hit in early 1959, but because Berry had leased it to a major record company his take wasn't as large as it could have been. That summer the Miracles' "Bad Girl" did well, but Johnson was Berry's hottest act, and "You Got What It Takes" and "I'm Coming Home" followed in 1960. In the meantime, two other men had joined the Gordy venture, Lamont Dozier and Mickey Stevenson.

On the advice of his protégé, Smokey Robinson, Berry started his own label, management firm, and studios. He'd already moved the operation into a two-story house that had been a photographer's studio on West Grand Boulevard, and now he set to work converting it into a recording facility and offices, with living space on the second floor for him, Ray, and her kids. It became a second home to all the writers. No one thought of it as a job; they just loved being there. There weren't yet deadlines to meet and orders to follow. Things just seemed to happen.

One evening, Richard Morris was listening to Barrett Strong, a young singer. "Barrett was trying to start his career," Richard recalls. "He hadn't made a record yet. I was in the control room putting some machines together, but I also had the monitor open so that I could hear because I always did enjoy Barrett.

"Berry came down and—I'll show you what kind of mind he had. 'So,' he said, 'what is that Barrett is playing?' Let's go down and listen to it.'

"So we went down to the studio and Berry starts nodding his head.

'Hey, man,' he says to Barrett, 'can you change that up just a little bit?' So Barrett started changing it up—just a little bit—and came up with a new rhythm. Berry said, 'That's great. Richard, go put this on tape,' which I did.

"The next morning Berry called Janie Bradford down for the lyrics. She had written something but it wasn't what he had in mind. 'See,' he said, 'I wanted something like I need a new pair of shoes. Well, give me a title of something that everybody wants.'"

"Janie replied, 'Money, that's what I want.' And there was Berry's first big hit."

And "Money" was an apt title. Berry's cohorts loved their work, but very few got paid, and those who did made maybe eight dollars a week. Coming from the ghetto these kids were hip that money was what they wanted—like all of us, they longed for the freedom they thought money would buy.

Gradually people on the local scene began to regard Berry as the man with the golden touch. Over the next decade, some of our generation's best writers, musicians, and performers would find their way to Berry. But not just anybody got in and not everybody stayed. From the start Berry surrounded himself with only the best and the brightest. Janie Bradford had her sights set on becoming an attorney; Eddie Holland was studying to become a certified public accountant. You had to have brains, energy, ambition, and a degree of class to pass muster with Berry.

By the time we returned in the winter of 1960, Motown was firmly established and running very much like a family. Loyalty, honesty, and obedience were demanded and often gladly given. In the days before people got paid, Smokey brought in Miss Lily, a woman who had cooked for him most of his life, to cook up hot meals. These big "family" meals were the closest thing to board meetings we had in those days. Projects were discussed, assignments given, gossip exchanged.

Not surprisingly, Berry's parents also became part of Hitsville. All of the Gordys seemed to have been born with the gift of gab, and I'm pretty sure they all inherited it from Mrs. Gordy. And Pops was a favorite. No one was immune to the Gordy charm, least of all the Primettes. Pops was a sweet gentleman fond of making wolfish remarks to attractive young girls. Flo was his favorite, and we'd tease her about Pops' flirting.

The making of Motown was not unlike the building of the pyramids. Countless people—some known and others long since forgotten —toiled literally night and day. Of course, most of us were teenagers still living at home, so we didn't make the same demands independent adults would. And Berry inspired and excited us. Berry himself was something of an outcast, still not being taken seriously outside the music business. Berry saw the bigger picture, grasped the importance of details, and often found ways of getting things done other people either couldn't or wouldn't tackle.

When Berry realized that he couldn't write great songs by himself, he used other people. As Motown expanded, he would take this approach one step further, seeking not only the best person for a job, but the best that person could offer. Berry was a perceptive judge of character and a quick study of almost anything. He knew how to get people to do his bidding. He knew their talents and weaknesses. After years of observing him, I believe he often knew more about us than we knew about ourselves.

# CHAPTER 8

When we got back to Hitsville everyone there seemed overjoyed to see us. We had been away only about four months, but the way our friends there carried on, it might have been years. Before we could fully explain our absence to anyone, we spotted Berry coming out of the control room on his way down to Studio A. He hugged each of us, we introduced him to Barbara, and then he told us to come into the studio with him.

Stepping down into that basement studio was like entering a whole new world. The musicians there who knew us gave us little waves and nods of acknowledgment. After that day, we could usually be found either sitting in the lobby or scrunched up together on the stairs to the studio, peering through the smoke at the musicians and singers working below.

Mary Wells was soon to become Motown's first premiere female artist. Although her first big hit was still a year away, she was cutting tracks regularly with Motown and was also a songwriter; Berry decided to sign her after she sang one of her own songs for him. Doing background vocals for her was one of our first assignments. We sang with her on a number of tunes, and though I can't remember all of them —especially since Motown's artists sometimes recorded many times the number of songs that were released—I believe they included "He Holds His Own," "Honey Boy" (which the Supremes later recorded), and "You Lost the Sweetest Boy."

Mary's voice had a sweet, sexy quality I admired. None of the songs we cut with her became hits, but I thought she had a certain star quality, and tried to learn from watching her. She was only eighteen, about a year or so older than we were, yet she was definitely more sophisticated.

"Can't that girl sing? Whoo!" Flo said as we left a Wells session.

"Honey," Barbara replied, "Mary Wells sounds real good."

As we'd sit on our favorite bench in the lobby, we'd catch people walking through. Many of the fellows, especially Brian Holland, would stop and remark on how beautiful we each were or tease us. Humorous come-ons would be matched line for line by Barbara, while Flo and I would laugh it off. Diane would play coy. Other girls who were friends of ours, like Janie, would comment on our clothes or make small talk. The Motown scene was completely new to Barbara and she tried acting nonchalant, but one look at her when a celebrity passed by or when she got to see a session in progress and you could see she was starstruck.

Out of curiosity, I once asked Janie what she thought of us, and was not entirely surprised when she said that she thought we were rather naïve. I knew Janie could be brutally honest, so I braced myself. But when she said that we were good, though "nothing to knock your socks off," I was stunned. Maybe she was right. She had no ulterior motive, and I generally valued what she had to say, but this was something else. My faith in the Primettes was unshakable, and after that I never asked anyone outside the group for advice about anything. What would they know, anyway? We'd stuck it out for almost two whole years and we were going to make it. What other people thought didn't matter anymore.

After a few weeks of being everyone's favorite prodigal daughters, the fuss over our return died down, and before long we were wondering when we'd finally get to make our own record. Fame wasn't our goal and money wasn't yet that important; we just wanted to make music. Despite our youthful impatience, we knew better than to pester Berry about this. We'd learned our lesson and weren't going to blow it again. It was enough that we made sure to catch Berry's attention whenever we saw him. I was sure he'd get around to us someday.

In late 1960 Mrs. Ballard used the insurance and Social Security money she received following her husband's death to buy a new detached house on the west side of town. Even though the new home was larger than the row house in the Projects, it was always filled with family. Because Flo was now technically living outside the Northeastern district, she enrolled in Northwestern High School. We were all in our junior year of high school, still wondering what the future might hold. As far as our parents knew, all of us were going to college, but we weren't so sure. We had school and the normal teenage responsibilities and headaches. I was still working at the record store, making next to no money but bringing home copies of all the latest records. I'd hole up in my room, doing my nails or setting my hair, and play my current favorite hit over and over again. "Girl," my mother would say as I played "Will You Love Me Tomorrow" by the Shirelles for the hundredth time, "you're going to play those grooves smooth." I'd just laugh. My little sister Cat would sometimes join me in dancing to the songs. My brother, like most young boys, was seldom around and hardly useful when he was. I adored them both.

Even with all the activities—school, chores, dates, rehearsals, sock hops, and the daily pilgrimage to Hitsville—I never felt tired or pressured. I'd go to West Grand Boulevard every day, never knowing what to expect but praying for a miracle. No one ever said anything about us hanging around. We were always ladylike and fashionably dressed. We spent so much time sitting on that bench that I'm amazed we didn't leave fanny prints in it. Everyone knew our names, but soon we were known collectively as "the girls."

One day Smokey popped into the lobby on his way to a session with Mary Wells. While we were all chatting, he suddenly got the idea to use us on Mary's record. We were so thrilled at the chance to record we almost thought we would die. Then Smokey told us that handclaps were all he had in mind.

By early 1961, more and more acts were migrating to Hitsville. Soon we were joined at Hitsville by our old affiliates, the Primes. A lot of things had happened since we'd last seen one another, and now Eddie Kendricks and Paul Williams, with Eldridge Bryant, and Otis Williams and Melvin Franklin of the Distants, were the Temptations. Over the years, the Tempts' lineup would change, with old friends like Richard Street joining later on.

Otis Williams and Melvin Franklin had first gotten together while both were attending Northwestern High. As Melvin recalls, he first knew Otis only by sight. When Otis first approached Melvin, Melvin ran like hell away from him, thinking he was a gang member intent on beating him up and taking his lunch money. Shortly after that, Melvin returned home one day to find Otis on his doorstep, waiting to ask Melvin's mother if Melvin could join his group, the Distants.

"In truth, I was really scared of Otis because he had a process and looked like a tough customer," Melvin recalls. "I would never have thought that he and I would be cut from the same cloth."

Melvin became a Distant and finagled a place in the group for his cousin, Richard Street. This version of the Distants broke up. Otis,

Melvin, and El Bryant, another Distant, got together with Eddie Kendricks, but Eddie refused to join unless they took his friend, Paul Williams, too. At this point in the group's history, it's unclear whether or not Richard was still an official member, but everyone recalls him being around. Somehow, though, the chemistry between Richard and Eddie just wasn't right, and Richard stopped hanging around with them altogether. Richard wouldn't finally join the Tempts until 1971, when Paul Williams quit.

Melvin's mother belonged to a ladies' club with Anna and Gwen Gordy. When Mrs. Franklin mentioned that her son was singing with a group, the Gordy sisters suggested that they audition for their brother. So Otis Williams and the Distants sang their repertoire for Berry, a cappella. Berry was very impressed with the group, but he didn't like their name. He wasn't ready to sign them right away, either, but the guys started hanging around Hitsville anyway.

Newly signed to Motown were the Contours. They would have only a few hits, and have been sadly overlooked in the Motown story, but they were good friends of ours and lots of fun, especially during the tours.

Billy Gordon, Billy Hoggs, Joe Billingslea, Sylvester Potts, and Hubert Johnson started out in 1959 as the Blenders. They would walk up and down Twelfth Street singing in bars for beers, just trying to perfect their harmonies. The first record company they approached was Flick and Contour studios. Wes Higgins wanted one of their songs, "Come On and Be Mine," but didn't want them. Next stop: Hitsville. Berry liked the three songs they sang; Raynoma liked the songs and the guys. But Berry didn't like the guys. They struck him as being too hardcore R&B, which wasn't Berry's taste.

Unbeknownst to the other group members, Hubert Johnson was Jackie Wilson's cousin. Hubert took them all to Jackie's home in Detroit, where Wilson kept them waiting for an hour and a half before he'd see them. Later, Wilson told them that he was just testing their patience to see how badly they really wanted to sing. After they explained their problem, Jackie called up his friend Berry Gordy and arranged another appointment for them later that day.

"We went right back to Motown," Joe remembered, "and sang the same three songs *again*, and signed the contracts."

Another future Motown star was also there by now. Martha Reeves was working as Mickey Stevenson's secretary in the A&R department. We knew Martha because she and her group, the Del-Phis, also rehearsed at the House of Beauty. The group had a different original lineup, but when we met them, it was Gloria Jean Williams, Annette Sterling, and Rosalind Ashford. After Martha told her boss Mickey about her group, they got into Motown as background singers. Because they had recorded with and were technically under contract to another label, they recorded as the Vels.

Gloria eventually left the group, and Berry decided to sign them, but first they needed a new name. Martha took "Van" from Van Dyke Street, and "Della," for the popular singer Della Reese, and came up with "the Vandellas." They backed Marvin Gaye on several of his early hits, including "Pride and Joy," "Stubborn Kind of Fellow," "Hitch Hike," and "Can I Get a Witness," and often toured with him. Like most of us girls at Motown, Martha had a crush on the handsome, soft-spoken young Marvin.

In December we got our first shot in the studio. Freddy Gorman —who'd been our mailman in the Projects—had written "I Want a Guy." We didn't care about what kind of song it was; we could make a hit out of anything, we thought. We spent days with Freddy, trying to perfect the harmonies, which was usually the hardest thing about learning a new song. We got to the studio early the day of the session. Berry was very excited for us; he thought "I Want a Guy" was a good song for the Primettes to record. He took us aside, offered some words of encouragement, and promised to come down later and see how we were doing.

The song was written to sound coy and girlish, so it needed a high lead vocal, and Diane did it. The recording went off without a hitch. Berry showed up later and suggested some changes to the musicians and discussed altering the tempo with Freddy; he also added and deleted a few words. Everyone agreed with everything Berry said.

Having finished the first track so quickly, we decided to go ahead and record the flip side, figuring that the sooner both sides were finished, the sooner the release. Diane also took the lead on "Never Again," a slower song in the style of the Chantels' "Maybe." When the four of us were all done, Freddy hugged each of us and praised us for our good work. He took us out for a bite to eat and then drove us home.

After "I Want a Guy" was finally released, Freddy complained to us in private that Berry had heard the song before we recorded it, changed a few words, and then took credit for co-writing it. Freddy's resentment was short-lived, though; we all knew we were lucky just to be able to make records, and the incident was forgotten.

One of our favorite people there was Smokey. He was also one of the busiest, but he was always sweet. "How are you young ladies doing?" he'd casually inquire on his way from an office to a studio and then back again, nonchalantly delivering news we hoped would change our lives: "I've got a song I want to use you on," or "This I just wrote would be perfect for you girls," he'd say just before disappearing again. Each time Smokey mentioned recording we'd eagerly pipe up, "Use us!" "We're ready!"

We weren't even signed to Motown yet; still, Berry assigned us to Smokey. We were all pleased that the first song we got to record with Smokey was a Miracles tune, "Who's Loving You." Because it was a ballad, I assumed I would be singing the lead, as I always had. I stood in the studio that day, expecting Smokey to hand the lead sheet to me. When he gave it to Diane instead, my heart sank. There was nothing I could say, and in the excitement of recording, I forgot my disappointment and turned my attention to singing the best I could on what I hoped would be our first hit record.

We were earnest and professional, but, being young girls, we started off the session laughing, with Flo and me teasing Barbara about her new boyfriend. We knew the song so well that we thought recording would be a breeze, but Smokey was a perfectionist, and he would stop us repeatedly because one of us was always too loud— usually Barbara. The technology then didn't make it easy for producers to do punch-ins—rerecordings of just the few seconds of a take that needed to be corrected—so a perfect recording had to be literally perfect from the first second to the last.

We had come to the session straight from school, and the studio —which we called the sweat shop—was so hot we just weren't concentrating. Diane was in one of the two vocalists' booths and the three of us were all crowded into the other. When we reached the part where Diane sings the words "My life, my love," and we had to repeat them, Barbara sang loud and flat. It was such a sad song, but the three of us stood in our booth cracking up. Of course Diane didn't see this happen, and we hoped that the goof wouldn't be so obvious on the playback. Today I laugh when I play that track from *Meet the Supremes*; it doesn't even sound that bad. We were certain "Who's Loving You" would be a hit. Diane's voice had lost some of its nasal tone and was developing a more confident, brassy sound.

One day in early January 1961, Berry called us into his office and offered to sign us. We were ecstatic. "But," he added, "you girls need

That's me at the age of three in Chicago. I was all dressed up to move to Detroit to live with my aunt and uncle, and I wasn't about to let go of my doll, or my Oreo cookie! (*Mary Wilson Collection*)

My brother Roosevelt, my sister Cat, and me in 1955. (*Mary Wilson Collection*)

Our first manager, Milton Jenkins,
before he started wearing his sharkskin suits.
(*Mary Wilson Collection*)

The Primes were our brother group
when we were starting out.
They named us the Primettes.
(*Mary Wilson Collection*)

The original Primettes in 1959, before the Motown Artist Development Department got a hold of us. Left to right: Betty Travis, me, Flo, and Diane. My little cousin Cynthia wanted to be part of the act too! (*Mary Wilson Collection*)

Before there were the Supremes, we were the Primettes. These were the dresses that Diane and I made with the help of my Aunt Moneva. Clockwise from the top: Diane, Flo, me, and Barbara Diane Martin, 1961. (*Mary Wilson Collection*)

My graduation photo from Northeastern High School, January 1962.
My goal: to one day write a book.
(*Mary Wilson Collection*)

Left: Florence and I always wanted to see our names up in lights, but on our summer 1964 tour, it looked like this was as close as we would come. Later that year "Where Did Our Love Go" became our first number-one hit. (*Mary Wilson Collection*) Below: Annette of the Vandellas and Flo sharing a room on the 1962 Motown tour. (*Rosalind Ashford*)

Above: Mary Wells and Diane on the first Motown tour in 1962. (*Rosalind Ashford*) Right: When Florence laughed, everyone around her laughed too. This was taken on the 1962 Motown tour. (*Rosalind Ashford*)

One of the Motown family's benefits for Beans Bowles, after the car accident on the 1962 Motown Revue tour. Beans is the tall one standing behind "Little" Stevie Wonder. (*Mary Wilson Collection*)

The "no-hit" Supremes at the Apollo Theater, New York City, 1962. (*Mary Wilson Collection*)

This was our first photo session as a trio.
(*Mark Bego Collection*)

On the bus: Diane sleeping next to one of the guys on Dick Clark's Caravan of Stars, 1964. (*Mary Wilson Collection*)

Below: Flo, Diane, and I get our first taste of fish and chips in London. (*Mary Wilson Collection*)

Left: The first time we went to England. We heard about "A Foggy Day in London Town," so we brought our umbrellas. (*Mary Wilson Collection*)

Below: Our first trip to London, 1964. Berry decided we needed chaperones, so he brought the whole Motown staff. Left to right: Butch Edwards, Diane, me, Barney Ales, Flo, Esther Edwards, and Berry. Ales was the man who made the Supremes a "pop" act on the record charts. (*Beans Bowles*)

While in Paris, Flo and I couldn't resist seeing *all* of the historical sights. (*Mary Wilson Collection*)

In London. (*Carl Feuerbacher Collection*)

The Motown Revue in England, 1965. Left to right: the Temptations, Stevie Wonder, Smokey Robinson and the Miracles, the Supremes, and Martha Reeves and the Vandellas. (*Mary Wilson Collection*)

On our 1965 tour to London to tape the *Ready, Steady, Go* show. I'm holding Florence's fox fur, and Diane's holding Smokey Robinson. (*Mary Wilson Collection*)

Flo, Diane, and I on one of our first television appearances, *The Bill Kennedy Show* in Detroit, 1965. (*Mary Wilson Collection*)

Below left: The Supremes on the TV show *What's My Line* in 1965. (*Allan Poe Collection*) Below right: Things go better with Coke! Diane, Flo and I singing a rewritten version of "Baby Love" as a Coca-Cola jingle. (*Mary Wilson Collection*)

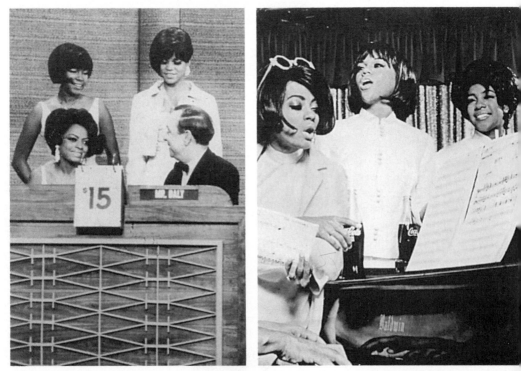

One of our early publicity shots. It wasn't long before our wigs became as famous as we were! (*Michael Ochs Archives*)

Many people thought that Florence should be the center of attention in the Supremes. Here she is proudly in the spotlight. (*Mary Wilson Collection*)

One of our early publicity shots. It wasn't long before our wigs became as famous as we were! (*Michael Ochs Archives*)

Many people thought that Florence should be the center of attention in the Supremes. Here she is proudly in the spotlight. (*Mary Wilson Collection*)

Florence and I checking out the crowd from the window of our limousine, while our chaperones weren't looking: "Girl, did you see that guy?" (*Mary Wilson Collection*)

Diane being interviewed in our hotel suite. By now, Flo and I were on our way to being seen and not heard. (*Mary Wilson Collection*)

This was one of our most famous publicity shots.
*(James Kriegsmann/Mary Wilson Archives)*

a different name. Primettes won't do." He told us to come up with suggestions. We didn't really want to change our name at all; we really liked Primettes. But Berry had already set the date for the contract signing, so we had about a week to come up with something new. The Primes didn't exist anymore, so we had no obligation to keep the "sister" tag. We thought of all the group names we liked—modern, smooth-sounding names like the Platters, the Shirelles, and the Chantels. The name we chose had to convey something about us—class, beauty, quality. We came up with countless suggestions, but none was perfect.

Flo was in charge of keeping a list of the names we'd collected. We were each pretty vocal about our favorite choices, but Flo kept her opinions to herself, dutifully writing down our ideas. The contracts were drawn up, so we had to decide about this soon. One day Flo read off her list: "The Darleens, the Sweet Ps, the Melodees, the Royaltones, the Jewelettes, the Supremes." None of them really impressed any of us, but Flo seemed to like one. After a minute she said, "I like this one—the Supremes."

We weren't exactly crazy about the name; I had my heart set on something that ended in "ettes." But we were anxious to sign the recording contracts, so even though we didn't all like the name, we were now the Supremes.

On January 15, the four of us, my mother, Flo's mother, Diane's mother, and Barbara's mother met with Berry, his sister Esther Edwards, and someone else from Motown to sign the contracts. None of us thought about hiring our own legal counsel. Our parents trusted that Berry and Motown would do only what was best for us. Berry reassured our mothers that Motown would not only work on our behalf, but manage all of our earnings as well. Everyone seemed happy with the arrangements.

Then, suddenly, Mrs. Martin announced that she had changed her mind, that Barbara could not be in the Supremes. We were very upset with Mrs. Martin because she had promised us earlier that she would sign for Barbara and now she was reneging. Furthermore, her attitude was somewhat condescending; she implied that her daughter was too good to be a singer.

After a few minutes, everything was smoothed out, and Barbara's mother signed. But even if she hadn't, we would have carried on without her. Even though we'd been together barely two years—a very short time compared to how long other groups were around before they got deals (i.e., recording contracts)—it felt like an eternity to us. We would not give up.

As I now look back, my first recording contract was fourteen pages of double-spaced type outlining my obligations to Motown as a "singer and/or musician" for the next year. Somewhere in all that legalese were some revealing terms: no advance, no salary, and permission for Motown to recoup any monies they'd advanced to us or spent on our behalf from the royalties we would be entitled to. The purpose of this was to reduce Motown's loss if our records didn't sell. Despite the fact that we formed and named our group, in the event one of us chose not to continue with the Supremes, her replacement would be chosen by Motown. Similarly, if someone was to be fired from the group, only Motown could do it. We no longer had any say. Ironically, however, the space in the contract where the name of the group should have been placed was left blank.

Furthermore, for records sold in the United States (and not returned) I was to be paid 3 percent of 90 percent of the suggested retail price for each record, less all taxes and packaging costs. What was especially interesting about that was the 3 percent royalty applied only when I cut solo records. I did not know the terms of the other girls' contracts, but my contract said that theirs were substantially the same as mine. Based on my figures, this meant that as a solo artist I would get approximately 2 cents for every 75-cent single sold. So, if I or any of the other Supremes had recorded a million-seller as a solo, that person's net would be around $20,000 *before* other expenses were deducted.

However, this was not the whole story after all. Ten pages further on in my contract is where the real deal was. There it states that the recordings we made as a *group* (which was the only way we ever recorded) were subject to a different royalty formula. Instead of each of us receiving the 3 percent royalty rate, we had to divide that 3 percent royalty four ways. So the real royalty rate for each of us was three-fourths of one percent (or .0075); thus, my earnings per 75-cent single would drop from two cents (the solo royalty formula) to about half of a penny. At this point a million-seller would earn about $5,000. Again, without knowing the exact amount for which Motown sold our records, these figures are based on the assumption, conservative I am sure, that the price for a single 45 rpm in the 1960s was 75 cents. This also assumes that Motown sold our records to distributors for one-half that price and then deducted another 20 percent for taxes, packaging, arrangements, copying and accompaniment, and all other related costs for each recording session, regardless of whether or not the particular record was released. I might add that, at the time of this writing, only very recently has Motown released some of the many unreleased records we cut back then.

Over the next several years the terms of my contract changed somewhat, but ever so slightly. In the next contract I signed, in 1965, I was also given $12.50 for every master (which the contract defined as a 2-sided single record) we recorded and a new royalty rate of 8 percent of 90 percent; but this royalty formula was based on the whole-sale price and not the suggested retail price of the record, as was the case in my first contract. So, during the very height of our career, we basically worked under the same terms as in the early days.

Looking back, people might wonder how Motown got away with this sort of thing or why so many artists just seemed to have accepted it. In truth, few of us knew anything at all about the business, and fewer still knew to have legal counsel for any business dealings or contracts. There was also the problem of how Motown was structured. Today most performers have an attorney-at-law, a booking agent, a manager, an accountant, a financial adviser, and many other professionals attending to their business. This forms an intricate and indispensable system of checks and balances, since each professional protects the performer's interests in his particular area.

Motown, however, did everything. Motown was your booking agent, your manager, your accountant, your financial adviser, and everything else. The corporation also made it difficult for outside people to ascertain the accuracy of its earnings reports, since, according to contract, there were two auditing periods per year, but an artist was allowed only one audit per year. In other words, even the most astute artist could only know the details of his finances for half a year. Without seeing the second period's figures, there was no way to know exactly what was going on, how much money you had earned, how much was being spent on you and deducted from your account, or how much you were entitled to. To this day, I still don't know exactly how many millions of copies any of our records sold, although I still receive royalties.

Our new official status as Motown recording artists made us more popular than ever at the sock hops and we were booked all over the area. Accustomed to always having someone like Milton or Richard around to handle the logistics of traveling, we were in for a rude awakening. Marv Johnson and Mary Wells not only had their own cars, but drivers as well; unbeknownst to Berry, we were hitching rides from friends and other artists to and from shows. We wouldn't dream of mentioning this problem to Berry for fear he'd think we were unprofessional or unable to handle the demands of a career. After Flo's rape, we had all become more leery about going out at night, and as the bookings outside Detroit proper increased, we faced having to decline offers.

Only a few weeks after our signing, we were sitting in the lobby discussing how we were going to get to a date on the other side of town. We were upset at the prospect of canceling. Little did we know that an angel was listening.

John O'Den was a big man who worked out daily and was into bodybuilding and fitness. He was fair-complexioned, had a deep, gruff voice, and on first sight appeared menacing. When we first met him, he was in his late thirties. Despite his appearance, he was very gentle, always smiling, and happy to help anyone who needed him.

John had met Berry when they were both boxers, and they also worked in the same auto plant in the late fifties. John was one of several old friends Berry brought into the Motown organization. John was Berry's personal valet and bodyguard; he also drove for Mary Wells. Even though Berry had a wife, John was responsible for his personal care.

"Disappointed about something? Y'all looking real sad." He was sympathetic, but teasing us, too.

"It's not funny," I mumbled, trying to hold back tears. "How are we going to get to the hops without a car of our own?"

"Well, how have you girls been getting around? I hear the Supremes are busy little girls. Mr. Gordy and Mrs. Edwards think you'll be moneymakers—just wait."

"We don't have time to wait," Diane interjected.

"We sure don't," Flo added. "We need a way to get to and from all these shows we're booked for."

"I'll be happy to drive you after work, and I'll wait around for you till it's over, too."

At this, Barbara jumped up and hugged John, as we followed, smiling with glee.

True to his word, John took us to the hop, and on the way home treated us to burgers and fries. We felt comfortable with him immediately, and he soon became our daily companion, driving us everywhere, covering little expenses out of his own pocket. There were many people around Motown like John. I remember Bobby Smith of the Spinners also driving us around. Some of these people weren't even on the payroll, yet they would help out whenever they could.

As we were coming in one day, we heard Berry ask the receptionist, "Where are the girls?"

Elbowing each other to beat a path to Berry's side, we cried, "Here we are!" We were now Berry's shadows; wherever he went, we followed. Our mentor had finally taken us under his wing.

# CHAPTER 9

The year 1961 was starting off as a great one for the Supremes, and within a few months it would prove to be a banner year for Motown. The Miracles' third Tamla release, "Shop Around," had gone to #1 on the R&B chart and #2 pop. This phenomenal showing was Berry's biggest crossover success so far and set a standard he would try to match with every release that followed. Smokey worked so hard with everyone, writing, producing, arranging—it's no wonder that in 1962 Berry made Smokey a vice president of the Motown Corporation, a position he holds today.

It was exciting to see all the different groups and artists who came aboard. Mary Wells finally hit with "Bye Bye Baby" (which she had written) and "I Don't Want to Take a Chance," and in December the Marvelettes' "Please Mr. Postman" became Motown's first pop number-one hit. The Miracles also released "Ain't It, Baby" and "Mighty Good Lovin'," which, while not as big hits as "Shop Around," kept their name in the public eye.

While acts were coming to Hitsville, Berry was assembling Motown's support staff; the producers, writers, musicians, and business people whose work behind the scenes was as important to the company's success as the biggest star.

The Motown musicians are legendary. How Berry acquired the services of the finest players in Detroit when it was common knowledge among them that Motown paid well below union scale was a mystery to me. When I learned that Mickey Stevenson was the scout who lured them in and that Thomas "Beans" Bowles was functioning as his backup, it all fell into place.

Beans Bowles knew the Gordys from his days as the sax player in the band at the Flame Show Bar. Like most local musicians, Beans had trouble supporting his family on his wages. In discussing Berry's plans for Motown with him, Beans was struck by Berry's enthusiasm and apparent willingness to do things that would really help his employees. Promising promotions and bonuses, Berry's sister Esther Edwards convinced Beans to join Motown. Most of the local musicians knew him, and when they would drop by Hitsville and ask what was happening, Beans would go into the spiel: "This is a young company that is still growing. It is the only company in America that you've got a chance to grow with . . ." and so on. And Beans believed it.

In 1960 Beans had toured with Marv Johnson, then Berry's hottest property. Functioning as Johnson's musical director, road manager, driver, and accompanist, Beans was doing the jobs of several people, which was impressive enough. But when he returned to Detroit and gave Esther a stack of meticulously neat and correct financial records, she and Berry snatched him up right away. Musicians were all over the place, but a musician with business and organizational skills was something they weren't going to see again for a while, if ever.

It fell to Esther to lure Beans into the fold. He was reluctant at first; he saw himself first and foremost as a musician. But after spending years on the road—which was a lot more uncertain and dangerous for blacks then—and never knowing where the next job was coming from, Beans decided to go with Berry. There was also the sense that something unique and wonderful was happening at Hitsville. For one thing, Berry promised Beans a company car. But more impressive were some of Berry's other ideas: plans to buy food, cars, and other items in bulk and form a cooperative plan for all Motown employees, were quite lofty and appealed to even the most cynical. Of course, these plans were never realized, and what ultimately won Beans over was the promise of a large starting salary.

Mickey Stevenson was another young writer/musician kicking around Detroit waiting for a break. Mickey was handsome and always very nice-looking. Years later, he married Kim Weston. "I used to work with Mickey's mother, Kitty Stevenson," Beans said. "I watched him grow up. He would come to my office and say he couldn't get anybody to listen to his songs. I said, 'All you have to do is stay on that porch [meaning the one at Hitsville], and when Berry comes out, just walk beside him and talk with him, because he is fast.'

"Mickey worried Berry to death, and that's how he got in—at least that's how I got rid of him," Beans recalled.

I remember sitting on that same porch and seeing Beans for the first time. Beans was a hip dresser in the fifties jazz style—dress slacks, turtleneck sweater, and a sports coat were standard attire. He was extremely tall—over six feet four—and very fair and handsome, with twinkling eyes. He was charming and well-spoken, and he always impressed people as an honest, wise man. Beans also had a charming smile. His confident, refined demeanor and aptitude for business would prove great assets to the company, especially out on the road.

Mickey started working for Berry in early 1961, and eventually he was put in charge of supervising everyone at Motown. Mickey made schedules, set up sessions, and enforced deadlines.

"I think Mickey started to recruit, and then they all started coming up," says Beans. "Earl Van Dyke got guitarist Robert White from Harvey and Gwen Fuqua's Anna Records. He also had Joe Tex at one time, but I don't think he stayed. Joe Messina, who was Italian, but who no one really considered white. There was Jack Ashford on percussion, and other guitarists as the years went by. Earl Van Dyke added Eddie Willis, Johnny Wah-Wah Watson, and eventually some other white boys got in there. Of course, bassist James Jamerson came in, too. Mickey would go to different places and hear their sound. Then they found out I was part of it. Mickey was working on them, and then he would refer them to me, and I'd corroborate everything he'd told them about working here."

Between the two of them, Beans and Mickey were turning 2648 West Grand Boulevard into more than just a big house. Though there were several bandleaders before him—including Joe Hunter, who brought in Hank Cosby, among others—Earl Van Dyke, a keyboardist, was the undisputed architect of the Motown sound. Jazz pianist Barry Harris was the leader of the young local musicians who would come together as Earl Van Dyke's Funk Brothers band. Many of them were, like me, alumni of Northeastern High. Almost all of these early players were well trained and had years of experience, mostly with playing jazz. Before they'd come to Motown, they'd each backed countless established stars. They knew their stuff. I've often thought that their mutual respect for one another kept the competition among them to a minimum. You never saw anybody trying to upstage anybody else. They were just there to do the best job they could.

Among my favorite musicians was Benny "Papa Zita" Benjamin, one of the greatest drummers ever. Everyone believed he was a musical genius. He didn't read music as well as some of the other players, so to get started he'd say, "Just give me the feeling, man." Sometimes he would be so into his drums he would miss a change, but whoever was producing would leave it on the recording because it still sounded great.

I was too young at first to really know what went on down in the Hitsville basement, so it's hard to say exactly what Papa Zita's thing was. I recall him being a chronic complainer; he never came in to work without something being wrong. He was late for sessions because his uncle died—over forty times. One incident I remember vividly occurred after he'd undergone an operation to have glass removed from his face. He had been thrown into the windshield in a car accident. Apparently, some of the glass was left in, and for months afterward he would come in and show everyone another piece he'd taken out himself. His poor face was a mess. Years later I'd learn that many of Papa Zita's little quirks were the product of drink, but everyone loved him all the same.

Another musician who will always have a special place in my heart is the bass player James Jamerson. He was young, good-looking, and one of the funniest men at Motown. He wrote all the fabulous bass lines that are the pulse of the Motown hits. I can just picture him, playing the bass, smoking a cigar, and grinning. No matter what was happening or how tired we all would get working for hours in that steaming studio, James still managed to throw out a funny line and get producers, engineers, singers, and the entire band laughing. James' wisecracks were the cause of many retakes. We'd all try to keep it in, but sooner or later someone would let loose, and we'd have to start all over again.

At the beginning, Berry still wasn't offering anybody much more than carfare to work with him. When union scale was approximately $47 to $60 per session for three hours' work, Berry was paying musicians $5 per side, and a side could take a whole day to record. An exception to that rule were the strings players whom a young Motown arranger named Paul Riser worked with; they were from the Detroit Symphony Orchestra. Though at first these classically trained musicians resisted some of the producers' ideas because they weren't "correct," once the records became hits, the symphony musicians were always proud to have been on them.

None of the early producers wrote out his arrangements—sometimes not even the basics of the melody. Because the musicians created and improvised from simple lead sheets, it was they who actually made the music. I've heard that lead sheets would be brought in for saxophone players with instructions that they play notes that weren't even on the horn. Nor was B.G., as we began calling Berry, known to write down musical notation on paper. Like many of us, Berry lacked formal musical training; I believe he played piano by ear. I must say that I've never met or heard of another man who did as much musically with so little. He'd walk into a session, hum a line or two of a tune, and say, "Play this. This is what I want to hear. Can you do this?" The musicians would take it from there. Then Berry would add, "Make me a riff back here," and so on.

Generally speaking, the musicians knew more about music, in the technical sense, than anyone else at Hitsville. When the producers and songwriters came into the studio with a new idea for a song, they had only what they heard in their heads, and maybe they could hum it or play a couple of bars. Not knowing that much about music, one of them might hum a part for, say, piano, that someone who really knew about music would have written for horns, or someone might ask for a rhythmic change or guitar riff that was technically impossible to play. Had a musician who knew of these limitations tried to write the same song, he probably would not even have considered these ideas. But as limited and rough as some of the early ideas were, the musicians rose to the challenge and tried to get the music they could play to fit the producer's or writer's original conception as closely as possible. This process entailed a lot of give and take, and in that exchange, possibilities not only doubled, but probably quadrupled. The products—the songs—speak for themselves.

Arrangements were the key to the Motown sound, for the arrangers provided the bridge between what the producers wanted to hear and what the musicians could play. Most of the early ones were done by Joe Hunter, who wrote them out and painstakingly structured each part. Organist Willie Shorter arranged all of the Miracles' earliest stuff. In the beginning, you could often find young Smokey watching Willie to learn how it was done.

The original recording facilities were limited, to say the very least. The basement studio's control booth was separated from the rest of the room by a plate glass window and elevated two steps higher than the rest of the room. Motown's famous echo chamber was actually the toilet behind the control room. Anyone who needed the toilet had to either run all the way to the top floor and use the facilities there or wait. Many takes were lost when someone knocked on the door, not knowing that the "chamber" was occupied. The vocalists' booths were no larger than telephone booths. And the band was often so close to the singers that it was ridiculous, but the excitement was infectious.

Working in such close quarters may have been cramped, but it was conducive to a better rapport between the singers and the players. Really making music, as opposed to making sounds, demands an emotional exchange among everyone involved. When the band got into a groove it inspired the singers, and vice versa. There was a real chemistry there, and I think the best Motown records—Mary Wells's "My Guy," Marvin Gaye's "I Heard It Through the Grapevine," the Four Tops' "Baby I Need Your Loving," and our "When the Lovelight Starts Shining Through His Eyes," which featured the Four Tops and Holland, Dozier, and Holland on backing vocals—have a spontaneous intensity to them. Today's records are often made by musicians and producers who are abetted by a plethora of technological gimmicks and tricks; to my ears, the sound is sterile and flat.

Though Berry and the Motown producers and writers did experiment with different methods of writing and producing, they were not, as is generally assumed today, looking for a specific sound. Berry had known as far back as his days with Erma Franklin that he wanted a smooth, clean, classy R&B-cum-pop style. One of the reasons Berry liked writing for Jackie Wilson was that Jackie could—and did—sing almost any style. Berry wasn't rejecting the earlier, rougher R&B style so much as he—and everyone at Motown—was formulating what could be more accurately described as the next step in R&B. What "experimenting" was done with individual groups was more a matter of fitting an act to the right material and right producer to achieve a sound that would appeal to all listeners. Still, virtually all the hits that came out of Motown—whether they were by the Supremes or the Contours—fell within the stylistic parameters Berry had set years before.

Handclaps, heavy drum accents, and repeated choruses and melodic hooks made Motown's sound unforgettable, even to people who didn't especially care to remember it. Every producer had his own trademark, and some of the best Motown songs have several kinds of hooks in each song, in the lyrics, background vocals, chorus, rhythm sections, and melody. People everywhere—all over the world—identified with that sound. There are as many interpretations and definitions of the Motown sound as there are people who love it.

Part of the credit for the sharp attack of the instruments on any Motown record goes to dumb luck. The acoustics in the first studio were so tacky, they amplified the sound of any instrument naturally. The room emitted a big, booming sound that Berry at first believed would mar the records. Instead, like so many other things in Berry's life, it had the opposite effect and worked to his advantage. This inadvertent recording ambience was so haphazard that it can't be duplicated today with millions of dollars of sophisticated equipment.

Of course none of this would have mattered at all if it weren't for the great songs. As a songwriter, Berry's great strength was that he didn't set out to write poetry, or make a statement, or pen a classic; he just wanted to tell a story. Berry's approach is summed up in this quote:

"Try and make it appear it's happening right now so people can associate with it. Not 'My girl broke up with me' but 'My girl's breaking up with me.' "

Quality Control, the division that screened every single track for release, was tough to please; their standards were high. Someone from Quality Control might tell a writer to his face that his song was "garbage" or great. There was nothing in between. Grading a song for the lyrics, title, arrangement, lead and backing vocals, style, and sound became standard procedure.

Many songwriters were upset whenever Berry started rearranging a tune or rewriting a line, especially since he would then take a co-writing credit, no matter how little he may have contributed. As it was, all Motown writers' songs was published by Berry's Jobete Music, so he was already getting a sizable cut of a song's royalties even when he didn't have credit on it. But Berry's input also turned many mediocre or borderline efforts into first-rate hits.

Another erroneous impression about Motown is that several acts recorded the same song, then the different versions "competed" for release. In fact, we recorded songs that other groups had hits with for our albums simply because Jobete—and Berry—earned the royalties on a record, no matter who sang it. The Supremes recorded the Vandellas' "Come and Get These Memories," and the Tops' "I Can't Help Myself" and "Shake Me, Wake Me (When It's Over)." These recordings were not considered for release as singles, they were just filler.

Artists were usually the first—and probably the only—ones to hear a writer's grumblings when he or she thought Berry had taken more than his share of credit. Lots of independent record companies were a lot less particular about these things; today they're all out of business. In its final form, any great Motown record was a product of equal parts artistic expression and quality control. Berry took this idea as far as it would go; soon, artists would be subject to another kind of quality control.

\* \* \*

In July 1961 "Buttered Popcorn" became our second release on Tamla. It was another sweltering summer, and of course the studio was hotter than hell. Each of us wore lightweight clothing, but by the end of the session we looked like we'd all been dunked. Capturing that carefree sound took a lot of hard work!

Flo sang lead on "Buttered Popcorn," a song written by Berry and Motown's vice president of sales, Barney Ales, and she really jammed with it as only she could. Everything about the record—the background vocals, the lyrics, the music—was upbeat and sassy. The song had a great dance riff, and I think "Popcorn" was the most raucous thing we ever released. The musicians were pleased with the session, and we all left the studio believing we had a hit.

Though Barney Ales wanted to give this record a big push, for reasons unknown to us it never got any real support from the company. The B side was "Who's Loving You," the lovely ballad we had recorded earlier with Smokey. Naturally we were proud of our first two singles. At last we felt we had the credibility we needed. Later I learned that Berry didn't care for "Buttered Popcorn"; though most people who heard Flo's voice loved it, Berry didn't think it had the commercial sound he was looking for.

It was such a thrill to go to the sock hops and sing our own songs, songs no one else had ever recorded before. This is where we learned to lip-synch, though very often we would be really singing along with our record with our microphones off. Standing up and singing songs that belong only to you is the most satisfying and exhilarating feeling on earth. We were legitimate. Finally.

About a month after we released "Buttered Popcorn" in the summer of 1961, the Marvelettes recorded their biggest hit, "Please Mr. Postman." The record was one of the few early Motown releases to be written by one of the singers (there were a couple of exceptions: Mary Wells's "Bye Bye Baby," and Smokey's tunes, of course). Seventeen-year-old Georgeanna Dobbins wrote it overnight after Motown talent scout Robert Bateman had suggested that her group, then known as the Marvels, work up some original material. It was Berry who changed the group's name to the Marvelettes. Of the original group —Georgeanna, Gladys Horton, Katherine Anderson, Wanda Young, and Juanita Cowart—only Wanda had graduated from high school when "Please Mr. Postman" hit.

The first time we saw them was a Saturday afternoon, and they were entering a studio as Mary Wells was leaving. They were new around and absolutely thrilled to see a big star like Mary. The office was buzzing about the fact that the Marvelettes had written their song themselves, so we were anxious to find out more about them.

We were awful, at first, whispering to one another about the fact that the Marvelettes not only looked square but were from Inkster, Michigan, in the sticks. Coming from the inner city, we considered ourselves far more sophisticated. The Marvelettes were always very down to earth; sometimes they even seemed unsure of themselves.

The Marvelettes had been rehearsing in the basement and Robert Bateman was walking around looking real proud. We were a bit jealous of this new girl group. There was a feeling of family at Motown, but they were still encroaching on our territory. After all, we had been the first girl group to join Motown. The four of us, however, were curious, so we introduced ourselves. Flo never stood on ceremony. She was always ready with compliments and encouragement for other singers, so when she overheard the Marvelettes practicing, she offered to help.

"I heard you girls practicing," Flo said to Gladys. "Why don't you ad lib a little bit more?"

"That's a good idea," Gladys replied. "What do you have in mind?"

"Like say, 'Plea-ea-ea-ea-ease Mr. Postman.' Or add some 'Oh yeah's."

"Great! Come downstairs and show me that part again. I think it will really work."

"Sure," said Flo as they all trooped down the stairs together.

Flo returned after a while, smiling. "Gladys can really sing," she said. "She is nervous because another girl named Georgeanna Dobbins wrote that song and was supposed to be singing the lead on it, but she dropped out at the last minute."

Flo was always willing to help someone, and she and Gladys soon became fast friends. (For the "Mr. Postman" session the drummer was none other than Marvin Gaye. The song's memorable backbeat wasn't written into it; Marvin had just started playing, and all the other musicians fell in.)

Like many other groups at Motown, the Marvelettes were recording for Berry before they even had a contract. Of course, the record was a smash, and Berry wanted to put them out on the road as soon as possible. But there were problems. Not only were the girls still in school, but Gladys was an orphan and a ward of the court. It was necessary for Motown to appoint a legal guardian for her, and Esther Edwards's husband, a Michigan state legislator, George Edwards, was called upon.

Esther Edwards recalls how obtaining this guardianship was almost impossible. "I had to talk to Jim Lincoln, judge of the probate court, who I knew because we both worked in Democratic politics. He was not enthusiastic about it; you know, nobody wanted their kids to be in show business. I explained the situation and told him I would be the chaperone with them while they were on the road for that three weeks. I also promised I would make the girls study. I handed him a copy of 'Please Mr. Postman.'

"Bright and early the next morning he called and said, 'Esther, let me tell you one thing. When I showed my kids the Marvelettes' records, they screamed and ran out of the house. I couldn't believe it! They ran all over the neighborhood telling the kids and everybody that their father was the guardian of the Marvelettes. I get more respect for that than for being a judge or their father.'"

The Marvelettes' first tour included a week in New York City at the Apollo Theater, a week in Philadelphia, and then on to Washington, D.C., for a week at the Howard Theater. True to her word, Mrs. Edwards saw to it that they rose early each morning and took in all the historical sights, even the U.S. Mint. She had promised not only that the girls would keep up their schoolwork while on the road, but that they would deliver oral reports on all the places they'd been once they got back to school.

"We thought traveling would be fun," Gladys said, "but all we had time to do was the show, go to bed early, and then get up early to visit all the sightseeing spots. You know, Mrs. Edwards was real hard on us."

We'd started traveling to shows outside the Detroit area on the weekends. Our first big show was in Cincinnati, followed by another in Pittsburgh. John usually drove us to the gigs in his trusty VW van, but because this was a longer trip John's wife, Lily Mae, was coming along with us, and Berry lent us his Cadillac. We were scared, nervous, thrilled, and happy to be playing real theaters, where we could sing live, which we hadn't been doing much of since losing Marvin Tarplin. Also, we weren't doing the cover tunes anymore. For these shows, the promoter in each town supplied us with a band, and each act on the bill sang just a few songs. Our repertoire included "Buttered

Popcorn," "Who's Loving You," "He's Seventeen," and "I Want a Guy," all records Barbara sang on, but for which she never received royalties.

Our first show was on a bill with Gladys Knight and the Pips. They were simply fabulous. We watched their performance from backstage and were so in awe of them. By then Gladys had been singing professionally for over a decade; the group's command of the audience made it seem easy. We wondered if we would ever be that good.

We were terrible! Without Marv, and singing with an unfamiliar band, we were lost. Barbara sang lead on "He's Seventeen," and from the downbeat, she was singing in one key and the band was playing in another. This was the first time Barbara had sung this song live, and she was terrified. We knew something was wrong from the first second, but this being the first time we'd ever sung live with a strange band, we didn't know what to do to correct this mistake. We were up there for what felt like an eternity. When it was over, the four of us ran off the stage in tears.

Gladys and the Pips were so kind to us, telling us not to worry, it could happen to anyone, and we would do better next show. Their encouragement helped us a lot, and we tried to put it behind us. For some reason, though, Diane just couldn't leave it alone, and was still complaining about the incident as we drove to Pittsburgh, where we would spend the night with her relatives. Barbara apologized to us, but there wasn't much any of us could do about it now except vow that nothing like it would ever happen again.

The next show was uneventful, and as we left Pittsburgh, Barbara begged John to let her drive Berry's car. John had been teaching all of us how to drive, but we took the wheel only when we were out on a highway, never in a busy town. At first he wisely told Barbara no, but she kept bugging him, so at the next light, he let her take the wheel. Of course, none of us had any business driving any car, let alone Berry's, and we all knew it.

When John parked, he'd turned the wheel at such an angle that the second Barbara pulled away, she rammed into a car on our left. We were in trouble. John's wife was the only female with a driver's license, so she agreed that she would take the blame for what happened.

The car was barely scratched, but because we were from out of town Barbara and John had to appear in court a few days later. Barbara was supposed to be Mrs. O'Den, but it slipped her mind. When the judge called out, "Mrs. O'Den, please step forward," Barbara just sat on the bench like a bump. The judge called her name a couple more times, and John kept nudging her in the ribs. She finally came to her senses and rose. It was all cleared up, and we were all certain that our secret was safe.

Once we were home, though, it wasn't long before the truth got back to Berry. We never knew who spilled the beans, but no one— except John—was above suspicion.

One evening Berry summoned us into his office, one at a time. I don't remember whom Berry questioned first, but he made it impossible for anyone coming out of his office to say anything to the others, so we had no way of knowing what Berry knew or who had said what. I was literally shaking as I entered the room. Speaking gently, Berry asked me all kinds of questions about what happened to his Caddy. The office seemed to be closing in on me until I felt like a prisoner in a cell. After a few minutes of this interrogation, I surmised that Berry might know the truth, but I'd promised to back up my friends, and that's what I did.

"Mary, who was driving the car when the accident happened?"

"John's wife—"

Before I'd even finished, Berry said, "I know who was driving the car, so you might as well tell me the truth! The one thing I hate," he continued in a firm voice, "is a liar, and for that reason, *you* are no longer in the group."

I couldn't take it. It was hard enough for me to lie to anyone, but to have it lead to this! I started crying.

"Yes, I lied to you, because we agreed to tell this lie. My loyalty is to my group. My girls are the most important thing in the world to me. And I'd lie to save them again, if I had to, because we can always get another manager. I may never get another group like this."

With that, I ran out of the office and into the darkened street. My eyes were almost swollen closed as I walked up and down West Grand Boulevard in confusion. At my age, what was I going to do—be a secretary? I regretted lying to Berry. My head was spinning and my eyes ached, but I continued pacing the block. Who had cracked? Why hadn't everybody stuck together?

Finally I was summoned back to the office. Flo, Diane, and Barbara were already there, and everyone had pretty much calmed down. Berry was sitting behind his desk, leaning back in his big, overstuffed executive's chair. For the longest time, he just stared at us the way a parent looks at a child who has learned his lesson.

"You girls shouldn't have lied to me," Berry said quietly. "I will not tolerate that kind of dishonesty, and you ought to know you will always be found out in the end, so what's the use? And Mary, don't worry—you're back in the group."

It's strange, but at that moment I was proud of myself, even though I had done something against my principles. I had stood up to someone who was bigger and stronger than me. Years later, I would have to stand up to Berry again, but he wouldn't confront me personally; he'd have the company do it for him.

This episode marked a real turning point in our relationship with Motown, for it proved that even though we didn't have a hit, we were still worth hanging on to. We were doing more hops and shows, and we were still *the* live local act, but we were anxious to get beyond that.

Though we were spending as much time as possible at Hitsville, we still liked hanging out with our friends. We weren't really stars yet, but we weren't exactly your typical teenagers anymore either. Being around our friends provided an escape from the responsibility and pressure, and we could be normal kids.

We were still running with a pretty wild crowd that included Tall George, Berry Fletcher, Silky, Willie Peeples, and Richard Street. They were mostly friends of mine, but Diane would hang around with us, and before long our friend Silky developed a crush on her. She wanted nothing to do with him, but instead of letting it drop, Silky decided to pursue her. Like many sixteen-year-old boys, he thought that by being obnoxious he would win her heart.

We were at one of those crazy parties when Silky yelled across the room to Diane, "Hey, come here, girl!"

"What do you want?" Diane replied indifferently.

"Come on, girl," Silky mock-pleaded as he grabbed her arm. "Do you want to fool around?"

"Oh, leave me alone!"

With that, Silky gave Diane what we called a body slam, which was actually a dance move. He grabbed her by the arms and pulled her up against him forcefully. Everyone roared with laughter. I was shocked but couldn't help but be amused by the look on Diane's face.

"What did you do, Silky," Tall George yelled, "get too close?"

Diane was furious. "Leave me alone!"

"Let her alone, Silky," I said, trying to sound as serious as I could without cracking up. I knew Diane was really angry, and I didn't want her blaming me and Flo for this predicament.

"Mary, I am going home," Diane said.

"Now see what you've done?" I said to Silky, giving him what I hoped was a meaningful look. Diane didn't like not being in control of a situation, and seeing her like this was amusing. Obviously she saw no humor whatsoever in the situation and was leaving. I helped her gather her things and followed her out. I wanted to stay because my new boyfriend Willie Peeples was there, but he came out right behind us.

"Do you girls want me to give you a ride?"

"No, thank you," Diane huffed as she began walking away rapidly.

"Oh, come on, Diane," I pleaded. I wanted to spend time with Willie, and Diane knew it, but because Diane and I were the only ones from our neighborhood at this party, we were pretty much obliged to travel together.

Willie had a white Dodge, which I thought of as our lovemobile. I knew he would want to drop Diane off first and then he and I would cruise around for a while before parking somewhere and spending a couple of hours in the backseat.

"If you don't let me drive you," he warned, "I'll follow you anyway."

With that, Diane finally gave in.

I could never convince her that Silky wouldn't bother her again, and she refused to go with me to any more of that crowd's parties.

Around this time, my family had the good fortune to move into one of the row houses, like the one Flo's family had lived in before her father died. Though still technically part of the Projects, the row houses were single-family dwellings, and moving into one of them was a step up.

All through school, I dated several guys, but didn't have a real boyfriend again until I met Ronnie Hammers. With him, my emotions were more intense than ever. I was madly in love.

Ronnie and I were true high-school sweethearts. Being older, he was set to graduate a year ahead of me. To my young, romantic mind, the only sure way to protect our precious love was to announce our engagement. I think what made him agree to it was that whatever we did after we became engaged would be overlooked, since we'd be practically married anyway. And we did "whatever" right away. Wisely, our parents kept their reservations about it to themselves. They must have known that our wedding plans wouldn't come to fruition and that forbidding the engagement would make us more serious than we really were.

We were nearing the end of our high-school years and beginning to feel very grown-up. We were all changing. I had the feeling that things had changed with Diane, too. Perhaps it was Richard Street, or someone else, but I could sense in Diane a different attitude toward boys. They weren't just cute anymore. Her tomboyishness had completely vanished, giving way to a more feminine style of competing. Suddenly, for no apparent reason, Diane would make some statement, comparing her figure and mine. Since Flo and Barbara were both referred to as "stacked," Diane could find little to remark on there. But when it came to me, it was another story. We were both skinny, and then thin was most definitely not in. Still, Diane found plenty to say about everything from my legs to my hairstyle, which I changed every other week.

Even at that young age, I could see that Diane was trying to build up her own self-confidence. Her haughtiness was just a front; deep down, she believed that she wasn't as pretty as the other girls. She craved attention, and in her attempts to get it, she could seem almost ruthless. Sometimes she would throw a childish tantrum, then moments later pretend it was all a big joke, that she was just being silly. Her bluntness could be disconcerting and feelings were hurt, but we saw Diane's actions as the product of thoughtlessness, not malice. If Diane ever criticized one of us in public, none of us would call her on it. It was more important to us then to be ladies than to settle some score. Besides, we knew where she was coming from. Diane was our friend, and we accepted her. At one time or another, each of us lost our patience with her, but compared to our main goal—the success of the Supremes—everything else was secondary. Forcing a confrontation with Diane didn't seem to be worth risking the group. Nothing did.

Most of the time it was easy to ignore Diane's behavior, but things took a different turn when she decided that she could borrow my boyfriend as easily as she borrowed my clothes. Diane was one to covet anything that belonged to anyone else, and, as we got older, those things could include men. Diane liked a challenge—whether it was to get into a sorority, make a team, or get a guy—and she never walked away, no matter how what the odds or who would get hurt. Toward the end of high school, Diane would complain about other girls not liking her, and we would all sympathize. But over the years, I began to wonder which problem came first: Did other girls treat her badly and force her to prove herself, or was her willingness to compete against them so obvious that they couldn't help but dislike her? In those pre–women's lib days, lots of girls thought fighting over men was what being a real woman was all about. Other women who weren't your friends were the competition; men were the prey and the prize.

Around this time Diane and Smokey's interest in each other was well known. We had cut a few records with him and we would see him around Hitsville. Everyone knew he was married to Bobby Rogers's cousin, Claudette, so I was surprised when one day Diane said, "Guess what? I went out with Smokey!"

"You did what?" Flo and I replied. She had been flirting with Smokey openly for some time, but we never suspected it would come to this. They were very discreet, never going out too much in public. Diane would tell us where Smokey had taken her to dinner, or whenever he had sent her flowers.

After Ronnie and I had announced our engagement, Diane began dropping hints that she wanted Ronnie for herself. Fluttering her eyelashes at him, she tried to charm him. If we were all out together, she would act as if he were her boyfriend. Ronnie and I would be dancing, and she would cut in. Not being very sophisticated, Ronnie didn't know what was going on. "Why is she always talking to me?" he'd ask. But all I could do was shrug my shoulders. I could never have said what I thought without looking bad, and, more than anything, I wanted Ronnie to see me as a nice girl, a mature young lady. When Diane made disparaging remarks about my thin legs or flat behind in front of Ronnie, I'd be torn between rage and fear that any rocking of the boat might destroy the group. Of course the Supremes were important, but standing up for myself was even more so. I was just too young to know how.

One afternoon, we were on a bus when we heard "This Magic Moment" being sung a cappella from the very last row. Five boys, who seemed younger than us, were straining to emulate the Drifters' sound. I smiled to myself, knowing we were on our way to make our own record, and I wondered if someday, somewhere, other young girls whom we would never meet would be singing along to our records and trying to capture our sound.

# CHAPTER 10

We had been officially signed to Motown for almost a year and a half now, and from where we stood it seemed everyone except the Supremes was forging ahead. Mary Wells' "The One Who Really Loves You," the Marvelettes' "Beechwood 4-5789" and "Playboy," the Contours' "Do You Love Me," and the Miracles' "I'll Try Something New" had been climbing the charts, while we had barely scraped into the Hot 100 with "Your Heart Belongs to Me"—and that had been the high point. In the fall we would release a light tango-tinged girl-group song, "Let Me Go the Right Way," but after it took four months to perch at #90, we were beginning to worry. Even the diehard optimists around Motown, who had thought everything we'd released would hit, were beginning to wonder.

By now, almost all of the artists who would make Motown great were on the roster. Of them all, I will always remember Marvin Gaye. He was one of the truly gifted.

They say behind every great man is a great woman. Berry Gordy had several women behind him, and among the first were his sisters Gwen and Anna. The pair can also be credited with having a hand in launching Marvin's career. Marvin arrived in Detroit with his mentor, Harvey Fuqua, after they both departed the Moonglows, a Washington, D.C., vocal group whose best-known hits were "Sincerely" and "Ten Commandments of Love." Harvey had been the group's lead singer, but in Detroit he was working as an independent producer with a couple of small labels, including his own Tri Phi and Harvey. In late 1960, he had married Berry's sister Gwen, and when their Anna Records folded, many of their artists came with Harvey over to Motown. Marvin seemed to flow in with that transition. Early on, he recorded a few unsuccessful singles—"Let Your Conscience Be Your Guide," "Sandman," and "Soldier's Plea"—and was still trying to find his niche.

"Who's the cute guy wearing the beret?" I asked the first time I spotted Marvin Gaye in the studio in 1961.

"Oh, he's a drummer. Used to be in the Moonglows," one of the musicians replied.

"Sure is cute. What's his name?"

"Don't know. Friend of Harvey's."

Overhearing this, Barbara stage-whispered, "Come on, he's got to have a name."

Somehow Marvin sensed that we were talking about him, and we saw him blush. It was rare to see that genuine shyness in a man, and it endeared him to us all the more. We giggled behind our hands about it, but from that moment, Marvin was very special to us. As I learned more about him, I attributed his lovely manners to the fact that he was a preacher's son.

Marvin was known around Motown for wearing kookie hats—tam-o'-shanters, berets, and jaunty fedoras, each perched slightly to the side of his head. His unusual appearance was probably his way of hiding his shyness; ironically, it only attracted more attention. We knew him from seeing him around in the studio, but we only got to know him well when he would sing just to us.

By coincidence, we all wore pedal pushers to the studio one day. Nothing was going on in the lobby or out on the porch, so we sauntered down to the studio, not knowing what to expect. The studio was very dim, and sitting in the middle, as if on a deserted, spotlit stage, was Marvin softly playing the piano. He surely heard us as we came in, but he didn't miss a note.

"You girls look real nice today," he said. Other guys would have said it one way, but Marvin spoke in a hushed tone that was very respectful and polite.

"Oh, these old things?" Feminine wiles!

"If I knew you'd be here, Marvin, I would have gotten dressed up."

"It was too warm to wear anything else."

In Marvin's presence, we became as shy and reticent as he was. Then everything began to fall into place like the most carefully blocked scene from a movie. We each took our places around the piano, arranging ourselves in what we thought were our most seductive poses. Maybe one of us would make eye contact with him, and that would be the most romantic thing in the world.

Times like this were so precious. Even though there were four of us, we each felt like we were in some beautiful dream with him. Other guys were cute or sharp; Marvin was beautiful. Other guys teased and joked around; Marvin was always considerate and solicitous.

"What do you girls want to hear next?" he would ask quietly, looking up at each of us in turn.

" 'Mona Lisa,' " Flo would say.

" 'Come to Me,' " Barbara always yelled.

" 'Tears on My Pillow.' " I loved hearing Marvin sing in that high register.

"Try something different," Diane suggested.

"We just love your LP with all the love songs," Diane said, referring to *The Soulful Moods of Marvin Gaye*, his first album.

"You all like it?" he would ask as if he couldn't believe anyone would.

Later, on our way home, we would daydream aloud about him. "How old do you think he is?" I mused.

"Nineteen or twenty," Flo guessed.

"Girl, can you just imagine him singing to you while he held you in his arms, in between kisses?" Barbara would say this while clasping her hands to her breast and rolling her eyes heavenward. Now this might seem a little silly, but we were all very serious. Being with Marvin was like having every girlhood dream come true. He was a prince, and there was just no one like him anywhere.

"He can't have a girlfriend. We would know about it, wouldn't we?" I reasoned.

"Not necessarily." Flo wasn't so sure.

"It doesn't matter," Barbara proclaimed, "I say Marvin Gaye is one of the best-looking men around here and I sure wish he was *my* boyfriend." At this time, Barbara was dating Willie Richardson, her future husband, but you could tell she wasn't kidding about Marvin.

Our attraction to Marvin was not really a sexual one. The minute we laid eyes on him we knew that we loved him in that pure, sweet way few people ever get a chance to love anymore. It was enough just to be around Mr. Gaye. Everyone seemed to enjoy being in his company. We were still in our early teens, and Marvin was twenty-three or so; no doubt he saw us as silly teenage girls, and our attraction to him must have been comically obvious to him and anyone else. But he never treated us as if we were silly, and so we continued to hang on his every word. In the next year or so, as Marvin's star rose with "Stubborn Kind of Fellow," "Hitch Hike," "Pride and Joy," and "Can I Get a Witness," I knew no one deserved it more.

\* \* \*

The biggest event of this most eventful year came early in October. We had arranged to rehearse at my house, and Flo and I were there, working with our friend Diane Watson, who was a great dancer. She was helping us put together some new routines, and we were practicing when Barbara called—she was pregnant! After I recovered from the initial shock, Flo and I started talking about Diane replacing Barbara. We still felt we needed four voices, and she seemed the most obvious candidate at the moment.

When Diane Ross showed up, we gave her Barbara's news, and we talked about it a bit, then all sat down to wait for Barbara. I was beginning to see how hard it was to keep a group together. It was one thing to be schoolgirls, with your lives pretty well defined, but now it seemed like everyone we knew was getting married or going off to college or work.

Finally I said, "We've got a new girl here; she can teach us to dance."

Diane didn't say anything for a minute. Flo was on the couch, drinking a soda, and Diane Watson just stood in silence.

We dropped the subject again and sat around waiting for Barbara, but she never showed up.

"I'll tell you what," Diane said, as she jumped out of her chair, "Barbara's out! If the three of us can't make it, then we won't make it. I'll see you later." Then she left.

The year 1961 slipped through my fingers before I had much of a chance to grasp all its lessons. I was so caught up in everything—every day seemed like a new adventure. I knew that I loved this lifestyle. Barbara Martin had married in December, but she planned to continue with us for a while, even though she was pregnant. Flo and I didn't want to see her go. Though her husband supported her in her decision to continue her career, we wondered just how long this would last.

At Christmas, none of us could afford gifts for anyone but our closest relatives, but we didn't care. The four of us spent our time together thanking God for all our blessings and thinking about what the future held in store. We always shared our daydreams, but now it was clear: we had to be stars. Part of this was all girlish musing, but suddenly it seemed that anything could happen.

There was much to look forward to, but nothing was as important to me as graduating from high school. During my time at Northeastern, I studied English with Mr. Boone, a very good teacher known for being tough. My first encounter with him wasn't entirely pleasant. Before he even had me in one of his classes, he pulled me aside in the hall one day to inform me that my thinking I was a "star" cut no mustard with him. I was a bit frightened of him and confused as to why he would even bother me. Sure enough, I did get his class, and the first time, he did fail me. But when I took his class again, I grew to know him better and he seemed to take a special interest in me.

I was a basically happy-go-lucky kid, and I never thought too much about my early childhood, at least not consciously. For our final exam in Mr. Boone's modern literature class, in the first days of January 1962, we had to write an essay. I don't remember exactly what the question was—it dealt with psychology—but whatever it was prompted me to write a short autobiography in which I revealed to my teacher thoughts I never knew I had, and, reading it years later, I would find answers to many questions.

*Psychology is the study of the mind. An individual who cares about himself may become a psychologist. This may seem strange, but if a person senses that he has a psychological problem, he can analyze himself and possibly overcome his problem. There are many ways in which people become mentally ill. Mentally ill persons may be what we call* crazy, *but there are some situations where a person has just a small problem and is disturbed, which causes a maladjusted personality. I am was [for some reason, I left both words] such a person." My problem began when I was a very young girl.*

Of my confusing early childhood with I.V. and my real mother, I wrote:

*Situations such as this cause people to react in different ways. I have developed a protective shell, which whenever I feel I may face a conflict, I draw into. Why? Is it because I subconsciously feel I might be snatched again? For a little girl, this problem can become so great that anything might happen.*
*. . . I try to cover up my deficiency by developing a pleasing personality. Actually, underneath this, I am still a young and*

*frightened girl. I also try to better my physical appearance, so
that, even though I might be dumb, I will be pretty, and this
might cause people to look over my deficiencies.*

*I recognized my problem but I still can't overcome this con-
stant veil of fear. . . . If many of the parents would realize that
children have feelings and that they need love sometimes, this
problem might be destroyed.*

A few days later, Mr. Boone told me privately that he had read
my paper before his church congregation. He told me that I was
exceptionally perceptive and suggested that I consider becoming a
writer. From that day on, I have kept a diary, in which I have recorded
my thoughts and feelings.

My mother was still clinging to the dream that I would stop singing and start earning a decent living as a secretary or go to college. All
I wanted was to wear that cap and gown and hold my diploma in my
hands. I had promised Mom that I would finish school, no matter
what happened with the Supremes.

I was also looking forward to taking my diploma with me when I
visited my relatives in Mississippi that summer. I especially wanted my
father to see it. A few years before, my father had married one of the
daughters of Big Daddy, my maternal grandmother's husband. and
they had a child, my half-sister Jerry Ann. When I'd seen him in the
summer of 1961 we had spent more time together, and I got to know
his new family. Just before I'd arrived that year my father suffered a
severe stroke. He was very weak, and I knew that he would never be
the same again. Still, like all children, I suppose, I could not accept
that my father, whom I'd come to know so late and grown to love so
deeply, would die. He was so proud of my accomplishments, and the
one thing he said to me over and over again was, "I just want to live
to see at least one of my children graduate from high school. Promise
me you'll graduate. I will send you money for your dress or anything
else you need. But, baby, I just want you to get a diploma. It will take
you a long way in life." I promised him I would be back the next year,
diploma in hand.

My father died one week before the graduation ceremonies. It
comforted me to think that at least he knew that I kept my promise,
and I have since wondered if my father didn't hold onto life, as some
terminally ill people have been known to do, until he was certain that
I would be all right. His passing didn't come as a complete surprise,

and though I was very sad, I was determined to go to Mississippi to bury him.

It was during my trip down South to arrange my father's funeral that I first encountered blatant prejudice. On previous visits down South, I'd never noticed too much difference between the way my family there was treated by the whites and the way I'd been treated in Detroit. When I was very little, tagging along with my older cousins Josephine and Christine, we all talked to and joked with the white kids outside the movie theater. Of course, we were separated from the white kids inside, but we never thought much about it. You grow up being taught certain attitudes and, not knowing any differently, you may never think about it. At that age, you don't see the evil behind such seemingly innocuous practices, and you are in no position to do anything about them. When I arrived in Greenville, however, I was a different person: confident, self-assured, and proud. I'd been around, and, as a result of my experiences, I had a sense of self few blacks in my father's community could imagine.

When I walked into one of Greenville's major department stores with my cousin Josephine in tow, I don't know what kind of reception I expected, but it certainly wasn't the condescending rudeness I got from a white redneck salesman. As the eldest child, it was my duty to select the clothes my father would be buried in. I had already purchased the shirt, tie, and white gloves. When I asked to see socks, the salesman showed me a cheap, shoddy pair.

As he casually flung them on the counter, he said, "Oh, these will be okay." I could hear in his tone of voice the unspoken words "for a colored."

"No, they won't! My father just died, and these are for him. I can afford the best and that's exactly what I want." I was stunned; I had never in my life been made to feel different or inferior because I was black, and in my grief and shock I was far more aggressive than I might have been. The salesman was taken aback, but he complied without another word. As soon as she could, Josephine hustled me out of the store and tried to calm me down. As we made our way back to Grandmama's house, I was crying and screaming, "It is ridiculous to be treated this way! Our money is just as good as anybody else's! These people have got their nerve!"

What I didn't know then was that down South I was the one with the nerve. I felt as though I had suddenly matured in ways I couldn't describe. I was anxious to go home, and Flo, Diane, and Barbara were happy to see me. They'd continued going to Motown each day, but all plans were on hold until my return.

We were at our usual stations in the lobby when we first saw Stevie Wonder.

"Flo, who is that boy Ronnie White is helping up the stairs?" I asked one day as we were lounging around the lobby.

"Looks like the kid is blind," she whispered.

"Oh," someone else said, "that must be be the little blind boy Ronnie was telling Berry about. He's nine or ten years old and really gifted in music."

Stevie's mother and brother led the him into B.G.'s office, and the four of them emerged minutes later. As Berry's shadows, the four of us fell in behind and followed them into the studio. The little blind boy—Steveland Morris, soon to be rechristened Stevie Wonder—played piano and every other instrument the boss requested.

"What else can you play, Stevie?" Berry would ask after Stevie had demonstrated his ability on one instrument. Stevie would jump up, find his way to something else, and start playing that—keyboards, horns, percussion. Nothing seemed beyond him. I especially remember him playing a harmonica he'd brought with him. Of course, we were all dumbstruck with amazement. At the time, the Supremes were still the youngest artists on the roster. To see someone as young as Stevie was something else.

"This Stevie is truly a young genius," Berry muttered. (In a recent interview, Berry says that he wasn't impressed with Stevie, but I was there. We were *all* impressed, to say the least!)

Stevie Wonder was immediately accepted into the Motown family, and he came to the studio all the time. Learning every inch of the place, he eventually got to the point where he didn't need help getting from room to room, and before long he was pulling his practical jokes. Everyone loved him, and that was a good thing, because he was full of mischief. Stevie seemed to always know who was standing near him, and one of his favorite pastimes was to run up and pinch young ladies on their bottoms. He would also tell one of us exactly what we were wearing—what color it was, and how it was styled. Some of us would act amazed, or at least feign amazement; of course, he was in cahoots with somebody. We all loved him.

Early in the spring of 1962, Barbara left the group. Her baby was due in July, and she was really showing. Having a child is a huge responsibility, and I was sure she made the right decision. We would miss her, but we kept in touch and attended her baby shower. Flo, Diane, and I decided it was just too hard keeping a fourth member. The Supremes would be a trio from now on.

Our career seemed to have stalled. Not much was happening for us, so when one of the Marvelettes turned up pregnant that summer, Flo was asked to replace her for a tour. Flo went to Hitsville and rehearsed with the other three girls every day. Their steps were pretty simple and their harmonies weren't all that complex, so it was easy for Flo. After all, compared to the Marvelettes, the Supremes were old pros, having been at it for over three years now. Their short tour followed the usual itinerary—Philadelphia, D.C., and some one-nighters scattered between.

During this tour, Flo and Gladys Horton became closer than ever. Years later Gladys told me about their talks. Gladys would explain to Flo why she felt that, after living in a series of foster homes, Motown really was her home. Flo felt comfortable with Gladys and told her things she would never tell anyone. They shared a room, and Flo told her about everything, including the rape.

The tour was rough; sometimes they'd do eight shows a day. No matter how tired they were, though, they'd lie awake in bed and talk until sleep overcame them.

"I wish I could be more outgoing," Flo said. "Do you think I act too stuck up or anything?"

Gladys replied no, then Flo continued.

"Well, the reason I act this way is because it takes me a long time to get used to guys because of what happened to me."

Gladys understood.

Flo could be friends with some guys, though, and one of her friends was William Knight of the Pips. Mrs. Ardeena Johnson, the girls' chaperone on this trip, caught the pair talking backstage and reprimanded Flo, saying "You can't get too serious . . ."

While Flo was out with the Marvelettes, the Supremes were on hold. Now if anyone around the studio were talking about "the girls," they were talking about the Marvelettes, not us. Diane and I were alone together, again. We became disillusioned and decided to run away from home.

I don't know exactly what went through our heads. Maybe we got nostalgic for the days when we'd just returned to Motown and were treated like we were really something special. Those days were over, and we were beginning to be known as the "no-hit" Supremes. My cousin Josephine had married a man named James Jenkins the summer before. The wedding had taken place at the Pippins' home on Bassett Street, and my family, Jackie Burkes, and the other three Supremes attended. The Jenkinses had since moved to the West Side of Chicago, so that was our destination. We packed our best clothes and took a Greyhound bus to Illinois.

Our parents knew we were going, so we weren't exactly running away from home, but we were running away from Motown and everything else. We were young ladies now, fresh out of school and ready for life. Besides, we needed to get away. We knew where we would stay, and we set out to have a good time. We loved the Chicago nightlife, and we even started dating a couple of the Dells.

Things were going pretty well, but Diane was getting on my nerves. We had to share my cousin's living room, and all she had was a couch, so one of us had to sleep on the floor. During the whole two weeks Diane was there, she never once offered to switch places with me, so I slept on the floor. She went home, but I stayed on for another month. Finally, I got homesick too, and returned to Detroit.

We resumed our old, familiar places in the lobby. Not only did we not get the kind of reception we'd received after our first extended absence, but we could see that Hitsville was crawling with new acts dying to get in.

Around this time, Diane decided to try and get a real job at Hitsville. On slow days, when there were no sessions and nothing for us to do, we got bored. Also, it was now obvious that Diane had a crush on Berry. "I'm going to get him," she'd say. I always liked Berry, but it was hard to picture him as a boyfriend. I thought nothing of it. Diane did land a job as Berry's secretary, but it was more—and less— than a real position. Her duties included keeping us posted on our assignments and bookings and cleaning Berry's desk. Many people around Hitsville thought the job was a joke, and Diane got her share of teasing about it. But she just ignored everyone else and did her work.

Through the years I've come to accept certain tenets of astrology, and I certainly saw them at work in the Supremes. Flo, a Cancerian; Diane, an Aries; and me, a Pisces—three completely different, insecure people. What each of us saw in the other two were the parts of herself she lacked or couldn't assert or tried to deny: Flo's earthiness, my nice-guy demeanor, and Diane's aggressive charm. We accidentally discovered that three separate, incomplete young girls combined to create one great woman. That was the Supremes.

# CHAPTER 11

In the fall of 1962 Motown began sending its artists out on extended tours across the country. Touring the South in those days, we learned more about people and the world than most of our parents ever wanted us to know. For many of us, being in the South allowed us to experience firsthand the hatred and bigotry that had driven many of our parents North years before.

At the same time, these tours were the most exciting thing ever. Not only did we have lots of fun, but we established friendships—and in some cases, love affairs—that have endured. We were thrilled to go on the tour, especially since the Supremes were just about the only act—except for Stevie—included that hadn't yet had a big hit.

That summer Esther Edwards and Beans Bowles organized a tour that would last from mid-October to Christmas 1962, and include the Regal in Chicago, the Howard in Washington, D.C., and the famed Apollo in New York. These theaters were part of the chitlin' circuit, a loosely organized group of venues that catered to the black audience in major cities. In those days, every black performer dreamed of playing the Apollo, and we were no exception.

Mrs. Morrison, a heavy-set woman who resembled singer Ethel Waters, was the chaperone for all the girls on the tour. She was the first of many official escorts who would travel with us in the early days. Esther Edwards had been the first woman to accompany us on the road, and after her strict, overbearing attitude, Mrs. Morrison seemed like an angel. Still, she lectured us.

"Now, girls, this is an opportunity for you that shouldn't be marred by an overeagerness to become intimate with the boys on this trip," she began. And then went on and on to tell us about the perils of impetuous affairs and the effect the consequences might have on our families, our futures, and—especially—our careers.

"Yes, ma'am," we all answered dutifully.

No matter how strict or easygoing our chaperones, each took every available opportunity to lecture us. The only chaperone who didn't lecture was Diane's mom, Mrs. Ross. She was my favorite of all the chaperones, because her expectations were realistic, and she was the most lenient.

The tour lineup consisted of the Contours, the Tempts, the Marvelettes, the Velvelettes (now best remembered for "Needle in a Haystack" and "He Was Really Sayin' Somethin' "), Stevie Wonder, Marvin Gaye, Mary Wells, the Miracles, and the Supremes. Thrown in for good measure was Singing Sammy Ward, a blues singer, and a comic; in this case it was Winehead Willie, my cousin by marriage, who also functioned as master of ceremonies. He can be heard introducing the acts on the first live recording from the Apollo. Willie and I are the only entertainers in the family, and we were excited to be sharing a bill.

Choker Campbell organized the band, all first-rate Detroit musicians who had been working sessions and club dates. Most of these players made more money playing on recordings than touring, and often in the middle of the tour or after a few stops, one of them would go back to Detroit to work, then meet up with us later on. For this reason, Choker sensibly contracted more than one player on the important instruments, such as drums, guitar, bass, and keyboards.

As was Motown's way back then, all agreements were oral. Neither the bandleaders nor the musicians ever signed papers. Though many people working for Motown complained—justifiably—about the money, I never heard a word from the musicians or leaders.

"No," Choker said once, "I never had a problem with Berry. Everybody was very happy. That makes me feel so good. Happiness, togetherness—that's a beautiful thing. Fifteen, maybe sixteen musicians—if they're happy, they're going to play happy." And Choker was right.

There were so many great musicians on the early tours. I remember sax players Tate Houston, Miller Brisker, Norris Patterson, Joe Collins, Willie Smith, who was also an arranger, and Choker; trumpeters Herbert Williams, Little John Wilson, and Tommy "Shaky" Perkson. The rhythm section included Benny Benjamin and "Swing" Lee, guitarists Marvin Tarplin, Cornelius Grant, keyboardists Teddy Harris and Joe Hunter, and of course, James Jamerson on bass. Trombonist James "Chips" Outcault could make his instrument sound like a person talking, which would have us all screaming with laughter.

Working with a sound of that magnitude behind you makes you feel that music really is bigger than life. The vibrations flowed up from the stage floor and through my whole body, dispelling any nerves or fear. I just couldn't wait to go on.

It was quite a mix of people on that first tour: proper, refined chaperones; young, eager kids; the old show-biz pros like the musicians, who couldn't be fazed by anything. We would all be living together in close quarters for up to four months. Forty-five of us squeezed into that rattling old bus, while others traveled in three cars and a couple of station wagons.

On the day of departure, everyone was in high spirits. It was as if we were all going off to Monte Carlo, or some other exotic place. Even those of us who were habitually late were punctual. A few days earlier, Berry made it clear that he wouldn't tolerate tardiness and that those who tested his rule would be left behind.

There were stacks and stacks of luggage—everything from old battered suitcases tied together with string to cardboard boxes. The Supremes had their fair share of pieces—probably more—and we got upset when some of the others complained that we were bringing along more than we needed. Clutching our cosmetic cases, which were filled to the brim with night cream, powder, mascara, eye shadow, eye-liner pencils, and every other conceivable necessity, we tried to ignore their gripes.

Minutes before we boarded the bus, Berry called all the guys in and warned them that he'd better not hear of any messing around on the road. The fellows promised to behave—if the girls wouldn't bother them! And then Berry said to the girls, "I want you girls to leave the fellows on this trip alone. Especially the Contours—they're nothing but trouble. Just leave them all alone."

With the last-minute instructions taken care of, we were all eager to hit the road. A head count was taken, and Beans Bowles checked to see that all the roadies and assistants were accounted for. That done, we all posed in front of the beat-up old bus with MOTOR CITY TOUR painted on the sides. Our smiles were genuine and filled with optimism, despite the wreck looming behind us. Had we been older and wiser, most of us would have wisely refused to board such a decrepit contraption. But fear never crossed our minds, and no one voiced concern about the vehicle's reliability. As we headed out of Detroit, I was sure I was embarking on the greatest adventure of my life.

As the bus chugged along, we all got situated. Once we got comfortable, we started chattering excitedly:

"What's our first stop?"

"Who cares as long as it's outside of this city?"

"Do we go on before you all do?"

"Depends. Who has the biggest hit record?"

"How come Smokey and them get to ride in their own private car?"

"They paid for it, didn't they?"

"Girl, do you think we'll ever have our own car?"

"Can you all sing good enough to get a hit that will buy you a car?"

"Can your mama?"

We were finally on our way.

Passions ran high and it had little to do with who got to sing lead or which group had top billing. We were only onstage a few hours a night; the real thrill was in the traveling and what was happening on the bus.

Despite Berry's last-minute admonishments, people were pairing off before we'd crossed the Michigan state line: Bobby Rogers of the Miracles and Wanda Young of the Marvelettes; Gladys Horton and Hubert Johnson of the Contours. Off the bus I saw Diane eyeing Smokey. Eddie Kendricks was my choice, and I took every opportunity to be alone with him. Frankly, Berry could have saved his breath. We were too young and too excited to care about consequences. For most of us, this was the first big trip away from home, and we were going to have a good time.

While most of the performers sat up in the front of the bus talking and singing, the musicians sat in the back, which they had designated as their private domain. They had what seemed like endless card games, and the gambling, joking, and storytelling went on through the night, but nobody minded. It was as if we could absorb the wisdom of the road, even in our sleep. Since they were older and a lot more savvy about touring and the South, we took comfort in having them around. Nothing seemed to bother these veterans, and their dry sense of humor about things could put otherwise upsetting situations into perspective.

Our first big stop was the Howard Theater in Washington, D.C., followed by seventeen one-nighters. Every few days we would stop at a cheap motel to bathe and wash some clothes. We seldom got to sleep one to a bed, but compared to sleeping sitting up on the hard bus seats, being able to lie on any mattress was heaven. Living in cramped quarters, eating irregularly, going days without the most basic comforts—this was baptism by fire, but none of us complained. With every bump in the road, bad meal, or sleepless night, we knew we were one step closer to being real professional performers, and we cherished every moment.

As we pulled into Savannah, Georgia, we were surprised to see the Staples Singers going into a motel. A number of the other artists with us had worked with them before, so we all jumped off the bus and were introduced to Pops Staples and his daughters Mavis, Cleo, Yvonne, and his son Pervis. Though the Staples weren't as well known as they would be after signing to the Stax label in the late sixties, their gospel style had been popular with blacks since the forties.

"Oh, I love your music," I told Mavis.

"Well, thanks. What is your group called?"

"The Supremes," I answered proudly.

"Well, if you girls sing as good as you look, you will really go places," she said, smiling.

"Thank you!" I was so thrilled. After that they talked with us a while, giving us encouragement and tips on how to deal with life on the road.

As we continued through the South, we ran into bigotry head on. These were the years when blacks were openly challenging the white supremacists, and with civil-rights legislation right around the corner, some racists seemed more determined than ever to keep what they considered "uppity niggers" in their place. Of course, I was no stranger to racism, but somehow I'd come to think that a troupe of artists like ourselves might escape confrontations.

I learned quite differently in Macon, Georgia, when a big barrel-bellied white sheriff stopped our bus. He introduced himself, then said, "I am the peace officer in this here town, and if you folks have any trouble, you just let me know. I'll take care of you."

As it happened, we'd just come from a local service station where the workers had refused to do some work on our bus. "Y'all go right on back down to that same fillin' station," he said. "I'll make sure they do the repairs y'all need."

We turned around and headed back. As we pulled in, we could hear the attendants loudly "muttering" about "them damn niggers."

Even if they had never said a word, we would have known what they thought from the looks of disgust and hatred on their faces. They stood around, just shuffling their feet and refusing to help us until the sheriff arrived.

"Hey, service that bus!" he yelled. "Don't y'all know a new integration law has passed?"

The attendants reluctantly gave in and did some minor repairs and filled the tank. A satisfied sheriff boarded our bus just as we were about to leave. At this point, we were all convinced that we'd found a champion.

"As y'all can see, the local folks down here are not adjusting too rapidly to the new laws and the change in customs. But never you mind. If you run into any problems, you just let me know. In this county, you are under my jurisdiction, and I will not fall short of my duty to uphold the law just because y'all are black and I'm white."

Once he learned our destination, he told us that the theater we were going to play had a "colored"-folks night where blacks were allowed to sit downstairs and the whites were relegated to the balcony. Since this was the opposite of the usual blacks-in-the-balcony arrangement down South, this was considered pretty progressive.

"Take the intermission time to let the people get settled before you start. Because if niggers and white folks get to fighting, I'll put the lights on so bright, it'll all be over. Do you hear me? The dance will be over." Then he added, "I don't want them blacks and whites together anyway."

At first we were shocked, but we were impressed that he put the law before his own personal prejudices, and not the other way around, as so many people did.

A few days later, as we headed out of town, we had many a laugh imitating the sheriff. He was the perfect prototype of the Southern lawman. Unfortunately, however, we didn't have too many more encounters with bigots that we would be able to laugh about. People like the sheriff were few and far between down there. Our biggest problems were always with restaurants. The bus driver would stop and check out the atmosphere, but most times he'd be told, "Yeah, sure y'all can eat here. Tell 'em to come around to the back."

Hearing this, we would all scream indignantly, "We're *not* going around to the back!"

Once, after being told to come in through the back door, Bobby Rogers of the Miracles jumped off the bus and told the owner, who was standing out in the parking lot, that he wanted to enter the place like everybody else—through the front door. "Hey," he informed the owner, "I'm Bobby Rogers of the Miracles!"

Unimpressed, the owner replied, "If you want to eat, you're going to use the back."

By this time, some of the other guys started shouting insults at the owner. A few had gotten off the bus and were practically up in the guy's face.

"Don't you know there's been a law passed against this kind of stuff?"

"Who do you think you are, anyway, honky?"

"I don't want to eat in your funky old restaurant—"

"You need your ass kicked by us niggers. That will show you—"

"Well," the owner said after a few minutes of this, "I'm gonna get my pistol and . . ."

With that he ran inside, and the fellows ran for the bus. The man was serious, and we expected shots to be fired any second. We tore out and after a few minutes all breathed a sigh of relief. As usual, though, the musicians found something to laugh about.

"What did that man say, Bobby?" a voice from the back of the bus teased. " 'You're going to need a Miracle to get your behind out of this'?"

Although our itinerary followed the chitlin' circuit and we performed in the larger black theaters, we also played other gigs, some in open-air arenas and smaller clubs. In Birmingham, Alabama, we were scheduled to perform at a ballpark—picture the bandstand set up over the pitcher's mound and you get the idea of how small-time and tacky it was. What made this particular show special was that it was the first time in the community that an integrated audience got to see a show.

I saw more blacks and whites mingling and certainly more integrated couples than I'd ever seen in Detroit. During the show I heard there had been some trouble in the crowd and that the police had shot someone, but that may have been only a rumor. The show itself went along quite smoothly.

James Jamerson passed a guard backstage and asked if he could use the rest room. As James was coming out, another guard was called, and he said to James, "Hey, nigger, what are you doing here?" James was understandably upset; after all, the promoter should have seen to it that there were accommodations. We seemed to have been put in the middle of a conflict between the townspeople and the promoter, but nothing was said. No one wanted trouble. We just wanted the show to be over so that we could get out.

We were pleased that the shows were a success and the crowd begged for encores, but it had been a long, tense day, and we had to go. We were slowly boarding the bus when we heard several sharp, loud cracks.

"Someone's throwing rocks," one of the Vandellas said as we all looked around to see where they were coming from.

"Them's bullets!" Choker shouted, and at that we ran for the bus. In her panic to board the bus, Mary Wells had fallen down on the bus steps and refused to get up, barring the entrance to the rest of us. Everyone tried to push her out of the way, but she was so big it was impossible.

"Get out of the way, girl!" we all shouted, but she just screamed back, "I am not getting up!"

Finally she moved, and we all got on board as fast as we could. Once the bus was loaded, we flew out of Birmingham. Only after we'd traveled quite a distance did the driver stop to examine the bus. Sure enough, there were bullet holes in some of the windows. None of us —not even the musicians—could find anything to laugh about this time.

The big problem with touring the South was that even when you weren't being shot at or called "nigger," you could never forget where you were. Bigots who were too smart to get violent used intimidation and insults to put you in your place.

One day we stopped at a motel in Miami Beach, where we were scheduled to play that evening. Beans Bowles went into the front office to book our rooms. Suddenly, from out of nowhere, there appeared fifteen police cruisers with dogs. They didn't make a move toward us; they just sat outside and watched us.

At first the owner didn't want any blacks staying at his motel, but once Beans explained our situation to him, he became a total businessman. "I'm not supposed to rent you any rooms," he said, "but this is my motel and I need the money. Come on and check in."

This motel wasn't the Ritz, but it was clean and comfortable. After days on the road, just being able to bathe and rest a few hours before the rehearsal and show was a luxury. It was also a relief to know that we would get a good night's sleep after the show.

But things could never be that simple down South. When we returned after the show, the same cruisers and dogs were waiting.

"You would think we're Martin Luther King on a freedom march," Choker remarked.

Beans decided that enough was enough and approached the police. As road manager, he was responsible for our safety and well-being. Always articulate and personable, Beans was invaluable in this kind of situation. He told the police who we were, what we were doing, and so on. After he'd finished talking with them, they took their dogs and left.

The other interesting thing about people in general is that they have two different standards: one for common blacks and another for entertainers and other famous blacks. I saw this clearly demonstrated once in South Carolina. We pulled up in front of a motel called the Heart of the South, and the whole time we were unloading our stuff and checking in, two rednecks stood outside making offensive remarks, which they made sure we could hear very clearly. It was hard to believe that they wanted to provoke a fight, especially since there were so many strong young men in our group, and one of them was old enough to be a grandfather, but they kept it up, ending their little tirade with this gem:

"By gosh, that's a shame. We gotta get rid of that President Kennedy 'cause he ain't doin' the right thing letting them niggers go and do whatever they want."

Of course, we were all insulted, but we regarded them as just a couple of backwoods fools and ignored them. As I entered the hotel, I saw Choker sitting on his horn case with his back to the two fools, cracking up. I could see that he didn't want them to see that he was laughing, and I can't blame him. But one look at Choker and I almost started laughing myself. After we'd checked in, Choker was still sitting there, wiping tears of laughter from his eyes. Here they were acting like they were so superior, yet talking like idiots. We couldn't help but laugh at them.

As soon as we were settled, we jumped into our swimsuits and headed for the pool. The minute we dived in, the white people started climbing out. They sat on the lounge chairs and stared at us for a while, but when they saw what good divers and swimmers some of us were, they eased themselves back in. A few minutes later, they started getting out again. It took us a while to figure out what was going on. Unbeknownst to us the local radio stations had been playing all of our records over the past few weeks. Once word had spread that they were sharing the pool with the Miracles, Little Stevie Wonder, the Marvelettes, and so-and-so, they ran to get paper and pens for our autographs and asked how they could get tickets for the show.

Our tours made breakthroughs and helped weaken racial barriers. When it came to the music, segregation didn't mean a thing in some of those towns, and if it did, black and white fans would ignore the local customs to attend the shows. To see crowds that were integrated —sometimes for the first time in a community—made me realize that Motown truly was the sound of young America.

As we should have expected, the tour bus finally broke down, in South Carolina. It was hot as hell inside the bus, so we all piled out, only to discover that we were standing next to a jailhouse.

"Hey, who are you guys?" came a voice out of nowhere.

It was obvious from the sound of their voices that most of the inmates were black. All we could see were black hands clutching at the iron window bars, and before long, they all started pleading with us to help them. We girls hung back, afraid to get too close, but the Miracles and the Tempts went up and shook hands with the prisoners through the bars. Once the men understood who we were and what we were doing, they opened up to the guys. The prisoners told their stories, and some of them broke down crying, asking us to talk to someone for them. It was so sad.

"Isn't there something we can do for these fellows?" I asked one of the musicians.

"Are you kidding?" he replied. "We'd better get this bus fixed and get out of here before they throw us in there, too. They don't care about no innocence or guilt down here. That's how they treat niggers in the South. Besides, to hear them tell it, all jailbirds are innocent."

The ugly realities of the South were becoming more evident to me the further we got past the Mason-Dixon line. By the time the bus was repaired and we were on our way, there was little talk and no laughter.

We were in the Carolinas, relaxing after a series of well-received shows, when we decided that we really deserved a big party. We were leaving the next day for Florida, but we stayed up partying all night, and then took off with just a couple hours' rest.

Usually Beans and his driver, Eddie McFarland, left either before or after us. Generally, they stayed behind a few hours to finish up business. This particular morning, Beans and Eddie left a few hours after us, in the Contours' station wagon.

When we arrived at the hotel hours later, there was a message saying Esther Edwards was on her way down by plane and that there had been an accident. We had no way of finding out what had happened to Beans and Eddie; all we could do was to wait.

Before we'd finished breakfast, Mrs. Edwards arrived. She called us all together in one of the rooms. We were anxious to find out what had happened, but before she would tell us, Mrs. Edwards asked us about the night before. Once she was satisfied with our answers she told us that Eddie had fallen asleep at the wheel and crashed into a semi. Beans had been in the back of the car, practicing on his flute. In the collision, the instrument had punctured his armpit and emerged through the back of his neck. Both of his legs were broken and doctors feared he would never walk again. Beans was alive. Eddie had been decapitated and had died.

We were stunned and saddened. Everyone was crying, but Mrs. Edwards kept her head. She got Choker to help her organize things and give her an update on all the business dealings. Somehow everything was settled, and the tour proceeded as planned.

I went back to my room speechless. That night, when the announcer called out "the Supremes," and we pranced onstage, flashing our biggest, sweetest smiles, the oldest cliché in show business ran through my mind: The show must go on.

Our last stop on this tour was New York's Apollo Theater. The manager there was Honi Coles, the ex-partner of Motown choreographer Cholly Atkins. We had been well received by all the crowds so far, but we'd heard that the Apollo was a tough venue. For one thing, if the crowd didn't like you, Coles would come onstage with a long hook and physically drag you off the stage. We won the crowd over from the first minute, though, and came off the stage thrilled to death—we had played the Apollo.

# CHAPTER 12

Diane always had enormous energy. She would flit up and down the aisle of the bus, teasing people and mussing their hair. Sometimes she'd sit quietly for hours, in deep concentration or listening intently to what was being said. But usually she had a mischievous playfulness that she thought was very cute but that most people—especially under the stress of touring—found annoying.

"You do so wear dirty underwear!" Diane, laughing, said to Marvin Tarplin.

Marvin took it as a joke, but Gladys Horton jumped to his defense.

"No, he doesn't!" Gladys screamed.

"I'm not talking to you!" Diane hissed.

Diane and Gladys seemed to be fighting all the time, most often over something silly. Gladys was a country girl and, like Flo, she could be very outspoken. She and Flo understood each other, partially because they both believed that you should speak out whenever you saw a wrong being committed, whether it was your business or not. This trait earned the two of them the occasional wrath of Motown management, but they didn't care. It was obvious they both enjoyed being the defenders of the underdog.

After any set-to with Diane, Gladys would come to the seat I shared with Flo and ask, "Why does Diane act like that?"

I'd shrug it off. "Don't pay any attention to her."

"That's just Diane," Flo would add philosophically. It was clear, though, that few people shared our forgiving attitude, and things could really heat up.

We were playing a show in Philadelphia and had just finished "Let Me Go the Right Way." The song ended abruptly, so the audience didn't start applauding right away. In the silence, I heard Gladys' voice from the wings: "Oh, her dress looks like a nightgown!" I didn't think anything of it. We were wearing long white dresses and there was some competition among the acts regarding stage costumes. The Supremes were always a little more sophisticated, so I just wrote the comment off to jealousy. It didn't mean anything. The three of us bowed and exited the stage.

Diane ran around to the other side, and she was steaming. "Flo, did you hear what she said? She said our dresses look like nightgowns!"

When Diane confronted Gladys, Gladys set her straight. "Diane, I didn't say *their* dresses—I said *your* dress!"

Diane was extremely thin before it was fashionable, and some people thought that our gowns looked nicer on fuller figures. But that wasn't what this was really about. Because Diane was known to have a very high opinion of herself and a low tolerance for criticism, no matter how well intended, some people liked to let her know that they didn't think she was so hot.

The spat continued, with Diane sending a girl who worked at the theater around to Glady's room to deliver a message: "Diane is going to kick your behind after the show."

Later that evening, as we were leaving the theater, Gladys was helping a little blind boy named Lee across the street. She was headed for the station wagon we all shared on this tour, and Diane was sitting behind the wheel. The minute Diane saw Gladys, she pulled out, hit the gas, and stopped just a few feet short of Gladys and Lee. Gladys left Lee standing in the street and ran over to the car screaming, "Go on and hit me!"

Diane gave Gladys the finger, rolled up her window, and sped off. Mrs. Ross, who was in the car, was shocked and reprimanded Diane for her behavior, but Diane didn't seem to be listening.

The next day Diane surprised all of us when she announced that she was going to Gladys' room to apologize. Diane told Gladys, "I called Berry last night and told him about our argument. He said I should apologize because you didn't approach me and you weren't talking to me individually, and I shouldn't get so upset."

Gladys felt very bad after that. This was Berry's way of getting to you psychologically. When he wasn't around, he wanted Diane to learn not to get caught up in petty fights. That was all well and good, but Diane had access to Berry none of us had, and the effect of her doing everything he said—and doing it just because he said to—was a little disconcerting. He was so paternal toward us because he believed that artists should never be allowed to think for themselves. It wasn't that he thought they were particularly stupid; he just thought they should stick to making music.

Over the years, Diane's spats with Mary Wells, Gladys, Dee Dee Sharp, Brenda Holloway, and especially Martha Reeves were company knowledge. If you ever asked Diane why she got into fights, she'd say, "They're picking on me." But that wasn't always the case. Once when Mary Wells suggested helpfully that Diane wear a girdle onstage, Diane flew off and started insulting her.

A few weeks into any tour, everyone got tense. Riding for days in that funky old bus, crowding more than a dozen girls into a tiny dressing room meant for one—it could all get to you. But no matter who was fighting with whom, each of us was loyal to our group. All the girls in the girl groups seemed to stick together that way. I noticed that it was different with the guys; they could be friends with whomever they wanted, and their "fights" were usually playful and full of teasing. With the girls, however, it could get downright vicious.

In addition, there seemed to be a lot of resentment toward the Supremes. Though we still hadn't had a hit, we did get special treatment—Diane's direct line to Berry being just one example—and other groups resented this. Flo, Diane, and I could be friends with other performers, but when it came to business, there was always the feeling that the Supremes were, in some way, different.

The next big event after we'd come home from the first tour was the Motown Christmas party. The Marvelettes were riding the crest of "Please Mr. Postman" 's success, and the Supremes were someplace much further down the totem pole, regardless of any "special treatment" people thought we were getting. We all received gifts. Artists who had sold lots of records got very expensive things; the Marvelettes were each given ⅓-carat diamond rings, which we thought were so extravagant. The rest of us got tiny transistor radios and tape recorders, but no one went away empty-handed.

Everyone in attendance was sharply dressed, and you couldn't tell the secretaries from the stars. Detroiters are flashy dressers to begin with, and people in the music community were even flashier than the rest. All the men wore suits; mohair was the thing then, and there was every color from beige to black. They also wore very expensive, classy ties. The women wore little jewelry except chic custommade pieces, and everyone wore hats. Hardly anyone wore beads or sequins. And, of course, all the girls wore pointed-toe shoes to match their dresses. None of us was making that much money, but almost every cent we did make went on our backs.

These were some of our happiest days. The fame and fortune to come would never replace the caring and true affection we felt for one another in the early years. Of course, we couldn't know that then, and so we were jealous of the attention being lavished on the Marvelettes. Feeling this way seemed out of character for me, but I couldn't help it. The fact that I liked each of the Marvelettes as an individual didn't change the fact that we were all in competition for the same things.

Besides the Marvelettes, the Vandellas were one of our favorite groups. Even as a young girl, Martha Reeves was one of the most soulful singers I'd ever heard. Over the next year, they had hits with "Come and Get These Memories," "Heat Wave," and "Quicksand," and were near the top of the Motown roster. Things happened faster for Martha and her group than they did for us, and this only fueled the rivalry between Martha and Diane. Both had drive and charisma, and neither would ever back down.

Flo and I would get caught in the middle, and though we both liked all the Vandellas—Martha, Rosalind Ashford, and Annette Sterling—our relationship with Martha was strained by her feuds with Diane. Flo and I would always admit—privately—who was right in a spat, and it wasn't always Diane. But she was in our group, and solidarity was crucial, right or wrong.

One time, we were on the bus and Gladys was talking to Hubert Johnson, her seat partner and would-be suitor. "You think you're the cutest one in the group."

"No, I don't," Hubert replied, obviously embarrassed.

Gladys then turned to Billy Hoggs, Hubert's fellow Contour, and said, "Oh, I think you have the prettiest gray eyes, Billy." She smiled, knowing she was driving Hubert wild. He looked over at her and said nothing, but you could see the hurt in his face. This was like watching a soap opera, and Hubert's love might have gone unrequited had it not been for Diane agreeing to speak on his behalf.

"Gladys," Diane said during one of their truces, "Why don't you give Hubert a chance? Hubert wanted to be my boyfriend, but I just didn't want to go out with him. I don't know why—"

"Really?" Gladys was shocked by Diane's revelation and surprised that she was trying to help her.

"Yes," Diane continued. "He's a swell guy. I used to like him a lot—"

"Diane, are you telling the truth?" Gladys was understandably suspicious.

"Yes. I used to like Hubert a while ago, and we didn't hit it off, and I really wanted to. . . . Hey, he's such a nice guy. You should be glad that he chose you."

You could have knocked Gladys over with a feather! Of all the people on the tour, Diane was the last she would have pictured playing Cupid. This was a facet of Diane's personality seldom seen, but Hubert knew exactly what he was doing. Diane's powers of persuasion were strong even then, and she pleaded his case to Gladys beautifully.

We were all sitting in our dressing room after a show, anxious to get out of our costumes and makeup and go out for dinner. Diane was still working on Gladys, and I removed my makeup a little more slowly, trying to hear every word. Whatever Diane said definitely worked, for Gladys and Hubert were soon an item.

Wherever we were, the three of us spent most of our spare moments practicing as quietly as we could, or talking about boys.

"Girl, that Bobby Rogers is good-looking!" Flo would say.

"Well, why don't you and he get together?"

"Mary, I think he likes somebody else."

It was sad that she was still so frightened of men. Flo was always more comfortable around other girls, where she could relax and laugh. We would all be backstage, coping with preshow nerves, running down our songs, or mending a stage costume, and always talking girl talk. There would be Mary Wells, Martha and the Vandellas, the Marvelettes, Claudette Robinson, and us, all squashed together in a tiny room. Flo would tease and joke around with everyone, good-heartedly offering pointers and suggestions about makeup and hair to the other girls.

We saw this side of her, but people who didn't often commented that she was hard to get close to, moody. And when she was uncomfortable, I suppose she was. We were all so involved with the shows and the tour that we paid little attention to things like that.

In between the four or five shows we did each day on these tours, we all looked forward to meeting at the local soul-food place and having a dinner of gravy-smothered steak, greens, and cornbread. For young kids far from home, the phrase "like Mother used to make" took on a whole new meaning. We especially liked the Uptown Theater in Philadelphia, because right outside the stage door was the house of a woman who made the best dinners I'd ever eaten north of the Mason-Dixon line. No restaurant license was displayed, and she never had to advertise. Word of mouth from veterans of the road kept the place packed. Eight people would crowd around a table meant for four, and some of the older musicians who didn't want to wait for a table would eat standing up.

Mealtime was the best time of the day. We could relax for a change and think about something else besides the shows. Flo would eat with Gladys, Rosalind, Annette, or any of the other girls. The guys would start up a card game, and we would fix our nails, touch up our makeup, or attend to our hair. We would turn on the nearest radio to keep abreast of the latest hits. If a Motown hit came on, we'd all stop talking, listen, then cheer at the end. There was such optimism in those days. We knew that our turn was coming, soon.

These were good times, and we never seriously considered doing anything else, but as we got older we started to realize that money would become a more important consideration than it had been. The allowance we received for travel was little more than spending change, and I remember looking to the back of bus and hearing the heated betting, and wishing I had learned to play poker.

One day we got a real surprise. We were sitting on the bus, getting ready to take off, when Berry came aboard and shouted, "I've come to take you suckers' money!"

"Man, where did you come from?" Choker howled before he doubled over with laughter.

"Hey, everybody, Mr. Gordy's here!" one of the girls yelled.

"How are you all doing?" Berry asked. We all said "Fine," but Berry wasn't really listening as he made his way to the back.

Choker was gleefully rubbing his hands together. They all stopped talking and the game was on. All the regulars sat in for the first few hands, but the number of players thinned out as the stakes rose.

After several hours it was down to just Berry and Choker. As he often did, Berry was chewing on his tongue as he concentrated. I always found it amusing that a number of the younger producers around the company, including Smokey Robinson and Brian Holland, adopted Berry's mannerisms; they would chew their tongues, too.

By the time we reached our destination, Berry was ready to catch the next plane back to Detroit. He'd lost $6,000 to Choker, and though I know Berry didn't necessarily mind losing, I'm sure he hadn't expected to lose that much. But Berry was a risk taker, and he taught us all not to fear taking a chance.

Whenever we were on tour, we would do our set, then we'd change into our street clothes so we could watch the rest of the show. Every night we'd watch to see if the Contours got a bigger response than the Tempts, or if the crowd favored Martha and the Vandellas over the Marvelettes. The lineup was determined by whoever had the biggest hit record out (they would go toward the end), and the order was arranged so that one act would leave the stage hot for the next one. When you hit the stage, you really had to go for blood, because everyone on the tour was so good. The polish and poise Motown acts were famous for came not only from practice but from watching other acts. I especially enjoyed watching Marvin Gaye and Stevie. They were always great.

Little Stevie Wonder never failed to get a crowd going. Though he was the youngest in the group, he had one of the best senses of humor and we loved him.

Motown went to great pains to protect Stevie and provide him with the best care when he was away from home. Because of the legal restrictions and labor laws regarding minors, Stevie had to finish his performance by a certain hour. This was a curfew, and the hour varied from state to state, as did our show times, so we would always have to juggle the lineup to accommodate Stevie. He also had to travel with a tutor. Like all young kids, Stevie would do anything to get out of doing his schoolwork, and during one trip he would feign sleep whenever he heard his tutor approach. His teacher was a kind, studious young man who took his responsibility for Stevie's education very seriously. Nonetheless, he could never bring himself to awaken this poor exhausted child, and Stevie got away with murder.

One night in Chicago, we were all standing around backstage watching the show from the wings. Stevie had just finished his set and Mary Wells was waiting to go on. Because of the curfew, Stevie had done an abbreviated set and then quickly left the stage. Each act had its own conductor; Mary had bass player Joe Swift, and Stevie had Clarence Paul. Stevie had just finished "Fingertips—Pt. 2" and left the stage. When the crowd demanded an encore, Clarence—an old show-biz veteran—pushed Stevie back onstage. It was a choreographed ploy designed to make the audience think that Stevie didn't know where he was. Joe Swift had already taken over the conductor's spot, and when Stevie started the reprise of "Fingertips," Joe was shouting, "What key, Little Stevie, what key?" Many people don't know that Motown regularly recorded our live shows, and has in the vaults countless unreleased live video and audio tapes, most of which I've never seen. Stevie's number was one of the few that was released, and in August 1963, it became his first number-one hit.

Like the musicians, the performers sometimes snuck away from Hitsville to do a little session work on the side, which was strictly forbidden. One day, Joe Hunter pulled me aside and said, "I can give you a hundred dollars to come with me to Chicago."

"Say no more!" Compared to the lousy five or ten bucks we got for every song we recorded, a hundred dollars was a fortune. I went to Chicago with James Jamerson, Hank Crosby, and anyone else Joe wanted to take along. Like many of the other bandleaders, Joe was very generous about sharing his freelance work with others. Also with us were the Andantes, Motown's in-house background vocal group— Jackie Hicks, Marlene Barrow, and Louvain Demps. These three appear on about three quarters of all Motown's releases, including those by the Four Tops, the Temptations, Marvin Gaye, and even the Supremes.

This was a session for Jerry Butler that Curtis Mayfield was producing for Vee Jay. We recorded a song called "A Teenie Weenie Bit of Your Love." I also worked on blues legend John Lee Hooker's "Boom, Boom, Boom."

Back in Detroit, we were always out of town on smaller tours, with just one or two other acts. The Motown groups would share the bill with other performers, such as Ike and Tina Turner, Dionne Warwick, Flip Wilson, Jackie Wilson, and Richard Pryor. When we were playing the Howard, there was another girl group, Patti LaBelle and the Blue-Belles, and everyone remarked that one of their members, Cindy Birdsong, looked a lot like Flo.

Instead of using a professional driver for these trips, the company relied on people who had approached them for jobs. Many of these people were aspiring artists or people who just liked hanging around. Among the upcoming artists who drove for us were the Spinners and the Dells.

The Supremes never missed any opportunity to practice our craft. Once while we were singing "Canadian Sunset," the Marvelettes were awestruck by our harmonies.

"I wish we could do that," Gladys said.

"Well, we've been at it a long time," Flo replied, trying to reassure Gladys.

We were riding in John O'Den's van to Virginia, and Diane was talking constantly. Before long, she almost had Gladys in tears, going on and on about the fact the Supremes still hadn't gotten a hit, and she was blaming Billie Jean Brown, who was in charge of screening all the recordings for Berry. Though Janie Bradford was still the queen of the lobby and there were many more secretaries around, Billie Jean was the one Berry seemed to have the most trust in. Billie Jean had attended Cass and was now the head of Quality Control. Some of the guys around Hitsville complained about how hard it could be to persuade Billie Jean to give their tapes to Berry.

"Gladys," Diane said, "we have all this great stuff, and Billie Jean will not let Berry hear it. She doesn't like me."

Gladys seemed shocked and sympathetic to our plight.

"We never did anything to her," Diane went on. "When Fridays come and they're playing all the records for Berry to review, she sticks our good stuff in the back, and Berry doesn't even listen to it."

Mrs. Edwards was our chaperone on this trip, and I'm sure Diane was saying all this as much for her benefit as for Gladys'. Mrs. Edwards said nothing.

"Don't worry, Diane," Gladys said, trying to reassure her. "You all will get a hit record. It just takes time, you know."

We knew.

# CHAPTER 13

By late 1963, we were getting tired of waiting. Many of the other Motown acts were doing great: the Miracles had "You've Really Got a Hold on Me," the Vandellas had "Heat Wave," and Marvin Gaye had "Hitch Hike." Though we were still the "no-hit" Supremes, we were working very hard doing numerous one-nighters and minitours. Coming to this point had been a long, happy struggle, and it seemed to be getting more difficult each year. We were working at a whirlwind pace, with our schedules for dates and recording sessions often in conflict.

Another thing that frustrated us was the amount of attention other groups were receiving. In the beginning, it sometimes seemed that the public didn't understand us. The songs we'd been recording were sweet and usually soft, and we found ourselves put in a "charm" bag. We complained to one another and to our friends, but we knew we were lucky to be with Hitsville, and we made the best of it. Being out of school, we were doing more out-of-town dates, and learning more and more about the world.

Once at the Royal in Baltimore we followed a very popular show called the Jewel Box Revue. It was a gay revue, something that I'd never even heard of then, and the show, complete with men in drag, attracted a largely homosexual audience. Perhaps because there were so few shows of this type anywhere, the crowd was extremely well integrated for the Howard, and they seemed to enjoy our show, too.

We were boarding the bus after the last show when a very masculine-looking lesbian ran up to the vehicle and started screaming for Martha Reeves. This woman had been following and bothering Martha the whole week we were there, and Martha was embarrassed and uncomfortable about it. Martha was sitting on the bus when the woman started screaming, "Martha, I love you," and pressing her face against the window. She was crying, and Martha was humiliated beyond words. Being young and wild ourselves, we all thought it was a big joke, and we teased Martha, but deep inside none of us really knew what to think of it either. Traveling around the country, there was no end to what you could see.

We played some pretty rough places. I remember a time in Cleveland when we did a show with Flip Wilson. Flip's material was as blue as Redd Foxx's, and Berry asked him to tone it down around us. What really concerned us was that the Supremes weren't generally considered as "soulful" as some of the others, and once we heard acts like Patti LaBelle and the Blue-Belles, whose style seemed more dramatic and histrionic, we knew we were in for a rough time. We didn't really look very soulful, either. We weren't yet wearing sequined chiffon gowns, but while the other girl groups were in cute, matching outfits that seemed designed to play up their sweetness and innocence, we were wearing the most sophisticated dresses we could find, short dresses with full, solid taffeta skirts covered by floral-printed nylon, usually in some pastel color. We also had one long black sheath; that was our first really elegant gown. The Supremes seemed to be everything a funky crowd would not like, but as we became more experienced we noticed that once we stepped onstage, everyone quieted down. They could see that we were different, and we rarely had a hard time.

Even though we were out of high school, we were still underage, so we never traveled without a chaperone. Up until 1965 or so, when we turned twenty-one, we'd always be accompanied on the road by an older woman. Of course, each had her own ideas and attitudes, but one thing they all shared was a love for lecturing us. "Now, girls . . ." was the standard opening phrase, and what followed could be answered only with polite "Yes, ma'am"s. Several, like Diane's mother, Mrs. Ross, were wonderful to have around, but there were others who were entertaining for reasons they would never have guessed. One woman, Mrs. Ardeena Johnson, was a friend of Moms Gordy and, except for Esther Edwards, was by far the strictest. Mrs. Johnson prided herself on being an educated woman, and she spoke and acted like an aristocrat. What was so funny about her was that, despite the hoity-toity façade, she loved to drink and was sure that no one knew her little secret.

The cardinal rule of chaperoning was never to leave your charges unguarded, and, as a result, we had some interesting substitutes. Once, when Mrs. Ross ran out for a bite to eat, she left us backstage at the Howard Theater under the watchful eye of Jackie Wilson. People who knew Jackie would equate this with leaving a kid in charge of a candy store, but Mrs. Ross had made him promise to keep us out of trouble. The minute she left, Jackie let us out, and we were down the hall, flirting with the Dells.

This was all great fun, but we needed a hit, and Berry Gordy was becoming obsessed with making us stars. The word went out to everyone at Hitsville: "Get a hit on the Supremes." We had worked with a couple of other producers, including Berry, but most of our records were done under Smokey Robinson's aegis. Still nothing. Berry decided in mid-1963 that there should be a "marriage" between the Supremes and writer/producers Brian Holland, Lamont Dozier, and Eddie Holland, or HDH. Although early indications weren't promising, by year's end this would prove to be a match made in heaven.

Brian Holland, Eddie Holland, and Lamont Dozier joined up with Berry the same way so many others did in the early days. Eddie was a sixteen-year-old aspiring singer when he met Berry at the Graystone Ballroom in the late fifties. Unlike many of the early Hitsville crowd, Eddie's love of music wasn't everything for him—he wanted money.

Eddie's younger brother Brian also had musical talent. "At an early age, Brian was much better at music than I," Eddie recalled. "I knew my brother was interested in music, so I told Berry about him. Berry asked me how old Brian was, and I told him Brian was about sixteen. Berry thought that he was too young, but I convinced him to listen to him."

By this time, Eddie had joined Berry and some of his collaborators in trying to create hits. Eddie recalls that at first Berry wasn't crazy about Brian; he thought he was a little fresh. Eventually, though, Brian was working with Berry's group, and writing with Janie Bradford.

Lamont Dozier had been singing around Detroit since the age of fifteen. He also met Berry in the late fifties and, like both Holland brothers, briefly pursued a recording career, under the name Lamont Anthony. Freddy Gorman (our producer and ex-mailman), Lamont, and Brian wrote together until about 1961, when Freddy dropped out. By then, it was clear that Eddie's singing career wasn't taking off, and he told his brother that he thought he had a feel for writing.

"Why don't you let me write the lyrics?" Eddie asked Brian. "If you and Lamont do the melody and I do the lyrics, you could move at a faster pace, and we could get more songs done quicker and deal with more people, and finally make a lot of money." Brian said okay, but Lamont hedged at first. Eventually, the three worked out a system: Lamont created the melodies, Eddie took care of the lyrics and working with the singers, and Brian was in charge of production and working with the musicians. Of course, there was some overlap—Lamont, for example, also knew a lot about production—and the chemistry was only perfected over time, but eventually the HDH style would be Motown's calling card.

After Diane's relationship with Smokey ended, she set her sights on another married man—Brian Holland. He was a real gentleman and he liked Diane a great deal. They would work late in the studio, and Brian would do little things like write notes to Diane and give them to Janie Bradford to deliver to her. Before long, of course, everyone at Hitsville knew what was up and Brian's wife Sharon soon got wind of it, too. Diane and Brian saw each other from late 1962 through late 1963, and Sharon made her displeasure about the subject quite public. She would come to the studio and say, "I know Diane Ross is messing with my husband, and if I catch her, I'm going to kick her butt!"

Sharon was not a small woman, and one night at the Twenty Grand, she decided to make good on her threat. We were all on our way in to do our show, when Sharon accosted us, the Velvelettes, and my friend Alice Fletcher. Sharon was shouting obscenities at Diane, and we all circled around Diane, with Flo stepping right in the middle. Sharon kept saying she was going to kick Diane's butt, and for a few minutes, we had to hold Diane back—she was raring to go. We could see that it would be no contest, but we were also concerned that Sharon might take a swing at one of us. We were relieved when finally, we got Diane in the car and away from Sharon. Soon thereafter, Diane stopped seeing Brian.

Though we hadn't yet scored the big hit, a few of our records did get regional and a little national airplay. In January "Let Me Go the Right Way," which Berry produced, went to #90, and "A Breath Taking Guy," one of Smokey's tunes, topped at #75 late that summer. As we traveled across the country we met countless people who were working hard on our behalf, the record promotion men and disc jockeys who liked our records and did everything they could to bring them to the public's attention. Among them were Bob King at WOOK, Bill

Johnson of WUST, Al Bell (who later founded Stax) of WUST, Kelson "Chop Chop" Fisher, Al Jefferson, Paul "Fat Daddy" Johnson, Long, Tall, Lean, Lanky Larry Dean, Butterball, Robin Seymore, Dave Shaffer, Eddie Castleberry, Bill Williams, and scores more. They would also see that our records got plenty of airplay right before we came to town, and as a result the crowds always knew our songs and made us feel welcome.

Eddie Bisco was a white record promoter based in the Baltimore-Washington area who worked especially hard on our behalf. When we met him in 1962, he was around our age, and we knew he had a crush on one of us; it turned out to be Diane. Because Marvin Gaye's family lived in the area, Eddie had become good friends with Marvin, and Marvin's father, the Reverend Gay (Marvin added the *e* to his name when he became a performer), often had Eddie to his home for dinner when Marvin was in town.

In late 1963 Marvin married Anna Gordy. News of the impending marriage came as quite a shock to all of us. I felt very close to Marvin, and we were all hurt and confused when he began avoiding us. Shortly before the wedding, our conversations with him started to center on business and recording; there were no more leisurely afternoons spent around the piano. Of course this match was the talk of Hitsville, for not only was Marvin marrying the boss's sister, but she was seventeen years older than he. Though we no longer enjoyed our special relationship with Marvin, he still liked us very much. When he found out that Eddie had a crush on Diane, he arranged for Eddie to come up to York, Pennsylvania, where we were all playing, and stay with him and Anna.

We were all delighted to see Eddie; whenever we got together, we'd sing a new song for him or try out new bits of choreography, and he would tell us what he thought. After this particular show, we were all walking back to the hotel. Diane and Eddie were holding hands. We were crossing a street when a car suddenly swerved, missing Diane and Eddie by just inches. It wasn't an accident, either; the driver didn't like the idea of a white boy walking with a black girl.

Being white, Eddie was sometimes stuck in the middle. There were still plenty of restaurants and hotels that didn't allow blacks, and black establishments that didn't want whites. These restrictions reflected the local attitudes, but rarely in our travels did we see these barriers carried over into show business.

Once back at the hotel, Diane and Eddie, Flo and Paul Williams, and Eddie Kendricks and I went back to our room to talk and listen to records. The single room was divided into three sections by curtains hung from the ceiling; it was hardly the place to get intimate, with four other people just feet away. But when Mrs. Edwards burst in, we could tell she didn't see things that way. According to the rules of the road, none of the boys should have been in the room, and we all deserved a good talking to, but Mrs. Edwards ignored Paul and Eddie Kendricks and zeroed in on Eddie Bisco.

"*You* don't belong here. Young man, you are in trouble. I suggest you get back to Washington, D.C., as soon as possible."

We were all embarrassed; Eddie was getting the brunt of it because he was white. He ran back to Marvin and Anna's room. They suggested he stay overnight with them and try to talk with Esther in the morning. When Eddie apologized and promised it would never happen again, Mrs. Edwards was all business: "Well, I hope not, because your distributors could possibly lose the line," she warned. Fortunately, nothing came of her threats, and I've often wondered if the incident was ever reported to Berry.

Diane and Eddie continued their long-distance romance for nearly a year; she would call him collect, until his parents put a stop to that. Whenever we were in his area, we'd get together with Eddie, and he became our cohort in devising schemes to sneak out of our chaperone's sight. We never did anything bad; after working all day, just being able to go to a restaurant, bowl a few frames, or play cards in our dressing room was bliss. Diane kept in touch with Eddie for years, and he was one of our greatest boosters, encouraging us to forge on even when things looked dim.

That fall we'd made our first record with HDH, "When the Lovelight Starts Shining Through His Eyes" backed with "Standing at the Crossroads of Love" (a song HDH would rework into the Four Tops' "Standing in the Shadows of Love"). When "Lovelight" hit #23—our best showing so far—we thought we were on the right track, but when "Run, Run, Run" (b/w "I'm Giving You Your Freedom") just barely slipped into the Hot 100, we were distraught. We had been certain "Run" would be our big smash, and we began to doubt that this "marriage" would endure. After three years of recording we were dying to get that elusive hit. We liked Brian, Eddie, and Lamont and had a great rapport with them. They'd been doing great work with other artists lately—"Come and Get These Memories," "Heat Wave," and "Quicksand" for Martha and the Vandellas, "Mickey's Monkey" and "I Gotta Dance to Keep from Crying" for the Miracles, and

"You're a Wonderful One" (on which we did the backing vocals) for Marvin Gaye. When would our turn come?

One day we were working in the studio and Berry came in. He said, "I know everybody in the group sings lead, but Diane has the more commercial voice, and I want to use her as the sole lead singer."

We were all surprised to hear this; there wasn't even a discussion. Berry had made up his mind. We still believed that having three lead singers made the Supremes unique, but that didn't seem as important to Berry as making more commercial records. Of course, Flo and I were disappointed, but we never thought the arrangement would be permanent. Certainly, when a song came along that either of us could do very well, we'd get our chance. At that moment, all we knew was that we wanted a hit—desperately. If this was how we were going to get it, fine.

HDH had worked up some new tunes, including "Where Did Our Love Go," "Come See About Me," and "Baby Love," but we were quite upset when we heard them. To our ears, they sounded childish, with just a few words or phrases repeated over and over. Besides, we wanted to do something soulful, something with spirit, like the songs Martha Reeves was doing.

"Hey, we want hits," I told them one day.

"Yeah," Flo added, "stop giving us these songs you know won't be hits."

"Trust us," they said, laughing.

I couldn't, though. I went into their office to give them a piece of my mind.

Eddie tried to console me. "You don't like these now," he said, "but—just wait. You will."

All I could say was okay; we were lucky to get anything at this point.

One day in late March 1964 Eddie Holland wanted us to record "Where Did Our Love Go," which needed a subtle lead. Since that was my forte and I'd been doing the ballads for as long as we'd been singing together, I was certain it would be given to me. As was the usual procedure, he'd played the song for Berry, the Quality Control people, and a few other singers to get an idea of who might be best for it. Berry suggested that he try the Supremes on it. He offered it to the Marvelettes, but they turned it down, opting to record a song Eddie had written with Norman Whitfield called "Too Many Fish in the Sea."

To my ears, "Where Did Our Love Go" was a teenybopper song.

It had childish, repetitive lyrics ("Baby, baby, baby, baby don't leave me, please don't leave me . . ."), a limited melody, and no drive. It was too smooth, and I couldn't imagine anyone liking it. Still, this was probably going to be my lead, so I decided to make the best of it. But it was soon clear just what Berry had meant by his announcement. I later learned that Eddie wanted me to sing it, but that his partners had convinced him that Diane had the more commercial sound and, besides, wasn't she the lead singer?

Flo and I went along with them, and Diane did the lead. Little did we know that neither of us would ever sing lead on a Supremes single again. HDH hit upon a special formula for the Supremes and, after a few hits, Diane's voice became as much a part of the formula as the arrangements or any other HDH trademark. The bigger we got, the less anyone at Motown wanted to tamper with what was beginning to look like a sure thing. This changed our sound in other ways as well. On our earlier records, Diane would do her lead, then sing with us on the background, but eventually the backgrounds were done by Flo and me. Besides being upstaged, Flo and I also felt that the records suffered; our three-part harmonies were so beautiful; we should have recorded more of them.

From this day on, we'd spend almost every day we weren't on the road or involved in some other business recording with HDH. Although no complete record exists, I'd say we probably recorded at least five or six tracks for every one that was finally released, everything from show tunes to gospel. Motown was careful to release only winners.

In early 1964 the Supremes became one of the first Motown acts to perform outside the United States when we played the Clay House Inn, a classy black supper club in Bermuda. After months on the road we were ready for a vacation, and we had one in Bermuda. The people there loved us, and we took every opportunity to swim, bicycle, or just lie around, so we were in good shape when we got back to Detroit and learned we were booked for another tour.

We were flattered to hear that Dick Clark, the young host of TV's *American Bandstand*, wanted the Supremes for one of his Caravan of Stars package tours. Tours like these—a roster of stars from various labels traveling around for up to three or four months—could never be arranged today. Traveling is too expensive, the logistics are too complicated, and performers now have savvy managers whose various conflicts make the kind of cooperation we had back then impossible to achieve, unless it's for a good cause, like Live Aid. For just $1.50, kids got to see maybe a dozen of their favorite stars. Those days are gone forever, and I am happy that I was part of it while it lasted.

The tours would run from Memorial Day to Labor Day, and the other acts on the bill were the Jelly Beans, Major Lance, the Velvelettes, the Shirelles, Bobby Sherman, the Crystals, the Dixie Cups, Brian Hyland, Mike Clifford, the Ripchords, Gene Pitney, and Dee Dee Sharpe. Dick, who will always be one of my favorite people, was a great promoter, too. He gave us support and encouragement, and, unlike many other business people, never acted as if he were above us. He rode on the same cramped, dirty bus we did, and treated us all as equals.

Like the Motown tours, the Caravan went through the South. Whenever we came to a restaurant that would not serve blacks, Dick put it to a vote. Every time, our white colleagues voted to wait until we found a place that would serve us all. As a result, we usually ended up eating at the local Greyhound terminal, but we were all together.

All three of us made lots of friends on this tour. Mike Clifford was a white singer whose hits, "Close to Cathy" and "What to Do with Laurie," made him one of United Artists' most promising young stars. He and I spent hours talking, but I knew he really liked Diane. Many men were attracted to her even then. She had a certain air about her, a coy shyness that they found intriguing. Having known Diane as a little tomboy, I was amazed by this recent transformation. Her mother was chaperoning on this tour, and Diane stayed very close to her. Mike would ask her to eat out with him, but Diane would always decline, saying that she was going to have dinner with her mother.

Flo, on the other hand, was having a great time flirting with all the guys. It was obvious that she did this to be friendly and wasn't looking for a serious relationship with any man, but all the boys ate it up.

"Where are you from?" Flo would ask, and no matter what the reply, she'd come up with a funny line about their hometown that would have them rolling in the aisles. "Baby, I am from the Motor City. You ever been there?" And when they'd say no, Flo would do her best Mae West-cum-Edie Adams imitation, putting on the sexiest grin and saying, "No? Then why don't you come up and see me sometime?" At times like these, Flo was the life of the party, and everyone loved her.

My heartthrob on this trip was the star, Gene Pitney. I fell in love the minute I laid eyes on him and spent every moment I wasn't sitting beside him figuring out the best way to discreetly move over to his seat. Despite his having a string of hits behind him—including "Town without Pity" and "Only Love Can Break a Heart"—he was modest and polite. This was quite exciting, even though Gene was engaged, and we never so much as smooched the whole trip. When Diane noticed that I liked Gene, she pulled me aside.

"Why do you like that white boy?" she asked incredulously.

Why not? I thought.

A tour was a tour, but we felt we'd taken a step up with this one. Dick was an experienced promoter, and because of his reputation he was able to get us booked into places that were nicer than ones we'd worked on the chitlin' circuit. Some of these places were just high-school gymnasiums, auditoriums, or roller rinks without stages or dressing rooms, but they were still nicer.

A few weeks into the tour, everyone started getting bored, and the bus became the target of our frustrations. Garbage of all descriptions littered the floor. Sleeping was usually impossible, and so the three of us would stay up and practice our tunes. Those who wanted to sleep yelled at us to quiet down, and in Dick's book *Rock, Roll, and Remember*, he refers to "dummies" who sang all night. He was probably talking about the Supremes.

We would sometimes have to change—boys and girls together—in minutes under a makeshift stage, and sometimes we had to do our dressing, hair, and makeup on the moving bus. We soon got into sharing everything with everyone else—Mike Clifford liked using our Max Factor foundation, because he liked the tan look.

No matter what the circumstances, the Supremes always looked great. We were always well dressed, neat, color-coordinated and fully accessorized. Our image was important to us even then. Once, when an angry bus driver took off with the bus and our stage clothes, we weren't sure what to do. After discussing it with Dick, we went on in our street clothes. Our two most popular outfits were red sleeveless spaghetti-strap dresses with tons of fringe, and a silver spandex costume, complete with tight pants, halter tops, and high heels. We looked hot.

Tensions did mount, and sooner or later there'd be fights. Diane always made friends with everyone on the tour; she often would do their hair for them. But this camaraderie never stopped her when she felt she'd been wronged or slighted. When that happened, Diane pulled out all the stops until her opponent was forced to concede. Brenda Holloway and Diane were getting along fine on this trip until Diane insisted that Brenda had stolen her can of hairspray. Brenda denied the charge, but the two of them went back and forth about it until the Shirelles came to Brenda's defense, confirming that Brenda had had the same can of spray since the tour started. As much as I sympathized with Brenda, I knew that Diane was out of line, there was no way I, or Flo for that matter, was going to side against her. Mrs. Ross talked to her, and she finally calmed down, but she had been so clearly mistaken that we were all a little embarrassed by the situation.

One of the most dramatic spats involved Diane and one of my favorite Crystals, Delores Brooks, whom we called Lala. We all liked Lala; she was friendly and outgoing, and she had even made friends with Diane. Then one night while we were en route to a date, Diane accused Lala of stealing a pair of her shoes. Lala denied it, but Diane carried on about it, crying and playing the victim. Not everyone liked Lala; some people thought she was a real pain. When the argument escalated, Diane and Lala were ordered off the bus. We were all sure it was going to come to blows, and this worried Mrs. Ross, who jumped in the middle. Lala, a real sight in her four-foot-high beehive hairdo, was screaming at the top of her lungs and ready to belt Diane. By this time even Flo was set to defend Diane, and I was sure she was going to punch Lala any minute. Finally, Ed McAdam, the tour manager, intervened and told them both to shut up, get back on the bus, and sit down.

We were all embarrassed, but probably no one was as embarrassed as Mrs. Ross. She would talk to Diane, but Diane would still do little things that drove other people crazy. For example, we often had to dress for a show in a school locker room, where there was only one small mirror on the wall. One of the girls would be standing in front of the mirror putting on her makeup, and Diane would come along, smiling and acting very sweet, and sort of work her way around whoever was standing there so that she would be in front of the mirror. It was all done so casually that, by the time you realized what had happened, it was too late.

Diane always had a temper, and while some people might have seen her actions as the result of conniving, her behavior was actually more like that of a spoiled brat. Once she made up her mind about something, there was no reasoning with her, and even being her best friend didn't ensure that what you said would be taken as it was meant. In Diane's mind, anything that wasn't a compliment was a criticism, which hurt her deeply.

Diane would fight with anyone, and often she would take a minor issue and keep on it until you reacted. Knowing Diane as Flo and I did, we understood that the best way to deal with her in these situations was to ignore her. Diane was like a child testing a parent. Over time, her tantrums and shows of temper became like bad habits, and Flo's and my responses became reflexes. When we saw it coming, we just tuned out.

One day, for a reason so trivial I can't even remember it, Diane jumped on my back and started pulling my hair. She was punching me and screaming at me. Flo was within seconds of intervening when Mrs. Ross appeared and pulled her off me. One of Mrs. Ross' finest qualities was her sense of justice, and she never sided with Diane blindly.

Ironically, Diane made the only truly profound statement I ever heard her utter in the middle of one of these spats. She was carrying on about something, goading me to respond, and I just refused.

"Mary," Diane said in her crisp, high voice, "you better let it all out. Because if you keep it inside, it's gonna hurt you."

She was probably right. The statement also revealed to me one reason why she didn't hesitate to make a scene, which was something Flo and I just would not do: She saw it as quasi-therapeutic.

When the Dick Clark tour started, the Supremes got the usual polite hand after each number. Maybe a few people in the crowd would know "Buttered Popcorn" or "Lovelight," but the response we got was a mere whimper compared to the screams Gene Pitney or the Shirelles elicited. In our absence, Motown had released "Where Did Our Love Go" sometime in June. We knew it was out, but we weren't yet sufficiently interested in the business side of music to be reading *Billboard* or *Cashbox*, and without a radio on the bus we had no idea who had a hit.

Slowly, though, we began to notice the applause getting a little louder and a little wilder in each city. When the audience screamed for us, we stood in the wings paralyzed with disbelief. They really wanted us! By the end of August 1964, the "no-hit" Supremes had the number-one song in the country.

# CHAPTER 14

We returned to Detroit in August, feeling like we had really made it at last. Having a number-one record proved to the world what Flo, Diane, and I had believed for years—we were the greatest. I couldn't wait to get back to Hitsville and find out how rich we were.

As long as we'd been with Motown I always seemed to be the one who spoke up for the three of us when it came to business. We couldn't wait to find out how much we'd earned, and I went to Esther Edwards' office feeling very proud. When I asked her how much each of us would get, she replied, "There is no money. Motown managed to get you on the Dick Clark tour only because he wanted Brenda Holloway. I told him to take you too, and he agreed."

"But, Mrs. Edwards," I said, "we've been on the road for three months, and most of the shows were sellouts. Surely, there must be some money coming to us."

"You were paid only six hundred dollars a week. Deduct from that the price of room and board and food for yourselves and Mrs. Ross and that leaves nothing." Then, as if to add insult to injury, she added, "It probably cost the company, but you needed the exposure." I tried to figure it out; where could the money have gone, especially when we so rarely stayed in a room anywhere?

I left the meeting crushed. Why did there always seem to be another hurdle? Up until now, we were having so much fun—it really was like living a fairy-tale. While most of our friends had gotten married, gone on to college, or were working at boring jobs, we were in show business and having the time of our lives. It seemed like we were living under a spell—and perhaps we were.

"Girls," Mrs. Edwards had said, "you know that what you're getting paid is important, but more important is how you project yourselves to people. When they begin to like you, they go out and buy your records, so think about your show."

Our "show" was our lives. We concentrated on what to wear, how to fix our hair, how to speak, what to say to journalists and other people we met, and so on. Even this early in the game, we were getting little messages that we wouldn't really understand until years later, like "Be careful about the guys you decide to marry, and make sure your husband has as much money as you. Because if he doesn't, he'll always be looking at your pocketbook."

The Supremes hadn't yet made their fortune, but judging by the way many of our colleagues at Motown (as Hitsville was now known) carried on, you'd think everybody else had. No one really knew how much anyone else was getting paid, but the general consensus was that the writers and producers were doing pretty well. I was sitting on the porch at Motown when I overheard this conversation:

"Man, I'll give you the money to buy a Cadillac," Brian Holland said to his brother Eddie. Brian had just bought his first Cadillac, and we were all admiring it.

"I don't want a Cadillac," Eddie insisted.

"Everybody here has a Cadillac. Don't you want one? I can afford to buy you one, no problem."

"I never wanted a Cadillac," Eddie continued. "I want a Buick Riviera."

"A Buick? Are you crazy?"

"That's what I want! I've never seen anything like it, and it's different," Eddie said finally.

This conversation took place against a backdrop that would be a familiar sight on West Grand Boulevard for years to come—a fleet of brand-new Cadillacs parked all over West Grand Boulevard. As soon as a writer, producer, or performer got his first check, it was as good as endorsed over to the local Cadillac dealership. Purchasers, intent on protecting whatever individuality they could enjoy when they were buying the same car everyone they knew had, would consult with one another about style, colors, and options, so that no two would be alike. Of course, no one would dare ask Berry about his preferences. One day Mickey Stevenson drove up in a Caddy the same color and style as Berry's new one, a light color, like gray. *Someone* would have to exchange his car; a few days later Mickey was tooling around in a black Cadillac.

All the money pouring in built the Motown machine. From the very beginning, Beans Bowles had made Berry aware that some of the artists on the roster, especially those with little or no previous show-business experience, needed some polish. Certain aspects of appearance, stage presence, and etiquette were not quite up to snuff, as far as Beans was concerned. Having worked with some of the classier acts, Beans knew what he was talking about. At a time when most record labels were content to just produce records, Berry wanted to produce stars. Eventually, the Artist Development department came under the guidance of Harvey Fuqua, who staffed it with the best people he could find.

Just what did Artist Development do for the artists at Motown? The most prevalent idea, which I like to call the Motown Myth, runs something like this: Berry took a bunch of ghetto kids with no class, no style, and no manners, put them through hours of grueling training in etiquette, choreography, and interview tactics, and then—voilà—stars rolled out of Hitsville like cars off an assembly line. Young "uneducated" blacks suddenly knew how to speak and which fork to use. And so the story goes.

Not only is this view incorrect, it's insulting. Yes, Artist Development played a role in preparing many of us to deal with a wide range of situations. However, in an age when top executives with graduate business degrees from Harvard are sent to special etiquette classes, it's safe to assume that most people—regardless of age, race, or class—would not know how to give a good interview or greet a president or a queen without some instruction. Motown's Artist Development department was patterned after the movie studio "charm" schools of the thirties and forties. In the sixties, when most young performers were rebelling against show-business conventions, Motown's approach seemed archaic.

The truth is that Berry never signed anyone to Motown who needed to be "remade." The uncouth, boisterous, and slovenly couldn't get a foot in the door anyway. Almost everyone who came to Motown wanted to move up in the world. None of us came from homes that didn't teach manners. We were all trying to get ahead, and it's always bothered me that some people have assumed that by accepting what some consider "white" values, we sold out. It's just not true.

Once we got back from the Dick Clark tour, Artist Development went into overdrive working on the Supremes. Although no one there knew how big a success we would become, Motown wanted us to be prepared for anything. The system was geared to give full support to whichever act was at the top then, so this month it might be the Supremes, and we would have first priority; next month it could be the Tempts or the Vandellas. All of us understood this, so there were no hard feelings, and everyone was very supportive.

One of our first chaperones, Mrs. Maxine Powell, was in charge of etiquette and grooming. She spoke and carried herself very properly. "Young ladies always . . ." was the stock opening phrase for Mrs. Powell's directions. Hats and gloves were mandatory attire for the girls around Motown, and she often lectured us about clothes. Since Flo, Diane, and I already had devoted years to creating our own unique and very sophisticated style, we quickly became Mrs. Powell's star pupils. Attendance in Artist Development was never mandatory. We went because we loved it. We spent only about six months working with Mrs. Powell, but anything that we learned would be incorporated into our behavior that same day. We would be out eating something, and if one of us accidentally picked up her chicken with her fingers, the other two would say, "Remember what Mrs. Powell said," and it would be corrected. It was like a little game to us.

Mrs. Powell was the expert in residence, and every day we reported to a studio that was set up in one of the buildings that Berry had just purchased adjacent to Hitsville. Mrs. Powell took her job seriously, and she would make us walk up and down the mirrored room while she critiqued our every move. She was always on the lookout for bad habits and would point out any flaw, no matter how minor. I can remember feeling her eyes upon me as I walked around with books on my head. Were my shoulders straight? Was my posture good? Was my makeup—the little I wore then—feminine and flattering—not too brassy? Which fork to use, how to greet people, how to hold eating utensils, how to enter a room, how to find a chair, and how to sit and rise gracefully were all part of the program.

Of course, not everyone was as receptive to the charm school course as we were. Those who were unaccustomed to thinking about their every move took any criticism personally, while others found the very idea of etiquette phony. There were some girls who thought that Mrs. Powell was just insensitive to their particular problems. Rosalind Ashford of the Vandellas, for instance, was left-handed, so she had problems following Mrs. Powell's right-handed instructions for handling flatware.

One thing that everyone working in Artist Development found, regardless of what they taught, was that some people just found learning these things much easier. Every group had one member who found the courses more difficult, and in the Supremes it was Flo. It wasn't that she didn't want to learn—she did. Flo's problem stemmed from her being a little awkward. She was always accident-prone, and she lacked what athletes call body sense. "Now, look, Florence . . ." became a familiar phrase. But Flo just worked harder.

Mrs. Powell's efforts paid some interesting dividends. Not only did we have a lot more self-confidence, but other people began treating us differently. This was true of all the Motown acts in general, but especially the Supremes. When Mrs. Powell accompanied us on the road, she would correct young men when they addressed us in a way that she felt was not quite proper.

Mrs. Powell had a great sense of humor. One day she was demonstrating to us the correct way for a lady to enter a car. She stood near a chair and pantomimed opening the car door, stepping sideways into the car, and sitting. When it came to the sitting part, she stuck her rear end out and said, "Now, girls, when you get into a car like this, *this*"—and she patted her fanny—"is what everybody sees. A lady, however, does it like this." And she showed us the proper way.

That afternoon, we were all standing on the porch when we saw her get into her car. The second she pulled away, we all fell down laughing, because Mrs. Powell had entered her car with her rear end protruding. Mrs. Powell was one of a few people around Motown, like Mrs. Ardeena Johnson, whose motto might have been "Do as I say, not as I do." Still, we liked them immensely and appreciated everything they taught us.

As beneficial as our grooming lessons were, there were some things that makeup and poise just couldn't help. Padded bras and falsies were all the rage, and even Flo, who definitely didn't need any more, was wearing them. Diane and I, still being beanpoles, used anything we could. Diane added hip pads, and I padded my backside as well. In my new curves, I was strutting around Motown with a vengeance. One afternoon I was chatting with some people in the lobby when, unbeknownst to me, Lamont Dozier stuck a long straight pin into what was supposed to be my derrière. When it was obvious to everyone that I hadn't felt a thing, they broke out laughing, and for a few seconds I fancied myself a very entertaining conversationalist.

A more serious aspect of Artist Development was the music classes we took with Maurice King, a veteran bandleader who'd worked at the

Flame Show Bar. Back when we were hanging out Milton's window, we would see Maurice, and later John O'Den snuck us into the Flame, where we met Maurice and Sam Cooke. John introduced us to Sam and Maurice as "his girls," and Sam Cooke wished us luck and told us to keep up the good work. We were so thrilled.

Maurice worked with most of the other Motown acts, including Mary Wells and the Temptations. We had worked with Maurice just prior to recording "Where Did Our Love Go." Maurice taught us various vocal exercises and more sophisticated arrangements. One day, we were working on "Where" when I said, "I hate this song!"

"Look, don't knock it," Maurice said. "Why don't you wait—you may be knocking something you will learn to love."

And, of course, when we got back from the Dick Clark tour, I knew what Maurice was talking about. After that I knew to leave picking the songs we recorded to those who knew best.

We also worked with choreographer Cholly Atkins, a well-known song-and-dance man whom we had met back at the Apollo in 1962. Cholly started in show business as a singing waiter in Buffalo, New York, and then worked with prominent stars—such as Bill Robinson, Ethel Waters, and Lena Horne—over the years. In 1945 he teamed up with Honi Coles, and the two of them worked as dancers with big-band leaders such as Duke Ellington, Cab Calloway, and Count Basie. He earned his reputation as a choreographer in New York, where acts would come to him so that he could "doctor up" their stage presentations. And that's how Harvey Fuqua met Cholly.

After Cholly joined Motown, he was very careful to always present a professional image, even in terms of his relationship with Berry. We were still a "big, happy family" then, but Cholly never attended the gatherings and Christmas parties. One day Berry asked Cholly why, and Cholly replied that he didn't see himself as being on the same social level as Berry, and that business was business, and personal time was personal time. I guess Berry respected Cholly's honesty.

Among the other people who worked with us in polishing our acts were Gil Askey, an arranger; and Johnnie Allen, a musician, arranger, and our rehearsal pianist. Cholly was in charge of scheduling, and he and the others kept copious notes and files on each group's progress.

Whenever we had time between recording and touring, we would be in the studio working out new steps, new arrangements, or anything else that needed practice. Flo, Diane, and I worked very hard, and it was clear to the people in Artist Development that we had something special. First, it was our music and our sound, which wasn't really rough or raucous and lent itself to the more sophisticated choreography and staging. Second, we had what Cholly called "built-in sophistication."

Motown's leading lady, Mary Wells, had just left Motown for a better deal with 20th Century–Fox, and Berry was looking for an act he would be proud to present anywhere in the world. Motown had already committed to a tour of Great Britain, which Mary was to headline; now, it was decided, the Supremes would assume what had been Mary's spot.

There was no question in anyone's mind now that the push was on the Supremes. Though we never attended production meetings, things that were said about us in them usually got back to us. Berry would say things like, "We're going to make a push on the Supremes," or "Hey, play the girls' record again," or "Well, the Supremes are who's going to make this company." And Berry meant every word of it. We were flattered to be "the girls" again.

We were local heroes. Wherever we went in our neighborhoods, people would call out to us and wave. In the Projects, "Where Did Our Love Go" could be heard coming out of every window. We gave copies of our hit to all our neighbors and relatives, and if one of our parents had a special friend over, we'd meet there and sing along to our record, doing our show in the living room. Everyone we knew was supportive of us. By now, even our siblings were friends: Roosevelt hung around with Fred and Arthur Ross and Billy Ballard, and Cat was friends with Rita Ross. They were all known in their schools for having a Supreme for a sister.

In August, we recorded a live album at the Twenty Grand Club, which was never released, and Motown released our second album, *Where Did Our Love Go.* The LP eventually went to #2, bolstered by our next two number-one singles, "Baby Love" and "Come See About Me."

On October 7, we embarked on our first English tour. The trip was off to a good start when we met Louis Armstrong at the Detroit airport. He gave us his autograph and then said, "I've heard so much about you girls. I hope I get to see you sometime soon. Good luck!" From the second we took off, things just kept on getting better and better. We knew our records were popular in England, but nothing could have prepared us for the reception we got at the airport from dozens of members of the Tamla-Motown Appreciation Society, which was headed by Dave Godin, a devoted fan who played a critical role in exposing our music to England. They carried placards bearing our photos and presented us with bouquets of flowers. We had all seen the reception the Beatles had gotten in New York earlier that year, and we were pleased to be so enthusiastically welcomed. This was the beginning of a romance with England and Europe that would last throughout our career and through my solo career, to the present.

During our two weeks in England, we did everything we could. Photographers and reporters seemed to follow us everywhere, and we were asked our opinions on everything from the British music invasion to fashion. The English press referred to us as "dishy," and their fascination with us was indicative of our relationship with the press for years to come. In the beginning they referred to the three of us as "Negresses," a term we had never heard. At first we were offended; we thought they had some nerve to insult us like that. As we began to understand the English, we saw that there was no offense intended. We were exotic darlings, sexy and cute, and all the more interesting because we were black and hailed from what the foreign press liked to portray as a rat-infested ghetto.

Every night, after we'd finished our work for the day, the three of us would sit in one of our rooms with all the latest papers and magazines spread out all over the bed. We would read some passages aloud and stare at the same pictures over and over again. It was incredible to us. Just a few months before, we were eating crummy road food in an old bus; today we were flying first-class, drinking champagne, and eating caviar.

After a week of touring, we were invited to London's Ad Lib Club as guests. Still young ladies ourselves, we were thrilled to meet Paul McCartney and Ringo Starr there. Earlier that day we had taped a spot for the pop music program *Thank Your Lucky Stars*, and by the time we left for home, "Where Did Our Love Go" was number two; by late November, "Baby Love" would top the U.K. charts.

We returned to the States, and within days flew straight to Hollywood to film the TAMI (Teenage Music International) Show at the Santa Monica Civic Auditorium. The show, which was directed by Steve Binder, stands today as one of rock's classics, with performances by us, the Rolling Stones, the Beach Boys, Marvin Gaye, Chuck Berry, Jan and Dean, Gerry and the Pacemakers, James Brown, Lesley Gore, the Miracles, and others. We performed "Where Did Our Love Go," "Baby Love" and "When the Lovelight Starts Shining Through His Eyes." The show was really great, but some of the best moments occurred backstage. The Rolling Stones and James Brown were both asking themselves and anyone within earshot essentially the same question about the scheduling: How did the Stones think they were going to follow Soul Brother Number One? The Stones weren't quite sure they could, and James Brown was pretty sure they couldn't!

Three days later, Motown released our third number-one single, "Come See About Me." When one of our promotion men, Jocky Jack, heard another version of the song by a group called the Nelodods, with exactly the same arrangement and backing, Motown rush-released ours. We were never sure if Motown knew that the Nelodods' producer was our friend, promotion man Weldon MacDougle.

Back in Detroit, we started recording A Bit of Liverpool, our "tribute" to the British Invasion. With this release and next year's Country, Western, and Pop, which we had recorded earlier, the Supremes started getting criticism for "selling out," because we weren't singing only "soul" music. In fact, we enjoyed singing all kinds of songs—everything from jazz to show tunes—and would do so throughout our career. We particularly liked the country material, since it lent itself to the complex three-part harmonies we loved to sing.

In December we returned to the West Coast to appear in Bikini Party, a movie that was never released. During our stay, Gil Bogas, a local promotion man, showed us the city. The big thrill of our stay there was having lunch with our idol, Sidney Poitier, at the Brown Derby. It had been arranged by a publicist, and we were as giddy as little girls, swooning all through lunch and making sure that he autographed photos for us, our families, our friends—everyone we knew, it seemed.

This most auspicious year ended with the Supremes making the first of many appearances on The Ed Sullivan Show. After watching the show every Sunday night for as long as I could remember, I found it hard to believe that we were actually going to be on it. This was the best Christmas present in the world.

Although the program aired live, performers arrived in New York a week early to rehearse with the orchestra and tape their segments just in case they wouldn't be able to appear. As it came time for us to tape our segment, we dressed in short, blue, softly tiered sleeveless dresses, the most elegant in our stage wardrobe thus far. We were pampered by the makeup artists, who spent about half an hour on each of us, meticulously applying powders and liquids to make us look perfect for television. We had always done our own makeup, which we kept light, and we were leery of letting them do ours, but we were novices to television—they must know best. Or so we thought. When we took one last look before going onto the soundstage we were shocked. We looked like black-faced singers in a minstrel show!

"Honey, I'm not goin' out looking like this!" Flo exclaimed.

"Oh my god!" I gasped.

"Let's get this stuff off our faces before it's too late," Diane suggested.

We ran to our dressing tables and removed the dark pancake makeup as quickly as possible. Our self-taught makeup expertise would stand us in good stead in the years to come, since in 1964 few makeup people really knew how to work with black skin. All three of us were black, of course, but the nuances of our individual skin tones had eluded our artist, who'd covered all of us with a dark Egyptian tone. In minutes, we'd applied our own makeup and were ready to go on.

The afternoon's taped performance went smoothly. When Sunday night rolled around and our live spot drew nearer, we were very excited. Millions and millions of people would be watching us. We were so happy that we didn't even think about being nervous. I heard Mr. Sullivan welcoming us to his "shew." We stood side by side, with Diane in the middle, and shared one microphone. Cholly had worked out a very subtle but sexy little shimmy step that worked beautifully. We smiled demurely and sang perfectly. Within a few months, with a few more national television appearances behind us, we were America's sweethearts.

The dreams we had shared for so many years were finally coming true now—overnight. Our good fortune was the answer to all our prayers, and I believed that this would bring us closer together. Instead, our personal differences were suddenly cast in a new light. The higher we ascended, the more Diane wanted for herself. Around this time, she began dating Berry, and whenever she was unhappy about something, she would let him know. It had been hard enough dealing with her when all we had to face was her temper; knowing that even the most personal argument or discussion—even if it had absolutely nothing to do with our work—would be relayed to Berry fostered an atmosphere of distrust. Now Diane's little tricks—like checking what Flo and I would wear so that she could be sure to wear something totally different, or refusing to share her clothes with me after I'd lent her mine—took on a whole new meaning. These things were, on the surface, really quite petty, but what upset Flo and me wasn't what she did but what it all meant. We'd been friends—for life, we thought—but now our friendship was a means to an end, a license for Diane to behave exactly as she chose. And that hurt.

Flo and I had been parts of Diane's life—and she of ours—for so long now, we weren't just dealing with a friend but a family member. The Supremes became partners in a kind of marriage; each partner sees the others' flaws but tolerates them, because divorce is out of the question and fond memories of the courtship and romance refuse to die.

One day we were eating out when Diane suddenly became very angry with me. I have always been a very slow eater, and usually finish last, something Diane and Flo knew.

"Mary," Diane snapped, "you did that just to make us look bad."

Flo had a wonderful, mock-haughty look that seemed to say, "Well, who is this?" that she would give me at times like these. I couldn't believe my ears, and the look on Diane's face was hilarious. Would someone deliberately eat slowly to make someone else look bad? I didn't think so, and neither did Flo, but obviously Diane did. Flo and I just gave each other our secret look and kept on eating.

Diane was being regarded as Berry's other half, and Berry made the Supremes his number-one priority. He saw in the Supremes his vehicle to prominence, the golden key to any door he wanted to open. We were now BLAPs—black American princesses.

# CHAPTER 15

Beginning in 1965, hardly a week passed that the Supremes were not featured on at least one television program. During the sixties, variety shows were extremely popular, and we appeared on just about every one of them. Motown had planned it so that we would debut our latest record on national television within a day or two of its release. We were seen on *The Ed Sullivan Show, Hullabaloo, The Hollywood Palace, The Tonight Show, The Dean Martin Show, The Red Skelton Show*, and countless specials. We usually did our latest release, which we often lip-synched—since it was the record being promoted—and then sang something else, like a show tune or a medley, live. Gradually, producers gave us more complicated production numbers, complete with intricate choreography and very sophisticated vocal parts. There weren't too many young performers interested in doing anything but their hits, so once the producers saw how much we loved doing these other numbers, they got more extravagant. We loved it.

Doing television was a lot of fun, and we met and worked with many great performers, such as Dean Martin and Johnny Carson. We always tried to look a little different for each appearance. Flo, Diane, and I loved to shop anyway, and now that we had to have not only new stage costumes but a large wardrobe of daywear for publicity appearances and luncheons, we took to shopping with a vengeance. Most of the television shows we did early on were taped from New York, so when we had even a two-hour break from rehearsals, we'd all jump into the limo and head over to Saks Fifth Avenue. We each had equal say in what outfits we wore onstage, and whenever any of us went shopping alone, she'd run into the others' rooms to show them what she'd bought.

The Supremes' image underwent its first major change at this time. Until now, we'd worn only the lightest makeup and maybe false eyelashes; Diane and Flo wore wigs. Soon after the first Sullivan show our itinerary was booked through 1965, so even I started wearing wigs. It was easier to change wigs than to change hairstyles. We each had dozens of them, all expensive, handmade human-hair pieces in a variety of styles ranging from Mod-ish Vidal Sassoon cuts to high, elaborate flips. In fact, the bulk of our luggage was made up of huge wig boxes, which were always carried on flights, never checked. Diane had been wearing long false nails for some time. Also, television work required heavier, pancake makeup, which we learned to apply ourselves. Soon the look involved more eyeliner, darker eyebrows—especially Diane's—and longer false lashes.

Next came the dressier dresses, which were still street length until mid-1965 or so, when we started wearing long evening gowns in performance. These first gowns were usually sleeveless, often with an Empire waist and made of soft fabrics, like chiffon or velvet. Motown went along with our sexy but wholesome image for the Supremes, but, contrary to what some people think, it wasn't foisted upon us. We really were those girls, and we never felt that what we were onstage was anything but an extension of our true personalities. When I had seen myself in the mirror years before in a homemade costume, I saw a girl every bit as glamorous as the one on television in 1965.

Of all the hosts we worked with, Ed Sullivan was my favorite. We were booked for his show so often that I began to think of it as *The Supremes Show*. Mr. Sullivan made no secret of the fact that he was crazy about us. The Supremes were the only act he let keep the special gowns from the production numbers.

Tapes of these early appearances reveal that while we were true professionals, there was still an innocence about us. Working in television and film gave us confidence and a chance to see how we looked. Strangely, because we traveled so much in those days, we rarely got to see ourselves on television, but when we did, we made mental notes about what looked good and what needed work. This was all great practice, and we applied to our live shows what we learned from seeing ourselves.

Motown was anxious to solidify its relationships with English and European record distributors, and so a tour was scheduled to begin in mid-March 1965. This was to become the infamous Ghost Tour. Though the Supremes had made a real splash in England just six months before, the Revue as a whole didn't fare quite so well. It was a strange turn of events for us. Just a year before, as the "no-hit"

Supremes, we'd been opening the Revue in the States, for the other acts—Marvin Gaye, Martha and the Vandellas, Stevie Wonder, and the Miracles—who'd all had huge hits. In England, however, it was another story: To date, only the Supremes had Top Ten hits there. Not surprisingly, some of the Revue veterans weren't entirely comfortable with the amount of attention the Supremes were getting. There were avid Motown fans all over England and the Continent, but it was clear that reporters in the smaller towns really didn't understand what the music was all about. And, for the first time in as long as many of us could remember, we were playing to half-filled houses.

The worst part of all, and the reason the tour was called the Ghost Tour, was what many of the foreign publications did to our photographs. One day we were scanning a local publication for a review.

"Oh, my God!" I exclaimed when I saw our picture.

"Who is that?" Flo asked.

"I don't know."

"We look like Martians!"

One of the Miracles looked over Flo's shoulder and remarked, "I think that's you, Flo."

"Me?" she shrieked. "Honey, I know I'm black, but this is ridiculous. We're all so washed out and smutty-looking, you can hardly see us. We look like ghosts."

Apparently the European photographer hadn't taken too many photos of blacks and the lighting was all wrong. We laughed about this the whole tour.

Beans Bowles and Mrs. Edwards, however, weren't laughing about much of anything. Financially the tour was a flop, but everyone at Motown saw it as a means of promoting the other acts and making the foreign distributors happy. We had left Detroit in high spirits, thinking that the Miracles, the Vandellas, the Temptations, and Stevie Wonder would conquer the English and European markets as easily as we had, but this was not to be.

Through it all, the Supremes received special treatment. Mrs. Edwards had divided all the travelers into three different groups, and we were in group A with Berry and his entourage. One of Mrs. Edwards' young protégés, Booker Bradshaw, knew England well, having attended Oxford, so he was put in charge of the tour.

We got a great welcome from fans at Heathrow Airport in London and then set out for the dates. We started out traveling by bus, but Berry got fed up with the length of time it took to travel through the

English countryside. When he complained about it, I said, "Now you know how we feel on those long tours."

He sort of grinned, then instructed his assistant, Don Foster, "Let's hire a limo."

So it was the Supremes, Berry, and Don traveling through Great Britain in a stretch limousine. We saw Bristol, Cardiff, Manchester, and Newcastle, and numerous small towns in between. The English cuisine was bland, as usual, and many of the fellows were surprised to find how easy it was to get drunk on warm ale. Whenever we asked for ice, people looked at us like we were crazy.

Though most of this came as no surprise to us, many of the other performers were appalled by such British things as the slick brown toilet paper, which was like heavy waxed paper. This wasn't anyone's idea of civilization, and people carried on about it like it was the end of the world. Now, after years of touring all around the globe, I shudder to think of their reactions had we been working the Middle East.

In London we stayed at the Cumberland, a luxury hotel near the Marble Arch, that offered a wide range of personal services, including overnight shoeshines. All you had to do was leave your shoes outside the door that night and the next morning they'd be back, nicely polished. Most of the guys put their shoes out one night, which inspired some wiseguy to go through the halls and switch everyone's shoes around. It took a couple of hours to get it all straightened out, and though we never knew for sure who the culprit was, James Jamerson, David Ruffin, and Bobby Rogers were prime suspects.

Everything moved rapidly. We barely became acquainted with one city before it was time to move on. The Supremes always got the biggest audience response. We had only three hits under our belts, and there was no guarantee that we'd do anything after that, so it's understandable that some of the other performers failed to see why we were getting preferential treatment. Frankly, I wasn't sure myself, and Flo and I did all we could to keep it from going to our heads.

Dusty Springfield, one of England's biggest female vocalists, was one of Motown's strongest supporters, and it was reported that she convinced the BBC to do a television special on our music. We taped "The Sound of Motown" during this trip. Dusty was the hostess, and I enjoyed working with her. She and the crew treated each one of us like a star, but it was clear that Martha and the Vandellas were their favorites. That was okay; I always thought there was room for all of us at the top.

For the opening number, we did "Shake" with the whole cast and wore those red fringed dresses Dick Clark loved. In our solo spot we did "Where Did Our Love Go," and later Flo commented on how square the English go-go dancers were. We then changed wigs, donned long white gowns, and sang "Stop! In the Name of Love." This number featured what is probably our most famous piece of choreography. Though no one recalls where the "stop" gesture came from, the Temptations worked with us perfecting the routine.

The finale included all of us and Dusty, with the Supremes standing alone on stage right. When the show aired in England the next month it received unanimous acclaim, and from that time on there'd be no more empty seats for any Motown act's show.

Soon after the show aired, Berry held a lavish birthday celebration for Diane. I remember this party especially because I was struck by how adeptly Diane played the star. Just months before we'd all been kids working at Hitsville. Suddenly Diane had ascended; she was now the first lady of Motown.

Following the TV special, we performed at the beautiful Wintergarden in Bournemouth. Berry was right there with us. This tour was a great opportunity for Motown and all its artists. We were getting booked in the most prestigious venues in the world, and we were all meeting important people from all walks of life. It was an exciting time.

Berry and I became very good friends. As we started traveling more, Diane chose to stay in her hotel room when we had time off. Berry and I would get up early and go out to see the city. We both wanted to learn as much as we could about everything we saw. For example, Berry and I would jump in a cab, then spend the whole ride asking the driver how to say things in the native language.

Berry and Flo also had a close relationship, but it was different. Berry was a different person when he wasn't being the president of Motown, and we liked him immensely. Flo, however, wasn't one to pal around, like I was. Her relationship with Berry was based on mutual affection and respect, and at this time we all felt like four very lucky good friends on a wonderful adventure.

Berry never let us out of his sight, and I began to think of him as the fourth Supreme. If he couldn't be with us, he had one of his executive assistants, such as Dick Scott or Don Foster, accompany us. We traveled with a huge entourage—a five-man band, a hairdresser, Gregory, and sundry personnel—and the logistics and business were complicated. Berry wanted to ensure that things would be taken care of.

We were all backstage in England one night when our publicist ran back to tell us that Lord and Lady Londonderry were in the audience, had loved our show, and invited us to visit their home. We were honored, and of course accepted.

"Maybe they live in a castle," I wondered aloud.

"Well, honey, if they do, it better be heated," Flo replied, "because some of these English places are too cold for me."

A few days later we rode in our limousine to the outskirts of London. When we arrived at our hosts' estate, I was dumbfounded. It was like something out of a fairy-tale; not exactly a castle but closer to it than anything any of us had ever seen before. The manicured grounds seemed to roll on forever, with beautiful gardens and a private lake. There was also a family chapel on the premises.

During our entire visit, Berry was right beside us. When we'd first met Lord and Lady Londonderry backstage, they were quite charming. His lordship was tall and handsome; I pictured him wearing riding boots and jodhpurs every day. But while the atmosphere at the estate was subdued, our hosts were very friendly and outgoing.

We stayed there a week and had everything at our disposal. We would leave at night to do the show, then return. One night we brought the English rock singer Georgie Fame back with us and had a blast. Our last day there we stayed up all night playing our records for them, and we even got them to sing along.

We were having the time of our lives. Back in Detroit, we were still living with our families in the Projects; here we were guests in a hundred-room mansion, dining amid antique china and crystal. Lord Londonderry got along great with Flo; she really kept him laughing the whole week we were there. Lady Londonderry seemed to like Georgie Fame, too. A few years later, she married Georgie.

This really was like living in a fairy-tale, not only for us but for Berry, too. We realized that we were going to make it—and bigger than we'd ever imagined. Berry never overlooked an opportunity; he had jokingly said that the Supremes would make Motown: now it was happening right before his eyes. Less than a decade before, Berry had been pushing his songs at the Flame. Now he was doing essentially the same thing, except the people he met were more important, the stakes much higher. How far could we go? No one knew. But we did suspect that there may not be a limit.

Even amid all this hoopla, I still cared more about the singing than anything else. Dozens of important people came to our shows, and the British press treated us like royalty. *New Musical Express* named the Supremes the number-three group in the world, and *Music Biz* named us the top female trio. We got a great reception in Germany and in France, where one of our more interesting adventures took place.

We were booked to play the Olympia Music Hall with the Miracles and Martha and the Vandellas. The show was going to be filmed for French TV, and, like most Motown shows from that period, it was recorded (and released in Europe as *Live in Paris*). Among those in the audience were Marlene Dietrich and singer Sarah Vaughan. That afternoon, someone came up with the bright idea of filming the three of us singing while skipping down the middle of Paris's busiest street, the Champs Élysées, during rush hour. Someone cruised ahead of us in a car, filming the action and blasting one of our records over a loudspeaker so we could get the lip synch right. The director didn't tell us that we didn't have official permission to do this, and after a few minutes of us merrily trotting down the street, traffic backed up for blocks.

Suddenly we saw gendarmes approaching us, yelling angrily. We didn't understand what they were saying, but the director kept screaming for us to keep going. We followed his instructions, and the next thing we knew, the policemen were grabbing at us and trying to forcibly remove us from the street. My arm was sore for days after, but as you can see in a film clip of the incident, we gamely proceeded as if nothing was wrong. Not knowing the story, you'd think it was staged.

After a few minutes we finally figured out what was wrong and that we might be headed to jail. The policemen weren't at all impressed with our explanation, and as we were being escorted away I said to Mrs. Edwards, "What are we going to do?"

"Yeah," Flo interjected. "If we go to jail, think of the bad publicity."

Mrs. Edwards replied, "It doesn't matter—as long as they spell your name right, there is no such thing as bad publicity." Fortunately we didn't go to jail, so we never found out.

In Paris Berry and Diane befriended a black French model named Ariane Sorps. Berry was taken with her, and Diane liked whatever Berry liked, so Ariane became her new best friend.

Berry always was a collector of interesting people, and Diane constantly craved new diversions. Ariane was different and exotic, and she was no doubt flattered by Diane's and Berry's attention. Whatever Ariane liked, Diane liked, and when we returned to the States, Ariane came with us. Back in Detroit, Ariane pranced around Motown like she owned the place. There was even a photo of her with us published in one of the local papers. A few weeks later, she returned to Paris, and I never heard of her again.

Coming home meant returning to a hectic schedule of appearances and recording dates and some great news: We had been booked to appear at the Copacabana in New York City, one of the most prestigious clubs in the country! Every moment of free time was devoted to preparation for this landmark event. In May we recorded several Coca-Cola commercials; one is based on "Baby Love," and there are two others, written by HDH, that incorporate musical phrases from other Motown hits. We were recording our hits in German and Italian, which we learned phonetically, recording new vocals over the original backing tracks, and were enjoying our fifth consecutive number-one hit, "Back in My Arms Again." *We Remember Sam Cooke*, our tribute to the recently deceased singer, was out (Flo was given the lead on "Ain't That Good News"), and we did several television specials, including "It's What's Happening, Baby," with the Vandellas, the Temptations, Marvin Gaye, and the Miracles, and a program about President Lyndon B. Johnson's War on Poverty. In May we were pictured on the cover of *Time*, and the following month we made the cover of *Ebony*.

Just eight months after our first big hit, the Supremes were Motown's greatest commodity. But as great as the Motown machine was, it could work only on a couple of acts at a time. As a result several other acts began receiving less attention than they deserved, especially since Berry was now spending so much time with us. Martha and the Vandellas, for example, saw their position erode at this time. Writers and producers still wanted to work with them, and they were still making great records. But Motown was still a small company, and our success was just too big for the setup. Before we hit, the company's promotional efforts would be concentrated on one act while it was hot; several weeks later, someone else would be hot. It all balanced out over the long run. The Supremes' constant success, however, threw a wrench in the works. I could see that it was happening, and I felt very bad about it. But I was too young to know how to approach my friends and tell them how I felt. It was all beyond my control.

Throughout; most of the artists had a genuine affection for one another; we really believed we were one big family. But success separated us from the other artists, and the industry started calling all the shots. We weren't just the Supremes—we were Motown's Supremes, not just the company's biggest act, but the company's public face as well.

In mid-1965, Flo, Diane, and I moved into homes on Buena Vista Drive in Detroit. Don Foster's girlfriend had done the preliminary search for us while we were gone, and when we returned we each made our final decision. It was only then that we learned that we'd all chosen houses on the same street. Having our own places was a dream come true, and the houses were tangible proof of our success. I bought one house for my mother, Cat, and Roosevelt, and a duplex for myself, half of which I rented out to Cholly and Maye Atkins. The house I chose was very modern, with a big backyard and spacious, open rooms, which I decorated in bright yellows and oranges. Flo moved many members of her family into a house a block and a half down the street from mine and across the street from Diane's. We both had our houses redesigned to include large kitchens. Flo's taste in decorating was classic, and she used lots of blue tones throughout. Diane didn't seem as interested in decorating her house. The one major renovation she made was to build a large mirror-lined room just for her clothes. Walking into this room was like entering a department store; all her clothes hung on professional racks, grouped by color. Diane didn't stay in her house long. While she was there, Mrs. Ross lived with her.

Berry, who had an almost sophomoric lust for competition, decided that we should hold a house-decorating contest, but we all declined; it seemed so silly. We were rarely in Detroit long enough to enjoy our places, but when we were, they were our private sanctuaries.

I first realized that the Supremes had grown bigger than the three of us after Berry heard through the grapevine that I was planning to install mirrors on my bedroom ceiling.

"I don't think it's a very good idea, Mary," he said. "It's not going to sound right."

Though I resented the idea of Berry having anything to say about what I did in the privacy of my home, I agreed with him. We often had journalists at our houses, and it would have looked bad. I knew then, though, that the Supremes were more than just another group.

The cost of purchasing, renovating, furnishing, and decorating our homes was certainly substantial, but I knew it represented only a fraction of what the Supremes had earned for Motown. Though Motown didn't submit its sales figures to the Recording Industry Association of America, the people who certify gold records, we knew that our records were selling in the millions worldwide. By now, we each received a weekly allowance of $500; anytime we needed more money, for example, to buy a car, we would tell Motown and it would be issued to us. In addition, our clothes and other travel expenses were deducted from our accounts. During my years at Motown, I never even saw my tax return. This would strike most people as hard to believe, but it was impossible to think that everything we were told wasn't true. If we hadn't made a fortune, how could there always be limos, champagne, thousand-dollar dresses, and a complete entourage at our beck and call?

The Four Tops—Duke, Levi Stubbs, Lawrence Payton, and Renaldo (Obie) Benson—had been together almost ten years when they signed to Motown in 1964. In the mid-fifties they'd recorded for several labels and, despite a lack of hits, they were always a popular supper-club act in Detroit and often played Las Vegas with Billy Eckstine. Around the time Duke and I met, Berry had matched the Tops up with HDH for their first hit, "Baby I Need Your Loving." The Tops were older than most of us at Motown, and they were always regarded as a class act.

When Duke and I had started dating in late 1964, he was separated from his wife and staying at Janie Bradford's house. Once my house was finished, he moved in with me, and we became known as the "sweethearts of Motown." Despite Berry's concern over what the public might think if I had mirrors over my bed, nothing was said about Duke and me living together. It was a time of true happiness. Duke liked the same things I did—entertaining, singing, decorating the house, collecting furniture, and having people around. Often other acts, such as the Miracles, the Temptations, and the Tops, would rehearse next door at Cholly's, then drop by.

Duke was a man's man, and many times when we were home he'd call and say, "Sweetpea, I'm bringing some of the guys over for dinner." I'd cook up a big meal, and we'd all hang out. Maybe a group would rehearse its new number in the den, and we'd all watch. Flo was at my house a lot then, and we had some great times. Duke was known for making a knockout punch, and we'd have what we called "sloopy parties." I can't count the mornings I woke up to find a guest lying face down on the black bear rug in the den. Diane rarely attended these gatherings; she kept pretty much to herself or spent her time with Berry.

We rehearsed for the Copa date for over four months. Our success there would be a milestone for Motown, and Berry wanted to be sure nothing went wrong. Once the Artist Development people finished with us, we were ready. Among the new tricks we learned was a classic hat-and-cane routine Cholly taught us for "Rock-A-Bye Your Baby with a Dixie Melody," which we loved doing. Cholly was also a master at devising routines especially so that we could all walk around the stage but never tangle our microphone cords.

There was some tension during these rehearsals. Both Cholly and Maurice thought that Flo and I weren't as ambitious as Diane, and we resented that. I caught on the quickest and once I learned something I knew it. Flo still would have to work at things to make them look smooth. If she made a mistake, it would upset her, but she would work at it until she got it right. Diane, however, proceeded very slowly and deliberately, and made sure everyone knew how hard she worked. Once on a television show she complained that she had a greater workload yet received the same pay Flo and I did.

For the Copa show, we all learned to twirl our straw hats. This was the trickiest part of the "Rock-A-Bye" routine, but we finally learned it and were all quite pleased. Diane, however, made sure that everyone knew she could do it. For weeks, she would stop anyone around the rehearsals and say, "Look!" and demonstrate the twirling.

As we got closer to the opening, Diane began refusing to comply with Maurice and Cholly's wishes. If they insisted that she do what they say, she would run to Berry. Before long, those working with us were handling Diane with kid gloves. We knew these people liked Flo and me, and I hoped they understood that it was Diane making the demands, not the Supremes.

Diane was making noises that she wanted to be set apart from us. She had Berry and never hesitated to hold that over the head of anyone who crossed her. What would come next was anyone's guess.

Flo, Diane, and I were being interviewed for an important European magazine feature when we heard Diane announce that her real name was Diana. This was the first Flo and I had heard of this. Apparently the name Diana was on her birth certificate, and she would start using it immediately. Flo and I couldn't believe our ears. We just stared at each other.

Flo and I continued to call her Diane. Of course, everyone has a right to change her name, and what Diane did was pretty minor. But I sensed that this was just one more step away from us, one more way of setting herself apart. The change bothered Flo most, not because of what Diane had done but because of the secret way she did it. Why surprise us? Why not just tell us about it privately first? It wasn't that big a deal. At this time, Flo and I were still hopeful that we might be singing more leads, or have solo spots in the live shows. Little did we know that our fates were sealed. The mass public that bought our hits never knew that Flo and I could sing.

Diane also started monopolizing interviews. Writers had always seemed to enjoy talking with all of us and writing about our different personalities. In the beginning we had been treated as three individuals and were quoted equally. Slowly, though, Diane started answering questions that were clearly directed at Flo or me.

During an interview in June 1965, the reporter said, "Florence, what's your most unusual experience while on tour?"

Flo said, "Hmm," and was getting ready to reply when Diane interrupted her and said, "She doesn't have to think long on that, because we know two that were really great."

This kept on until, after a year or so, no one would even bother to ask us, assuming that Diane alone spoke for the Supremes.

The company was buzzing with activity. The Copa's owner, Jules Podell, had booked our first appearance there for the summer, when most of the club's regulars were out of town. Most new acts were booked during this period; there was less money to be made—and lost —if they didn't work out. Though Ed Sullivan had predicted our success and we'd received nothing but raves for all of our shows, Mr. Podell took no chances. After all, the Supremes were the first black pop group of the sixties to play the Copa, and one of the youngest.

Having performed all over the world, we felt ready for the big time, but Motown wasn't taking any chances either. We moved into a New York hotel, joined by Cholly, music director Gil Askey, and arranger Johnnie Allen. We would get so tired, but we'd snap right to whenever Gil would say, "We have to work on this until we get it right." Cholly was more blunt: "I don't care if we work until we're blue in the face." We'd go back to the hotel for a few hours, then we'd be back at rehearsal. We sang the same notes, made the same moves, recited the same lines hundreds and hundreds of times.

Motown went into action like an army on maneuvers, and pretty soon everyone had something to do with the Supremes. Berry's youngest sister, Gwen Gordy Fuqua, helped with our wardrobe. After our sound, our clothes were the most important component of the Supremes style. We were still picking our gowns, but for this occasion a friend of Gwen's designed some special things for us. We—along with everyone else—approved the sketches but didn't see the actual dresses until opening night.

There were people all over the place, giving us instructions and taking our orders. I began to feel as if I could just stand still and everything would be done for me. All I'd have to do was walk onstage and sing. It used to be just the three of us; now we didn't have a minute alone without someone hovering around somewhere.

Opening night found me as excited as ever. I always thought going onstage was the greatest thing, and nothing ever flustered me. HDH called me "cool Mary." Backstage it was us; our hairdresser, Gregory; and a bodyguard, Joe Shaffner. When we realized that some of the people who were supposed to help us, including Mrs. Powell, were late, Diane started biting her false nails.

"Our new dresses are not here," she said.

"Well, some of our old dresses are here," Flo said, perusing the gowns, "but I know these aren't the ones we're going to wear tonight."

"I know they'll be here soon," I said, hoping.

"We've got to know which of these gowns we're supposed to put on," Diane insisted. Of course, we all knew that, but she was starting to get this wild look in her eyes.

We were relieved when Cholly's wife, Maye, came in and tried to help. She was like a mother to us, and she knew it was close to curtain time. As she was standing near the gowns, Mrs. Powell rushed in.

As always, Mrs. Powell had to be in control. She dismissed Maye curtly and started unwrapping the new dresses. With just minutes before curtain, we got dressed and were ready to go.

The club was packed. Eddie Bisco was in charge of making sure that everyone was comfortable and that the important people—disc jockeys, industry heavies, promotion men, press—had anything they wanted and good seats. He also had to be sure that everyone from Motown was taken care of. Among the celebrities at our debut were Ed Sullivan, columnist Earl Wilson, Sammy Davis, Jr., disc jockeys Murray the K and Frankie Crocker, and countless sales reps and distributors. And Motown spared no expense. Don Foster told me that the opening had cost Motown $10,000 (we were paid $2,750 for the week), and later Eddie Bisco revealed that he'd signed tabs amounting to $4,000 just for drinks.

It was a gala opening, and we started the show with "Put on a

Happy Face," which we sang in unison. The songs, dance routines, and patter went smooth as silk. We sang "Come See About Me," "Make Somebody Happy," "The Girl from Ipanema," "You're Nobody till Somebody Loves You," "Rock-A-Bye Your Baby with a Dixie Melody," "Somewhere" from *West Side Story*, and Cole Porter's "From This Moment On." The only problem was our stage gowns. The designer Gwen Fuqua chose usually made costumes for dancers, so these dresses were very soft and plain, in soft blue. They were nice, but we thought that the artificial flowers made of feathers were too much. Once we got onstage, we looked gaudy. For another show our gowns had feathers around the neck, which fluttered all over the stage whenever we moved.

"Get these feathers off my neck!" Diane panted as we entered the dressing room after a show.

"I think the flowers should come off, too," Gwen added, trying to be helpful.

"Do something," Flo said sarcastically as she stepped out of her dress. "Honey, these dresses are a mess, aren't they?" she asked me. I agreed.

Alterations were made, and, after a short rest, we were on for the second show. Since the Broadway shows were over, many stars were in this audience, and I felt like we were just getting better and better. All the hassles were forgotten, and even the gowns weren't a total loss; at least Motown knew to leave the costumes to us. We were cooking, and after the show we all hugged, knowing we had been a real smash. Now everyone in the entertainment world knew the Supremes had what it takes, and we weren't just girl singers anymore. We had arrived.

Right after the opening, Berry met with Harvey Fuqua and Mrs. Edwards and others. Berry wanted to see a few things changed and tightened up, especially our vocals, since he wanted to record a live album. Harvey then relayed Berry's instructions to Cholly and Maurice. Before, Berry would talk to everyone directly; now there was an official hierarchy and channels to go through.

Before we opened at the Copa, we had rehearsed two different openings for the show. Berry liked one of them, and Cholly and everyone else liked the other. But Berry was the boss and insisted that we do it his way first. After the opening night Berry decided that his way wasn't the best, and so we used the other. Regardless of what other people thought, Berry would always insist on seeing every second of an act, then he would make changes. The Artist Development people would go crazy, and we always wondered why Berry didn't make his changes earlier. But he didn't care; he wanted things to be perfect. Nine times out of ten, he was right. Also, I think he was trying to keep everyone on their toes, and he succeeded at that.

As the recording date for the live album drew near, we had to finalize our repertoire. Despite our joy at our success, Diane was becoming moodier. The pressure was really on all of us. Starting around this time Berry encouraged anyone in the Motown family— including relatives, road managers, and other performers—to keep a pencil and pad on hand and jot down anything they saw in the show that should be changed or improved. Berry would then come back and tell us what to change, often at the last minute. These switches would make Diane nervous, but she kept it to herself and did it.

Things came to a head, though, when it was announced that Flo would no longer be doing her solo number, "People," from *Funny Girl.* We had included the song in all of our nightclub appearances, and audiences loved it. Opening night at the Copa, Flo had just re- covered from a week of the flu and was a bit hoarse, but she still sounded great. A couple of nights later, however, Diane was singing it. No one in Artist Development was ever given a clear explanation of why; Harvey Fuqua announced the change one day, and that was that.

We all suspected that Berry had taken the song from Flo, but Flo was thoroughly convinced of it and she was crushed. How much more of the spotlight did Diane need? Everyone knew that Flo was very sensitive and that this meant a lot to her. Berry's taking it away from her like this was just vicious. It was impossible to know for sure who had instigated it—Berry or Diane—but neither of them acted as if they were sorry. From that moment on, Flo regarded what was in fact the highest achievement of our career as a disaster. She was sad and moody, and I could see the three of us being torn apart.

I didn't have a featured solo spot, but, ever the optimist, I was still pestering Berry to let me sing a lead now and then, when one day he jokingly said, "Oh, Mary. You know you can't sing!" I was so devastated by his words that it would take me years of music therapy to overcome my gradual loss of confidence.

Flo responded to these events in a way that would become habit- ual for her. She would get defensive, and no matter what Berry said, she would disagree. Unlike Berry, Flo could not separate the personal from the professional. You were either her friend all the way in everything or you were her enemy; there was no in between. I couldn't beat this system, and, judging from the past few months, there was nothing the Supremes couldn't do. This whole situation would probably pass, or so I thought. Flo, however, was a firm believer in action, and she started bucking Berry at every turn. I wondered how long my two friends could keep this up. Certainly Diane would have to slow down some day, and things with Berry and her would cool off. I decided to wait until I had some answers.

But I was wrong. Diane was obsessed not with being *a* star, but *the* star. During the Copa date, she complained to Cholly about the choreography for "The Girl from Ipanema" because she didn't want to stand between Flo and me. Cholly refused to move her to the end and flew back to Detroit on business. When he returned to New York a few days later, Diane was on the end.

"Diane, you made that number look terrible. Go on back to the center," Cholly said angrily.

"No!" Diane replied. "You'd better talk to Berry."

Diane had called Berry, and he had agreed with her. The matter was settled, and when Cholly called Berry, he was told the same thing.

After our three weeks at the Copa, the Supremes were welcome to play any club in the world. Shelly Berger, a young Jewish actor turned agent, was hired by Berry and put in charge of us. He helped us in many ways: writing monologues, for example, and teaching us how to deliver lines. With his help, our fee for future Copa engagements would be raised each year until we were earning $20,000 a week, a sum equal to what performers such as Dean Martin and Sammy Davis, Jr., commanded. Because we never saw the accounts, we had no idea how much of the Supremes' fee was spent on drinks, complimentary tickets, and other promotional items. Shelly once said, "You couldn't pay enough commissions in four years to cover what Motown spends on you each time you play the Copa." Berry saw this as a trade-off—Motown had carried the "no-hit" Supremes; now the Supremes were going to carry Motown for a while.

But as the Copa had been the scene of several disappointments for Flo, it also put her into the spotlight. I heard through some of the agents that during a later show some movie people contacted Motown executives because they were interested in casting Flo in a film. Flo always had a natural flair for comedy and a wonderful delivery. Her lines, which she always rewrote from the script we were given, were classics: "Just give me the money, honey, and I'll do the shopping," was just one that had the audience screaming with laughter. Another of her famous lines was a reply to Diane's introduction of her as "the quiet one," was, "That's what you think." People laughed, but Flo, Diane, and I knew Flo wasn't kidding.

Standing onstage, I could see that many men regarded her as the sexiest one, and critics never failed to mention her beautiful voice or brilliant timing. Flo could have gone far, and she knew that. Looking back, I suspect that Berry and Diane saw it, too. But Flo needed support, and all she got from Motown were constant reminders to stay in her place.

To the world outside, the Supremes had everything, and Berry spared no expense in creating and maintaining that image. Berry instructed Motown employees to do our bidding and supplied limos, champagne, and unlimited funds. Money was no longer an object, and we never asked the price of anything.

# CHAPTER 16

As long as I had known Diane, she would pursue her goals until she achieved them. With the Supremes' new stardom, this characteristic took on new proportions. When I'd see her threatening to tell Berry about something or hanging on his every word, I'd flash back to years before, when she'd said to me, "I'm going to get him." At that time, I didn't understand why she would want him; he wasn't sexy. But he had power, and as I would soon see, that is perhaps the strongest aphrodisiac in the world.

Diane stepped up her self-improvement program, but in secret. Instead of us all going out shopping for clothes together, Diane would go out alone and then refuse to show us what she had bought. She took makeup classes at John Robert Powers, and when Flo and I found out about it, tensions mounted. Again it wasn't what Diane did, it was the way she did it. The public's perception of us began coloring our personal relationships, and Diane kept stepping further and further away, returning to us only when there was no one else around.

Flo and I wanted to further our educations, and with more than just charm classes. We had all planned to attend college, but now that we were stars we had no idea when—or even if—we would get to go to school. As busy as we were touring, there were countless idle hours. We wanted to get our educations, and so I approached Berry about perhaps making some arrangements so that we could. I suggested that Motown contact Wayne State University and make plans to have professors join the entourage and tutor us privately. For example, a French professor might travel with us for a few months, then a physics teacher would come aboard, and so on.

For some reason, however, the plan never materialized, though Diane's "special" studies accelerated, and Berry was learning as much as he could about an array of subjects.

＊　＊　＊

We were celebrities in our own right now, and meeting other stars soon became routine. When we were in London, the British rock group the Animals invited us up to their hotel. These boys were wild. I would go out alone, without a chaperone, and I dated Hilton Valentine, the group's guitarist. He took me to his apartment to listen to records, and I was amazed at his collection of American R&B and blues recordings. Strangely, he was just as amazed that I hadn't heard of most of the artists.

Times were really changing, and, compared to almost any other pop stars around, we probably seemed like nuns. We always felt a little out of place when we'd meet other stars who were either dressed like slobs, were stoned or drunk, or were using a lot of profanity. Knowing we were black girls from the inner city, many of our colleagues, especially those from England who liked to romanticize the plight of the disadvantaged, were surprised to discover that we dressed well offstage and comported ourselves like ladies. I shuddered to think what they were expecting.

One of the most memorable meetings took place in August 1965. We were in New York to tape Ed Sullivan's show, and our publicity people and the Beatles' publicity representatives thought it would be great to get the world's number-one and number-two pop groups together. When we'd met Paul and Ringo at the Ad Lib the year before, we hadn't really gotten a chance to talk with them in the noisy club, so we looked forward to a real meeting.

We wore smart, elegant day dresses, hats, gloves, high heels, and jewelry, as well as fur jackets—Flo in chinchilla, me in red fox, and Diane in mink. When our limo pulled up in front of the Warwick Hotel, the crowds of screaming girls—thinking we might be the Beatles—charged the car. Once we stepped out and they saw through our bodyguards that we were only the Supremes, they lost interest and went back to standing watch by the hotel door.

We entered the Beatles' suite, perfectly poised. Apparently other people had been up to visit them earlier, including Bob Dylan and the Ronettes. The first thing I noticed was that the room reeked of marijuana smoke, but we kept on smiling through our introductions. It was difficult to be gracious and friendly in the face of what we could only see as the coolest reception we'd ever received. We felt that we had interrupted something. Paul was nice, but there was an awkward silence most of the time. Every once in a while Paul, George, or Ringo would ask us about the Motown sound, or working with Holland-Dozier-Holland, then there would be silence again. Someone might crack a little joke, but we never knew what they were laughing about. John Lennon just sat in the corner and stared.

After a few moments, we wanted out. Years later, I was visiting George Harrison at his home in England. Recalling that first meeting, he said, "We expected soulful, hip girls. We couldn't believe that three black girls from Detroit could be so square!"

We were back on the road, booked to appear at the Michigan State Fair, on Dean Martin's show, and doing concerts at JFK Stadium in Philadelphia and the Safari Room in San Jose. Recording sessions, rehearsals, wardrobe fittings, interviews, and personal appearances were squeezed into every free minute. When we would sweat in some stinky bus or race through eight shows a day on the early Motown tours, we'd fantasize about how easy things would be once we made it. Well, here we were, working harder than ever—and I loved it.

Of course, most things were better—a lot better. Limos were now de rigueur, and there was always one waiting with its motor running. We seemed to always be racing for the airport; I never understood why the company didn't just give us phony schedules so we'd be on time even if we thought we were late, but they never did. Somehow, we always got where we were going. We had packing down to a science. Each of us always took along at least five pieces of luggage, but the only ones we couldn't live without were the makeup cases and wig boxes. Our arrival in any city would be quite a sight—us, the musicians, road managers, and the wardrobe and hair people (including our wardrobe mistress Miss Marjorie Wooden), each with a big wig box in hand. Days off would find me lounging around wearing a mudpack that would horrify anyone. Hours of flight time were devoted to manicures and pedicures.

Berry kept us pretty well insulated from the rest of the world and the business, it is said. But around this time, we stopped traveling with chaperones. Diane, tired of Mrs. Powell's lectures, had called Berry and had her taken off the road. Then Mrs. Ross stopped traveling with us. Before she stopped, she and Maurice King, our musical director on the road, made quite a pair. When we were in between shows or traveling, he and Mrs. Ross often played cards together.

Like her daughter, Mrs. Ross was quite a kidder, and if Maurice didn't look out, she'd hit him over the head. But Maurice seemed to enjoy it, and having those two with us made it feel like we were a real family. Mrs. Ross would talk to Maurice about Diane. Once she even told us, "Ever since Diane was a child, she's been stubborn and wanted her own way. Then when she gets her way, it isn't what she really wanted at all." Insights like these helped us all deal with Diane's tantrums, and Maurice seemed to have a way with Diane. She could be in the worst mood, and Maurice would still kid her, saying he'd spank her—even if they were sitting in an executive meeting. He was one of the few people around whom Diane would let down her guard.

The last of our chaperones was Doris Postle. Mrs. Postle was another Gordy family friend but quite different from Mrs. Powell or Mrs. Johnson. Mrs. Postle liked to have fun and she gave us free rein. "You young ladies are grown now," she'd say, "and I trust you."

"Yes, ma'am," we'd reply, all the while thinking of about a dozen reasons why she shouldn't.

Now we traveled with our own entourage of road managers, business managers, wardrobe people, and hairdressers. The days of scrunching up three to a lumpy bed, sleeping and changing on moving buses, and worrying about whether or not a restaurant would seat us were over for good. We had individual rooms in the best hotels, and we ate in the finest restaurants. When money was no object, neither was color. I found myself living in scenes that I'd only seen in movies. At every hotel, we'd open our doors and find baskets of fresh flowers and fruit, fully stocked bars, and every conceivable touch of luxury. The first thing I'd do was to unpack, then put out photos of my family and current beau, arrange all my makeup and perfume on the dresser, and try to make the room as much like home as I could, even though I knew I wouldn't be spending more than a few waking hours there.

Berry usually had a suite of his own near our rooms, and he kept an eye on us. Diane would have an adjacent room. Later the entourage was joined by Chris Clark, a white female singer Berry had signed and whom he was also dating. Often one of the road managers would really have to do some fancy footwork—including paying hotel guests to move to another room—so that Berry's room would be in between Chris's and Diane's. The road managers and musicians were my friends, so I got the scoop on these things.

In all-night towns, such as Las Vegas, we would party until dawn. The innocent image got harder to maintain as we traveled and met more men who were smitten by us. More often than not, once back from the show, I'd throw off the wig, peel off my stockings, wrestle my way out of the gown, and take off. No matter how hard we worked, I was determined to live my life. I had a boyfriend in every town, all around the world, and I couldn't wait to meet new people and really enjoy myself. What was the point of traveling around the world if you were just going to stay up in your room?

As curtain time approached we and our entourage would head for the dressing rooms to prepare for the show. We would decide on wardrobe changes, see that all the last-minute repairs had been made on our dresses and shoes, be sure that all the accessories were accounted for and that the flashy jewelry pieces were at hand. Our assistants had to be careful to hide our "beauty secrets"—the wigs, lashes, and falsies—which they smuggled in and out. Around this time, Winnie Brown, a niece of Flo's by marriage, began traveling with us as our hairdresser. Winnie was one of the few people whom Diane opened up to, and she was also the only person, it seemed, who could tease Diane out of one of her funks. She was a great storyteller and was known for her cute but naughty jokes. If she sensed some tension, she'd just come out with a line, and we'd all laugh. One of her favorite pranks was to walk to the wings with us, then when we were announced, to hold Diane's arm. We'd all walk onstage, but Diane would be held back by Winnie, who would be making faces the whole time. It was hard not to come on laughing.

There would be countless guests coming backstage to meet us, and no matter how harried things were, we were always gracious. Berry would also want to be back there, and always seemed to have some urgent news for us that had to be delivered when we were stark naked.

"I don't want to see what you have anyway, so you might as well let me in," Berry would say.

"Lock the door!" Flo always cried. "I don't want any dirty old man in here!" Diane would just giggle.

Berry was a riot at times like these. When my sister Cat and Diane's sister Rita graduated from high school, we flew them to New York to stay with us and see the show. Berry had them sequestered up in a hotel room one day, teaching them to sing and harmonize, claiming that he was creating "the little Supremes." Everyone got a big kick out of that.

Back home, we were really living in the material world. We could now indulge in our lust for clothes, and Saks Fifth Avenue in Detroit

Local girls make good: The Supremes return to the Brewster Projects.
(*Paul A. Begler Collection*)

From left to right: Florence, Diane, me, Sammy Davis, Jr., Cher and Sonny Bono rehearse for Sammy's March 4, 1966, show. (*From the NBC-TV/ Sammy Davis, Jr. Show archives, reprinted courtesy of Jeffrey Wilson's Hot Wax Music archives*)

Above: Recording "My World Is Empty Without You" at Hitsville U.S.A. studios in Detroit, 1966. The session was recorded for the TV documentary "The Anatomy of POP." Duke Fakir is standing in the doorway waiting to take me home. (*Allen Poe Collection*)

Right: In the 1960s we were "Berry's girls." (*Mary Wilson Collection*)

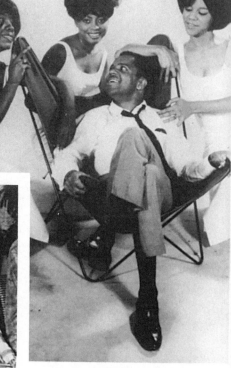

On our first trip to the Far East in 1966, fielding questions from the press. (*Mary Wilson Collection*)

No camera ever captured us like this!
(*Mary Wilson Collection*)

Here we are with the fourth Supreme: Berry Gordy. (*Paul A. Begler Collection*)

In a 1966 photo session with Berry Gordy. In the beginning, we all shared the leads, but Berry soon chose Diane—in more ways than one. (*Murray Laden*)

Facing page, top: After one of the shows at the Roostertail in Detroit with "the Motown family" in 1967. Left to right: (standing) Billy Davis, Gwen Gordy Fuqua, Mr. Edwards, Nate McAlpine, Levi Stubbs, and me; (seated) Mrs. Stubbs, Anna Gordy, Berry Gordy, Bobby Darin, and Diana. (*Mary Wilson Collection*) Near right: They called me "the sexy one." (*Mary Wilson Collection*) Far right: When the British Invasion hit our music charts, Diane, Flo, and I invaded the shops on Carnaby Street. (*Nick Strange Collection*)

Before we had sequinned gowns, we had miniskirts. (*Mary Wilson Collection*)

One of Flo's last photo sessions with us. We were still wearing our million-dollar smiles, but Flo and I were crying inside. (*Carl Feuerbacher Collection*)

Above: The first time Cindy stood in for Flo, at the Hollywood Bowl, April 1967. (*Mary Wilson Collection*) Below: Performing "Thoroughly Modern Millie" on *The Ed Sullivan Show* in 1967. (*Carl Feuerbacher Collection*)

On *The Ed Sullivan Show*, May 5, 1967. It would be Florence's last appearance on the show. (*From the CBS-TV/Ed Sullivan Show archives, reprinted courtesy of Jeffrey Wilson's Hot Wax Music archives*)

Tom Jones and me in Las Vegas. (*Allen Poe Collection*)

Cindy, Diane, and I exchange medleys with the Temptations on the Sullivan show, November 19, 1967. (*From the CBS-TV/Ed Sullivan Show archives, reprinted courtesy of Jeffrey Wilson's Hot Wax Music archives*)

The Duke and Duchess of Bedford show off their historic artwork, and Cindy, Diane, and I show off our Motown charm school stances . . . thanks to Mrs. Powell. (*Mary Wilson Collection*)

In the receiving line to meet the Queen Mother in 1968 with Diane (left) and Cindy (right). We are wearing our beaded gowns that Michael Travis designed, and they weighed 35 pounds each! (*Allen Poe Collection*)

At the funeral of Dr. Martin Luther King, in Atlanta, 1968. (*Nate McAlpine*)

Cindy, Diane, and me in our Michael Travis gowns on the "TCB (Taking Care of Business) Special" in 1968. (*Mary Wilson Collection*)

This was from my blond wig days. I think I saw too many Doris Day movies. (*Michael Ochs Archives*)

A never-released shot from one of our most famous photo sessions with
James Kreigsmann, 1968. (*Michael Ochs Archives*)

When we rehearsed "Love Child" for our appearance on the Sullivan show on September 19, 1968, Cindy and I were given "Love Child" shirts like Diane's. When it came time for the show, though, we were given street clothes instead. (*From the CBS-TV/Ed Sullivan Show archives, reprinted courtesy of Jeffrey Wilson's Hot Wax Music archives*)

How's this for impersonal? (*Mary Wilson Collection*)

WESTERN UNION
TELEGRAM

SYMBOLS
DL = Day Letter
NL = Night Letter
LT = International
Letter Telegram

CLASS OF SERVICE
This is a fast message unless its deferred character is indicated by the proper symbol.

The filing time shown in the date line on domestic telegrams is LOCAL TIME at point of origin. Time of receipt is LOCAL TIME at point of destination

330P PDT AUG 9 69 LD214
L HDA172 (L BHA083 LY) DF NL PDB FAX BEVERLYHILLS CALIF 9
MISS MARY WILSON
1820 RISING GLEN HOLLYWOOD CALIF(DY)
PLEASE JOIN ME IN WELCOMING A BRILLIANT MUSICAL GROUP THE JACKSON
FIVE ON MONDAY, AUGUST 11, 6:30 TO 9:30PM AT THE DAISY, 326NORTH
RODEO DRIVE, BEVERLYHILLS THE JACKSON FIVE FEATURING SENSATIONAL
EIGHT-YEAR-OLD LEAD SINGER MICHAEL JACKSON WILL PERFORM LIVE
AT THE PARTY. PLEASE COME AND LISTEN TO THIS FABULOUS NEW MOTOWNROUP
RSVP 275-4588
DIANE ROSS

Toasting the end of a dream. After the "farewell" show with Diane at the Frontier Hotel in Las Vegas. (*Mary Wilson Collection*)

Embarking on a solo career in 1979. (*Mary Wilson Collection*)

Me in the 1980s. And I've never felt better! (*Marc Raboy*)

would open especially for us and have special shoppers accompany us through the store. During this time, I began treating myself to jewelry, like the dome-shaped diamond cluster ring I bought in New York City and wore on every single album cover. Being back home was great, because it was now almost the only place left where we could walk around and go about our business without being accompanied by security.

That summer, we released "Nothing but Heartaches" and *More Hits by the Supremes*. In September, NASA's mission control played "Where Did Our Love Go" for the *Gemini* V astronauts, Pete Conrad and Gordon Cooper, as they orbited the earth. By the end of the month, we were back in Europe.

We attended the Grand Gala du Disque Festival, an international music event held in Amsterdam, Holland, as the official United States representatives to the celebration. A Dutch disc jockey named Peter Fellerman was our host and escort, and we had a wonderful time. He took Berry and us all around and told us about his country's history and culture. Like us, he was open and curious about things, and we remained friends for many years. By now we were all but ready to move to Europe for good, something I still think about.

One night in Holland, Diane, Flo, and I dined together in one of our rooms.

"And what will the mesdames have this evening?" the waiter asked.

"Chateaubriand, please," Diane answered, "Well-done."

"And you, madame?"

"The same, please," I replied.

Before he could ask Flo, she said, "I think I'll have this steak. Tartare?"

"Certainly." The waiter smiled and took our menus. For a second we wondered why he hadn't asked how Flo liked her meat cooked, but we figured they knew what they were doing.

A while later, the waiter returned to our suite with a rolling cart on which were placed a little mound of fresh raw ground meat, some finely chopped vegetables, an array of seasonings, and an egg. He put on quite the show, adding ingredients and stirring the concoction with all the flair of a magician pulling a rabbit from a hat. I began to wonder if I shouldn't change my order. Flo's dish looked great. Just then, Diane and I were served, and Flo's waiter molded her meat into a little patty with a "nest" in the middle, and then he broke the egg into it and proudly placed the dish before Flo.

"What's this?" Flo was mortified.

"Your steak tartare, ma'am." The waiter was as confused as we were.

"You don't expect me to eat it like that!" Flo was incredulous.

"Well, madame, that *is* steak tartare."

"Honey, you better take this stuff back and cook it!" Flo exclaimed.

Diane and I died laughing. After the waiter returned with the meat cooked, Flo said, "That's better."

A few days later we went to Brussels, then on to England, where we taped segments for *Top of the Pops* and *Ready, Steady, Go,* then traveled on to New York, where we appeared in Sybil Burton's "Very, Very In" at Arthur's. Two days later, we became the first pop group to play New York's Philharmonic Hall in Lincoln Center. The Spinners opened for us there, and the poster, designed by Eula, is now a collectors' item.

In November we did a benefit at Madison Square Garden called "USO A-Go-Go," with Sammy Davis, Jr., Joan Crawford, Carroll Baker, Robert Vaughn, and Johnny Carson. That month, "I Hear a Symphony" was at number one, and we returned to Europe with the Motown Revue for a show at the Olympia Music Hall.

Back in the States in December, we performed at the opening of the Houston Astrodome. Also on the bill was one of my childhood idols, Judy Garland. Though we had met many famous people, it was always different meeting someone who meant something to you. We couldn't wait to meet her, but every time we'd ask someone when we could, they'd just tell us "later." We snuck around, and finally she stuck her head out of the door of her dressing room and said, "How are you? It's nice to be on the show with you," then went back inside. I'd seen *The Wizard of Oz* dozens of times, and it was strange to meet "Dorothy" and see how frail and sad she was. We also got to meet a number of the astronauts, and after the show we went to a club where Glen Campbell was playing and sang a couple of songs. The day before we had appeared on Larry Kane's show, a local television program. We hadn't discussed wardrobe, and were surprised when we got there to see that Diane had really outdone herself, with big earrings, long fake lashes, and a big wig, while we were in our usual attire—considerably more modest—for daytime publicity appearances like this.

At the end of the year, we were guests at the Orange Bowl Parade in Florida, where we were booked to play in Miami, which became an annual tradition for us. That Christmas, Berry gave each of us a fur coat. We had a party in Berry's suite at the Eden Roc, and Aretha Franklin and her husband attended. It was a blast.

Professionally things just got bigger and better every day. Privately, though, it was a different matter. In just over a year Diane had become a new person, and with an entourage to do her bidding, there was no reason for her to think about anyone but herself. Road managers would bear the brunt of Diane's demands from now on. Once when we were in New York she told a new road manager, Phil Wooldridge, that she was hungry and wanted pizza. It was one in the morning, and Phil ran all over New York until he found a place that was open. When he got back to the hotel, though, Diane was asleep.

Another time, Flo, Diane, and I were playing Las Vegas but had gone to Los Angeles for dental work. Flo and I were already back in Vegas, and Diane was having special work done to close a gap near her left upper molar. Don Foster was to pick her up from the dentist's and take her to the airport for the flight back. Diane was still recovering from the dentistry and wasn't quite herself. Everything was running smoothly until she and Don went to check in. Western Airlines refused to let her bring on a huge wig box as carry-on luggage; she would have to check it. Diane had a fit and made such a scene that the airline refused to let her on with or without the box.

Don did everything he could, including bribing the counter attendants with the promise of free tickets to one of our shows. Finally they relented and Diane and the box got on the plane. The minute she was gone, Don ran to the phone to call Joe Shaffner, the person who would be picking up Diane in Vegas, to warn him.

"Listen, Joe, be at the airport—at the plane—on the tarmac, because when Diane gets off—she's mad as hell and she's all upset, and whatever she wants . . ."

Joe got there, but it was too late. Diane had landed and called Berry. Though it was clear to any logical person that Don made the best of a bad situation he'd done nothing to create, Diane was not happy, so Berry was not happy, and no explanation could change that.

"You're ridiculous," Berry told Don, using one of his favorite words. "What do I have you out there for if you can't handle things?"

After this, Don stopped traveling with us, but he was in charge of whoever did. He called constantly to be sure things were all right, because he knew that if one little thing went wrong, Diane would be on the line to Berry and that would be it. Sometimes it was quite embarrassing to be around her when these things happened, and we felt the way parents feel when their child throws a tantrum in public. We were public figures now, these scenes made us all look bad.

Shortly after it was announced that we had been booked to play the Flamingo in Las Vegas, rumors began flying that Diane would leave the Supremes. The first time we heard them, Diane was as upset as we were. We knew we weren't as close as we used to be, but we thought that we'd always be together. Well, maybe not always; we used to talk about which of us would marry first (me), and who would have the most children (me), and how it would be to settle down. They all thought that I was so boy-crazy that it was only a matter of time. But all that was in the future. As always, we looked to the future to fix what was wrong with the present. We'd still be happy when a show went well, and cry together when something went wrong. But these days less and less went wrong, and the fairy-tale got grander every minute. I took my place between my two best friends, waiting for one of them to give and for this phase to come to an end. Everything was so good now, certainly everything would be fine. Soon.

# CHAPTER 17

We started 1966 with "My World Is Empty without You" in the Top Ten, a Grammy nomination for "Stop! In the Name of Love" (which we didn't find out about until months later), and a short tour of West Germany and Scandinavia. We maintained our usual frantic pace, appearing on a television special called "The Anatomy of Pop" and returning to the Copa for two weeks in March.

Things could not have been better, except that my relationship with Duke was ending. The Four Tops were doing very well, and after living with me for about two years Duke decided that he should give his marriage another try. At this point our schedules were always in conflict and sustaining a relationship with both of us so busy was nearly impossible. I respected his decision; he had a young daughter to think about. Still it hurt me deeply to lose him. We would see each other now and then, but it was never the same. Around this time Flo was ending her on-and-off relationship with another Top, Renaldo "Obie" Benson. We each provided the other with a shoulder to cry on.

Though none of us was really happy with what was going on inside the group, we still managed to have plenty of fun touring and performing. When we appeared on Sammy Davis, Jr.,'s show, we did a number with the Andrews Sisters. When we were all little girls we'd loved their songs, and I remembered sitting down in the basement on Bassett Street, singing along to their records. The producers had us perform a medley together, in which the Supremes sang such Andrews chestnuts as "Don't Sit under the Apple Tree," while they sang "Baby Love" and "Where Did Our Love Go."

We liked one another immediately, and we paired off: Maxine with Flo, Patty with Diane, and Laverne with me. In rehearsals, we had a great time. They taught us their parts and how to sway gently, and we taught them our routines. If someone made a mistake, everyone on the set would crack up. In fact some of the goofs were so funny —especially when they would tackle our choreography—that Sammy would make them repeat the mistake for anybody who dropped by. We seemed to be laughing the whole time.

Later that spring Supremes White Bread went on sale in the Detroit area. Some people thought this was an odd product for the Supremes to lend their name to, and it looks even stranger now that the expression "white bread" has come to mean "plastic" or "phony." At the time, though, these connotations weren't yet widespread, and besides, decisions about product endorsements were made by management. Certainly we would not have endorsed anything we deemed offensive, and loaves of bread seemed pretty innocuous. At this point we had done the Coke commercials as well as spots for public-service organizations. Our next venture into advertising would be an Arrid deodorant commercial, featuring our armpits.

Through everything, what really kept us—especially Flo and me —going, were the fans. In the days when we traveled so much, their methods of finding us were ingenious. Only years later would one fan reveal to me the intricate work involved in finding us.

A few days before we would arrive in New York, a series of phone calls would be placed.

"Hello, Waldorf-Astoria Hotel. May I help you?"

"Yes," the fan would say. "I'm calling from the Supremes' office and we would like to cancel the reservations they are holding."

"Just a moment, please. I'm sorry, but I can't find a reservation for the Supremes."

"Oh, excuse me. There must have been a mix-up here. Good day."

Then another call.

"Hello, Sherry Netherlands."

"Yes. I'm calling from Motown Records, and we have decided to change the reservation you are holding for the Supremes."

"Just a moment, Miss. I'm afraid I don't see them listed here."

"Forgive me. I've just remembered that they have been changed. Sorry to bother you. Good-bye."

Then another call.

"Thank you for calling the Warwick."

"Yes. This is Motown Records and we have to change the arrival time for the Supremes."

"One moment. Yes. They are to arrive here on Sunday, the fifteenth. What date would you like to change to?"

"Hold on one moment, please. Could I get back to you on that? In the meantime, please just hold it as is."

And so it would go. I don't know how many telephone calls were made, but the feminine voice was neither from Motown, nor was it female. It was Tony Turner, an eleven-year-old boy whose sleuthing led him to us whenever we were in New York.

"How did you know we'd be here?" we would scream when we saw him in the lobby. He'd just smile. Tony had fallen in love with the Supremes after his parents took him to see us at the Apollo. Though he loved us all, he was devoted to Miss Flo, as he called her. Tony was not the only one who could find us every single time, and of course he was not the only one trying. There were hundreds like him all over the country.

Though Motown kept up a tight security system, fans like Tony —who were always well behaved—were permitted to see us. There was a lot of competition among the fans, and the fact that it was friendly made it no less serious. The fans divided themselves into two groups: the B fans—just anyone—and the A fans, like Tony, who always got through. Within the fan community the As were stars in their own right (so the As told us), and one reason they were allowed to be around us was that it was known that a good A fan would throw the other fans off our trail. We were rarely mobbed, but could always count on a lively, vocal contingent of kids and teens waiting for us wherever we went.

I was touched by these shows of affection, especially from the little ones. It took a lot of stamina to stand outside a stage door, sometimes in freezing weather, just to catch a glimpse. All of us would sign autographs, but Flo and I would stay out and talk to the fans. Flo also made the younger fans her little pals, and soon Berry was criticizing both of us.

"Mary, you know I think you're making yourself too available," Berry said. I knew he wasn't referring only to the fans; he thought I had too many boyfriends, too.

"I like to be out," I replied.

"You should be more like Diane—untouchable, unreachable. You're getting too familiar."

But Flo and I didn't see any harm in what we were doing. Hundreds of times I saw her standing outside a stage door while a limo was waiting, motor running. She'd have her hands on her hips and be chatting away. "How are you all doing?"

"Fine," they'd all reply.

"How long you kids been standing out here? Probably all day, huh? You must be hungry. Let's go get something to eat."

Then she'd lead the kids down the street or around the corner to the nearest fast-food place. Flo would always be beautifully dressed, and on winter days her long fur coat would sort of billow as she marched along briskly, looking like a Pied Piper with a couple dozen young kids jogging behind her. She'd quickly get the proprietor's attention, order pizza or burgers and sodas or cocoa for everyone, then sit with the kids for a while. Once they were engrossed in their snacks, she'd slip out the door.

Sometimes she'd bring Tony or some other starstruck kid up to her room. On days when she was tired or didn't feel well, Tony would stand outside her door, and she would pass autographed pictures and dollar bills for treats to him, making him always promise not to reveal her room number and to bring back her change. This kind of accessibility, as limited as it was, irked Berry no end. The more Flo and I dealt with the fans, the more Berry complained about it, but he couldn't stop it and he didn't try. Once, when we were rehearsing for Ed Sullivan's show, dozens of kids were standing under the window of the studio screaming for us. When Flo saw what was going on, she threw a paper bag full of money down to them from a third-story window. It was about $20, which in those days bought a lot of hot dogs.

Another time we were taping a segment for the Sullivan show on West Fifty-seventh Street. Across the street from the studio was a large building under construction. When the workers on the site saw our limo waiting, they assumed someone famous would be coming out, so they kept watching. When they saw the three of us emerge, they started screaming for us. Diane, of course, rushed into the car, and I had started to get in, when Flo suddenly strutted into the middle of the street. She stopped right on the white line and raised her arms up as if she were on a stage. Everyone on the street, even people in cars, were cheering for her. Their love for Flo was so obvious. The minute Diane heard everyone applauding Flo, she tried to get the driver to take off and leave Flo standing there.

In May 1966, *Look* magazine profiled us for a feature entitled "From Real Rags to Real Riches." Each of us was interviewed separately for our profiles. Though this feature story should have been one of the high points for us, Diane managed to taint it by stating for publication that her mother had had tuberculosis. Diane didn't mean it maliciously; she loved her mother dearly. But Diane always was a chatterbox; she simply loved to talk, and it wasn't always clear how many of her slips were inadvertent. This time, though, she'd gone too far. When Mrs. Ross confronted her, she was hurt and angry beyond words. In those days having had tuberculosis still carried a stigma, and there was no reason for Diane to have mentioned it at all. Berry was also furious.

"Now," Berry said to Diane, "maybe you will learn to think before you open your mouth!" Ironically, Diane is quoted in the same piece saying, "Everyone knows to this day they can tell me secrets and I won't tell."

Along with this jet-set life came the jet-set life-style. Wherever the three of us went, we were fêted in grand style—at lavish receptions, gala parties, meals in the most exquisite restaurants. Of course, no occasion would be complete without the best liquor and the finest champagne. None of us had ever been what you would call a drinker, but once we had really made it, there was nowhere we could turn without finding someone poised to refill our glasses. During our first trip to England in 1965, we were introduced to fine sherry, and we adopted the custom of sipping a glass whenever people were drinking just to appear more worldly.

Diane and I could drink without suffering any ill effects, but Flo's tolerance for alcohol was almost nil. After just one beer, she would be unsteady; any more than that and she was clearly intoxicated.

As our schedule of club bookings, international tours, television appearances, and recording dates accelerated, so did tensions within the group. By now Diane was given her own dressing room, while Flo and I shared one. Seeing Diane and Berry together, I never knew exactly who was directing whom; when changes occurred, we never knew which of them had instigated them. But Flo and I could see that whatever Diane wanted, Diane got. In Flo's mind this was unfair, and her resentment began to consume her.

Despite this internal turmoil, the three of us never let the public know about our problems. Part of the Supremes' magic came from our ability to make the real world and its problems stop at the edge of the stage. When we sang together—no matter what had happened backstage or in private—we were as close and as happy as we had been singing in the Projects or sitting in the Hitsville lobby. Although I had believed that the group would survive anything, seeing the friction between Flo and Diane and Berry, I began to have my doubts. Sadly, Flo found it harder to ignore Diane and Berry's maneuvers and more difficult to maintain the façade.

Around this time Motown began engineering appearances to emphasize Diane's role and diminish Flo's and mine. In the beginning the three of us would enter a room together, followed by Shelly Berger or Berry. Before long, though, it was Diane who walked in first on the arm of a Motown honcho, while Flo and I followed behind like bridesmaids in a wedding procession. When Diane's name showed up in columns preceded by the words "leader" or "spokesperson," Flo and I were crushed. It was apparent that neither Diane nor Berry gave a damn about what we wanted, and Flo made no bones about feeling betrayed and lied to.

Things began to crack while we were touring the Far East that fall. We visited Tokyo, Okinawa, Taiwan, Hong Kong, Manila, the naval bases at Yokosuka and Kajikawa Naval Base, Medina Air Force Base, and the U.S.S. *Coral Sea*. We enjoyed touring the military bases, especially since earlier plans to do a tour of Vietnam had been canceled when the U.S. Government informed us that they could not provide adequate security. When we visited hospitals we were saddened to see so many young men injured, but grateful that our visits could cheer them up. Almost all of them had been in Vietnam, where my brother Roosevelt was stationed.

We made a special stop at a military hospital that had a large burn unit, where many of the most badly hurt soldiers were sent for treatment. Against the advice of our military escort we visited the burn victims. It was one of the most emotional experiences of my life; I had never imagined that human beings could be so brutally injured and live with so much pain. It was all we could do to keep from crying in front of them.

When we got back to the base to do our show, we were late. As we rushed to get ready, the military official in charge of the show told Don Foster that if we weren't ready to go on in five minutes—which was impossible—we couldn't go on at all, and we wouldn't be paid.

"What's your name?" Don asked.

"Why do you want my name?" the official replied.

"Because I'm going to go out there and tell the people who have been waiting for two hours to see the Supremes that the girls can't go on because they were late getting here, and that the reason they were late was that they were visiting those men's comrades in the burn center."

With that, the case was closed, and we went on to give one of our best shows ever.

Though we were world travelers, the Far East was so unlike any-place we'd ever been, we were instantly captivated. Berry commissioned Milton Ginsberg to make what amounted to a very expensive home movie of our trip. Included in this footage (which remained in Motown's vaults until the mid-eighties) are some of our numbers and the usual posed stuff, like the three of us dressed as geishas (how telling!), talking to people working in rice paddies in the countryside, and pulling rickshaws into the above-ground sewage ditches.

There are also some behind-the-scenes sequences. Though nei-ther Diane nor Berry could have foreseen this, the "intimate" scenes are by far the most revealing. One scene takes place in our dressing room. Diane languidly lays her head down and pretends to be sleep-ing, all the while keeping her face to the camera. Flo and I are chat-ting in the background, then Flo sits down to brush her hair. From the look on Flo's face, you know that she sees through Diane's ploy, and she proves it by acting like she's about to throw her brush at Diane. Of course Diane immediately picks her head up and opens her eyes in alarm. Then the film cuts.

In another scene, a reporter at a press conference asks us to sing "You Can't Hurry Love" a cappella. Berry very nicely says that he doesn't know if we can do it, since we've never done it before, but Diane says that she thinks we can. Once we indicate that we're game, Berry tries to help us along by snapping his fingers to the beat. We were prepared to do anything for the public, no matter what.

Back home, we continued with our itinerary, opening at the Fla-mingo in Las Vegas toward the end of September. By now, anyone who'd missed our shows could see us—and Berry—at the gambling tables. Gambling fever had always been rampant among the men at Motown, where there were probably as many all-night games upstairs at Hitsville as there were on the Strip. As the money had started rolling in, most of the male producers, writers, and performers took their turns being high rollers, usually with disastrous results. Women were rarely admitted into this male bastion, so we only knew what we heard, but it was no secret that money it had taken—or would take—years to earn was disappearing at the turn of a card. The stakes were also pretty outrageous—the keys to a brand-new Cadillac, thousands of dollars, and once even the right to produce an up-and-coming female lead singer, bet by a producer and won by Berry.

Sitting at a table, Berry was in heaven. Flo never especially liked to gamble, but Diane and I would go out with Shelly Berger's wife, Eleanor, and take over a table. Losing $5,000 a night wasn't unusual. We were all pretty lucky—blackjack was my game—but Berry and Diane did take some pretty big losses. I remember walking into Berry's suite after he'd had a particularly bad night and seeing everyone in his entourage acting like they were at a wake. When the boss was unhappy, everybody was unhappy.

In late 1966 I began to notice that Flo's drinking was becoming a habit. She never drank before a show, but after we finished our set we would change and go out to partake of the local nightlife or attend private parties. This was when Flo drank. A normal person leading a normal life could have slept it off and carried on. But we were not leading normal lives. After a show we might fly to another city to finish a recording or prepare for our next engagement or television appearance. Virtually every new record release or promotional appearance was preceded by a press conference and interviews, followed by a luncheon with local politicians or record business people, then rehearsals, then hours in makeup and wardrobe, then the show, then the parties, then the same thing all over again. Many nights we were lucky to get two hours' sleep before facing the public again. And we were never less than perfectly gracious and beautiful. To the public Flo was still the same.

But Diane and I knew differently. We tried to influence Flo to limit her drinking by curtailing our own. We would nurse a single glass of sherry for hours. Flo wasn't dumb, and she was touched by our efforts. "Don't worry," she'd say, "I'll be all right." As time passed, our little ploy became less effective. Though we were too young to consider it then, it is clear to me today that the unresolved emotional problems Flo suffered after the rape were making it more difficult for her to cope with what was happening now. She was sinking. Everything in her life seemed to be coming apart at the seams. Flo's rage over having her solo spot taken from her and the public's new Motown-inspired obsession with Diane was consuming her. Diane's blatant scene stealing could not be ignored, and my two best friends were starting to act as if they hated each other.

In the fall of 1966, while touring to promote our latest album, *Supremes A-Go-Go* (which featured my lead on "Come and Get These Memories"), we did a record signing at Stern's department store in New York City. The room we were in was divided in the middle by a models' runway that sloped upward at the back. We were seated at the top, and the fans gathered at the other end of the runway, held back by ropes and several security guards.

After we'd signed a bunch of records, the master of ceremonies, a local disc jockey, urged us to get up and walk down the runway so that the fans could get a closer look. When I hesitated, Flo got up and strolled down the runway, smiling politely. The fans always loved Flo, and as she neared them they reached out to her and applauded. After Flo sat down, I walked about halfway down and got my share of wolf whistles and applause. But when Diane's turn came, she held back, coyly shaking her head no and acting as if she hadn't a clue what the fans could possibly want. She kept it up until the fans were screaming wildly. In a flash, she jumped up, dramatically spread her arms so that the wide dolman sleeves of her sweater resembled a giant bat's wings, and charged down the ramp, flashing a brilliant smile. She turned and ran back up the ramp. The crowd tore through the ropes to get at her. The security people rushed to protect Diane, but she reassured them, cooing, "That's all right. They love me!"

Flo and I gave each other our secret look. I just let a smile freeze on my face, but Flo made no secret of her displeasure. This did not endear her to the fans, who were mesmerized by the Ross razzle-dazzle. Later, when Flo and I were alone together, she cried to me, "I can't take it anymore! Why does Diane always do this?"

During our trip to the Far East, Flo and Tommy Chapman had fallen in love, and they were now as inseparable as our schedule would allow. Flo now seemed happier when she was away from the Supremes. Tommy was very nice; he seemed to empathize with Flo, and he loved her. But people at Motown talked; in their eyes, Flo was one of the label's three leading ladies, and Tommy was just Berry's chauffeur.

Knowing how difficult it was for Flo to be intimate with a man, I was happy that she had Tommy. Whenever Tommy was around, she stopped obsessing about Berry and Diane, whom she'd come to regard as a single entity. As Diane moved further toward the front, Flo became not only defiant but bitter. Diane and Flo's bickering had become incessant, and I knew there was nothing I could say or do to revive our childhood friendship. Flo would be late for press conferences and rehearsals, and while I understood Flo's problem, we were all on the same crazy schedule. She was not only making us look bad, but hurting her own cause. I tried to reason with her. These things often happened early in the day, but rather than confront Flo then and risk a scene before a show I'd wait until we were off and back at our hotel.

"Flo, why were you late to the press conference today?" I asked. One look and I knew she was already on her second beer.

"Honey, I am not working myself to death to make Diana Ross a star." We always referred to Diane as Diane, and when Flo said "Diana" the bitterness cut through me like a knife.

"But, girl," I said, "can't you see that you are only making yourself look bad? You should have heard Diane carrying on. She was trying to get Berry on the phone, and you know she's going to tell him everything. Why are you doing this to yourself?"

"Because I don't give a damn about Diane or that jive Berry!" Flo screamed. "And don't think for a minute that they give a damn about me or you!"

Flo believed Diane and Berry were using her to make Diane a star. Unfortunately the only way Flo knew to fight back was to fight in any way she could. When Flo thought she was right, she was right, even if what she did was wrong. If she felt she was justified, that was it. An injustice was being committed, and Flo wasn't going to tolerate it.

Her defiance was coming to be regarded as a serious problem by Diane and the higher-ups at Motown. Though she would get much heavier over the next few months, she had already gained a little weight, which was enough to affect how our stage costumes fit. Sometimes Diane would want to wear one outfit for a show but couldn't because Flo's no longer fit her.

One night Flo ran into Berry at the Twenty Grand. In front of a bunch of people from Motown and some of the other performers, Berry said, "I agree with Diane. You have to do something about your weight. You are much too fat."

"I don't give a damn what you think!" she replied. Then she threw her drink in his face and stormed out of the club.

Though Flo had never been comfortable maintaining the Supremes' glamour-girl image, she had enjoyed it at first. Lately, however, she had come to regard it as phony and fake, and the rigors of touring, of being a star, seemed to overwhelm her.

"Mary, I can't do those interviews again and fly out tomorrow," she said. "Are those fools crazy?"

"I'm pretty tired, too," I would admit.

"I'm telling you, we need a vacation," s⌐

"And I'm telling Berry that. Who does he thir

In these complaints, I could hear the f

out—out of the Supremes, out of this lif

down. Her concerns were valid, and I was ∿

that even if Diane left, we could go on, and if we a⌐

probably be the lead singer. I would try to tell Flo thⱱ

the hopes that she would cool down and stick it out a litⱱ

longer. But as time passed it became increasingly evident that ⱱ

would not.

Strangely, even when Flo was angry with Diane, she still worried about her, thinking, for instance, that the reason Diane was so thin was that Berry was working her too hard. Though Flo and Berry had gotten along, they now seemed to clash, and she alternated between seeing Berry as the force pulling Diane away from us and as Diane's ally in her power plays. Once Flo said, "Why doesn't she leave him? He doesn't care about her. She doesn't get anything that we don't get." Flo paused, then added, "Well, almost."

Still, Flo kept her sense of humor, especially onstage. It was around this time that she began replying to Diane's stage patter line, "Thin is in," with "Yeah, but fat is where it's at," which always brought down the house.

In their desperation, both Diane and Flo established lifelines to the outside world. Diane had Berry, and when he wasn't around she was on the phone with him, telling him who was doing—or not doing —what, and getting his advice and assurances. Flo had her family, whom she would call every day from wherever she was. She would talk with them for hours and tell them all her problems. Sadly, her family could not offer much constructive advice, nor give Flo sorely needed perspective. Her complaints about Berry, or Diane, or touring, elicited only support and encouragement. They believed she should express herself and not let "them" push her around.

That fall we had another number-one hit with "You Can't Hurry Love," and were booked up for the next year. We cut records when-ever we could, and sometimes we did our vocals on different days. Though the records were still important, they were not our primary concern. The Supremes had transcended the "pop group" categori-zation and were now firmly embedded in the entertainment establish-ment. We were secure, and without having to worry about whether or not we could maintain our position, it seemed likely that we could

y concentrate on some of the internal problems that needed
ng.

Then the final wedge was driven. In our travels we talked to
countless journalists. Toward the end of 1966 they all seemed to be
asking the same question: Was it true that we were changing our name
to Diana Ross and the Supremes? Flo and I always denied it. No one
from Motown—not even Diane—ever said a word to us about it.

Over time we learned that the name would indeed be changed,
and, when it seemed certain, Flo went over the edge. The underhand-
edness of it all was more than she could bear. She missed a couple of
shows. To her credit, she never came onstage drunk, and, as always,
we were consummate pros. When Flo didn't make a show, Berry
would send out Marlene Barrow, one of the Andantes, and, frankly,
few people in the audience were ever the wiser. But something had to
give.

"You can't do this, Flo," I told her once after she missed a show.

"I don't care," she replied, lying. "Berry hates me, and I hate him.
That fool!"

Flo was getting further and further away from me, and I found
myself anxiously awaiting each day. Would she make the show? And
even if she did, would she plummet back into this self-destructive
depression afterward? Flo was threatening to quit the group. I could
see that she didn't care what happened to herself. Flo was not a small
woman, and with the drinking, she continued to gain weight. Soon
the svelte, revealing stage costumes were tight and unflattering. Flo
had always cared so much about her appearance that, when I saw that
she was just letting herself go, I knew something was seriously wrong.

There wasn't much anyone could do. When Berry wasn't around,
Diane would corner me and try to get me to side with her against Flo.

"Did you see how Blondie looked at that last show? I called Berry
and told him. Flo makes us look bad, and I'm not going to stand for
it!"

It had gotten to the point where Diane and I were hiding bottles
from Flo, and the road managers saw to it that my room was always
next to Flo's. Diane and Berry started avoiding Flo, which only enraged her. I sat in Flo's room with her all the time, it seemed. Flo
would start griping about Diane and Berry, then she would threaten
to call them and give them a piece of her mind. I would talk her
out of it and stay with her. I'd tried to reason with her, but it was
impossible.

For my part I just wanted to keep the group intact and keep Flo from going to pieces. Coming from my background, I never thought to suggest to Flo that she needed a psychiatrist. Perhaps if I had, things might have been different. We needed each other, but while I saw the situation as something that might be resolved one way or another, Flo saw it as the last straw. I knew that I needed an ally and I tried everything to get Flo to stay, but she wanted to go.

Weeks later in early 1967 Berry held a meeting with some upper-level people at Motown, Diane, and me. It was decided that the search for Flo's replacement would begin. Cindy Birdsong of Patti LaBelle and the Blue-Belles was everyone's choice, largely because she and Flo had a similar look, and she was contacted. In the meantime Flo stayed on the road, but things were touch-and-go. I never knew for sure if Flo knew about Cindy; if she did, she wouldn't have let on, I'm sure. I still prayed Flo would straighten up, but as the days passed, the possibility of that happening seemed less and less likely.

Our lives at that time were such that, even though we met hundreds of people, we really saw only each other. I had witnessed Flo's deterioration and it had been so gradual that I really had no idea how bad it was. One night I was walking back to my room with Stevie Wonder's drummer, Hamilton Bohannon. Flo opened her door and was so drunk she could barely stand. Hamilton was amazed. "What's wrong with Florence?" he asked. I knew then that it was all over.

It all blew up in Memphis. We were doing a series of one-nighters and were leaving for New Orleans, where we were scheduled to appear that evening. We were all sitting in the cars, ready to go, but no Flo. When she didn't come downstairs to leave with us that morning, Don went up to check on her. He found her sitting up in her bed drunk. She'd been talking to her family long-distance all night, and refused to go with Don. He got her up, washed her face, helped her dress, and finally got her into the car. As we drove to the airport, Diane was furious, and I was sad and disappointed. Flo was digging herself into a hole so deep she would never get out.

All during the flight, Flo refused to speak with us, and as I watched her from across the aisle, I could see how desperately she wanted out of what she viewed as an impossible situation. She knew that if she walked out she'd have to bear the responsibility for what might happen to the group, so she chose another way. Her attitude was, "Let them put me out!" And she made it easier and easier for them to do just that. She knew what she was doing, and there was no way anybody could stop her. Diane called Berry the minute we checked in at our hotel. Berry then instructed Joe Shaffner to send Flo home.

It had finally happened. It had been one thing for her to show up late for rehearsals and interviews, but that she'd allowed herself to lose so much control that they would take her away was incomprehensible to me. Before she left she was saying things like, "I know everybody is looking at me, and I don't care," but I knew she did. Where was my best friend, who was tough, strong, and proud? My friend whose dreams had all come true? Why was she throwing herself right into their hands?

As they bundled her up and got her ready to catch a plane back to Detroit, I took one last look at her. She gave me a big smile, and then laughed, as if the joke was on them.

That night Diane and I were the Supremes. We put on our best smiles and carried on as a duo. I was so shaken by the day's events, I could hardly think, but the show went on. Marlene Barrow was flown in for other shows. When Flo was back on the road with us, things weren't much better. Now it was worse than before because Flo wouldn't even pretend that she wanted to be there, and Diane wasn't pretending that she wanted her there. The minute Flo took a drink, Diane would be on the phone to Berry. I knew this couldn't go on forever.

And it didn't. One day in mid-April we were all summoned to Berry's home on Outer Drive. As I drove there, I recalled the past months' events and hoped against hope that Flo would say something or do something this afternoon to save herself. She'd given Berry, Diane, and me every reason to want her out of the group, but I believed she still might be the old Flo I knew and fight for her place in the Supremes.

When I arrived I found Flo and her mother, Diane, and Berry. We sat in the living room, where there was a huge grand piano. Diane and Berry sat together, Flo and her mother sat together, and I sat to one side by myself. With one look at Flo, I knew that dreams don't die, people just stop dreaming. As I sat there staring at Flo, Berry spoke calmly but firmly about how important the Supremes were, and how important each of us was to the group. Then in a somber tone, he told Flo that she had been messing up and was not upholding her end of the deal. Berry limited what he had to say to the facts. There were no insults or accusations; he knew better than to provoke Flo. She had a violent temper. It was clear that he just wanted to get it over with. Flo said nothing.

Then Flo's mother said, "But Mary still wants Flo in the group," and looked straight at me.

Suddenly everything got tense. I realized that Diane and Berry had come to this meeting not knowing what I was going to say or whose side I would take. For a second I thought to myself, why doesn't Flo speak up? Then I realized that Flo was waiting for me to rescue her, waiting for me to tell Diane and Berry how they'd mistreated Flo, and how wrong they were. But to what end? While Flo no doubt would have appreciated me defending her, she had refused to defend herself. She wanted out more than anything else, and she knew that I knew it.

As I stared at Mrs. Ballard I drew upon every ounce of courage I had. I loved Diane and I loved Flo equally, more than anything else in the world. But my two best friends had each taken a different course, and this is where it led. It hurt me, but I said, "Mrs. Ballard, Flo no longer wants to be in the Supremes. Yes, I want her with us, but she no longer wants us."

In those few seconds, I saw nine years of work and love and happiness fade away. Although I was an adult, the Supremes still stood in my mind as a dream from childhood, a wonderful dream that had come true. I believed the Supremes would last forever. Now I knew that even dreams that come true can change.

The real meaning of changing our name to "Diana Ross and the Supremes" became clear to me as I looked across the room at Berry and Diane. All of a sudden, I was alone. There wasn't a group anymore. This was the worst thing that had ever happened to us, yet Diane and I would never speak about it. Though Flo would do a few more dates with us, on a kind of probation, this was the last time the three of us were really the Supremes.

Flo's response was frighteningly cold and distant. She was detached, yet seemed satisfied with the outcome. Flo and her mother left, with Mrs. Ballard in tears. I stood at the window and watched them get into Flo's Cadillac and drive away. Turning my attention back into the room, I saw that Diane and Berry both looked relieved. In fact, within minutes, Diane was almost giddy, and she looked uncannily like she would onstage during our tribute to Martin Luther King, Jr., when she'd cry, "Free at last, great God Almighty, free at last." No one said a word about Flo; she was gone. I wondered, How could they be so happy?

Within minutes of Flo's departure, Cindy Birdsong came into the room, and we started making plans for rehearsals with the new Supreme. If I was going to stay with the Supremes—which I was—there was nothing for me to do but dig in and get to work. Suddenly I didn't feel like just one of the Supremes—I felt like the only Supreme.

# CHAPTER 18

Of course no one could ever replace Flo, and I admit that at first my feelings toward Cindy were neutral. For Cindy, becoming a Supreme was a great opportunity, and she worked hard to fit in. Berry and Diane liked her a lot, and her jovial air was a welcome change, but instead of cheering me up, it only reminded me that Flo wasn't there.

We were scheduled to play a benefit sponsored by radio station KHJ for the United Negro College Fund at the Hollywood Bowl on April 29, which was only a few days away. Flo's fate was still up in the air—maybe she would be back; maybe she would not. What we did know was that Cindy would be singing at the Bowl, and so we got right to work, rehearsing and going over vocal arrangements for hours each day. Diane had not rehearsed with us in a while now, so the job of getting Cindy ready fell to Cholly and me. In Berry's living room, though, Diane stood up and started to show Cindy the steps Flo and I did, but it was obvious she didn't know what they were. Since Cholly still lived next door to me, we set to work at his place, and Cindy stayed at my house. Cindy was a fast study, and we were pleased with her progress, but we knew the real proof would be in the performance.

The Hollywood Bowl show went like a dream. Because the stage is so far from the audience, it was even harder for people to see that Cindy was not Flo, and in fact many reviewers were fooled. Cindy was very excited. We had also worked very hard to get our sound right. Flo was a first soprano, and Cindy a lower, second soprano, so I had to make some adjustments in my singing. The night before the show, Cholly made a point of telling Diane not to mention to the audience that Cindy was replacing Flo.

The show was such a success that the next day the three of us went on a shopping spree. An exclusive Rodeo Drive shop in Beverly Hills opened up just for us. Diane and I strolled through, picking up anything that caught our fancy, but Cindy just watched us. Though

Cindy had been performing for many years, she was still a little awkward around us, especially Diane.

Though it seemed that Cindy would be joining the Supremes, she was committed to the Blue-Belles for the next several months. Soon after the Hollywood Bowl show, Cindy left us to meet her other group, and so Flo was back. Flo's pride wouldn't let her beg for her place in the Supremes, but I could see that she was glad to be given a second chance. I believed that once Motown made it clear that they meant business, Flo would either leave for good or shape up.

Rumors that Diane would be leaving the group were now common, though like the name change, it was never discussed with any of us. It was obvious that her being thrust to the forefront was part of that plan. Though I knew better, in my heart I still retained the smallest hope that when and if Diane left, Flo would be made the lead singer, and that was certainly worth holding out for. Flo, however, couldn't see that.

There were many other people whose interest in us was as great as Berry's, among them General Artists Corporation, our booking agents. Sure, the Supremes were the top act, but if we continued having to use stand-ins for Flo, or if we ever worked again as a duo, our image would be shattered. I did not want the name changed. Berry, sensing that I might be a problem on this issue, explained to me that the name change would benefit all of us because we would actually be two attractions—the Supremes and Diana Ross—and so would earn more money. "Don't worry about it, Mary," he promised. "I will always take care of you." Believing Berry and feeling I had no choice, I went along.

In late May, when Flo was back with us for a few appearances, we made what would be Flo's last appearance on *The Tonight Show*. As always, Diane sat next to Johnny Carson, while Flo and I were relegated to the couch, and Diane did most of the talking.

In the course of the conversation Johnny Carson mentioned that there had been a stand-in for Flo at the Hollywood Bowl and asked if this meant we were breaking up. Of course we denied the rumors and made a few jokes. Carson then went on to another topic, but Diane interrupted him to say, ". . . just like in a Broadway play . . . we have a stand-in. The show must go on. Except for me. They can't stand in for me. But Florence and Mary, we have two young ladies that will stand in in their place."

That was news to me! I didn't know they had one for me, too. After this Flo monopolized the entire interview, interrupting Diane to give clever and honest answers to the rest of Carson's questions. The audience loved her, and for a minute I could see the old spunky Flo, but it really wasn't her. Though she didn't drink in public, she had been drinking so much and so often that her emotional problems got worse. It seemed that whatever bravado she got while she was drunk would carry over to when she was sober.

The times Flo was back with us, it was obvious how much she had changed. Her drinking had escalated. When we were on the road, she shunned the rest of us and stuck with Tommy. After our shows at the Copa, we would all ride back to the hotel in our limo, while Flo and Tommy walked back alone, holding hands.

There were other dramatic changes in Flo's behavior, such as her treatment of the fans, whom she now avoided, and her appearance. Flo's facial features were delicate and naturally beautiful. Suddenly she was wearing very harsh, dark eye makeup and keeping her sunglasses on all the time. She was also heavier than ever, and Diane, who was never known for her diplomacy, never let Flo forget it.

That July we played the Flamingo Hotel in Las Vegas. This was an important occasion for several reasons, not the least of which being that this was the first time the marquee would read "Diana Ross and the Supremes." Berry was in all his glory, and we knew there were many important people in the audience. For one of our first numbers, we wore two-piece tuxedo pantsuits. Unlike our long, flowing chiffon gowns, these fit very snugly, and Flo barely squeezed into hers.

For the first time Flo drank before the show and came onstage tipsy, with her wig awry and her costume too tight. At one point, Flo moved in such a way that the waistcoat of her outfit rode up over her belly and her flesh was exposed. Berry ran backstage the second the show ended and in front of a small crowd of Motown and Flamingo people, he calmly ordered, "Get her off the stage. Now."

Back in the dressing room I knew this was it. Diane, Berry, and I were upset, but Flo just acted like she didn't care.

"You're too fat!" Diane said to Flo. "Why don't you stop drinking so much? Look at yourself! You're as big as a house!"

Next to my size 7 and Diane's size 4, Florence's 10/11 looked huge. Worse, she was out of shape.

"Florence—" Berry said.

"Berry, you better get out my face!" Flo snapped back.

"Listen to me, girl. You look terrible onstage! Look at the other girls. You're not holding up your end," Berry replied.

"Oh, I don't care. Leave me alone!"

There was nothing left to say; Flo was told to leave. She packed
and went back to Detroit, and Cindy, who had been discreetly sequestered down the street at Caesar's Palace, stepped in the next night, for
good.

In July we released "Reflections," the first single released under the
name Diana Ross and the Supremes. Because we recorded our singles
so many months in advance of their release, this is the last hit single
Flo appears on. We also played Forest Hills Stadium with Cindy. The
announcement that Cindy was now a Supreme prompted much speculation from the press as to the exact circumstances of Flo's departure.
Officially, Flo left because of exhaustion and a desire to settle down,
and people seemed to accept that. The real story was kept under
wraps, and Flo, despite everything that had happened, chose not to
divulge the truth.

I stayed in New York for a couple days after the Forst Hills date.
One day in early August I received a telegram.

*Mary*
*Stick by Florence. It may happen to you. Think about it.*
                                                    *—Tempts*

That August we were in Los Angeles, where we performed at a fun-
draising dinner for President Johnson. Though we had never met him,
we were impressed by his social policies, especially in the area of civil
rights, so we were happy to help him. After we had finished singing,
we were getting into our limousine when we saw the president running
toward us, leading a trail of Secret Service agents, and with his daughter Lynda in tow.

"I was supposed to rush away from here and head back to the
White House before the show was over, but I refused to leave until I
got to talk to the Supremes." He told us how much he liked "Somewhere," which contained a love monologue, and his daughter also
complimented us. We were quite thrilled about this meeting, and it
was reported in newspapers all over the country the next day.

Later that month we performed at the Steele Pier in Atlantic City,
where Diane and Cindy were robbed of furs, jewels, and other items
from their hotel room. Security was tightened up, and we carried on
with our schedule, playing the Cocoanut Grove, the Michigan State
Fair, and doing the now-routine guest spots on *The Ed Sullivan Show*,

*The Hollywood Palace,* and other television programs. By September, *Diana Ross and the Supremes' Greatest Hits* was the number-one album.

Motown was only too happy to broaden our audience and consolidate our show-biz appeal, and so we flew to Las Estacas, Mexico, in October to film an episode of *Tarzan,* a weekly series starring Ron Ely in the title role. In a case of truly bizarre casting, we were to play three nuns. Our makeup was so natural, it seemed almost nonexistent, and the long, dark habits were an interesting contrast to our usual stage attire. After the makeup people had finished with us, we'd sneak back into our dressing rooms and put on more makeup. Of course Diane had the most lines, but we all spoke, and even sang "Michael Row the Boat Ashore" and "The Lord Helps Those Who Help Themselves" (we had recorded some other gospel songs at Motown, but they've never been released). Also co-starring in this episode, "The Convert," was James Earl Jones. Berry, Shelly Berger, and Mike Roshkind, Motown's newest expert in corporate public relations, were also on hand.

Cindy was very excited about the show, and Berry seemed very attentive. He couldn't seem to compliment her enough. I was pleased that things were going so well for Cindy, but as time passed, I realized that she had come to the group believing—as did the public—that Diane was the leader. Nonetheless, Cindy and I gradually became good friends, and in her I had a confidante and buddy, which I needed very badly.

After Flo left, my relationship with Berry was a little strained. No one was quite sure what to say to me, or what I might do. Maybe I wanted to leave, too. They shouldn't have worried, though; I'd outlast them all. But we had a great time in Mexico, far away from the usual bustle, and Berry and I were pals again.

We became friends with the other cast members and crew, and Ron Ely and I were real chums. We were all staying in a beautiful hotel, where we'd lie around the pool on our days off, or go shopping in town. We all got Montezuma's revenge, and even that became a source of humor. There were plenty of reporters and photographers on the set, and they got some funny pictures of us, including one of me sitting with my habit pulled up over my knees, smoking a cigarette and drinking beer. When the show aired in January 1968, it was the highest-rated episode in the series.

\* \* \*

Back from Mexico, we hit the road again. "In and Out of Love" had just been released, and in early November we played UCLA's Pauley Pavilion with trumpeter Hugh Masekela.

Cindy was many things—a great singer, a good buddy—but no ally when it came to standing up to Diane and Berry. I had no idea what they had said to her before she joined, but it was clear to me that she believed that just because Diane was the lead singer she called all the shots inside the group.

"She's not the boss. I've told you that. We're a group, and everything comes up for a vote, okay?"

"Okay," Cindy would reply.

"The same thing happened last week with the blue dresses. Don't just go along with everything she wants. If you don't want to speak up to her, wait until I get here."

"Okay."

"There won't be any group if you and I don't stick together. Please, Cindy."

"Okay."

Suddenly the Supremes seemed bigger than all of us. I began to feel like that little girl on Bassett Street, waiting at the picture window for somebody or something. Until then, I just drew into myself. I wasn't depressed, but I knew things weren't as good as they could have been. But how to change it?

Throughout 1967, one of our booking agents, Norman Wise, had been telling me about this wonderful new singer he thought I should get to know. Each time Norman mentioned him, I sort of half-listened. I had been pursued by countless men, and at that point Norman's latest choice—a guy named Tom Jones—struck me as just another celebrity who wanted to meet one of the Supremes. There were plenty of those. One day, though, when we were discussing a trip to Europe, Tom's name came up again. I had bought some of Tom's records and, besides being shocked to find that he was white, was impressed by his great looks. When Norman tried to play matchmaker again, I went along with it. He arranged a meeting between us, to take place in Munich, Germany, at the Bambi ceremony—the European equivalent of the Academy Awards—at which he conveniently booked us to perform.

As the date drew closer I became giddy as a schoolgirl. With Flo's departure I'd been thinking about my own life and career. Loneliness seemed to come with the turf. I remembered going to see Diahann Carroll when she was playing the Elmwood Casino in Windsor, Ontario. After the show, I went backstage to invite her to a party, and that night we talked a lot about how lonely life could be for a female performer. It was about ninety-five percent hard work and five percent glamour, but I still loved every minute onstage. When I was singing, I saw my purpose and direction clearly. Offstage, though, I felt very much alone. Since my breakup with Duke, I had dated a bodyguard from Puerto Rico, Brian Holland, Fuller Gordy (Berry's older brother), and a wonderful English producer named David Puttnam. This little rendezvous was just what I needed.

Shelly Berger arranged to go with us on the trip, and I let him and Cindy in on my little secret. She was as excited about it as I was. Diane and I were no longer chitchatting about everything like we used to, and I feared that if she knew the real reason we were going, she'd refuse, so I kept it a secret from her. This was unlike me, but I have to admit that after being in the dark about so many of her and Berry's plans, I sort of liked having a little intrigue of my own for a change.

The three of us and Shelly flew from New York to Milano, where we were to catch a connecting flight to Munich. Somehow, though, we missed our plane by fifteen minutes. I was crushed, but couldn't act too disappointed. Deep inside, I wanted to pound on the counter and get put on some flight—any flight—but that was not my way. We decided to stay over. Berry wasn't there, so Diane was talking to us, and we were having a great time.

That night we dined at Alfio's, an Italian restaurant we'd discovered on one of our previous trips. We each ate a dozen escargots and drank lots of red wine. On the way home, our cab driver insisted on keeping all the windows open. It was freezing, and in my broken Italian (based on my broken Spanish, which sounded like German and Japanese), I tried to convince him to close the windows, saying "Cerra la ventana" and pantomiming the motions for him. All he'd say was something that sounded like "ajo." Finally it dawned on me what he was trying to tell us: He had to keep the windows open because we all reeked of garlic. We laughed all the way to our rooms, then settled in for a night's rest.

The next morning I was up bright and early, rushing everyone to make our flight to Munich. Once we arrived there we had to head straight for our dressing rooms, since we had missed our rehearsals. I tried my best to stay calm as we got dressed. Every once in a while I'd catch Cindy's eye, and we'd both grin. Diane was taking her time getting ready, oblivious of the fact that I was ready way ahead of time, which was rare. She was barely dressed and didn't even have her wig on when there was a knock at the door.

"Who is it?" I asked, my heart pounding.

"It's Tom Jones," he replied in his beautiful Welsh accent.

Diane screamed, jumped up, and ran into another room. I had been waiting for this moment for weeks and wasn't going to blow it. I opened the door and there he was, dressed in a ruffled white shirt, black tuxedo, and—of course—skin-tight pants. Sparks flew; he was gorgeous. Why had I waited so long?

"What's the matter with her?" he asked, gesturing toward the door where Diane had disappeared. "I didn't come to see her anyway."

Fortunately Diane was out of earshot. I introduced him to Cindy, and we spoke for a few moments, making plans to meet after the show at a dinner party. When he left, I was speechless. A second later Diane huffed into the room, obviously miffed.

"Did you guys know he was coming?" she asked.

"No," Cindy lied.

"No, we did not," I added, pretending to be insulted that she would suggest such a thing. Apparently it worked.

The show went well, and though I was into it, my mind was on Tom. At the dinner I saw him seated across the room from me at a table of beautiful women. I tried not to be too obvious, but every time I looked over at him, our eyes would meet. He sent messages to me through the waiters, saying that he was sorry for the delay, but he would speak with me as soon as he could. When he finally made it over to my table, he said, "Look, I'm going to be traveling in a limousine with Richard Burton and Elizabeth Taylor, so we can't go together to the next nightspot, but go on, and I'll meet up with you."

When I arrived at the next destination, he had already left, but there was a message waiting for me, telling me where to meet him. I got there, only to find another one: "I'm on my way! Don't leave! Tom." After waiting a while, I decided to go back to my hotel. I should have been disappointed, but I wasn't. I was already in love, and I knew that somehow we'd be together.

Back at my hotel a grand celebration that involved every guest there was in progress. People were drinking champagne by the bottle. I went into one of the large rooms and joined the fun, drinking champagne and having a ball. Suddenly he entered the room, and for a moment I felt like we were living out a scene from a musical, with "Some Enchanted Evening" playing in the background. Within moments we were throwing back glasses of champagne and having a wonderful time. I could see instantly that Tom was like no man I had ever met. He was extremely down-to-earth and passionate. We talked, then we cuddled, then we kissed, and by the time the evening had ended I knew I was in love. When we finally parted to go back to our separate rooms I was already thinking about when I would see him again.

This was really love at first sight, but much more. Tom loved women, and his reputation as a sex symbol preceded him, but he was a man's man. Despite his recent ascent in show business, he retained the basic values of his working-class Welsh upbringing and always spoke his mind, no matter who was around to hear it. I think that many other stars, after years of being surrounded by people who worshipped them, found Tom's attitude refreshing. Elvis Presley, for one, always sought Tom out and spent as much time as he could with him. These characteristics also made Tom a great friend, in addition to being a fine lover, and our relationship was wonderful. It was wildly romantic, and yet we could spend hours and hours just talking, which is something Tom rarely did with a woman, or so he said.

After that night I was consumed by thoughts about our next meeting. Since we both had hectic schedules, we would fly to each other whenever we could. I truly believed I had found my love at last.

During this trip we also went to England, where we appeared on the Palladium television show (which also included Tom). It seemed that every time we went to England we were treated better and better. This time the Duke and Duchess of Bedford held a party in our honor at a Chelsea restaurant/disco called the Club Dell'Aretusa. Among the invited guests were Vanessa Redgrave, Mick Jagger, Marianne Faithfull, Brian Jones, John Paul Getty, Michael Caine—Cindy's idol—and Tom. We were later also invited to the Duke and Duchess's estate, Woburn Abbey, an ancient home filled with antiques, art, and other treasures. We were tickled when they told us that they kept entire sets of our albums at both Woburn Abbey and their Paris flat.

A few days later, in early February 1968, we played what was the English debut of Diana Ross and the Supremes at London's Talk of the Town. Cindy and I rehearsed as much as possible, and the show was really tight. Gil Askey was there and we had our own rhythm section, which seemed to impress many of the British pop singers, who didn't have these luxuries. Our band included Bob Cousar on drums, Jimmy Garret on bass, Napoleon "Snaps" Allen on guitar, and Bobby Jenkins on percussion. The show was structured around several medleys—"Thoroughly Modern Millie," a tribute to Sam Cooke, and our greatest hits—and included "Unchained Melody," "You're Nobody till Somebody Loves You," "Michelle," and "Yesterday." The latter two we especially enjoyed singing, since Paul McCartney was in the audience that night. Also there were Samantha Eggar, Michael Caine, Laurence Harvey, Tony Blackburn, Engelbert Humperdinck, the Shadows, Cat Stevens, Shirley Bassey, and Sharon Tate and Roman Polanski.

We went onstage after having been up for two days without sleep and having just arrived in London from Cannes. We were a smash. The British press loved us and made a point of mentioning our rendition of "Somewhere" and Diane's monologue. Frankly, I found it a bit on the mushy side, but the audience always ate it up.

Following the show, Paul McCartney joined us and others at the Speakeasy and we celebrated until four in the morning. Paul was always one of my favorite people and we became friends. Despite being a big star, he was always very sweet and open. In fact, when it was later officially announced that Diane would leave the group, Paul telephoned me to ask how I felt about it.

The next day we had a press conference at EMI, the English distributors of our records. There were at least fifty photographers and writers, all asking us the kinds of questions we had never been asked before: How were our love lives? What kind of pajamas did we sleep in? What were our exact measurements? What did we think about the Vietnam War? The Black Power movement? And what was the truth behind Florence's leaving the group?

We weren't sure what this was all about. It wasn't that we minded answering questions. But before this, the press had gone along with the Motown PR program, sticking to such topics as the music, our gowns, whom we had met recently, what our homes were like, and so on. The next day we saw the headlines: SUPREMES MOBBED AT EMI, and the answers were in the copy. Though some critics called us "sensational," others were claiming that we had gotten away from our "roots." "Get back to church, baby!" one writer pleaded.

At this point, the English journalists were far more critical than Americans about what they perceived as our "selling out." The English held on to the misguided notion that a black who was singing and didn't sound like Aretha Franklin or Otis Redding must have been corrupted in some way. And what was this church business? None of us had ever sung in church. This segment of the press completely disregarded the fact that our roots were in American music—everything from rock to show tunes—and always had been. We weren't recording standards because they were foisted upon us by Motown; we loved doing them and had since we were fourteen years old.

But the times were definitely changing, and being accomplished, world-famous black women, the Supremes were caught in a cross fire between standard show-business conventions and new, more radical ideas about performers as political spokespeople and leaders. And, of course, now everyone was a critic. Though we'd never shunned political or social issues, we were starting to take a beating for being glamour girls in a "relevant" age. The press would accept some other pop stars' cries for revolution at face value, never bothering to note that these stars lived as lavishly as we did. But the Supremes were right out there, and before long we'd be attacked in the press for not being "black" enough. I still wondered what exactly they had meant. Did they mean to say that blacks could only sing "soulful" music? Or that to sing Cole Porter, you could only be white? These kinds of ideas struck me as a new kind of racism, but no matter. It would soon be clear that being the Supremes wouldn't be enough.

# CHAPTER 19

Soon after we returned to Detroit I learned that Flo had married Tommy Chapman in Hawaii on February 29. It was a civil ceremony, with no guests. I was very happy for Flo. Things seemed to be looking up for her, and about two weeks after the wedding she signed a two-year recording contract with ABC Records.

As part of her settlement with Motown, she was forbidden to even mention that she had been in the Supremes. It seemed petty and ironic, since everyone knew she had been a Supreme and she had picked the name. With Tommy acting as her manager, Flo hired an attorney named Leonard Baun, who negotiated a better deal for Flo than what she was originally offered in July. Just before the wedding, Motown gave Flo approximately $160,000, which represented all of her earnings for her work with the Supremes. She and Tommy turned this money and some other funds over to Baun, who was supposed to oversee them for her. With some of the money Flo rented an apartment in Manhattan, and she and Tommy started a management firm, with Flo as the sole client.

As always, we were busy, but in the few weeks since I'd met Tom I managed to fly to London, New York—anywhere to be with him. Only later did I discover that Tom was married. I couldn't believe it. Maybe Tom figured that since every other woman in the Western world knew that he was "unavailable," I should have, too. At first I felt like a fool, then I felt betrayed, as if I had been the one cheated on. My pride wouldn't let me be treated like this; I didn't have to be any man's mistress, and after my experience with Duke I had vowed never to get involved with a married man again. I resolved to break it off the next time I saw Tom, but when that time came, I realized that I couldn't. It was too late.

Tom was living in London at this time, and whenever I could manage four or five days off, Cindy, Dick Scott, and I flew there and stayed at the Mayfair Hotel. Tom would come to my suite and spend the evening, then go home in the morning. Traveling around the world to meet my lover for just one night was the height of romance. When I'd come into London, Tom would send his Rolls-Royce to pick me up. Any time I met him in a large city, where there might be lots of press around, I dressed plainly and kept my sunglasses on.

I treasured every moment with him. We would laugh and talk, and just be so happy to be together. The way he pronounced my name in his Welsh accent, rolling the *rs*, made it sound like music. He loved to take me to his favorite pubs in London, and later, when we got bolder, we ventured out into some of the nicer restaurants, like Mr. Chow's in London. Eventually we were spotted, and it made the gossip columns, but no one at Motown ever said a word to me about it. In the fan magazines I was the femme fatale tearing Tom's home apart. But at this point, I didn't care about what anyone thought. I was young and in love. Whenever one of us would think about the other, the phone would ring; it was as if we could read each other's minds across the miles. If one of us missed the other's call, we would leave a coded message saying that a "Jimi Hendrix" had called, which must have kept people in our entourages buzzing.

It was nice to be with someone who thought the world of me. When we were together, I was in heaven, but when Tom was away, I would wonder if I had not traded one problem for another. Not only was Tom married, but he had a child, and even if he'd been single, I would have had the gaggle of other women who followed him wherever he went. And Tom loved women too much to say no.

Whenever I could I went to his shows, and Tom would always sing songs just to me. In Las Vegas he once sang "Green, Green Grass of Home," then segued into "That Old Black Magic." I was both flattered and embarrassed to have such a private tribute paid so publicly.

Whenever Tom and I talked about singing, which was often, I would urge him to give up the sex-god shtick and play it straight. He had one of the most beautiful voices I had ever heard, and I often told him that he had the makings of the next Sinatra. Of course these suggestions weren't especially appreciated by Tom's manager, Gordon Mills, but I didn't care. Gordon wasn't crazy about me anyway. The more I talked to Tom about his singing, the more I thought about my own, and so I started taking vocal lessons from Teddy Hall in New York. It was at Teddy's studio that I met Margie Haber, a wild Jewish girl from Long Island who soon became my best friend.

Margie became my lifeline to the outside world. She didn't really think too much about me being a Supreme or a star. We would just get together whenever we could and have a great time doing those things that girlfriends do. If I were playing in the New York metropolitan area, I'd call Margie to come get me, and we would go out or go see Tom's show, stopping en route at a McDonald's. For the first time I realized how far I'd gone beyond what anyone would consider a normal life.

In February 1968 Motown released "Forever Came Today," the first in a series of Supremes songs I did not sing on. When the song was recorded in mid-1967, we were so rarely in Detroit that we heard little of the company gossip, but it was clear that HDH weren't entirely pleased with their deal there. Motown was changing. Berry had his sights set on the West Coast; he wanted to get into movies and television, and he liked hanging out with the entertainers, such as Sammy Davis, Jr. and Sidney Poitier, and other VIPs he'd met. He was spending less time in Detroit, and some people—particularly those like HDH who'd thrown their lots in with Berry during the lean years—now wanted to share in Motown's success. It was no longer enough just to be part of the company: This was especially true for those who had built the company, many of whom remembered Motown's promises of profit-sharing plans and other "extras."

The issue had been raised in 1966, when Clarence Paul held a meeting of disgruntled Motown artists and producers at his house. They discussed ways to get together and support one another in dealing with Motown. All of that went the way of the wind when people heard rumors that management people were sitting in parked cars, taking notes on and photographs of who went into Clarence's house. But Motown's success then was nothing compared to what it was now. Motown had expanded into several other buildings and had even taken over another black-owned label, Ric-Tic/Golden World.

HDH had tried to get a better deal from Berry, and when things didn't work out to their satisfaction, they instituted a work slowdown. HDH were determined to get what they wanted from Berry or not work for him at all. So few artists succeeded after leaving Motown that many people there saw Motown as all-powerful. But Eddie, Brian, and Lamont's situation was different. They were an integral part of the Motown machine, and Eddie felt that he knew the business inside-out. That was one reason they wanted to be more involved on a corporate level, which Berry refused to consider. Their contribution to Motown's success—and the Supremes'—was incalculable, and when it was clear that they had stopped working, Berry went into action.

In August Motown sued HDH for $4 million in damages resulting from their not writing and producing hits. Motown also sought to restrain HDH from going to work for anyone else. HDH countersued Motown for $22 million. The cases dragged on for years and were finally settled privately, out of court. But long before that, as early as spring 1968, the damage was done—at least as far as the Supremes were concerned.

The sound HDH created for us was what set our records apart. Their songs were made for us, and after this we bounced from producer to producer. When "Forever" hit in April, at #28, our lowest-charting single since 1963, it was our last HDH hit.

Though the Supremes were at the top of Motown's roster, other acts were doing well. The Temptations and Marvin Gaye were soon playing the Copa and the Latin Casino, and Berry started talking with people in television and working on plans for producing television specials. Although Berry had long employed whites in upper-management positions, around this time he started signing more white artists as well. The most profitable black-owned business in America was also one of the most thoroughly integrated.

Despite some of the criticism the Supremes got for being too "glamorous," we were fortunate to come along when we did. Blacks and whites were making efforts to change things, and music helped bridge the gaps. Touring the South had opened my eyes to racism, and as the Supremes got bigger, we would be confronted by people saying the funniest things. Of course they meant well, and, fortunately, we knew where they were coming from, but these comments said a lot about what the Supremes meant. In Miami, where we usually performed over Christmas and New Year's Eve, a middle-aged Jewish woman came up to us and said, "You know, I usually don't let my children watch Negroes on television, but the Supremes are different." We were living examples of the slogan "black is beautiful."

We were playing the Copa on April 4 when we learned that Dr. Martin Luther King had been assassinated in Memphis. Like so many Americans, we were stunned. We canceled our show, and the next night appeared on *The Tonight Show*, where we talked about Dr. King. Many performers were going on radio and television to pay tribute to

Dr. King and to do whatever they could to inspire people to channel their grief and anger into something positive. This evening we performed "Somewhere," which had long been in our repertoire, substituting for the "love" monologue a short, dramatic speech about unity that Diane, Berry, and Shelly Berger had written. Unfortunately, efforts of this type couldn't quell the violent riots that broke out in several major cities, including Detroit. Dr. King was a man of peace, and it saddened us to see his death used as an excuse for rioting and looting.

We made arrangements to fly to Atlanta immediately, where along with such celebrities as Marlon Brando, Sammy Davis, Jr., Eartha Kitt, Diahann Carroll, Harry Belafonte, and others, we were to walk those last miles with Dr. King.

As we rode into town with Junius Griffin, an associate of Dr. King's who also worked with Berry, we noticed a commotion in the street and saw a man up on a telephone pole. We couldn't figure out exactly what he was doing, but one of us mentioned that we thought he was cute. Junius replied, "Oh, that's Jesse Jackson."

The funeral arrangements were made by a committee of prominent blacks, including the Reverend Ralph Abernathy, Jesse Jackson, Sidney Poitier, and Julian Bond. Harry Belafonte was chairing the meeting, and when he was called away by other business, he asked Berry to keep things running until he got back. Apparently when Harry returned about half an hour later, the meeting was in chaos. When we later heard the various accounts of who did what and what was said, we were embarrassed that such a solemn occasion was marred by such pettiness, since we were all representing peace.

On the day of the funeral, Diane, Cindy, and I walked with thousands of others, and as we made our way to Dr. King's final resting place, I hoped his work would live on and that every person there would keep his memory alive.

Not long after the funeral, Mrs. Coretta Scott King organized the Poor People's March on Washington, D.C. Mrs. King asked Berry if he would provide entertainment at a benefit in Atlanta, where the march was to begin. Junius Griffin helped Berry get this together. Mrs. King called Berry on Tuesday, and by that Thursday, it was all arranged down to the last detail. The Supremes, Stevie Wonder, Gladys Knight and the Pips, and the Temptations performed for over thirteen thousand at the Atlanta Civic Center. At the end of the show, the Reverend Ralph Abernathy of the Southern Christian Leadership

Conference presented Berry with a plaque. Mrs. King then gave Berry a leather-bound set of Dr. King's books, which she had inscribed. It was a proud moment for all of us.

Back in Detroit, though, the rioters had done incredible damage, and this event marked a turning point for Motown. The Supremes had been recording so frequently in Los Angeles that I was spending more time there than at home, and I had considered moving there. After the riots my decision was firm. Every time I was on the West Coast, I'd scout around for the perfect house.

On July 23 we endorsed Democratic presidential candidate Hubert Humphrey. We had met him earlier and were convinced that his policies were sound. Humphrey's platforms included a continuation of President Johnson's social policies. Though it didn't always make the front page, the Supremes had long been contributing to Democratic causes, usually as performers at fund-raising functions. For example, we sang at a benefit to clear Senator Robert Kennedy's campaign debts after his assassination. The Gordys were always politically active, especially Esther Edwards, and when the idea of endorsing Humphrey was presented to us, we thought it over carefully and were glad to do it. We certainly could have refused, and we would have if we had been asked to endorse someone we did not believe in.

For some reason, though, the press had a real field day with our endorsement, and some writers treated it as if it were a joke. In several published accounts, more space was devoted to what we wore than what we said. Humphrey wasn't the most popular candidate to come along, and his sincerity was ridiculed. We were hurt by this, but thought better of speaking out. We just hoped that we had helped his cause. The next day we performed at a fund-raising dinner for him at the Waldorf Astoria.

Despite knowing that it was hopeless, my affair with Tom was more intense than ever. We were staying at his cabin in Bournemouth when his wife called. She told Tom she suspected that he had a woman there and that she was coming up to see for herself. Tom and I decided that I should leave. He put me in his limousine and kissed me goodbye. I cried all the way to London. Ironically, Tom's devotion to his wife and child was one of the things about him I admired most. Never once did he even hint that he would leave her, but I couldn't let go. Sometimes I'd been so foolish, going so far as to telephone his home in England, only to hang up when his wife would answer.

Between all our work, I kept in touch with Flo through my cousin Josephine, who was living in my house in Detroit and had been friends with Flo for years. Flo was expecting her first babies—twins—and her record, "It Doesn't Matter How You Say It," had been released in the spring. She was still my best friend, and I wasn't comfortable with the way things had been left between her and Diane. She was out of the group now and never coming back. I felt it was time that things be settled. Everyone at Motown loved Flo, and I thought it would be good for her to see them. Berry was holding a huge party at his poolhouse, and I had been invited. This was, I thought, the perfect chance for Flo to see some of her old friends from Motown and see how much she meant to them. Her departure had been so abrupt; no one had really said good-bye.

When I suggested the idea to Flo, she flatly refused. As the day drew nearer, I kept insisting that she go.

"Mary," Flo said, "you know this is a bad idea. You know Berry and Diane won't like the idea of me coming there. Forget it, will you?"

But I continued pestering her until she reluctantly agreed to go with me. We drove up together in my car. Flo was a little nervous, but everyone from the company welcomed her so warmly that we both forgot about Diane and Berry. We were having a great time, but there was an undercurrent of tension, and I knew that Flo and Diane were each watching every move the other made.

Finally Diane left Berry's side and sauntered over. She wasn't especially warm to Flo, but she was pleasant, and they talked for a while. Then she left and went back to Berry. A while later Diane came back to Flo and asked, "How have you been? What have you been doing?" Things seemed to be going very nicely, and I was pleased with myself for having engineered this meeting.

Several minutes later Diane came back over and made a comment about Flo's weight. Flo bit her tongue, and we kept talking. Diane went back over to Berry, then came back again. Each time Diane would walk toward us, I could see Flo tense up, and as the evening wore on, Flo drank a little—which was all it took—and the exchanges got louder and less pleasant. The last time Diane ran back to Berry, Flo turned to me and said loudly, "What does she keep coming over here for?"

Everyone stopped talking and looked at Flo. I knew then that Flo had been right: She shouldn't have come. All I could think of was getting her out of there as quickly and gracefully as possible. But once Flo got to drinking and things got hot, she was the last to walk away from a good fight, and the last time I saw Diane coming over, I knew that was exactly what was in store. Flo had had three or four drinks by now and could barely stay on top of her stool.

"If she comes back over here one more time," Flo proclaimed loudly, "I'm going to kick her."

I could tell that everyone felt sorry for Flo. They looked from Diane to Berry to Flo. Something had to give.

"Flo," I said quietly, "I think it's time to go."

"No, Mary. You stay; I'll go," she replied.

A second later Berry said, in a voice that everyone could hear, "Who brought her here?"

Berry knew damn well who did, and I knew I'd have to go, too. "Get her out of here," he said calmly but sternly. We left.

The minute we got into my car, Flo turned to me and said, "Mary, I told you I shouldn't have come. I don't know why I let you talk me into it." Flo didn't let me forget this night for a long time. Diane and Berry, on the other hand, never mentioned it.

Regardless of Diane's or Flo's motives for behaving the way they did, it took me months to get over my own anger. I was still singing with Diane, and Flo was still my best friend. I was miserable, but maybe I was just being selfish. I had always been in the middle, and here I was again, trying to make us all friends again. I had always admired Flo's outspokenness and Diane's aggressive nature, but things would never be the same. We had all suffered wounds that would not heal.

In addition to the changes I had witnessed in Diane, I could see that Berry was a new man, too. The roles were clearly shifting, and, at least in public, Berry seemed to be doing Diane's bidding as often as she did his. Sometimes, though, Berry surprised her.

Once when we were in Miami Billy Davis, Berry's personal aide and a friend who traveled with us (and no relation to Berry's early songwriting partner) and I stayed out all night long. We walked back to our hotel along the beach, certain that we were going to run into Diane and Berry on their way to breakfast. When I got upstairs I breathed a sigh of relief. I had just put my key in the door when Diane popped out of her room and said, "Well, where have you been all night?" I walked into my room and closed the door.

That night my singing wasn't great, and after the show Diane,

Berry, and I were in the dressing room when Diane decided that Berry should know why.

"Mary, you see? That's what happens when you're out all night. You lose your voice."

"Look, Diane," I replied, "I do my job here, and as long as I do, my private life is none of your business!"

Berry never said a word.

Diane now really was the star of the Supremes, and this was something of a problem when we started working with new producers. Even people we had worked with before, such as Smokey Robinson, approached the Supremes differently, choosing to emphasize a lighter, middle-of-the-road style, and Diane's voice at the expense of any good harmonies. Nick Ashford and Valerie Simpson had been successful with a series of duets they'd written and produced for Marvin Gaye and Tammi Terrell—"Ain't No Mountain High Enough," "Your Precious Love," and "Ain't Nothing like the Real Thing." But the song Diane cut with them (using the Andantes, not Cindy and me, on backing vocals), "Some Things You Never Get Used To," barely scraped into the Top Thirty.

Berry was always fascinated by people, and every once in a while he'd bring someone new into Motown. While we were in New York, working at the Copa, Cindy introduced him to her friend Suzanne de Passe. Suzanne was the talent coordinator for a New York club called the Cheetah, and she and Berry hit it off right away.

Before long Suzanne was walking around wherever we were working, with a little notepad and pen in hand, jotting down notes. She made suggestions to Berry about everything. She soon became one of his top assistants, but unlike so many bright newcomers Berry would hail as geniuses and then discard after he realized they were as foolish as everyone else had known they were from the start, Suzanne stayed.

Things were changing, and I felt like I was in limbo. I had no real home and felt that I needed to get away. I said to Berry, "I need a vacation—a real one. Not one of those little breaks you give us, where we still have to come in to record or do publicity. I've been working too hard."

"Mary, you had better work while you can," he replied in that paternal tone of voice he liked to use. "There may come a day when you will wish you had taken advantage of every working day offered to you."

"But, Berry, I deserve a real vacation."

"Mary, we're getting ready to write and record a new single. Don't you want to be in on it? It could be important."

"I'm going for only a week, and you know I have business on the West Coast. Can't you wait until I get back to record? I'm not a writer; you don't need me for that anyway."

My arguments didn't seem to be working. Berry acted as if I were doing something foolish, but he knew that I knew that they didn't need me to write a song. This was just a game. I took the time off and went to Los Angeles to take care of some details regarding my upcoming move there and then went on to Acapulco. Duke's marriage had ended, so we decided to give it one more chance, just to see if we could make things work.

I found my home, a large, modern place in the Hollywood Hills, complete with pool and sauna, and we had a wonderful time in Mexico. I came back to Detroit refreshed and ready to get to work, only to find that they had gone ahead and recorded the new song without me. Berry had wanted a song written, so Pam Sawyer, R. Dean Taylor, Frank Wilson, and Deke Richards had composed "Love Child." Although I was angry and hurt by being left out, I did like the song. Though its story line was not autobiographical for any of us, we knew girlfriends and relatives who had babies out of wedlock, and we knew what a hardship it was. "Love Child" was quite explicit, and the message was, I felt, important. It would be our only number-one record in 1968, and the first major hit I had not sung on. When we performed it on Ed Sullivan's show in September, we lip-synched; still, the words caught in my throat.

After Flo left, HDH had begun recording Supremes records with just Diane and someone else on backing vocals to keep to the release schedule when we were touring. What happened with "Love Child" seemed designed to send Cindy and me a message; namely, that Diana Ross was all that they needed. Diane and Berry were together all the time, usually working on something. It was impossible for me to know what they were doing when, and by now it was clear that they didn't want me to.

Looking back, I suppose I shouldn't have been surprised that things turned out the way they did. But I also knew that I had worked hard, and the Supremes were still the hottest thing Motown had. I knew Diane would leave the group eventually, but in the meantime it seemed stupid of Motown to make things harder for us as a group.

After all, the name would have a value for years to come, and up until then, most artists who left groups to go solo usually failed.

That fall we were also working on our first television special, "TCB," which starred Diana Ross and the Supremes and the Temptations. Since our appearances on *Tarzan*, Berry had been cultivating a working relationship with people at NBC, so this was quite a coup for him. It was produced by Motown Productions in conjunction with George Schlatter and Ed Friendly, who were responsible for *Laugh-In*. Mark Warren was the director, and Donald McKayle, who had worked on *Hullabaloo*, was the choreographer. The set was a modern, multilevel Plexiglas platform, and we wore beautiful gowns, designed for us by Mike Travis.

We all knew there would be at least one solo spot for Diane, so that didn't ruffle anyone's feathers. However, once we got down to rehearsing and taping, it was clear to all of us that seven of us were extras. It was "Miss Ross this" and "Miss Ross that." Paul Williams grumbled, "This must be the Diana Ross show." "Where will Miss Ross be?" was the only thing the crew seemed to care about. It was bad enough that none of us had any input regarding the show, but the fact that a newcomer had more influence than we did indicated how drastically things at Motown were changing. Suzanne de Passe didn't mind telling us what to do, but she didn't dare cross Diane. At one point, designer Mike Travis and Diane were discussing gowns when Suzanne burst into the room, frantic about something.

"Wait just a moment," Diane said. "I am talking to Mike and I will talk to you later."

"Sorry, Miss Ross," Suzanne replied, embarrassed.

I wasn't sure if Diane was as confused about Suzanne as we all were. Of course this was another little game; Diane and Suzanne couldn't be nice enough to each other when Berry was around.

The Temptations were as upset about things as Cindy and I were. One of them even remarked that, since Motown knew the Supremes weren't really accepted by blacks and the Temptations were, they were being used to draw black viewers. We felt better when Otis, Eddie, Cindy, and I were featured in a production number of the Brazilian hit "Mas Que Nada." We did a good job, but then one of the production people came over and told us that it might not be in the show. And, no surprise, it wasn't. Why put us through all the work, then? The whole situation was a mess, and it seemed to get worse every day.

I'd read the script, so I knew Diane had a special spot, the "Afro

Vogue" number. I didn't realize just how special it was, though, until I saw the set. The entire background was made up of hundreds of still photos of her, and she had several costume changes. Diane was great, but I couldn't stop thinking about how little any of the rest of us knew about what was going on.

Having worked with Diane for so many years, I knew she'd be tense and anxious. No matter how she might have acted toward other performers, she always carried her weight and worked hard to see that everything she was responsible for was as close to perfect as she could make it. The Tempts, however, hadn't worked with her as closely, and since some of them had known her as a kid, they found the "Miss Ross" business ridiculous. They weren't going to defer to her; they thought it was a joke.

Besides being one of my biggest heartthrobs, Eddie Kendricks is one of my best friends. He and Diane had been buddies from way back too, but as the plans to launch her solo career starting taking form, some of her earlier Motown friendships had lapsed.

During a break one day, all of us went out to eat, except Diane, who rarely went with a group of us, and Eddie, who had something he wanted to do. Although Eddie hadn't asked anyone to, someone in the group was thoughtful enough to bring back some food for him. When Diane found out about it, she walked up to Eddie and said, sarcastically, "Oh! How do you rate that?" It was absolutely absurd; we couldn't believe our eyes. A minute later, she came over and playfully slapped Eddie across the face. Ever the gentleman, he did nothing. Having an attitude was one thing, but this had gone too far. It was getting harder and harder for me even to want to be around her.

Amazingly, the show was great. When we were all singing together it was just like old times. When it aired in early December, we got rave reviews, and an album we cut with the Temptations was on its way to the top of the charts, along with a single, "I'm Gonna Make You Love Me." Despite all the tension and unhappiness, the special was a great boost to all of us, and plans were put in motion for a second program with the Supremes and the Tempts.

In early November we traveled to Stockholm, Sweden. There Sweden's Princess Christina came to each of our shows at Bern's Cafe, bringing along lots of her friends and even dancing on the tables. After the shows she would hang out with us at one of her friends' homes. Berry, who was with us, of course, seemed especially to like these meetings. After Sweden, we went to Copenhagen, Brussels, Hamburg, West Berlin, Munich, Frankfurt, and then London, where we did a show at the Palladium. The real highlight of this trip was the Royal Command Performance we gave before Princess Margaret and Lord Snowdon, the Queen Mother, Princess Anne, and Prince Charles at the London Palladium.

In the middle of "Somewhere," Diane gave the little monologue we had been doing since Dr. King's death:

"There's a place for us. A place for all of us. Black and white, Jew and gentile, Catholic and Protestant. So was the world of Martin Luther King and his idea. If we keep this in mind, then we can carry on his work."

A tear rolled down Diane's cheek as we picked up the song again. After we'd finished, there was a two-minute standing ovation, and the Royal Family cheered wildly. Though the British press still adored us, a few writers were critical of our having subjected the Royal Family to something so "political." But they had loved it, and in interviews for a long time thereafter Diane eloquently defended the speech.

The event also had its lighter moments. Though we had enjoyed doing the show, because we were meeting royalty and had memorized all the protocol, we weren't exactly loose. Everything was quite proper and formal; we knew not to speak until spoken to, and not to address a royal, and so on. We stood in line, with Diane first, then me, then Cindy. Princess Margaret walked up to me, extended her hand, then —so quietly that no one else could hear—she whispered in her prim, high-pitched voice, "Is that a wig you're wearing, Mary?" I did all I could to suppress a giggle. When I realized that she was very serious about it I thought how bizarre it was that a member of the Royal Family could be so candid. Here I'd grown up in the Projects and I had more sense than to ask someone a question like that. But then I thought how great it was to have these experiences, and how glad I was to be a Supreme.

# CHAPTER 20

In November of 1968 Flo gave birth to her twins, Nicole Renee and Michelle Denise. They had been born prematurely, but they were healthy, and Flo seemed anxious to get her career going. I had heard her first single, and though I loved Flo's voice, I didn't think the material was right for her. I hoped she would find success.

Nothing that had happened in the last year could erase my years of friendship with Diane, and I decided to let things ride. I knew she would be leaving the group soon, and I wanted the Supremes to go on. I would be the last original member, and I wasn't about to throw everything away, like I was beginning to fear Flo had. The Supremes were going to continue, and I tried to prepare myself for what lay ahead as best I could.

The success of "Love Child" prompted Berry to want another release in a similar vein. I didn't sing on "I'm Livin' in Shame," which I thought was melodramatic and lacked a message. From this point on, I would not be on any other singles except those we recorded with the Temptations. "The Composer" and "No Matter What Sign You Are" are surely among the worst things ever released under the Supremes' name, so not singing on those wasn't too bad. That these records charted so poorly compared to our biggest hits was due in part to the fact that, as several critics have since pointed out, they did not sound like "Supremes records." However, when the Supremes' "farewell song," "Someday We'll Be Together" was recorded without Cindy or me, I knew it really was over.

On February 1 we opened at the Frontier Hotel in Las Vegas. As Diane's leaving the group drew near, everything seemed to revolve around her, and Cindy and I became "just" the Supremes. When I read interviews where Diane said things such as "I am leaving the Supremes," it hurt.

One night during this engagement I was standing backstage when

I happened upon Diane and Berry. They didn't notice me, and, as I stood there, Berry said to Diane, "Now, Diane, you go out there and ignore everything. Forget about the girls—all of it—and just think about yourself."

I could tell by the look on Diane's face that she was shocked, and in that moment I was reminded of the Diane I knew and loved. For a moment I believed she still did care about me. It was one of those rare instances when I could see that she must have wrestled with her conscience, too.

Despite this, though, she did exactly as Berry said. From the moment we were announced, she ignored us. There was none of the usual interplay, and she barely made eye contact with either Cindy or me. I understood her so well, perhaps too well. Maybe if I'd reacted the way most people would have, things would not have gone this far. This slight was the last blow. I suspected that things would probably get worse before they got better, and I'd either have to ride it out or leave. My friends from the Club Bravo (Dionne Warwick, Leslie Uggams, Mira Waters, Lola Falana, Yvonne Fair, and Nancy Wilson, with Lena Horne as den mother) often gave me refuge.

My friend Nancy Wilson was also performing in Las Vegas, and when she heard that we were in town she invited me to dinner at her hotel suite. I was grateful to spend some time with another woman whom I didn't see every day. Of course I didn't discuss any of my problems with Nancy; that was group business. When I got there, Nancy's beautician had just finished doing her hair. I asked if she could do mine, and she happily obliged. She gave me a hair-relaxing treatment and seemed to know what she was doing. Later, when she rinsed off the solution, my hair started falling out, breaking off near the root. I was mortified, and the poor beautician was afraid she'd done something wrong.

"Oh my God! I'm so sorry," she kept saying. "I only did what it said to do. I've done this so many times. I don't understand—"

But I couldn't be consoled. I was hysterical, crying, "What am I going to do? I've got shows to do! What am I going to do?" I knew that my hair was falling out as a result of stress and exhaustion. Nancy didn't know what to say. She took me back to my hotel, and someone in the entourage sent for my mother and my doctor, who both flew in immediately.

When my mother got there she didn't say a word; she just held me and I cried my eyes out. This was the first time I really thought everything was getting to be more than I could handle. When my friend and doctor, Herbert Avery and his wife, Monaloa, arrived from Los Angeles, we talked. I told him all about what was going on with the Supremes and my personal life with Tom. I'd been running around the world, having the time of my life, I thought. This episode made me realize how much of a mess my life was. Dr. Avery gave me some advice, and I resolved to straighten things out. I knew the relationship with Tom had to end and that I had to stop holding everything inside. There was only a short while to go before Diane left. I had to hold on.

I threw myself into decorating my new home in Los Angeles, giving parties and entertaining friends whenever I had a chance. Cindy moved to L.A., too, and we became closer than ever. The two of us would go to private clubs in Beverly Hills, such as the Daisy, the Candy Store, and Pips. We were at one of these clubs when I met a new neighbor, Jim Brown, the football player. He introduced me to a young basketball player from UCLA named Mike Warren, and the two of us hit it off right away. He was still in college when we met, but that didn't stop me from falling in love with him. He came into my life like an angel.

I had just brought my adopted son, Willie, out to live with me. Willie is my cousin Christine's eldest child, and, ironically, I adopted him under circumstances similar to the Pippins' taking me. Christine had several children, and she and I agreed that Willie would have more opportunities living with me than were available to him in Detroit. Besides, I had always loved children and had a strong maternal streak. I was happy to have Willie, but it was quite an adjustment. Mike was there with me every step of the way.

"Mike," I often said to him, "with your good looks and charm, I think you have the potential to make it in this business."

"Do you really think so, Mary?" he would ask shyly.

"Heck, yeah. You should give it a try. You have charisma. You'll find your niche. Wait and see."

Now, whenever I see Mike on *Hill Street Blues*, I always think that few people are more deserving of success than him.

Diane and Berry were still an item, though it was hard to see where the relationship was going. They didn't seem any closer to marriage, and yet they still seemed fascinated with each other. This didn't stop Diane from seeing other men. For a while she was dating Tim Brown, a football player with the Philadelphia Eagles. Whenever we would play in the area, he would come to see Diane, sometimes he would bring along one of his teammates, and the four of us would double-date. Everyone in the entourage knew about Tim, except, I assume, Berry. Of course, Berry had been having his fun, too, bringing Chris Clark on the road while he was seeing Diane.

Years before, Flo and I had started traveling with our dogs. When we were out on tour once, we had seen two little Yorkshire terrier puppies from the same litter, and we each took one. They were our constant companions and soon became as good at traveling as we were. I had never known Diane to be particularly fond of animals, but when she saw the amount of attention ours got she decided to get not one but two dogs, a Maltese named Tiffany and a Yorkie named Little Bit. When Cindy joined the Supremes, she got a Boston terrier. It was quite a menagerie.

Cindy and I kept our dogs on their leashes at all times, or locked in the hotel or dressing room. Diane, however, preferred to let her dogs roam free, no matter where we were. We had all of the dogs with us at the Latin Casino in June 1969. This was one of our bigger engagements, and the dates had been sold out for months. There were plenty of industry people and celebrities in the audience, and the show was a success. The standard procedure was that we would do our "last" song, then Diane would exit to one side, and we would exit to the other. After a few moments of applause, we would return to do the encore.

As Cindy and I were making our false exit, we heard Diane, who we thought was standing backstage, let out a blood-curdling scream. I rushed backstage to see what had happened. The audience had also heard the scream, and they immediately expected the worst. Before I got to Diane's dressing room, I heard someone ask, "Is there a doctor in the house?" Had something happened to Diane? From backstage I could hear people in the audience talking.

"Something must have happened to one of the girls."

"Oh, no! This is awful! I wonder what it was."

"Are they coming back?"

As I ran to her dressing room, I could see people standing around and Diane in the middle of the crowd, jumping up and down and screaming at the top of her lungs. At her feet Tiffany and Little Bit were walking very shakily and vomiting violently. By now a crowd had gathered around, and in the chaos people were calling out suggestions.

"Let's get them to the hospital."

"Joe," Diane screamed at our road manager Joe Shaffner, "this is your fault! You should have kept an eye on my dogs!"

"Let's just get them to the hospital," the first voice said again. "We're wasting time."

"They must have eaten the rat poison that was out," another voice added.

"Yeah," someone else said. "She should have kept them on a leash."

At that, Diane started screaming again, "I'm going to sue this place if they've poisoned my dogs! How dare they lay poison down when animals could be around!"

Everyone was doing their best to calm Diane down, but she just got wilder by the minute.

"I'm getting out of here and I am never in my life going to appear here again. I want to leave at once!" She ran into the dressing room, and a group of people followed her. A few made timid suggestions, but nothing was really getting accomplished. The dogs had been rushed to a hospital, and Diane was yelling, "Pack my things! Let's get out of here!" as she flung gowns around the room.

"I want to be taken to the hospital where my dogs are! Immediately!"

As people were talking, trying to decide who would travel in which car, someone from the club said, "Now the other two girls can go on without her."

"Oh no," someone from Motown replied, "you cannot send them on alone."

And this went on for several more minutes. The phone rang and Diane answered it. Everyone fell silent. Diane said, "What's going to happen? I don't know . . ." We figured that the dogs must have died. A second later, she said, "We are leaving!"

One of the club owners, Dave Dushoff, had heard enough. "Well," he said, "I don't see why you can't do the show. We had a very famous singer here recently, and his mother died and he still did the show. It's only your dogs. Come on."

"I'm canceling the show," she proclaimed, "and we're going to sue this club. And we'll never be here again!"

"I've never heard of such a thing," someone else from the club said. "You shouldn't have let your dogs run loose."

"Well, *you* should have had signs up!" Diane retorted.

"You let them roam! And it is not our fault if they got sick."

This was a mess. Berry was right there, but he did nothing to stop Diane. Berry and Diane were getting ready to leave when she spotted Joe.

"This is all your fault," she screamed. "It's your responsibility to look after my property!"

Joe was silent. Diane was furious, and I could see that there was more going on than just the dogs. Several people suspected that Berry had found out about Tim. Unfortunately, it wasn't just Diane who was canceling, it was the Supremes. I was ashamed at how unprofessional it looked to everyone.

"Miss Ross has to leave. She is very upset," Berry told the club people as he helped Diane to the door. In front of us, he was kind and understanding. The next day, however, he was livid. He believed that Shelly Berger had straightened everything out with Dave Dushoff, one of the Latin Casino's owners. When the other owners heard about it, however, they refused to accept the cancellation. All four thousand of the house seats had been sold for every night of our two-week engagement. In addition, the Latin Casino was a supper club, so there were thousands of dollars in food that would go to waste.

During July we were booked at the Copa, so I had plenty of time to spend running around New York with Margie. I invited her to stay with me at the Sherry Netherland Hotel, and since Tom was also in town, we would go to see his show.

The night the Apollo astronauts landed on the moon, Margie and I were in Tom's dressing room, waiting for him to change so that we could go out for a bite. When he emerged from his shower, barely covered by a towel, he cried, "Oh, Mary," and started hugging and kissing me. I was so engrossed watching the moonwalk that I shooed him away. Margie later told me that the whole time I stared at the screen, Tom stood there staring at me. I was really in love, but I knew it had to end.

Whenever I could, I brought Margie along with me to all our shows. She would be with me as I dressed, would sit in the front row for the show, then come backstage, and we would usually leave together. Diane seemed to resent her, which I thought strange, since Diane and I weren't that close anymore. What was there to be jealous about? Still, Diane would make a point of being catty to Margie.

One evening we were riding in the limousine from Manhattan to the Westbury Music Fair on Long Island. On the way out, Diane was debating whether to come back into New York after the show or to stay overnight in a hotel near the Music Fair. Margie, who knew the area well and was trying to be helpful, said, "Even though it doesn't seem far away, the drive from Long Island to Manhattan can be very long, because the traffic on the expressway gets backed up."

After the show, we drove back to Manhattan, and the ride went smoothly. Diane, however, couldn't resist making a dig at Margie.

"It's so typical of you, Margie. There is no traffic problem. I knew we didn't have to stay overnight on Long Island. I'm certainly glad I never listen to you."

Margie took it the right way; she ignored it. But I couldn't. At the same time, I didn't confront Diane about her behavior, either. Looking back now, I've often wondered if I was such a good friend to her, never telling her off at times like these. It seemed to me that we were both locked into patterns that were unbreakable, and getting more destructive with time.

In October we hosted *The Hollywood Palace*, which meant that Diane hosted, and we just sang. On this show, Diane introduced the Jackson Five in their first national television appearance.

Everyone at Motown knew that Bobby Taylor of the Vancouvers had discovered the Jackson Five and had told Berry about them. Berry didn't have time to see them audition in person, so he had asked Bobby to take them over to the Graystone Ballroom, where Berry kept a whole batch of video equipment, and tape their act for him to look at later. Bobby taped the Jackson brothers, and Berry signed them immediately. Many artists had come through Motown, but few of the newer acts had made it big. Berry knew the Jackson Five would be big money-makers, and Motown set out to promote them from the very start. Part of the promotion was that Diane had discovered them. A few weeks later, Diane hosted a party in the Jacksons' honor for three hundred guests at the exclusive Daisy Club in Hollywood. I didn't know anything about it until I received my invitation via telegram.

Knowing that Motown's plans for Diane's solo career had been the force behind much of the unpleasantness of the first TV special made doing the second one a bit easier. We weren't treated any better, but at least we knew why. I also knew that this phase would end when Diane left, and that wasn't too far away now. None of us were upset at the taping of our second special with the Temptations, "G.I.T. on Broadway." Diane's departure was announced in early November; the word had been out around Motown for some time.

Strangely, we never talked about her leaving. I mean, Diane and I never said two words to each other about it. Like everyone else in the world, I read about it in the papers. Speculation was that I would be taking over her spot as lead singer; Diane had said so in interviews. But it was never really discussed, and if Berry had asked me to, I am sure I would have declined. I had been singing in the background for so long that I doubted I could sing lead well enough. My standards for the Supremes—whoever they were—were too high to let my ego run amok. After years of being denied the chance to sing more leads and being told over and over that I couldn't sing, my confidence was shot. I was taking singing lessons with the best teachers in the world, but in my heart I knew I wasn't ready to make that step.

Once it was an open subject, Berry and I discussed possible replacements, but there didn't seem to be too much of a rush to decide. Fan magazines were holding polls to see who readers thought should take Diane's place, and Tammi Terrell seemed to be their favorite. Sadly, Tammi was nearing the end of her long struggle with a fatal brain tumor and was never considered. Other names were suggested, but I was in no rush. If nothing else, the last three years had made me more determined than ever to keep the Supremes alive, with or without Diane. I was here for the long haul, and I had to feel comfortable with my new partner.

One day Berry said, "I found somebody." When I met Jean Terrell, the sister of the boxer Ernie Terrell but no relation to Tammi, I liked her immediately. She was a great singer, and her voice was higher and totally different from Diane's. She seemed happy to be in the Supremes, and I was happy to have a real group again. We started rehearsing for live shows together in the fall and had begun recording that winter. Though it was obvious from the beginning that Jean had a mind of her own and wasn't nearly as much a team player as Cindy and I were, I overlooked it. Things would be worked out, and I was just happy to know that the Supremes would go on.

My relationship with Tom was coming to a close. We both realized that our feelings were too serious for us to keep chasing each other around the world. We were at my home in Hollywood and I was throwing one of my usual parties. There were people all over the place, and Tom and I were alone in my room. We both knew what was coming. "Mary," he said, "I don't think this is fair to you. There is no future for us, and I think we should break away from this affair now."

I had to agree. He wasn't going to leave his wife, and I had always known that. I was crying, but when we said good-bye at my door, I knew we were doing the right thing.

After that, we kept in touch, and deep inside I still nurtured the faintest hope that things might change. I finally accepted that they never would when he brought his wife backstage after one of our shows and introduced her to me. She was very nice. After I was married and got to experience firsthand what she had gone through, I understood the pain and humiliation she must have suffered. Still, Tom remains one of the very special people in my life. I fell in and out of love after that, having affairs with Steve McQueen, Flip Wilson, and Jack Lucarelli.

In early December, Cindy was kidnapped from her Hollywood apartment by the building's maintenance man. She escaped from him several hours later by jumping from his moving car on a freeway. The incident upset all of us. I had to stop keeping my front door open whenever I threw big parties after a couple of suspicious characters turned up. While some of my nervousness probably had to do with the brutal murder of Sharon Tate, there was no question but that things were changing, and everyone I knew felt the same. (I had to use Lincoln Kilpatrick to house-sit while I was on tour.) The end of the sixties seemed to bring an ill wind. I sensed that this was the end of an era. As a Supreme I had spent so many years traveling with chaperones, bodyguards, and other people whose job it was to look after me, that I had rarely thought of being in danger. Cindy's kidnapping was just an extreme example of how mixed a blessing fame could be.

Later that month "Someday We'll Be Together" was at number one, and we were caught up in a flurry of "farewell" publicity. It was hard to know exactly what to feel.

On December 21 we did our last show with Ed Sullivan, performing a greatest-hits medley and "Someday." It was strange to think how far we'd come since our first appearance on that stage just five years before. By this time I had spent so much time with Jean and Cindy that, in my mind, they were the Supremes. This was just a formality. I felt like I'd said good-bye already. It was sad and yet triumphant at the same time, and as we walked down a ramp, Diane kept moving further and further away.

On Wednesday, January 14, 1970, Diana Ross and the Supremes gave their final farewell performance at the Frontier Hotel in Las Vegas. Looking back over the past couple of years, I could see that everything had been leading up to this, and, professionally, this was the only way things could go. Diana Ross was going solo, and the Supremes would continue—Jean, Cindy, and me. We even had our first single in the can, "Up the Ladder to the Roof," which I was sure would be a hit.

People must have asked us how we felt over a million times, and there were a hundred different emotions, but for me the main one was relief. In the public's eye, every group—no matter how "equal" the members—has its star, and that's fine. But in the day-to-day work, a group has to function as a team, and that was something we hadn't done for a long time now. Diane's status at Motown and her relationship to Berry made it impossible for things to be otherwise, and if she hadn't left the group, something would have had to change. Working with Jean and Cindy was a joy. Maybe we weren't as close as Flo, Diane, and I had once been, but we were starting fresh. After years of hard work, I felt I was embarking on another wonderful adventure. I had been blessed to have been in the Supremes the first time; now it could happen all over again.

Deep inside, in the part of me that still believed in dreams, I couldn't deny that I was also very sad. This was, I thought then, not the end of the Supremes, but the end of the dream Diane, Flo, and I had shared. The three of us were who we were today because of a dream we all had nurtured a decade before. There were plenty of people behind us; I wouldn't deny that for a second. But the three of us had created the Supremes; we'd made ourselves into our image of what we could be, in our homemade dresses and fake pearls. Now, here Diane and I were, dripping in real diamonds and adorned in black velvet and pearls by Bob Mackie. And this was the end.

The farewell performance was scheduled to begin at midnight. I sat in my dressing room, sipping champagne and quietly putting on my makeup, doing the same things I had done a thousand times before. As showtime drew nearer, I felt exhilarated, and I went out onstage determined to enjoy myself.

The moment I heard the laughter die and the applause begin, I knew Willie Tyler and his dummy Lester had finished their act, and within minutes we would be standing on that stage. I was reminded of our school concerts where Flo and I sang our opera solos; Willie Tyler and Lester were on those shows, too. It was so long ago. It felt funny to realize that though I was now, at twenty-five, more experienced, I still felt like the same little girl. I could hear the band—Gil Askey with Jimmy Garrett, Napoleon "Snaps" Allen, and drummer Curtis Kirk, who had replaced Bob Cousar and Bobby Jenkins. As I walked toward the backstage area, I felt looser than ever. This was it. Diane would be free to follow her own dreams, and I would be free to make the Supremes a real group again.

As we stood in the wings awaiting our cue, Diane and I just glanced at each other in silence. There were no "good-bye"s or "good luck"s; not even a hug. We could have done those things, but we both knew it would have been a farce. We had said our farewells long before this.

When the curtain went up, the roar of the crowd was so loud the floor vibrated under my feet like an electric charge. Though our arrangements were exactly the same, each note seemed to come zooming at me faster than ever. We started with a lengthy medley of hits, including "Stop! In the Name of Love," "Baby Love," "My World Is Empty Without You," "Come See About Me," "Love Is Here and Now You're Gone," and "I Hear a Symphony."

Diane did a bit of patter, then we sang a very suggestive version of "Hey Big Spender." I got my recent solo spot singing "Can't Take My Eyes Off You." I sang it with all my heart, thinking of Flo, and wishing she were there with us. Diane then did "I'm Gonna Make You Love Me," which she sang right to Berry, and he loved it. From this point on, she continued punctuating her performance with what one writer later described as "out and out hints about her close-guarded relationship with Berry Gordy."

I knew there would be no stopping Diane tonight, and I wasn't disappointed. She upstaged us, which was nothing new, but for the first time it didn't really matter, because this would be the last time. Throughout the show, she would step into the audience and sing to people. This was the only show we did where Diane got two solo spots. When she began "Didn't We," she almost broke down crying, and after the song she made a reference to the fact that Berry's family had "accepted" her. Her next song was another solo, the old torch song "My Man." Few people could guess how important this moment was to Diane. She was grateful to Berry—as we all were—and this performance was her way of saying thank you to him in front of the whole world.

When Diane got to "Aquarius/Let the Sunshine In," she walked around the audience, putting the microphone in front of people so that they could sing along. In the audience that night were Steve Allen, Jayne Meadows, Dick Clark, Lou Rawls, Bill Russell, Hugh O'Brian, Shirley Eder, and, of course, the Motown family, including Marvin Gaye and Smokey Robinson. Everyone screamed when Marvin got up to sing along. We had sung the chorus about fifty times before it finally ended. In the middle of it, Diane asked that our mothers stand up. My mother stood, then Cindy's, but Diane's was nowhere to be seen.

"Mother, where are you?" Diane cried out, looking crushed.

"She's probably trying to make it the hard way," someone at Berry's table called up, using a term familiar to anyone who plays craps. Everybody laughed, and Mrs. Ross later returned.

Finally the show was winding down. As the first chords of "Someday We'll Be Together" were played, Diane said, "We won't be together on stage as a team, but we'll always be together in our hearts." The three of us were teary. This was sad. For the finale, we sang "The Impossible Dream" to Berry. It was fitting.

After several standing ovations, the Frontier's entertainment director, Frank Sennes, presented us with a plaque from the hotel—the first for their Wall of Fame—and flowers. Diane's were said to be black roses from Berry. He read a telegram from Ed Sullivan and another from the mayor of Las Vegas; then he gave each of us a gold watch. The people at the Frontier had gone all out for this occasion. The room, which seated fifteen hundred, was packed to the rafters, and they had named drinks after us: Diana's Delight, Mary's Mystique, Cindy's Sin, and Jean's Jubilee.

At the end Diane brought Jean onstage and introduced her, touting her good looks and fine voice. She graciously conceded that the Supremes would go on without her. We received seemingly endless ovations. Then it was over.

Paul Block and the public-relations staff at Rogers and Cowan had really outdone themselves. The Frontier gave us a lavish party in their cabaret room which was attended by every celebrity in Vegas. There was also a large cake inscribed "Someday We'll Be Together." Right after we arrived at the reception the three of us and Berry and Pops Gordy sat together in a booth, toasting one another with champagne, while writers and photographers from around the world recorded every second of it. All the other Motown people came over and congratulated us, gave us hugs and kisses, and wished us the best of luck.

After a while, I quietly left the party to go to the tables. I loved gambling, and Margie and I spent a few hours there. I was being paged all the while we were gambling, but I just ignored it. I knew that they wanted me back at the party; there was probably more press or other celebrities on hand. Motown had worked overtime to make everything about the farewell and Diane's departure seem friendly, and I had cooperated. I was happy for Diane, but now I needed to be by myself, or at least with a real friend.

During the show Cindy was very excited and professional, and I had a ball, and reporters wrote about how I clowned around, and "teased Diana Ross, much like a sister would, toying with the spotlight —a demonstration of the girls' closeness." That the world still believed we were the best of friends seemed the perfect ending.

Margie and I went to my room with several bottles of champagne, and sat up until dawn, talking and laughing, toasting to happiness and freedom and true friendship. Every fifteen minutes, the phone would ring, and there'd be someone from Motown on the other end.

"Mary, why aren't you down here?"

"Because I'm in my room," I'd reply, giggling.

"Don't you want to come down here?"

"I'm having a party up here!" Then I'd hang up. Margie and I would laugh some more and then go back to our conversation.

When I couldn't keep my eyes open another minute, I crawled into bed, certain that I would sleep like a baby. Years of tension and stress had disappeared magically; tomorrow my career would be my own again, and a whole new chapter in the history of the Supremes would begin. I drifted off to sleep, feeling better than I had in months.

Just barely an hour later, the phone rang.

"Hello?" I mumbled into the receiver, which I couldn't even see. "Who is this?"

"Mary?" I knew it was Berry.

I couldn't believe my ears. He knew I slept late; what could he possibly want at this ungodly hour?

"What?"

Berry spoke briefly about the farewell celebration, then he dropped the bomb:

"I don't like Jean Terrell," he proclaimed.

"What are you talking about?" I had to be dreaming.

"I want to replace her with Syreeta Wright."

We'd been over all this already. Jean was in; she had been introduced to the world last night as the new Supreme. Was he mad? I had noticed that Berry was having a harder time getting Jean to follow his directions to the letter than he'd ever had with Diane, but he was in love with Diane. I didn't think Jean's attitude was that big a problem, and besides, I would be dealing with her more than Berry would anyway. What was wrong with him?

All I knew was that I couldn't let him get away with this. Our first single was set for release; the Supremes were what had kept me there all these years. Berry wasn't going to ruin it now.

"Mary, do you hear me?" Berry asked when I was silent for a minute. "I want to replace Jean with Syreeta."

"No!"

"All right," Berry replied. "Then I wash my hands of the group."

Berry hung up, and I decided that the Supremes were going to work. I'd make it happen.

# EPILOGUE

Despite Berry's lack of interest in our career, the Supremes went on to have several more major hit records—"Up the Ladder to the Roof," "Stoned Love," "River Deep, Mountain High" (with the Four Tops), "Nathan Jones," and "Floy Joy." Cindy left the group in 1972 and was replaced by Lynda Lawrence. The next year, when Lynda and Jean decided to quit the Supremes, Cindy returned and Scherrie Payne (Freda's sister) took over the lead spot. When Cindy left for the second time, in 1976, Susaye Green stepped in. Finally, in 1977, the Supremes were officially disbanded.

Through the years, Flo and I kept in touch. I was living in Los Angeles with my husband, Pedro Ferrer, and touring the world with the Supremes, so I rarely saw her. We talked on the phone, and my cousin Josephine, who lived in my old house on Buena Vista, saw Flo often.

After her twins were born in November 1968, Flo did a few college dates and made a couple of television appearances, but her career hadn't really taken off. One of the last good moments was her performance at one of President Nixon's inaugural functions in January 1969. After that, things went downhill.

Though he loved her very much and gave it his best effort, Tommy Chapman didn't have the experience or the knowledge to guide Flo's career. After working with Berry for a while, he had surmised that there was nothing to it, and Flo had taken part of her settlement money from Motown and set Tommy up in his own management company, Talent Management, Inc. Cholly Atkins and arranger Fred Norman helped Flo put together an act. She was willing to play smaller venues, just to get her confidence back and to get used to working again. Though there was no way she could have been booked into the same places the Supremes had played, Flo should have been working small but classy establishments, not the little bar and grills Tommy booked for her. In some places, the bands were so bad that they could not read music, and one night in Atlantic City Flo was forced to sing tunes she had never sung before just because it was all the band there knew. Word around was that Tommy also made outrageous demands of ABC Records, which were not well received.

Flo was no fool, and certainly she saw that Tommy was not qualified for the task, but it was too late. That March her attorney, Leonard Baun, informed her that all of her funds—the $160,000 settlement from Motown plus Flo's other assets—were exhausted. Flo was stunned by the news and would spend the next year, with the help of her brother Billy, trying to find another attorney to take her case against Baun. In the press, Baun called her charges that he had mismanaged her funds "ridiculous," then added, "She will be flat broke after she pays her taxes." Years later, Baun would be disbarred. Until then, no local or state government official Flo or Billy contacted about the case would touch it.

When Flo was with the Supremes, we would sing "You're Nobody till Somebody Loves You." When Diane sang the line, "Gold won't bring you happiness . . .," Flo would break in and quip, "Now, wait a minute, honey. I don't know about that." When I later read interviews with Flo, where she said, "One day you're on top of the world and the next day you're broke," that line came back to me.

By mid-1969, Flo was worse than broke; she had gained more weight and become so depressed by her situation that she refused to leave the house. She continued in this state for some time. In early 1971, she filed an $8.7 million lawsuit against Motown and the Supremes, alleging that in late 1967 Diane had "secretly, subversively, and maliciously" plotted to oust her. She also revealed that while she was in the Supremes she had received a $225 weekly allowance and had never seen an accounting of the Supremes' income. (I had never seen an accounting either.) Based on this lack of information, she requested that her earlier agreement with Motown—which forbade her to bring future suits against anyone or anything related to the Supremes or Motown, and in which she signed away her rights to any future income from the Supremes, such as royalties from records she sang on—be declared nonbinding. In 1973, the case would be thrown out of court.

She had also instituted another suit against Leonard Baun, charging him with gross negligence, malpractice and breach of fiduciary duties and obligations." No one in Flo's family is sure when or if she ever received any kind of settlement from this suit.

Flo had always been a fighter, but that never made the fighting any easier. Flo had given birth to her third daughter, Lisa, in 1971. My cousin Josephine often called me in L.A. to tell me how Flo was doing. She would bring her daughters over to visit Josephine almost every day. She and Jo would sit around chatting and drinking beer. Sometimes Jo would have to help Flo get home, then she would keep the girls until Flo sobered up.

After the management firm went under, Tommy went to work as a road manager for a recording group, then as a chauffeur for a local minister. In order to keep her house, Flo pawned her jewelry and other valuables, but finally she was notified by the bank that foreclosure was imminent. Flo went to another recording artist, who agreed to lend her $700. When she went to the artist's business office to pick up the money, she was told to sign an agreement outlining the method and amount of the repayment and several blank sheets of papers. Flo wisely refused, but the decision cost her the house.

"Why my house?" she would cry to friends. "Why couldn't I at least keep my house?"

Our houses were more than just homes; they were the symbols of our success, and owning a home meant that you were secure, or so we all thought. During this time, Flo and Tommy separated. At first he provided child support. No matter what happened between them, Flo always defended Tommy; she still loved him very much. After she lost the house, she and her three children moved into a two-family apartment with her mother and sister Pat. When Tommy stopped sending support money, Flo's sister convinced her to apply for Aid to Families with Dependent Children. Flo finally went. Later she said of the experience, "Being a star, going there would mean I'd reached the bottom. But the children are important. I had to think about the children."

Flo always felt responsible for everyone, and this was no doubt a contributing factor to her problems. When we were making money, she would instruct Taylor Cox to send money to members of her family from her account. Over the years, she took great pleasure in helping her family, and there seemed to be no end to their requests. She could never say no, and so withdrew far more money from her account than either Diane or I. Taylor Cox, who worked at ITM, would keep us up to date on our accounts. Word of Flo's financial plight didn't reach me until she had lost the house. She never asked for help.

One of the few people outside her family that she confided in was Maye Atkins, Cholly's wife. Cholly and Maye were still living in the other half of my house on Buena Vista, so they saw Flo often. Flo had gotten up to around two hundred pounds. Though she had lost most of everything else she owned, she held on to the Cadillac. When her kids were asleep at night, she would make herself up, put on what was left of her finery, and drive around Detroit for hours, singing along to tapes in the car. Many nights she would go to her old house on Buena Vista, which had not been resold and was boarded up and vacant. She soon lost the car, too, but she made regular pilgrimages to the house, often with her three children in tow.

One day before Christmas 1974, Maye saw Flo and the three girls standing in the snow outside the old house. She went out and asked Flo to come in. When Maye asked her what she was doing, bringing three little ones out in such bad weather, Flo couldn't give a coherent answer.

"I don't have anything for Christmas for my kids," Flo said. "You know, that's a shame, Maye. After all the money I made. I was a big star, and here I can't even afford a few gifts for my kids this year. When Christmas comes, I might be in heaven with my children."

Maye was alarmed by Flo's last statement. When some friends of the Atkinses dropped by, Maye asked them to give Flo and the girls a ride home. Flo agreed to go, but once she'd got into the car, she demanded to be let out. The couple gave Flo cab fare, but when Maye looked out again, Flo was sitting on the porch of her house.

Maye decided to make Flo's plight known, in the hopes that public interest might spur Flo to pull herself together. Maye told the story to a reporter from the *Detroit Free Press* on the condition that she remain anonymous and that Flo be treated with dignity. The next day the story was on the front page. *The Washington Post* picked up the story and sent two writers to Detroit to get an exclusive interview. Days later, the story of the ex-Supreme living in poverty was all over the wire services.

The story did what Maye hoped it would. Fan mail poured in from all around the world, Flo was asked to appear on several talk shows, and there were rumors that Flo had been offered a role in a Broadway play. A local day-care center wanted to employ Flo for $85 a week, and a New York club called the Riverboat wanted her to play there. Flo considered taking the day-care job but refused to perform. She was afraid.

In June 1975 she made her final concert appearance in Detroit at a benefit for Joann Little, a black female prisoner who was charged with killing a prison guard who allegedly had raped her. Also on the bill were comedienne Lily Tomlin and the feminist rock group Deadly Nightshade. Flo received a standing ovation. It was so obvious that the public loved her. Yet that just wasn't enough.

In August 1975 Flo came to visit me at my home in Los Angeles. We both felt it would be a good change for her. I knew of her performance in Detroit, and I set out to convince her during her stay that she should be singing. She helped me prepare a birthday party for my husband and never let my daughter Turkessa who was then four months old, out of her sight.

One night while she was there, Cindy Birdsong, Scherrie Payne, and I were playing Magic Mountain. Just before the last number, I said, "Ladies and gentlemen, I have a surprise guest—Miss Florence Ballard!"

The audience went crazy. Cries of "Flo, we love you!" went on for minutes. It had been eight years since Flo had stood onstage as a Supreme, and her fans' devotion was stronger than ever. Flo and I were teary-eyed, and I could see that Scherrie and Cindy were also moved. Even though she did not sing with us, I hoped this would show her how much the fans still cared. As we walked backstage, I could sense Flo's excitement. I decided then that I would tell Flo how I felt, no matter how much it hurt.

It was a very hot night, and we drove back to my house in silence. Once we got inside, I tried to express my feelings. We were sipping wine and had wound down from all the excitement.

"Flo, you see they love you. You can sing again."

"But, Mary, you just don't know."

"Girl, get yourself together. Florence, you are one of the finest singers I have ever known. Do whatever you have to do to get some work and maybe a record deal. At least try, Flo," I pleaded.

"I can't, Mary," she replied. "There's nothing I can do about it."

My plan had backfired; it seemed that the longer I talked, the more depressed Flo became. When we'd first arrived home, Flo seemed happy, but after a couple of drinks she was the saddest person I had ever seen.

"Flo," I said slowly, "you have got to do it. You love to sing, and you see the fans love you. You only need to find the right producer and some good songs. Flo, dreams don't just die—people can change them."

I believed in what I was saying, but when I looked into Flo's eyes, I could see that she didn't. There was no hope left in her, and for a moment I felt that my friend was gone, far, far away. She just looked up at me, like a child who'd been beaten. "Mary, leave me alone. Don't you realize that it's over? I don't want to do it anymore. Just leave me alone."

I wanted to shake her and scream, "Wake up, Flo!" I became angry with her for falling to pieces. "It's time for us to go to bed," I said.

"I don't want to go to bed!" Flo was like a stubborn child.

"Flo, if you break anything, I'm going to be upset." She could barely walk. "Suppose you were like this and you were alone with your children? What if you were at home and you accidentally started a fire? How are you going to help yourself or your children? Look at yourself, Flo!"

"Now, you see?" she cried. "You see?"

Flo went back to Detroit a couple of days later, and I didn't see her until Thanksgiving. When Flo heard that I was holding a family reunion in Detroit she knew she would be welcome. Everyone knew of her problems, but she maintained her dignity, always smiling and happy—the old Flo. That was the last time I ever saw her.

Sometime in late 1975, Flo received a large settlement from a lawsuit, mostly likely one she brought against the owners of a property where she had fallen on the ice and broken her leg the year before. Wherever it came from wasn't important. Flo and Tommy were back together, she bought a new house, and paid cash for a brand-new Cadillac. This seemed to be her second chance. Several people who knew her said that the minute she got the money, she went back into her "Supremes bag," by which they meant that she started taking care of herself again.

In 1975 Cholly and Maye moved to Las Vegas, where Cholly choreographed shows for the stars. Neither of the Atkinses had heard from Flo for months, when one night in February 1976, she phoned. It sounded to Maye as if Flo had been drinking, and all Flo seemed to want to talk about was the old days.

"Why did Diane have to act that way?" Flo asked Maye over and over. Flo had never got over that, and Maye just listened. Then Flo said, "Maye, I don't feel so well. I have a pain in my chest."

"Flo, baby," Maye replied, "you'd better get to the hospital."

"No," Flo said, acting as if it was no big deal, "I'll be all right." Then she hung up.

Five minutes later, Maye's phone rang. It was Flo. This time she wanted to talk about me and my mother.

"After they put me out," Flo said, "Mary was the only one who stuck by me." Then Flo started to ramble on, sometimes incoherently. Maye began to worry.

"Flo, honey," Maye said, "why don't you go to the hospital?"

"Yeah. Okay. Maybe." Then the line went dead.

A few minutes later, Flo called again.

"Thanks, Maye."

"Thanks? For what, Flo?"

"I know you called the *Detroit Free Press* about me."

"Now, why would I do that, Flo?"

"Because nobody else in Detroit cared enough about me, except you, Maye."

Flo hung up again. The more Maye thought about what Flo had said, the more worried she became. She decided to call Flo and see that she was okay, but then she realized that she didn't have Flo's new number.

At 3:30 A.M. on Saturday, February 21, Flo called her mother and told her she was experiencing shortness of breath. "Mama, if anything happens to me, I want you to keep the children," Flo said.

"Oh, baby, nothing is going to happen to you."

During the night, though, Flo seemed to get worse, and her daughter Nicole called Flo's sister Maxine to tell her that something was wrong. Maxine and some of Flo's other siblings dismissed Nicole's calls as another one of Flo's attempts to get attention. Tommy was at work, and Maxine's car wasn't running. She promised to come over first thing in the morning and check up on Flo then.

Years later Maxine said she had had a premonition of Flo's death. Two weeks earlier, Flo was visiting Maxine and her mother. The whole time she was there, she drank glass after glass of water.

"Why do you keep drinking so much water?" Mrs. Ballard asked.

"I'm hot inside," Flo replied. "I can't get rid of this hot feeling."

Flo had high blood pressure and was taking medication for that and more medication to lose weight, and her family might have assumed that her various aches and pains were caused by that.

When Maxine got to Flo's the next day, she found her lying on the floor, unable to move. She was paralyzed from the waist down and could barely speak. When she did, the words sounded like a mechanical whisper. Maxine and Flo's daughters managed to get her on a couch, and Maxine called an ambulance.

Flo was rushed to Mount Carmel Mercy Hospital, where she died the next morning of a heart attack, the result of a blood clot in a coronary artery.

I was at my assistant Hazel Bethke's house in Glendale, California, with Scherrie Payne and Susaye Green, picking out old Supremes gowns to take on tour. Hazel came into the storage room and said, "Mary, your mother just called. She said Flo passed away."

I couldn't move. All I could say was, "I knew it, I knew it," and cry.

My husband, relatives, and friends helped me pack for the trip to Detroit. Hazel took care of my travel arrangements. All I could think about was Flo and how much I loved her.

Once I got to my old house on Buena Vista, I had the comfort of my family, all of whom had known Flo for years. I called Flo's family and spoke with some of her sisters. Everyone was in shock; it had all happened so suddenly, and just when Flo seemed to be getting herself back together. Maybe she never would have sung again, but at least she could have been happy. Only then did I realize that simply being happy in life was more than enough.

Jesse Greer had married my friend Diane Watson, the girl I had wanted to replace Barbara Martin in the Primettes. Jesse and Diane drove me to the funeral home to view Florence the night before the funeral. Winnie Brown, our former hairdresser and Flo's niece and good friend, did Flo's makeup and hair. Flo was dressed in a flowing, light-blue robe. They had positioned her so that she appeared to be almost sitting up, and when I first saw her I was surprised at how heavy she was. Still, she was beautiful.

There were crowds surrounding the funeral home, and when we arrived and I was recognized, people started banging on the car. I was in the backseat with Diane Greer and could see people trying to get my attention. Inside, and outside the home, I heard people talking, blaming Diane and Berry for Flo's death. Though Flo had played along with Motown's version of her departure, things were out in the open after the 1971 lawsuit. But still no one really knew the full truth. Flo was the tragic heroine; I guess people had to find a villain.

The next day I was driven to the New Bethel Baptist Church in a Rolls-Royce. I never knew for sure who supplied the classic cars used in the funeral procession. My mother, my sister Cathy, and Diane Greer accompanied me. As we neared the church, we saw thousands of people lining the sidewalks. Policemen did all they could to keep the crowds back, but it was near impossible. Earlier that day, I had met with Flo's family. It had taken all I had not to break down in front of her three girls, but here, I knew this was the last time I would ever see Flo. I just wanted to be alone with her, but I knew that I would not be.

I spotted dozens of people I had known from the Projects and school. When Motown had moved to Los Angeles in 1975, part of Detroit had died. Today, though, the city was alive for one more day. People had started lining up in front of the church before dawn. Some of the mourners wore mink coats and evening gowns, while others were in housedresses and tattered streetclothes. There were over five thousand people standing outside when I got to the church. The police were trying to hold the crowd back, but every time a celebrity stepped out of a car, someone would shout, "Here comes somebody!" and bodies would press forward. When we arrived, we were asked to stand with Flo's family and my family in the line of mourners entering the church. A few minutes later, a limousine pulled up next to the church steps and Diane jumped out, flanked by four bodyguards. The crowd booed her, and I saw the pain on Mrs. Ross's face as she stood in the line with us. Diane looked stunning, and I watched as she was quickly ushered in. She came down the center aisle of the church, and people were pushing and shoving to get a glimpse of her; the scene caused quite a commotion. Diane was seated in front next to Tommy and Flo's mother and held Flo's youngest girl, Lisa, in her lap.

When I got in a few moments later, the first thing I was struck by were the floral arrangements. Every act from Motown had sent one, as had Berry. Diane's said, "I Love You, Blondie." I took my seat a few rows back from Flo's family, but this wasn't like any funeral I had ever attended before. The crowd was wild, and there were flashbulbs popping every other second.

Reverend Franklin nearly lost his patience, asking people to sit down, be quiet, and show some respect for the dead. I was listening but thinking about Flo. For some strange reason I recalled this gorgeous white fox stole Flo had. She knew that I loved it, so whenever she wore it I'd always say, "Flo, if you ever die, will me that coat, honey." And then we'd laugh. Why was I thinking about this now? Because I never thought Flo would ever die.

Right after the reverend finished, Diane jumped up and said, "Can I have the microphone, please!" Then she said, "Mary and I would like to have a silent prayer."

At first, I was stunned, then shocked. Diane and I hadn't spoken to each other in months. I was furious that I was being dragged into this. My grief was personal and private. I didn't want to get up, but I was so taken aback by Diane's words that I felt I had no choice. Declining would have made a bad situation worse. There were things I wanted to say, but to Flo, by myself. But I got up and stood beside Diane, who said, "I believe nothing disappears, and Flo will always be with us." Then she handed me the mike. "I loved her very much," was all I could say. Diane and I walked past Flo's coffin, and I looked down at Flo and gently touched her cheek. She looked so pretty.

As we filed out, the organist played "Someday We'll Be Together" —a Supremes hit neither Flo nor I had sung on—over and over. We got into our cars to go to Detroit Memorial Park for the burial. The pallbearers—Duke Fakir, Obie Benson, Levi Stubbs, Lawrence Payton, Marv Johnson, and Thearon Hill (Stevie Wonder was an honorary pallbearer)—had to be ushered out by attendants. At the sight of Flo's coffin, the crowd got even wilder, and in an attempt to keep onlookers away from the coffin, all of her floral arrangements were thrown out to the mob. Within minutes, the only proof that the flowers had ever existed were the bare wire and Styrofoam frames left lying on the sidewalk.

When we reached the cemetery, it was just Flo's family, the pallbearers, the Four Tops, and me. After Flo's body was lowered into the ground, everyone made their way back to the cars. This was it. Suddenly I realized that Diane wasn't there. Regardless of what had passed between us, we were the only two people who had shared Flo's greatest moments. For that reason alone, Diane should have been there. But she was gone.

A wind blew through the cemetery, and in just a few moments a thousand thoughts came to me. How did three talented little girls come to this? What turn of fate made one friend a household name, while the other struggled for years in poverty? When did our dream die? And what else could I have done to help Flo? I thought back to the night after Magic Mountain, when I looked into Flo's eyes and realized that she was beyond all of this now. There probably weren't any answers to my questions, and if there were, they came too late.

I finally threw my flower down on Flo's coffin.

"Don't worry, Flo," I said aloud, because I knew she could hear me, "I'll take care of it." Then I repeated one of Flo's favorite lines from our happy days: "Honey, we is terrific."

# APPENDIX I:

## A SUPREMES ITINERARY

Here are some of the highlights of our career, as compiled from my personal diaries and scrapbooks. Asterisks indicate information that is missing or unknown. All chart positions are from *Billboard* magazine.

### 1961

| | |
|---|---|
| January 15 | The Supremes sign with Motown. |
| March 3 | "I Want a Guy" backed with "Never Again" released (recorded late 1960). |
| July 21 | "Buttered Popcorn" backed with "Who's Loving You" released. |
| September* | Recorded "Those DJ Songs" (on *25th Anniversary*, 1986). |

### 1962

| | |
|---|---|
| May 8 | "Your Heart Belongs to Me" (recorded December 1961) backed with "He's Seventeen" (recorded August 14, 1961) released, #95. |
| November 5 | "Let Me Go the Right Way" (recorded August 30, 1962) backed with "Time Changes Things" released, #90. |

## 1963

| | |
|---|---|
| February 2 | "My Heart Can't Take It No More" backed with "You Bring Back Memories" released. |
| June 12 | "A Breath Taking Guy" backed with "(The Man with) the Rock and Roll Banjo Band" released, #75. |
| July* | Recorded "Come On Boy" (on *25th Anniversary*, 1986). |
| October 31 | "When the Lovelight Starts Shining Through His Eyes" backed with "Standing at the Crossroads of Love" released (recorded October 1963), #23. |
| December* | *Meet the Supremes* released. |

## 1964

| | |
|---|---|
| * | Recorded "Penny Pincher" (on *25th Anniversary*, 1986). |
| February 7 | "Run, Run, Run" backed with "I'm Giving You Your Freedom" released, #93. |
| May* | Recorded "Send Me No Flowers" (on *25th Anniversary*, 1986). |
| June 17 | "Where Did Our Love Go" released (recorded April 8, 1964), #1. |
| July 3 | Recorded "With All My Heart" (unreleased). |
| July 6 | Recorded "The Truth Does Hurt" (unreleased). |
| July 24 | Recorded "In His Eyes" (unreleased). |
| August 13 | Recorded "Darling Baby" (unreleased). |
| August 17 | Recorded *Live! Live! Live!* (unreleased). |
| August 18 | Recorded "Ooowee Baby," released on *The Supremes 25th Anniversary* (1986). |
| August 20 | Recorded "Put Yourself in My Place" (released on *A Go-Go*, 1966) and "Across the Road" (unreleased). |
| August 31* | *Where Did Our Love Go* released, #2. |

| | |
|---|---|
| Summer | Dick Clark's Caravan of Stars tour with Gene Pitney, Brenda Holloway, and others. |
| September 17 | "Baby Love" released (recorded August 13, 1964), #6. |
| September 12–21 | Brooklyn Fox Theatre, New York, New York, with Dusty Springfield, the Shangri-Las, the Temptations, Jay and the Americans, the Contours, the Ronettes, Martha and the Vandellas, Little Anthony and the Imperials, Marvin Gaye, the Miracles, Millie Small. |
| September 29 | Recorded "Blue Memories" (unreleased). |
| October 7 | Leave Detroit for English promotional tour. |
| October 15 | Met Ringo Starr and Paul McCartney at the Ad Lib Club, Birmingham, England. |
| October 24 | Filmed *The T.A.M.I. (Teenage Awards Music International) Show*, Santa Monica Civic Center, California (filmed in electronovision) with the Beach Boys, Chuck Berry, James Brown, Marvin Gaye, Gerry and the Pacemakers, Lesley Gore, Billy J. Kramer, the Miracles, the Rolling Stones, hosted by Jan and Dean. Released 1985, Media Home Video. |
| October 27 | "Come See About Me" released (recorded July 13, 1965), #1. |
| November | *A Bit of Liverpool* released, #21. |
| November 14 | Dick Clark tour, Holy Cross College, Worchester, Maine. |
| November 24 | Recorded "The Only Time I'm Happy" and "Who Could Ever Doubt My Love" (on *More Hits by the Supremes*, 1965). |
| December 1 | Recorded "I'm in Love Again" (on *More Hits*, 1965). |
| December 12 | Recorded "Bikini Party" (unreleased). |
| December 16 | Recorded "Take Me Where You Go" (on *From the Vaults*, 1979, 1982). |
| December 24 | Rehearsal for *The Ed Sullivan Show* (CBS) *The T.A.M.I. Show* movie shown in Michigan Theatre. |

| December 25 | Motown Revue, Brooklyn Fox Theatre, New York, with Marvin Gaye, the Miracles, the Marvelettes, Stevie Wonder, the Temptations. |
| December 27 | First appearance on *The Ed Sullivan Show* (CBS), performed "Come See About Me." |

## 1965

| January 8 | Recorded "I Just Want to Make You Happy" (unreleased). |
| January 11 | Rerecorded "Take Me Where You Go" (unreleased). |
| January 11/13 | In England *New Musical Express'* readers voted the Supremes the #3 group; *Music Business Magazine* names them the #1 female group. |
| January 18 | Recorded "You've Been a Long Time Coming" (unreleased). |
| January 25 or 26 | *Hullabaloo* (NBC). |
| February 2 | "Battle of the Stars," recorded 3 sides live (unreleased). |
| February 8 | "Stop! In the Name of Love" released, (recorded January 5, 1965), #1. |
| February 17 | Recorded "Big City Babies Don't Cry" and "Fancy Passes" (unreleased cuts). |
| February | Nominated for Grammy Award for best R&B Vocal Performances, "Baby Love." |
| February 18 | Filmed *Go-Go*, in Palm Springs, California; a Dick Clark production. |
| February 23 | Recorded "There's No Love Left" and "It's All Your Fault" (on *25th Anniversary*, 1986). |
| February 27 | *The Hollywood Palace* (ABC). |
| March | *Country, Western and Pop* released (recorded February 6, 17, and 26, 1963), #79. Recorded "Sleepwalk" (on *25th Anniversary*, 1986). |

| | |
|---|---|
| March 3 | Recorded "Rock-A-Bye Your Baby," "You're Nobody 'til Somebody Loves You," "Little Miss Loser," and "Something for My Heart" (for unreleased *There's a Place for Us* LP). |
| March 12 to mid-April | Motown Revue in Europe with the Temptations, the Miracles, Martha and the Vandellas, Stevie Wonder. |
| March 18 | Motown Revue taped *The Sound of Motown*, BBC special, London, England. Hosted by Dusty Springfield, air date April 21. Released on Sony Video, 1985. |
| March 21 | Winter Gardens, Bournemouth, England. |
| March 26 | The Venue ABC, Kingston on Thames, England (Motown Revue first U.K. visit), with Martha and the Vandellas, Stevie Wonder, the Miracles, Earl Van Dyke. |
| March 30 | Manchester, England. |
| April | *We Remember Sam Cooke* released, #75; *Elegant Teen* cover story "Supreme Supremes." |
| April 1 | Recorded "Love is like a Heat Wave" (on *The Supremes Sing Holland-Dozier-Holland,* 1967). |
| April 15 | "Back in My Arms Again" released (recorded December 1, 1964), #1. |
| April 19 | Recorded "He's All I Got" (on *I Hear A Symphony,* 1966). |
| April 21 | "The Sound of Motown," BBC special airs in England. |
| April 27 | Rerecorded "Put Yourself in My Place" (on *A Go-Go,* 1966). |
| May* | Steele Pier Memorial Day show this month. Recorded a tribute to Berry Gordy, "We Couldn't Get Along Without You" (special lyrics to "My World Is Empty Without You," on *25th Anniversary,* 1986). |
| May 2 | Leave for New York to tape *Hullabaloo* (NBC). |

| May 7 | Recorded "It's the Same Old Song" (on *The Supremes Sing Holland-Dozier-Holland*, 1967). |
| May 12 | Recorded two Coca-Cola commercial themes ("Baby Love" and "When the Lovelight Starts Shining Through His Eyes" variations). |
| May 21 | *Time* Magazine cover story with other pop artists. |
| May 25 | Recorded "Love You Forever" (unreleased). |
| June | Cover of *Ebony* Magazine. |
| June 2 | Recorded "Mother Dear" (on *More Hits*, 1966). |
| June 10–11 | Taping President Lyndon Johnson's "War on Poverty" special, CBS Greenfield Village. |
| June 16 | Rerecorded "Fancy Passes"; recorded "Sincerely" and "Mr. Sandman" (unreleased). |
| June 25 | Recorded "Don't Let True Love Die" (unreleased). |
| June 28 | "It's What's Happening Baby," special (CBS) with Johnny Mathis, the Temptations, Martha and the Vandellas, Marvin Gaye, the Miracles, airs. |
| June 28 | "War on Poverty," special (CBS) airs. |
| July | *More Hits by the Supremes* released, #6. |
| July 7 | Recorded "Too Much a Little Too Soon" (unrecorded). |
| July 16 | "Nothing but Heartaches" released (recorded May 13, 1966), #11. |
| July 21 | Tape *Jackie Gleason Summer Show with Al Hirt*. |
| July 24 | *Al Hirt Show* airs (CBS). |
| July 28 | *The Tonight Show* (NBC). |
| July 29* | Copacabana debut, New York, New York, recorded *Live at the Copa*. |
| August | Bill Billikin Parade, Chicago, Illinois. |
| | Recorded "Things are Changing" (NARA's equal-opportunity campaign song, produced by Phil Spector). |

| August 27–<br>September 9 | The Michigan State Fair. |
|---|---|
| August 29 | *The Dean Martin Show* (NBC). |
| September | Motown announces that the group is booked through September 1966 (at Flamingo Hotel, Las Vegas, Nevada—rumors that this would be Diana's last engagement with group). |
| September 2 | Rerecorded "Mother Dear" (possibly for single release, cut already on *More Hits*). |
| September 10 | JFK Stadium, Philadelphia, Pennsylvania. |
| September 13 | *Hullabaloo* (NBC). |
| September 14 | Recorded "Noel" (on *Merry Christmas*, 1965). |
| September 17–26 | Safari Room, San Jose, California. |
| September 30–<br>October 8 | European tour. |
| October | *The Steve Allen Show*. |
| October 2 | Holland's Grand Gala du Disque Festival, Amsterdam. |
| October 6 | "I Hear a Symphony" released (recorded September 22, 1966), #1. |
| October 7 | *Tops of the Pops*, Manchester, England. |
| October 8 | *Ready, Steady, Go!*, London, England. |
| October 9 | *Michigan Chronicle* announces a tour of Vietnam that will run from January 6 to January 22, 1966, with the Four Tops. (Later cancelled.) |
| October 10 | *The Ed Sullivan Show* (CBS), performed "I Hear a Symphony" and "You're Nobody 'til Somebody Loves You." |
| October 13 | Sybil Burton's "Very, Very In," Arthur's, New York, New York. |
| October 15 | Lincoln Center, New York, New York, with the Spinners. |
| October 18 | *Hullabaloo* (NBC). |
| October 20–25 | Boston. |
| October 27 | Recorded "Heaven Must Have Sent You" (unreleased). |
| October 28–<br>November 3 | Latin Quarter, Philadelphia, Pennsylvania. |

| | |
|---|---|
| November | *Live at the Copa*, #11, and *Merry Christmas* released. |
| November 3 | Recorded "Here I Am Alone in Life" (unreleased). |
| November 7–14 | Oklahoma. |
| November 14 | Oklahoma State Fair arena, with the Lovin' Spoonful. |
| November 14 | USO a Go-Go Benefit, Madison Square Garden, New York, New York, with Sammy Davis, Jr., Joan Crawford, Carroll Baker, Johnny Carson, Robert Vaughan. |
| November 15–16 | Recorded *I Hear a Symphony*, Los Angeles, California. |
| November 18 | Dean Martin special (NBC). |
| November 24 | Recorded "(I Know) I'm Losing You" (unreleased). |
| November 29 | Motortown Revue recorded live at Musicorama, Olympia Music Hall, Paris, France, with the Miracles, Martha and the Vandellas, and Stevie Wonder. |
| December 3 | University of Bridgeport winter formal. |
| December 4–11 | Twin Coaches, Pittsburgh, Pennsylvania. |
| December 6 | *Hullabaloo* (NBC). |
| December 13 | *Hullabaloo* (NBC). |
| December 15 | *Where the Action Is* (ABC). |
| December 16–18 | Houston. |
| December 16 | Shamrock Hilton DJ party, Houston, Texas. |
| December 17 | Went Christmas shopping. |
| December 17 | Tape Larry King Show (air date December 18) performed "I Hear a Symphony." |
| December 17 | Opening of the Astrodome, Houston, Texas, with Judy Garland. |
| December 18 | *Larry Kane Show*, performed "I Hear a Symphony." |
| December 23– January 1, 1966 | Pompeii Room, Eden Roc Hotel, Miami, Florida, with Jack E. Leonard. |
| December 29 | "My World Is Empty Without You" released, #5. |
| December 31 | Orange Bowl Parade. |

# 1966

| | |
|---|---|
| January 9 | *The Ed Sullivan Show* (CBS). |
| January 17–29 | Roostertail, Detroit, Michigan. |
| January 19 | Rerecorded "Mother Dear" (possibly for single release, already on *More Hits*). |
| January 25 | *The Red Skelton Show* (CBS). |
| January 25 | Tape Washington Hilton Grand Ballroom performance; CBS to televise gala party. |
| January 30 | Leave for San Juan, El San Juan Hotel. |
| February | Nominated for Grammy Award for Best Group Vocal Performance, "Stop! In the Name of Love." |
| February 5 | Civic Arena, Pittsburgh, Pennsylvania. |
| February 9–28* | Tour of West Germany and Scandinavia. |
| February 11 | Recorded "He" (on *We Remember*). |
| February 12 | Holy Cross College, Mount St. James Field House, Massachusetts. |
| February 12 and/or February 13 | Waltham-Branden University, Massachusetts. |
| February 15 | "Anatomy of Pop: The Music Explosion," special (ABC), performed "My World Is Empty Without You." |
| February 17* | Open at the Copacabana, New York, New York. |
| February 18 | *I Hear a Symphony* released, #8. |
| February 20 | *The Ed Sullivan Show* (CBS), performed "My World Is Empty Without You" and "Somewhere." |
| February 27 | "Anatomy of Pop," rerun as ABC Sunday afternoon special. |
| March | *What's My Line?* Recorded "Who Can I Turn To" (on *25th Anniversary*, 1986). |
| March 3–16 | Copacabana, New York, New York. |
| March 4 | *Time* Magazine article. |
| March 4 | *The Sammy Davis Show* (NBC), with the Andrews Sisters. |

| | |
|---|---|
| March 11–12* | Recorded in Los Angeles, California, "On a Clear Day You Can See Forever," "The Wheels of the City" (all unreleased), and "Blowin' in the Wind" (on *Cream of the Crop*, 1969). |
| March 17 | Recorded "One Way Out" (unreleased). |
| March 17 | *The Dean Martin Show* (NBC). |
| March 22–April 3 | Blinstraub's, Boston, Massachusetts. |
| March 23 | Recorded two sides for *The Supremes Sing Holland-Dozier-Holland*. |
| March 24 | *The Dean Martin Show* (NBC). |
| March 24 | Supremes White Bread on the market. |
| April | Press conference at Roostertail, Detroit, Michigan. |
| April 8 | "Love Is like an Itching in My Heart" released, #9. |
| April 13 | Recorded "Deep Inside" (unreleased). |
| April 19 | Recorded "Until You Love Someone" (unreleased). |
| May | *Look* Magazine. |
| May 1 | *The Ed Sullivan Show* (CBS), performed "Love Is Like an Itching in My Heart." |
| May 19–June 8 | Fairmont Hotel, San Francisco, California. |
| June 1 | Recorded "Together Again" (unreleased). |
| June 2 | Recorded "Hurtin' Again" and "It's Summer" (unreleased). |
| June 11 | Recorded "Hurtin' Bad" (unreleased). |
| June 14 | Recorded/rerecorded five *Holland-Dozier-Holland* sides and "Baby I Need Your Loving" (on *A Go-Go*, 1966). |
| June 15 | Rerecorded "Baby I Need Your Loving" (on *A Go-Go*, 1966). |
| June 20–25 | O'Keefe Center, Toronto, Canada. |
| June 28 | Recorded "Moment of Weakness" (unreleased). |
| June 30 | *The Today Show* (NBC). |
| June 30 | Recorded "Misery Makes Its Home in My Heart" (on *Reflections*, 1968). |
| July 1 | Recorded "Many Good Times," "Mother Tell Me What to Do," "Just a Little |

| | |
|---|---|
| July 1 (*cont.*) | Misunderstanding" (all unreleased), "What Becomes of the Brokenhearted" (on *Let the Sunshine In*, 1969), and "Come On and See Me" (on *25th Anniversary*, 1986). |
| July 7 | *The Mike Douglas Show*, with the Temptations.* |
| July 8 | Recorded "With a Child's Heart" (on *Let the Sunshine In*, 1969). |
| July 9 | Rerecorded "Put Yourself in My Place" (on *A Go-Go*, 1966). |
| July 11 | Recorded "Just a Smile Away" (unreleased). |
| July 16 | Recorded "Here Are the Pieces of My Broken Heart" (unreleased). |
| July 20 | Co-host *The Mike Douglas Show*. |
| July 24–30 | Steele Pier, Atlantic City, New Jersey. |
| July 24 | *The Ed Sullivan Show* (CBS). |
| July 25 | "You Can't Hurry Love" released, #1. |
| August | 17 Magazine. Music Circus, Lambertville, New Jersey. Colonie Summer Theatre, Lathan, New York. Recorded "If I Ruled the World" (on *25th Anniversary*, 1986). |
| August 9–14 | Circle Star Theatre, San Carlos, California. |
| August 11 | Recorded in Los Angeles, California, seven unreleased sides including "The Sound of Music," "If I Ruled the World," (on *25th Anniversary*, 1986), "I've Been Blessed," "Tender Is the Night." Also recorded "Love (Makes Me Do Foolish Things)" (on *Reflections*, 1968). |
| August 10–16 | Rehearsal/taping "Rodgers and Hart Today" special (ABC) Los Angeles, California. |
| August 18 | *The Tonight Show* (NBC). |
| August 19 | Civic Center, Virginia Beach, Virginia. |
| August 20 | Forest Hills Tennis Stadium, Forest Hills, New York, with the Temptations and Stevie Wonder. |
| August 25 | *A Go-Go* released, #1. |
| August 26–30 | State Fair, St. Paul, Michigan. |
| September | In Los Angeles this month to tape "Rodgers and Hart Today." Mary and Florence visit |

| September (*cont.*) | the Temptations at The Trip, Los Angeles, California. |
| September 2 | Arrive in Tokyo. |
| September 3–22 | The Far East Tour: Tokyo, Okinawa, Taiwan, Hong Kong, Manila, Philippines. |
| September * | Yokosukso Naval Base, USS *Coral* (4,000 men). |
| September 14 | Leave for Manila. |
| September 15 | *Soul* Magazine cover story "Surprises from the Supremes." |
| September 23–25 | *The Ed Sullivan Show* (CBS), performed "You Can't Hurry Love." |
| September 25 | Recorded live LP (unreleased) at Roostertail, Detroit, Michigan. |
| September 29– October 19 | Flamingo Hotel, Las Vegas, Nevada. |
| October | Recorded "Manhattan" and "The Blue Room" (on *25th Anniversary*, 1986). |
| October 12 | "You Keep Me Hangin' On" released (recorded June 30, 1966), #1. |
| October 13* | Recorded "My Guy" (unreleased). |
| October 19 | Recorded "Leave It in the Hand of Love" (unreleased). |
| October 21 | Taped *The Hollywood Palace* (ABC) (air date October 22 or October 29). |
| October 21 and 24 | Recorded in Los Angeles sides for *Rodgers and Hart* LP (twelve sides were unreleased). |
| November 27 | *The Ed Sullivan Show* (CBS), performed "You Keep Me Hangin' On." |
| December | Deauville Hotel, Miami, Florida. |
| December 4 | *The Ed Sullivan Show* (CBS), performed "You Keep Me Hangin' On." |
| December | Helped commemorate the independence of Barbados. |
| December 25 | Open at the Eden Roc Hotel, Miami, Florida. |
| December 31 | New Year's Eve King Orange Jamboree Parade. |

## 1967

| | |
|---|---|
| January 6–7 | Recorded sides for unreleased *Disney* LP in New York, New York. |
| January 11 | "Love Is Here and Now You're Gone" released, #1. |
| January 12, 14, and 20 | Unreleased *Disney* LP recording in New York, New York. Among these recordings is "When You Wish Upon a Star" (on *25th Anniversary*, 1986). |
| January 22 | *The Ed Sullivan Show* (CBS) performed "Love Is Here and Now You're Gone." |
| January 22 | *The Andy Williams Show* (NBC). |
| January 23 | *The Supremes Sing Holland-Dozier-Holland* released, #6. |
| January 23–27 | Elmwood Casino, Windsor, Ontario, Canada. |
| January | *Playboy* annual reader's poll: voted #1 group (the Beatles, #2; Peter, Paul and Mary, #3). |
| February 13–25 | Roostertail, Detroit, Michigan. |
| February 13 | "Ice Capades" special (NBC). |
| February 16 | *Soul* Magazine cover story "Good Things Come in Threes." |
| March | Deauville Hotel, Miami, Florida. |
| March 20 | "The Happening" released (recorded March 2, 1967), #1. |
| March 22 | "The Happening" released to coincide with film premiere Adams Theatre, Detroit, Michigan. |
| April 1* | Opening at Eden Roc, Miami, Florida, with Sonny Sands. |
| April 29 | Hollywood Bowl benefit for UCLA School of Music and United Negro Fund, Los Angeles, California, (first appearance with Cindy Birdsong); receive KHJ Radio award. |
| May 7 | *The Ed Sullivan Show* (CBS) performed "The Happening" and "Millie/Rose/Mame" medley (Florence's last appearance on Sullivan Show). |

| | |
|---|---|
| May 11 | "Rodgers and Hart Today." special (ABC) with Bobby Darin, Petula Clark, the Mamas and Papas. |
| May 11–24 | Copacabana, New York, New York. |
| May 19–20 | Recorded live album at Copacabana (unreleased). |
| May 21* | *The Ed Sullivan Show* (CBS), broadcast from Expo '67 Theatre, Montreal, Canada. |
| May 22 | *The Tonight Show* (NBC), performed "The Happening" and "The Lady Is a Tramp" (Florence's last TV appearance). |
| May 26 | University of Cincinnati, Ohio. |
| May 27 | Southern Illinois University, Carbondale, Illinois. |
| May 28 | Hara Arena, Dayton, Ohio. |
| May 29 | Minneapolis Auditorium, Minnesota. |
| May 30 and/or May 31 | Arena Auditorium, Duluth, Minnesota. |
| May | *The Supremes Sing Rodgers & Hart* released, #20. |
| June 1–10 | Shoreham, Washington, D.C. |
| June 8 | *Soul* Magazine cover story, "A Smash at the Copa." |
| June 11 | Symphony Hall, Washington, D.C. |
| June 13–18 | Cocoanut Grove, Los Angeles, California. |
| June 22 | Recorded "Lonely Boy" and "Ask the Lonely" (unreleased). |
| June 23 | Presidential Ball, Las Vegas, Nevada, Presidents Club of California, Citizens for Johnson-Humphrey. |
| June 28–July 19 | Flamingo Hotel, Las Vegas, Nevada. |
| July | Met President Lyndon Johnson. Cocoanut Grove, Los Angeles, California. |
| July 14 | Invited by Johnny and Joanna Carson to party, Las Vegas, Nevada. |
| July 18 | Invited to Milton Berle screening of *Who's Minding the Mint*, Las Vegas, Nevada. |
| July 24 | "Reflections" released (recorded March 2, 1967), #2. |
| July 29 | Forest Hills Stadium, Forest Hills, New York. |

| | |
|---|---|
| August 5–9 | Allentown Fair, Allentown, Pennsylvania. |
| August 8 | St. Moritz Hotel, New York, New York. |
| August 12 | *American Bandstand* (ABC), performed "Reflections." |
| August 13–19 | Steele Pier, Atlantic City, New Jersey. |
| August 20 | In Montreal, Canada. |
| August 21–23 | Expo '67 Theatre, Montreal, Canada. |
| August 25–28 | "Showcase '68" Motown's first national sales convention Hotel Pontchartrain, Detroit, Michigan, debuted Supremes' *Greatest Hits*. |
| August 26 | Two-hour "Motown Showcase," Hotel Pontchartrain, Detroit, Michigan, with Stevie Wonder, Gladys Knight and the Pips, the Spinners, Chris Clark, and Earl Van Dyke. |
| August 27 | Recorded live at the Roostertail album, Detroit, Michigan (unreleased). |
| August 28–30 | Ohio State Fair, Columbus, Ohio. |
| September | *Cosmopolitan* Magazine article "The Supremes: They Make You Believe Again," by Rona Jaffe. Recorded "Heigh-Ho" and "Someday My Prince Will Come" (on *25th Anniversary*, 1986). |
| September 1–4 | Michigan State Fair, Michigan. |
| September 11–17 | Farmington Music Circus, Farmington, Massachusetts. |
| September 17 | Rhode Island Auditorium, Providence, Rhode Island. |
| September 23 | *The Hollywood Palace* (ABC), performed "Reflections," "I've Got You Under My Skin," and "I Get a Kick out of You" (Cindy's TV debut*). |
| October 29 | *Diana Ross and the Supremes Greatest Hits* released (double album), #1. |
| October* | In Mexico this month to film *Tarzan*. |
| October 2–14 | The Cave, Vancouver, Canada. |
| October 6* | Recorded "Heaven Must Have Sent You" (unreleased) and "Stay in My Lonely Arms" (on *Motown's Brightest Stars*, 1986). |
| October 11* | Recorded* "Then" (on *Reflections*, 1968). |

| October 14 | Recorded "Up, Up and Away" and "Ode to Billie Joe" (both on *Reflections*, 1968). |
| October 25 | "In and Out of Love" released (recorded April 20, 1967), #9. |
| October 27 | University of Oregon, Oregon. |
| October 28 | Coliseum, Portland, Oregon. |
| October 29 | Coliseum, Spokane, Washington. |
| October 30 | Arena, Seattle, Washington. |
| November 3 | Coliseum, Oakland, California. |
| November 4 | UCLA Pauley Pavilion, Los Angeles, California, with Hugh Masekela, Sandy Baron. |
| November 6–12 | Rehearsal/taping "The Tennessee Ernie Ford Special" (CBS), Los Angeles, California (air date December 3), with Andy Griffith, Danny Thomas. |
| November 19 | *The Ed Sullivan Show* (CBS), with the Temptations, performed "In and Out of Love." |
| November 27 | Recorded "What a Friend We Have in Jesus" and "Everytime I Feel the Spirit" (both unreleased). |
| December 3 | "The Tennessee Ernie Ford Special" (CBS), performed "Reflections," "The Happening," and medley of hits. |
| December 18 | Recorded "I'm Gonna Make It" (on *Reflections*, 1968) and "Treat Me Nice John Henry" (*25th Anniversary*, 1986). |
| December 22–31 | Deauville Hotel, Miami, Florida. |

## 1968

| January 8–9 | Milano TV show. |
| January 10 | Lunch with the Duke and Duchess of Bedford, London, England. |
| January 11 | Paris TV show. |
| January 12 | *Tarzan* "The Convert" episode (NBC), with James Earl Jones, airs. |

| | |
|---|---|
| January 13 | Berry "Pops" and Bertha Gordy's fiftieth wedding anniversary, renewed vows at Bethel A.M.E. Church, Detroit, Michigan, entire family and Motown artists attended. |
| January 14 | "The Supremes in Berlin" TV show. |
| January 16 | TV show in Amsterdam. |
| January 17 | TV show in Madrid. |
| January 18 | TV show in Paris. |
| January 19–20 | Bal Paree, Munich Bambi Film Festival. |
| January 21 | Miden Festival, Cannes. |
| January 22–February 3 | Talk of the Town, London, England. |
| January 28–February 9* | In London, England. |
| January 28 | Duke and Duchess of Bedford give party honoring group at the Club Dell'Aretusa, Chelsea, London, England. Guests included Tom Jones, Mick Jagger, Marianne Faithfull, Michael Caine, Lynn Redgrave. |
| January 28 | Palladium TV show. |
| February 3 | "Live at London's Talk of the Town," BBC hour special (shown live*). |
| February 4 | Eamon Andrews TV show. |
| February 5–11 | Berns Restaurant, Stockholm. |
| February 10 | Recorded "Am I Asking Too Much" and "He Loves Me So" (both unreleased). |
| February 12 | TV show in Geneva. |
| February 13 | Recorded "Don't Forget I Love You" (unreleased). |
| February 17 | Recorded "I Can't Shake It Loose" (on *Love Child*, 1968) and "You'll Never Cherish a Love So True" (unreleased). |
| February 22 | Florence signs her general release from Motown, a nine-page settlement. |
| February 24 | Recorded "Can't Take My Eyes Off You" (unreleased, Mary lead). |
| February 29 | Recorded "A Little Breeze" (unreleased). |
| February 29 | "Forever Came Today" released (recorded April 21, 1967), #28. This is the first single |

| February 29 (*cont.*) | on which no other Supremes except Diane appear. |
| March | *Reflections* released, #18. |
| March 6 | Florence sings with ABC Records, $15,000 advance, two year exclusive contract. |
| March 7 | Recorded "When It's to the Top" (on *Cream of the Crop*, 1969) and "You Made Me Feel Like Everything Was Alright" (unreleased). |
| March 9 | Recorded "Honey Bee" (on *Love Child*, 1968) and "The Beginning of the End" (on *Cream of the Crop*, 1969). |
| March 14 | Recorded "Sweet Soul Music" and "If You Should Walk Away" (unreleased). |
| March 15 | Recorded "A Place in the Sun" (on *Join the Temptations*, 1969) and "Believe in Me" (unreleased). |
| March 18 | Recorded "Growing," "The Nitty Gritty," "The Boy from Crosstown," "For Once in My Life" (unreleased). |
| March 24 | *The Ed Sullivan Show* (CBS), performed "Forever Came Today" and Fats Waller medley. |
| April 4* | Copacabana, New York, New York. |
| April 4 | Recorded "Will This Be the Day" (on *Love Child*, 1968). |
| April 5 | *The Tonight Show* (NBC), performed "Somewhere." |
| April 12 | Recorded "You've Been So Wonderful to Me" (on *Love Child*, 1968). |
| April 20 | "Crusade '68" special (CBS). |
| April 24 | Recorded "Touched by the Hand of Love" (unreleased). |
| April 29 | Recorded "Hey Hey" and "Honey Babe" (unreleased). |
| April 30 | Recorded "He's My Sunny Boy" (on *Love Child*, 1968) and "Ain't I Gonna Win Your Love" (unreleased). |
| May 4 | *The Hollywood Palace* (ABC). |
| May 4* | Open at the Copacabana, New York, New York, with Lewis and Christy, Copa girls. |

| | |
|---|---|
| May 5 | *The Ed Sullivan Show* (CBS) performed "Some Things You Never Get Used To." |
| May 10 | Recorded "Uptown" (unreleased). |
| May 11 | ABC Records lists Florence's "It Doesn't Matter How I Say It" as coming product, *Billboard*. |
| May 13–18 | Westbury Music Fair, Long Island, New York. |
| May 21 | "Some Things You Never Get Used To" released (recorded April 15, 1968), #30. Recorded two unreleased sides, rerecorded "Honey Bee" (on *Love Child*, 1968). Appeared at Fisher Theatre, Detroit, Michigan |
| May 27–31 | Fisher Theatre, Detroit, Michigan. |
| May 31 | Recorded "Don't Break These Chains of Love" (on *Love Child*, 1968). |
| June 20 | Recorded *Funny Girl* LP sides in New York, New York. |
| June 24–30 | Carter Barron Amphitheatre, Rock Creek Park, Washington, D.C., with Stevie Wonder, the Little Step Brothers. |
| July 19 | Recorded "Ain't No Sun Since You've Been Gone" (unreleased). |
| July 20 | Forum, Los Angeles, California, with Stevie Wonder, Shorty Long. |
| July 22–27 | Garden State Arts Center, New Jersey, with George Kirby, the Little Step Brothers. |
| July 23 | Endorsed Hubert Humphrey, Waldorf Astoria, New York, New York. |
| July 24 | Waldorf Astoria, New York, New York. |
| July 25 | Recorded "Weak Spot," "Soul Appeal," "Double or Nothing," "Operation Teamwork" (unreleased). |
| July 26 | Recorded "This Is Where I Came In," "It Only Happens When Love Is Gone," "The Girl that Was," "I Feel Love" (unreleased). |
| July 28 | Recorded "How Long Has That Evening Train Been Gone" (on *Love Child*, 1968) and "I Can't Give Back the Love I Feel for You" (same cut that's on Diana's solo *Surrender* LP*). |

| | |
|---|---|
| August 1 | Recorded "You Ain't Livin' Until You're Lovin'" (on *Love Child*, 1968). |
| August 2 | Recorded "Make Me Yours" with the Temptations (unreleased) and "This Is Where I Came In" (unreleased). |
| August 5 | Recorded "You've Got the Love" (unreleased), rerecorded "I'll Set You Free" (on *Love Child*, 1968). |
| August 9 | Recorded "Those Precious Memories" (unreleased). |
| August 19 | Recorded "I'm So Glad I Got Somebody (Like You Around)" (on *Let the Sunshine In*, 1969) and "For Us Both I'll Be Concerned" (unreleased). |
| August | *The Supremes Sing and Perform "Funny Girl"* released, #150. |
| | *Live at London's Talk of the Town* released, #57. |
| September* | Carousel Theatre, Framingham, Maine, with the Temptations, one week engagement. |
| September 1 | Baltimore Civic Center, Maryland. |
| September 6 | Recorded "I Get Lost" (unreleased). |
| September 12 | Recorded "Love for a Lifetime" (unreleased). |
| September 14 | Recorded "Where the People Live," "Won't You Come Fly with Me," "Don't Say You Love Me" (unreleased). |
| September 17 | Rhode Island Auditorium, Providence, Rhode Island, with the Temptations. |
| September 18 | Recorded "Seeing Is Believing" (unreleased). |
| September 23 | Recorded "It Could Have Gone Either Way" (unreleased). |
| September 29 | *The Ed Sullivan Show* (CBS), performed *Funny Girl* medley and "Love Child." |
| September 30 | "Love Child" released (recorded September 17, 1968), #1. |
| October* | Florence's second 45, "Love Ain't Love," released. |
| October 1–14 | The Grove (Cocoanut Grove), Los Angeles, California. |

| | |
|---|---|
| October 2 | Recorded "Does Your Mama Know About Me" (on *Love Child*, 1968). |
| October 8 | Recorded "The Shadows of Society" (on *Cream of the Crop*, 1969) and "Give Back the Good Things" (unreleased). |
| October 13 | Florence gives birth to twin daughters, Michelle Denise and Nicole Rene, at Henry Ford Hospital, Detroit, Michigan. |
| October 16 | Rerecorded "I'm So Glad I Got Somebody (Like You Around)" (on *Let the Sunshine In*, 1969). |
| October 23 | "Bing Crosby Special" (NBC), performed "You Keep Me Hangin' On." |
| November* | *Soul Illustrated* Magazine cover story (winter '68) "The Beauty, the Soul, the Style of . . ." |
| November 4 | Recorded "My Love for Your Love" (unreleased). |
| November 5 | Recorded "I'm Lost" and "It's Unbelievable" (unreleased). |
| November 8 | *Love Child* released, #14. |
| November | In Europe. |
| November 8 | Olympia Theatre, Paris, France. |
| November 11 | London Palladium, London, England, meet royalty. |
| November 12 | Stockholm. |
| November 13 | *Diana Ross and the Supremes Join the Temptations* released, #2. |
| November 13 | Copenhagen. |
| November 14 | Malmö, Sweden. |
| November 16 | Brussels, Belgium. |
| November 16* | Rerecorded "The World Can't See Through the Eyes of Love" (unreleased). |
| November 17 | Royal Command Performance, London, England. |
| November 18 | London Palladium, London, England, members of Royal Family in attendance. |
| November 21 | "I'm Gonna Make You Love Me" (with the Temptations) released, #2. |
| November 21 | Dublin, Ireland. |

| | |
|---|---|
| November 23 | Manchester Odeon Free Trade Hall, Manchester, England. |
| November 24 | London Palladium, London, England. |
| November 26 | Hamburg, Germany. |
| November 29 | Munich, Germany. |
| November 30 | Frankfurt, Germany. |
| December* | Still in Europe. |
| December 2 | *TCB* soundtrack LP (with the Temptations) released, #1. |
| December 3* | Rerecorded "I'll Set You Free" (already on *Love Child*, 1968). |
| December 5 | Recorded "The Young Folks" (on *Cream of the Crop*, 1969) and "I Just Can't Carry On" (unreleased). |
| December 6 | Rerecorded (for third time*) "I'm So Glad I Got Somebody (Like You Around)" (on *Let the Sunshine In*, 1969). |
| December 9 | "TCB (Takin' Care of Business)" special (NBC) with the Temptations. |
| December 28 | Recorded "Are You Sure Love Is the Name of this Game" (released on *25th Anniversary*, 1986). |
| December 28 | Host *The Hollywood Palace* (ABC). |

# 1969

| | |
|---|---|
| January 5 | *The Ed Sullivan Show* (CBS), performed "Love Child" and "I'm Livin' in Shame." |
| January 6 | "I'm Livin' in Shame" released (recorded December 26, 1968), #10. |
| January 10 | Trinity University Earl C. Sams Memorial Center, San Antonio, Texas. |
| January 13 | Recorded "Sunshine Days" (unreleased). |
| January 17 | Recorded "Why Am I Lovin' You" (unreleased). |

| | |
|---|---|
| January 21 | Recorded "Everyday People" and "Western Union Man" (both cuts on *Let the Sunshine In*, 1969), "Hey Jude" (on *Cream of the Crop*, 1969) "Stormy" (unreleased), rerecorded "For Once in My Life" (unreleased). |
| January 24 | Recorded "Son of a Preacher Man," "Chained to Yesterday," "Nothing from Nothing," "Witchi-Tai-To" (unreleased). |
| January 25 | Recorded "I Had a Dream" and "The Onion Song" (unreleased). |
| January 29 | Recorded "You're Gonna Hear from Me," rerecorded "Witchi-Tai-To" (unreleased). |
| January 30–<br>  February 12 | Frontier Hotel, Las Vegas, Nevada. |
| February 15 | Recorded "Memories" and "A Little Too Much" (unreleased), rerecorded "For Both of Us I'll Be Concerned" (unreleased). |
| February 17 | "Bob Hope Special" (NBC), performed "Coronet Man" and "Sam, You Made the Pants Too Long" (both from *Funny Girl*). |
| February 20 | "I'll Try Something New" (with the Temptations) released, #25. |
| February 24 | Recorded six sides for *Together* LP with the Temptations. |
| February 27 | Recorded "The Paper Said Rain" (unreleased). |
| March 8 | *The Hollywood Palace* (ABC). |
| March 18 | *The Tonight Show* (NBC). |
| March 20 | Recorded "Discover Me" (on *Let the Sunshine In*, 1969), rerecorded "The Beginning of the End" (on *Cream of the Crop*, 1969). |
| March 24 | Recorded (with the Temptations) "Why (Must We Fall in Love)" (on *Together*, 1969). |
| March 25 or 27 | "The Composer" released (recorded December 28, 1968), #27. |
| April* | $1,000-a-plate concert/fundraiser to help clear Robert Kennedy's political debts, Beverly Hills, California. |
| April* | Announced that Diana would make her film debut in Walter Zeltzer's *Darker than Amber*. |
| April 1 | Recorded "Make the Most of It" (unreleased). |

| | |
|---|---|
| April 4–13 | Casanova Room, Deauville Hotel, Miami, Florida, with Scoey Mitchell. (Motown artists appearing across the country paid tribute in their concerts to Dr. Martin Luther King, Jr., on this first anniversary of his death.) |
| April 7 | Recorded "I'm Just a Little Bit Nothing When Love Falls" and "Love What Have You Done to Me" (unreleased). |
| April 10 | Recorded "Since You Came Back" (unreleased). |
| April 13 | "Like Hep!" special (NBC) (Diana solo) with Dinah Shore and Lucille Ball. |
| April 19 | Recorded "Will I" (unreleased). |
| April 22* | O'Keefe Center, Toronto, Canada, with O. C. Smith, the Little Step Brothers. |
| May 9 | "No Matter What Sign You Are" released, #31. |
| May 11 | *The Ed Sullivan Show* (CBS), performed "No Matter What Sign You Are." |
| May 14* | Waldorf Astoria Empire Room, New York, New York. |
| May 19 | Recorded "Though Love Has Gone," "The Unwanted," "Look at Where We Are" (unreleased). |
| May 26 | *Let the Sunshine In* released, #24. |
| May 31 | *The Hollywood Palace* (ABC). |
| June* | Jean Terrell signed to Motown as a solo artist. |
| June 3 | Recorded "I Wanna Go Back There Again" (unreleased). |
| June 10 | Recorded "My Heart's on a Trip" and "Mr. Loneliness" (unreleased). |
| June 23 | Recorded with Jean Terrell "Take a Closer Look at Me" (on *New Supremes' Right On*, 1970) and "Standing Ovation," "Baby Don't You Go," and "While They Watch" (unreleased). |
| June 30–July 6 | Carter Barron Amphitheatre, Rock Creek Park, Washington, D.C. with Julius Wechter and the Baja Marimba Band. |

| | |
|---|---|
| July 8–12 | Carousel Theatre, Framingham, Massachusetts, with Stevie Wonder. |
| July 17 | Recorded "Honey Take Me" and "I'm Getting Married" (unreleased). |
| July 18 | Recorded "Another Lonely Night" (unreleased). |
| July 25 | Recorded (with the Temptations) "Everyday for a Lifetime" (unreleased). |
| July 31 | Rerecorded "I Wanna Go Back There Again" (unreleased). |
| July 31 | *Top of the Pops* (BBC), London, England, with Donovan, the Rolling Stones, Billy Preston, Cilla Black, host Alan Freeman. |
| August 11 | Daisy Club, Beverly Hills, California, Diana Ross threw a party for Jackson Five. |
| August 16 | Forum, Los Angeles, California, with Edwin Starr, the Edwin Hawkins Singers, Jackson Five. |
| August 21 | "The Weight" (with the Temptations) released, #46. |
| August 25 | Recorded "I'm Going Crazy" (unreleased). |
| September* | *Together* (with the Temptations) released, #28. |
| September 7 | *The Ed Sullivan Show* (CBS). |
| September 16 | Recorded "Then I Met You" (on New Supremes' *Right On*, 1970). |
| September 22 | Rowan and Martin's *Laugh-In* (NBC). |
| September 23 | *Look* Magazine cover story "The Supreme Supreme" (Diana solo article). |
| October 12 | "Someday We'll Be Together" released, #1. (last 45 release with Diana). |
| October 18 | Hosts *The Hollywood Palace* (ABC), with Sammy Davis, Jr., the Jackson Five, performed "Someday We'll Be Together," Mary solo "Can't Take My Eyes Off You." |
| November | *Git on Broadway* soundtrack (with the Temptations), #38, and *Cream of the Crop* (last with Diana) released, #33. |
| November 5 | Recorded "These Things Will Keep Me Loving You" (on Diana's first solo LP). |

| | |
|---|---|
| November 8 | *Billboard* Magazine carries official confirmation: Diana leaving the Supremes, Jean Terrell her replacement. |
| November 11 | *The Tonight Show* (NBC). |
| November 12 | "Git on Broadway" special (NBC) with the Temptations. |
| November 14 | Recorded "Bill, When Are You Coming Home" (on New Supremes' *Right On,* 1970) and "I Can't Wait 'Til Summer Comes" (unreleased New Supremes cut*). |
| December 2 | Cindy Birdsong kidnapped from her Hollywood, California apartment. |
| December 18 | *Greatest Hits, Volume 3* released, #31. |
| December 21 | *The Ed Sullivan Show* (CBS), performed medley of hits, "I Hear a Symphony" and "Someday We'll Be Together" (last TV appearance with Diane). |
| December 23– January 14, 1970 | Frontier Hotel farewell engagement, Las Vegas, Nevada. |
| December 31 | Recorded "I Got Hurt (Trying to Be the Only Girl in Your Life)" (on New Supremes' *Right On,* 1970) and "The Day Will Come Between Sunday and Monday" (unreleased New Supremes cut). |

## 1970

| | |
|---|---|
| January 2 | Recorded "Up the Ladder to the Roof." |
| January 6 | Recorded "I Wish I Were Your Mirror" (on New Supremes' *New Ways but Love Stays,* 1970) and "Lovin' Country" (on New Supremes' *Right On,* 1970). |
| January 9 | Recorded "Three Day Journey of Me" (unreleased). |
| January 12 | Rerecorded "Then I Met You" (on New Supremes' *Right On,* 1970), recorded "That's How Much You Made Me Love You" and |

|  | "I'll Never Let You Get Away" (unreleased New Supremes*). |
| January 14 | Frontier Hotel, last day, last performance of Diana Ross and the Supremes. |
| January 15 | Recorded "Stepping on a Dream" and "Wasting Time" (both unreleased). |
| January 16 | Recorded "Thank Him for Today" (on New Supremes' *New Ways but Love Stays*, 1970) and "I Almost Had Him (But He Got Away)" (unreleased New Supremes cut*). |
| January 23 | Rerecorded "I Can't Wait 'Til Summer Comes" (unreleased New Supremes cut*). |
| January 30 | Rerecorded "Up the Ladder to the Roof," "Na Na Hey Hey Kiss Him Goodbye" (on New Supremes' *New Ways but Love Stays*, 1970), and "Didn't I Blow Your Mind This Time" (unreleased New Supremes cut*). |
| February | New Supremes' "Up the Ladder to the Roof" released, #10. |
| April 13 | *Farewell* three-record boxed set released, #46. |

# APPENDIX II:

# SUPREMES DISCOGRAPHY

The following is a discography of all albums and singles by the Supremes—as the Primettes, as the Supremes, and as Diana Ross and the Supremes—up through the departure of Diana Ross from the group in 1970. Solo albums and singles by Florence Ballard and Mary Wilson are included; Diana Ross' are not, because her solo career is well documented in several other sources. Also included is a partial list of songs recorded by the Supremes but never released, as well as a videography. Asterisks indicate information that is missing or unknown.

| | |
|---|---|
| 1959–1960 | _The Primettes_ |
| | Florence Ballard |
| | Betty McGlown |
| | Diane Ross |
| | Mary Wilson |
| 1960–1961 | _The Primettes_ |
| | Barbara Martin |
| | Florence Ballard |
| | Diane Ross |
| | Mary Wilson |
| 1961–1962 | _The Supremes_ |
| | Barbara Martin |
| | Florence Ballard |
| | Diane Ross |
| | Mary Wilson |
| 1962–1967 | _The Supremes_ |
| | Florence Ballard |
| | Diana Ross |
| | Mary Wilson |

1967–1970                    *Diana Ross and the Supremes*
                            Cindy Birdsong
                            Diana Ross
                            Mary Wilson

## *Singles*

| *The Primettes* | *Label* | *Released* |
|---|---|---|
| "Tears of Sorrow"/"Pretty Baby" | Lupine 120 | 3/59 |

| *The Supremes* | | |
|---|---|---|
| "I Want a Guy"/"Never Again" | TAMLA 54038 | 3/9/61 |
| "Buttered Popcorn"/"Who's Loving You" | TAMLA 54045 | 7/21/61 |
| "Your Heart Belongs to Me"/"He's Seventeen" | Motown 1027 | 5/8/62 |
| "Let Me Go the Right Way"/"Time Changes Things" | Motown 1034 | 11/5/62 |
| "My Heart Can't Take It No More"/"You Bring Back Memories" | Motown 1040 | 2/2/63 |
| "A Breath Taking Guy"/"Rock & Roll Banjo Band" | Motown 1044 | 6/12/63 |
| "When the Lovelight Starts Shining Through His Eyes"/"Standing at the Crossroads of Love" | Motown 1051 | 10/31/63 |
| "Run, Run, Run"/"I'm Giving You Your Freedom" | Motown 1054 | 2/7/64 |
| "Where Did Our Love Go"/"He Means the World to Me" | Motown 1054 | 6/17/64 |
| "Baby Love"/"Ask Any Girl" | Motown 1066 | 9/17/64 |
| "Come See About Me"/"Always in My Heart" | Motown 1068 | 10/27/64 |
| "Stop! In the Name of Love"/"I'm in Love Again" | Motown 1074 | 2/8/65 |
| "Back in My Arms Again"/"Whisper You Love Me Boy" | Motown 1075 | 4/15/65 |

| | | |
|---|---|---|
| "Nothing But Heartaches"/"He Holds His Own" | Motown 1080 | 7/16/65 |
| "I Hear a Symphony"/"Who Could Ever Doubt My Love" | Motown 1083 | 10/6/65 |
| "Children's Christmas Song"/ "Twinkle Twinkle Little Me" | Motown 1085 | 11/18/65 |
| "My World Is Empty Without You"/"Everything's Good About You" | Motown 1089 | 12/29/65 |
| "Love Is like an Itching in My Heart"/"He's All I Got" | Motown 1094 | 4/8/66 |
| "You Can't Hurry Love"/"Put Yourself in My Place" | Motown 1097 | 7/25/66 |
| "You Keep Me Hangin' On"/ "Remove This Doubt" | Motown 1101 | 10/12/66 |
| "Love Is Here and Now You're Gone"/"There's No Stopping Us Now" | Motown 1103 | 1/11/67 |
| "The Happening"/"All I Know About You" | Motown 1107 | 3/20/67 |

*Diana Ross and the Supremes*

| | | |
|---|---|---|
| "Reflections"/"Going Down for the Third Time" | Motown 1111 | 7/24/67 |
| "In and Out of Love"/"I Guess I'll Always Love You" | Motown 1116 | 10/28/67 |
| "Forever Came Today"/"Time Changes Things" | Motown 1122 | 2/24/68 |
| "What the World Needs Now"/ "Your Kiss of Fire" | Motown 1125 | 1968 |
| "Some Things You Never Get Used To"/"You've Been So Wonderful to Me" | Motown 1126 | 5/21/68 |
| "Love Child"/"Will This Be the Day" | Motown 1135 | 9/30/68 |
| "I'm Gonna Make You Love Me"/ "A Place in the Sun" (with the Temptations) | Motown 1137 | 11/21/68 |

| | | |
|---|---|---|
| "I'm Livin' in Shame"/"I'm So Glad I Got Somebody like You Around" | Motown 1139 | 1/6/69 |
| "I'll Try Something New"/"The Way You Do the Things You Do" (with the Temptations) | Motown 1142 | 2/20/69 |
| "The Composer"/"The Beginning of the End" | Motown 1146 | 3/27/69 |
| "No Matter What Sign You Are"/ "The Young Folks" | Motown 1148 | 5/9/69 |
| "Stubborn Kind of Fellow"/"Try It Baby" (with the Temptations) | Motown 1150 | 1969 |
| "The Weight"/"For Better or for Worse" (with the Temptations) | Motown 1153 | 8/29/69 |
| "Someday We'll Be Together"/"He's My Sunny Boy" | Motown 1156 | 10/14/69 |

## Albums

### The Supremes

| | | |
|---|---|---|
| *Meet the Supremes* | Motown 606 | 12/63 |
| *Where Did Our Love Go* | Motown 621 | 1/65 |
| *A Bit of Liverpool* | Motown 623 | 10/64 |
| *Sing Country and Western and Pop* | Motown 625 | 2/65 |
| *More Hits by the Supremes* | Motown 627 | 7/65 |
| *We Remember Sam Cooke* | Motown 629 | 5/65 |
| *At the Copa* | Motown 636 | 11/65 |
| *Merry Christmas* | Motown 638 | 11/65 |
| *I Hear a Symphony* | Motown 643 | 2/66 |
| *A Go-Go* | Motown 649 | 8/66 |
| *Sing Holland-Dozier-Holland* | Motown 650 | 1/67 |
| *Sing Rodgers & Hart* | Motown 659 | 8/67 |

### Diana Ross and the Supremes

| | | |
|---|---|---|
| *Greatest Hits Volumes I and II* | Motown 663 | 8/67 |
| *Reflections* | Motown 665 | 8/68 |

| | | |
|---|---|---|
| *Love Child* | Motown 670 | 11/68 |
| *Sing and Perform "Funny Girl"* | Motown 672 | 8/68 |
| *Live at the Talk of the Town* | Motown 676 | 8/68 |
| *Join the Temptations* | Motown 679 | 11/68 |
| *TCB (with/the Temptations)* | Motown 682 | 12/68 |
| *Let the Sunshine In* | Motown 689 | 5/69 |
| *Together (with/the Temptations)* | Motown 692 | 9/69 |
| *Cream of the Crop* | Motown 694 | 11/69 |
| *On Broadway (with the Temptations)* | Motown 699 | 11/69 |
| *Greatest Hits Volume 3* | Motown 702 | 12/69 |
| *Farewell* | Motown 708 | 4/70 |
| *Great Songs and Performances* | Motown 5313 ML | 1985 |
| *Motown Legends* | Motown 5361 ML | 1985 |
| *Sing Motown* | Motown 5371 ML | 1986 |
| *Anthology* | Motown 794 | 5/74 |

Also:

| | | |
|---|---|---|
| *Live at the Apollo*—Volume 1 (1 cut) | Motown 609 | 4/63 |
| *Motortown Revue in Paris* (3 cuts) | Tamla 264 | 1965 |
| *In Loving Memory* (1 cut) | Motown 642 | 8/26/68 |
| *Motown at the Hollywood Palace* (3 cuts) | Motown 703 | 8/70 |
| *From the Vaults* (1 cut) | Natural Resources NR4014T1 | 1979, 1982 |
| *Superstar Series*—Volume 1 | Motown M5-101V1 | 1979 |
| *All the Greatest Hits*—Diana Ross (1 medley) | Motown M13-960C2 | 1981 |
| *Motown's Brightest Stars*—The 1960's (1 cut) | Motown 538ML | 2/86 |
| *The Detroit Girl Groups* (2 cuts) | Relic Records Lupine 8004 | * |

## Guest Appearances

| | | |
|---|---|---|
| *Four Tops Live!*<br>(1 cut) | MS 5654 | 1966 |
| *Temptations—Getting Ready*<br>(1 cut) | Gordy 918 | 1966 |
| "You're the Wonderful One" by<br>Marvin Gaye | * | 1964 |
| "You Lost the Sweetest Boy" by<br>Mary Wells | * | 1963 |
| "Fancy Passes" by Barbara McNair | * | * |

## Florence Ballard

| | | |
|---|---|---|
| "It Doesn't Matter How I Say It"/<br>"Goin' out of My Head" | ABC 11074 | 1968 |
| "Love Ain't Love"/"Forever<br>Faithful" | ABC 11144 | 1968 |

## Mary Wilson

| | | |
|---|---|---|
| "Red Hot"/"Midnight Dancer" | Motown 1467 | 1979 |
| *Mary Wilson* | Motown M7-927R1 | 8/79 |

## Promotional Singles

| | | |
|---|---|---|
| "The Only Time I'm Happy"/<br>"Supremes Interview" | Motown 1079 | 1965 |
| "What the World Needs Now"/<br>"Your Kiss of Fire" | Motown 1125 | (unreleased) |

## Unreleased Recordings

Currently Motown has in its vaults countless unreleased recordings. Since no official record of these recordings has ever been released or published by Motown, it is impossible to compile a complete list. However, here are a few more memorable recordings in addition to those listed in the Itinerary.

"Supremes Sing Ballads and Blues"
"Live! Live! Live!"
"There's a Place for Us"
"A Tribute to the Girls"
"Pure Gold"
"Our Day Will Come"
"Can't"
"All I Want to Do"
"Send Him to Me"
"Davy Crockett"
"The Tears"
"I Idolize You"
"Bye Bye Baby"
"Mr. Blues"
"Silent"
"Whistle While You Work"

For the RIAA (the Recording Industry Association of America) to certify a record gold (sales of $1 million wholesale before 1976; 500,000 copies after 1976) or platinum (one million copies; this award established in 1976), a record company must submit its accounts to an audit. Because Motown, among other labels, refused to do this throughout the sixties, only the Supremes three-album set *Anthology* (1974) was ever officially recognized by the RIAA as a gold record. Although no official figures have ever been released by Motown, it is certain that any Supremes release that entered the Top Thirty sold in the millions, and many releases continue to sell today, in some cases, over two decades after their original release.

## Videography

The following is a list of all performances or interviews of Mary Wilson or the Supremes currently available on home video.

*The Girl Groups*, MGM/UA Home Video: interview with Mary Wilson, various clips of performances by the Supremes.

*Ready Steady Go: The Sounds of Motown*, Sony Video: three performances by the Supremes.

*Mellow Memories*, USA Home Video: performance of one song by the Supremes.

*That Was Rock: The TAMI/TNT Show:* performance of four songs by the Supremes.

*Motown 25: Yesterday, Today and Forever,* MGM/UA Home Video: various performances and clips of the Supremes.

# INDEX

ABC Records, 212, 240
Abernathy, Ralph, 216–217
Abner, Jimmy, 44–45
Ales, Barney, 97
Allen, Johnnie, 153, 170
Allen, Napoleon "Snaps," 210, 235
Andantes, 134, 196, 220
Anderson, Katherine, 97
Andrews Sisters, 185
Animals, 177
Anna Records, 92, 106
Ant, Adam, 1–2
Armstrong, Louis, 154
Ashford, Jack, 92
Ashford, Nick, 2, 220
Ashford, Rosalind, 83, 130, 132, 151
Askey, Gil, 153, 170, 209, 235
Atkins, Cholly, 126, 153–154, 157, 167, 168–170, 172, 201, 239, 242, 244
Atkins, Maye, 167, 171, 242, 244–245
Avery, Herbert, 227
Avery, Monaloa, 227

Baker, Carroll, 182
Ballard, Barbara, 29
Ballard, Bertie, 29
Ballard, Billy, 29, 64, 154
Ballard, Calvin, 29
Ballard, Cornell, 29
Ballard, Florence, 2, 4, 26–30, 31, 32–36, 38–41, 43–50, 52, 54–55, 58, 60–72, 77, 79–80, 84–85, 88, 97–98, 101, 103–105, 108–109, 112, 114–115, 127–132, 134–135, 139–140, 142–144, 146–148, 151–153, 157–159, 161–165, 167–170, 172–177, 180–183, 185–205, 212, 218–219, 221, 225–228, 234, 239–249
Ballard, Geraldine, 29
Ballard, Gilbert, 29
Ballard, Hank, 37
Ballard, Jesse, 28–29, 80
Ballard, Jesse, Jr., 29
Ballard, Linda, 29

Ballard, Lurlee, 28–29, 62–63, 64, 66, 68, 80, 85, 198–199, 241, 245
Ballard, Maxine, 29, 245–246
Ballard, Pat, 29, 241
Ballard, Roy, 29
B&H, 70, 72
Barrow, Marlene, 134, 196, 198
Basie, Count, 153
Bassey, Shirley, 210
Bateman, Robert, 52, 55, 76, 97, 98
Baun, Leonard, 212, 240–241
Beach Boys, 155
Beatles, 155, 177–178
Belafonte, Harry, 216
Belestrieri, Guiseppe, xi
Bell, Al, 140
Benjamin, Benny "Papa Zita," 69, 92–93, 117
Benson, Renaldo "Obie," 168, 185, 248
Benton, Brook, 73
Berger, Eleanor, 192
Berger, Shelly, 174, 192, 205, 207, 216, 230
Berry, Chuck, 24, 25, 155
Bethke, Hazel, 246
Billingslea, Joe, 82
Billy Ward and His Dominoes, 74
Binder, Steve, 155
Birdsong, Cindy, 1, 2–3, 134, 197, 200–202, 204–209, 212, 216, 220–221, 225–228, 232, 233–234, 237, 239, 243
Bisco, Eddie, 140–141, 171
Blackburn, Tony, 210
Blenders, 82
Bogas, Gil, 156
Bohannon, Hamilton, 197
Bond, Julian, 216
Boone, Mr., 110–111
Bowles, Thomas "Beans," 75–76, 90–92, 116, 118, 123–124, 125–126, 149–150, 161
Bradford, Janie, 55, 57, 74–75, 77, 80, 135, 138, 139, 168

Bradshaw, Booker, 161
Brando, Marlon, 216
Breaux, Mrs., 44
Brisker, Miller, 117
Bristol, Johnny, 59
Brooks, Delores "Lala," 146
Brown, Billie Jean, 135
Brown, James, 155, 156
Brown, Jim, 227
Brown, Tim, 227–228, 230
Brown, Winnie, 180, 246
Bryant, Eldridge, 81
Burkes, Jackie, 21, 71, 115
Burton, Richard, 208
Burton, Sybil, 182
Butler, Jerry, 134
Butterball, 140

Caine, Michael, 209, 210
Calloway, Cab, 153
Campbell, Choker, 117, 123, 124, 126,
    132–133
Campbell, Glen, 182
Carroll, Diahann, 207, 216
Carson, Johnny, 159, 182, 202–203
Castleberry, Eddie, 140
Chantels, 83, 85
Chapman, Lisa, 241
Chapman, Michelle Denise, 225, 239
Chapman, Nicole Renee, 225, 239, 245
Chapman, Tommy, 193, 203, 212, 239–
    241, 244
Charles, Ray, 33–34
Christina, Princess of Sweden, 223–224
Clark, Chris, 179
Clark, Dick, 3, 143–148, 150, 153, 163,
    236
Cleftones, 24
Clifford, Mike, 144, 145
Coasters, 24
Cole, Nat "King," 25
Coles, Honi, 126, 153
Collins, Joe, 117
Commodores, 3
Conrad, Pete, 181
Contours, 68, 95, 106, 117, 118, 119, 133
Cooke, Sam, 24, 25, 37, 73, 153, 166, 210
Cooper, Gordon, 181
Cosby, Hank, 92, 134
Cousar, Bob, 210, 235
Cowart, Juanita, 97
Cox, Taylor, 241
Crawford, Joan, 182
Crew, Eugene, 69
Crocker, Frankie, 171
Crystals, 144, 146
Curley, Mr., 43

Davis, Billy, 73–74
Davis, Homer, 59
Davis, Sammy, Jr., 171, 174, 182, 185–
    186, 214, 216
Day, Doris, 24
Dean, James, 25
Dean, Larry, 39, 140
DeBarge, 1
Dells, 115, 134, 138
Del-Phis, 59, 82–83
Demps, Louvain, 134
de Passe, Suzanne, 220
Dietrich, Marlene, 165
Dixie Cups, 144
Dobbins, Georgeanna, 97, 98
Dozier, Lamont, 76, 95, 138–139, 141,
    152, 214
Drifters, 24, 33, 105
Durham, Frantic Ernie, 23, 39, 64, 68
Dushoff, Dave, 229–230

Earl Van Dyke's Funk Brothers, 92
Eckstine, Billy, 168
Edwards, Esther Gordy, 72, 85, 88, 91,
    99, 116, 126, 135, 137, 141, 148, 161,
    165, 172, 217
Edwards, George, 99
Eggar, Samantha, 210
Ellington, Duke, 153
Ely, Ron, 205
Eula, 182

Fair, Yvonne, 226
Faithfull, Marianne, 209
Fakir, Duke, 168, 185, 207, 212, 221, 248
Falana, Lola, 226
Falcons, 59, 68, 69
Fame, Georgie, 164
Fellerman, Peter, 181
Ferrer, Pedro, 239, 246
Fisher, Kelson "Chop Chop," 140
Flamingos, 24
Fletcher, Alice, 139
Fletcher, Berry, 102
Flick and Contour Studios, 68, 70, 82
Floyd, Eddie, 69
Foster, Don, 163, 167, 171, 183–184, 190,
    197
Four Freshmen, 50
Four Tops, 1, 47, 69, 95, 96, 134, 141,
    168, 185, 248
Foxx, Redd, 137
Frankie Lymon and the Teenagers, 23,
    26, 38
Franklin, Aretha, 23, 26, 40, 73–74, 183,
    211
Franklin, Carolyn, 22–24, 73

Franklin, C. L., 22, 73–74, 247–248
Franklin, Erma, 23, 73–74, 75, 95
Franklin, Melvin, 3, 41–42, 44, 81–82
Freed, Alan, 26
Friendly, Ed, 222
Fuqua, Gwen Gordy, 72, 73, 74, 82, 92, 106, 170–172
Fuqua, Harvey, 3, 92, 106–107, 150, 153, 172

Gabrielle, Charlie, 69
Garland, Judy, 182
Garret, Jimmy, 210, 235
Gay, Reverend, 140
Gaye, Anna Gordy, 72, 73, 82, 106, 140–141
Gaye, Marvin, 1, 3, 54, 83, 95, 98, 106–108, 117, 133, 134, 136, 140–141, 142, 155, 161, 166, 215, 220, 236
General Artists Corporation, 202
Gerry and the Pacemakers, 155
Getty, John Paul, 209
Ginsberg, Milton, 191
Gladys Knight and the Pips, 71, 100, 114, 216
Godin, Dave, 155
Gordon, Billy, 82
Gordy, Berry, xi, 1, 2, 4, 5, 52–58, 72–80, 82–85, 88–101, 106, 113, 115, 117–119, 128–129, 132–133, 135, 137–139, 141–143, 149–151, 153–154, 157–158, 161–169, 172–176, 179, 181, 183–184, 187–201, 203, 205–207, 214, 216–221, 224–228, 230–232, 234–239, 247
Gordy, Berry, Sr., 72, 77, 236
Gordy, Bertha, 72, 77, 137
Gordy, Fuller, 72, 207
Gordy, George, 72
Gordy, Loucye, 72, 73, 74
Gordy, Raynoma Liles, 75–76, 82
Gordy, Robert, 72
Gordy, Thelma, 73
Gore, Lesley, 156
Gorman, Freddy, 83, 138
Grant, Cornelius, 117
Green, Susaye, xi, 239, 246
Greer, Diane Watson, 109, 246, 247
Greer, Jesse, 46–47, 49–50, 64, 68, 73, 246
Griffin, Junius, 216

Haber, Margie, 213–214, 230, 237
Hall, Teddy, 213
Hammers, Ronnie, 103–104, 105
Harris, Barry, 92
Harris, Teddy, 117
Harrison, George, 177–178

Harvey, Laurence, 210
HDH, 70, 138–139, 141–143, 166, 168, 171, 178, 214–215, 221
Hicks, Jackie, 134
Higgins, Wes, 82
High Inergy, 1
Hill, Thearon, 248
Hoggs, Billy, 82, 130
Holland, Brian, 57, 75, 76, 95, 132, 138–139, 141, 149, 207, 214
Holland, Eddie, 57, 59, 75, 77, 95, 138–139, 141, 142, 149, 214
Holland, Sharon, 139
Holloway, Brenda, 129, 146, 148
Hooker, John Lee, 134
Horne, Lena, 153, 226
Horton, Gladys, 97, 98–99, 114, 119, 127–132, 135
Houston, Tate, 117
Huckleby, Oscar, 51
Humperdinck, Engelbert, 210
Humphrey, Hubert, 217
Hunter, Joe, 76, 92, 94, 117, 134
Hyland, Brian, 144

Isley Brothers, 59

Jackson, Jesse, 216
Jackson, Michael, 3, 4
Jackson Five, 231
Jagger, Mick, 209
Jamerson, James, 92, 93, 117, 122, 134, 162
James, Rick, 1
Jan and Dean, 155
Jefferson, Al, 140
Jelly Beans, 144
Jenkins, Bobby, 210, 235
Jenkins, James, 115
Jenkins, Josephine Pippin, 112, 115, 218, 239, 241
Jenkins, Milton, 30–35, 37, 38–39, 48, 52, 55, 69, 73, 87–88, 153
Jobete Music, 96
Joe and Al, 59
John, Mabel, 58
Johnson, Ardeena, 137, 152, 179
Johnson, Bill, 139–140
Johnson, Hubert, 82, 119, 130–131
Johnson, Lynda Bird, 204
Johnson, Lyndon B., 166, 204, 217
Johnson, Marv, 57, 76, 88, 91, 248
Johnson, Paul "Fat Daddy," 140
Jones, Brian, 209
Jones, James Earl, 205
Jones, Tom, 206–209, 212–214, 217, 227, 230, 232–233

Kane, Larry, 182
Kendrick, Betty, 69, 70
Kendricks, Eddie, 30, 33–34, 81–82, 119, 140–141, 222–223
Kennedy, John F., 124
Kennedy, Robert, 217
Kilpatrick, Lincoln, 233
King, B. B., 73
King, Bob, 139
King, Coretta Scott, 216–217
King, Martin Luther, Jr., 124, 199, 215–217, 224
King, Maurice, 152–153, 169, 172, 178–179
Kirk, Curtis, 235
Kitt, Eartha, 216
Knight, Gladys, 71, 100
Knight, William, 114

LaBelle, Patti, 134, 137
Lawrence, Lynda, 239
Lee, "Swing," 117
Lily, Miss, 77
Lincoln, Jim, 99
Little Richard, 24, 25
Lucarelli, Jack, 233
Lumpkin, Henry, 58

McAdam, Ed, 146
McCartney, Paul, 155, 177–178, 210
MacDougle, Weldon, 156
McFarland, Eddie, 125–126
McGlown, Betty, 31, 32–35, 40–41, 44–45, 49, 54–55, 57–58, 60–62, 69, 70, 72
McGuire Sisters, 24
McKayle, Donald, 222
Mackie, Bob, 234
McPhatter, Clyde, 25, 74
McQueen, Steve, 233
Martha and the Vandellas, 83, 96, 123, 130, 131, 133, 136, 141, 151, 161, 162, 165, 166
Martin, Barbara, 71–72, 79, 80, 84–85, 88, 100–101, 104, 107–109, 112–114, 246
Martin, Dean, 159, 174, 178
Martin, Mrs., 85
Marvelettes, 90, 97–99, 106, 114, 117, 119, 124–125, 129–130, 131, 133, 134, 142
Masekela, Hugh, 206
Mathis, Johnny, 59
Mayfield, Curtis, 134
Messina, Joe, 92
Mickey & Sylvia, 24

Mills, Gordon, 213
Mills Brothers, 30, 50
Miracles, 3, 53–54, 55, 75, 76, 84, 90, 94, 106, 117, 119, 121–122, 124, 125, 136, 141, 156, 161, 165, 166, 168
Moonglows, 106–107
Moore, Peter, 53
Morris, Richard, 52, 54, 55, 58–61, 68–72, 73, 76–77, 87–88
Morrison, Mrs., 116
Motown, xi, xii, 1–6, 52–55, 57–58, 72, 75–80, 82–98, 102, 106, 113–114, 116–117, 125, 127, 129, 130, 132–134, 136, 143, 147–150, 154, 156, 159–161, 163–164, 166, 168, 170–171, 175, 178, 186, 187, 194, 197, 205, 210, 212–215, 221, 231, 240, 247
Murphy, Mrs., 49
Murray the K, 171

Nelodods, 156
Nixon, Richard, 239
Norman, Fred, 239

O'Den, John, 88–89, 99–101, 135, 153
O'Den, Lily Mae, 99–101
Osborn, Kel, 30, 33
Otis Williams and the Distants, 41, 82
Outcault, James "Chips," 117

Page, Patti, 24
Patterson, Norris, 117
Patti LaBelle and the Blue-Belles, 134, 137, 197, 202
Paul, Clarence, 133, 214
Payne, Freda, 38, 239
Payne, Scherrile, xi, 239, 243, 246
Payton, Lawrence, 168, 248
Peeples, Willie, 102–103
Peppermints, 41, 46–47
Perkson, Tommy "Shaky," 117
Pickett, Wilson, 59, 69
Pippin, Christine, 115, 227
Pippin, Ivory, (I.V.), 10–16, 18, 20, 21–22, 35, 61, 70–71, 110
Pippin, John L., 10–16, 21, 35, 70–71
Pitney, Gene, 144–145, 147
Platters, 24, 75, 85
Podell, Jules, 170
Poitier, Sidney, 156, 214, 216
Polanski, Roman, 210
Postle, Doris, 179
Potts, Sylvester, 82
Powell, Maxine, 151–152, 171, 178, 179
Presley, Elvis, 24, 25, 209
Primes, 30–34, 37, 38, 42, 48, 81, 85

Primettes, 32–35, 38–43, 45, 48–49, 53, 55, 58–62, 65–66, 68–72, 77, 80, 85, 246
Pryor, Richard, 1, 2, 134
Puttnam, David, 207

Raelettes, 34
Randolph, Barbara, 69, 70
Rayber Voices, 58, 76
Redding, Otis, 211
Redgrave, Vanessa, 209
Reese, Della, 73, 83
Reeves, Martha, 1, 2, 3, 59, 82–83, 129, 130, 131, 133, 136–137, 142
Richards, Deke, 221
Ric-Tic/Golden World, 214
Ripchords, 144
Riser, Paul, 93
Robinson, Bill, 153
Robinson, Claudette Rogers, 53, 105, 131
Robinson, Smokey, 1, 3, 53–54, 75, 76, 77, 81, 83–84, 90, 94, 97, 105, 119, 132, 139, 236
Rogers, Bobby, 53, 105, 119, 121–122, 131, 162
Rogers, Sonny, 53
Rogers, Tommy, 26
Rolling Stones, 155, 156
Ronstadt, Linda, 1
Roshkind, Mike, 205
Ross, Arthur, 154
Ross, Diane, xi, 1–5, 26, 31, 32–36, 39–52, 54–56, 58, 60–63, 65–66, 68–72, 80, 82–85, 88, 100, 102–105, 108–109, 112, 114–115, 117, 119, 127–131, 135, 139–148, 151–153, 157–160, 163, 165–167, 169–185, 187–199, 201–210, 216, 218–232, 234–237, 240, 246–248
Ross, Ernestine, 35–36, 85, 117, 128, 137–138, 144, 146–147, 148, 149, 178–179, 189, 236, 247
Ross, Fred, 35–36, 50–51
Ross, Rita, 154, 180
Ruffin, David, 162

Sawyer, Pam, 221
Schlatter, George, 222
Schofield, Willie, 69, 70
Scott, Dick, 163, 212
Sennes, Frank, 236
Seymour, Robin, 39, 140
Shadows, 210
Shaffer, Dave, 140
Shaffner, Joe, 171, 183, 198, 229–230
Sharp, Dee Dee, 129, 144
Sherman, Bobby, 144
Shirelles, 25, 81, 85, 144, 146, 147

Shorter, Willie, 94
Shufeldt, Mrs., 13
Silhouettes, 53
Silver, Mr., 44
Simpson, Valerie, 2, 220
Smith, Bobby, 89
Smith, Willie, 117
Sorps, Ariane, 165–166
Spinners, 89, 134, 182
Springfield, Dusty, 162–163
Staples, Cleo, 120
Staples, Mavis, 120
Staples, Pervis, 120
Staples, Pops, 120
Staples, Yvonne, 120
Staples Singers, 120
Starr, Ringo, 155, 177–178
Stax Records, 120, 140
Sterling, Annette, 83, 130, 132
Stevens, Cat, 210
Stevenson, Kitty, 91
Stevenson, Mickey, 76, 82–83, 90–92, 149
Street, Richard, 3, 41–42, 44, 71, 81–82, 102
Strong, Barrett, 55, 58, 76–77
Stubbs, Joe, 69
Stubbs, Levi, 168, 248
Sullivan, Ed, 157, 160, 170, 171, 188, 233, 236
Swift, Joe, 133–134

Tall George, 102
Tarplin, Marvin, 3, 37–38, 42, 48, 52, 53, 55, 58, 69, 99, 100, 117, 127
Tate, Sharon, 210, 233
Taylor, Bobby, 231
Taylor, Elizabeth, 208
Taylor, R. Dean, 221
Temptations, 1, 2, 33, 81–82, 117, 125, 133, 134, 151, 161, 163, 166, 168, 204, 215, 216, 222–223, 232
Terrell, Ernie, 232
Terrell, Jean, 232, 233–234, 238, 239
Terrell, Tammi, 220, 232
Tex, Joe, 92
Travis, Mike, 222
Turner, Ike and Tina, 134
Turner, Tony, 187–188
Tyler, Willie, 51, 234

Uggams, Leslie, 226
United Artists, 144

Valentine, Hilton, 177
Vancouvers, 231
Van Dyke, Earl, 92
Vaughan, Sarah, 25, 73, 165

Vaughn, Robert, 182
Vee Jay Records, 134
Velvelettes, 117, 139, 144

Ward, Singing Sammy, 117
Warren, Mark, 222
Warren, Mike, 227
Warwick, Dionne, 134, 226
Washington, Dinah, 25
Waters, Ethel, 153
Waters, Mira, 226
Watson, Johnny Wah-Wah, 92
Webster, Arnett, 44
Wells, Mary, 57, 58, 79, 81, 88, 90, 95, 97,
    106, 117, 123, 129, 131, 133, 154
West, Robert, 68–69, 70
Weston, Kim, 91
White, Robert, 92
White, Ronnie, 53, 113
Whitfield, Norman, 57, 142
Wiley, Richard "Popcorn," 58
Williams, Bill, 39, 73, 140
Williams, Gloria Jean, 83
Williams, Herbert, 117
Williams, Otis, 41, 81–82, 222
Williams, Paul, 30, 31, 33–34, 62, 81–82,
    140–141

Willis, Eddie, 92
Wilson, Cathy "Cat," 19–20, 36, 46, 81,
    154, 167, 180, 247
Wilson, Earl, 171
Wilson, Flip, 134, 137, 233
Wilson, Frank, 221
Wilson, Jackie, 25, 61, 74–75, 82, 95, 134,
    137–138
Wilson, Johnnie Mae, 7–10, 18–21, 31–
    32, 34–35, 39, 85, 110–111, 167, 226,
    236, 247
Wilson, Little John, 117
Wilson, Nancy, 226
Wilson, Robin, 111
Wilson, Roosevelt, 10, 19–20, 22, 26, 36,
    46, 81, 154, 167
Wilson, Sam, 7–10, 20–21, 111–112
Winehead Willie, 117
Wise, Norman, 206
Wonder, Stevie, 1, 3, 4, 113, 116, 117,
    124, 133–134, 161, 197, 216, 248
Wooden, Marjorie, 178
Wooldridge, Phil, 183
Wright, Syreeta, 238

Young, Wanda, 97, 119

*My* mother and me in the early '90s just before she started to show signs of Alzheimer's disease. Two years later she wasn't sure who I was. Mom passed away in 1997 when I was in Sweden. I didn't go to the funeral. I wanted to remember her like this.

*F.*A.M.E. (Friends Against Musical Exploitation) board members who are working to stop bogus groups from using established names. Background left to right: Herb Reed (Platters), Brian O'Connor, Pat Benti, me, Chuck Blasko (Vogues). Foreground: Gene Hughes (Casinos).

*A vintage Supremes photo with the Jimmy Wilkins Band. These gowns belong to my "Mary Wilson Supreme Gown Collection" (M.W.S.G.C.). They and many other early Supreme gowns have ended up at the Motown Museum in Detroit (these black striped gowns mysteriously ended up at the Hard Rock Hotel in Las Vegas). I am told by the Motown Museum that if I want them back I have to prove that they are mine.*

*M e and Tommy Nillson in the Swedish musical* Supremesoul.

*L*eft to right: Fellow singers
Rita Coolidge, Brenda Russell,
and me in Mexico at the Rene
Enriquez Celebrity Tennis
Tournament for Orphaned Children.

*T*op left (TV actress and announcer for this affair) Tamara Tunie and me
with some of the young skaters at the Figure Skaters of Harlem's Second Annual
Ice Show, Supreme Ice, *featuring a skating tribute to the Supremes.*

*Left to right: Jaid Barrymore, Sherri Goldner (who gave me her part as a Jewish Yenta), and me during the successful run of the interactive off-Broadwy play* Grandma Sylvia's Funeral.

*Me and Michael Jackson backstage at the British Awards show in London. Michael was very sweet and I was surprised when he softly asked me if I remembered when he and his brothers used to come and play with my adopted son Willie when they were young.*

*A fan's photograph capturing me hitting my stride: in my fifties, a bit overweight, but happy because I don't have too many hot flashes.*

*My son Rafael Ferrer in his St. Catherine's uniform in the 1980s.*

*L*eft to right: Pedro Jr., Pedro Sr., and Rafael. This photo was taken during Christmas vacation, just before Rafael passed.

*L*eft to right: Son-in-law Anthony Babich, my mother, my daughter Turkessa, and me at Anthony and Kessa's 1996 wedding. Mom asked me all night, "Who is the girl getting married?"

*L*eft to right: Beverly Todd (actress), me, Jackée (actress), Linda Green (businesswoman), and Freda Payne (singer/actress) at Kessa's wedding reception.

*L*eft to right: Anthony's mother, Anthony, Kessa, Kessa's father Pedro Sr., Linda Green, and me at Kessa's wedding reception.

*M*e with my granddaughter Mia Marie (born September 7, 1998) at nine months.

# SUPREME FAITH

## *Someday We'll Be Together*

[Co-written with Patricia Romanowski]

*I dedicate this book to my four children—Turkessa,*
*Pedro, Jr., Rafael, and Willie—and to all the people*
*who have come in and out of my life,*
*giving me the love that is my soul's existence*

*In Memory of*

*Florence Ballard (Supremes)*
*Paul Williams (Temptations)*
*Tammi Terrell*
*Marvin Gaye*
*Sandra Tilley (Vandellas)*
*Georgeanna Dobbins (Marvelettes)*
*Hubert Johnson (Contours)*
*Shorty Long ("Function at the Junction")*

# ACKNOWLEDGMENTS

*T*hrough the grace of God, I have lived a full and contented life even though many of the hurdles I had to jump over came fast and unpredictably. But during all the hard times, there have been people there, when I have reached out to them.

First of all, I thank my children, Turkessa, Pedro Jr., and Rafael, for giving me the space to take on such a huge project. To my publicist Jay Schwartz: I truly owe my public image to him, for it was he who directed that part of my career and kept me in the limelight. Gill Trodd from England was the best road manager, nanny, chauffeur, and wardrobe mistress any star could have. She was invaluable. Work has never been a problem for me; I have Ira Okum, Abby Hoffer, and Barry and Jenny of Marshall Arts to thank for booking me all over the world in the seventies and eighties.

I'd like to thank my thousands of English fans—like Kevin Medville, Terry and friends, Steve, Doug, John, Lee John, and Pat Ross (for loaning me all her scrapbooks); Paul

Delapeñna and friends, who made me feel welcome while on tour there; Margie Wooden and Tony Turner for taking great care of my gowns and hair on the road; Greg whom I can't find and who styled all those wigs we carried around in wig boxes; Howard Porter for chasing all around London to find my *Dreamgirl* manuscript, which I had left in the back of a cab while enroute to Heathrow Airport. Can you believe he found it? Thanks to my godson Allen Poe, for always being there for me, and designing all my eighties gowns. Thanks Angela.

To Anthony for his creative Christmas cards, and to my chauffeur, Kenny, for his wonderful dependability.

A very special thanks to Hazel Bethke Kragulac for her contribution to my life. To Glenn McGuire for coming up with that divine subtitle "Someday We'll Be Together." Ted LeMaster for the wonderful portraits. Norwin Simmons for giving me his entire Supremes collection (sans Diana Ross). And special thanks to Charlie Murdock. A huge thanks to Maxine Powell, Cholly Atkins, Maurice King, and Gil Askey who gave the Supremes the class and charm that helped them become a class act.

The Supremes have thousands of fans all over the world, many of whom have sent me photos and clippings for my research for both books. I feel very grateful for the fans who do not appear in this book but who have sent cards and letters, and who supported us throughout the years during ups and downs, changing members, and hit records. To put every single name on these pages would leave no room for the story, so forgive me, but you are here, in every line, in every thought, and in my heart. My love to my new brother and sister, Duke and Lynda Greene, and to Mr. Boone for inspiring me to write.

All artists are indebted to their fan clubs, and I too have my fan club, under the direction of Carl Feuerbacher. I want to thank him, along with a few folks like Tom Ingrassia and Nick Strange, for their day to day assistance.

My heartfelt thanks to Mark Bego, my assistant, for sitting and working along with me to remember all those happy and tragic moments of the seventies and eighties. And, last but not least, to my manager, Chip Lightman, for taking a chance on managing me.

# PREFACE

*O*n January 1988 I stood on the stage of the Waldorf-Astoria Hotel's grand ballroom, proudly accepting an award for the Supremes. We were being inducted into the Rock and Roll Hall of Fame, alongside the Drifters, the Beach Boys, Bob Dylan, and the Beatles. Again it was me and me alone representing my group.

For the past two decades I had made it my job to keep the legend and the memory of the Supremes alive. Florence Ballard had died tragically a dozen years before, and my other singing partner, Diana Ross, had decided that she was far too busy to even acknowledge the group that had made her a household word. Like our millions of fans worldwide, I was proud of the Supremes and our accomplishments. I believed and feared that no one would ever care as much about the Supremes as I did. Today, over two decades later, I know that for a fact.

As I accepted the crowning honor of my long and exciting career as a Supreme, I found myself apologizing for Diane's unexpected absence. But I wasn't totally surprised. Since she left the group in 1970 to become the legendary "Miss Ross," she's gone out of her way to pretend that the Supremes never existed and that our phenomenal success was hers alone. Diane, Motown Records, and its founder, Berry Gordy, Jr., thought they could just sweep the Supremes under the rug, and the world would forget us. But the world did not. This pitiful charade was an insult, not only to me but to everyone who loved the Supremes.

The Supremes' story was a beautiful fairy tale and a dream come true. I cannot idly stand by as Diane, Motown, and Berry try to crush all I have worked so hard to preserve. Everywhere I go, people tell me what the Supremes meant to them, and I am gratified to know that we touched millions of lives. They remind me of what Diane and Berry seem to have forgotten: that the world first fell in love with *three* young black girls from the Detroit projects, not just one. Yes, there was Diana Ross, and before that Diana Ross and the Supremes. But it all began with the Supremes. It reminds me of the old question: Which came first, the chicken or the egg? Well, I'm one chick who is damn proud of the egg she came from.

Whatever happened to the Supremes? What went wrong? What killed the promise, and the group? These are questions I've been asked time and again, but which I've never been able to fully answer. Until now.

Contrary to popular belief, or Motown's version of the story, the Supremes didn't just wither after Diane left. In spite of Motown's deliberate lack of support and its scheming against us, we had several hit records and continued to be a top draw around the world. In those years I was the group's manager, the sole original member, and along with several talented young ladies, I kept the group alive.

In 1979 I took the long-overdue plunge into my solo

career. I set about discovering who I was, both publicly and privately. My discovery process hasn't always been pleasant. While I strove to keep the Supremes on top, I faced other personal challenges: enduring a physically abusive marriage, raising my adopted son and my three natural children, regaining my self-esteem, being a working mother. I realized that not all of my enemies were external. Some were deep inside of me. There were insecurities and fears that for years my success had eclipsed and repressed, but never erased.

When I began singing I was just a happy, confident little girl. Bit by bit certain events and people began chipping away at what I felt was the real Mary Wilson. The way I thought about things like success, money, and fame were different from the way other people I encountered in show business thought about them. Many of them based their self-image on the money they earned or the trappings of success they collected. Inside, some of them were really sad and lonely people.

*If I'm already a happy person,* I thought, *I don't need all of these things to make me happy.* Many people, particularly at Motown, interpreted my attitude as ambivalence. Because I didn't assume the lead singer's role right after Diane left and instead did what I felt was best for the group, some saw me as unambitious. Since I grew up with the Motown family, I listened to these people and saw myself through their eyes. As my self-confidence plummeted, fear took its place.

When I finally took charge of the group in the midseventies, I became mired in petty squabbles and group politics. Although I was sorry to call it quits with the Supremes, I knew that it was time. Not only did I have my eye on recording as a soloist, but I also began taking acting classes and eventually performed in movies and the theater. Through all my trials and endeavors, one thing has never faltered: what I call my "Supreme Faith." I prayed to God for a life filled with challenges, lessons, and happiness, and I have gotten just that.

When my first book, *Dreamgirl: My Life as a Supreme*, became a huge success in 1986, it made me truly realize how important the Supremes were to so many people. I also realized how much the public longed for a real reunion of the Supremes. Motown's corporate machinery robbed our fans of a proper worldwide farewell tour, or a satisfactory end to our glorious career together. I too have dreamed that, as our song says, "Someday We'll Be Together." While the odds on that remain somewhat questionable, my hope and faith—though sorely tested—never falter. As I've learned, anything is possible.

The hope that Diane and I might again be friends is only a spark of a dream I once had. In 1983, during the Supremes' highly publicized reunion at the "Motown 25: Yesterday, Today, Forever" TV taping, I was the victim of Diane's volatile temper. I stood shocked as she tried to push my microphone down and then shoved me onstage during the only song we sang together that night. When the television special aired, Motown included mere seconds of the so-called reunion. It had to protect the "Motown family" image and hide Diane's shameless shenanigans.

Since then and my book's publication, Diane's behavior toward me has alternated between warmly cordial and maliciously cold. When I have attended Diane's concerts and attempted to wish her well backstage, she's rudely snubbed me. The frosting on the cake came in 1989 while Diane was on her "Working Overtime" tour. She refused to set foot outside her dressing room until I had been expelled. I never dreamed that Diane, my daughter's godmother, could be so vindictive. Typically, I publicly apologized for *her* immature behavior.

I can no longer pretend that these incidents haven't occurred. While Diane hurt me deeply on a personal level, Berry and Motown caused me endless pain by deliberately misleading me, and causing me to relinquish my rights to the group name.

Two decades later, I'm still fighting for the Supremes, even though they are long, long gone. Until Diane left, I'd never thought about the business side of my career. My knowledge was limited to the music, the stage, the recording studio, the wonderful people I'd met, and the great places I'd been. I signed my contracts, did my job, had my fun, never once even considering that there was something else making the wheels of Motown spin besides talent, camaraderie, and love. In my heart I—and my fellow performers—were just adults blessed with the ability to continue living in the dreamworlds we'd spun as teenagers when we watched our favorite acts on the stage of Detroit's Graystone Ballroom. We had music and magic and success. To me, that was a beautiful miracle, a blessing.

What turned everything so sour in the seventies? Did Motown actively conspire to kill the Supremes? Were all of the company's efforts centered so totally on Diane's career that it felt compelled to destroy my group? In reality, the dream that was the Supremes began to unravel the very night that Diane left. I'll never forget that emotion-filled evening of January 14, 1970, a night that really put my supreme faith to the test.

Although I wouldn't realize it for many years, that night I began a very hard journey. On it I learned that Motown's heart didn't beat to the driving backbeat the world danced to. Corporate politics and the bottom line called the tune. I'd put my faith in Motown not just because of what it had stood for, but for what it was; the most successful black enterprise in history. Of course, other labels treated their artists badly; we all knew that. We also thought Motown was different.

Once upon a time, I believed that machine worked for me. In truth, my talent—along with almost everyone else's at Motown—was just the grist for that mill.

# CHAPTER 1

*P*ass me your lipstick," I said to Cindy Birdsong, glancing into the dressing-room mirror. "Are you wearing that curly wig tonight? I sure wish I had brought my blond wig."

"I can't seem to make up my mind," she replied, sipping from her glass of champagne.

Just then someone knocked on the dressing-room door.

"Who is it?" I asked.

"Gil Askey," our musical director replied.

"Come on in, Gil."

"Hey girls, what's going on? Is everything all right? You guys should see out front—every star from Hollywood is out there! Marvin Gaye, Bill Russell, Steve Allen and Jayne Meadows, Smokey Robinson, Lou Rawls, Dick Clark . . ."

Behind Gil walked a delivery man with another bouquet of flowers to add to the dozens already there. Our huge makeup mirror was encircled with congratulatory telegrams from around the world.

*Another* knock: "Five minutes, Miss Wilson and Miss Birdsong!"

Diana Ross and the Supremes' final farewell performance took place at Las Vegas's Frontier Hotel, beginning near midnight on January 14, 1970, and ending in the wee hours of the following morning. Coincidentally, January 15 also marked the ninth anniversary of the original Supremes signing our first contract with Motown. As I wrote in my first book, *Dreamgirl: My Life as a Supreme*, what appeared to be an emotional send-off was a true show in every sense of the word. Yes, Diane's leaving signaled the end of an era; no one could deny that. But after having spent the last several months working whenever possible with her replacement— Jean Terrell—and Cindy Birdsong, I felt nothing but optimism and hope.

The final show started with "T.C.B.," a rousing opener, segueing into a hurried greatest-hits medley, followed by "The Lady Is a Tramp," "Let's Get Away from It All," "Love Is Here and Now You're Gone," and "I'm Gonna Make You Love Me." I then sang my solo, "Can't Take My Eyes off of You," after which Diane playfully said, "Thank you very much—now get back to your microphone!" Everyone laughed.

We sang "Reflections," and then Diane had two solo numbers, "My Man" and "Didn't We." Cindy and I returned for "It's All Right with Me," "Big Spender," "Falling in Love with Love" (from our *Rodgers and Hart* LP), and "Love Child." Next came "Aquarius/Let the Sunshine In" from the musical *Hair*. Diane moved through the room, coaxing celebrities in the audience to sing along. Smokey Robinson and his wife, Claudette, Dick Clark, Lou Rawls, Steve Allen, and other stars good-naturedly joined in on what nearly became a marathon sing-along. The show hurtled to a close with "The Impossible Dream" and, fittingly, "Someday We'll Be Together."

Toward the end of the last show, Diane officially introduced Jean as the next Supreme. Then Nevada Senator Howard Cannon read aloud a beautiful congratulatory telegram from Ed Sullivan, in which he praised us for having made it "without backstabbing and hypocrisy" and "working as a team." (If only he knew . . . ) He continued, "As of tonight, one of the greatest attractions of the sixties becomes *two* of the greatest attractions of the seventies." How I hoped he was right. Everyone cheered, tears were shed, and we were presented with huge bouquets of roses. Then it was over.

A huge, crowded party was held in one of the hotel's private lounges. After putting in an appearance there, I moved to the casino. Sitting at the blackjack table, I gave one of the greatest performances of my life. I'd left the farewell celebration because I couldn't stand being the forgotten star. It was really Diane's moment. Inside, it hurt me more than anyone knew. That I could feel such pain and yet happiness all at once surprised me even though I've always believed that because of my Piscean nature, I'm able to see both sides of an issue and to feel two seemingly contradictory emotions simultaneously.

"Hit me," I said. The dealer turned up my five of hearts. I looked at my cards; I had ten in the hole.

"Mary, you'd better stay in!" someone shouted from the side of the table. The casino was buzzing with excitement. I looked at my hand and knew my staying days were over. A fifteen would mean that I'd lose this hand of blackjack. I took a chance.

"Hit me." The dealer turned up a six. Blackjack! Everyone cheered.

"Mare, how are you doing?" It was our manager Shelly Berger's wife, Eleanor.

"Winning," I replied with a smile. Looking up I saw a tall, handsome man step out from the crowd. "That was a great show you girls put on tonight. Why aren't you back in there at the party with everyone else?"

I didn't answer but smiled politely. Most everyone was still inside, toasting Berry and his star Diane, congratulating them on their success and wishing her the best in her solo career. I was happier right where I was, being myself, having a great time.

"Hey, baby." It was my friend Marvin Gaye. As always, he had that shy, sexy smile. He touched my shoulder gently and gave me a kiss. "You were really jammin' up there tonight," he said softly. He was right. While Diane was in the audience, I was wailing loudly, as is very evident on our live farewell LP.

"Yeah, well, you really tore up the place when Diane gave you the microphone," I replied. Marvin had sung a chorus of "Let the Sunshine In" so beautifully that I, like every other woman in the room, thought we'd die. It had come toward the end of Diane's last performance with the Supremes, a tremendous moment. It also marked the end of the most exciting part of my musical career. But that isn't what I was thinking about then. I was looking ahead, ready for whatever came my way.

Lots of people assume that Diane's departure hurt me or made me bitter, but that's not how it was. Motown began engineering the change as far back as four years earlier. Despite Diane's persistent claims that she, Cindy, and I "discussed" her going solo, it was never mentioned. In fact, I first learned of Motown's plans while the Supremes were touring Europe in 1968. I'd seen the stories in the press, and after Berry changed the group name to Diana Ross and the

Supremes, speculation as to when she would leave swelled. Maybe I was naive, but it didn't occur to me that these were more than rumors until a reporter from an English music paper asked me point-blank, "What about Diana Ross leaving? What are you going to do?" He looked at me as if I knew what he meant.

"As far as I know," I replied honestly, "she's *not* leaving."

I thought back to spring 1967, when Berry said, "Mary, changing the name doesn't really mean anything, except that you girls will be making twice as much money. It won't affect your position in the group." As we stood in a recording studio, Berry had his arm around my shoulder and spoke in an even, paternal tone. "Now we have two entities: Diana Ross, and the Supremes. And people will pay more money to see you girls."

He had just fired Flo (though, to be honest, it was her fault too). Knowing that she and I were close friends, Berry wisely tried to assuage my fears and draw me back into the fold. His charming grin reminded me of a mischievous little boy. "And I want you to remember, Mary: no matter what happens, I will always take care of you."

In the last dozen years I'd lived two lifetimes, the first between 1958 and 1964, when Flo, Diane, and I became friends. We started singing together and, in our homemade stage costumes, set our hearts on a dream. This was the happiest time of my life. We were learning our profession, on the road, in clubs, and in the recording studio. It was like being in school. In 1964, when "Where Did Our Love Go" went to Number One, it was like we had graduated at the top of our class. Another life began for us, one of promise, wealth, and security. We toured the world, meeting everyone from ardent fans to royalty. Like most young people, we lived for today and thought it would last forever.

When Berry replaced Flo with Cindy, I began to grow up. I started to see that the world wasn't always good, life wasn't always happy. And being happy today didn't guarantee that you would be happy tomorrow, or ever again. Yet I did not really understand that the Supremes' success was about much more than simple dreams. There were also unchecked ambition, hard work, money, greed, and company politics. I was too much in the middle of it all to see how this would ever affect or change me.

Once I knew for sure that Diane would go, I experienced a whole range of emotions: anger, hurt, sadness, and, finally, acceptance. My decision to carry on with the Supremes and replace Diane was logical and right. The Supremes obviously needed a third member. And Motown, which had invested countless millions in creating both a group institution and a solo star, knew there was still money to be made from both acts. To the public, the Supremes were more than the label's flagship, the personification of Motown. We led the roster in Number One hits, commanded top personal-appearance fees, and continued to maintain our still-undisputed position as the most successful female singing group in history. Diane's leaving changed none of that. Even before Jean Terrell was introduced to the public, we were booked well into the next year, all prestigious rooms in Las Vegas, New York, San Juan, and Miami.

Motown officially announced Diane's plans in late 1969, and everyone wondered who would take her place. Reporters kept asking, "When will you step up to the front, Miss Wilson?" That seemed a natural move, but the mere thought of it filled me with fear. For years I'd done my solo spot in the show, "Can't Take My Eyes off of You," and always to enthusiastic applause. But as I've learned, having the voice to sing and having the talent to be a lead singer are two vastly different things. After years of being pushed into the background, told I lacked drive and a voice, I'd started believing it. I could have taken over the lead if I'd asked Berry, but I decided to put the group first. A new lead singer who could really handle the job was best for the Supremes, and that's what I wanted.

Fan magazines ran contests asking readers to nominate singers for the job. It was rumored that Florence Ballard might rejoin as a lead singer, something Motown would never have gone for. Other nominees were Tammi Terrell, by then suffering from the brain tumor that would claim her life the following year, and Syreeta Wright, a singer under contract to Motown. Because Syreeta's style and voice were similar to Diane's, she seemed an obvious choice to Motown, but I thought the "obvious choice" was a mistake. Everyone knew that Syreeta wanted a solo career, and I refused to bring in someone who saw the Supremes as a stepping stone. The Supremes had to be a team again. Berry decided on a singer he'd happened to hear in a Miami showroom in mid-1969, Jean Terrell.

Motown was following the standard procedure for replacing group members, except that unlike with the more quiet personnel changes—Flo's ouster from our group, David Ruffin's departure from the Temptations—it made this a grand occasion. This was what Diane wanted and what Berry wanted, but amid all the hoopla, *Motown* was the star. In Berry's mind, no single member was greater than any act, and no act was greater than the label. Not Flo, not me, and in the very end, not even Diane.

Today people say it was obvious that Diane was unique, that she had done all she could with the Supremes. But in fact, both within and outside the industry, many—including some people at Motown—predicted she would fail when she went solo. Not me. I believed in Diane and knew that anything she set her sights on would be hers. And while this might surprise you, I also thought she deserved it.

That night at the blackjack table, I flashed back in time to Hitsville, the original Motown building on West Grand Boulevard in Detroit. It was September 1961, nine months after we'd signed our first recording contract. Diane, Flo, and I had just finished a Smokey Robinson song called "Those D.J. Shows," a hard-driving, soulful track with a wailing sax and Flo and me singing out clearly in the background. The three of us tumbled out of the studio, laughing and hugging one another, and ran through the hallway singing, "I'm gonna be diggin' that rock and roll . . . If I don't, I'll go insane, when I'm too old to walk around with a cane, I'll still turn on those DJ shows." We really did think we'd still be singing rock and roll as a trio even when we were ninety. Now Flo was gone, and soon Diane would be too. Only I remained to hold the Supremes together.

Once, when I was very, very young, I prayed to God that he would make the Supremes a success, and my prayers were answered. Did I dare to dream again? The realization that I was no longer a carefree young girl struck me time and again. Here I was, a twenty-five-year-old woman, the single adoptive mother of a young boy, my son Willie, and the sole support of my wonderful mother, Johnnie Mae. Being the last original member of the Supremes also brought new challenges. I loved the Supremes and what we stood for. We were at the pinnacle of our career, and I was determined to keep us there.

The world in 1970 was very different from five years before. Politically, socially, musically, everything was changing. The Supremes would have to keep in step with the times, something we'd had a little trouble doing the previous two years. When Diane left, we had a Number One hit, "Someday We'll Be Together." How funny to say "we"; the record featured only Diane and Motown's house background singers, the Andantes. Despite that, this song became our anthem, because it expresses the Supremes' spirit.

As much as the Supremes were loved all around the world, the last couple of years with Diane we'd lost something of our winning form on the singles chart. Our historic run of five consecutive Number One hits was three years behind us. While "Love Child" and "I'm Livin' in Shame" were big hits, there were disappointments too: 1968's "Forever Came Today" and "Some Things You Never Get Used To," and 1969's "The Composer" and "No Matter What Sign You Are," none of which made the Top 25. For an act so often in the Top 10, those records hinted at an imminent commercial decline.

When I couldn't stand smiling anymore, I left the casino and went up to my suite with my best girlfriend, Margie Haber. I had champagne on ice, and we sat up for hours, drinking, talking, and laughing. Every once in a while, the phone rang. "You're being paged downstairs, Miss Wilson." I'd just laugh and hang up. Margie, who is Jewish, told me that I was "meshugana"—Yiddish for "crazy." I finally fell asleep around four-thirty in the morning.

A few hours later I was startled awake by the shrill ring of the telephone. I was so tired that when I opened my eyes, I couldn't even recall where I was.

"Mary? Mary? This is Berry."

"What?" Didn't this man ever sleep? It always irritated me that Berry called very early in the morning to discuss important matters, knowing he would probably wake me out of a sound sleep.

"I don't like Jean Terrell," he stated abruptly. "I don't think Jean is right."

I bolted up in bed, pushing my hair out of my face. Was this a nightmare? "What are you talking about? Didn't we just tell the world that the Supremes had accepted Jean as our new lead singer?"

"I've worked with Jean and talked with her," Berry replied, ignoring my questions, "and I am sure she won't work out." My head spun as I thought of all the work of the past half-year. By day Cindy, Jean, and I rehearsed, recorded, had gown fittings and photo sessions. By night Cindy and I sang all over the world with Diane.

"I want Syreeta Wright in the group."

I couldn't believe he was saying this. We were booked to make our national television and live-concert debuts with Jean in just weeks. I was speechless, feeling angry and betrayed. If Berry really didn't want Jean, he should have known it before. Just a few hours before, I had known, for the first time in years, where I was going and with whom. Now with a wave of his hand, Berry threatened to destroy everything.

"No way!" I answered. "Jean stays."

For a few seconds, Berry was quiet, probably as surprised as I was to hear me stand up to him. Berry Gordy might have been the lord of the manor, he might have made me a star, and he certainly could do lots of things for me. But he wasn't snatching this away.

"Mary, do you hear me?" Berry demanded. "I said Jean is wrong for the group, and I want her out."

"I heard you. And the answer is no!"

"All right," Berry replied sternly, "then I wash my hands of the group!" He hung up. I looked around my luxurious hotel suite and began to cry.

# CHAPTER 2

I left Las Vegas certain Berry would call any minute to say that Jean Terrell had to leave the group. Oddly, neither he nor anyone else at Motown ever mentioned the subject again. Still, I did fear that when Berry said he was washing his hands of the Supremes, he meant it.

Just days after the "farewell" show in Vegas, we were in the studio recording as the "new" Supremes. I found myself standing in front of the microphone with Jean and Cindy. As I looked at this new grouping of world-famous Supremes, I reflected on the first time Diane, Florence, and I were together in the studio. It dawned on me how much the three of us had accomplished. At first it felt very odd without Diane, but I realized that my life must go on and that there was no sense dwelling in the past. Jean, Cindy, and I were recording "Up the Ladder to the Roof," our first single together. Our producer, Frank Wilson, had already recorded the music for three songs: "Up the Ladder," "But I Love

You More," and "Everybody's Got the Right to Love," all for our first album, *Right On*.

As the three of us listened to the instrumental tracks over the huge studio monitor speakers, we beamed with happiness. We'd spent part of the past six months working with several great producers, but no one had created a sound as fresh and well-suited to us as this. Cindy, who had been in the Supremes since spring 1967, was smiling broadly, her eyes twinkling, and Jean looked like she couldn't wait to start singing. We knew this was going to be something very different for the Supremes, and we were ecstatic.

That day, Frank said, "Mary, you know Suzanne dePasse [Berry's chief assistant] has been pushing the idea of Motown developing more concepts for our albums. So I've come up with this for you girls. It's a world-peace concept, a higher ideal about humanity."

I was delighted that Motown was working with us to give the new Supremes an exciting new sound.

"If the few songs I produce on this LP are hits," Frank continued, "I'll have a chance to produce your next LP." I had known Frank since he joined Motown in the mid-sixties, and we were good friends. Frank's work, like that of his fellow Motown producer Norman Whitfield, represented a very clear departure for Motown and the Supremes.

In song selection and performance, *Right On* was very strong. It opened with our first gold single, "Up the Ladder to the Roof," an invitation to love, and closed with Smokey Robinson's beautiful "The Loving Country," which also expressed Frank's love concept. These new songs were more soulful than earlier Supremes tracks. As you can hear on "Up the Ladder," Frank favored an almost ethereal vocal sound, with layered voices and harmonies far more complex than in our later work with Diane, but all driven by a pulsating, bass-heavy groove. He also experimented with modern studio effects, such as the electronically phased vocals on "Nathan Jones."

One of the most exciting things for us was Frank's approach to our singing. Not only did he come up with great chord structures and harmonies that went beyond the typical I-III-V progression, but he also had Jean singing background, which gave the songs a richer vocal sound. This was something we had not done since our early days with Diane.

By the end of the session, we were flying. I sat down in the control room while Frank discussed a few points with Jean. "This is a very straight song," he said. "You don't have to oversing it." With Cindy sitting beside me, we listened as Jean glided through the harmonies we'd just put down. She made one vocal run so glorious that when I closed my eyes I thought I was back listening to a soloist at the First Baptist Church in Detroit.

Frank pushed a button, and the music stopped. "Jean, I want you to keep it simple. You're making it too soulful." When I talked to Frank later, he confessed that he hated doing that, but he had no choice. Frank didn't ascribe to the company's long-standing attitude that artists were the least important link in the creative chain. He would fight for what he believed was right for his artists and their records. He made great strides on our behalf, but even he observed certain limits and kept to the established Motown Sound.

Jean seemed a little confused, so Frank went into the studio and sang the part for her. He was so patient and good to work with. Jean, whose recording experience was limited, tended to do a lot of runs, which are the long notes singers hold while running up or down the scale. These are common in r&b because they do add soul. I was disappointed that these were being cut, but I knew what we had was perfect.

Our new sound not only celebrated the refined pop the Supremes were known for, but was more contemporary and soulful—in other words, black.

How Jean came to the Supremes is a Cinderella story. It was early 1969, and Berry and our manager, Shelly Berger, were in Miami. One evening they wandered into the Fontaine-bleau Hotel and caught a show by Ernie Terrell and His Heavyweights. Ernie, the former World Boxing Association heavyweight champ, had retired in 1967 and put together the five-piece group, which included two of his brothers. The lead singer was his twenty-one-year-old younger sister, Jean. As she later told me, "Berry immediately began taking notes on me, and after the show Ernie and I talked to Berry and Shelly until morning." Clearly, Berry was impressed with Jean's silken soprano, as anyone who heard her would be.

Several months later Jean and Ernie traveled to Detroit, where they met with Motown, but for whatever reason, nothing happened. That April Berry called Jean and asked that she come out to Hollywood, and there, the following month, she signed with Motown. Not to slight Jean, but it struck me as odd that the search for Diane's replacement would end so quickly, especially considering what was at stake: the continued success of Motown's top group. There had to be hundreds, or at least dozens, of young women who might have been Supremes. But Berry saw Jean Terrell and chose her.

Even after nine years with Motown, I still knew too little about the actual business of our career. Jean's contract was a solo contract, and from this point on Motown signed each successive Supreme individually. In effect, the label was "subletting" memberships, a development that would create problems for us in the years to come. This was another variation on Motown's "divide and conquer" method of control.

When Berry happily announced to me that he had found Diane's replacement, I was very surprised at how excited he seemed. "Mary, she's great," he enthused. "You'll love her." For a while I hadn't been so sure that he wanted the Supremes to continue without Diane. I didn't trust Motown completely but decided to wait and see. When I heard how enthusiastic Berry was, I was relieved. If Berry was behind something, then everyone at Motown was behind it too. Berry's office called to set up a time for Cindy and me to meet Jean. Berry played us a tape, and I was impressed immediately with her voice.

Jean was Diane's complete opposite. At five feet six, she was taller than both Cindy and I. In her conservative outfit, medium-length Afro, and minimal makeup, Jean was anything but a kittenish glamour girl. Instead, she projected strength and confidence. Though not beautiful in the classic sense, she had undeniable presence. Everything about her, the way she spoke and carried herself, seemed to say, "I am proud to be a black woman."

*This is wonderful,* I thought. Some critics regarded the Supremes as a "white" group; why, I'll never know. Although many of the business people and our social acquaintances were white, my success had drawn me closer to black people and black ideals. I embraced the burgeoning awareness of black culture, history, and pride. Like many blacks of my generation, I felt it important to show my blackness in every aspect of my life, especially our music. Cindy felt the same. Jean's presence provided a refreshing change.

Berry asked me my opinion of Jean. I agreed he'd found the right person, and I could see he was happy that I liked her. Over the years I'd known Berry, we'd differed many times. He knew that the group meant more to me than anything else and that my loyalty would always be to my girls and not to him or to Motown. I first made this clear to him back in 1960, when the fourth Primette (as we were originally known), Barbara Martin, wrecked his Cadillac and everyone—except one person (I've always suspected Diane)—told Berry the lie we had all agreed on.

When Berry called me on the lie, I said, "My loyalty is to my group. My girls are the most important thing in the world to me." I was sixteen, and I was crying my eyes out. From then on, Berry liked and respected me but never felt that I was, as he often said, "on his side."

The Supremes were a real group again, three equal partners all committed to a goal, just like in the beginning. Not only did we work well professionally, but personally we all got along beautifully. For me this was a rebirth.

Cindy had been a Supreme for two and a half years. An original member of Patti LaBelle and the Bluebelles, she knew Diane, Flo, and me from our days touring the black chitlin circuit. Cindy was always the consummate professional, a hard worker, cooperative and flexible. *Everyone* likes her. She also had a great deal of self-confidence and brought her unflagging enthusiasm to everything she did. Cindy never had a negative thing to say about anything, which, when you're out on the road working the way we were, is a tremendous asset. Our fans thought she was the greatest. In the beginning, some people thought she was trying too hard to be like Flo, but Cindy eventually found her place in the group and became one of the public's favorite Supremes. Today people still ask me, "Where is that Birdsong girl?"

When she first joined, Cindy, like most people, naturally assumed that because Diane was lead singer, she was also boss. It was a while before I convinced Cindy that, business-wise, we were three equals. (Unless Diane threatened, "I'm gonna tell Berry on you.") I was still very sad over Flo's departure, and I'm sure this colored my attitude toward Cindy at first. As time passed, though, we got to know each other well. She soon found that no matter how much she tried buttering up Diane, by then "Miss Ross" didn't pay much attention to either of us.

Cindy helped so much with Jean, showing her the dance steps, taking extra time with her, drawing her out. Like every young woman who would join the Supremes, Jean was both excited and awed by her new position. To be suddenly thrust to the top was a little disconcerting. Before, Jean had lived and worked in relative obscurity; now everyone would be watching every move she made, both onstage and off.

In many ways Jean was different from Cindy and me. She was one of ten children born to Lovick and Annie Terrell, who moved to Chicago from rural Mississippi when Jean was six years old. Jean's family had much in common with Flo Ballard's. Both were large, and in each everyone stuck closely together and was wary of "outsiders." Unlike Flo, Jean often spoke to reporters about her family's closeness and the fact that her older brother Ernie and her mother inspired each of her siblings to have and work toward a goal.

Anyone could see that Jean Terrell had a mind of her own. Having worked all my life with strong, outspoken women, like Diane and Flo, I respected that.

One of the happiest times I recall from these early days was when we were trying on our gowns. Jean, Cindy, and I laughed and joked as we took turns seeing which costumes fit whom. At up to $2,000 each, the gowns represented a sizable investment, and we weren't about to replace all of them. Jean joked about Diane being so thin, and Cindy said, "Mary, I guess you'll have to wear hers." Cindy struggled into my dresses, Jean ended up in Cindy's, and I took Diane's.

These were all the newer designer gowns we'd had made since Flo's departure. What happened to all the gowns before Cindy joined the Supremes is a mystery. When Diane left in

1970, all music and gowns were to be turned over to me. I am still looking for them.

Our fans finally got to "meet" Jean when we appeared on *The Ed Sullivan Show*, Sunday, February 15, 1970. Having been on this program with the Supremes approximately twenty times since late 1964, I'd come to think of the CBS studios in New York City as a home away from home. Jean had never done network television and was nervous, as we all were. But I believed our true fans and the public would love us.

Before the show, several fans came backstage. From inside our dressing room, we could hear them shouting for us to come out and sign autographs. Most were in their young teens, and we knew many by name. No matter how big the Supremes got, we always made time for our fans, because they were important to us. I'm happy to say that loyalty continues today. As fans go, ours were different; opinionated, outspoken, they let us know if they thought we were doing something wrong. One fan said, "Mary, I'm sorry, but I don't like Jean Terrell at all."

"Please just give her a chance," I replied. "Maybe we can change your mind."

I figured he was one of the fans who decided they weren't going to like anyone taking Diane's place, no matter what. Diane's leaving had split our fans into three camps: those who followed us, those who followed her, and those who loved both Diane and the new Supremes.

For this important appearance, we followed a format we and Motown had established years before: sing a standard, or a medley of standards, to show that our repertoire extended beyond our hits; then debut our next record, which, thanks to this broad-based exposure, would most likely become a hit. Motown's acts were such popular guests on any number of television variety shows that records were usually premiered sometimes just hours before release.

Dressed in identical red-sequined pantsuits, Cindy and I stood in the wings while Jean took her place onstage and began singing, "If they could see me now, that dear old gang of mine, eating fancy chow and drinking fancy wine." We joined her after the first few lines of the medley, which included "Nothing Can Stop Us Now," and fell into the routine as if we'd been doing it together forever. Jean appeared serene and confident, and Cindy and I felt more certain about her with every note.

Next we lip-synched, or mouthed the words, to the prerecorded track of "Up the Ladder to the Roof," set for release the following day. As we glided and swayed, the studio audience rocked in their seats. Even before the rapturous applause swept over us, I knew we'd won them over.

Mr. Sullivan then called us over for one of his "chats." He introduced Cindy as "Cindy Birdstone" and for a moment looked as if he wasn't sure which of us was Jean. I "helped" him out and thanked him for the beautiful telegram he'd sent us in Vegas. Mr. Sullivan wished us good luck, and as we waved good-bye, the audience went wild. The next day we got word that "Up the Ladder to the Roof" was selling out at record stores across the country. Things couldn't have been better.

By week's end we were opening at the Fairmont Hotel in Dallas. The Fairmont chain was prestigious, and we had always enjoyed working there with Diane. It also had the greatest china of any hotel we'd ever stayed in, so each time we played there, we "augmented" our "collections." Cindy had the most extensive by far, and in later years, when I had trouble booking my solo act there, I wondered if someone had gotten hip to the disappearing dishware.

As always, Motown provided a small army of professionals—arrangers, choreographers, designers, musicians, writers—to put together our new act. But as good as we were in
rehearsals, it was impossible to predict the live audience's
response. Audiences could be quite fickle, as indiscriminate
in their approval as in their criticism. Even with Diane in the
group, I knew there were nights when we weren't "on." Notes
fell flat, cues were missed, and we were not at our best. Yet
most people only had to hear the opening chords to one of
our hits, and we could do no wrong.

This engagement was important for other reasons besides it being our live debut. The Supremes now were regarded as more than a mere pop act. We had become what
our detractors called a "Vegas act," a term that didn't bother
me. Back then there were few venues for black artists outside
the chitlin circuit. With greater success, we moved up in show
business, and that meant moving into better clubs.

The Supremes were among the first rock and roll acts to
appeal to adult club-goers, and we brought black audiences
to these clubs. In 1965 we broke racial and stylistic barriers
by playing New York's Copacabana. At the time, nightclubs
were *the* hip places to be. While conquering the club circuit
was part of Motown's overall strategy to attract a more adult
audience, we wanted to achieve that as well. It meant status,
money, and career longevity. The Supremes' ascent dove-
tailed with Berry's plans to push Diane further to the front of
the group and then out on her own. Everyone benefited, but
to some critics, fans, and the record industry, club success
was a handicap, mainly because clubs attract adults, and
adults don't buy as many records as teenagers. We were
fortunate that as a rock and roll act, we were loved by *both*
the older generation and the younger record buyers.

By nature, club acts are extravagant and showy. Glamour and the Supremes were by then synonymous, so we had

no qualms about the sequined gowns, the elaborately coiffed wigs, and the glittery chandelier earrings. It was a part of performing I especially enjoyed. I loved being a woman and a star, and I loved all the dazzling trappings. Now, that's not to say it wasn't a lot of hard work. Some of those gowns weighed up to forty pounds each, and you could fry under the wigs and the stage lights. Fans expected all the glitz, and we happily obliged. From the start, it was the Supremes who demanded the gowns, not Motown. We wouldn't have had it any other way.

But what was considered an admirable accomplishment in the mid-sixties—three black girls from Detroit's inner city conquering the Copa, Las Vegas, London's Talk of the Town—now seemed like a sellout. To younger people especially, glitz plus glamour equaled white equaled phony.

With Jean and *Right On,* we expanded the Supremes' image, keeping the sequins but reviving the soulfulness some people thought we'd lost since the early records. The distinctly black rhythm & blues influence in our music was so much stronger prior to "Where Did Our Love Go," and you could really hear it in Flo's singing. Sadly, few people heard her before Berry appointed Diane lead singer. Thank God for recordings, because today people can hear Flo's wonderful voice on "Ain't That Good News" (*We Remember Sam Cooke*), *The Supremes Sing Country & Western,* and the recently released "Silent Night" (now on the CD *Never Before Released Masters*).

As I viewed our itinerary for the coming year, I saw it was filled with the same great venues we had played in the past and was every bit as hectic. Our new live act still included our two Supremes medleys with all our hits. Plus we sang "Reflections," "You Keep Me Hangin' On," and our new hit, "Up the Ladder to the Roof," as well as such standards as "Once in a Lifetime," "MacArthur Park," "Something," and "If They Could See Me Now." We threw in a few surprises: Janis Joplin's "Mercedes Benz" and a country-and-western-style medley of songs about Texas.

What excited the fans was that the formula of our act had changed. Instead of there being only one lead singer, Jean and I now shared leads. *Why shouldn't a group have more than one lead singer?* I wondered. Over the years there had been many groups that did, such as the Temptations, the Pointer Sisters, and the O'Jays.

Inevitably this lineup was compared to its predecessor, and Jean compared to Diane. Jean anticipated reporters' questions about Diane: "How do you feel about taking her place?" "What do you think of her?" "Are you and Miss Ross friends?" Their interest was understandable. Berry and Motown had been vigorously promoting Diane as the first superstar of the seventies. As uncomfortable as it may have made Jean, it couldn't be avoided.

Because it was opening night, and the crowd was dominated by show-business people and writers, we were a little nervous. Some industry people believed that Diane was making a big mistake by leaving us, and others felt that we were making a big mistake by going on without her. It seemed unthinkable to them that both the Supremes and Diane could continue successfully. I didn't see it that way at all. She was great, we were great, and there was plenty of room for us both. From the moment we swirled onstage, the audience loved Jean. As we took our bows to a standing ovation, I saw Jean smile, and I felt her anxiety about comparisons to Diane dissolve.

In those two hours, the Supremes seemed to have stepped out of Diane's shadow. But during our second show that night, the emcee announced, "Please welcome Miss Diana Ross!" A spotlight found her, Diane rose from her seat in the audience, and the crowd applauded wildly. Every newspaper made a big deal out of the "reunion of Miss Ross and her former partners." Apparently Diane had checked into the hotel that afternoon under an assumed name. Inexplicably, she never contacted me or anyone else in the group; the only time we saw her was during the show.

In April Motown released *Farewell,* a lavish, boxed, double-album documentary of Diane's last show with us. Charting at just Number 46, it wasn't one of our top-selling LPs. A couple of months later, our first album with Jean, *Right On,* was on its way to a solid Number 25; not the best showing the Supremes ever had, but certainly better than our last releases before Diane left.

The next big date looming for us was New York's Copacabana. It was so inspiring to stand on the stage where the Supremes had made history, and to feel we could do it again. Dionne Warwick, a good friend for many, many years, Glen Campbell, and Flip Wilson, whom I'd begun dating, were among the celebrities attending our opening night. We had critics eating out of our hands. The consensus was that Jean was certainly different from Diane, but it was a welcome difference. In most comparisons, Jean came out on top, especially as a singer; they felt her stage presence was more natural.

Over the next few weeks we appeared before sellout crowds in Washington, D.C., and San Francisco. A writer for the *Miami Herald* stated the general critical view of us: "Miss Ross has been replaced by Jean Terrell, a singer who, if not quite so unique, is a much better singer. . . . For the first time in years there is a true attempt to produce a really elegant harmony. And the two remaining members . . . [are] no longer merely hooting owls for a lead singer." This was what the Supremes were in the very beginning, and I couldn't help wondering how things might have been different if we'd returned to this format before Flo left. This is not to say that I objected to Diane as lead singer; I am happy for all the hits with her as lead. We should have been allowed, however, to share more on album cuts and in concerts.

Another reviewer applauded Motown's taking us in a new direction: "Instead of slipping in a Xerox copy [of Diane], Motown has mainlined quality and class into the act, mostly abandoning the old Supremes sound and creating an entirely new concept instead." Although only a handful of writers came out and said it, what they meant was that with Jean the Supremes were once again "black enough."

Considering all the positive signs, I almost forgot about Berry's threat to wash his hands of the Supremes. In only a few months we had proved ourselves on television, on stage, and on the charts. "Up the Ladder to the Roof" was on its way to Number 10 here and Number 6 in England. I felt stronger every day. *No*, I thought, *nothing—not even Berry—can stop us now.*

# CHAPTER 3

New York City and Los Angeles are the centers of the entertainment world, and as the original Supremes started doing more television work, we often found ourselves on the West Coast for weeks at a time. Motown even established an office there in 1965. My main reason for moving west in 1969 was to have a private life away from Motown and its chaperones. Initially, Cindy and I stayed at the Beverly Comstock Hotel; we felt like two kids running away from home.

In 1965, when Diane, Flo, and I each bought our first house on Detroit's west side, I never imagined that I wouldn't live there for the rest of my life. This was my home. But when the Detroit riots hit, everything changed. I came home one day from a tour to see the city in flames. I was driving on the Edsel Ford Expressway when an Army truck packed with armed soldiers pulled alongside my car. Through a bull-horn one announced: "Please get off the streets! No one is allowed in the streets!" I hurried home.

From my kitchen window I watched in disbelief as men, women, and little children carried radios, televisions, stereos—even stoves and refrigerators—they had taken from the burning stores. All day long gunshots crackled in the distance. The hometown I loved was dying.

Flo stopped by to visit that day; her house was just two blocks down the street from mine. She had only recently left the Supremes. I told her that I planned to move to California soon, and she replied, "Mary, girl, if I could, I would too. But I've got my family, and I belong here with them."

As much as I hated to leave my hometown, my mind was made up. We were stars, and I was going where the other stars lived. Though I had to leave my family and friends, in late 1968 I happily packed all my belongings and watched the van as it disappeared down the street—heading west.

I initially rented a house in Nichols Canyon, in the Hollywood Hills. Isolated by trees, it felt like you were living out in the country, and I loved the solitude. I'd grown up idolizing Doris Day and in love with Hollywood, and the very idea that I now lived there thrilled me. The very look of the place was exciting. The sun always shone, so you never had to wear winter coats and boots. I saw palm trees instead of smokestacks, flowers in the winter instead of snow, rolling hills instead of skyscrapers. To me this was paradise, and I swore I'd never leave.

On any given day, you could run into stars on the streets in Hollywood, or in Beverly Hills. It was a haven for fun and drama in those days. In Los Angeles I discovered a whole community of people who did the same kind of work I did, who understood this lifestyle. I loved it from the beginning and started making new friends very quickly. Today Hollywood is much more casual about its stars; but when I moved there it was every bit as glamorous as what I'd seen in the movies.

MARY WILSON

Everything about my new life was so eye-opening. People were walking around in shorts, conscious of their health, and on self-improvement kicks. I too joined in, immediately taking Yoga and acting classes, becoming a vegetarian, and reading self-awareness books. I had my astrological charts done, and read about nutrition and different philosophies. Everyone wanted to improve their lives, and I did too. I loved this new freedom. The lure of Hollywood had gotten to me: driving up and down Sunset Boulevard, stopping into Schwab's Drug Store, shopping on Rodeo Drive, and basking in the sun year-round. I had arrived in "Surf City U.S.A." And, if I had been the local party giver in Detroit, I really blossomed in L.A. Since the Supremes were the rage, people flocked to my parties in the Hollywood Hills, to see what the Supreme glamour and glitz was all about.

Part of my new lifestyle included perfecting my craft. Probably the single most important thing I did was to start taking vocal lessons. Back in Detroit, none of us ever thought about taking voice lessons, but in L.A. it was the thing to do. My first teacher was Seth Riggs, with whom I made great improvements in just a short time. But, one night I went backstage to see my friend Freda Payne. She told me about her teacher Giuseppe Belestrieri, whom everyone calls "the Maestro." He is responsible for turning my voice into the strong instrument it is today. Once I learned from him how much of my singing problems could be solved simply through physically strengthening my vocal cords, my confidence began to return.

Less than six months after moving west and living in a rented house, I found my dream home, tucked away in the Hollywood Hills on Rising Glen Road. It was a beautiful ranch-style house that overlooked the entire city. The view of Hollywood was fantastic, and on a clear day you could see all the way to Catalina Island. It was truly a dream come true. I particularly loved the gigantic swimming pool. Between that, the fireplace, and the sauna I was sold. I set about designing everything in the home to suit my casual personality. There were only two actual chairs to sit in; everything else consisted of huge pillows, low coffee tables, plush green velvet draperies throughout, and a mirror-lined hallway that was twenty feet long. Often I would sit there and meditate when I wanted to be alone. My bedroom was all done in red velvet draperies and red carpeting, to match the oversized round bed that I bought—to make sure that I never woke up on the wrong side of the bed. Because we had done so much traveling in Japan in the sixties, I fashioned my kitchen in an oriental style. Guests were always amazed that they had to sit on the floor when I invited them over for dinner. Also in true Japanese style, I requested that everyone remove their shoes upon entering my house.

It was a fantastic house, and at first I filled it with dogs and cats and friends. Now that I had a secure, promising future, I longed for someone to care for, someone with whom I could share the life I'd built, a husband and children. At the time, my older cousin Christine had several children. Her eldest son Willie was eleven and seemed to need more attention than her other kids. Whenever I was in Detroit, I'd make the rounds, visiting all my extended family. Willie's grandmother told me that he had a discipline problem and that they were considering placing him in a reform school.

I firmly believe that in Willie, God gave me a chance to do something for someone in my own family. So I asked Christine if I could perhaps have Willie come live with me, so that I could give him the attention he needed. Because I had seen so many children in my travels around the world whom I would have loved to adopt, I felt that here in my own family was someone who needed some special care and could benefit from the love that I wanted to give. In California he would live in a more pleasant environment, attend special schools, and experience a different life than what he knew in Detroit. Although I never adopted him legally, Willie was, and is, my son. I believed that I could really help him through the sheer force of my love.

He moved out to California with me, and I assembled a household staff that included a woman to take care of him while I was away. Having grown up poor, I knew nothing about having maids or other servants, except for what I'd seen on television. In Detroit I'd always done my own house-keeping, with my mother or cousin Josephine helping, but now I was living the life of a star. I hired a wonderful young manservant/personal secretary named Harry Pondichelli, who waited on me hand and foot. A single woman would never dream of having a manservant in Detroit. Hollywood was just different.

The situation with Willie paralleled my own early child-hood. Because my natural mother was unable to care for me, when I was three her sister, my Aunt I.V., and her husband, John L. Pippin, took me to Detroit. I lived with them until I was ten. In a way, I tried to re-create for Willie the good parts of my experience with I.V. and John. I showered him with love and many of the luxuries he didn't have at home. Willie's bedroom in the Rising Glen house was decorated with a big bed that looked like a stagecoach, and he had a pet boa constrictor, which kept unwanted visitors away. The rare times when I was home, we spent hours together, lying by the fireplace and playing chess. He was wonderful, play-ful, and sweet when I was around. But like most kids, he resented my being away. Being a career woman and a mother was hard at first, but I loved the new responsibility.

I found "instant motherhood" fulfilling. Caring for Willie gave my life balance. No matter what else you've accom-plished, learning to handle a child is a unique, rewarding challenge. Not all of it was easy. I was a single working mother with many hats—or in my case, wigs—to juggle. Whenever possible, I took Willie along with me. He had some wonderful experiences, such as meeting royalty in England and counting among his friends some of the Jackson 5. However, growing up in Hollywood had its drawbacks too, and I'm afraid that he was also exposed to things most kids don't see until their late teens. Like any working mother, I wondered if I was doing the right thing for my son by continuing my career instead of staying home.

When I was growing up I had always heard about wild Hollywood parties. I started frequenting popular exclusive private clubs in Beverly Hills, such as the Candy Store, the Daisy, and Pips, where on any given night you could run into Peter Lawford, Liz Taylor, Tom Jones, Joe Namath, and countless others. It was at this time that I really got into the Hollywood night scene. I loved entertaining friends. Soon my house was filled with people like Diahann Carroll, the Dells, the Pointer Sisters, Ron Ely (TV's "Tarzan"), Brock Peters and his wife, Lola Falana, Glynn Turman (who later married Aretha Franklin), and Lincoln Kilpatrick, just to name a few.

When I threw parties, I always did my own cooking. I would go down to Chalet Gourmet for beluga caviar and stock up on cases of champagne and white wine—which were very "in" at the time. Hard liquor was un-chic, because everyone was on such a health kick. Often the parties were impromptu get-togethers after an evening of dining and dancing at the Candy Store. If someone like Frank Sinatra was holding court there, just getting into clubs like this—of which I was a paying member—was a hassle. It was bizarre to see celebrities waiting in line for hours just to get in. The Candy Store was set up like a 1920s speakeasy, with a peephole for the doorman to see the patrons.

I had been protected from the devastation of the psychedelic drugs that were prevalent in the late sixties and became so popular with the counterculture. The Supremes were considered goodie two shoes compared to Jimi Hendrix, Sly and the Family Stone, and Janis Joplin. Because marijuana had gradually crept into all walks of life, it was something that I would tolerate, but had no desire to indulge in. Even doctors and lawyers would smoke a joint after a hectic day. One day in early 1969 I told one member of a very popular singing group, "If you have to smoke that, go out in the backyard, because I do not want it in my house." I was square!

To say that I was naive about drugs is an understatement. For several months I dated a guy who—unbeknownst to me—smoked marijuana regularly. I never understood why he simply smiled at me whenever I offered him a drink and told him to "loosen up." When I ran into him a few years later, he laughed because he said, "It was so funny. I used to just die laughing, because you were trying to loosen me up with a drink, and I was already mellow from the joint I'd just smoked!"

One night, while I still lived in my rented house, some friends and I decided to play Bullshit. This is a verbal game that we used to play with our Motown cronies like Gladys Knight and the Pips while touring. However, as the night got later and the drinks flowed, we turned this already crazy game into an even hotter and more exciting event. This time around my roommate, Gina, said, "Why don't we make each person who loses strip?" I hesitated, while Marvin Gaye stammered and blushed profusely. So, it was agreed that we would remove only our outer garments—like shirts, pants, and skirts. No, it didn't get any further.

When I did encounter drugs in Hollywood sometime in the early seventies, it was not as I'd imagined. Marijuana usage had long been widely accepted. Cocaine was another story. However, the way it was presented in the Hollywood scene, it wasn't perceived as something done in a back room or a dark alleyway, or by junkies.

It was usually served in a private study or bedroom. The best parties were usually given by movie producers, and a group of elite partygoers would be invited to indulge. It was served with the formality of having champagne in a champagne bucket.

When I first started attending Hollywood parties I wasn't aware of what went on behind closed doors. There was always the general party and then a more exclusive "private" party going on in another room. After I'd been in Hollywood a while, I was allowed to enter those back rooms.

There, cocaine was served on a Waterford crystal dish with a sterling silver spoon, like an exotic spice to be indulged in by the elite. It wasn't presented like the taboo and degrading substance I had heard about. It was the crème de la crème of Hollywood indulging in its own opulence, and most of us didn't realize the danger that it would hold in the future because of the glamour that surrounded the scene. We had all been convinced that we were enjoying a better, safer high than pot or champagne—myself included. It had gotten to the point where people were wearing expensive "coke spoons" on gold chains around their necks. In the coming years, too many people would be ruined by the very things we thought were so harmless in that era.

For years in the sixties Berry warned me that I was "too available" to the public in general and to men in particular. "If you keep more to yourself and stay in your hotel room instead of going out, you'll have more of a star mystique," he would say. "Be more like Diane."

I saw his point, but I wasn't out there only to be a star; I was out to live my life too. I knew how men were, and that's what *I* would call loose. They slept with as many women as they could handle physically. When the Supremes were on tour, we saw women prowling backstage, in hotel lobbies, and in hallways—everywhere—for male stars. Men don't run after women like women run after men. As a woman in show business, I had precious few opportunities to meet men.

Stars from the music business now mixed with people in film and with sports figures as well. The handsome football player-turned-actor Jim Brown lived just up the street from me. I'd known Jim for a couple of years, and it was he who introduced me to Mike Warren around 1969. Mike was then a star basketball player for UCLA. Mike and I started dating. He and I danced many nights away at the Daisy in Beverly Hills, and he took me to all of the UCLA games where I watched him, as the team's captain, play with Kareem Abdul-Jabbar (then Lew Alcindor) and Magic Johnson in their last years of college basketball.

After my relationship with Mike Warren ended, I met and fell in love with Mike's best friend, actor Jack Lucarelli. He was very gregarious and fun. Jack and I took acting classes together and he was wonderful with Willie. Jack invited himself to move in with me, which was fine, but I learned from this experience that I was naturally sort of laid back when it came to assertive men. I needed to speak up for myself more, but how? It was something I vowed to work on.

Not all the men I met were lovers. One of the first people I encountered after moving there was Dr. Hurbert Avery, a successful black physician a few years older than me. He and I checked each other out, but we decided that being friends would be better than being lovers. We have remained friends all these years, and he not only delivered all three of my children in the seventies but was always someone I could turn to. It was Hurbert who helped me when I suffered a bout of depression when I learned Diane would be leaving the Supremes, and he stood by me when I was going through the last stages of my affairs with Tom Jones and the Four Tops' Duke Fakir. When he married, his wife, Mauna Loa, and I became best friends too.

The men I did fall in love with were often other stars. In the mid-sixties I had ended my long relationship with Duke Fakir. I suppose because in my first book I wrote so much about Tom Jones, people assume that he was *the* love of my life. He was certainly one, but the real one was Duke. We still saw each other on and off through the late sixties and early seventies. He is a wonderful person. And by then, my affair with Tom was over, even though we remained friends.

Hollywood offered many more opportunities to meet men, and I'm not ashamed to admit that by the 1970s I was definitely husband hunting. I was at a Hollywood party with Bob Jones, Motown's publicity director, when across the room I spotted actor Steve McQueen. Deep inside I was still an old-fashioned girl, and so I often asked a male friend to introduce me to another man. Even in that era of changing mores, I felt awkward approaching strangers.

After sneaking a few glances Steve's way, I was certain he was looking at me too. Bob introduced us, and we hit it off from the start. He had undeniable charisma. Like many movie stars, Steve was interested in and intrigued by people from the music business.

Despite Steve's reputation for being wild, he was very, very quiet and didn't like being around too many people. He was very gentle, sensitive, and could spend hours talking about anything: animals, comic books, the music business, or weighty philosophical issues. He could be very childlike and sweet. We usually met at his house in Malibu, where we smoked grass on the beach. Steve kept our relationship a secret. It was more an intense friendship than an affair, but there was a physical side to it. He called me his "exotic doll."

Even though I was looking for a husband, several otherwise good relationships ended whenever the subject of marriage came up. This is what happened with Flip Wilson. I first met him in the sixties, when we were playing Leo's Casino, a popular Cleveland club and chitlin-circuit landmark. At the time the Supremes had a couple of hits. Flip was a stand-up comedian in the Redd Foxx mold, performing and recording sexually explicit material.

One evening at Leo's, Diane, Flo, and I were standing in the wings, blushing at Flip's act. After the show, Berry, who was always very protective of "his girls," cornered Flip backstage. "Listen, man, you're going to have to clean up your act, because my girls are good girls. We can't be on a show with acts like yours." The three of us stood out of sight, giggling as Berry threatened to cancel our dates there if Flip didn't tone down his material.

Flip did clean up his act enough to finish the gig, but Berry kept us away from him as much as he could. Flo, Diane, and I still snuck out to see Flip between shows, though. Our paths crossed dozens of times over the next few years, and Berry's warnings aside, we hung out with Flip whenever we worked together. At the time, Flip and I became close friends, but nothing serious. I just thought he was a terrific guy.

Like most people, I'd always thought of Flip as a very funny man. But as I got to know him, I learned that he rarely cracked a joke offstage. At first I found this strange, but I grew to respect his ability to separate private life from public life. I've always been drawn to creative men, but few are secure enough to share their creativity with a woman.

You wouldn't necessarily look at Flip and say, "Hey,

he's sexy," but I can tell you he really was. Flip was terribly romantic and loved women, not just for their bodies or their feminine qualities, but for their intelligence. That was something I always liked in my male friends, and to have it in a love relationship made it even more special.

Flip would sit for hours, writing jokes and working out different situations for material, then say, "What do you think of this?" He'd perform the material for me as if he were on stage. I'd be nearly convulsed with laughter, and with a totally straight face, he'd ask, "What do you think?"

"That was hilarious, Flip!"

"Oh. Okay. Great." Then he'd resume his writing.

After I moved to Los Angeles, Flip and I spent more time together. Willie liked Flip a lot too. He would talk and joke around with Willie, and was a very positive influence.

Flip and I took long, quiet walks, and I loved cooking for him. He would call me up and say, "Make sure you have my dinner ready." One day I decided to make him my famous lemon meringue pie and ended up severing a finger tendon trying to catch the glass pie plate as it fell off the counter. My finger still doesn't straighten out completely. If anyone asks, I say that Flip cut my finger. Or the devil made me do it.

At the time, black people were pulling together, socially and politically, but intermarriage between successful blacks and whites was on the rise. Interracial dating was basically accepted, but any mixed couple would always get second looks wherever they went. Many blacks, myself included, felt it was important to marry within the race. I thought that marrying a black man would complete my life. I was proud of being black and believed that as a black public figure I should set an example. Many black men I knew felt the same way. It wasn't only because of the times; I saw it as a very natural impulse, an expression of blackness.

MARY WILSON

36

Flip and I had finished dinner one evening when he became very serious and said, "Will you marry me?" Though I cared for him deeply, I had to say no. There was real love between us, but not the kind I thought went into a marriage. When I told Flip that I didn't think we should marry, he became very upset. "You black women," he grumbled, "when you find a good man, you turn around and marry a white guy."

"Flip, I really do want to marry a black man, but I can't marry you just because you are black."

"I'm a nice guy. I've made something of myself," he implored. "I love you."

I don't know if Flip understood that I was as hurt as he was, but I couldn't see us having a solid marriage. I thought then that only a passionate, all-consuming love could make a marriage. Today, I know differently. Unfortunately, I didn't convey my thoughts to Flip as clearly as I might have. For several months he was very angry, and I respected him for reaching out for the same ideal I too was searching for. Eventually we got to be friends again, but not without some awkwardness.

On May 24, 1970, Cindy became the first Supreme to marry while still in the group. Her husband was a debonair white guy named Charles Hewlett. They met a couple years earlier when he came backstage to see us in Las Vegas. The ceremony took place in the Crystal Room of the San Francisco Fairmont Hotel during one of our engagements. It was a small wedding, with just close friends and family, as well as our band and other people we worked with. The reverend said some beautiful words, very much in the spirit of the times—"God, help us to be groovy people so that our minds will be open"—and read from Kahlil Gibran's *The Prophet*. I was so happy for Cindy and believed in my heart that I would find that same happiness for myself. Someday.

Cindy, Jean, and I were having a ball traveling the country. Our friendship was growing, and everything looked bright for the new Supremes. Throughout the summer we performed live and on television. Prime-time variety shows were still a staple of TV programming, and we appeared regularly on most of them (*The Flip Wilson Show, The Ed Sullivan Show, Glen Campbell's Goodtime Hour,* and later, *The Sonny and Cher Comedy Hour*). In addition, we were popular guests on television specials hosted by Bob Hope, Kate Smith, and other stars, and on talk shows such as David Frost's.

I particularly remember a summer appearance in Central Park, one of our best dates ever. We had special stylists, and a young black designer named Stephen Burrows created for us short, stretchy, white gowns. As Stephen dressed us, he remarked, "Everyone's going to just die when they see you ladies slither out onstage with these sexy dresses. They even get to see your legs!"

Rather than wear our usual elaborate wigs, we had our own hair styled very simply, just pulled straight back off the face and adorned with silver hair ornaments. Standing in the wings, Jean, Cindy, and I looked at one another. We did look fabulous. *And yes,* I thought, *we're going to do it all over again.*

When we strode onstage, the audience went wild. I guess it had been many years since anyone saw a Supreme in anything but a flowing gown or an elegant pantsuit. The sun was just setting; grand old trees surrounded the entire Wollman skating arena; and behind us loomed the old, graceful buildings of Manhattan's Central Park South. It was one of those thrilling moments when everything a performer gives out comes right back tenfold. The ecstatic crowd wouldn't let us leave.

We returned to the Frontier in Las Vegas, scene of the big farewell eight months earlier. Comedian George Carlin opened for us. George wasn't the only comedian we worked with in those days. Rodney Dangerfield, Herb Eden, and Stiller and Meara were just a few of the great ones who were our opening acts.

This particular night in Vegas was fantastic. Ed Sullivan and his wife visited us in our dressing room, and exclaimed how great the group was. Sensing that he still wasn't sure who was who, I said, "Hello, Mr. Sullivan. Mary Wilson." He looked relieved to see that I was one of the girls he'd known since 1964, and that he wouldn't have to guess who was Cindy and who was Jean.

We now knew that the early enthusiastic reviews weren't just flukes. One critic wrote, "The Supremes with Diana Ross were great; without her they're just as good, sometimes better." When we got home from a series of one-nighters through Texas and the South, I was tired but very pleased.

Because I led such a hectic life, I found it comforting to write in the diary I'd kept since I was a teenager. My diary was like my best friend, and in it I expressed a quieter, more vulnerable side of myself than the world usually sees. I wrote:

November 3, 1970

The tour is over, and I am glad. It was one of those decadent tours (private jets, private dinner affairs, etc.), but working in Texas was hell. For example, one show was in a jet hangar. It was over 100° on stage every night, and it was all one-nighters. Sometimes when you're building a career as we are, you have to do extra work. I thank God for this chance to accomplish great things again.

We don't hear more cracks about Diane when we're onstage, so they have accepted us without her. But we need a smash to put us directly on top again. I think "Stoned Love" and the LP will do it.

I put all my hopes on our second album, *New Ways . . . but Love Stays.* The performances were uniformly strong, especially our Top 10 hit "Stoned Love." The dramatic orchestrated intro dissolved into a gritty, danceable groove, topped by strings and joyful harmonies. It and many of the other songs on this album captured us as we presented ourselves live: three identifiable vocalists. The record includes beautiful versions of Simon and Garfunkel's "Bridge Over Troubled Water" and the Beatles' "Come Together."

Frank Wilson's contribution to the Supremes at this point was invaluable, and in many ways analogous to Holland-Dozier-Holland's work with the original group. Though the Supremes recorded with several producers before and after H-D-H, it was their songs that initially defined our sound: "Baby Love," "Where Did Our Love Go," "Come See About Me," "I Hear a Symphony," "Stop! In the Name of Love," "You Can't Hurry Love," "You Keep Me Hangin' On," "Back in My Arms Again," "Love Is Here and Now You're Gone," "My World Is Empty Without You," and others. The team's defection from Motown in 1967 was a major blow to the label, but no group felt its impact as acutely as the Supremes.

Frank was one of Motown's younger producer-writers. Along with Berry, Hank Cosby, Deke Richards, and R. Dean Taylor, he had coproduced "Love Child" and "I'm Livin' in Shame," both of which he also cowrote. Aside from his work with us, Frank is best known for producing ex-Temptation Eddie Kendricks ("Boogie Down" and "Keep On Truckin' "), the Four Tops ("Still Water [Love]"), and the young Michael Jackson ("Got to Be There"). Although Frank was not as well known outside of Motown as were some other writers and producers, he was an influential figure. Marvin Gaye credited the Tops' album *Still Waters Run Deep* as the inspiration for his *What's Going On.*

In those days Motown always recorded us on the run. We made our first records with Frank in the little time we could grab between shows. We hurried into the studio, learned the songs, rehearsed them, then recorded our vocals over a prerecorded instrumental track. Today I regret not always being more involved with the writing of our records, especially our albums.

The original Supremes made it when singles counted most, and albums generally consisted of a hit or two, plus eight to ten tracks of "filler." By the early seventies, however, LP sales had become more important. Yet except for albums by writer-artists Marvin Gaye and Stevie Wonder and Norman Whitfield's work with the Temptations, Motown still relied on hit singles. Those of us who didn't compose our own material had less input when it came to our albums. That isn't to say we made no creative contributions (even in the sixties, Diane, Flo, and I helped arrange some of our harmonies), but it wasn't enough.

Cindy, Jean, and I posed for a group portrait in naturals, scant makeup, and black turtleneck sweaters. It was simple, classy, and the shot that I strongly believed should have been the album's front cover. What Motown put out instead was a hodgepodge of little round pictures of us in various stage costumes. At this point in our career, every aspect of our presentation was critical. The baby-pink background with hot-pink girlish type looked outdated: the wrong image at the wrong time.

Even worse, Motown decided the LP couldn't be titled *Stoned Love.* Yes, albums were important, but it took smash singles to draw public attention to them. The country was then in the midst of an antidrug hysteria, with self-appointed experts "discovering" drug references wherever they looked, even in the old Peter, Paul and Mary children's song, "Puff the Magic Dragon"! Our singing "Stoned Love" was actually edited out of a national television show for this reason. Sure, there were drug references in music, but not in *our* music.

When Frank wrote of a stoned love, he meant a real love, a solid love. Just one listen to "Stoned Love," and you knew that it was about love, peace, and faith in God, not getting stoned on drugs. Strangely, Motown didn't hesitate to release the single "Stoned Love" into this hysterical climate, yet worried about an LP with the same title.

I still maintain this album should have been the record to put the Supremes back on top. I think that through its neglect and carelessness, Motown squandered our big chance. *New Ways* settled at a very disappointing Number 68, a poor showing for an album bearing a gold single.

My dismay with the label was eased by the Top 20 success of "River Deep—Mountain High," which we recorded with our friends the Four Tops. (The single came from *The Magnificent 7*, the first of three LPs our two groups did together.) Since Diana Ross and the Supremes enjoyed two phenomenal albums and two historic television specials with the Temptations in 1968 and 1969, pairing us with the Four Tops was a natural. "River Deep—Mountain High" was an exciting record, and Levi Stubbs's and Jean's voices a dynamic combination.

As 1970 ended, we could look back on our first year with pride: two gold singles, four Top 25 hits, and a tour schedule fully booked into 1972. Unfortunately for Diane, she hadn't made quite the solo splash she and Berry had counted on. Her first single, "Reach Out and Touch (Somebody's Hand)"—now her theme song—stopped at Number 20. (I've read that she previously recorded the song while with the Supremes, but that's not true. Even so, we often got

requests to sing it; people thought it was a Supremes song.)
That fall Diane's cover, or remake, of the Marvin Gaye–
Tammi Terrell classic "Ain't No Mountain High Enough"
went to Number One, but it would be nearly three years
before another Top 10 single.

Partly, this was no doubt due to the fact that Diane's
decision to leave the Supremes was not popular with everyone. Many people also blamed her personally for Flo's ouster.
When Diane opened solo at the Frontier Hotel, the room
wasn't even sold out. So much for the misconception that
Diane rocketed to superstardom after leaving the Supremes,
while we floundered. Berry must have been puzzled; this
wasn't how it was supposed to be.

# CHAPTER 4

No matter how enthusiastically the Supremes were received onstage or how many records the group sold, in the eyes of the corporate powers at Motown, we were employees, plain and simple. Except for Diane, none of us was treated like a star. As the Motown myth got retold and reinvented, Berry and the machine loomed larger and more important than the writers, producers, musicians, and performers. I noticed that with each year Motown assumed more credit for making the artists what they were. Whenever we were billed for a concert or television appearance, it wasn't "The Supremes," but "Motown Presents the Supremes" or "Motown's Supremes."

By the early seventies Motown began its transition from the local label, where everybody was family, to an impersonal business. Most people see the early-1968 crosstown move from the original Hitsville building on West Grand Boulevard to a large office building on Woodward Avenue as the big change, for Hitsville had been home.

In the late sixties, whenever we had a few days off in Detroit and found out the Tops or the Tempts were recording, Cindy and I went down to Hitsville and stayed all day. By the time we left, we'd seen everybody who was in town. Then a group of us would head over to my house for a party, where we'd dance, sing, and laugh all night. Motown's choreographer, Cholly Atkins, still lived in part of the duplex I owned. He'd be rehearsing some other acts in his basement, and so the party would grow. Some people believe the artists weren't as close as we thought we were. But whenever we got together, it was like a family reunion, and it's still like that today.

That first move symbolized a big change, but we would never guess how big. I was just becoming confident with my new life in California when I got the news. "Did you hear Motown is closing down its offices in Detroit and moving to Hollywood?" someone asked me. I couldn't believe it.

Without any emotions involved, it did make sense. Berry had moved there to live and found the West Coast preferable to Detroit. Business was in Los Angeles, and with Berry interested in television and movie production, the relocation made sense. The 1967 riots were a factor too.

Motown's West Coast move didn't become official until 1972, but our home base was already being dismantled. Not all those who had worked and made Motown their life were invited along; many were left in Detroit, where they had to find new jobs after years of service. Some stayed behind by choice. For the most part, the Motown family as we'd known it was over.

The biggest changes in Motown, however, were taking place behind closed doors. Once on the West Coast, Berry began turning over the day-to-day operation to handpicked assistants such as Suzanne dePasse, Ewart Abner, Barney Ales, and Mike Roshkind.

Suzanne dePasse, in her twenties, was the youngest. She'd been booking talent at a New York City club called the Cheetah and was introduced to Berry by Cindy in the late sixties. Suzanne moved up rapidly and before long was Berry's protégée. Once Berry appointed anyone, that was who everyone had to impress, even though they might talk about the person behind his or her back. Many of the old-timers wondered whether Suzanne could handle everything Berry threw her way, but she did. She also brought aboard a new way of thinking about artists and records. I must say that of anyone at the label, she seemed to be the person most behind the Supremes. Today she is the executive director of Motown Productions.

Ewart Abner, a short, fair-skinned black man, had been president of the Chicago-based independent Vee-Jay Records label. Initially he was director of Motown's management division, International Talent Management. Of all Berry's assistants, smooth, personable Abner had the best rapport with the artists, creating the impression that he was on their side. If you went to him, no matter how upset you were, he was reassuring and sympathetic, always saying that he would take care of it. Whether he actually did was an entirely different story.

Barney Ales, the head of sales, had worked with Berry almost from the beginning and in 1960 was appointed vice president of sales and distribution. Barney had a hand in writing "Buttered Popcorn," one of our early singles in which Flo sang lead.

Mike Roshkind joined Motown in 1966. Many artists referred to him as "Berry's hatchet man." On a personal level, Mike and I generally got along well. He was a very effective executive who knew how to get things done, and with Berry gradually abdicating his role as Motown's leader, the company badly needed someone like Mike. Tall and distinguished-looking, Mike, like many of Berry's upper-echelon people, was white. His friendly manner never compromised his directness, and he could turn ice-cold in an instant. Mike was the heavy, the iron fist in Motown's otherwise velvet glove.

In the early days, you always saw Berry around Hitsville and could call him on the phone. Now if you needed to reach Berry, you had to go through Mike. While Berry pled ignorance about whatever went on in his absence, we all suspected differently. Rather than delegating full authority to the executives and staffers, in truth, Berry still needed to control things. Accordingly, the new Motown was set up so that even those with titles and the trappings of power still needed Berry's approval. Everything came down to Berry Gordy. I think this was Motown's biggest problem: it relied on the personal vision of a leader who was largely out of the picture.

In Los Angeles Berry was among his peers—other big-time wheelers and dealers—and he fully enjoyed it. The first time I visited his new home, it was graphically clear that Berry was a success. His house, formerly owned by one of the Smothers Brothers, had underwater tunnels and bridges in and around the pool. Among his guests were the biggest stars in Hollywood. Berry was obviously very, very happy.

Berry's team—dePasse, Abner, Ales, and Roshkind—was pleasant enough to deal with. But it was becoming increasingly difficult to get the simplest thing taken care of. Not only was the family feeling gone, but the artists had to deal with strangers and a whole new set of rules. It was the beginning of the end for many of us. We'd come off a three-week tour and go straight from the plane to the studio, only to find that someone in charge was too tired to work or didn't feel like it. That *never* would have happened at Hitsville.

True to her word, Jean Terrell maintained her individuality and was always completely honest and forthright with the press. Motown had abandoned its long-standing policy of overseeing (basically controlling) press access, so we were freer to say what was really on our minds. And Jean did.

Like Flo, Jean was incapable of pretending to believe in something she didn't. She felt very strongly that entertainers should address political and social issues. This seemed quite a switch for a Supreme, and some people couldn't reconcile our female fantasy image with some of Jean's blunt statements. The funny thing was that Cindy and I also began commenting on political issues when appropriate, but because we were viewed as friendly and outgoing, the same statements were perceived a little differently. Maybe they didn't take us as seriously.

Jean knew that joining the group meant conforming to our image on *and* off the stage. Being a Supreme really was a twenty-four-hour-a-day job. You not only had to look your best wherever you went, you had to be your best. This meant always being a lady: dressing stylishly, being friendly to everyone, and never leaving the house without your eyelashes. After so many years, and having been a clotheshorse my whole life anyway, this was second nature to me, and to Cindy as well. Looking back, I'm amazed at how many column inches writers devoted to discussions of the big question: When would the Supremes stop wearing wigs and sport naturals, which to many symbolized black pride.

At first Jean found our whole glamour dimension fascinating, but it wasn't long before its thrill wore off. Little by little she took less of an interest in dressing up around the clock. If the three of us had to make a special appearance or go to an interview, Cindy and I wore clothes that were casual but chic. Jean, in contrast, preferred dressing simply, which was fine. It just wasn't what people expected. I saw no contradiction in being proud of my blackness and being glamorous. She did.

Jean admitted that some people interpreted her shyness and nervousness the wrong way. She didn't mean to appear unfriendly, but that was how many of our fans took her, which was too bad. If the three of us were together, Jean often sat by herself. She had a special friendship with Cindy, and I came to rely on Cindy and our wardrobe mistress, Jan Dochier, to communicate with her.

With the start of 1971, I resolved to take greater control of my life. As with most Motown artists, the label had always handled my business and personal finances. It rankled me to have to ask Motown's permission before I made major purchases. All I knew about how much money I had was what Motown told me; I never saw any statements.

When I finally hired outside accountants to look into my personal business and the Supremes', I was shocked to discover that the "hundreds of thousands of dollars" Berry and Motown had repeatedly assured me were in my account actually amounted to *one* hundred thousand. And when I asked that it be released to me, I was told I needed Berry's signature!

My first reaction was anger; I'd been betrayed, fooled. After I calmed down, I dialed Berry's number.

"Hello, Berry. This is Mary. Look, I want to handle all my own money now."

"What do you mean?" he asked, surprised. "Mary, you can't take it out. This is one hundred thousand tax-free dollars. My name is on it for your protection."

*Protection from what?* I wondered. I was also a little mystified by this "tax-free dollars" business. Of course at this point it was tax-free; I'd already paid the taxes on it years ago when I earned it!

Berry finally gave in reluctantly. This was a positive first step, but it still hurt me. Motown had always told us it was investing the money for our own good. What I had were a few stocks and an investment made purely for its tax write-off value. Before, I knew that I didn't fully understand my own business; now it hit me how much I didn't know. For example, I didn't know how many records the Supremes sold, what expenses we'd paid over the years, or what I was entitled to. People at Motown had led me to believe I had made millions, and why would I have doubted them? *After all,* I thought, *the Supremes have made Motown many millions.*

I remembered all the times journalists asked, "How are you girls set for the future?" I'd smile and proudly say, "Oh, Motown is investing for us. Plus all of our taxes are paid on time. We're being well taken care of." I guess the laugh was on me. Now, this isn't to say $100,000 is small change; it's not. But put it in perspective: an artist with a midlevel hit makes that amount on a single record. When I think about our twelve Number Ones—more than anyone in our time except the Beatles and Elvis Presley—plus the hit albums, the television specials and appearances, the sold-out concerts, and then see what I have to show for it all, it makes me sick, and, believe me, I was not a big spender.

As I probed more deeply into my finances, I realized I needed an expert's help. Chuck Barnett from the William Morris Agency told me of a young Englishwoman named Hazel Bethke who might fit the bill, and she did. Hazel brought order, friendship, and a spiritual love into my life that endured for many years. Although she left me in 1989, I will never forget her tireless efforts to keep my personal and professional lives running smoothly in the early days. She worked around the clock, was available for any emergency, whether it was taking care of Willie or dealing with the banks or Motown. With Hazel's help I could really begin to direct the

Supremes' career and oversee business details that would have been unthinkable otherwise.

On January 20, 1971, Diane married Robert Silberstein (known professionally as Bob Ellis), a white public-relations executive, in Las Vegas. It was a surprise to a lot of people. When I heard the announcement on the radio, I smiled to myself and recalled how Diane used to ask me, "Mary, what do you see in all those white guys you date?" She always thought she would wed Berry someday, so I guess the question of marrying a white man never crossed her mind back then. Exactly why she did not become Mrs. Berry Gordy has never been totally clear. Only a year before at the farewell show in Vegas, Diane had said from the stage, "I am now part of the Gordy family; I am a sister." But as much as Berry may have loved Diane romantically, his primary attraction to her was—and would always be—professional.

In February we began work on our last album with Frank Wilson, *Touch*, probably our most rock-oriented work and, I think, our best. We recorded it all over the country, wherever we happened to be performing. The first single, "Nathan Jones," was the most unusual hit of our career, with its unorthodox blues-based structure and unison lead singing. Jean's vocals are pulled out of the mix ever so slightly, then our three voices break into harmony. As with almost everything Frank did for us, we loved this the minute we heard it. The psychedelic electric guitar and electronically treated vocals made "Nathan Jones" a great, unique record, and it reached Number 16, our fifth consecutive single to go Top 25.

This album was the first Supremes LP to be reviewed by *Rolling Stone*. As much as I've always taken critics with a grain of salt, the review showed me that we could reach a new, wider audience. "*Touch* is an unqualified success and the final proof that the Supremes will continue without Diana

Ross," Jon Landau wrote. Other critics continued to note our new concept and direction.

For reasons I could only guess at then, Motown simply didn't push the LP or the follow-up single, "Touch." The latter was different for us, because while I was singing some leads on each album and in our shows, this was the first 45 we'd released with Jean and me sharing leads. The lyrics were very sexy; this was a real soul love ballad. Still, nothing. It was our first flop, stalling outside the Top 40. Perhaps Berry's threat was rearing its ugly head.

Not long after *Touch* we stopped seeing Frank Wilson around. He was deservedly proud of the three albums he'd made with the Supremes but understandably disappointed with how poorly they charted. Jean, Cindy, and I felt the same way. The unfortunate thing about Frank's not working with us again after *Touch* was that our new sound was finally beginning to evolve.

The Supremes' releases began having trouble just as black music was entering a state of flux. Even during the golden sixties, Motown's records could not have crossed over to white record buyers without airplay on rock-and-roll-dominated Top 40 AM radio stations. In the late sixties album-oriented "progressive" FM radio drew away millions of AM listeners. While the new FM rock stations might play records by Marvin Gaye and Stevie Wonder, most of Motown's current singles-oriented acts—us, Diane, the Jackson 5, the Four Tops—suddenly "didn't fit."

Radio, since the late fifties the great ground of musical racial integration, was again segregated. Disc jockeys, who in the fifties and sixties picked what they played, lost programming control to consultants. The reviving force of black radio would be disco, which, it turns out, was another nail in the coffin for those of us who believed there was more to black music than dance music.

Beginning with "Up the Ladder to the Roof," I noticed a distinct difference in what having a hit single meant. In the sixties a Top 20 hit was played everywhere, and people couldn't help but know about it. That all changed. Suddenly you could have a successful hit that an average audience would not immediately recognize, or, worse, might not have ever heard.

In the sixties, even though not everyone in our live audience bought all our records, at least they recognized the hits. Now we would perform one of our four million-sellers—"Up the Ladder to the Roof," "Stoned Love," "Nathan Jones," and later, "Floy Joy"—and maybe receive just lukewarm applause. They didn't know our songs anymore.

Another, more insidious, reason behind this was that Motown stopped promoting our records the way it had in the past. People assume that hits "just happen," but that's not true, not even for the biggest stars. Each year thousands of records are released, yet only a few hundred get heard at all. If two acts are equally talented, the biggest difference between the unknown and the star is promotion: radio play, advertising, television appearances, print publicity. In fact, besides manufacturing the record, promotion is a record company's key job. Record promotion to radio stations is so integral to artists' careers that the government investigates instances of its abuse: payola, or play for pay. A record without promotion is like the proverbial tree that falls in the woods. Without Motown's clout behind us, we drifted.

While the Supremes were starting to struggle, Flo's solo career had quickly gone down the drain. Since leaving the group, she kept in touch with me; we called and wrote whenever we could. She was still in Detroit, married to Tommy Chapman, and the mother of twin girls. ABC Records, which signed Flo in March 1968, dropped her after her first two singles failed. Her last moment in the spotlight was a performance at President Richard Nixon's 1968 inaugural. By March 1970, when she came to see us perform at the Elmwood Casino, across the bridge from Detroit in Windsor, Canada, it was the beginning of the end of her solo career.

Only a month before, Flo became the first Motown artist to publicly break rank. She filed a $8.7 million lawsuit against the label, charging, among other things, that her firing from the Supremes was part of a conspiracy. Among the codefendants were me, Diane, Berry, Mike Roshkind, Ralph Seltzer (another Motown executive), Cindy, and Jean. As part of her original 1968 settlement, Flo received about $160,000, but her attorney misappropriated all of it. The judge had no sympathy for Flo, ruling in late 1971 that because she was unable to return any of the money and hadn't "done what she should have done" under the law, her suit wouldn't even be tried.

Flo had to name me in the suit, but I didn't take it personally, as some people thought I should. When it comes to business and law, sometimes you must do things you may not want to. I understood this, and I wrote Flo a letter telling her so. The post office returned it to me, unopened, claiming it could not deliver the letter. Flo never saw it.

While the press focused on Flo's provocatively worded charge that Diane had "secretly, subversively, and maliciously plotted and planned" to run her out, the suit raised another point that would be of increasing interest to me as the years passed: the issue of who owned the Supremes' name. Her attorneys contended that because she coined the name *Supremes,* she was entitled to share in its commercialization. They stood by this claim, even though part of the settlement she worked out with Mike Roshkind forbade her to ever identify herself as a former member of the group. For example, the word *Supremes* could not appear in her artist's biography from her new label. In addition to the $8.7 million, Flo's suit called for the Supremes name to be taken off the market.

Flo and I talked about the suit. She was extremely angry and knew that she had been terribly wronged. With little else happening in her professional life, she focused on her fight against Berry. I worried that her anger would consume her, but I also understood that you can't keep your pride and self-respect when people treat you this badly. Despite the suit's charges and all Flo's talk, she never wanted to hurt any of us, and, surprisingly, least of all Diane. Berry was a different story. She hated what he had done to her, and I don't blame her. Because now, slowly, it was happening to us.

I tried to help Flo channel her anger constructively. My main concern was that she do things right: research everything, find the right attorney, know what's going on. Instead she seemed obsessed with the very idea that she was suing Motown. She couldn't see the kinds of games they were playing, and believed that right would take care of itself.

Throughout the summer we kept up our frenzied pace, criss-crossing the country. Because the Supremes lacked a monster hit, initial enthusiasm for us started to fade. Sometimes standing onstage, even amid the cheers and applause, I sensed the skepticism of some people in the crowd. It was as if we had to prove ourselves, over and over again. There always seemed to be someone sitting out there in the dark, arms crossed, whose face said, "Show me." I fully believed we could.

For years I had been begging Berry and our managers to devise some kind of long-range plan for us. Especially once I took in Willie and Cindy married, we needed schedules where we worked six months a year, with the rest off. But now we depended more on touring to make up the money we weren't earning from records. It was a vicious cycle with just one way out: a Number One record. If we had that hit, it would be like getting sprinkled with fairy dust. Cindy and I had experienced years of professional ups and downs; we understood the business. For Jean, however, it must have felt like her gilded carriage was turning into a pumpkin before she got halfway to the ball. By mid-1971 all three of us were doing something unimaginable in Motown's earlier days: complaining publicly about our record company.

In August we teamed up with the Four Tops for a run at the Carter Barron Amphitheatre in Washington, D.C. One goal was to promote our second joint album, *The Return of the Magnificent Seven,* but, as it turned out, the album got no higher than Number 154—an embarrassment for all of us. Its successor, *Dynamite,* placed six positions lower. Within the year the Tops would be among the first of Motown's major groups to abandon Berry and his gang for another label. As Duke Fakir said, "We left Motown because we felt they were killing us, and we wanted to survive."

On opening night in Washington we made our standard fake exit and then waited in the wings, expecting the applause that would bring us back for the last number. Nothing. After a few seconds, we returned to the stage and stepped into a performer's nightmare: the audience was out of their seats, heading for the door. Jean announced, "We've got one more song we'd like to do," then we went into our rendition of the theme from *Exodus.* It was a painful, mortifying moment. How could this happen to the Supremes?

I still hadn't found Mr. Right, so although I was dating less, I was looking. In Las Vegas I met and had a brief flirtation with Bill Medley of the Righteous Brothers. Bill always struck me as a very sexy guy. He is also one of the kindest, gentlest men around. We remain friends. In fact, in 1989 he and I shot a pilot for a possible television series.

Even when we weren't working Vegas, I'd go there on

weekends and see friends' shows around town. Diahann Carroll was performing, so I caught her show. I'd known her for many years. To the public, she is a classy, beautiful woman, but among her friends she's also very friendly, soulful, and down to earth. At this time, she was dating David Frost, the English talk-show host. Seated at our table was George Hamilton. Later George and I went out on the town and had a wild time. I'd always thought he would be smug and square, but take it from me, he was anything but.

In November we embarked on a triumphant tour of Great Britain. Ever since the first transatlantic Motown Revue hit England in 1965, it's been one of my favorite places in the world. I've always appreciated that the British respect performers for what they have to offer, with or without current hits. That's why countless performers move or spend large parts of each year there and in Europe.

Our stateside lack of the elusive big hit did not diminish our British fans' love for us. In fact, as many British writers pointed out, Diane's leaving mattered very little there, and our records always charted higher and did much better in the U.K. than they did in the U.S. This was interesting, because with Diane, only one of our singles went to Number One there, compared to twelve here, and of those, only half made the British Top 10. Our track record there since Jean had joined was great: "Up the Ladder," Number 6; "Stoned Love," Number 3; "Nathan Jones," Number 5.

We played sold-out houses everywhere, which was very heartening. The highlight was a show at the Royal Albert Hall before Princess Margaret and Lord Snowdon. It was a charity event, with the Four Tops headlining. I had met Princess Margaret before, and so at the after-show party, Obie Benson of the Tops and I chatted with her at length about politics. This was one of the tours I took Willie on. Everywhere we went, he was the perfect little gentleman.

When we returned to the States in December, it marked the end of almost eighteen continuous months on the road. I decided to work even harder. Jean became more critical of Motown. She declared that she would no longer record whatever she was given but would "veto" and refuse to sing material she did not like. Some of her remarks sounded quite defensive, and writers ate it right up. She told one English reporter, "The Supremes were a status group before I came in, and my joining them didn't take away any of the status, as far as I'm concerned. But maybe in people's minds it did."

We were also growing weary of answering the same questions about Diane. Were we still friends? How often did we see her? How did it feel to go on without her? How did Jean feel stepping into her shoes? I loved and cherished the connection to the old Supremes and our—*my*—past, but I was torn. I had to be loyal to the new group, or they would feel I was a traitor. Through no fault of Diane's, her spectre still hung over us like a dark shadow.

Considering this, it came as no surprise that Jean began withdrawing from us and stating her position more strongly. Sometimes when I heard her comments or later read them, I winced. There was nothing the press loved better than a feud.

When Jean first came in she made it clear to everyone that she was not about to be one of three singing puppets. She was a true individualist, and this was why Berry wanted her out of the group following the farewell show. But instead of continuing to insist that we replace her or just firing her outright—which he could have done—he played it cool. He seemed to know that if he gave the Supremes enough rope, we might hang ourselves. Without realizing it, Jean grabbed it and ran, and so did I.

# CHAPTER 5

O kay, baby," Smokey said, "try it like this."
I sang, "Floy, floy, floy—floy joy, you're the man. I hope in some way, form or fashion I fit in your plans." He smiled. "That's great, Mary."

Cindy, Jean, and I were recording our fourth album, *Floy Joy*, with Smokey Robinson. Besides singing with his group, the Miracles, Smokey is one of the world's greatest songwriters and producers. He also has been a vice president at Motown since the early sixties. I was so surprised and thrilled when I learned we'd be working with him.

Things had come full circle. Smokey was one of the first producers to record the original Supremes; the song was "Who's Loving You," a ballad. I'll never forget the moment in 1960 when Smokey handed the lead sheet to Diane and not to me. I'd always sung our ballads and was sure I'd be doing this one too. (This was even before Berry designated Diane lead singer.) My heart broke, but I put aside my personal feelings, something I'd do a lot over the years.

While from 1964 on Holland-Dozier-Holland pretty much had the Supremes to themselves, we recorded a number of Smokey's songs, especially in the beginning. Though none was a big hit, Smokey remains one of my favorite producers to work with. He was always perfectly organized and had everything—the arrangements, the lyrics—worked out down to the tiniest detail. Being a performer himself, he really understood singers. He also gave me a great surprise: Smokey had written the album's title track with me in mind. During the sessions, he was so supportive and patient, guiding me through my lead lines on "Floy Joy." It was an experience and a kindness I will never forget.

Smokey came up with some beautiful, sexy, close harmonies, especially for "Floy Joy," and the album really sparkled. Suprisingly, while "Floy Joy" became a Top 20 hit in spring 1972 and remains a perennial favorite among our fans, few people know that it was a duet between Jean and me. A second single, "Automatically Sunshine," on which I sang lead, didn't do as well, though it did hit Number One in some local markets, including Washington, D.C., and Honolulu.

Because it was the first time I'd been in a studio with Smokey since the early sixties, we did a lot of talking, about Diane and her career (we both agreed she deserved all the good things that came her way) and about everybody else we knew, but mostly about what was going on at Motown with the Supremes. Thinking that Smokey would be more understanding than the corporate people, since he was an artist as well as an executive, I gave it a shot.

"You know, Smokey, I don't understand what it is. We're making good records and working hard, but Motown isn't giving us the push," I said. "I just don't know what we should do about it. I feel like we're getting good material but going nowhere."

Smokey thought for a minute, then said, "Why don't you talk to Berry about it? I'm sure if you do, he'll take care of it. Everything will be all right."

Smokey meant well, but he was like Diane: totally blinded by Berry's razzle-dazzle. Because Berry always treated Smokey and Diane differently than the rest of us, they see him differently than we do. Unlike most everyone else at Motown, Smokey and Diane could take Berry at his word. It wasn't Smokey's fault.

Everything about *Floy Joy* gave me hope. These tracks were the realization of what I'd felt the Supremes should be. Smokey achieved a beautiful blend of our voices, especially on "Automatically Sunshine." Again I was sure that we'd found a match as perfect for the Supremes as Holland-Dozier-Holland were in the sixties. And after losing Frank Wilson, having Smokey now was the best thing that could happen to us, and I wanted him to be our producer forever.

Cindy was expecting her first child in the fall and didn't plan to return to the group after that. She had always been very open about whatever was on her mind, and many times she mentioned that she might leave. Still, it was a surprise when she finally announced she was going. Whatever Cindy was into, she gave it her all. Her new family was no exception. Cindy's husband Charles often traveled with us, and they really enjoyed the show-business life. But once a baby enters the picture, things get complicated.

One evening in Washington, D.C., the three of us caught Stevie Wonder's show and noticed a great singer in his backing vocal group, Wonderlove. Sandra Tucker came to audition for us in Detroit and brought along her sister Lynda, whom we'd also seen in Wonderlove. Once we saw Lynda we realized that even though Sandra was a great singer, Lynda was who we wanted in the group. (Coincidentally, Sandra had replaced Cindy Birdsong in Patti LaBelle and the Bluebelles when Cindy left them to join the Supremes in 1967.)

The three of us had an instant rapport. Lynda was very outgoing and lively. When she was around, someone was always laughing. Her basic attitude was extremely positive, and that was something we desperately needed.

"You know, Mary," she said, "we have a friend in common."

"Oh, who?"

"Cholly Atkins."

As it turned out, she had rehearsed with Cholly at my house many times. Then she said, "I'm a Pisces," and I said, "I am too." That sealed it for me. When I learned that her father was Ira Tucker of the esteemed gospel group the Dixie Hummingbirds, I told her about how on our early bus tours the Temptations often broke into Hummingbirds songs a cappella. All this seemed to point to Lynda being the girl I was looking for.

Lynda adopted the stage name Lynda Laurence (or Lawrence; she later married musician Trevor Lawrence). A native of Philadelphia, she began performing with her father's group as a child. In her teens she formed a band with her brother and two friends, and then moved to Detroit, where she performed as a solo artist. Lynda met Stevie Wonder, and along with her sister Sandra and a cousin joined Stevie's backup group. Her first recording with Stevie was his 1970 hit "Signed, Sealed, Delivered." The trio, later rechristened Wonderlove, remained with Stevie until we "discovered" Lynda.

As Lynda told reporters afterward, she was thrilled to be a Supreme. We began rehearsing her immediately, and she worked every day with Cholly Atkins to learn the steps. Lynda came to our shows in Windsor, Canada, and studied tapes of us. We were scheduled to embark on an extensive tour of Australia soon, and I wanted her to go with us.

The shows in Windsor went well, and many people came to see us, including Berry and Flo. I was very happy that Flo was out, because she'd started withdrawing from the world ever since a judge threw out her lawsuit against Motown in November 1971. When Flo met Lynda backstage, she said, "That girl is really going to be good. She'll add some personality to the group."

The night Berry attended was one of the very few times he returned to the Detroit area after moving to Los Angeles. Back in the dressing room, he remarked, "I'm really pleasantly surprised at how good your show is." Then we got on to the subject of his new film venture, and he boasted, "Diana and I are going to make it."

"Berry," I said, "I know you and Diane are going to make it, but I am too."

"Yeah, but Diana and me are going to *fly*, and you'll have to go door-to-door."

Heart-to-heart talks between Berry and me were rare these days. When we did have them, there seemed to be another motive at work on his part. As he spoke proudly about his future plans, I recalled playing blackjack with him to pass the time on the road many years before. Once, in 1965, we stopped a game, and he owed me $4,000. "Oh, Berry," I said, "you know you don't have to pay me. It's just a game." His face lit up with relief.

"Okay, Mary, great!"

A few days later Berry beat me hand after hand. We kept score in dollars, but I really didn't think that he was playing for real. Finally, when I was in the hole $6,200, Berry said, "Okay, pay up. Give me my money."

"But Berry, the other day I let you go—"

"That was *you*, Mary," Berry interrupted. "It's a lesson

you have to learn." I ended up paying him every cent of the $6,200 over time. I suppose he wanted to teach me that not everyone was like me; certainly not Berry Gordy.

Around this time we started recording with Jimmy Webb. Though Lynda wasn't yet officially in the group, she sang on this album. (Some people assume she was on *Floy Joy* because Lynda is pictured on the cover, not Cindy. Due to her pregnancy and imminent departure, Cindy declined to appear in that photo.) I remember Jean, Lynda, and I staying up almost all night at my place after a session and talking. I was so happy and felt that we were on our way. Again.

Jimmy was the Supremes' first non-Motown producer, and it struck some people as an unusual pairing. Working with Jimmy was the idea of our latest manager, Wayne Weisbart, assigned to us by Motown. I was surprised but thrilled that the label let us use an outside producer. Jimmy had written such hits as "Up, Up and Away," "MacArthur Park," "By the Time I Get to Phoenix," "Wichita Lineman," and "Galveston," and produced Thelma Houston's beautiful album *Sunshower*. Interestingly, he had also worked briefly as a house writer for Motown's song-publishing division, Jobete Music, some years before. Jimmy released a few solo albums, but his performing career was eclipsed by his outstanding work as a writer and producer.

Jimmy was extremely quiet, and we got along very well. He struck me as one of those rare people who don't just make music, but have the music inside them, much like Marvin Gaye. One thing we liked about Jimmy was that he respected us and listened to our opinions. His approach differed from what we were used to. While he worked out all the musical details beforehand like most Motown producers, Jimmy encouraged our input. He taught you the melody, but then expected you to do your own thing.

The resulting LP, *The Supremes Produced and Arranged by Jimmy Webb* (originally titled *Beyond Myself*), was radically different from *Floy Joy*. Once again we were back to being a lead singer with two backup vocalists. I did sing one song, "I Keep It Hid." (In 1989 Linda Ronstadt covered this on her album *Cry Like a Rainstorm*.) The other selections included Joni Mitchell's "All I Want," Harry Nilsson's "Paradise," and the rock oldie "Tossin' and Turnin'." Stephen Schwartz's "I Guess I'll Miss the Man" from the Motown-financed Broadway musical *Pippin* was the first single. It was the LP's only cut not produced by Jimmy.

As much as I loved this album, several things about it were not in the Supremes' best interest. For example, Jimmy brought in additional background vocalists. After Smokey's having achieved that perfect vocal blend, I saw this as another big step backward. Except for Jean, the group on *Floy Joy* and the group on *The Supremes* might have been two different entities. Still, *The Supremes* received many very positive reviews, all commending our willingness to experiment. It was a great disappointment when "I Guess I'll Miss the Man" sold poorly, and the album became only the second in the Supremes' history not to enter the Top 100 (the first had been 1968's *Funny Girl*).

We hadn't set a definite date for Cindy's departure, but proceeded with our schedule. She sang with us live, and Lynda recorded with us. We had some time off after the March date in Windsor and were looking forward to the upcoming April tour of Australia. Unfortunately, Willie and I had to attend my maternal grandmother's funeral in Mississippi. We got home the day we were to leave for Australia. The minute Willie and I walked in the house my housekeeper Geneva said, "Mary, there's some bad news. Jean is in the hospital." My friend Dr. Hurbert Avery was caring for her, and while it was not clear to me exactly what her problem was, he was emphatic that she not work for as long as eight weeks. Did that mean the tour was off?

After a couple minutes the magnitude of the crisis seeped in. I started crying. It seemed that whenever I thought that everything was fine, another problem arose. Willie put his arms around me protectively, and I plopped down on a large floor pillow and started making calls. Soon our staff people arrived to discuss our options.

Our manager Wayne had left for Australia earlier, assuming we would follow. When we finally reached him, I said, "Even without Jean, we should do the tour. Lynda's been recording with us, she knows the show, and she can step right in." Wayne disagreed and wanted to cancel but said he'd talk to the promoters and see what they thought. On Sunday, however, we were still in limbo. I visited Jean in the hospital. She was in good spirits, but her health was still in danger. "Jean, we're going to try to go ahead with Lynda singing lead," I said.

"Whatever you have to do is all right with me; I understand," she answered.

After talking to the rest of the staff and to Lynda I became excited; I knew we could do it. I phoned Mike Roshkind, who agreed it was best to go ahead and promised to get right to work on the details. Yet shortly after that, someone else called and said, "Mary, Mike has officially canceled the tour." I was devastated and confused. Over the next couple days I tried to put the tour back together, but Motown had decided, and that was it. We did, however, manage to do a couple of the tour's last few dates, in Hawaii, with Lynda, and she was great. Still, the idea that people who did not have my best interests in mind were controlling and making decisions about my life bothered me. They weren't paying my bills anymore; who were they to say whether we would perform or not? I knew I had to take more control, and I proceeded to do just that. I could no longer delude myself that Motown was on my side. It was me against them. They didn't care what happened to me, but I did. And I knew I had to survive.

Jean recovered sooner than expected, and we resumed our schedule, opening at New York's Copacabana on June 1. We were doing three shows a night, which was tiring but exhilarating. Toward the end of our first week, Lynda called. "Mary? Jean is very sick again, and she's on her way back to Los Angeles."

"She's what?"

"She's going back to Los Angeles. She's on her way to the airport now."

"What's wrong?" I asked.

"I don't know."

"Okay," I said, stunned. "I'll see you later."

I sat back in bed, feeling guilty for what I was thinking. This was beginning to strike me as a little bit fishy. No one would ever tell me exactly what Jean's health problem was. Coincidentally, it seemed to crop up when she was unhappy. I didn't really believe this, of course, but I couldn't help thinking it. Well, there was nothing I could do but put it out of my mind and tackle the problem at hand. Would we cancel the shows or go on, just Lynda and me, as a duo? Copa owner Jules Podell was not pleased with either choice, and Motown and our agent wanted to cancel.

Cindy came in and did the shows with us on Saturday and Sunday, with Lynda singing lead. We had only the gowns we'd brought with us, and Cindy's pregnancy was showing, so the fit wasn't perfect. Cindy was happy to be back, and I was thankful for her flying in on a moment's notice. Then on Tuesday, Jean was back, and I got sick, so for the first and only time the Supremes performed without a single original member on the stage. And I'm sorry to say, I doubt anyone in the audience noticed or cared. Were we really that interchangeable, after all?

Later that night, I wrote in my diary:

I've always prided myself on being able to stay happy regardless of any misfortune. Maybe I was too young before to totally understand problems. Now when I look at people, I see things that I've never seen before.

Tonight I realize that I cannot be totally happy through my career alone. It's been a long time since I've had a boyfriend. I decided that after my one love, I'd work hard on my career and give up my love life and stop being so free with the men I dated. I realize I cannot substitute my career for love. I even tried to use little Willie to be completely happy. My career was always enough to keep me happy.

Actually, with Jean being ill on the last show, I should be in tears. Whatever was wrong has made her cancel out of tomorrow's press conference. Plus, the fans really missed her. Well, the day is over, and I lay here in the tub, soaking. After working these two shows, I reek like a truck driver. They just ran a lot of our old records on the TV oldies-but-goodies record commercial. I realize how much I have at stake.

In June we switched managers and started working again with Shelly Berger, who'd managed Diana Ross and the Supremes in the sixties. All during a meeting to discuss our upcoming summer tour with the Temptations, the managers and Motown people talked around Lynda, Jean, and me as if we weren't there. Then we discovered that not only were the Supremes the opening act, but we were billed under the Tempts. They were selling more records and had some big hits recently, like "Just My Imagination" and "Superstar," but still, this was a real blow to us. After we saw the itinerary, the only conclusion we could draw was that Motown was trying to kill us by working us to death.

We started rehearsals for the tour, and in some ways it was like old times, especially with Melvin Franklin and me. Melvin and I had crushes on each other when we were teens, and we've been dear friends ever since. But things were different, too. David Ruffin had left the group back in 1968, then Paul Williams and Eddie Kendricks in 1971. It was interesting, though, that despite all the changes, the Tempts still seemed stable. This I credit to cofounders Melvin and Otis Williams always supporting each other. Seeing them reminded me how much I missed Diane and Flo. I compared the Tempts' situation to my own: I would always be "outnumbered" by new girls.

We opened with the Temptations at the Now Grove in Los Angeles to great reviews. Many people from Motown attended the show, and afterward Berry invited us to a party at his home, but I declined. At the time, he and Diane were making *Lady Sings the Blues*, the film biography of singer Billie Holiday. "Hey," Berry suggested, "why don't you come down to the studio and see the rushes?"

My first impulse was to say no, but Berry insisted. We met at the Paramount lot, and he showed me some outtakes. I knew that Diane would be good, but I was surprised how great she was. I'd assumed you had to take acting lessons to know how to act. I was very proud of her and still think *Lady Sings the Blues* is the best thing she ever did.

The whole time with Berry I couldn't help but feel that he was doing more than just sharing his new work with me. He beamed as he talked about how great Diane was. His whole manner seemed to say, "I told you, you should have stuck with me." Berry was the winner, and he made sure that I knew it.

After Diane left the Supremes, I was always very proud of her and proud that she'd been a Supreme. Contrary to what most other stars might say publicly, there was scant support for Diane in Hollywood. Most of them said she would never make it alone, or if she did, she wouldn't be as big.

When word got out that she was going to portray Billie Holiday, some stars laughed at her behind her back, mimicking the way she hunched her shoulders and rolled her eyes when she sang, or the way the veins in her neck bulged as she reached for high notes. Part of this was anger and jealousy. There were many black performers who'd worked twenty or thirty years and could sing their butts off, but couldn't get the breaks Diane did.

One time Diane's name came up, and one star said, "That Diana is just too pushy for me. I mean, she acts like no one's important but her."

"Mary, I don't know how you put up with her all those years," another added. "You know that child is just a bitch."

This talk embarrassed me. It was like when people tell dirty jokes because they think you'll like them too. They were jealous of Diane and thought I should have been too. But I honestly wasn't.


August 1972

The review we received in D.C. was terrible. The critic said, "They lacked a gutsy, down-home sound." We "should give up giggling and act natural . . . background insufficient . . . parodies of a former time." But I'm not going to give up because something has gone wrong. We are going to make it work. We've got to get our people at Motown to see that music has changed, and we want to keep up, not die. Boy, we've been working our cans off. It's been almost two years now.

Replacing girls in the group has definitely hurt. But

when people feel they want to do other things, you can't stop them and say, "Hey, my life and career are at stake too." Flo, Diane, and Cindy? "Everyone's gone to the moon."

That summer and fall, nothing could distract me from the sadness and emptiness I felt. Since "Floy Joy" earlier in the year, our last three singles had fared progressively worse: "Automatically Sunshine," Number 37; "Your Wonderful, Sweet Sweet Love," Number 59; and the new "I Guess I'll Miss the Man," Number 85. Instead of making us a hit recording act that toured, Motown had let the Supremes become a road act without a hit. I felt like I was on a treadmill, running and running but getting nowhere.

I went back to Detroit to see my mother, as I did almost every fall. I loved my new life in California, but I also felt cut off from my roots: my Motown family, my blood relations, and friends. To compensate, I made extra efforts to keep in touch with childhood friends like Flo, Alice, and Ella, and to go home whenever I could.

It was so nice to sleep in my old round bed. After moving to California, I'd given my mother my house, and Willie's family and my Aunt Moneva moved into her old home. The drapes were drawn, so even though the sun was shining, inside my room was dark as night. I'd been out late, talking with Cholly's wife, Mae, and I needed my sleep. The phone rang.

"Mary, it's Flo!" my mother called. I picked up the phone.

"Hey, girl," she said happily, "come on over when you get up. The twins are waiting for you. I've told them all about their Aunt Mary."

"Okay, but first I have to get just one more hour's sleep."

"Oh, Mary, girl, get up. You sleep too much anyway. Girl, why do you sleep so much?"

"I have a lot on my mind, Flo. Sleep helps me work things out. But I promise I'll walk down to your house as soon as I get up."

Just then the smell of bacon, grits, and eggs cooking hit me. It was beginning to look like a conspiracy between my mother and Flo to get me up. I wandered into the kitchen and had a great home-cooked breakfast, then set out for Flo's house.

Whenever I walked through the old neighborhood, I recalled how Diane, Flo, and I each bought a house on this street and didn't even know it until after we'd closed our deals. That's how much alike the three of us were. Diane's house was directly across from Flo's, and mine was a couple blocks down the street.

When I rang the doorbell, Flo came flying down the stairs to open the front door. Her fair complexion was red, as it always was when she was excited. Her hair was now blond, so we both laughed when she opened the door and I blurted, "Blondie!" It was a nickname only her family, Diane, and close friends used, though I rarely did. Now it really fit. We hugged each other tightly.

Inside, the house was just as she'd originally decorated it, all blue, and her twins were all over the place. They were as different as night and day. Nicole was fair like Flo, and Michelle was chocolate brown like Flo's husband Tommy. I held them while we talked about babies. Flo was so proud of her children, and they loved her with that perfect love I believe only mothers know. It was the kind of accepting love Flo had never known before, and when she held her babies, it transformed her. All the friends and relatives I saw in Detroit kept asking me when I was going to have a baby; I wondered too.

Inevitably the conversation turned to Motown. "Mary, I've been hearing about your problems. I told you, girl, they weren't going to do anything for the group after Diane left. It's about time you woke up. Motown's only out for themselves."

Flo was right, but I changed the subject. I felt that my problems with Motown would only burden her. And this was a sore spot for both of us. Why Motown apparently wanted the Supremes to fail was beyond me. It hurt when anyone, including Flo, mentioned it. The situation was so depressing, I wanted to forget it for a while.

I sensed Flo's fear of where her life was going; she didn't want that to happen to me, too. I don't think Flo ever understood that while it was very easy for other people to say, "Leave the group," I fully understood that there was no place for me to go, just as there had been no place for Flo.

In October *Lady Sings the Blues* premiered in New York. It was the culmination of Diane and Berry's dream. Though they were no longer an item, he was as dedicated to her career as ever, if not more so. Diane was Berry's vehicle to his next conquest: Hollywood.

While some critics complained that too many liberties were taken with the facts of Holiday's tragic life, the film was a commercial success and a triumph for Diane, who chose to sing Holiday's music rather than lip-synch to the actual recordings. I particularly enjoyed Diane's singing, since most vocalists dream of singing jazz and blues like that. Later Diane was nominated for an Academy Award for Best Actress. The evening of the Oscars, I prayed she would win, but she didn't. Some in the industry believed that Berry, a Hollywood outsider, had overdone the pre-Awards publicity, and that Diane lost because of industry politics. Still, this was Diane's most definitive step to superstardom and away from all that had come before, including the Supremes.

That fall we played an all-star benefit for the Rev. Jesse Jackson's Operation PUSH. Taped in Chicago and later released as the feature film *Save the Children*, the show included Gladys Knight and the Pips, the Temptations, Marvin Gaye, the Staple Singers, the Jackson 5, the Chi-Lites, the Main Ingredient, the O'Jays, Bill Withers, Curtis Mayfield, Isaac Hayes, Smokey Robinson, Valerie Simpson, Roberta Flack, Jerry Butler, and Thelma Houston. The highlight was the young Jackson 5. Every one of us stayed to catch their set. No matter how many times I saw them, they were amazing. With four Number One hits behind them, they were now Motown's brightest stars.

We sang "Stoned Love" and "Up the Ladder to the Roof," among other songs, and got a wonderful response from the crowd. Everyone working on the film said we were great. Yet for some reason, our sequence got cut, something we didn't discover until the movie's release. I was crushed. Why did there always seem to be obstacles in our path? And who was placing them there?

In November we had a great run at New York's Apollo Theatre, where Eddie Kendricks appeared with us, and worked through the end of the year, even on Christmas Day. One highlight of the season was receiving the NAACP Image Award as Best Female Group. Diane won Best Actress, and several other Motown acts were also honored. For the first time since Diane left the group, we were honored as equally successful entities. This award meant a lot to me, since the original Supremes had never even won a Grammy.

While I had been worrying about the Supremes "missing something," we generally went over well live and had audiences dancing and shouting for more. Maybe my ideas about what the group should be were based on an unattainable ideal, the original Supremes. The realization of where we might be headed if I didn't keep my eyes open hit me when we arrived to play six days at a small Canadian club. It looked exactly like a Ramada Inn dining room, with a little portable stage. That was bad enough; then I learned that we were making $13,000 for the week, a far cry from the $30,000 to $50,000 we'd earned just months before at the Copa or in Vegas. Out of this our booking agents and Motown recouped their percentages, about one quarter of the gross, and expenses and payroll claimed anywhere from 50 percent to 90 percent of the remaining gross. Jean, Lynda, and I were paid out of whatever was left, which was unpredictable, sometimes amounting to just pennies.

It seemed pointless for us to be out on the road earning so little. It actually *cost* us money to play dates like this, when that time should have been spent at home, refining the act, cutting some good records, and, by our absence, creating a demand. Our contract with Motown was coming up for renewal. For the first time, I didn't automatically assume we would re-sign.

One morning Willie woke me up with the radio blasting. The disc jockey posed a trivia-contest question about the Supremes: "Who were the Grand Honorary Marshals in the Santa Claus Parade?" This was an old Hollywood tradition, where many stars appear in a Christmas parade down Hollywood Boulevard, and this year it had been the Supremes. It had been televised, and Jean, Lynda, and I had been thrilled to participate. We had ridden on a float, smiling and waving.

*Great,* I thought, *some more publicity.* But as I listened to the disc jockey chat with the winner, I couldn't believe my ears. He sarcastically remarked that we were "all new faces" in the Supremes, and "no one" knew who we were anymore, and where had we gone, anyway? Years later, after I saw

Rob Reiner's farce "rockumentary" about a fictional rock group on the skids, I'd classify this as one of those "*Spinal Tap* moments" in which even I saw the irony.

I couldn't control my anger. I phoned the station and after several tries finally got through. When the disc jockey answered, I snapped, "I'm Mary Wilson, and I am still in the Supremes, and have been since the very beginning. We are not all 'new faces.' "

"Miss Wilson, I'm so sorry," he said nervously, before apologizing profusely.

"Okay," I said. "Would you please then play something from our latest album, *The Supremes Produced and Arranged by Jimmy Webb?*"

After a second's silence, he answered, "Well, I don't think Motown sent it to us. Or maybe someone stole it. But if I find it, I'll play it."

"Thank you," I said. Half an hour later he played "Tossin' and Turnin' " and dedicated the Box Tops' "Sweet Cream Ladies" to the Supremes.

Even with all the work, our group shared some great, happy moments. Once we were in Mexico doing a photo shoot on top of some ancient ruins. Because it took so long to climb to the top, the three of us changed our outfits on one side of the pyramid, neatly laying down our clothes and undergarments on the stone. We were posing when a great gust of wind blew, and suddenly our bras, panties, slips, and stockings went flying through the air and fluttered down to the ground. Down below, several shocked tourists were amazed to witness this bizarre lingerie shower falling from the sky. We nearly fell off laughing, and the bewildered tourists continued to stare as we watched my bodyguard Benny chase our clothes.

Money was getting tighter. In December we opened in New Orleans to a half-filled room. It was getting harder and harder to maintain momentum. We never knew what we were going to find, and the unpredictability of it all began wearing on us. Jean took it the hardest, or at least showed it the most. There were nights onstage when she just wasn't into it, and the fans knew it. People remarked to me that she seemed cold and distant. Now I see that a lot of what she was experiencing was fear. She sometimes looked as if the weight of the Supremes was crushing her. Every once in a while a wiseguy in the audience yelled, "Hey, where's Diana Ross?" which would shake her confidence. (People still do this to me today.)

I was on Jean's side, but I still wonder if she realized how much I wanted her to stay and be happy—not just for the Supremes but for herself. If I tried talking to her about anything, such as being more discreet with the press, she took it personally. I wasn't attacking her or her beliefs, I was only trying to help her. If I asked her to just give in a little bit, she would say, "I can't do what they're asking. It's okay for you, Mary. But it's not good for me."

Lynda was still new enough to be excited just being there. I knew that whether there were ten thousand people in the audience or ten, you had to be "on." Each person in the room has to believe not only that you're happy to be there, but that you're happy to be there for him or her. It's a giving of yourself. Jean sometimes felt that simply being there was all she could give.

In early 1973 I went to the Now Grove to see the Four Tops, a group that I never miss seeing. They'd recently signed with ABC Records, and after two years of flop singles on Motown had a Top 10 hit with "Keeper of the Castle." Similarly,

Gladys Knight and the Pips bolted from Motown to Buddah Records and immediately went to Number One with "Midnight Train to Georgia," launching a string of gold records.

We wished them all the best, but until then no ex-Motowners ever did as well or better anyplace else. Among record companies, Motown was unique, and most of the artists who left found they needed its extensive support system. Mary Wells, Berry's first female star, had four Top 10 hits, including the Number One classic "My Guy," but after leaving Motown in the mid-sixties never had another. There's been lots of speculation why: some thought her head got too big; others contend that Motown's arms were too long. Whatever the reason, Motown pointed to her example whenever someone asked too many questions or got out of line.

For years most of us had overlooked or minimized how badly Motown treated us; as they say, you can't argue with success. But now the label's golden touch had started to tarnish. Acts that got attention, such as Diane, the Jackson 5, the Temptations, and Stevie Wonder, did well. As the Motown ship began sinking, the rest of us went down with it. In 1972 the label placed only four singles in the Top 10, a far cry from the heady success of the sixties. But few of us were brave enough to abandon "the family."

This night at the Grove everyone from the Four Tops' new label was out in force. You could see that ABC was behind them all the way. The Tops had two more hits on the heels of "Keeper of the Castle"—"Ain't No Woman (Like the One I've Got)" and "Are You Man Enough"—making 1973 their most prosperous year since the mid-sixties.

Jean, Lynda, and I began talking about what to me was unthinkable: leaving Motown. I admit I was very reluctant. They didn't really appreciate the value of the Supremes' name, which we might lose if we left. In the meantime, we arranged a meeting with Ewart Abner, now Motown president. Since

I'd always regarded Abner as the one company executive with some compassion for the artist, maybe there was a chance.

*How strongly do Jean and Lynda feel about sticking with the Supremes and Motown?* I wondered. I found out as I sat in my home with Abner, waiting for them to show up. They never did. As ever, I looked on the bright side. Frank Wilson had a song for us, Abner said, and top Philadelphia producer Thom Bell had flown in to discuss a possible future project. Either of these possibilities might work. If I could be optimistic, why couldn't they?

I served Abner a cocktail and we made small talk, then I said, "Abner, we are really tired of constantly touring. We are women out on the road. We all want a decent home life, like other women." Abner listened attentively.

"Motown has not followed up on any of our records to date," I continued, "and, Abner, you know we've made some very good records."

"Yes, Mar-ry," Abner replied, pronouncing my name as only he could. "I know you ladies have done a fine job of keeping this group together. But what do you want?"

I was a little confused; I thought it was obvious, but I repeated, "We need more and better promotion. *The fans* are doing a better job of promoting our records than Motown is."

"Yes, you're right, Mar-ry." Abner agreed with everything I said. Yes, they had to get us the right writers, and then Motown had to put the push behind us. Whereas Mike Roshkind would simply say, "We've done all we can do, and that's it," Abner assured me it would be taken care of.

Earlier that year Lynda, Jean, and I were discussing our trouble getting a decent record out, when Lynda suggested, "Why don't I talk to Stevie about it? We're still great buddies. He'll write us something." When Lynda proposed the idea to Stevie Wonder, he accepted immediately and gave us "Bad Weather."

Stevie had come a long way from the little boy who played harmonica on our bus rides in the sixties. In 1971, soon after his twenty-first birthday, he demanded Motown grant him full creative control or he would go to another label. He also became eligible to receive the monies Motown was holding in trust for him; the company turned over an astounding $1 million in royalties and advances. I can only imagine what went through Berry's mind as he wrote out that check.

Motown had lost performers before, but never anyone it really wanted to keep. In addition to his long line of hit singles, Stevie was one of the few Motown acts to develop a broader audience. The contract Stevie finally agreed to granted him the greatest freedom of any Motown artist. Not only was he freed artistically, but financially; for once, Motown permitted an artist to control his own publishing, the key source of income for songwriters. The album he'd worked on between contracts was the groundbreaking *Music of My Mind,* followed later in 1972 by *Talking Book.*

His new contract allowed him to produce other artists, enabling him to work with the Supremes. As he later told reporters about "Bad Weather," "I've been listening to Jean Terrell for a long while and feel the way she's been handled isn't right. She's got those certain riffs which sound great, but she's not been given the material on which to develop them."

Stevie was a dream to work with. He was very attentive, and he worked quickly and efficiently. We never felt rushed. As Stevie taught us the song, I thought, *He really is a genius.* I don't know if Stevie wrote it specifically for us, but the original title was perfect: "I Think I'm Going to Run into Bad Weather." When we heard its first few chords, with its unusual progressions and African beat, I knew this was our ticket. All Motown had to do was get behind it.

We recorded "Bad Weather" in Detroit during a run at the nearby Elmwood Casino. Believing this style would put us back in good standing with the disc jockeys, I encouraged Lynda and Jean to do some informal promotion, but they refused. I understood their thinking that Motown should be doing more. But it wasn't, and I figured that was all the more reason for us to get out there. Whether Motown was right or wrong wasn't the issue. Our careers were at stake.

I'd tried rekindling the offstage camaraderie I'd shared with Flo, and later, Cindy, but Jean was never one to go out, and Lynda declined my offers, saying she didn't feel she had the right clothes to wear, and so on. Further driving me apart from Jean and Lynda was their recent conversion to the Jehovah's Witness faith. Before, after, and between shows, the two of them closed themselves off and studied the Bible. Jean claimed that since she and Lynda had started reading the Bible, she was honest and guided by God. Like most Jehovah's Witnesses, Jean believed her way was *the* only true way, and that was that. I promised myself I would try to join them. Not only for whatever comfort it might bring me, but I was tired of being left out. Maybe this would help bring us together again as a singing group. Despite everything else, we still had a wonderful sound.

At this point, I guess you could say that I had everything, and I felt happy. Nothing really bothered me for more than a moment. As I got older, however, I realized that there were a few things in life I didn't have, like a husband and my own children. I was sure, though, that in time these things would be mine. I certainly didn't go around moping and thinking about what I was missing.

This eternally optimistic personality I'd developed as a

child helped me cope with the few problems I did have, just as it had seen me through the pain of having been given to my Aunt I.V. and Uncle John L. Pippin in Detroit while my mother remained down South with my younger sister, Cat, and brother, Roosevelt.

The Pippins treated me like a princess, dressing me in expensive, pretty dresses and making sure that I wanted for nothing. My Uncle John L. was a gentle, kind man, but my Aunt I.V. was strict and stern. I now understand that it was for my own good. She was only trying to raise me to be the best I could be. But deep inside, my little heart ached. I felt misunderstood and afraid. But strangely enough, I was still happy. Before I was even in my teens, I'd use my sunny, outgoing face for the world. I swore never to let anyone take that away from me. By the time my mother moved to Detroit to reclaim me at age ten, the die was cast.

My mother worked very hard to care for the three of us. She got no support from our natural father, Sam Wilson, who remained down South until he died in 1962. One of my few regrets is having never known any of my father's people. I know they must be out there somewhere. Despite being deprived of a decent education, my mother, Johnnie Mae, did a great job of raising me. One of our happiest days came in 1956 when we moved into our new home, in the Brewster Housing Projects.

Intellectually, I understood my life: growing up in the projects, loving to sing, meeting Florence and Diane, forming our little singing group, hanging around Motown, all the while praying to be noticed. Then the success of the Supremes, and how stardom changed my life and those of the people I'd grown up with, like Marvin Gaye, the Four Tops, the Temptations, the Marvelettes, and so many others. But once I moved to California, I began to see my childhood differ-

*F*lo, Diane, and I at Big Bear Mountain in 1965, taping a Dick Clark TV show. We used a photo like this for the Supremes' Merry Christmas album. (Photo: Mary Wilson Collection)

*T*he Supremes in Holland in 1965. (Photo: Paul Hux / Mary Wilson Collection)

*O*ne of the rare wrappers from a loaf of "Supremes Bread." How many other rock stars have had a bread named in their honor? The thing that really shows its age is the price: 27 cents. (Photo: Mary Wilson Collection)

*F*lo, Diane, and I with Hubert Humphrey. We were one of the first pop groups to become involved in politics by endorsing his campaign for the presidency. (Photo: Mary Wilson Collection)

*O*nstage at Holy Cross College in Worcester, Massachusetts. (Photo: The Worcester Telegram / Tom Ingrassia Collection)

*T*aking time to fool around with one of our favorite trumpet players, Herb Alpert. (Photo: Jeffrey Wilson's Hot Wax Music Archives)

The Tamla Motown team arrived in Britain well prepared for any extremes the weather might bring — and DISC WEEKLY was on-the-spot to greet them.

TOP THIRTY WINNERS!

*The Temptations, Smokey Robinson and the Miracles, the Supremes, and Martha and the Vandellas in London as part of the Motown Revue in 1965. (Photo: Disc Weekly)*

*Displaying the youthful innocence that made the Supremes the toast of the globe. (Photo: Paul Hux / Mary Wilson Collection)*

*W*hen Flo left the Supremes she began a solo recording career that included the song *"Love Ain't Love."* (Photo: Jim Lopes Collection)

*F*lorence Ballard, who was the heart and soul of the Supremes. (Photo: Mary Wilson Collection)

*With one of the great loves of my life: Tom Jones. (Photo: Mary Wilson Collection)*

*Diane, Cindy, and I being greeted backstage by Michael Caine and his wife (second from left) at London's famed club the Talk of the Town, in 1968. (Photo: Marc Henrie / Mary Wilson Collection)*

*Obie Benson of the Four Tops and I chatting with Princess Margaret after one of our many command performances to raise money for one of her favorite charities. (Photo: Mary Wilson Collection)*

**Diana Ross And The Supremes.
Where do they go from here?**

Funny how Diana Ross and The Supremes always come up with something fresh and vital. And far from tired. Funny like smart. That's what's made them get to the top and that's what's kept them there. The pace is a grueling one. Living out of a suitcase when they're on tour, making up on a plane, traveling from one coast to the other without batting a false eyelash. More often than not, it's a hot dog and a Coke sandwiched in between. The reason it's Coke is simple. Coca-Cola has the taste they never get tired of. No matter where or when they have one. They say it makes things go better all the way around. (The girls, left to right: Cindy Birdsong, Diana Ross, Mary Wilson.)

*T*he Supremes were among the first black artists to endorse Coca-Cola. This was years before Michael Jackson and Madonna were paid millions to promote Pepsi. (Photo: Bob Williams Collection)

*B*elting out a song with Ethel Merman on The Ed Sullivan Show in 1968. We were performing an Irving Berlin medley with Ethel on that particular show. (Photo: Jeffrey Wilson's Hot Wax Music Archives)

*C*indy, Diane and I as Indian princesses on the 1969 "G.I.T. on Broadway" special. Otis Williams of the Temptations is behind us dressed as a Mountie. We are wearing one of our outfits that burned in the famous Mexican fire, which claimed many of our trademark gowns. (Photo: Mary Wilson Collection)

*C*indy, Diane, and I showing off our wonderful legs! We were usually seen in floor-length gowns, but for this particular Bob Hope TV special we wore mini-dresses. (Photo: Jeffrey Wilson's Hot Wax Music Archives)

*C*indy and I in our "farewell" show with Diane, at the Frontier in Las Vegas, January 14, 1970. (Photo: Mary Wilson Collection)

*J*ean Terrell, new to the group, joined us onstage for the final bows that night. Little did I suspect that Berry Gordy would try to oust her from the group before the night was over. (Photo: Jeffrey Wilson's Hot Wax Music Archives)

*C*indy, Jean, and I onstage in Toronto. We made a hot trio, and for a while our recording career was much more successful than Diane's as a solo artist. (Photo: Collection of James Smith)

*A*t the Elmwood Casino in Windsor, Ontario—one of the few times that Berry came to see us after Diane left the group. (Photo: Mary Wilson Collection)

*T*he new Supremes—high above the Las Vegas strip in
1970. (Photo: Foster & Kleiser / Mary Wilson Collection)

*C*indy Birdsong, Glen Campbell, me, Flip Wilson, and Jean Terrell backstage at New York City's Copacabana, after a wonderful run at the club.
(Photo: Mary Wilson Collection)

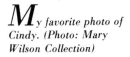

*M*y favorite photo of Cindy. (Photo: Mary Wilson Collection)

*J*ack Lucarelli and I in our seventies hippie outfits. (Photo: Mike Paladin / Mary Wilson Collection)

*T*aping the TV special "Festival at Ford's Theater." Left to right: *Dionne Warwick, Henry Mancini, Bobbie Gentry, James Stewart, Pearl Bailey, Andy Williams, Jean Terrell, Tennessee Ernie Ford, me, and Cindy Birdsong.* (Photo: Jack Silver / Mary Wilson Collection)

*M*y early-seventies "Black Pride" look. Photo session paid for by an admirer who prefers to remain anonymous. (Photo: Mary Wilson Collection)

*We recorded three albums with the Four Tops in the early 1970s and had a ball. They called us "The Magnificent Seven," and we also toured together. In these photos I'm standing next to the main love of my life, Duke Fakir (far left). (Photos: Hendin / Mary Wilson Collection)*

*W*ith Willie and the Jackson 5, giving out Christmas
gifts to needy children. (Photo: Mary Wilson Collection)

*T*his photograph was taken for the cover of our album New Ways but Love Stays, and I always thought that it was the most dramatic portrait we ever had taken of the Supremes. (Photo: Mary Wilson Collection)

ently. I began to question the constantly happy person the world knew as Mary Wilson. Was I really always happy?

These are questions most people ask themselves in their teens or early twenties. I'd traded that part of my life for the success Diane, Flo, and I had been blessed with. From the moment the three of us, with our friend Betty McGlown (who was replaced by another friend, Barbara Martin), decided to form a group, my career consumed every waking moment. The Supremes were everything to me, more than just me and Diane and Flo. It was a separate entity, something greater and more important than any one of the three of us, and no matter what occurred—whether our records hit or missed, whether we flew or flopped—I dedicated myself to doing the best I could. There were rewards, of course, but there was also a price.

Around this time I often found myself thinking back to 1962, when I turned down marriage proposals because of my singing. What would my life be like now if I'd married my high-school sweethearts Willie Peeples or Ronnie Hammers then and had never known stardom? How many children would I have? While I wouldn't have traded my life for anyone's, I suppose it was only natural to wonder about the path not taken.

In 1973, when I was twenty-nine and still single, my mother's warnings—"Don't end up an old maid"; "When are you going to give me some grandchildren?"—began getting to me. Family has always been very important to me, and I desperately wanted to have children, but I also knew that I could never bear a child out of wedlock. I wanted to settle down, finally.

Opening night in Puerto Rico, I looked out from the stage of the Flamboyan Hotel and spotted the most handsome black man in the audience. It was funny, because I made it a point not to date fans and had never noticed anyone before when performing. But this man, with his deep brown eyes and gorgeous features, was different. We made eye contact several times, or at least it seemed that way to me. You never can tell at those distances.

After the show, the phone rang, and Lynda answered. "Mary," she said, "it's for you. It's a 'Pedro.' "

"I don't know anyone named Pedro. Ask him where I know him from."

"He says he met you in Las Vegas, but that he was at the show tonight too." I didn't recall meeting him, but that didn't mean it hadn't happened. He asked me to have a drink with him, and at first I hesitated. Jean and Lynda, both seriously dating their future husbands, egged me on. "I can't go out with a man I don't know," I protested. Yet for some strange reason, I said yes.

When we met face-to-face in the hotel lobby, I realized Pedro was the man in the audience. He said, "Hi," then French-kissed me. I couldn't believe any gentleman could be so forward! I was turned off . . . but somehow fascinated too. For one of the first times in my life I decided to take a chance. And as I wrote in my diary several days later, "He took me out, and that was it. We've been together ever since."

It was the beginning of a dream romance, except for one hitch: I had just started dating a wonderful man named Freddy, and I could see that for him the relationship was becoming serious. Here I'd gone all year worried because I had no one in my life, and now I had two men.

Freddy was stable, sincere, and not in show business. I met him in New Orleans, and we hit it off very well. He had visited me in Los Angeles, and Willie seemed to like him too. We met in Puerto Rico to discuss our future. He was very anxious for me to decide one way or another. Freddy and I enjoyed being together, but I wasn't sure it would work out. We were on different levels financially and from different social worlds. I explained to him that my career was taking up all my time and energy. He was understanding, but hurt. As he left Puerto Rico he warned me that someday I'd wake up all alone. It was something I'd thought about often myself and feared.

Pedro Ferrer told me that he came from a very wealthy, politically powerful Dominican family, and that his father, a Mr. Roig, was a banker in Puerto Rico. Pedro dressed impeccably, and was intelligent and articulate. All the friends he introduced me to were obviously from privileged backgrounds. Pedro grew up and was educated with children from the rich ruling class. He was a model child, incredibly bright and well adjusted. An excellent scholar, Pedro had an IQ of 150 and a burning ambition to make something of himself. I had never known anyone quite like him.

The next couple weeks Pedro and I were together almost twenty-four hours a day. I thought I was fairly sophisticated when it came to men, but a total stranger was sweeping me off my feet. Several years later I realized that the only men I really understood were entertainers. Other men were a great mystery to me, and I was far more naive about them and their motives than I knew. This fling was so strangely wonderful, right out of a romance novel. Having always read fairy tales as a child, I suppose I was always waiting for my knight to carry me away on his white steed.

The entire time I spent in Puerto Rico was pure ecstasy. Pedro drove me all over the island, impressing me with his knowledge of its culture and history. During one of our excursions he pointed out a gorgeous, expansive home and said, "My uncle lives there." He stopped the car, got out, and talked to the gardener, who seemed to know him. Yet Pedro never rang the doorbell or attempted to introduce me to his "uncle." It seemed odd, but I put it out of my mind. Maybe no one was home.

We were inseparable. He took me to the airport, and as he held me, I felt my heart break. When he kissed me good-bye, I knew this was the man for me. By the time I left Puerto Rico for New York, Pedro was talking about our getting married in two years. That didn't seem so unusual, but that I agreed to this plan was—at least for me. From the very first moment, I believed that being with Pedro was my fate, and I was so tired and feeling so beaten down and defeated, I wanted to believe in something. Whether this was going to be the love of my life, something permanent, I still didn't know. I just wanted to be happy.

# CHAPTER 6

*F*alling in love with Pedro made me so happy, but I still had the group to deal with. Cholly Atkins had been Motown's staff choreographer since the early days. Although his dance steps are an integral part of the Motown style, he had lived a whole life before coming to the label and never considered himself part of Motown like I did. Cholly was in his fifties by then and over the years had become something of an uncle to me. He was hip to everything and didn't say too much, but when he did, I listened. I could always count on him. After I told him of our problems and of how we had little money to hire people, he agreed to come with us for our next dates in Puerto Rico.

We were rehearsing one day when Cholly said, "Look, baby"—he always called me "baby" when about to offer some fatherly advice—"people are starting to talk about Lynda, saying she's too bossy and outspoken. Now, you know you're the leader of the group. You've got to take charge."

"Okay, Cholly, I will," I replied. "But I don't want the girls to feel I'm too bossy."

"Mary, you know that if you don't start acting like the boss, they will take over."

He was right. When I recalled how I felt when Diane threw her weight around, I cringed, but I knew that I had to do it. I knew that people—inside and out of the group—were taking advantage of me, and in my heart I hated it. I resented people for forcing me to be something I was not and never wanted to be. Honest, caring advice, like the kind Cholly offered, was rare around Motown. I appreciated his concern. Too many others who influenced my life worried more about kissing Motown's butt than looking out for me and the Supremes.

Once back in the states, Cholly rehearsed us on the choreography for "Bad Weather" between our shows with the Temptations at the Latin Casino in Cherry Hill, New Jersey. I thought about Pedro every moment. He phoned me at all hours. I knew he loved me, but I became a little peeved when he insisted on showing up in New Jersey—I honestly thought he was kidding. We spent six days together, and while the romantic aspects were wonderful, I was relieved when he went back home. To say the least, this romance was whirlwind; I couldn't figure out how things had heated up to this point so quickly.

I looked forward to our upcoming monthlong tour of England, on which I planned to take Willie. I was home so rarely these days because of the Supremes' hectic schedule that I wanted badly to spend more time with him, even if it was on the road. Willie was the one thing in my life that was truly real.

I liked taking my son overseas and exposing him to different cultures. Once there Hazel arranged for Willie to stay a few days with her mother in the village of Eye. There he learned the proper way to drink afternoon tea and to eat scones with clotted cream.

MARY WILSON

One evening after visiting one of Hazel's younger relatives, Willie decided to cut across a field on the way home. It was a small village, and the local constable knew everyone in town, so it's no wonder that the sight of a young black boy racing across the field caught his attention. The bobbies picked up Willie and detained him. When he explained that his mother was Mary Wilson of the Supremes, one officer replied, "Right. And I'm the king of England." It was all cleared up, but not before it made the papers.

England is my second home, and I had so many friends there that it wasn't long before the phone was ringing off the hook. David Frost invited me to join him for drinks. He was off to the Middle East and offered to bring me back some exquisite silk. We had a great time together, catching up on the latest news. The press reported that David and Diahann Carroll had broken up and that he and I were dating. Really, it was only one date, hardly the big romance columnists tried to make it. After that, however, we did see each other briefly.

Unfortunately, there weren't enough hours in the day for me or for Willie. And, as if I didn't have enough on my plate, one morning at five Pedro called, waking me.

"Mary, guess what. I'm coming to England to see you!" I almost dropped the phone. I protested, but he was so pushy; it annoyed me. "I'll be there on the third. And could you also make hotel reservations for some friends of mine?"

"Sure," I answered uncertainly.

"So give me a kiss," he said.

When I didn't comply right away, he hung up on me. For not giving him a kiss? I felt like I was being dragged away on a wild adventure.

March 1973

I love Willie; he's growing into a fine young man. I hope he can lose that deep, angry mess he has inside him. I thought this new life would help him. And I love Pedro. Thank God I've finally fallen in love. I see myself beginning to feel for real. It felt good. I think I must let my heart go to Pedro. He's everything I'd want in a man: he is handsome, dashing, warm, sexy, he has a large Afro, and he digs me. At first I went out on the trip that he's after my money. But that just seems obsolete now. I am not used to a man so persuasive. Anyway, regardless of all that, my common sense has been overruled. As in the case of T.J. [Tom Jones], I have decided to pursue the situation. I am sticking my neck out. Willie says he doesn't like Pedro, but Pedro will win him over. I talk like I have no doubts. I do . . . however, I am throwing away my inhibitions. I want to dash into this affair.

This week I saw Tom [Jones]. Although I still love him, and always will, I find that my feelings have changed. I no longer have the heartache of someone who has loved and lost. My love for him is now more of a loving friendship—which is perhaps what the relationship should have been to begin with—a beautiful friendship. Still, it was great seeing him again. This same thing happened to my affair with Duke Fakir. In both cases, I believed that I had found the love of my life. But I was wrong. With this realization came a little sadness but also a sense of security and peace. At one time I never would have imagined I would stop loving either of them, but that time has come.


Our elaborate beaded gowns were so famous that they were the the talk of seven continents. They were so legendary that they somehow inspired some of our most outrageous male fans to dabble in drag. In fact, during an engagement in San Francisco, while one of our designers, Pat Campano, was repairing one of our sets of sequined pantsuits, they mysteriously disappeared—never to be seen again.

During the English tour we were the victims of a widely reported theft. After doing interviews most of the day, Jean, Lynda, Hazel, Willie, and I went to the dressing room to prepare for the show. Jean, Lynda, and I were putting on our makeup when someone asked, "Where is the other gown? I see only two."

"It was there when we left last night after the show," Hazel said.

We turned the tiny dressing room upside down looking for the gown, but it was gone! Willie and our road manager complained to the club manager and Hazel called the police. These gowns cost over $2,000 each. Within several days, they tracked down the culprit, who was tried and fined five pounds. The thief turned out to be one of our flamboyant, ardent gay fans who'd come to the show with a group of his most outrageous friends. They brought each of us a beautiful bouquet. Over a dozen years later I received a letter from one of the young man's companions, now a schoolteacher. It remains one of my favorite fan letters:

Dear Mary:

When we got upstairs, you, Jean, and Lynda were having a meal. We went back to our table, where my friend appeared. He had a big smile on his face, and I said, "You look like the cat that's got the cream." He said, "I have," and from his lap pulled up one of those bags we had brought your bouquets in, and there was one of your gowns. He had managed to steal something that we were all secretly dying to possess—one of those beautiful and priceless sequined gowns . . . As we were sitting there, one of the waitresses spotted the dress, and my friend gave her £5 to keep quiet. Anyway, the dress came back to our home with us, and—it fitted us all perfectly!

Jean's attitude grew unbearable during this tour, poisoning everything. The Temptations were in England too, and we jumped at the chance to see them. All through the Temptations' concert Jean talked loudly and critically of them from the front row. Later, at a dinner given in their honor, she continued to behave rudely.

Later that week Jean refused to rehearse for our upcoming appearance on Great Britain's most influential pop-music television show, *Top of the Pops*. We were going to sing our new single, "Bad Weather." The show's producer held this incident against me and the Supremes for the next several years, long after Jean was gone.

Jean and I stopped speaking. Out of frustration, one evening between shows I scribbled her a note, saying we were scheduled for a quick photo session. Her back was turned, and after I handed it to her, she angrily threw it to the floor. I should have grabbed the broad by her bugle beads and throttled her! Around this time she also told us that she didn't like singing the old Supremes hits, either.

Despite Jean's taxing behavior, and her and Lynda's obvious intentions to exclude me from their lives offstage, onstage we were still the Supremes. We continued dealing with one another as business partners, and we all wanted what was best for our business. We agreed to seek new management with no connection to Motown. We interviewed new managers and companies, and were most impressed by Allan Carr, who managed Ann-Margret. He had great ideas and seemed excited by the prospect of working with us. Before long, however, he expressed concern over Jean's attitude. I couldn't blame him, yet I knew that with someone like him on our side, things might look up, and Jean would be happier.

Jean and Lynda still tried to convince me to leave Motown. The failure of "Bad Weather" was the last straw; despite glowing reviews, the record went nowhere. Even Stevie Wonder was upset. He complained to Abner, who promised the company would "get on it." The record had been out since March, and here it was May. The time to have "got on it" was long past. It was too late.

An impulsive break from Motown would surely fail. Jean, and to a lesser degree, Lynda, read my caution as indecisiveness. But I knew, better than anyone, what was at stake and how Motown would respond. The big problem, which would haunt me for years, was the name *Supremes* and who really owned it. Morally, it should have been ours, but it wasn't that simple.

Jean and Lynda couldn't have cared less about the name, and, as I soon saw, they resented it just as they resented the constant questions about Diane. Both believed we would do just as well, if not better, without the name. I remember thinking, *Just wait until you wise up and see how hard it is to make it out there without a gimmick or a name like the Supremes. You'll wish you hadn't given it up.* (Ironically, fifteen years later Lynda and Jean would be touring with another seventies Supreme, Scherrie Payne, as the FLOs: Former Ladies of the Supremes.)

Every day I was finding out more about my business, though never from anyone at Motown. During a short tour with Sammy Davis, Jr., he told me that he'd asked our managers to let us perform with him. No one ever told me about this or, as I would learn, similar offers from many other established stars.

The intergroup tensions were taking a toll. Opening night at the San Francisco Fairmont, we received one of the worst reviews of our career. As a matter of fact, I think it's one of the few times an act has ever called a press conference to reply to a review. Our press conference was also "reviewed," under a headline that read: WHEN THE SUPREMES GET ANGRY. The *San Francisco Examiner* graciously allowed us to address its critic's views, which boiled down to his feeling that we were "not black enough." This issue would remain a no-win for us.

At the press conference, I said, "I'll probably be disliked by whites and blacks alike for what I'm going to say, but I went into show business to entertain. I'm not saying, 'Hey, look at me, I'm black.' I'm saying, 'Hey, listen to me, I'm a singer.' I'm an artist first and a black woman second. I don't feel that the people who come and spend their money to see the Supremes perform should be primarily concerned with our blackness. They should be concerned with how much we are giving them for their entertainment dollar." Jean, not surprisingly, felt that she was representing "every black person."

Then my worst fear was realized when Jean announced privately, "I want out of the group." It became a race against time. Which would come first—a new deal, or Jean's leaving? Shortly thereafter, Lynda revealed she was expecting a baby; a few weeks later I had a false alarm.

June 1973

I called Diane to tell her I thought I was pregnant, but she had changed her number. An hour later she called me. That was really funny, because we hadn't talked to each other in over ten months.

"Hi, Mary!" Diane said brightly. "How are you doing? I'm going to Japan soon, and I know you've been there lately. Tell me, what's the style there? What's happening? And I need to borrow your huge wardrobe trunk.

"Also, there's that beaver hat I lent you years ago. Could you return it?"

"Diane, I'm sure I have returned it."

"No, you haven't." (Years later I found the hat stuffed behind some others in my closet.) "I know. Let's go out shopping together. Come over here."

Diane was upbeat and happy, as if we'd just spoken yesterday. We went shopping in Beverly Hills, the whole time making small talk. Diane breezed through one exclusive store after another; in one she tried on dozens of pairs of shoes. We talked about Motown and how poorly it was promoting the Supremes. It was like we were girlfriends again.

"You know, Diane," I said, "I'm glad we got together today. I feel that we're better friends now than we were before."

Diane turned to face me, her large brown eyes wide with disbelief. "Mary, we are *not*," she said. "I don't know how you could say that."

Stunned, I felt she'd taken what I'd said the wrong way. Her reaction was so strong, I didn't even try to explain myself. The rest of the day passed slowly. From then on, Diane made me feel that I was not her friend, but her dearest devoted fan.

Later that night I wrote:

> It was as I had expected: we still can't communicate or be honest with each other. It's not that we don't like each other. It's more that we're just on different planets since she grew up. She seems to always be pretending. If anyone knows her, I do. Still, she talks to me as if I am a stranger. Maybe time will help us to talk freely with each other. She still tries to compete. Why? She doesn't have to.

This is a classic example of what I found most frustrating about Diane: her ability to hurt me without even knowing it. I knew that if I said one word in my defense, she would feel that she had been wronged. As long as I'd known Diane, whenever I confronted her, she always took a defensive stance and acted like the innocent victim. Berry taught Diane everything she knew. The difference between the two of them was that Berry could charm a snake. No matter how he really felt, he could still pretend to like you. Diane could not. Even today people Berry's hurt still think he's basically a nice guy. I don't think Diane ever understood how Flo and I were hurt by her and Berry's shutting us out of their lives and using the Supremes to advance themselves. I knew our relationship wasn't going to be the real friendship of our teens, I just hoped we could be friends today. Years passed before I would stop reaching out for Diane.

That June Pedro visited me in Los Angeles. His flight was due in right after midnight, and I spent the whole day getting ready. I wore a beautiful dress to the airport and was all smiles until I saw Pedro come through the terminal with loads of luggage and a huge Saint Bernard named Sky. *It looks like he's doing more than coming for a visit,* I thought to myself. *It looks like he's moving in!* I was right.

We had pretty much agreed to marry in the near future, so at first I didn't mind. After just a couple weeks, however, we ran into trouble. He was a little too bossy with Willie and possessive of me. One day he announced he was going back home.

"I'm sorry. Mary, I do love you."

That might have been the end of it, but a strong attraction kept drawing us together. Two clichés pretty well sum up our relationship: "Love is blind," and "Oil and water don't mix." The more Pedro stayed around, the less sense it made. I saw his shortcomings, but I believed I could help him and that together we would make things work. He was the only person besides my family, friends, and fans who loved me and was on my side. Between Motown's abandoning the Supremes and the press virtually ignoring us, I felt like a failure. There had to be something I could succeed at. It would be love.

In July 1973 Jean called to inform me she was about to ask Berry for her contract back. Even though I wasn't totally surprised, I was nevertheless dismayed. I'd always wondered if Berry lured Jean into the Supremes with promises of a future solo career. As her unhappiness grew, Jean let little things slip out to the effect that he had. She was frustrated and angry; we all were. But couldn't she see I was trying to hold things together? From her tone of voice, her mind was made up.

Within the hour, who should call but Berry. We hadn't spoken in months. In the sixties he and I had been buddies. Now that the Supremes were no longer "his girls," we rarely saw each other.

"Mary, it's Berry," he announced chipperly. "Billy Davis told me you're getting married. I just wanted to say congratulations, and I'd really like to give you away at your wedding."

What? Here my career was crumbling, and Berry wanted to give me away at my wedding! "No thank you," I replied curtly. "My son is giving me away." What I wanted to say was something along the lines of "the nerve of you, Berry," but I couldn't. Something was up; I had to stay on my toes.

"Well, what's happening?" he asked. This was a typical Berry ploy. I found his condescending attitude so insulting, I went off on him.

"Berry, what's happening to our group? The records aren't being promoted, and we're being run ragged with this schedule."

"What do you mean? You're working, aren't you?" he asked.

"Yeah, Berry, I'm working—for pennies, so I have to go out there every day. I've already been working all my life, fighting for time off, and now I can't take a good vacation without worrying that there'll be nothing in my bank account when I get back."

"But you're planning to get married," Berry said. So that was it: Berry probably thought I was going to wed, retire, and get out of his hair. "Besides, Mary, I've done so much for you and the girls. What I've been doing—the movie [*Lady*

*Sings the Blues*]—is going to help you and all the other acts in the future."

Berry saw Motown Records as a chess game, and we were all just pawns. Sure, he could walk away and do something else until he was ready to start working the puzzle again. But he forgot that our lives and careers went on, whether he was there or not. Now that Berry was back on the scene, he felt I should be grateful for his interest.

"What about us now, Berry? We can't get into Vegas, we can't get a record played."

"Mary, I have priorities."

I thought back to Berry and his priorities. When the Supremes became hot, earlier "priorities" like Martha and the Vandellas and the Marvelettes dropped down on the list. Then we benefited; now the Supremes were topped on his list by the movie business and Diane.

"Priorities? Well, my priority is the Supremes," I said. "And I'm paying you fifteen percent of every penny to make us a priority."

Typically, Berry agreed on every point. This was his way of making people feel good without him actually having to do anything. He admitted I was right, but it didn't change what he thought about the Supremes: that we were finished, and if we weren't quite finished yet, we should be.

"You know, Mary, when you girls were all babies, I used to tell you, a little knowledge can be dangerous.'

*Yes*, I thought, *and you also said, "I'll take care of you."*

"Mary, we have an idea for an outside manager for you."

"Well, Berry, that's something I've been asking for for a while and something I've been working on now for several weeks."

"Oh, really?" He tried to sound surprised. He had to have heard that I'd taken over much of the group's business, that I was looking for an independent manager, that I was making demands at Motown. I felt that the real reason for this call was to see where I was at, to see whose side I was going to take. That night I wrote:

> I do hope this is a start for the Supremes to be free of Motown. Even though I am ready to walk away, I am not ready to just let Motown have the name *Supremes*. And that may force me to stay.
>
> Is Jean giving me a chance to step up and take the lead? I don't want to lose Jean. But supposing the choice is to go with Jean or to stay with Motown and the name *Supremes*? Being that those are the only two outs I have, looking deeper, I suppose this is the time I should just stop the Supremes. Sometimes I get angry with myself because I can't make a decision. Jean made a decision, right or wrong; Flo made a decision; Cindy made a decision; Diane made a decision. I am the only one still hanging on (pardon the pun). Or maybe I have made a decision: to stay.

"A little knowledge can be dangerous." Berry's words stuck in my mind. The Supremes were in this precarious position *because* I had no knowledge. Our new manager Bill Loeb's first job was to explore our options for leaving Motown and obtaining rights to the name. In each of our contracts since the very beginning, Motown's position was clear: it owned the name the *Supremes* and could replace members at will. But just because it had slipped that clause into the contract didn't necessarily mean it legally owned it. There had to be more to it.

I wondered, *Does somebody own a name just by virtue of saying they do and getting you to agree with them? Isn't there something else involved? If there isn't, does that mean a company like Motown—or anybody—can just say whatever it wants and make it so? Even if it's a lie?* Flo's agreeing to never refer to herself as a Supreme in her press once she left the label hurt her career tremendously. The name was Flo's idea, no one else's. More to the point, she was a Supreme, just as I was. The way Motown exploited Diane's connection with the Supremes all the time only proved that it understood its value.

This was something I needed to think about, but before long Pedro and his things—*all* of them—arrived from Puerto Rico. I was too surprised to protest. My choices were to either live alone or let him stay. At first I chose the latter. One day after an argument I told Pedro he should go back home, and when he tried to convince me otherwise, I lost control and slapped him. I'd never slapped anyone. He slapped me back, and I stood there stunned. No man had ever raised a hand to me before. I started hitting him back. For those moments I felt like a stranger standing outside my own body, watching it all happen. When it was over Pedro wrote me a long note, saying he was wrong and sorry. He wrote, "Let's try one more time."

There were so many positive things about Pedro, such as his kindness and his boyishly romantic ways. Almost every day he brought me flowers or penned sweet little love notes. In fact, most of the time Pedro was remarkably gentle and thoughtful.

He was one of the first people to convince me that I could accomplish whatever I set my mind to. He really believed in me. He taught me to be strong. It bothered him that I feared so many things, including, at times, him. He showed me that my contribution to the Supremes wasn't like Diane's or Flo's. What I had uniquely contributed to the group was my gentleness; my love. However, in the atmosphere after Flo left, I found myself deeply hurt and vulnerable, so I retreated within myself. I felt I must survive at all costs. As strange as it sounds, Pedro helped me to reclaim that part of myself Motown had beaten down.

---

I was relieved to go back to Detroit that weekend for Mary Wilson Day, on July 21. The event was set up by Dick Scott, one of the Supremes' managers in the sixties. During the ceremony, held at the newly redeveloped waterfront downtown, a city councilwoman praised me as an example of the power of black women everywhere. I gave a brief speech, thanking everyone, and introduced my mother. Then the singing group the Originals dedicated a song to me. I had a wonderful time, seeing so many old friends from the Brewster Projects days.

Late Sunday afternoon I went over to Flo's house. She said she was very happy for me, but that I needed a man in my life. Her twin girls climbed all over their "Auntie Mary," and one threw up on my shoulder. The rest of the day I could think only about how badly I wanted my own baby. I returned to the street fair and gave another speech, this time to black women, telling them how beautiful they were and how proud they should be. When I got home I read the Bible for a while, then fell asleep.

Eddie Kendricks came by the next day, and we drove over to visit David Ruffin. Eddie has always been one of my favorite people, and I was happy to see that both his and David's solo careers were taking off. Eddie and I were lovers for a brief time, but our relationship had evolved into an enduring friendship. Like any two Motown artists when they got together, we compared notes, talked about what was happening, and dished a few folks.

Eddie was a rebel who spoke his mind. When I told him what was happening to the Supremes and how I was beginning to take over the business, he said, "Mary, you have to keep at it and don't give up, no matter what happens."

Before I left for Los Angeles, Mom pulled me aside. Though she rarely interfered in my life, she said, "I like Pedro very much, but I don't think you should marry him.

For one thing, he doesn't have his own money, and, baby, you need someone who can afford to take care of you. I don't want to meddle in your business, but why don't you just wait awhile?" She wasn't the only person with reservations; several friends remarked that Pedro was just using me. Still, I knew him better than they did, and I loved him.

In August Jean, Lynda, and I opened at the southern California amusement park Magic Mountain. It was one of our best engagements ever. Knowing that Jean was quitting, and possibly Lynda too, made it a bittersweet occasion. The irony was that they didn't want to leave the Supremes so much as leave Motown. I knew from experience that once someone's mind was made up, that was it. Flo taught me that. All the disappointment and struggle had soured Jean and Lynda, and I couldn't change that.

Jean was finished with me. No matter what I said or did, she took it the wrong way. When I couldn't take any more rejection, we stopped talking. I wrote her a letter, which, though I never sent it, expressed my feelings:

August 26, 1973

Jean:
I can't for the life of me see why you are venting your frustration at me. I feel that we—you and I—could take the Supremes and put them back at the top where they belong. You have a tremendous talent that I admire, and to be very candid, I went to bat for you with Berry. I don't know what he promised you when he first signed you to Motown. Did he say he'd make you a star? I've heard that before.

It's Motown that is constantly causing the problems by not doing its part as a recording company. You should be angry at them, not me.

Please, let's stop these childish games and go about achieving success while we are still young.

—Mary

Bill Loeb kept quietly making calls to other labels, and I talked to accounting firms about auditing Motown's books on the Supremes. I'd been considering an audit for a while; it was something Jean felt very strongly about. She once said, "They're not even keeping an accurate accounting. Don't tell me you can give me two pennies just because I was only making one at first, and that I'm supposed to be happy with it." Coming into Motown as an adult, Jean asked more questions, and she was right.

I knew, though, that an audit wasn't something Motown would take lying down. Once you started it, you had better be prepared to finish. If I proceeded, I would be one of the first artists in the label's history to audit. So many people had been hurt by the Motown system, and I saw what might well happen to me if I didn't get in there before it was too late. Here I was, having made millions for Motown—but out of the tiny fraction of the profits it gave me, I was terrified to spend a penny.

Around this time several disc jockeys and radio-station music directors (who determine playlists) started revealing to me that they didn't always get our records, and that Motown no longer pressured them to play them or offered them promotional favors if they did. Fans organizing campaigns targeted at radio stations often heard the same thing: Motown wasn't providing the records.

Through it all, our fans were always there cheering us on. The Supremes have always had one of the largest, most active fan clubs in the world, and I was grateful that the membership stuck with us. Many of the fans who joined in their teens were now young adults. They formed a national network and undertook several massive letter-writing campaigns on our behalf. They phoned radio stations to request our records and contacted other media to ask for press coverage. Almost every major city had its dedicated Supremes fans, and occasionally they were quoted in stories about us. It helped to know somebody still cared. In a couple of cases, fans were single-handedly responsible for our records hitting big in major markets.

Their activities encouraged me but infuriated Motown. I heard that Motown was angry and blamed me for the rumors that we were leaving and the press stories denouncing Motown's mistreatment of the Supremes. I said, "Berry, the fans are angry because they aren't hearing us on the radio, they don't see us on TV like they used to, and they don't see any publicity about us." He disagreed, maintaining that I was behind it all, that it was my plan to embarrass him.

He was half correct, but the fans acted on their own, doing what they believed was right. The real source of Berry's anger was that nearly four years after he'd "washed his hands" of the Supremes, we hadn't died. He intended for us to fade out quietly, and instead we had four gold singles and piles of rave reviews. Now Berry didn't know what to do. He couldn't ignore the fact that even without hits or exposure, the public still loved us. The Supremes remained high on popularity polls around the world.

From our talks, I managed to get some concessions from Motown: promises of special promotion men to work our future releases and some important contract changes. It all looked fantastic on paper. I didn't know, however, that Motown would arrange things so the Supremes could not release another record for almost a year and a half.

# CHAPTER 7

I clung more to Pedro as our romance became hot and furious. We were now together twenty-four hours a day. He and I had recently returned from Dionne Warwick's celebrity tennis tournament in Aspen, Colorado, when Ewart Abner called. "Mary," he said, "I have some bad news."

My mind racing, I thought, *Is it my mother? Flo? Diane? Is the label dropping us?*

"Paul Williams was just found shot to death in his car a few blocks from Hitsville."

"Oh my God." I felt my knees buckle. Not Paul. I thought back to the last time I'd seen him, at a 1970 taping of Smokey Robinson's first prime-time television special. It was like a wonderful family reunion performing again with Paul and the Temptations, Smokey and the Miracles, and Stevie Wonder. Just being around them all, especially the Tempts, brought back lots of great memories. Paul and Eddie

Kendricks had been in the Primes, and way back in 1959 they convinced our parents to let us become their sister group, the Primettes. Paul helped us choreograph our early act. Melvin Franklin, his cousin Richard Street, and Otis Williams were friends from those days too.

On Smokey's special the Temptations performed "The Impossible Dream," one of the rare songs that Paul sang lead on. Paul was the Tempts' true leader, creatively speaking. He'd been the group's guiding spirit and developed their trademark choreography. He was also a great singer, as you can hear on many of the Tempts' early records, like "I Want a Love I Can See" and "Don't Look Back." Because most of the later leads went to either David Ruffin or Eddie Kendricks, the public saw Paul as "only" a background singer. Motown turned the group's choreography over to Cholly Atkins, who, of course, was the best. It was typical of Motown to take ambitious, talented people and relegate them to the background, never acknowledging their contributions. Like Flo, Paul felt stifled and frustrated, and he quit the group not long after this taping. He had so much more to offer, but also, like Flo, he kept his pain inside.

Everyone around Motown knew that Paul had been drinking heavily for some time. As he sang the line, "To beat the unbeatable foe," he was shaking. It was sad to watch him struggle to put across the words; they held a lot of meaning to him. In that moment I recalled all the beautiful moments Diane, Flo, and I had shared with Paul. How dapper and suave he'd looked that day he came to my house to persuade my mom to let me be a Primette. His natural elegance and grace were really something back then.

Since I couldn't attend the funeral, I gave Abner a message to deliver from me.

I wrote in my diary:

I've been thinking an awful lot about Paul, the way I think about Flo. I've always had a love in my heart for both of them. Just mentioning the funeral on the phone, Abner and I had to hang up because we both started crying.

I've been asking for strength because I see it's so easy for a person to be bumped off, smothered, or just to end it all yourself. I tried to sleep tonight but I couldn't, so I placed a call to Eddie Kendricks. He and I talked for an hour and a half. It was very nice. We talked of Paul and Flo. Eddie sounded very optimistic about the future and how Paul's tragic ending has given us strength. I agree. It's funny how certain events can bring people closer. I've always known Paul and Eddie were special to me, just as Flo and Diane are. I am glad to know, as Eddie told me, he and Paul felt the same about me. I asked Eddie to say good-bye to Paul for me.

Paul's death was ruled a suicide, but in many minds there will always be a question as to the real cause.

On August 25 we appeared on the "Model of the Year." This was a TV special broadcast live from the old Ed Sullivan Theatre in New York, the site of Jean's television debut three and a half years before. I was pretty sure this might be Jean's last appearance, but I didn't know it would be Lynda's as well. We had a few more commitments before year's end, and Cindy had agreed to step in if we needed her. That way Lynda and I would share leads. Less than a year and a half away from the business, and Cindy was eager to come back. As always, I could depend on her, and I felt thankful.

No matter what happened, Bill Loeb had already decided that the act should be revamped around me. It was getting harder to keep a consistent lineup, and since I was the only original Supreme left and the only person *I* could count on, I agreed. Secretly, I wondered if I could do it. But I had to.

As we stood separately in the theater waiting to rehearse, Jean turned to our road manager and snapped, "I'm going to sing my solo." When he told me of Jean's remark, I was furious and stormed over to them.

"No," I replied, "that's not possible. Weeks ago I asked both you and Lynda what songs you wanted to do for this show, and all I got in reply were blank stares." Since we had no new single to promote, we ended up singing "Touch" and "Bad Weather."

While we were in New York, word leaked to the press that Lynda was pregnant and planning to leave. At the time, I blamed her lack of enthusiasm on what was happening with the Supremes. Now I realize that like any mother-to-be, she was understandably preoccupied with that, and it made her moody. I offered to throw her a baby shower, and she declined. I was so hurt. With Jean on her way out, not knowing what Lynda was going to do threw me off balance.

Lynda was trying to up her position in the group, demanding a larger percentage and special concessions like extra money for singing solos. Several Motown execs told me they didn't think Lynda was much of a team player. Between her pregnancy and the people at the company warning me "Mary, this Lynda is something else, you'd better watch her," I didn't know what to think. I was looking for a new girl to take Jean's place, without knowing if I should be trying to fill Lynda's spot too. The executive who criticized Jean and Lynda never owned up to how the business drove these woman to be that way. I understood where Jean and Lynda were coming from, perhaps too well. They were just rebelling. But I couldn't go on letting other people run my life.

The next week Pedro and I were going to Santo Domingo to meet his parents. As the date of departure drew nearer, Pedro became increasingly restless. The night before our trip he told me the truth about his parents' identity. Pedro confessed that Mr. Roig was indeed a banker, but *not* his real father. Apparently Roig had taken Pedro under his wing when he was a young man, and for whatever reason, Pedro contrived an extravagant fantasy about who he really was. In many ways he reminded me of the hero of F. Scott Fitzgerald's *The Great Gatsby*, a poor boy who recasts his life in the mold of a wealthy mentor.

In truth, Pedro was raised by his mother and stepfather, a politically powerful Dominican. The Dominican Republic occupies roughly two-thirds of an island, Hispaniola; Haiti makes up the other third. The country has a long history of colonial rule and dictatorship alternating with revolutions and democratic movements. In 1930 Generalissimo Rafael Leónidas Trujillo Molina took over and ruled the nation with absolute power until his assassination in 1961. Countless thousands who spoke out against him before his death were executed or died under mysterious circumstances.

Democracy eventually came to the Dominican Republic, but not without civil unrest and violence. Even now there are areas of shocking poverty. Pedro's family belonged to the professional class that worked to make possible the country's first free election in almost four decades, in 1962. They exerted a great deal of influence, which in the Dominican Republic was more valuable than money.

The few days we spent with his mother, stepfather, sister, and brother were pleasant but awkward. And in one sense, surprising. Pedro was so dark-skinned, I'd assumed he was black and expected his family to be as well. Imagine my shock when I saw that they were white! Pedro was not black, or at least not an Afro-American black person. He had black skin, but underneath it he was a true Latin. Boy, did I feel like a dummy, especially in view of how strongly I felt about marrying a black man. There went my perfect fairy-tale ending! Well, it was too late to worry about that now. We were in love.

Visiting Santo Domingo was fascinating. His family took me all over the small island. We swam in the crystal clear water of the Atlantic, strolled through the swank hotels and casinos. Pedro was the island boy who'd come home and made good. After all, I was a great catch: a wealthy singing star.

His mother prepared all the exotic Latin dishes of their region, one of which was a soup made of cow's intestines. I tried to eat it and found myself almost gagging. It was like our Southern dish chitlins. It was very funny because his mother, who doesn't speak a word of English, broke out laughing hysterically. That broke the ice, and they immediately considered me part of the family.

I liked Pedro's family very much. His little brother Rafael was a huge Supremes fan, and his sixteen-year-old sister Malvena and I hit it off from the start. His parents were initially taken aback by me—or, I should say, by Pedro's plans to marry me. They wanted him to marry within his own culture, preferably to a more traditional Latin type, not an entertainer, and probably not a black American Baptist, or, as I like to say, a BLAP (Black American Princess).

For the first time, I really got to see the man I was engaged to. I also saw how different Pedro and I were. In his society men and women observed strict social codes: the man was the undisputed leader, the boss, the provider, while the woman was the queen of the home. In public she always deferred to her husband. This struck me as backward and quaint, and yet some things about Pedro's way appealed to me. Some of my values were old-fashioned too, but American traditions are pretty progressive compared to what Pedro was used to. I was an independent single woman. As my career consumed more time and energy, I longed for a man to be strong, to fight for me. During these years there was nothing I liked better than to be in my home, cooking, entertaining, and taking care of Willie and our many pets. Pedro completed the picture.

En route to Santo Domingo we had stopped off in Puerto Rico, where I had met Pedro's friends. Most were well-to-do, handsome, and on the make. They hung around the San Juan casinos and hotels, providing "company" for rich, lonely women. I discovered that I wasn't the first famous woman whose path Pedro had crossed. Part of me couldn't believe it, but part of me did.

On the flight back to Los Angeles I had one last impulse to dump Pedro and save myself. On the plane, I wrote:

> Today at the airport I saw what I was afraid it would be. The young, boyish face. At first he did not accept anything from me. Slowly, he's taking. Boy, I let him reel me right in. A real con job. Willie and others saw it. I played into Pedro's hands so easily. I really thought we had a chance. Now the problem of discarding him; it'll be messy.
>
> When he's around I feel like I'm being smothered by a dark, heavy cloud, or a windbag. Now suppose I take him back and try it for a while? I'll be the loser. I need someone who's going to lighten my load. I don't care how often he has played the game. This is one he won't win.

After several months of waiting for promised jobs to come through friends, Pedro finally decided to finish his law education here in the United States. Willie and Pedro were at each other constantly. Willie, then fourteen years old, was trying to establish his own identity and rebelled; he didn't want me to marry Pedro. Having suffered a strict, unreasonable upbringing myself, I was sensitive to Willie. Although I firmly believe in discipline when appropriate, it has to be mixed with understanding and love. And Willie was not an average child. He was bright and caring but needed extra time and patience. I knew when I took him there would be special challenges ahead for us both, but I really believed in my heart that love would help us overcome them all. Now I wondered.

One evening my sister Cat, a friend, and I went out to the Candy Store. We got in late, and Willie and his brothers were still up. They playfully jumped on me, and Willie got too rough. Seeing that he was trying to hurt me, I lost my temper and hit him. He tried stabbing me with a ballpoint pen. My bodyguard Benny, who lived at the house, broke it up. I wasn't physically hurt, but emotionally I was devastated. How could this happen? I loved Willie so much, but I'd seen this day coming. He was a young man trying to flex his muscles. He was to begin attending military school that fall, and I prayed it would help.

When it came to Willie, Pedro's ideas were almost completely opposite to mine. He was raised in the old-fashioned Latin tradition where the father ruled. Pedro's family had explosive, often violent, arguments. I'd become very upset after witnessing one of these scenes, but an hour or so later Pedro and his family would go on as if nothing had happened. This he brought to our quiet little family.

Pedro was determined to control Willie and did not brook the smallest infraction of the rules he set down. Naturally, part of Willie's reaction to Pedro was simple jealousy over having to share me with someone else. Willie had always liked my other boyfriends, and they all liked him. I had never had a serious relationship with a man who didn't spend time with Willie or take him places. Freddy, whom I nearly married just before I met Pedro, flew Willie and his friend Brian to Mardi Gras in New Orleans one year.

Had I looked carefully, I'd have seen the first sign of Pedro's violent nature. Instead, all I could see was a man who needed my help, a man who I could love into becoming the person I thought he should and could be. I knew all the reasons why I shouldn't love him, yet I couldn't stop. By month's end Pedro and I were back in Hollywood, planning our engagement party.

Pedro loved the nightlife, and Hollywood certainly offered a surplus. Because of work, rehearsals, or simple exhaustion, there were times when I didn't go out. Pedro hung out and talked to other men, the way guys do. For all its glamour, Hollywood is basically a small town. I knew everybody, and when my name came up, guys I knew, however casually, usually said something to Pedro just to be polite. If a man said he thought I was nice or pretty, Pedro assumed I'd slept with him. What was actually said, I never knew. I only know what happened when Pedro got home.

After one evening out he stormed in with his brown eyes flashing, and I knew immediately someone had said something to set Pedro off. Still, there was no way I could be prepared for what happened next.

"You fucking whore!" he screamed.

"What?"

I trembled as he stepped closer. He flapped his arms as if he were about to strike me, but changed his mind at the last millisecond. He was right up in my face. "You lied to me! How many men did you sleep with?"

"But that was all before I met you!" I cried.

"I thought you were pure!"

*Pure?* I couldn't believe that in 1973 two adults were having this conversation. Suddenly Pedro slapped me several times hard across the face, as if he hated it. He tore off my clothes and then shoved me outside to the pool area and locked all the doors. It was fall, hot in the day, but very cold at night. I was crying so hard I could barely breathe. I looked out across the shimmering pool and down on the lights of Hollywood. How did this crazy man get into my life? Why couldn't I stop it? Maybe I could. As I sat on a cold lounge chair, hugging myself against the autumn breeze, I kept asking myself, *Why is this happening to me?* It was very hard, but we made up again.

A few weeks later I went to the Dorothy Chandler Pavilion to see my good friends the Pointer Sisters. Their act was fabulous, and their singing was great. I felt very happy for them but left the show feeling sad and a touch envious. It was like the Supremes were old and on the way out. The past couple of years had brought a modest girl-group revival. With acts such as Barry White's Love Unlimited, the Three Degrees, and the Emotions, there was competition. While I knew we couldn't copy anyone else's style, the Supremes needed something new and fresh. Unfortunately, we couldn't accomplish anything artistically until the most basic question— namely, Who was still in the Supremes?—was answered.

All my career crises faded into the background as Pedro and I prepared for our engagement party. We threw it at our house, and over two hundred people attended, including Flip Wilson, Lamont Dozier, Brian and Eddie Holland, Lola Falana, Jim Brown, Gail Fisher, Yvonne Fair, Robert and Fuller Gordy (Berry's brothers), Bob Jones, Raymond St. Jacques, Ron Townson, Sammy Strain of Little Anthony and the Imperials (now with the O'Jays), Johnny Taylor and his wife, Richard Roundtree and Cathy Lee Crosby, Herb and Mauna Loa Avery, Ruth Pointer, Chuck Jackson, Smokey and Claudette Robinson, Mike Roshkind, and Bill Loeb. Everything was beautiful. The tables were dressed in yellow, and there were large bouquets of daisies everywhere you looked. I cooked black beans, corn bread, ham hocks, and although I was tired by the day's end, I was very content.

Everyone was dancing and having a great time. Mauna Loa started acting kind of crazy and walked up to Cathy Lee Crosby and lifted up her top. Cathy had nothing on underneath! She swore she'd never talk to Mauna again. Meanwhile Benny and Willie entertained us with a karate demonstration in which they broke some bricks. It was a great party, and before it ended, I made a date to meet with Smokey.

During dinner a few days later, Smokey and I talked. "I want to sing lead now, Smokey," I said. "I know that I'm going to stick with the group, which is something I can never be sure of with anyone else. There has to be some consistency. It's getting to the point where people don't even know who we are."

"You're right, Mary," Smokey replied. "It's time you took that step."

Smokey discussed my idea with some Motown executives, but they didn't think I could carry the whole lead alone. They did, however, want me to assume part of the lead if we found a third girl who could carry the rest. That was pretty good news.

"I'll start recording an album with you," Smokey offered, "and then when you find your third girl, you'll share the leads."

I was so elated. I called Cholly in Detroit to tell him what I'd done.

"Well, Mary, you know it's about time you started speaking up for yourself, because nobody else will."

"Yeah, Cholly. I guess I had to find that out the hard way."

With just a few weeks before our next dates, the pressure to replace Jean intensified. I had auditioned many singers, but I liked Shelly Clark the best. A beautiful girl with a great personality, she'd been in the group Honey Cone, which had had a Number One record in 1971, "Want Ads." But Shelly declined due to other personal commitments.

I desperately called everyone I knew in the business to see if I'd missed any great singers. On a whim I called Lamont Dozier. "Hi, Lamont, it's Mary Wilson."

"Hey, girl. How are you doing?" It was typical Lamont, warm and friendly. "Lamont, do you know any great female singers?"

"For who?"

"For us." I sighed. "Jean is leaving, and probably Lynda too."

"Wow!" He laughed. "I know Scherrie Payne, and I think she would be good, because she grew up with the Supremes. She's pretty, and I know personally that she digs the group." Lamont went on to say that she was Freda Payne's younger sister and that, by the way, he and Scherrie were dating. That was enough recommendation for me. As one-third of the Holland-Dozier-Holland team, he'd produced hundreds of hit records. If he thought Scherrie was great, she must be.

Next I called Scherrie in Detroit. When I told her who I was and why I called, she was very excited. "Mama, it's Mary Wilson!" I heard her shout. I explained our predicament, and she seemed willing to help. When I asked if she'd like to come out to L.A. and audition, Scherrie said she'd be honored to. A few days later she was there, and I was sold. She was pretty, easy to get along with, and her voice was phenomenal. As far as I was concerned, she was in.

Scherrie and Freda Payne grew up in Detroit. We'd

worked the circuit with Freda in 1970, the year of her first hit, "Band of Gold," on Holland-Dozier-Holland's Invictus Records. Scherrie was asked to join the label as well, and she took over the lead spot in Glass House, a group that recorded only a few records.

My timing was perfect, as Scherrie was considering taking a regular job (she had studied medical technology and taught school) when I called. Her eagerness was refreshing, and she and Cindy hit it off. Like Jean and Lynda, Scherrie was opinionated and outspoken, but tactfully and with a sense of humor.

I'd hired Cindy assuming that Lynda too was leaving. Neither she nor Jean had come to my engagement party, and I heard from Lynda only through our manager, who kept me posted on her latest demands. She wanted a full one-third financial share of the group, which was unrealistic. I didn't see how it could be settled, and, besides, I figured to replace her in a few months anyway because of the baby.

Once we accepted Scherrie, Cindy and I began rehearsing right away in my living room. Cindy, as always, was a great help. Because she'd put on a little weight, though, her gowns had to be altered. We had only a handful of days to get ready, so it was going to be tough. But I was so hopeful and confident that I wrote my New Year's resolutions for 1974 in October:

1. Conserve money.
2. Check business.
3. Learn to sing and act.
4. Love Willie.

I decided to hire an outside lawyer. I needed someone good and strong, someone Motown couldn't intimidate or sway. For me or anyone with Motown, this was a big step.

One night at a show I ran into one of my favorite singers and close friends, Nancy Wilson. She introduced me to a tall, handsome black gentleman accompanying her and her husband. "This is my lawyer, David Williams."

David was one of the very few black attorneys coming up then. His father was a judge, and after talking with him, I felt that he was the right person for me and the Supremes. I could no longer ignore the ominous signs that Motown was abandoning us. I had to fight back.

A week after Scherrie joined the group, David and I met with Motown's lawyers, Abner, and Bill Loeb to review the Supremes' situation. When Abner heard that I had hired Scherrie on my own, boy, was he upset. He went through the ceiling. But Motown hadn't lifted a finger to replace Jean or Lynda. Why was the company mad at me for doing what had to be done?

"Mary," Abner said firmly, "you have overstepped your bounds. Besides, it's impossible for you to hire a new Supreme, when none of you are Supremes."

"Wait a minute, Abner," I said. "I *am* a Supreme."

"Well, Mary, you haven't even signed your new contract yet," Abner replied.

It was then that I knew I was right to instruct David Williams to have my new contract include a clause saying that I was a Supreme for life, unless I was disabled. How could Abner claim with a straight face that just because I hadn't signed a piece of paper I wasn't a Supreme? It was ridiculous. The stakes were suddenly clear. If I didn't start playing their games, I was going to lose.

On Halloween Cindy, Scherrie, and I played our first date together, at the Phoenix State Fair. The fans were thrilled to see Cindy back, and they loved Scherrie from the start. This was the first night I sang lead on most of the songs, and my performance was good, though I missed some notes on

"Somewhere." Between shows, some local reporters came for interviews. All the questions were directed to me, and all evening the promoter spoke only to me, as if Scherrie and Cindy weren't there. I hated this and told Bill Loeb to make sure that people knew there were three Supremes, not just me. Everyone was beginning to see me as "the boss," but in my heart I still wanted to be just one of the girls.

Two days later we did a Cincinnati show where only a few people came specifically to see the Supremes, with most of the audience there for Bloodstone and Donny Hathaway. I was thrilled to share the bill with Donny. His rendition of Leon Russell's "A Song for You" inspired me to perform a medley of it and "How Lucky Can You Get" a couple years later. Donny complained that the crowd was cold, but they certainly responded to us. When Cindy addressed the audience, fans screamed, "We're glad you're back, Cindy!" Tears came to my eyes. But that was about the only thing that went right.

We'd gone to Cincinnati thinking the promoter had sold five thousand tickets, only to find it was more like a few hundred. After the show the police tried to arrest him because he couldn't pay the acts. The sound was terrible, and we had to perform without a bass player, which the promoter was supposed to supply. These things never happened when Motown took care of us. No one was looking out for the Supremes. No one cared.

Afterward I went back to Detroit to visit Mom. Although she can neither read nor write, she is very wise. I respected her so much for her love and compassion, and I was happy to provide for her. She never asked me for anything, but on this day she said, "Mary, I would like you to get me a car."

"*What?*" Obviously she'd been talking to her friends, and one of them must have remarked that they thought I should buy her a car. I was a little annoyed, and without thinking snapped, "No. For one thing, you can't drive. And you can't read, Mom. How would you get around?"

"You could get someone to drive for me," she replied innocently. I felt so sorry for her. She was right; I should have had the money to give her a car and a driver, but money was getting very tight. I felt a twinge in my heart for having hurt her feelings.

I'd never thrown up her illiteracy to her before, but maybe I did on this day, because for years I feared that I might grow up to be just like her. I always secretly feared that ideas and information eluded me. And with the games Motown was playing, I was beginning to doubt my abilities to think and reason. I guess my Aunt I.V.'s constant harping when I was little about how sorry I'd be if I didn't learn had sunk in. To this day I regret lashing out at Mom. I was beginning to feel like a loser; I was beginning to unravel.

As usual, I went over to Flo's. She had lost a lot of weight and was looking better than she had in a while. In addition to her adorable daughters Michelle and Nicole, there was now a third child, sixteen-month-old Lisa. For several hours we talked about a little bit of everything. Flo was still very unhappy, though. Outside of lending a sympathetic ear, there was not much I could do.

In late 1973 the Supremes technically had no contract with Motown, but because I didn't own the name, we stopped shopping for a new label. I had told my attorney David Williams my whole story, starting from when Flo, Diane, and I signed with Motown in 1961. We were sixteen, and each signed a recording contract with Motown Records and a management contract with Berry Gordy, Jr. The day of the signing we still hadn't come up with a new name, hoping that would force Berry to accept the *Primettes.* Our mentors the Primes (Eddie Kendricks, Paul Williams, and Kell Osborne) had given us the name, and we didn't want to change. But

Berry stood firm, so we became the Supremes. Flo picked the name the Supremes, which we didn't think was as pretty as our former name, the Primettes. But Berry said, "Look, I don't like the name *Primettes.* Change it before you sign your contracts," and we did. Short of sleeping with him, we'd have done everything Berry wanted if it would get us a record deal.

When we signed our contracts, we didn't fully understand the clause stating that Motown owned the name the *Supremes.* Diane, Flo, and I *weren't* dummies. We *were* three enthusiastic, idealistic minors signing contracts without competent, independent legal counsel. God forbid if one of our parents—our only representatives there that day—decided not to sign for us. We lost our fourth member, Barbara Martin, when her mother refused, saying she didn't like the terms of the contract. From the beginning, our parents saw our signing as the best alternative to running the streets. In Motown they saw our Big Chance.

Meanwhile, no one at Motown said anything about a contract for Scherrie. They never indicated whether they liked her or thought she should be in the group. It was November; I decided that New Year's Day 1974 was my "deadline." We had to have a group, we had to know who was in it, and their contracts had to be in order. The Supremes had not recorded in almost a year, a period during which we'd normally have released two LPs and three or four singles. Remembering Smokey's promise to produce us, I started pushing Motown. We needed a new record out, and soon. Without contracts, Scherrie and I, along with Cindy, hit the road: another new group of Supremes.

December 1973

The shows here at Bachelors III in Fort Lauderdale have been going over very well. Scherrie and Cindy are doing an excellent job. Our reviews were great. Thank God for that. I know people are asking, "Just what are the Supremes trying to prove? Why don't they give up?" But if we did, what would I do? Could Pedro take care of me? Could I lean on his shoulder then? Would he stay with me? God, no, I must keep working.

December 13, 1973

*5:30* A.M.—Well, I was lying down, trying to sleep, when the phone rang. Pedro sounded drunk or strange. He called me a prostitute, saying he was tired of hearing things about me, and no wonder no one liked me. He started talking about the photo of me on the couch. He said the next time I see him, it will be with someone else. I guess it's over. I was hoping so much that we could make it, but I've lost again.

*11:00* A.M.—Pedro has called me three times already. At first I got the impression that we were finished, but when he called back he started asking if there were any other men. He brought up other names, some of whom I never had anything to do with, like Berry and Marvin Gaye. But trying to tell him now wouldn't matter because he has it in his head that I am a prostitute. Now he's even bringing up the fact that I went to bed with him the first week. I finally told him that he'd have to live with my past or get out.

While cleaning out some papers a few months earlier, Pedro had come across a photograph of me and Tom Jones. Tom had his arm across my chest so that although I was wearing a two-piece bathing suit, it looked like I was topless. Without a word, Pedro stalked into the kitchen and swatted a tray of food from my hands. He shoved the photo at me and screamed, "You fucking whore!"

I was beginning to see a pattern. Pedro always caught me off-guard, then made outrageous accusations and carried on so wildly I couldn't think fast enough to answer him. I knew he was wrong, but each time he came at me I became frightened little Mary, afraid of everything.

"Tell me everybody you've ever slept with, you fucking whore!"

Pedro yelled and waved the picture in the air. "I don't remember," I stammered, fearing for my life. His eyes looked like those of a madman.

"Tell me! Tell me who you slept with, you whore! I want you to write down their names on this piece of paper!"

When reason failed, I said, "Okay, okay," and he pushed me down into a chair by my shoulder. Suddenly I was a little girl again, being forced to recite my ABCs, or being reprimanded for wetting the bed. I started writing: Duke, Flip, Tom . . .

"Who else?" Pedro shouted, reading over my shoulder.

My mind raced to recall everyone. I knew that if I overlooked anyone, there would be hell to pay later. I listed my true loves, I listed some one-night stands. Tears streamed down my face, and sobs racked my body. Long ago, my mother told me, "Mary, never tell your husband everything; you'll live to regret it." Now I knew what she meant. I tried keeping my list to just those men whose names were well known.

When I finished, Pedro snatched the paper, read it, then said, "And you've got your fucking boyfriends' pictures all over the house." He was referring to some cocktail tables Willie and a few friends had helped me make. The tabletops were made of resin in which I had embedded dozens of mementos: photos, hotel-room keys from around the world, foreign coins, and other little tokens. Pedro tore through the house, shattering the tabletops and tearing up every photo he found as well as many of my diaries and scrapbooks.

"You think you're so great!" Pedro said derisively. "Who do you think you are? You never display your family's pictures. How do you think that makes them feel?" I was speechless with fear. When he finally calmed down, he left for Mexico. As he went out the door, he warned, "Mary, don't you dare leave this house!"

What was wrong with him? How could he accuse me of "hiding" my past when almost every man I'd dated was mentioned in the world press? He also knew that I was over Duke and Tom. Still, whenever I insisted on going to see the Four Tops perform, Pedro got moody and angry. He was the same way about Eddie Kendricks, although I told him many times that Eddie and I were only friends now. Nothing I said mattered.

Despite his hateful words, on his way to Mexico Pedro phoned from San Diego. He wanted to know, would I still marry him? Days later, he was back.

November 22, 1973

When I returned from acting class, Pedro poured champagne and said that he wanted to talk. He said he had read my diaries and now understands me. That was really a shock, because, as you know, I write everything. Well, he said that he found out that I had been very right in everything and that people just didn't understand me. As he was talking, I thought, *Wow, if my diary was that explanatory, then I must really have been writing well. Maybe I should write a book.* We talked for hours. I couldn't believe that just by reading my diaries he would really understand me. When he first said he had read them, I was ready for him to go into a tantrum and call me all kinds of names. Also, he said he had torn out the pages where there was something with a man. That hurt, because now I'll never know what I wrote. He said he was sorry about that and asked if I would forgive him. Plus, he said he will keep those photos so that he can control me and possibly use them . . .

Instead of seeing what was wrong with Pedro or with our relationship, I found myself more often looking for what was wrong with me. Instead of thinking about how to get away from Pedro, I blamed myself for falling in love with him in the first place. Pedro was stronger than me, and before long I was writing in my diary about how I should change, how I should improve, and how I should be more of a real woman, one who sacrificed for her man. In other words, be more like what Pedro wanted me to be. It was easier for me to stand up for the Supremes than for Mary Wilson. I'd opened myself up to Pedro, and in return he was destroying my self-respect.

I was really looking forward to Christmas this year, my first in my adult life I'd be spending with my own family. Having everyone together and the group's suddenly brighter prospects combined to lift my spirits. I'd usually been on the road during the holidays, so I rarely got to celebrate the way I wanted. I remembered how as a teenager all I wanted at Christmastime was a big, fat, beautiful tree flocked in pink artificial snow. It wasn't traditional, but to me that was how the other half lived.

On a day off I decided I'd surprise everyone. I went out and found *my* tree, then I unpacked boxes and boxes of angel hair, tinsel, glass balls, electric lights, and other ornaments I'd collected over the years. While trimming, I flashed back to when I was a kid in Detroit, and we would put anything we could find on the tree, including earrings and ornaments we'd made in school. When it was done, I stood back and admired my tree—which looked like the one I remembered from Hudson's Department Store—happily thinking how surprised Pedro and Willie would be. Oh, how beautiful it looked to me. This would be the best Christmas ever.

Pedro walked into the living room, and I stood there, waiting for him to smile or reach to hold me. Instead he began screaming, "What is this? This isn't a Christmas tree! It's cheap and trashy! Like everything here in Hollywood!"

As I watched silently, Pedro pulled down the tree. The

glass ornaments and lights made muffled tinkling sounds as they shattered on the floor. As Pedro clawed at the branches and threw the tree around, tufts of pink flocking settled on the carpet like little clouds.

Pedro had made his point. Christmas in my house—now *his* house—was to be celebrated not with the gaiety of the southern black holiday traditions I knew, but with the solemnity of his Latin, Catholic upbringing. More disturbing, the object of Pedro's rage wasn't just his perception of my pink-flocked tree, it was me. That tree symbolized everything about me and my life. I saw that who I was, what I was, threatened him.

I promised myself I would change.

# CHAPTER 8

*E*ven today I still believe that of all the Supremes'
seventies lineups, Jean, Cindy, and I had the most
potential to make it. But this new lineup with Scherrie and Cindy had the most glamour and pizzazz, an opinion
shared by fans. Visually we were perfect, and vocally, fresh
and dynamic. Scherrie was more than a terrific singer; she
had that indescribable something that makes audiences sit up
and listen. Scherrie and Freda were vocally similar, like
Dionne Warwick, Dionne's aunt Cissy Houston, and her
cousin Whitney Houston. You know that their talent was genetic, honey!

Although she was only a petite five feet one, Scherrie
was very sexy, and several writers dubbed her "the devil in
the red dress." With her unique, powerful blues-and-jazz-
inflected style, Scherrie, like Jean, was a great singer. No one
would ever compare her to Diane, for which I was grateful.
Scherrie had a fire, a spark, that the Supremes had been
missing.

For the first time in a couple years, writers were taking a renewed interest in the Supremes. Local critics unimpressed by our latter-day appearances with Jean and Lynda noticed us now and raved. We could not have asked for better, more encouraging reviews, but we still had no new record out.

We spent New Year's Eve performing at the Contemporary Hotel in Disney World, ringing in 1974 after singing the O'Jays' "Love Train." Following the show, Scherrie invited us to go with her to a party at a nearby cabaret. When Scherrie came out wearing a simple cotton pants set, I told her tactfully that we just couldn't go around looking however we wanted.

"I don't care what people think," Scherrie replied. "I hadn't planned on going out tonight; this is what I'm wearing."

"People don't care if you planned to go out or not, Scherrie," I said shortly. "All they know is that we are the Supremes, and we have to look like it—all the time."

"Yes," Cindy chimed in. "We do have to be sure we look our best wherever we go."

Scherrie changed into something more appropriate. *Not this again,* I thought. Every group had one person who always swam against the tide. First Flo, then Jean. Right or wrong, the image mattered and had to be maintained. Cindy promised me she would keep an eye on Scherrie.

The cabaret was a lot like the little places we used to go to in Greenville, Mississippi, where my mother and cousins came from. Everything was very informal, and everyone was so friendly and "real down-home," as I wrote in my diary. Pedro enjoyed it because it reminded him of his homeland. It was the first good New Year's Eve I'd had in years, with my husband-to-be, my son, and Scherrie and Cindy.

In the past few years, I'd been approached by a number of people either connected to or part of what I think of as the record industry's underworld. Often, these were not even face-to-face meetings with the alleged Mr. Big, but cryptic messages passed to me orally by someone who *knew someone* who *had heard that someone* was interested in "helping" the Supremes. One time I got the "word" while flying to a date with a very prominent entertainer. He advised me that it might be "better" for me and the Supremes if I was on the "right side." *The right side of what?* I wondered.

A casual acquaintance familiar with the music industry once outlined for me an elaborate and incredible scenario about who controlled the business. Most of it was so blatantly outrageous, I couldn't believe it. But then this person said things that only someone with connections could know, things I won't even talk about today. Some things he said about the Supremes were plausible: that our records weren't being played because "someone didn't want them played," a situation that could be "rectified" if I would align myself with the right "important people" and stop fighting. But who? No one was about to answer me unless I first agreed to go along with the secret agenda, whatever it was, whoever it involved. In the past couple of years, I'd heard through the grapevine that "someone" wanted the Supremes and could get me the name. As far as I knew, no one had the name. I ignored these offers of "help."

Shortly after one of these encounters, I went to see a famous psychic, something I did now and then in those wild days of the seventies. The psychic said that my father was my guardian angel and was looking after me. I wouldn't make the wrong move, and I would succeed eventually. I was warned not to let anyone stop me or pull me down. He also said that I would have very bad times, and fifteen years of bad luck. That turned out to be true.

Over the past few years, I had gradually set up and controlled a separate corporation that handled all the Supremes' business. Motown had no objection; if anything, it was probably relieved. Before, the company handled every business and financial detail of our lives, professional and personal. Every expense—meals, gowns, car rental, salaries for musicians, conductors, road managers, assistants and the required payroll taxes, dry cleaning, storage, wigs, makeup, recording sessions, *everything*—was managed and paid for through Motown but out of our pockets. When I started going over the books, I was amazed to see just how much it cost us to work.

One big expense was our stage wardrobe. Our designers included Mike Travis (who also designed for Dionne Warwick and Liberace), Bob Mackie, Mike Nicola, and Pat Campano. We spent hours reviewing designs, picking out colors, fabrics, and other materials. Our outfits were some of the most lavish in show business. Many of the sequins and beads were imported, and all were applied by hand. Diane once remarked to Johnny Carson, "Little old ladies have gone blind trying to sew on all those beads." Some costumes contained tens of thousands of them. The red-beaded jumpsuit we wore for our first appearance on Ed Sullivan's show cost over $1,000 in 1970, and it was one of the cheaper ones.

Before long, each costume had its own name, and audiences had their favorites, such as a thirty-five-pound, bead-and-rhinestone-covered "Pink Chiffon," the green, lime-green, and white "Swirl" gowns from "T.C.B."; or the beige, beaded "Chandelier" gowns. Each fit us so snugly that a pound gained spelled disaster. If any of us got the least bit out of shape, costumes were returned to designers for painstaking, complicated alterations and whatever rebeading was needed.

Certain parts of the outfits required special care, and there was a perpetual stream of costumes on their way to and from designers so that seats, underarms, crotches, and other well-worn areas could be rebeaded. Because of all the handwork, the delicacy of some fabrics, and the unique dyes used, cleaning and storing them was yet another expense. Some outfits cost over $100 each just to clean. The cost of shipping trunks of thirty- to forty-pound gowns and suits all over the world was exorbitant. We probably worked several weeks each year just to keep our costumes alive!

Years before I'd never given a second thought to what it cost to put together a show. Just making changes each year to incorporate new songs (which required new arrangements, new choreography, new costumes, maybe new musicians, and weeks of rehearsal time) cost a minimum of $40,000 and as much as $100,000. Every date meant at least a dozen round-trip airfares for us, staff, musicians, and whoever else we needed, a dozen hotel rooms, three dozen meals a day, and other incidentals. On some dates, the "miscellaneous" un-foreseen expense was a local hairdresser or a series of long-distance calls; other times, it was renting several cars or sound equipment, flying in and paying last-minute replacement musicians, or something even more costly.

In the sixties and early seventies we traveled with our own hairdresser, for example. Now we couldn't afford more than a skeleton staff: five musicians and three assistants. Meanwhile, back at home, we had people on staff, such as Hazel, Benny, and maids, drawing salaries whether the Supremes worked or not.

Retaining top musicians, however, was one major expense I never regretted. No matter how small the venue or how little the pay, I was determined to sound great. Cutting corners with second-rate players would only hurt us in the long run.

I'd decided that each Supreme receive a percentage of the corporation's income after all expenses were paid. I learned more than I ever wanted to know about unscrupulous or undercapitalized promoters, contract breaching, and the natural tendency for money to mysteriously disappear on its way from the box office to the Supremes, Inc., bank account. I found falsified receipts—a $60 piano-tuning bill with a suspiciously placed extra zero added, making it $600—and evidence of countless other ruses. It was impossible to keep on top of every single detail, and this is where Hazel proved a godsend. She examined, checked, and questioned every bill, check, statement, and contract that crossed my desk. She found countless errors and oversights, and, now and then, outright stealing.

Motown still had not finished our contracts or reached a settlement with the Hollands on Scherrie's contract, or so it claimed. Technically, she still "belonged" to Invictus, but the label wasn't doing much with her, so it's hard to figure out why Motown was having so much trouble getting her released. When I questioned one executive about why we weren't in the studio, he said the company couldn't record us without a contract. What a joke: in the early days, Berry recorded most of us without contracts. Something else was going on. Why weren't we recording?

After not hearing one word from Smokey about his promise to record us, I knew I was on my own. Not that I had really expected all that much from him. I love Smokey dearly, but his first loyalty will always be to Motown and Berry.

Because I still felt so close to the Motown clan in those days, I thought nothing about asking my few friends in the business to produce us. Marvin Gaye was one I approached over the years. When we got together, I described to Marvin what was happening, and he promised to stop by. When I told my housekeeper Ethel to expect Marvin Gaye, she looked as if she were going to faint. "Mary, should I make lunch for Mr. Gaye? Do you think he'd like some of my sweet-potato pie?" I told her I was sure he would. I had to laugh. Marvin was the sweetheart of every woman in the world, young or old.

It was a couple hours after Ethel's regular quitting time when Marvin arrived, and he didn't let her down. First he hugged me warmly, then after I introduced Ethel, he hugged her too. I know she will never forget that.

As we sat in the living room, Marvin ate a piece of Ethel's pie and drank a glass of milk. One of my cats climbed onto his lap, and we sat for quite a while in front of the fireplace.

"How do you feel about what's happening for Diane?" Marvin asked me. Because Marvin was Berry's brother-in-law and had fought so bitterly for his creative freedom, I knew that he—like most Motowners—had mixed feelings about her. Marvin was always Hitsville's rebel, and always, in his way, an outsider.

"I don't even think about it," I said. "I don't think she's the cause of my problems with Motown. I'm so busy trying to get my own life together, I hardly have time to think about anything."

"Well, baby," Marvin said softly, "you'd better slow down. Don't let anybody drive you crazy."

He promised he would write for us and produce us. I believe he really meant it, as he would mention it several more times over the years. None of these plans was realized, though, because Marvin had enough problems of his own.

Scherrie, Cindy, and I were up at Motown, finally picking songs for our next record, when we heard there would be yet another delay with the contracts. Berry was in his office, so I decided to stop in with Scherrie. The minute I saw him I felt like an old shoe he had tossed away.

"Hey, Mary, how are you doing? Scherrie, what's happening? Have you two signed your contracts?"

"No, Berry, we haven't," I said. "There are still all kinds of legal problems, and we are getting nowhere. We have to record, and this is really holding us up."

"Okay, okay," Berry said. "Let me call Abner and see what's going on."

He called Abner, and after speaking briefly, Berry hung up. "I've given Suzanne dePasse a lot more authority," he said, "and you can work with her when the contracts are all signed.

"You know," he added, "Diane's opening in Las Vegas."

"Yeah," I replied. "Tell her I said hello and good luck."

Scherrie and I were partway out the door when Berry suddenly remarked, "Mary, you know you're the one responsible for all the other girls leaving the group. You're always giving all the other girls too much power, like Diane and Jean. You really did it with Jean. That's why she left."

"It wasn't me, Berry. Especially not with Jean. It was you giving her all those lines, promising her the moon, and then letting things drop."

Berry said nothing.

"Berry, we're going to sign our contracts. I just want you to know that this time I'm going to be sure to read mine. *Very carefully.*"

"Well, Mary," he replied in all seriousness, "you know, if it weren't for me, you never would have had a contract."

So that's what Berry truly believed: everything that I was—everything that everyone there was—was only because of him. Sometimes I wanted to point out to him that everything he was, was because of *us*. I wanted to say, "You stole our name, and now I want it back!" Or, better yet, "Kiss my you know what," and walk away. But I didn't. I was caught in an invisible web.

In the meantime we got the go-ahead to sign our contracts. Mike Roshkind called me to say that, yes, Motown would delete the clause saying I waived all rights to the name. Within an hour of phoning Scherrie and Cindy with the good news, I got another call from Mike. This time he said, no, they could not do it.

When Bill Loeb, David Williams, and I met Mike at his office, he seemed surprisingly grim. "I have just spoken with . . ." he said, naming some other attorneys, "and they advised us not to let you sign the contract unless you waive all rights to the name."

Mike and I went back and forth, firmly but politely, for a while. Mike saw that I wasn't about to capitulate, so he went into what I called his hatchet-man bag. David Williams became so agitated that Mike asked him to leave.

"Mike, I am not signing under those terms," I said. "That's it."

"Fine," he replied evenly. *"We'll just have to get three other girls."*

The velvet glove was off, just like Flo had said it would be. But I wasn't going to be beaten down.

"You just try," I said, rising to leave. "Good-bye!"

Not long after *Dreamgirl* was published, I found myself on a plane sitting across from Mike and Smokey Robinson (whom he now manages) in first-class. Smokey was on a promotional tour of England. Between my first book and the "Motown 25" debacle, my relationship with Motown was nonexistent, so at first things were a bit awkward. After a while we got to talking, and I was surprised when Mike said he liked my book but felt I'd been too kind to many of the people in the story. "Mary," he said, as we sipped champagne, "you should have been harder. No one likes to hear all nice things." I smiled to myself, knowing my second book was in the works.

We talked some more. It was Mike who'd negotiated Florence's departure from the Supremes and presented her with the outrageous terms of settlement, including that she could never use the name *Supremes* again. "Mike," I asked, "how could you have done some of the things you did at Motown, those horrible things that really hurt people?"

"I was younger then," he replied. "But that was my job. One of the reasons I'm managing now is that I want to do something positive."

I was surprised at his frankness, but it did little to dull the memory of what he and other Motown executives had put me and the Supremes through in the seventies. I guess it goes to show that business, money, and power can make people do strange things.

This day in 1974, however, I saw Mike in a much less charitable light. I drove home nearly blinded by tears. As I turned off Sunset Boulevard and onto my street, my neighbor Johnny Mathis waved to me; I waved back, hoping he didn't see my face. I was a mess. My hands were shaking. All I could think was, *How can Mike do this to me?* By the time I pulled up my long driveway, I was weeping uncontrollably.

"What's wrong?" Pedro asked. I didn't answer as I ran down the mirrored hallway and into my red-velvet bedroom.

It was over. *Over.* Everything I'd worked for was gone. The one thing that had given Diane, Flo, and me the chance to make something of ourselves, to have something more than what our parents had, was gone, dead.

When I calmed down I told Pedro everything. Despite his persistence, I'd never let him see any of my business papers, until now. He read the contract Motown was offering and pointed out that it was essentially the same as the old one. I depended on Pedro's judgment. In fact, I began to feel that I could trust no one except him. Now I see that it was so simple; I was running from Motown and into my lover's protective arms.

I had no choice but to leave Motown. But then what? At moments like this a paralyzing fear crept over me. I could study all the facts, put together all that I knew, and know what was right for me to do. Still I was so afraid. Poor Flo's face loomed in front of me. *Oh God—don't let this happen to me,* I thought to myself, *I've never done anything to hurt a soul, I just want to sing, and be happy.* I felt so small and frightened. Somewhere deep inside me, though, was a powerful belief that I would do the right thing, that my life would eventually turn out all right, one way or the other. God would come to my rescue. There wasn't any real reason for me to believe this, but I did. That's the supreme faith that always seems to pull me through, even when all around me seems lost.

Early the next morning Berry called. "I spoke with Mike Roshkind and heard about the problems," he said quietly. Berry didn't sound like himself. He actually seemed concerned. "Mary, just what is it you want?"

Without thinking, I blurted out, "Fifty percent of the name *Supremes.*"

There was a second of silence, then Berry said, "You

got it. I'll have my people get right on drawing up those papers."

Was it that easy? I'd expected a hard time. As he spoke, I said a silent prayer of thanks to God for saving me and my family. *At least now,* I thought, *I won't end up destitute like Flo.*

In late February 1974 we went to Mexico City to appear at the Casino Real. We were all looking forward to working, because we needed the practice, the exposure—and the money. We attended a charity concert given by the Fifth Dimension.

Our trip to Mexico started out nicely enough, but soon we could only conclude that there was a hex on us. First we had trouble getting our luggage to the plane on time, then Cindy lost her passport. A week later our dressing room burned down, destroying tens of thousands of dollars' worth of gowns. The club owner signed a statement claiming that the full extent of the damages amounted to $250. Two hundred fifty dollars! We had costume jewelry that cost more than that. We lost nine sets of gowns, so the actual loss was more like $30,000. I phoned Hazel back in Los Angeles, and four more sets of gowns were shipped, but only one set fit all three of us. A few days later we were making a publicity appearance at a club. Suddenly the police broke in and, for some mysterious reason, arrested everyone. After being detained for three hours, we were set free. When we finally finished the engagement, we were glad to be home.

While we were gone, our manager and attorney tried to quietly interest another record company in us. ABC Records, which had done so well by the Four Tops, expressed the strongest interest, but later declined. I heard that the label got cold feet because Motown threatened legal action over the name the *Supremes.*

While all this madness was going on, I was still touring, mothering Willie, cooking meals, and planning for my wedding. Against my better judgment, several months earlier our manager had booked us to coheadline with Joel Grey at the Riviera Hotel in Vegas. So Pedro and I thought, *Why not get married there?* Vegas was still very glamorous. I became very excited about this great event. For a while I got so caught up in the happiness of picking out fabric for the wedding gown, finding the right wedding chapel in Vegas, making up the guest list, and so forth that all fears were forgotten. Now that I had decided to marry Pedro, it was just all too exciting.

During this time Pedro and I were just like two lovebirds. Plus, since I had allowed him to become more involved in my business affairs, he was happier, but I noticed that the more I allowed him, the more he took. The wedding was on, the cake ordered, the gown and the guest list were ready. I couldn't stop the wedding now.

Scherrie, Cindy, and I had to work our tails off to get ready for Vegas. We had to be a hit there. Since the Supremes now earned most of our income from performances, we needed to be in the top venues. For two days in mid-April we tried out our show at the Sahara in Lake Tahoe. It was a last-minute booking, so we weren't fully prepared, and it showed. The only bright spot came when, during her show at Harrah's, Liza Minnelli introduced us from the stage as "three entertainers I have admired and respected." She was one of those stars, like Cher and Dionne Warwick, who were always friendly toward me and never passed by without stopping to say hello and chat.

We got very bad reviews, all driving home the point that we could not take this same old show to Vegas. We needed the money and the exposure, true, but why embarrass ourselves? The constant pressure to be out working, even to our reputation's detriment, was a sore point between me on one side, and our manager and Motown on the other. They couldn't have cared less what happened to the Supremes, as long as they got their cuts. We should have been reworking the show or recording a hit. Couldn't they see that they were running the Supremes into the ground?

With just six days before the Vegas opening, we brought in Cholly Atkins and some other professionals to put together a new production. It was an impossible task, but we had to try. New songs, new steps, new group, new everything. We rehearsed every day until we couldn't stand up.

Phil Moore, an arranger, conductor, and pianist who had worked on Broadway and with such stars as Dorothy Dandridge, Marilyn Monroe, and Lena Horne, came in. He told us which songs we'd be doing, but when Cindy realized she had no solos, she became upset. She ended up getting a solo part in one number, which was fine, and fair. What bothered me, though, was her saying, "If I don't look out for myself, no one else will."

It never dawned on me that she wanted to sing lead; we'd never discussed it. If she had said something about it, I wouldn't have objected. I was crushed and, for a moment, quite angry. *After all*, I thought, *no one told her to leave the group the first time.* Now she was back, and all that time off showed. She still hadn't lost the weight. I begged her to take classes with my voice teacher, and she did for a while. More than anything, though, I was deeply hurt that my efforts on her behalf went unnoticed. I knew she wasn't that kind of person, but it made me think how things had changed.

It felt strange to do a thirty-five-minute opening set instead of our usual hour. Richard Roundtree, Cher, and Lamont Dozier came to see us. Everyone was complimentary and kind, but I knew we weren't as good as we should have been, and it was sad.

The important people at Motown knew that Pedro and I were getting married in Vegas. I still didn't know what the label was up to; it seemed a strange coincidence that Motown chose this time to send out Abner to work on me about the contract.

Abner had the agreement stating that I owned 50 percent of the Supremes' name ready for me to sign. The same day that Pedro and I got our marriage license, David Williams gave me the bad news: he'd heard from the Trademark Office that Motown owned the name. It was odd that it had taken him months to find that out. I was beginning to lose my grasp of all the legal intricacies. I did know, though, that I needed the name. Since getting 50 percent was better than getting nothing, I signed, against Pedro's advice. He told me that I would regret signing this deal, and he was right. The ink had barely dried on the new five-year contract when Abner said, "Look, Mar-ry, Motown should be managing the Supremes. Why don't you let us take over?"

"For nearly four years now I've held it together while Motown's done nothing," I answered. "There's no record out, and we are an opening act."

Motown's "giving" me 50 percent ownership of the name came with so many restrictions that it was essentially worthless *except* in one case: if Motown ever sold the rights to the Supremes' name, I would be entitled to half the proceeds. I'm sure Motown thought this "fine-print" restriction was quite clever. And it was. At that time, I'm sure it never occurred to Berry or anyone else that he would ever sell the name, or Motown. However, in 1988 he did.

Although I felt something was fishy about all of this, I couldn't figure out what. I had doubts and questions, but I wasn't an attorney. Short of getting a law degree myself, all I could do was listen to and trust my advisers. I'd tried my best. But besides my suspicions about the deal itself, I had questions about how it all came down. For one thing, Motown had been taking its sweet time with the contracts and hadn't recorded us for months. Suddenly, the day of my wedding, there was a big rush. What had made it so urgent that Motown flew in people from Los Angeles to get me to sign the paper? Why couldn't it have waited a few days? I was crushed at these new developments on the eve of my wedding.

Most of my family had flown in for the wedding, and many of our friends were there, too. Pedro and I were getting on each others' nerves, but that was normal. The morning of my wedding, my mother, my sister Cat, and my Aunt I.V. helped me get dressed. We were to be at the chapel at three o'clock, but by two my gown still had not arrived from Los Angeles. I was beginning to get nervous, wondering if Pedro really wanted to marry me, wondering where my dress was.

"I think I'm about to cry," my mother said.

"Mommy, please don't." I knew that if she did, I would too, and I'd already cried enough that day. I'd just finished applying my makeup, and I had to look gorgeous. After all, this was the day I'd waited for since I was a little girl, with the whole works: the church, the white gown, the handsome prince. But was I happy? At that moment, Mom and I *both* started crying, probably for the same reason.

At two-thirty my gown finally arrived. It was made from a Spanish-style pattern and trimmed in white lace and pearls. I put it on, and when I turned to look in the mirror, I began crying again. I didn't know why. The gown was perfect, and there I was, finally a bride. Maybe they were tears of happiness.

---

I arrived at the chapel before Pedro in "Grace," my Rolls-Royce. I had to wait in the back until he came, as the bride is not supposed to arrive before the groom. Then it was time.

I was taken to the front of the chapel. Pat Campano, my dress designer, pulled my veil over my face, telling Willie how to pull it back. I could feel the sun beating down on my head, and I could see the few remaining people hurrying inside the chapel. As Willie and I started down the aisle, I felt spaced. Our rhythm-section guys were playing my wedding march, "I Hear a Symphony." Cat walked in front of me, a beautiful bridesmaid. Pedro's sister Malvena, a flower girl, looked radiant, and Joey and Dax, Pedro's friends from Puerto Rico, were best men. Willie (who'd stepped on my gown coming down the aisle) pulled back my veil. He and I laughed as he squeezed my hand.

Pedro and I stood side by side. The lady nondenominational minister spoke to us. I felt like I was in a movie: the beautiful girl marrying the handsome man. I noticed Pedro had shaved off his mustache, which I despised because it made him look like a hard black militant. His eyes looked big and warm, his face as soft as a baby's. We held hands. His was shaking and a little cold, but firm. As I listened to the minister, I felt very happy. Pedro started repeating after her in his heavy Spanish accent. Most of the words he didn't say correctly. I started repeating after her and didn't say them correctly either. My voice was so quiet, it seemed to be coming from someone else. Pedro couldn't get the ring on. I laughed. The minister started reading from Gibran on marriage . . .

Then we kissed. I couldn't believe it: Man and Wife. As we turned to leave, my eyes brimmed with tears. Everyone kissed us and wished us well. We went outside to take photos and throw the bouquet. My sister caught it. Now on to the reception. It was nice. However, I had to paint the miniature couple on top of the cake brown with Hazel's eyeliner.

In addition to our relatives, other guests included Jim Brown, Joel Grey, Berry Gordy's mother, Cindy and Charles, Scherrie, Hazel, Bill Loeb, David Williams, and Ewart Abner and Bob Jones from Motown. Pedro and I left the reception around four-thirty and went up to our room, where we opened our gifts and jumped into bed. At eight that evening we were awakened by the phone. Our show started in fifteen minutes! Pedro and I ran around like crazy trying to get ready. When I got to the stage, everyone was waiting, and I was so embarrassed, holding up the show for ten minutes.

Our honeymoon was spent on the road with the Supremes. From the end of May through June we toured Hawaii, Hong Kong, Australia, and Japan. While in the last country, we taped a television program that aired there as a prime-time special and received great reviews. We planned to release the soundtrack here as a live album, and our manager sold the tape to ABC Television, which was going to broadcast it as part of the network's *Wide World of Entertainment* series. Somehow, the tape "disappeared." The soundtrack album was released in Japan, then suddenly and inexplicably withdrawn.

The weeks of work and travel took their toll on everyone, but especially on my marriage. I had been pretty much alone since leaving home at seventeen. Now I had a constant, domineering companion, my husband. The honeymoon was over almost as soon as it began.

A lot of problems started because, now that Pedro was my husband, he became the boss not only of me, but of the group as well. We were three women alone out there, and he took over. The one thing that bothered me was that he spent money as if it were his own—paying for everyone's dinner and buying "drinks on Pedro." He was the big shot, at least in his mind. Then, he began openly ordering me around. I was so tired of fighting now, after losing to Motown, that I just went along with this outlandish behavior.

I resigned myself to my situation. Whereas before I promised myself that I would try harder to make everything in my life better, now I accepted that I was different from the person I had been before. One night in Australia, I was lying in bed when suddenly I felt the sensation that another woman was taking over my body. She was all those things I fought so long to not be: negative, frightened, suspicious. All my courage and confidence disappeared. When I tried to picture myself now, I saw someone very small and cowardly.

I felt ashamed. But why? I tried to reason with myself. I promised I would stop being suspicious of people, although many of my problems stemmed from not being suspicious enough before. I wondered if other married women also felt they were being absorbed by their husbands, washed away. For a minute I thought I should see a psychiatrist.

In Hollywood, nightlife still retained a certain stylish cachet, and Pedro and I went out on the town like other people did. We partied hard. I had grown accustomed to "behaving" in public so as not to arouse Pedro's jealousy. We frequented private clubs where we saw many friends. I stopped dancing with men, even such old, close friends as Billy Davis. Billy didn't care for women, but that didn't prevent Pedro from acting insanely jealous toward him. The tension of having to monitor my every move was too much. Around this time I pretty much stopped going out at all. Unless I was on a stage, I was at home.

One of the few close friends I had was Teddy Pendergrass. He was still singing with Harold Melvin and the Blue

Notes, and Pedro knew them from their days playing clubs in Puerto Rico. The Blue Notes had been together since 1956, but their big hits began after Teddy became their lead singer in 1970. By 1976 or so, the Blue Notes had a solid string of hits ("If You Don't Know Me by Now," "The Love I Lost," "Wake Up Everybody"), and Teddy began to consider going solo. He and Pedro were running buddies from way back, so he often came to our house, and we'd talk.

That day Teddy said, "I really need to talk to you. I'm thinking about getting out of the group and going on my own. But I like the guys, and they gave me my start. Still, I feel like I can do other things too. I just don't know what to do."

"Teddy, if you truly feel that you have done all you can with the group and that you can do more on your own, you should go," I said. "But if you do leave, be honest and forthright about it." I must have been thinking about Diane and the Supremes. "Do it the right way, so there won't be any bad feelings."

"Do you think I could really make it alone?" he asked.

"I'm sure you can, Teddy. But remember: you've got to do it the right way."

"Thanks, Mary. There weren't many people I could talk to who would understand this."

Of course, Teddy went solo and became a sex symbol known to his female fans as "Teddy Bear." In 1982 he was paralyzed from the neck down in a freak car accident. We'd kept in touch, and I visited him at his home. One day he said to me, "You know, Mary, of all the people I've known, you're one of the few who's come to see me. It really means a lot to me."

Nine months after Scherrie and Cindy joined the group, they were still technically without contracts. These delays caused a lot of friction, because Cindy and Scherrie were essentially working for Supremes, Inc.; in other words, me. Despite my efforts to reignite the group spirit, I was the boss, and that made it hard.

I didn't like the fact that our husbands were suddenly so active in the business, either. Charles and Cindy's baby, David, traveled with us, so it made sense to find something for Charles to do for the group. Pedro had already pressured me into naming him road manager; we created a similar position for Charles. Even though I had reluctantly let Pedro work with us, I still felt that I could keep him out of my professional life. Before long, though, both were asking our manager about our business. The meddling husband is an occupational hazard for any female entertainer. I admit that while Pedro did push his way in, I wanted him there because he was strong, and I needed him. Cindy probably felt the same way about her man. Shutting out Charles would only have caused hard feelings, and besides, he and Pedro got along well and kept each other company on the road.

I loved Cindy and loved having her in the group, but her personal problems were affecting her performance. At times Cindy appeared quite happy to be back; then there were moments when she seemed ambivalent. "I want you to take some time and get yourself together, mentally and physically," I told her. Cindy cried a little bit, and my heart went out to her. Like me, she had marriage problems. Neither of us could accept not being able to give everything to both our careers and our marriages. I was beginning to see, though, that the only way many men can deal with successful women is to stifle their ambition and undermine their confidence. That's what Pedro was doing to me, and from what I saw, I believed that's what Charles was doing to Cindy. When I suggested to Cindy that she indulge herself and make herself as beautiful as possible, she gave me a sad, blank stare. There was nothing else I could do; the rest was up to her.

Diane was appearing in Los Angeles, and I really wanted to go see her. Even though we didn't talk very much anymore, I still enjoyed her concerts. When I asked Mike Roshkind for tickets, he said there were none. Funny: in all my years with the label, I'd never been denied tickets to see another Motown act; it was one of the perks. Later in the day, however, I got two tickets through Abner.

As I watched Diane sing, I thought of how far she'd come. Her inconsistent chart showings (only one of eight singles released since 1971 had made the Top 10, and her latest, "Sleepin'," had struggled to Number 70) did nothing to tarnish her stardom. She was far beyond all that, it seemed. The following year she starred in her second film, *Mahogany.*

Whatever exasperation I'd felt toward her had dissipated. As a grown woman, it was easy for me to see that many of the original Supremes' problems simply grew out of our youth and the pressures of our careers. Flo, Diane, and I responded as best we could. Not to say that I didn't think each of us could have handled certain situations differently; there's no one alive who couldn't be a better person. But through my recent dealings with Motown, I was coming to see that much of what I'd believed was Diane's doing back then was really Berry's. Ultimately, Diane was just like the rest of us working for Berry—only she didn't know it.

I'd never seen Diane give a better show. Once the curtain fell, I hurried backstage to compliment her. As I walked toward the dressing rooms, a guard stopped me and refused to let me pass. Several fans were standing nearby, and one said, "But she's one of the Supremes! You've got to let her go back!" The guard laughed in my face. Abner walked right past me with Stevie Wonder, making no effort to intervene on my behalf. I was speechless.

When I finally got back to her dressing room, Diane seemed happy to see me, but surprised. "Hello, Mary, how are you?" We embraced, talked about our families, and that was it.

Berry said, "Hi, Mary. You sure look good." And then he and Diane turned away. After having lied about the tickets, Mike was obviously embarrassed to see me there. I held my head high, but inside I felt like nothing. I wished Pedro were there with me. I felt so alone. It goes to show, you're only as hot as your latest project.

We began an eventful run at Magic Mountain, one of my favorite places to play because it always attracted lots of fans. This was our third year back, and tickets sold out so quickly that several shows were added. We had several special guests the first few nights: Freda Payne, Johnny Taylor, Berry's mother and sister Gwen, and Stevie Wonder. Stevie came onstage and did a song with us, which the crowd loved, and then afterward came backstage to visit.

I always remember this night, because it was the first time I really felt that Stevie was my friend. While guests and visitors poured into the small dressing room, Stevie and I sat back in a quiet corner and had our first—and last—deep conversation. He seemed concerned about what was happening with the Supremes and Motown's other groups. With the possible exception of Diane or Smokey, no one was happy with what Motown had become.

Stevie asked why I thought Lynda had left the Supremes, how I felt about the possibility of the Holland brothers producing the Supremes again (he thought it was a bad idea), and remarked that in his opinion Cindy lacked something onstage. I found this last point interesting, considering Stevie couldn't *see* her. He just heard something in our show and suggested that we might think about replacing her. He added that he'd written some new songs for us. Although he was very upset about what had happened with "Bad Weather," he said it didn't bother him that much anymore.

A couple days later Flo arrived from Detroit. We'd talked on the phone several times over the past months, and somewhere in the back of my mind I entertained the idea that she might rejoin us. Realistically, I knew it was a long shot. As I wrote in my first book, Flo drank quite heavily during this visit. We talked about her problems, and I was surprised to hear her say that most of the things that had happened to her were her own fault. She said she would stop listening to her family, and that now that she was broke, they wanted nothing to do with her anyway. All this time I'd been concerned about Flo because of her all-consuming anger over what her life had become. But now she seemed to have accepted her fate, and that killed me. I didn't know which was worse: to fight a losing battle or to never fight at all.

The first night, we agreed it might be better if she stayed home instead of coming with us to Magic Mountain. Flo said she looked forward to having some time alone. When I returned home, she was already asleep, and my house was a mess: liquor stained the rug, a statue lay broken on the floor. I cleaned up, and before I went to bed wrote in my diary, "If only I could save the world. But I can't even find the solutions for my own problems."

We talked for hours and hours, but never resolved anything. The trip's one bright spot was the night she joined Cindy, Scherrie, and me onstage at Magic Mountain. The fans cried out, "We love you, Flo!" She seemed happy for that moment, but a few days later she returned to Detroit, and I knew she was lost forever.

Having seen both Diane and Florence within a few weeks of each other, I thought about how different their lives were and how much we had all changed. I believed that deep inside, we were still the same girls we'd been back in high school, that all the changes everyone else saw in us were just external. *If we ever sat down together and really talked,* I thought, *it would be all right.* In their own ways, though, Diane and Flo said something else. Flo all but told me to give up on her. And Diane seemed so preoccupied with her stardom that I might as well not have existed. There didn't seem to be room in either of their lives for what we had been or for me. For very different reasons, Diane and Flo wanted to leave the Supremes far behind. But I couldn't, and it hurt.

After Magic Mountain, there were no live dates, no recording sessions, nothing. I entertained friends, went to parties, tried catching up on things around the house. Even though I was relaxing, I felt very, very tired. I couldn't even imagine going to Las Vegas with Pedro for a weekend, something I'd always loved to do. Was I depressed, physically exhausted, or what? Then one day my doctor called and said, "You'd better start knitting baby booties." I hung up the phone and cried for an hour. It didn't seem real to me. I was finally going to have a baby!

Pedro was thrilled, and I was walking on clouds. But the reality of having a baby soon hit me. I had to start planning for time off, and this gave our unresolved problems with Motown a new urgency. Now we had to get some work to pay the bills, and Pedro and I had to find a new, larger house.

Besides Willie, we had Pedro's younger brother and sister, Rafi and Malvena, living with us. Pedro worked, but as our road manager; he'd quit law school. Still, in his mind he was boss. While he felt no compunction about reprimanding and even disciplining Willie, I was not to raise my voice to either of his siblings, even though I supported, fed, and clothed them, and paid their tuitions. Our different ideas about how the kids should behave was a constant source of conflict.

September 1974

Well, it finally happened: Pedro beat me up. It all started when I wouldn't take Rafi with me to see Al Green in concert. Boy, Pedro looked like he hated everything about me. He said I wasn't going unless I took Rafi. Of course I said no, because Rafi had been bugging me all afternoon. When I refused, Pedro went off. I took a good look at him. His eyes became like steel. He was like a stranger, very unreasonable. He kept repeating that Rafi was his brother. He slapped me around, onto the floor. At one point, I couldn't believe this was happening. Why can't we be happy? I thought of the baby, especially when I fell to the floor. I didn't want him to hurt me, so I fought back. The times before, when Pedro broke the windows, threw me in the pool, I was very afraid, because I've never been around someone who completely lost control. But this time, with the physical beating, I felt it was too much for me to handle. I mean, is love worth all this?

October 1974

*A Married Woman's Poem of Sadness*

Love comes in many varied shapes, forms, and
degrees. I have had many different kinds since
my childhood, but I have never had one as
confusing as this one. Most of the love I have
experienced brought me varied degrees of joy and
pain, but never this complete numbness.

It smothers me. It's like being in a room with
no windows, like what I'd imagine solitary
confinement to be. It's like being under a heavy

MARY WILSON

152

blanket. I can neither see nor breathe. I have
no freedom. Love shouldn't be so restricting.
One should still have the freedom of being one's
self, maintaining one's own beliefs. It's hard
being completely blanketed by someone. It makes
you want to fly away.

# CHAPTER 9

The early months of my pregnancy were wonderful. I enjoyed being pregnant, finally having my own baby to dream about. If anything, I was tired all the time because of the constant travel. The postshow parties and dinners went on, and Pedro went out, while I stayed in my room. I wished that I could just stop and rest for a while.

In October the Supremes went to Japan at the invitation of Princess Shimazu and her husband to host an international celebrity tennis tournament. Also with us were actresses Janet Leigh, Claudine Longet, and Barbara Anderson, composer Burt Bacharach, Peter Lawford, and Davy Jones and Mickey Dolenz of the Monkees. We paired off in different combinations to play tennis. I was pitted against the top Japanese tennis pro. Of course I lost, but I was awarded a kimono for being the most enthusiastic player.

We gave a dinner concert for over five hundred politicians, entertainers, other VIPs, and the princess. The concert raised $20,000 for UNICEF and was a huge success. During our extended version of "Love Train," I invited the princess's husband to "come up on stage, honey, and join my love train." He politely declined, and later I learned that this wasn't exactly proper protocol. The Japanese are far more reserved than Americans. Still, I think everyone had a good time, and the show was later broadcast as a prime-time television special in Japan. The Supremes were still stars everywhere—everywhere but America.

When I got home I called Florence, who was living with my mother for a few days. She'd lost her house to foreclosure. Unfortunately, none of her brothers and sisters could take her and the three little girls in. There was even talk among people who knew Flo that her family wanted to put her in a sanitarium.

Despite all the misfortune that had befallen Flo, I was surprised that she sounded better than she had in years. She was relieved to be staying with Mom, and Mom was happy to have her. Flo and I spoke very honestly to each other. "I told you years ago, Flo, that you gave your family too much," I said. "It's a sad thing to realize, but when it comes right down to it, family is just like other people. They're there for you when things are good, but when things get rough they may or may not be able to hang around." There wasn't very much I or anyone could do for Flo. While I was advising Flo about spending too much money on her family, I should have listened to some of my own advice. I now barely had enough money to support my husband, his siblings, Willie, my mother, and the Supremes; in fact, I was in debt.

We remained on the road almost constantly through November. Pedro wasn't always with us, so his paranoia increased. All through the night, he would call to carry on about some "rumor" he claimed to have heard about me. After a night of this I'd wake up feeling like a zombie. This couldn't have been good for my baby, and now, three months pregnant, I worried more and more about my health.

One evening I came into the dressing room crying my eyes out. By now Cindy and Scherrie knew that Pedro often beat me. Like most battered women, I said nothing about it. Cindy held me as I cried on her shoulder. "Everything will be all right, Mary," she said softly. "Don't cry." Neither of them mentioned Pedro's cruelty; they just made me feel cared for. After this, their problems with Pedro escalated, and Scherrie seemed to disagree with him on almost everything.

Pedro was determined to become someone important and powerful in Hollywood, just as he had in Puerto Rico and in his homeland. Besides a failed film company he'd launched with Jim Brown, Pedro always seemed to be "making deals." Pedro was nothing if not charming and smart, and he knew how to get things going. Unlike me, he wasn't afraid to meet new people or try new things.

For example, he gave a luncheon at our home for a young Muslim leader named Louis Farrakhan. Mr. Farrakhan espoused black financial independence and wanted to meet all the black entertainers in Hollywood. In exchange for Pedro setting up introductions, Mr. Farrakhan promised to see that Supremes records were played on the Muslim radio stations in New York and Chicago. Many people dropped by to meet him, including Stevie Wonder, Lola Falana, football-star-turned-actor Bernie Casey, and Paula Kelly, the first black *Playboy* playmate. I felt it was important to publicly support black causes and blacks who were making positive contributions. This is one reason I had so many qualms about saying anything against Motown, a black-owned company.

In the last decade the civil rights movement had brought so many changes, but there was still a long way to go. Yes, there were more successful blacks than ever, but racism was something we all contended with daily. Pedro and I went to Las Vegas with our friends Herb and Mauna Loa Avery for the weekend. One morning Mauna Loa and I got word that our husbands had been arrested. Pedro and Herb had stopped by a local club off the main strip and were just talking. Or so they told us. Because they didn't buy any drinks, the owner called the police and had them arrested for trespassing. We bailed them out, and they had to stand trial at a later date.

It was outrageous and unjust. Even though black performers brought millions of dollars into Las Vegas, if you were a black man walking around town too late at night or happened across someone who didn't like you, you were suspect. The whole episode was upsetting for everyone, but especially for Pedro and Herb. Both very proud men, they were angry about their treatment. This wouldn't be the last time the two of them got into a scrape because of their color.

After a period of relative calm, Willie began having trouble in school. He was now fifteen and a half, and I suspected that he was smoking cigarettes behind my back. Hollywood wasn't a great place to raise a kid, and in our neighborhood there were few children to play with. I tried talking to him but sometimes felt I couldn't reach him. If I'd raised him from birth, maybe things might have been easier. It broke my heart to see how hard things were for Willie, despite all the time spent tutoring and helping him.

Around this time, my brother Roosevelt briefly reentered my life. We really didn't have that much to say to each other. He was very easygoing and seemed to take life as it came. He also smoked what I considered far too much pot, but I said nothing. Who was I to lecture him? Back then everyone still thought of marijuana as safer than alcohol. From our few conversations on the subject, I knew that Roosevelt's experiences in Vietnam were never totally out of his mind. In Willie and my brother I saw two proud young black men whose futures were dimming, through no fault of their own.

Pedro was still talking to Marvin Gaye about working with us, but things never came together. We visited Marvin in his studio once. He was singing in the control room instead of the vocal booth, because it made him more comfortable.

When he saw me, he said, "Hey, baby," and kissed me on the cheek, carefully leaning toward me so he wouldn't crush my swollen stomach. I was alarmed at how exhausted and run-down he appeared. I don't think he'd slept in days. After this meeting we stopped pursuing the idea of working with Marvin.

In December we finally started recording with Terry Woodford and Clayton Ivey, two writer-producers from Muscle Shoals. The songs included "Give Out, but Don't Give Up," "You Turn Me Around," "Color My World Blue," and "You Can't Stop a Girl in Love." These appeared on our next album, *The Supremes;* its other tracks were produced by a number of producers: Brian Holland, Greg Wright, Mark Davis, Michael Lloyd, and Hal Davis. I sang lead on four of the nine songs and shared a lead with Scherrie on the first single, "He's My Man."

Pedro insisted that I be given more leads, which created a degree of tension. Some people saw this as me just flexing my ego, but it was a matter of survival. I finally accepted the responsibility to prepare myself for future personnel changes and possibly the end of the group. After all my years in the Supremes, I was still the least known of the originals. Record buyers and club-goers assumed there were no original Supremes left. That hurt.

As I prepared to sing my leads, Scherrie grew very quiet, and Cindy acted strangely. We'd rehearsed for days, but wouldn't you know it, once in the studio I lost my voice! It was totally psychological; I was scared to death and felt guilty taking leads meant for Scherrie. I wasn't ready to really step out as a full lead singer.

Pedro and I met with Cindy and Charles and pleaded with her to apply herself. She had started taking voice lessons, then dropped out. Now that we were officially signed and recording again, Motown took a keener interest in our internal affairs. I heard that Motown was secretly looking to replace Cindy. I hated them for that, but I was angry at Cindy for giving them an excuse. Scherrie and I felt that Cindy could make herself great again and told her so often, but nothing worked.

January 1975

Pedro said I should realize by now that my career has gone downhill. I've known it's been slipping, but I keep assuring myself I'll make it to the top again. Each night I cringe as we walk onstage. The audience is all young kids. Plus, this place is out in the dumps, and it's wintertime, to make it worse. My gowns are getting too short in front as my baby gets bigger, and I am finding it very difficult to move as rapidly on stage. I must admit, though, I look very pretty being pregnant. In fact, I feel beautiful.

Pedro said he feels hurt when he touches me and I reject him. Of course I don't openly reject him. I know he's speaking of those fears I have that creep up on me. I don't know why I still walk around like a frightened kid. But Pedro feels it. He thinks of them as something personal against him, but it's more than that. It's the fear within me of losing everything. I've tried to rid myself of it by working hard, but it's still there.

When not working, I was getting things ready for the baby and trying to salvage our working relationship with Motown. Not long after Diane and Berry returned from Rome, where they were filming *Mahogany,* she called me. We had an interesting chat. I was surprised to hear from her. But, typically, she just rang me up as if we talked on the phone all the time.

She asked me what was happening, and I told her that I thought Motown could be doing more for us. This wasn't any secret; I had been widely quoted in the industry trade papers as saying the same thing months before. It was the talk of Motown for some time. Diane was surprised. "Well, Mary, you just have to go to Berry and tell him. You can do it, I know you can. You just get them to do what you want."

"Diane," I replied, "you don't understand. Motown is doing nothing for us. I've done all that I can do alone."

Diane knew that my baby was due soon, and she promised she would come by the house to visit, but she never did. I could never figure out what prompted these calls. I sometimes wondered if she felt the way I did, like there was some unfinished business we should address, like she missed me. But I never knew.

I treasured my happy moments and could separate the good parts of my life from the bad. Whenever I had cause to feel happy or blessed, I accepted it. I am the same way about people. For better or worse, I tried to love those around me as they were and help them. I could not write them off or turn them away.

As my birthday approached I began to feel forgotten. Here it was just weeks before my baby was due and still no baby shower. The weekend of my birthday Pedro and I went out to dinner, although Peter Lawford had invited us to a party. I couldn't understand why we weren't going to the party, but Pedro was very insistent about this dinner. We had a wonderful meal at La Scala, then headed over to Peter's party at the Candy Store.

When we got to the private club, a woman at the door checked a list and then said haughtily that she wouldn't admit us. I felt my temper rise and began to say, "Of course our name is on the list—" Suddenly I heard yells of "Surprise!" There were all my friends, including Peter, Cindy, Herb and Mauna Loa, Richard Roundtree, and the Fifth Dimension. Even Lynda Laurence and Jean Terrell were there. I received so many beautiful gifts, and after the club closed the party moved to our house.

That Sunday I went to a luncheon at Scherrie's house, and there was another surprise: a baby shower. Cindy, Hazel, Jayne Kennedy, Dionne Warwick, Natalie Cole, Freda Payne, and some other friends were there. More beautiful gifts and happiness. Not long after, we attended a party that Berry's sister Gwen gave for our mutual friend Billy Davis. Earlier that day I had felt my first labor contractions. Berry hugged me warmly. He seemed a little awkward, but it was nice to be together. All night people came over to rub my stomach and wish me good luck. For a short time everything seemed so wonderful.

A couple days later, though, I was back in a blue funk. Pedro and I were fighting. My mother was there, waiting for her grandchild to arrive, and when she wasn't looking, I cried. This was supposed to be the happiest time of my life.

That day Herb instructed me to go to the hospital; the baby was coming. I was so thrilled. My elation lasted until I got to the hospital room, where the real nitty-gritty of childbirth hit me right between the eyes. Two nurses came into my room arguing.

"I'll do the shaving," said one, brandishing a razor.

"No, you do the enema," replied the other.

Then a laboring woman in the next bed screamed out, cursing her unborn baby's father. Well, that turned me around. My contractions started slowly, but I made steady progress, with Pedro at my side. We weathered six hours of labor, and even though Pedro had attended only a few of the natural-childbirth classes, he was supportive. Unfortunately, he'd missed the classes about when things go wrong, so he didn't fully comprehend what was happening when Herb said, "Your baby's heart rate is a little funny. We may have to take it."

"What do you mean, 'take it'? " Pedro asked, turning pale.

"It may have to be caesarean," Herb explained, trying not to alarm us. "That means we cut the abdomen and take out the baby."

"What? Okay, Herb," I said, "whatever it takes."

Pedro sat beside me, trying to put up a brave front, but I could see his fear when they began to cut. It seemed like no time at all before Herb peered over the sheet and announced, "It's a girl!" A few more seconds, and I think Pedro would have fainted right there. Herb laid my baby across my chest, and I knew what being blessed truly felt like.

My next thought was, *What will Pedro say?* I knew he wanted a boy. In fact, I had been afraid to even pick a girl's name. But suddenly it didn't matter. I had my baby. While I lay in the recovery room, Pedro and Herb drank champagne, and when I saw them several hours later, they were in fine shape.

Pedro brought me a beautiful plant. I asked him was it was called. *"Turquesa,"* he replied, "Spanish for *turquoise.*" So we named our daughter Turkessa. She was the most beautiful baby. I spent hours looking at and holding her. She was an angel to me, a gift. My mother was so excited, she stayed over in my room, sleeping in a chair. Everyone visited, and by the time we received all the flowers and fruit baskets, my room looked like a florist's shop. Diane and her husband Bob tried to visit one evening but arrived too late; they promised to come by the next day, but never made it. Lola Falana and Mira Waters also dropped by, along with Scherrie, Cindy, and Hazel. Herb, Jim Brown, and journalist Walter Burrell were Turkessa's godfathers.

With all the euphoria came the physical reality of having a baby, which every mother knows. After major surgery I needed plenty of bed rest, but sitting around the house wasn't for me. I had to save my energy, though, because Motown planned to release *The Supremes* next month, and in three weeks we were to tour Japan again.

Having a baby brings many couples closer together; that wasn't the case for us. I'd be breast-feeding Turkessa, and Pedro would dash in and dash out, going here and there, never stopping to talk. When we did talk, we fought. I'd become more worried about money. Our commitments to our employees and Cindy and Scherrie continued, even without money coming in. We had to stop spending, but Pedro would not. Even though he brought in little money, he'd long ago gotten into the habit of spending as much as he wanted.

Pedro was now our manager. He'd been pushing me for months, and I gave in reluctantly. When I told Berry, he didn't say much, but I could tell by his expression that he didn't think it was a great idea. "I'll be here to guide him," I said. "I can tell him what to do."

"Mary, you can't," Berry replied. "And it won't be the way you want it to be."

Needless to say, I didn't listen. I needed Pedro because I felt he was the only person I could trust, so I overlooked everything: the flashy clothes, the fast talking, the bravado. Berry, and everyone else at Motown, saw right through it.

Could Pedro do a worse job managing the group than

anyone else had? The answer was no. At least he could offer the one thing no one else could, and that was concern for what happened to me.

Cindy and Scherrie were opposed to this change. When Pedro told them that he was taking over, they said nothing, and that said it all. I knew what they were thinking: the same things Flo and I used to think about Diane and Berry.

It was very obvious that Pedro had a lot to learn, but he refused my help, and his flaws as a manager were soon apparent. We went to Las Vegas in May 1975 to sing the National Anthem before the Muhammad Ali–Ron Lyle heavyweight title fight. The live national broadcast began, and Cindy, Scherrie, and I stood in the ring, waiting for the music. After a few interminable seconds, I spotted Pedro outside the ring.

"Where's the music?" I mouthed to him.

"There is no music."

*Oh, no,* I thought. Scherrie hummed a note, and we sang "The Star-Spangled Banner" a cappella. Happily, we rose to the occasion, and Howard Cosell even commented on how good we sounded.

Three weeks after Turkessa's birth we arrived in Tokyo to kick off our two-week tour. Hardly any fans were waiting for us at the airport. Every year it seemed that fewer people came to greet us; even the number of reporters at the press conference dwindled. My mother and mother-in-law came along to help with the baby, and Herb and Mauna Loa were there too. The crowds were okay, and most of the shows were fine, but some of the clubs we played, like one in Manila, were small and dirty. It was demeaning to be in places like that, especially when people would say, "Oh, you're at *that* club? You really should be at . . ." As if I didn't know that.

Pedro was out almost every night. He insulted me when

we were together in public. He made me hate myself. I began thinking that if all I could have was my career, and Pedro could help me put that together, fine. Sometimes I saw my situation very objectively: I'd made a mistake, and it was my job to fix it. At other times, though, my insecurities overwhelmed me. Then all I wanted was for Pedro to love me and care for me. It was almost schizophrenic. Because Pedro could be like two different people, I began to think like two different people just to deal with him.

In June Motown finally released the Supremes' first single in two years, "He's My Man," a sexy disco number. Scherrie and I traded off leads, and although I was never fond of disco, I loved this song. The single and the album got very positive reviews, and the renewed interest in the Supremes garnered us lots of press and many television appearances on such shows as *Soul Train, American Bandstand,* and Dinah Shore's program.

The industry treated *The Supremes* as a comeback album. Working with so many different producers kept the LP from achieving the kind of cohesiveness our albums with Frank and Smokey had, but maybe that wasn't so bad. There was a little something for everybody, as they say. In the year and a half the Supremes hadn't recorded, times had changed, and several girl groups came on very strongly, particularly the Three Degrees (especially in England) and Labelle.

Labelle was Cindy's old group and the Supremes' former cohorts, Patti LaBelle and the Bluebelles, but totally revamped with futuristic costumes and a sassy style. Their recent Number One "comeback" hit, "Lady Marmalade," was fresh and daring. Interestingly, the song's writer-producer, Allen Toussaint, had dated Jean Terrell years before. At the time, Jean didn't think it was important that he produce us, even though I suggested she ask him. I'm not one to speculate, but in this case it is tempting. Labelle took a drastic step, and it worked. Now if we could just find the right person with the right ideas for us, the Supremes could be on top again.

That August we attended the first annual Rock Music Awards show, Don Kirshner's answer to the Grammys. Diane and Elton John cohosted the nationally televised event, and performers included Kiki Dee, Chuck Berry, and Labelle, who won best r&b single for "Lady Marmalade." After the show, we went backstage to visit Diane and Labelle. When we got to Diane's dressing room, she was leaving with her two daughters and Mike Roshkind. She seemed very distracted and only waved as she walked right past me. I made a silent vow not to visit her backstage again. It wasn't worth the humiliation.

Next we went with Cindy to visit Labelle. She had stayed in touch with Sarah Dash, Nona Hendryx, and Patti LaBelle, and was understandably proud of their great success. Like me, she was hoping to rekindle some kind of warmth among them, but when we got there, the three of them acted coolly toward us. Cindy was her usual friendly, outgoing self, but it wasn't being taken the way she meant it. An unspoken rivalry between our two groups seemed to color the conversation.

Show business is hard, and sometimes performers struggle for so long that it makes them hard too. I realized that the reason I didn't regard other groups as competition was because the Supremes had been on top for so long. Once some of those performers who'd been second, third, fourth, or fiftieth to us made it, they let me know it. Now that the Supremes had fallen on lean times, the tables were turned.

In interviews I spoke frankly about where we stood with Motown. I've been accused of being foolishly optimistic about the group; if only I could have been. By summer all signs indicated that we weren't going to have a hit. "He's My Man" wasn't out more than a couple of weeks before we could tell it wasn't receiving adequate promotion. Despite all the promises to promote us, many key radio stations across the country didn't receive the record, much less get pushed to play it. I took heart, though, because without any help from Motown, the album and the single made respectable showings. "He's My Man" was a Number One disco hit and reached Number 69 on the black singles chart. Our other 45s, "Where Do I Go from Here" and "Early Morning Love," were picked up on by club DJs, spurring more record sales.

Motown's ideas about what our problems were and how they could be solved differed radically from mine. In one of the Supremes' monthly fan club letters, an upper-level company staffer was quoted (anonymously, of course) as saying, "The Supremes' troubles started when they went independent . . . We at Motown are a family and we, as any family does, like to deal with members of our family. We work well together. When someone brings an outsider in and tries to force him into our family, the family is apt to rebel. Now, I'm not saying we rebelled against the Supremes, but the fact that we did not like their independent management was to the disadvantage of the Supremes. We could not communicate.

"I'd be the first to admit," the mystery spokesman continued, "that Motown hasn't always been fair with the group. But by the same token, the group has not always been fair with us."

I'm still trying to figure out just what we did to Motown that was so "unfair." I could only take perverse pleasure in noting the label's problems: the Jackson 5 had just split to go to Epic, Diane and Marvin were having trouble with their singles, and Stevie Wonder was beginning another lengthy holdout for a better contract.

That summer we hired Phil Moore and Geoffrey Holder to redo our act. Phil did the music, and Geoffrey choreographed our routines. Geoffrey, who was responsible for the Broadway hit *The Wiz* (and who had become a familiar face as the man in the 7-Up TV commercials extolling the virtues of the "un-cola nut"), had a million ideas. They wanted to give us a good repertoire as well as an exciting, new visual image. It was a huge expense, over $60,000 coming out of our pockets, but it was now or never.

Phil and Geoffrey spent a lot of time talking to us, explaining how they saw our personalities and how we presented ourselves onstage. We felt they had the right ideas. The syncopated choreography we'd done for so many years was changed. One new number, "Body Heat," was very suggestive, with us caressing ourselves—tastefully, of course. For another bit, a fantasy sequence, a genie granted us wishes to be anyone we wanted. Scherrie played Bessie Smith; Cindy, Marilyn Monroe; and I chose Josephine Baker, the legendary black diva. Growing up, I had idolized Baker. She was beautiful, sophisticated, exotic, and sexy, scandalizing Parisian audiences in 1926 by coming onstage wearing only a single pink flamingo feather.

Before we started doing this routine, Geoffrey said to me in his resonant Jamaican accent, "Mary, you *are* Josephine Baker. I think you should play her in a movie." He later introduced me to Miss Baker, in Hollywood on her last U.S. tour. It was such a thrill for me.

"Jo," Geoffrey said to her, "this is Mary Wilson of the Supremes."

Miss Baker studied me carefully for a moment, then said to Geoffrey, "You were right. She does look like me."

That made my day.

Opening night in San Francisco basically went well, but I was tired and at points lost my voice. Still, we got very nice reviews, and the new show and new gowns gave us a lift. While we were there, *Billboard* was holding a convention, and

Flip Wilson invited us to his cocktail party. I declined, fearing what Pedro would do. He'd already torn up all my pictures of Flip and destroyed all my diary entries containing his name.

Scherrie, Cindy, and I were outdoors in a nearby garden, posing for a magazine cover, when someone told me that my son and Pedro's sister were at Flip's party. I ran up to the suite, grabbed Willie and Malvena, and told them they had to leave immediately. The whole time I looked over my shoulder, hoping Flip didn't see me.

We were almost out the door when Flip approached us. He was very happy to see me, but all I could think about was getting out before Pedro showed up or someone there saw us. I knew Pedro would go crazy if he found out I'd seen Flip. Flip didn't understand why I acted so strangely; I think his feelings were hurt.

That night Pedro came home and gave me the third degree, asking over and over where I'd been that day, what I'd done. I'm a poor liar, and Pedro knew this. He questioned Malvena, and she told him the truth, so he immediately assumed that I'd gone up there to see Flip, to sleep with him. Pedro went out, came in late, and the next morning announced, "Now you and Flip can be together. I'm filing for divorce, and I'll get custody of Turkessa too."

Silly as it sounds now, I took his threats seriously. Although my mother had raised me with many old-fashioned ideas about sex and men, I had disregarded much of her advice. After all, this was a new era. I was never ashamed of how I conducted my life or my relationships, but some deep-seated, residual guilt left over from my upbringing seeped into my consciousness. Furthermore, I believed that when you married and had a family, you stayed together for eternity and worked out whatever problems you encountered. Whenever Pedro harped on how I was trying to attract men,

I reviewed my every word and gesture, wondering, *Did I really do that? Did it really look like that?* At first I easily dismissed his accusations as silly. But soon the guilt about sex my mother had passed on to me mixed with Pedro's archaic ideas, and I began to believe I'd done something wrong. I didn't even bother arguing with Pedro. He acted like an irate, powerful parent, and I reacted as the child I had been so many years ago.

Pedro's paranoid obsession with my (nonexistent) affairs escalated over the years, so that before long I was afraid to look any man in the eye. I rarely left the house alone, and if I did I had to report my every move. My baby and my work were the only escapes from my prison of fear. I had lost most of my friends; either Pedro had scared them away, or they felt uncomfortable witnessing the abuse. Many of my women friends called and tried to be helpful by hinting at Pedro's infidelities, but I didn't listen to them. Almost all my male buddies were either out of my life completely or, like Herb, Jim Brown, and Marvin Gaye, had become Pedro's friends too. No one ever called me anymore. I felt truly alone.

I see now that the main reason I continued fighting the losing battle for the Supremes was that I felt alive only when I was with my daughter or singing. Performing was like therapy to me, the stage my home away from home. At least there I knew who I was and that people loved me. Having my career and Turkessa gave me faith that my life would eventually work out. My heart breaks for women who are totally alone in an abusive marriage. It's a hell you cannot emerge from unless you have some hope, no matter how slight. I thank God I had that.

Like most abused women, I protected myself by learning to deal with my husband's insults and outbursts. I knew what upset him, so I did all I could to prevent those things from happening. With each abusive act or cruel word I lost another bit of myself. Only after reflecting on the awful experience years later did it become clear what had happened to me and how it had happened.

Pedro's power over me was complete. You can be presumed guilty for only so long before you begin to act and feel guilty. I walked around full of shame for nothing. In my heart I truly believed that if Pedro went before a judge, I would lose Turkessa. My husband could be so convincing, so smooth. In my worst dreams, he would produce that photograph he'd found of me and Tom Jones; then everyone would see what a bad person I was. I remembered when Pedro forced me to write that list of men I'd slept with. Those names now haunted me like ghosts.

Turkessa meant everything to me; I couldn't lose her. To prevent that, I'd do anything, including staying with Pedro.

# CHAPTER 10

By late summer Pedro had made headway with some of Motown's top people, especially Suzanne dePasse, who then headed the creative division. Of everyone, she put forth the most effort on the Supremes' behalf. Suzanne saw to it that we got good material, the best photographers, and so on, and she and Pedro worked well together.

Pedro tried to ingratiate himself with the label's higher-ups, sending flowers to their secretaries, for example. He began believing he'd turned Motown around. Pedro thought it would be great to throw a dinner for Suzanne and Abner. He invited other guests, rented tables, and got me to cook a lavish buffet-style dinner. I knew these people were just playing with him; they weren't going to show up, and I told him so. Sadly, I was right.

The company line—one that many Motown historians and journalists have accepted unquestioningly—is that Pedro caused the Supremes' downfall. In truth, Motown had ruined the group before he came on the scene. If nothing else, Pedro made it possible for us to continue. Though making many mistakes, we recorded some great music during that time. He got us the best booking agents, publicists, accountants, and attorneys.

I saw through Pedro's games, but I also knew his other side. No one had ever believed in him. I felt that if Pedro accomplished something real, like making the Supremes a success, he would stop all the make-believe and settle down.

Part of Pedro's campaign to get around Motown included asking Mike Roshkind to be a godfather of one of our kids. I vetoed that one right off. Then one day he asked, "What do you think about asking Diane to be Turkessa's godmother?"

Growing up, I'd always thought that each of my children would have two godmothers, Diane and Flo. But so much had changed. Asking someone to be your child's godmother is a very personal thing. "I don't think it's a good idea," I said. "We aren't close anymore." I felt Diane would think I was using her because she was a star.

Pedro badgered me until I relented. Patching up things between Diane and me was important to him. Frankly, I was surprised and very touched when she accepted the invitation to be Turkessa's godmother. In 1979, when Turkessa was four years old, she was baptized at St. Patrick's Cathedral in New York City. Diane stood as her godmother and Herb Avery became her godfather.

In early September we took our new act to England, where the press roundly criticized us for being "too slick." The British had tired of us too, it seemed, and "He's My Man" did not even chart there. Making this all the more frustrating was that even our sharpest critics made a point of mentioning how much better we looked and sounded. There was something about our presentation, our approach, *us*, I guess, that missed the mark. We were not the *Supremes*.

Soon after arriving in England, I had to undergo painful surgery for a chronic health problem. While I could work, I was miserable with pain and should have been home resting in bed. Then someone connected with the Irish Republican Army set off a bomb in our hotel lobby, killing two people and injuring sixty-three. We were all up in our rooms, getting ready to go out sight-seeing with some record-company representatives, when we got a call saying they would be about half an hour late. Had it not been for that call, we might have been down in the London Hilton lobby at the moment the blast occurred.

Pedro awoke me from a nap. The elevators were out, so we rushed down twenty-five flights of stairs with Turkessa bundled in our arms. In the lobby bells rang and sirens screamed. Every window was blown into a million fragments, injured people lay everywhere, and blood splattered the floor.

As we stood across the street in Hyde Park, I took a head count and discovered Scherrie missing. She turned up later that evening. Because she'd gone back upstairs for some personal things, the police held her for questioning. Since no one was permitted back in the hotel, she stayed at another nearby hotel. We all worried about her as we spent the day wandering around the park.

It was an off day for us, so I hadn't dressed too well. Still, people were coming up to me and asking if I was Mary Wilson of the Supremes and would I please give them an autograph. One person said, "I've been a fan since you started. By the way, where's Diana?"

"Where have you been?" I said, laughing. "She's been gone since 1970." It was a strange day.

Cindy walked up to me and, grinning, said, "Mary, come here."

She had on a brown trench coat wrapped tightly around her. "You have to come *real* close," she added mischievously, "I have something to show you." Cindy opened her coat and closed it quickly, revealing that she had on nothing under it. We all laughed. It was the one bright spot in an otherwise miserable day.

Later we found out that our assistant, Gill Trodd, just missed being in the blast, and that she and Hazel had seen the woman suspected of planting the bomb minutes before the explosion. By the time we were let back into our rooms at around seven, we were all exhausted.

It was during this trip that we purchased ex-Beatle John Lennon's custom-made stretch Mercedes limousine from George Harrison. Pedro was very sociable, striking up fast friendships with people I had known for years and yet never been close to. In England Pedro went out a lot with Peter Lawford, Ringo Starr, and George Harrison, who invited Pedro and me to visit him and his girlfriend (now wife) Olivia at their home.

It was one of the most beautiful places I'd ever seen. George's grounds were like a huge park. I recall one especially beautiful swan-filled lake. The house resembled a small palace, decorated with precious objects from all over the world. Except for George's extensive guitar collection, everything reminded me of a scene out of a fairy tale. George had just finished building a recording studio in the house, and he proudly gave us a tour of it.

While Olivia prepared dinner, he asked me countless questions about Motown and how we made our records, how we got that sound. It was a very relaxing day. What struck me about George was how happy he seemed. It made me realize how few people I knew, especially performers, who were content and at peace. After this I became a great fan of George's music, especially its spiritual aspect.

George showed us the Mercedes limousine that had been custom-built for John Lennon. The moment Pedro saw it he had to have it. That it had belonged to John Lennon meant nothing to me or Pedro. It was a beautiful, rare car, that's all. Although we got it for a very, very low price—cheap, actually—it was still more than we could afford. I tried persuading him not to buy it. We already had the Rolls. What did we need with two luxury cars?

As fate would have it, the Mercedes limousine later assumed a life of its own too. We brought it back to the States, but after a year returned it to England because we were there so often and could use it for touring. Following John's assassination in 1980, anything connected with him skyrocketed in value. I stored the limo in a garage, from which it was stolen in 1984. Next thing I heard, it was up for auction. After retrieving it from the selling block, the British High Court ruled that I was the rightful owner, and I had it auctioned off at Christie's in London in 1989. I can honestly say I wasn't all that sad to see it go.

Just as we were leaving for the States, our European Motown affiliate asked that we stay an extra week to do more radio and television shows. Everyone's nerves were shot, and some of our musicians got angry and left. Cindy and Scherrie complained bitterly that Pedro was disorganized and never told them anything until the last minute. For example, we were scheduled to perform at the Shubert Theatre in Los Angeles toward the end of the month, and Pedro hadn't bothered to tell Cindy and Scherrie that we were giving a benefit performance, for which none of us would be paid. They were upset, and understandably so. Everything was coming apart. When I mentioned these problems to Pedro, he always snapped, "Sing, and don't worry about the business."

"But I have to work with these people. You cannot do things behind everyone's backs, including mine."

Pedro ignored me unless he was lecturing me on what I was doing wrong. During this trip he complained a lot about our love life. I had a typical new mother's responsibilities and then some. Pedro couldn't fathom why after performing sometimes two shows a night, taking care of Turkessa, and overseeing the group's business, I had neither the energy nor the interest in a wild, romantic sex life. I was failing at everything except being a mother.

After stopping off in Santo Domingo to visit Pedro's family for a few days, we returned home and immediately went to work publicizing the upcoming Shubert date, a benefit for the Citizens Action to Help Youth and the University Community Health Services. Herb Avery was actively involved in these organizations, and he and I appeared together on many local talk shows to promote the work these groups did in the community. I've always felt that performers have an obligation to devote time and energy to worthwhile causes such as these.

This was our first performance in Los Angeles in nearly three years, so we were psyched. When we walked onstage to a half-filled house, my heart sank. We made a few minor mistakes here and there, but the audience loved us. We did the basic show Geoffrey Holder and Phil Moore had developed for us, including the Josephine Baker/Marilyn Monroe/Bessie Smith number we'd just broken in, in England.

Moments before we went on, Pedro informed me that Diane was in the audience and that I should introduce her, which I did. She received a thunderous ovation. I still hadn't fully recuperated my energy, and the show really knocked me out. Before going into my dressing room, I specifically instructed my assistant not to allow anyone backstage until the three of us caught our breaths and freshened up. No sooner did I sit down than I heard a knock, and in walked Diane. She was friendly, but that didn't make up for such a breach of courtesy, especially after she hadn't said more than a handful of words to me the last two times I'd visited her backstage. I was growing weary of constantly turning the other cheek.

Pedro insisted that I go straight home and skip the after-show party, which, of course, he attended with Cindy, Scherrie, and assorted other guests, including Gladys Knight, Natalie Cole, Sarah Dash, Lola Falana, Freda Payne, and a group of Motown VIPs.

The next morning we left Los Angeles for Miami, our first stop on the way to London and our final destination, South Africa. Once word had gotten out that we were going to South Africa, the Supremes became the focus of a national controversy. I admit, I wasn't surprised that our going there provoked such a heated reaction. Cindy, Scherrie, and I were keenly aware of how South Africa's black majority lived separate, impoverished lives under the nation's racist apartheid laws. After careful consideration, however, I decided we should go; Scherrie and Cindy, while voicing reservations, agreed.

One provision of our appearing in South Africa was that all our audiences be fully integrated. In South Africa it was customary to present shows for either all-black or all-white audiences. While in America we are especially aware of the conflict there between blacks and whites, South Africa is home to other ethnic groups, such as Indians and Orientals, and also maintains a very strict caste system that groups people of mixed blood in a clearly defined hierarchy. Our promoters promised to secure the required permits for mixed audiences and to sell tickets on a "no-barriers" basis, so that anyone could see us.

I can speak only for myself, but I felt very strongly that as a black I should witness firsthand what was happening. I was opposed to apartheid before I went there, and my experiences only reinforced my belief that the system must be abolished.

*In 1972 Lynda Laurence replaced Cindy in the group. I'll never forget these dresses: bugle beads for days! (Photo: Mary Wilson Collection)*

*O*ur newly appointed manager, Wayne Weisbart, wanted to get into the picture. He was responsible for putting us together with producer Jimmy Webb. (Photo: Mary Wilson Collection)

*J*ean and I and Lynda on tour in Japan, after dinner with our Japanese promoter, Tats Nagashima. (Photo: Bruce W. Talamon / Mary Wilson Collection)

*S*eated between Lynda and Jean on the cover of my
favorite Supremes album, Floy Joy, which Smokey
Robinson produced. Although Lynda (left) appeared
on the cover, it was Cindy who was singing on every
cut. (Photo: Mary Wilson Collection)

*O*nstage with Lynda and Jean in Los Angeles, 1973. (Photo: Allen Poe)

*He turned on the charm, and the rest is history. (Photo: Mary Wilson Collection)*

*B*etween the champagne and Pedro's smooth style, I was swept off my feet.
*(Photo: Mary Wilson Collection)*

*O*ne of my fun moments with Pedro. (Photo: Mary Wilson Collection)

*I*n 1973 Jean and Lynda left the group, and I re-formed the Supremes with Scherrie Payne (left) and Cindy Birdsong. (Photo: Harry Langdon / Mary Wilson Collection)

*I*n 1974 Flo came out to visit me in Los Angeles, and she joined us onstage at Magic Mountain. Here she is with Cindy that night. (Photo: Lee Valvano)

*M*om and I, moments before I tied the knot at
Caesars Palace in Las Vegas. Our suite was donated by
Caesars Palace. (Photo: Mary Wilson Collection)

*T*he family wedding shot: Dax Diaz, best man; Malvena, Pedro's sister;
Rafaela, Pedro's mom; Pedro; me; Johnnie Mae, my mom; Cathy, my sister;
I. V. Pippin, the aunt who raised me; and my adopted son, Willie. (Photo:
Mary Wilson Collection)

*C*utting the cake. (Photo: Mary Wilson Collection)

*P*edro looking on as I receive a congratulatory kiss from Joel Grey, while actor Jim Brown (right) waits to congratulate us. (Photo: Las Vegas News Bureau / Mary Wilson Collection)

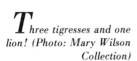

*C*indy and Scherrie had to cover me with themselves as well as with flowers on our 1975 LP, simply titled The Supremes, *because I was pregnant with my first child, Turkessa. (Photo: Mary Wilson Collection)*

*T*hree tigresses and one lion! (Photo: Mary Wilson Collection)

*I* think I was Japanese in a former life! With Scherrie and Cindy in Japan. (Photo: Tom Ingrassia Collection)

*S*cherrie Payne (left), Susaye Green (center), and I formed the final Supremes incarnation from 1976 to 1977. (Photo: Sam Emerson / Mary Wilson Collection)

*The front of the final album.*

*S*usaye and I and Scherrie among the California redwoods in 1976 for the back of the final Supremes album, Mary, Scherrie & Susaye. *(Photo: Sam Emerson / Mary Wilson Collection)*

*S*cherrie, Susaye, and I watch as Turkessa remixes our album in the recording studio. (Photo: Mary Wilson Collection)

*S*usaye and I rehearsing with Geoffrey Holder. (Photo: Mark Bego)

*T*he poster for my solo debut, in August 1979, at the Manhattan nightclub New York New York. This poster was done by the famed artist Eula, who painted the well-known Supremes poster from our Lincoln Center concert in 1965. The Supremes poster from 1965 is reprised at the bottom of this carica-ture, by my feet. (Poster: John Christe Collection)

*A* truly rare shot: me singing a duet with Diane at my New York New York solo debut, August 28, 1979. She told the audience that night that we were still the best of friends. (Photo: Charles Moniz)

*F*lashing a supremely triumphant smile after my opening night at New York New York. (Photo: Robin Platzer)

After reading the hundreds of letters and telegrams imploring us to cancel our trip, I understood our critics' arguments. They advocated a full cultural boycott of South Africa, of all its people, both white and black. The parallels between the black struggles for freedom in South Africa and in the United States are obvious, although the repression in South Africa is much more extreme and brutal. When considering all these facts, I kept recalling the racism I experienced during the fifties and sixties in the South. While we blacks who lived in the North didn't agree with what went on down South, we didn't boycott those places or those people. We went there by busloads and carloads. Just because the South African blacks are across the ocean doesn't mean we can't help them.

I always believed that by confounding racist expectations and being a source of pride to blacks, in some small way I had helped in that struggle. My brother Roosevelt criticized me in the early seventies for not using the Supremes as a platform for political comment. I reminded him that I wasn't a marcher or a speech-maker, and that we each contribute to change in our own way.

This argument didn't cut it with our antiapartheid critics. In 1985 Artists United Against Apartheid brought the issue to national consciousness with the hit "Sun City." Many people don't know that American black entertainers and prominent people were organized against South Africa and apartheid as early as 1975. We received letters from organizations who had the support of some of our friends—Bill Cosby, Sammy Davis, Jr., Richard Roundtree, Diahann Carroll, Brock Peters, Wilt Chamberlain, and others—begging us not to go. Interestingly, once we returned to the States, none of those I knew personally whose names appeared on the antiapartheid organizations' letterhead and petitions ever rebuked me publicly about our trip. The wire services picked up the story and it ran for several days all over the country. I think it probably goes without saying that, careerwise, going to South Africa was not the most prudent decision.

As soon as the plane landed in Johannesburg, we were swamped by reporters. On the car ride from the airport, a black South African journalist interviewed us. We were so exhausted from the long trip and the jet lag, all we wanted to do was sleep. But the first night, after a brief nap, Pedro and I were guests of honor at a dinner given by our promoter and Motown's affiliate there.

The next day we gave at least fifteen interviews, with an hour off for lunch. Our publicity people there were white, and from the beginning I detected a dismissive, rude attitude toward their black journalists. Our press person wanted the writers to avoid political issues and stick to the same old topics, such as how the Supremes started in Detroit, etc., etc. As this was my opportunity to learn something, I always ended up asking more questions of the black reporters than they asked of us.

One PR woman got very perturbed with me and reprimanded a black reporter for "wasting time" with questions she didn't believe were "pertinent"; namely, those concerning oppression of South African blacks. Her attitude toward him was unacceptable, and I called her on it. She replied that the blacks were "ridiculous people," then left the room and sent her partner in to deal with me. That was it.

I recounted this incident to Pedro, who didn't seem to understand my outrage. I tried explaining to him that while I hadn't been born into a world as repressively racist as that of my parents or grandparents, they had passed on to us their feelings of inferiority, their fears, their insecurities. No matter how successful any black of my generation might be, these "messages" we'd received all our lives about how the world was and where we fit in it affected us, whether we knew it or not. Pedro, coming from a Latin background, never understood American blacks' problems.

In Johannesburg we canceled some interviews so that we could visit a black school. Our promoters, the Quibell brothers, were very polite; in fact, almost all the South African whites we encountered were. This was in stark contrast to how they regarded the native blacks. We were taken to see a number of sites, but they pretty much took us to all the tourist traps, steering us away from seeing too many black South Africans. Finally, through a black connection, we were able to arrange a trip to Soweto, the all-black township outside Johannesburg.

As we drove into the township, it was as I imagined it would be: dirt roads and poverty everywhere. It was very hot, but still hundreds lined the streets to see us. At the school a crowd of youngsters, the principal, and the teachers greeted us in the courtyard. The children ranged in age from five or so to eighteen and wore clean, crisply pressed uniforms. A little program had been prepared in our honor, at which the students sang songs in English and in Zuto. One little boy recited a very beautiful, moving poem. Following the children's presentation, Cindy, Scherrie, and I talked to them about education, hygiene, anything we thought might be helpful. Many times when we bent down to speak to the children they touched our faces and exclaimed with awe, "You are so beautiful!"

We took lots of pictures, and many of the children talked into a tape recorder we'd brought. When I asked "What do you think about your black American brothers and sisters?" the children cried out in unison, "We love our black American brothers and sisters!"

During our run in Johannesburg, we did a benefit concert for an organization called TEACH (Teach Every African Child), and with the proceeds three badly needed classrooms were built. It was a multiracial audience, and we were honored by the white mayor of Johannesburg and the black mayor of Soweto. The Coliseum where we performed didn't sell out, so only $6,000 of an expected $10,000 was raised through ticket sales; Pedro suggested we donate the balance. I too was determined to make our visit to South Africa yield positive results. By helping to build the three classrooms, I felt we'd accomplished something constructive.

It was a moving, gratifying experience. This was not discussed with the girls, and when they heard, they were furious. Then Pedro got into an argument with them. Scherrie and Cindy were upset to learn I'd turned over my share of the group to my husband, giving him full control of the Supremes.

"If you have control over the group, and you are managing us, isn't that a conflict of interest?" Scherrie asked. "Couldn't you be sued?"

I don't think Scherrie meant this in a hostile way, but Cindy, who had been pretty unhappy throughout most of the trip, jumped right in.

"I should be told who the boss is around here!" she said angrily.

"How soon people forget," Pedro sneered, obviously directing his comment to Cindy. He'd been after me to let her go for almost a year, but I couldn't do it. The meeting ended with Scherrie and Cindy threatening that we'd hear from their lawyers. I sat in the corner, watching it all and saying nothing. I was wrong to have given control of my ownership in the group to Pedro without telling them, and I understood that they deserved to know where they stood.

In Johannesburg we made an appearance at a new department store. From the moment we pulled up we could see it wasn't well organized. Many black people gathered to see us, and as we sat up on a platform, the emcee kept pleading with people to stop pushing. But no one was trying to form orderly lines or help the situation. Outside were policemen with vicious dogs, which they threatened to turn loose on the crowd if it didn't settle down. One organizer only exacerbated things by tossing out records and photographs. This caused people to push and shove one another, resulting in an ugly riot.

By the time Pedro finally took charge and established some semblance or order, it was too late. I'll never forget the hateful expressions on the white people's faces. They really didn't care what happened to our black fans and were on the brink of violence to stop the noisy surge. When it seemed that the platform might collapse, we left, reluctantly. Most of the whites blamed the blacks because of the way they behaved. I saw it as the responsibility of the people in charge—black or white—to make things run smoothly. That the black people were in danger of being injured or crushed didn't seem to enter anyone's mind. It was as if all blacks were invisible.

During our stay a black South African woman named Susan took care of Turkessa, now six months old and beginning to crawl. Susan was very kind and intelligent, in her early thirties, and she was wonderful with Turkessa. From the moment we met, I insisted that she address me by my first name. A look of fear crossed her face, and she politely explained that she could not do that, even though I was black too. Even among blacks, the South Africans drew distinctions. We discovered that the reason we could go places and do things that black citizens could not was our "honorary white" status. This did not come to our attention until toward the end of the tour, and it upset all of us. I didn't see why Susan and I could not relate to each other as equals, not as a boss and a slave. It hurt me to see how living in South Africa had stripped Susan of her pride and self-worth, and brainwashed her into believing that she had no right to such things. In the weeks we spent together, I tried to change some of that.

Susan was in the room during one of my many heated discussions with our PR people. When I spoke up to the white publicist, she became visibly shaken. Later she confided timidly that she was worried about what would happen to me, how I might be punished for addressing a *white woman* that way. I explained that the white woman worked for *me* and that she'd done something I disagreed with. There was no reason why I should be afraid to address anyone—regardless of color—as I chose. Susan understood my words, but her experience was so different from mine, she really didn't know what they meant.

The full extent of the constant fear blacks live with there became clear one evening when Scherrie, our conductor Teddy Harris, and some others from our entourage dined in Cape Town. Now, Cape Town was one of the more "liberal" areas, or so we'd heard. One of our party asked his black waiter to find out from the chef when his meal might be ready. The waiter went into the kitchen, and the white chef slapped him simply for *addressing* him. When the waiter returned to the table, everyone was furious about what had occurred. Naturally, everyone's first reaction was to do something about it, but the frightened waiter pleaded, "Please, please, do not say anything, because I will lose my job."

Another time I was in a beauty salon getting my hair done, and a white beautician chattered on about how it was such a shame the way black South Africans were treated in her country and how wrong it was. Not a moment later, a black hair washer politely asked her if she might use the telephone; she was ordered to use the phone in back. Racism was everywhere.

The tour was plagued by mix-ups about what type of

audiences our promoters had permits for. In Johannesburg the shows were mixed, although this had not been officially sanctioned. During the part of our show where we invited people on stage to dance with us, integrated couples seemed to come from everywhere. It was a beautiful thing to see, and something many Johannesburg newspapers commented on favorably.

In Durban, however, reporters tipped us off that, despite what we might have been promised, the shows planned there were not for mixed audiences. The promoter swore he'd applied for the permits over two months ago but that the bureaucracy was stalling, which I believed. The situation became front-page news for several days running. Our white promoter gave out free passes to blacks, who could not buy tickets at the box office. He assured us he was doing everything possible, and Pedro kept reminding him of our contract's stipulations that we play only for mixed audiences.

Finally, the day before our first show, things appeared to have been worked out. The local paper heralded it as "a major breach in the apartheid barrier," and I felt certain everything was settled.

I was walking through the hotel lobby when a group that included Indians and blacks approached me. They begged me not to let the Supremes go on that night. Whatever integration was reflected in our audience was token at best, they claimed. I was very embarrassed and told them to purchase tickets at the box office. If they couldn't, I promised we would not go on. It was sad to see their resignation. I guess they didn't think it was worthwhile to even bother.

Each night before the shows, we made sure the audience was integrated. In addition to the preshow feature stories and postshow concert reviews, our tour there prompted many antiapartheid, pro-integration editorials. Despite our efforts to ensure that our audiences were mixed, it came to our attention toward the end of the tour that not all the audiences we had believed were integrated really were. In some cases, just enough blacks and other nonwhites were put in the audience so that when we looked out from the stage, it appeared fully integrated. For having performed before one such audience in Durban, the Supremes were roundly criticized by local black leaders.

This upset all of us. But Cindy and Scherrie, obviously very angry, went public with their feelings. Scherrie said that the country was beautiful but that some of its people were "bigoted and ugly." Cindy said that she was insulted to be considered an honorary white. Both vowed that once they returned to the States they would tell everyone what they saw and discourage other black performers from coming over. I shared their basic belief that the government and the promoters of South Africa could not be trusted, but did not go to the press.

The story was picked up by papers all over South Africa, and almost immediately the government there demanded that the Supremes leave the country, which we did. Before we left I gave Susan a wig, which looked very pretty on her, and a dress, which she said she would give to her daughter for Christmas.

As I looked into Susan's eyes, I saw a spark of hope. I prayed that one day soon the bonds of apartheid would be broken.

# CHAPTER 11

The South African tour drew Cindy and Scherrie closer. Once again I was the outsider. I needed the Supremes to be a group again, but everything was working against that, namely, lack of money. Everyone knew that whatever monies we earned first went into the corporation, and that's how we paid ourselves weekly salaries, as well as musicians, assistants, travel expenses, stage wear, public relations, photographs, and various professionals, like choreographers, to work with us. Whatever remained at year's end was divided among us by contractually set percentages. The real cream—the only way any of us would make Big Money—was to have a hit record. As that possibility slipped away, everyone started to become edgy.

Scherrie and Cindy had very different reasons for sticking with the Supremes. Scherrie and I were splitting our solos pretty evenly, and while Scherrie was a stunning, gifted singer, I was getting progressively better notices. Cindy, though, had changed since the last time she was in the group.

She seemed unhappy; things had come to a head with Charles, and her divorce from him was finalized the day of our Shubert Theatre show, but I think she still loved him. As a mother, she had to feel torn between her career and her child, as I did.

Cindy couldn't seem to lose the weight she'd gained, and on stage she appeared to be just going through the motions, occasionally flubbing cues. I kept encouraging her to change, for her own good. Cindy took any comment I made defensively. She kept missing a certain step, and when I mentioned it, she replied, "I didn't know that's what we were supposed to do."

"This is how Geoffrey had us do it, Cindy," Scherrie chimed in.

Cindy felt we were ganging up on her. Staring at me, she snapped, "All right, Boss!" It hit me right between the eyes. *Diane*. How I'd hated feeling pushed aside by her ambition. Now the shoe was on the other foot—my foot—but it didn't fit. Scherrie always tried to come to the rescue, imploring us not to fight, and not to go onstage mad at each other. But she too snapped whenever Pedro was around.

It was getting harder for me to disguise my impatience with Cindy. I thought back to all the years I had gone out of my way to make excuses for other people. They had probably laughed at me behind my back then, thinking I was such a soft touch. Those same girls would probably someday go around saying they had been one of the Supremes.

I started admitting to myself what I had known in my heart all along: no one would ever care about the Supremes more than I did. I started looking at everything with a colder eye. Rather than accepting things at face value, I became more skeptical. Before, I would have silently hoped Cindy would lose the weight; now I said something to her about it.

We had put off the decision to ask Cindy to leave long

enough. Pedro wanted to replace her with Thelma Houston, who had enjoyed moderate success with "Save the Country." Her big break would be 1977's Number One "Don't Leave Me This Way." I often caught Thelma's show in Vegas and thought she was a great singer, with an incredible gospel voice. But I knew that she would never want to be part of a group.

Turkessa and I spent two weeks in Detroit, and I could see that she was beginning to resemble my mother. As always, all my friends dropped by, and I went around visiting. I looked into selling the houses I owned there because we needed a bigger place in Los Angeles, and I didn't have the money to buy one. It was so distressing to learn how little my properties were worth. When I'd moved onto Buena Vista in 1965, it was a beautiful area; now I was told I'd be lucky to get what I paid for those homes. Detroit had really changed.

I went to our old hangout, the Twenty Grand, with a bunch of friends. Stepping into the nightclub was like entering a time warp. It was there that Diane, Flo, and I had decided to pursue a record deal. This night the Four Tops were performing, and they had people out of their seats, dancing. People kept coming up to me, asking, "Hey, girl, when did you get back in town?" I couldn't really relax or really enjoy myself, though, because I kept glancing at the door, expecting Pedro any moment. He was in Los Angeles taking care of business but planned to fly in for Thanksgiving. When I got to my mother's later, he was there, obviously peeved that I hadn't met him at the airport.

Flo came over, and she looked so different. She had put on a lot of weight again and after only a few beers was very high. During dinner she asked, "Mary, can you help me? I want to get back in the business."

As Flo spoke, I realized that my whole attitude toward her had changed in the past year. Things had gone wrong for her; things were going wrong for me too. Life is unfair, but there comes a point where you have to face where you are and do something about it. Diane had made a statement that she wanted to shake Florence. She'd been widely criticized for saying that, but I understood how she felt. Eight years after she'd left the group, Flo still couldn't get on with her life.

I told Pedro that I'd seen the Four Tops, and as I expected, he took it badly. He was perfectly charming at Thanksgiving dinner, then without a word went upstairs and packed. I followed him up the stairs, trying to reason with him. When I told Flo that I had to take Pedro to the airport, I could see that she was hurt.

After I got home from the airport, Flo called, sounding tipsy.

"You're a good girl," she said. Then, after a long pause, she added. "You're very nasty . . . and I'm listening to the Jackson 5. . . . I'm sorry if I hurt your feelings."

"Hurt my feelings about what?" I asked.

"I'm confused, Mary. I can't talk to you now." The line went dead.

There was always something left to say.

November 30, 1975

We are playing a Hotel Executive Inn in Evansville, Indiana. The first night there was no one in the audience. The next five nights there was close to no one. It's such a letdown. Scherrie fell off the stage one night. It was one of those little portable stages they roll out for the show, then roll back later so people can dance. One minute she was there, the next minute she was gone! But she pulled it off beautifully, like a pro.

Now when I go onstage, I don't think we're good. I know that Scherrie is a wonderful singer, but I feel like I am not good. I sound awful. I don't have any soul or technique.

I can't even look people in the eyes without feeling fear and uneasiness. Oh God, where am I? I never used to be this negative.

In late January 1976 Scherrie, Cindy, and I played at a small club in Toronto, to wonderful reviews. This turned out to be Cindy's last show with us, and soon after we got home her departure was announced. Animosity between her and Pedro had worsened since South Africa, and he asked her to leave. Once again, another singer; the fifth new lineup since Flo had left.

Earlier, Pedro and I had discussed the idea of me going solo, but I felt that I owed the Supremes one more chance. And, besides, I was scared to death. When Pedro said bluntly, "The Supremes are dead," I hated him. He was only trying to do what was best for both of us, but I didn't see that; I felt like everyone was trying to take the group away from me.

Cindy, Scherrie, and I had already begun work on our next album, *High Energy*, for which Motown teamed us up with Brian and Eddie Holland. The brothers now collaborated with Harold Beatty in place of Lamont Dozier. They cowrote and produced the entire LP except for "I Don't Want to Lose You," by Thom Bell and Linda Creed.

Pedro and I were driving through Beverly Hills, and he was excitedly telling me about a great new singer he'd found, Susaye Green. A meeting was arranged with me, Pedro, Brian and Eddie Holland, Scherrie, and Susaye. I was surprised by how short she was, even shorter than Scherrie; at five feet four and a half inches, I still towered over them. My first thought was, *All Cindy's gowns will have to be cut down.*

Susaye had been in show business most of her life, attending the Professional Children's School and the High

School for the Performing Arts (the real-life setting for *Fame*) in New York City. Her mother taught voice, and so Susaye was exposed to all manner of formal training from a very early age. She first worked as a singer with Harry Belafonte and for a number of years toured with Ray Charles as a Raelette. She and Ray also dated during that time. More recently, she'd been a member of Stevie Wonder's Wonderlove (like Lynda Laurence).

It's interesting to note that as time went on and our records became less successful for a variety of reasons, one thing the Supremes never wanted for was talent. Ironically, as time passed and fewer people got to know the group, we were better than ever technically and talentwise. Susaye, who composed music as well, was a very good singer, with a five-octave range. We took her on the spot.

Although *High Energy* was already completed, we over-dubbed Susaye's voice on two tracks: "High Energy" and the first single, "I'm Gonna Let My Heart Do the Walking," which made respectable showings on the pop (Number 40) and black (Number 25) charts.

I was at Hazel's home with Scherrie and Susaye, trying on some gowns that needed to be altered, when Hazel told me that Flo had just died. Her last year had not been a happy one. At one point she'd checked into a hospital, apparently on the verge of a nervous breakdown. Flo's nerves, weight problems, and high blood pressure were all being treated with different prescription drugs. On Saturday, February, 21, 1976, she was admitted to Mt. Carmel Mercy Hospital, complaining of numbness in her arms and legs. She'd been drinking while on medication. The next day a blood clot blocked a major artery, and her heart stopped.

I left immediately for Detroit, where I went straight to Flo's house to see her family and children. Flo was laid out at Stinson's Funeral Home, and over the next couple days thousands stood in line to pay their last respects. All Detroit seemed to mourn Flo's death. The *Detroit Free Press* reported that the funeral would be held the following Saturday, under such headlines as EX-SUPREMES TO ATTEND BALLARD RITES and DIANA EXPECTED. The ceremony threatened to become a media circus, so at the last minute it was decided to have the funeral a day early.

Shortly before noon that Friday Flo's body was moved from the funeral home to the New Bethel Baptist Church, where Aretha Franklin's father, the Reverend C. L. Franklin, presided. Despite all attempts to keep the funeral plans secret, word leaked, and even before the flowers were arranged around Flo's coffin, a thick line of fans wound around the corner and down the block. Within the next two hours over 2,200 fans, mourners, family, and friends filled the church to capacity.

The police presence outside was doubled, and inside a dozen uniformed nurses stood by to help the overwrought. It began to seem more like a show than a funeral. Around two-thirty someone announced from the altar, "The stars have asked you not to take pictures of them in the church," which only fueled the crowd's anticipation. When Stevie Wonder was led up the aisle to the front of the church, a wild round of applause erupted.

"Clear the center aisle!" Reverend Franklin ordered, and suddenly Diane appeared, surrounded by bodyguards. She started down the aisle, then let out a loud sob, dramatically swooning and stumbling until her bodyguards swept her to her seat. Now the crowd was on its feet, hundreds of flashbulbs popping.

"Would you please clear the aisle so that we can get the family in!" someone pleaded over the public-address system. Flo's family quietly entered and took their places in the front pews. Her six sisters, four brothers, mother, husband Tommy, and three daughters were in the church, so that by the time my mother and I arrived, all the seats down front were taken, and we had to sit farther back.

Finally, around three o'clock the choir began singing, and Reverend Franklin delivered the eulogy. "We have experiences that are not always good and true," he said. "Sometimes they are frustrating and crushing, but positive good comes out of negative situations. . . . Even though some of you were not as orderly as you could be, I know that you are here in a gesture of respect for this deceased young lady, Florence Ballard."

After nearly an hour of song, prayer, and sermon, Reverend Franklin was bringing the funeral to an end when Diane got up and asked for his microphone. She said, "Mary and I would like to have a silent prayer." I hadn't spoken to her in months and had no idea that she had prearranged a tribute to Flo. My grief was personal and private; I didn't want to get up. She said, "I believe nothing disappears, and Flo will always be with us." As I stood beside her, stunned, she passed me the microphone. All I could muster through my tears was, "I loved her very much."

I looked down at Florence one last time. They closed her coffin, and the procession slowly headed for the door while "Someday We'll Be Together" poured from the huge pipe organ. We proceeded to Detroit Memorial Park, and I was surprised to see that Diane didn't come to the grave site, as I'd assumed she would. Flo's death is another subject we have never talked about.

Now, years later, when I think about Flo's death, I think most about the promise I made to her at her grave: "Don't worry, Flo; I'll take care of it." I don't concentrate on the events that struck me so deeply that day: the packed church, the people tearing at the floral arrangements, Diane's grand entrance and her "incorporating" me into her tribute to Flo,

Berry's conspicuous absence, the sight of her three little girls, Michelle, Nicole, and Lisa, so young, not really comprehending the awful fate their mother had met.

All those things remind me that Flo actually died, and they become harder for me to focus on these days, because Flo's spirit is not dead for me. I can still feel her now as I did when we were young together, and that's how she will always remain in my heart. When I'm down, all I do is think of her hearty laugh, or imagine her rolling her eyes, planting her hands firmly on her hips, and saying, "Honey . . ." like she's about to let me in on the greatest secret in the world, and I get shivers. Her spirit is so alive for me now, I know that all the things we deal with every day that seem so urgent are external things. The *real* us is our spirit, and this non-physical part that so many consider "unreal" is probably the only real thing we have.

Flo had more soul in one little finger than anyone I ever knew. I see her spirit especially in a familiar Supremes film clip of us singing "Back in My Arms Again." Flo's sassy expression as she watches Diane sing, ". . . And Flo, she don't know, that the boy she loves is a Romeo," is priceless and uniquely Flo.

Unlike Diane and me, Flo couldn't slip between the black world we grew up in and the white world we later seemed to have conquered. She was honest and direct, and not always when it was the wisest thing to be. But Flo didn't think things out that way; she didn't connive or have ulterior motives. She was what she was, and she stuck to her principles, even when it wasn't to her advantage. She had so much pride—probably too much for the likes of people like Berry and those who wanted to manipulate her.

To this day I'm totally mystified by the claims of some people, including several members of Flo's family, that Diane or I could have done something to save Flo. Would money (assuming I had it to give) have saved her? What Flo needed more than anything, I now realize, was serious psychological therapy for the lingering aftereffects of her rape at age seventeen. Today this is such an obvious solution, but it wasn't then. The alcohol, I have contended all along, was to ease the emotional pain of that rape.

Pedro and I moved into our new home, a beautiful mansion in Hollywood's exclusive Hancock Park district. The classic Tudor was designed and owned by the preeminent architect of this old Hollywood style. To give you an idea of how things change, when Nat "King" Cole moved into a home across the street back in the fifties, he was threatened by bigots.

This was my dream house, and although we probably shouldn't have bought it when we did, Pedro and I fell in love with it. It had twenty-two rooms, seven bedrooms, ebony wood paneling throughout, a large library, an office, a magnificent winding staircase that looked like something out of *Gone with the Wind,* and a built-in, three-story-tall pipe organ. Because the chief architect built this house for himself, it had all sorts of little features and improvements (pool, tennis court, full basement) that made it very special. Whenever in England and Europe, Pedro and I shopped for antique furnishings and paintings with which to decorate our new home. It made me feel the star people thought I was. Yes, Pedro and I were living high on the hog, but to keep all the staff, such as Hazel and two servants—including a driver—I had to work constantly. As soon as the money came in, it went out.

This new home was more than a house to me. Like the first houses Diane, Flo, and I bought in Detroit, this one symbolized something. Inside the walls I felt safe and secure, and I remember seeing it and thinking that this would be the house I'd raise my children in, the house where I hoped Pedro and I would settle our problems and grow old together.

Pedro continued to come and go as he pleased, while I stayed home decorating, cooking, planting a garden, and playing with the baby. I'd seen so many other women get themselves into this situation; I remembered looking at some of them and knowing what everyone was saying about their husbands, thinking it could never happen to me. But it had.

One of the things that attracted me to Pedro was his need to control: his single-minded determination to get what he wanted. The first few times I'd seen his more dangerous side—when he pushed me outside in the cold, when he beat me while I was carrying Turkessa—I made myself deal with it. Wives who are in this situation are very misunderstood. People think that one day you fall in love with a man, the next day he beats you, and then leaving him is the obvious choice. When I was young, I heard pimps beat up on whores right down the street from where I lived in the projects. But that seemed so removed from my life, and I'd never seen it for myself. I had too much pride to let that happen to me. Or so I thought.

Instead of helping to build me up emotionally and showing me how to love myself, Pedro exploited my insecurities. It was this part of him that I found very strange and confusing, because at tender moments he was so kind and concerned. These were the times I was sure of his love, and I let it eclipse the pain that he caused. Long before he ever raised a hand to me, I sensed he was dangerous. Why didn't I walk away then, or at any time along the way?

Obvious question; difficult—maybe impossible—answer. I still don't know, except to say that the subtle, almost imperceptible steps toward that living hell were far behind me when I finally realized where I was. A part of me needed to see firsthand how people who needed power operated. I felt by staying with Pedro I could learn.

I decided to have one more go with this new group of the Supremes. If this didn't work, I would take Pedro's advice and go solo. Susaye made her debut with us in April at the Royal Hawaiian Hotel in Falls Church, Virginia. Vocally the act was very exciting. Nearly half the solos were mine, and Susaye and Scherrie both had featured solo numbers as well. Finally the Supremes were back to three lead singers like on the *Meet the Supremes* album in 1963. I was determined to give this new group 150 percent of my time and energy.

The reviews for our initial shows were very positive, and it looked like we'd made the right choice. We appeared on several national television programs during this time—*The Dinah Shore Show, Soul Train, American Bandstand, The Merv Griffin Show*—and "I'm Gonna Let My Heart Do the Walking" went Top 10 in discos across the country. We also appeared (but with Cindy, not Susaye) in a series of commercials for the American Heart Association, of which we'd been named ambassadors. None of this could counteract the effects of Motown's lack of support. There was again evidence that the label had not supplied review copies of the album and the single to the industry trade magazines.

In May we toured England, then went on to Germany, Italy, and France. English fans and critics who'd found our last tour too Vegas-y loved the new show. Susaye drew notice for her voice, and during a performance in London her rendition of "He Ain't Heavy, He's My Brother" got a five-minute ovation.

One of our shows was taped at the Jazz Festival in Montreaux, Switzerland. Right before the taping, I decided to change dresses. The one I put on was a sexy, see-through, covered in all the strategic areas—nothing outrageous. When Pedro saw it, he exploded, beating me up and blackening my eye before we went onstage. Hazel and I tried to cover it with makeup, and I pretended nothing had happened. But everyone knew.

The European tour was a success. However, when we got to Bachelors III in Fort Lauderdale, Florida, ticket sales were so slow that some nights we did only one show instead of two. I hadn't wanted to come back here to begin with, but I knew we had to. It was the old story: we needed money. About the only thing that cheered me up was Turkessa, who was beginning to talk. Fortunately, she was a very easy child to be around, and Scherrie and Susaye really liked her. Willie too was with us, working as assistant road manager.

The summer was uneventful; then in August we had a great engagement at the Roostertail in Detroit.

It's nice coming back to Detroit to perform. Everyone here seems to genuinely like the Supremes, even though we are not the same hometown girls. The name *Supremes* really carries a lot of weight. I've been having dinner over at Aunt I.V.'s house every day. It feels nice to spend time in my hometown without being rushed. I even went to see Daddy [J. L. Pippin] in the old neighborhood where I grew up. All the houses looked so small. As a child, everything looked so big. Even some of the same people were still living there. The family I stole fifty cents from still lived on Bassett Street. I brought it up to them so I could get it off my conscience. All these years I had been ashamed of that.

Well, the show was a success, and everyone loved us. I was getting standing ovations every night. It really made me feel great. Scherrie was her usual great self, and Susaye also got standing ovations. She has been the catalyst in making Scherrie and me free with our singing, especially me.

I've really been getting a great response to my tribute to Flo. I am glad. Sometimes I feel guilt, using her for my own gain. But everyone has loved it. Many people have told me they were close to tears because of it, so I think it's good. At least her name is out there.

One guy gave me a standing ovation after "How Lucky" and shouted, "Thanks for Flo, Mary." It's amazing how many people know Flo. I've been with the group eight years more than (or after) her, and they're just starting to know me. But they all knew Flo.

One evening Pedro was up at Motown and happened to run into Berry. They went into the studio, and Berry listened to some tracks from our new LP, *Mary, Scherrie & Susaye,* our second with the Hollands. He seemed very pleased and told Pedro it was the high quality we needed. The signs seemed encouraging, but it was so hard to know what Berry really thought. Berry had recently told us that Motown wanted to manage the group again. Pedro was very hurt; I didn't know what to do.

The album, our last, came out in early fall. Initially it got more of a push than the others; we were on the cover of the trade magazine *Billboard,* for example. But after a promising start—the single "You're My Driving Wheel" bowed on the national disco chart at Number 29—sales fell off.

August 1976

Susaye, Scherrie, and I arrived in San Francisco to perform at the Fairmont Hotel for two weeks. Lucky for us it's the middle of the convention season, so it has been packed every night. In fact, we went into percentage (earning a part of the take at the door) the first week. Anyway, nice to be on the plus side instead of always being in the red.

Hazel told us that the bank will not honor any more checks unless the money is there. We have been operating on pennies, always behind, these past three years. It's finally catching up with us. I am glad I never really let it get me down. However, we've got to start making that big money again, because we are too far in the hole. The Supremes have to repay me the $30,000 I lent them. The bank's screaming about bouncing checks. All our employees want raises. Several of them have threatened to quit. But fortunately, we are at a time when maybe the cards are in our favor. So it always seems to be its darkest just before the dawn. I'll get it together. I'll give myself and the Supremes another chance.

I firmly believe we'll be greater than ever, even though somewhere in my mind there are doubts. But I am going to do what I believe is right and face the future when it gets here. As Pedro said the other night, we can only go so far wrong because it's in us to be big. We are big. We'll always find a way.

After a lot of thought, Pedro and I decided to move the Supremes' booking to the William Morris Agency, something we'd considered for quite some time. One of our new agents there mentioned that there was a December opening in Las Vegas on a bill with the comedian Alan King. It was a great break; it was also just two weeks away.

At Pedro's insistence, Motown finally came across with money for a new stage act, and we rehearsed furiously in our new home. Gil Askey worked out arrangements in the basement, while George Faison, a popular Broadway choreographer in charge of staging, had his secretary and various assistants and technicians running in and out all day. For a full week it was utter chaos from noon until night, but we were excited and happy to be working.

George suggested, "Since everyone always mimics the Supremes' choreography, like the 'Stop! In the Name of Love' hand gestures, maybe you should do something like that." We talked about the Broadway play *Hair*, which had a sequence that parodied the original Supremes. Three girls sang together à la the Supremes, but at the end of the number you saw that they were wearing a single gown. In the early seventies one of my girlfriends had appeared in the L.A. production, so I'd seen it countless times and thought the takeoff was cute.

"Look, Mary," George said. He stood up, all six feet one of him, and sashayed across the room in a perfect imitation of how the Supremes moved. Scherrie, Susaye, and I laughed out loud. "Now, wouldn't it be funny to see you guys mimic the three black girls in *Hair* mimicking you?"

"Great!" I said. We all thought this was a wonderful idea, a good chance to show that while we loved the Supremes image, we also knew that it was extreme. I was always looking for something new and were sure that this routine was a winner. We worked up an arrangement of greatest hits to sing with it. Who wouldn't like that?

In the middle of rehearsals Mike Roshkind called, demanding that Pedro and I attend a meeting at Motown that afternoon. Besides being logistically inconvenient, it was insulting to be ordered around like that. When we arrived, Mike was there with Suzanne dePasse, chief publicist Bob Jones, company lawyer Lee Young, Jr., and Susaye's mother, who was also her manager. The gist of the meeting concerned Scherrie and Susaye's dissatisfaction with Pedro's management, which annoyed me. This had all been planned behind my back. I'd brought those girls in, and now they were conspiring against me. Joining the Supremes is like going into a job in a department store. You follow their rules or you leave. They didn't come into the Supremes as owners, but as employees. They knew that. I felt that someone there wanted Pedro *and* me out of the way. As I learned later, Motown was promising Susaye and Scherrie that it would give them creative freedom and label support if only it weren't for Pedro and me.

Our opening in Las Vegas, which should have been fabulous, was another all-time low. There was no talk about "coheadlining"; we were clearly the opening act, with a meager thirty minutes to perform. However, I was very excited that we were playing Caesars Palace, one of the top hotels. Mike Roshkind, Suzanne dePasse, Thelma Houston, and Bob Jones were all there, along with dozens of industry friends.

From the minute the curtain rose, we knew the set wasn't right. George had had to make so many changes in so little time, we looked and felt like amateurs. Then came the medley of Supremes hits, with the three of us in one dress. It was an unmitigated disaster. People in the audience just didn't get it, or if they did, they didn't think it was funny. Where there should have been laughter, there was stony silence. Once the number ended, we struggled to get out of the one big dress, but we couldn't get it off before the lights came back on. What an embarrassment!

At our opening-night party, I ran into Mike Roshkind and Bob Jones. Mike barely said hello; his expression was so cold I shuddered. Bob was pleasant enough, but I could read his mind. No one would say what we all knew was the truth: we were awful.

Over the next several days, we spent every free minute with George, revamping the show. Everyone had a very negative attitude. Conductor Teddy Harris was annoyed that we'd brought in other arrangers to work out certain numbers, Susaye was behaving like a petulant child, and Scherrie was joining her. Every time George made a suggestion, those two shot him down. As I sat there, watching this, I thought despairingly, *This is it.* At one point, George approached me and apologized for Scherrie and Susaye's attitude. That was very kind of him, but I knew that it should have been me apologizing to him.

Pedro decided right then to notify Motown that I was going solo. I'd been fighting it for a long time, though not for sentimental reasons, as many people thought. I wanted to leave the Supremes with a hit record. To top it all off, over the years I'd lent the group tens of thousands of dollars from my personal account. If I left now, or if the Supremes were dissolved, I could kiss that money good-bye.

One night our show was so bad that people got up and walked out in the middle. We had rearranged the hits medley, but it was worse than ever. "Baby Love" went by so fast, we literally missed it, or so we thought. We started singing the next song, "Where Did Our Love Go," before we all realized the band was still playing "Baby Love."

Pedro came into the dressing room before the second show and announced, "Mary is leaving the group. This is it."

Scherrie and Susaye seemed genuinely shocked. "Mary, is that what you want to do?" Scherrie asked. I think she was trying to see if this was my idea or Pedro's.

"Yes, Scherrie, I am leaving." I was tired of the constant bickering, the pettiness, the embarrassment of failing. From our dressing room we could hear the crowd roaring with laughter at Alan King's jokes, so the audience wasn't the problem; it was us.

The rest of the run, cut short because of poor attendance, just dragged on and on. One bright spot was a show when, no matter what we did, we received a very loud, enthusiastic response from one corner of the room. Onstage, you can't see more than a few rows into the crowd, so we had no idea who these rabid fans were until after the show, when the Pointer Sisters came backstage to visit. It turned out that they were the ones. Now, that's what I call true friends. We spent hours talking, playing cards, and being real crazy.

With Pedro and me on our way out of the picture, Scherrie and Susaye must have wondered what Motown had in store for them. Surprisingly, they seemed to believe everything the company said. They were promised an album deal and Motown's full support. Pedro and I pointed out how the label hadn't adequately promoted the Supremes since Diane left. We warned them to be careful. Naturally, Susaye and Scherrie were suspicious of everything we said; nothing penetrated. They were two very headstrong women, determined to carve out their own careers from the Supremes.

Since having Turkessa, I'd tired of the whole party scene, but on occasion I missed it. Hollywood was no longer a truly glamorous place; there didn't seem to be the same magic. Even the private clubs, like the Candy Store, weren't what they used to be. Everything I'd loved about Hollywood in the late sixties and early seventies was dying.

Also, the music scene had changed. All the clubs played only disco. Whereas the music of the O'Jays, the Temptations, and the Four Tops made me want to jump up and dance, disco's soulless, mechanical thumping made me want to cover my ears and run.

Almost every time Pedro and I went out, there was trouble. One evening we were at a club, and I was speaking to a television producer, thanking him for how well the Supremes had been treated at a recent taping. As far as I was concerned, this was simply good business. But Pedro became upset, so we left a few minutes later, and at home it was a familiar scene. As I wrote in my diary:

December 1976

We silently got in bed, then he started talking about it. What could I say? He had his own point of view. Then when he wanted to make love to make up, I wasn't ready for that. It takes me a long while to get over a quarrel. He became very strong, and that turns me off even more. Those are the moments when I know I am closer to hating him. When I wouldn't return his advances, he slapped me and slapped me. Why does he think his strength will make me love him more? I need tenderness and understanding. He told me a friend of ours has found a girlfriend because he is tired of how his wife has become. Somehow I feel that Pedro is talking about us, although he said if he ever did that, he would tell me in some way. Maybe that was a hint.

# CHAPTER 12

had all but accepted that Pedro and I would divorce eventually, and, to be honest, I'd stopped loving him. My career was another question. Anything might happen: we could get that hit record and be on top again, or we could continue our slide downhill. Our financial situation was bleak, my confidence was shaken, but I still had faith.

My diaries from these years are filled with entries that alternate between utter despair and soaring optimism. As always, there were two—or three or four—sides to every story, and I saw them all. Instead of becoming embittered and cynical, I kept looking for and believing in what was good about people and life. Despite all that had gone wrong, I had my family, my baby, my talent, and my friends. I didn't need to have everything; I didn't even want everything, just happiness.

The idea of going out alone during the coming year was exciting and frightening. I felt like both a mother leaving her child, and a little bird leaving the nest. It was agreed that the

Supremes would continue with Scherrie, Susaye, and a third girl. I had mixed feelings about that. On one hand, I felt I owed it to Scherrie to let her continue. She'd given the Supremes so much. In my heart, though, I knew it was time for the Supremes to end, with or without me. Susaye was another story; she'd been in the group such a short time and had caused so much dissension. I also wondered whether the fans would accept a group with no original members, and I worried about Motown. Would it offer me a solo contract? Would it kill the Supremes, but openly this time? What was going to happen?

The main thing I can credit Pedro with is pushing me. Left to my own devices, I wonder if I'd have made the decision to go off on my own then. But he was right: I could not go on fighting like this.

It's funny how Pedro was so supportive of me professionally and yet treated me so badly in our marriage. I think he saw me as two different people: his client and his wife. When it came to my career, he showed all the characteristics that I loved. He was smart, strong, shrewd, and reasonable. I believe that he truly wanted to do what was best for me.

But at home or in social situations, I was just his wife, and he treated me like even less than that. His obsession about me cheating on him was out of hand. He told me he was having an affair with one of my best friends, a famous star. I didn't believe him, but I had to know, so I called her. When I told her what Pedro said, she replied, "Mary, that is a lie." I was so relieved. At one point, he told me that he was going to start dating other women. My first reaction was to say that I wouldn't stand for it, but then I looked at my situation: the baby, the career, the house, the image, the future. A famous advice columnist says to ask yourself, "Am I better off with him or without him?" In many ways I still needed Pedro.

Two people who felt they did not need Pedro were Scherrie and Susaye. The tension among us broke into open hostility. Both women hated Pedro and showed it at every opportunity. Susaye and her manager mother had their own ideas about the Supremes, and while Scherrie wasn't as bad as Susaye, she became her partner in crime. Soon Scherrie was as rebellious as Susaye.

While I was not happy with the way Susaye and Scherrie treated us, I understood. And to be fair, their futures were as uncertain as mine, despite Motown's assertions to the contrary. I tried not to take the cold glares and heated words personally, but it hurt nonetheless. I couldn't wait to leave, but there were still concert dates to fulfill.

We spent most of early 1977 overseas. By late March we had played Germany, El Salvador, San Juan, Mexico, and England. Ironically, our shows were getting better all the time. At last the contracts were signed for the Supremes' final "farewell" show: Sunday, June 12, 1977.

Motherhood was the most rewarding thing in my life. Even today I consider my children my real gold records. But as every mother knows, there are limits to how much mothering a mother can give. I was beginning to realize that society's double standards applied to parenthood too. Before it was fashionable, I was a working mother, and, in a sense, my daughter was a working child. She came with me wherever I went, and even amid all the chaos Pedro and I tried to keep our family intact. Even with all the help I had on the road, there was still only one "Mommy" as far as Turkessa was concerned. Others could hold her, change her, put her to sleep, but only I could nurse her. Of course there were alternatives, but I'd waited all my life for my baby, and I was determined to do everything right.

One night we were getting ready to go onstage in England at the Hammersmith Odeon. Turkessa was almost two years old, but because it was so much trouble carrying formula and bottles on the road, she still nursed. My usual routine was to dress, make up, then feed Turkessa right before the show. This way she'd stay calm until the show was over. As I stood in the wings, I held Turkessa in my arms, pulled down one side of my gown, and nursed her. Just then we heard the announcer introduce our band, and Teddy start our opening number. Gill Trodd, who also assisted with Turkessa, ran up, agitated. "What's going on here?" she asked.

I started toward the stage, gently pulling Turkessa away, only to find that she wouldn't let go. Gill took the baby in her arms and tried to coax her off while I kept walking, but no go. Turkessa was there to stay. The emcee was introducing the Supremes now, and there I stood, my bronze-sequined dress down to my waist and a baby stuck to me like glue. Finally, Gill and I gave Turkessa one strong (and, for me, painful) yank, and I was freed. Milk splattered up in my face, but I managed to get my dress up a split second before the curtain rose, and we began singing "Everybody Gets to Go to the Moon."

Returning stateside we had a successful run at Bachelors III in Fort Lauderdale, where just the year before we'd played to half-empty houses. One evening Pedro and I were invited to dinner by Bobby Van, one of the club's owners. We were having a wonderful evening until he received a phone call, and then the whole restaurant started buzzing: *Tom Jones was on his way over.* Everyone knew that Tom was in town to open a new theater, and I suspected that Pedro had brought me here because Tom might show up. In the next minutes, Pedro gave me an in-depth lecture on how I should behave: I should not approach Tom or seem too eager to talk with him.

I was in the ladies' room when two of Tom's backup singers, the Blossoms, came in. We had known one another for a long time, and we spent about fifteen minutes chatting. They both told me they were so proud of me, that Tom talked about me often and always with great respect.

When I finally emerged from the restroom, the restaurant fell silent, and it seemed like all eyes turned to me. Not everyone there knew about our relationship, but many of the same people in his entourage had been there in the sixties, and the affair had been reported in newspapers around the world. Tom walked toward me, extended his hand, and said, "You all right?" I felt my knees go weak.

"Sure, I am fine," I replied shakily. "Is your son Mark with you?"

What was wrong with me? My love for him was a thing of the past, so that wasn't it. I guess it was my guilt. Everyone was looking at us, at me, at Tom, at Pedro. They all knew what I'd done.

We sat at a long table, drinking champagne, ostensibly having a good time. I was a nervous wreck. Every time Tom tried making casual conversation, I could feel the heat of Pedro's searing jealousy.

The Blossoms attended one of our shows that week and told me that they knew Tom planned to come see us. One evening as I started "A Song for You," I looked out from the stage, and there he was, sitting in the first balcony, right in front of me. The line "I've made some bad rhymes" took on a whole new meaning. I glanced at Tom and thought to myself, *Clean up your wicked ways, girl.* Tom came backstage later, and we all stood around, awkwardly making small talk. When we left Fort Lauderdale for Nassau a few days later, I was relieved.

Months after our breakup and as I'd started maturing more, in the back of my mind I always feared that I would have to pay for that affair. Still, until now, I believed I'd been forgiven. Not Pedro, though. He said that I was a sinner who'd done something terrible, and I believed it. Pedro used guilt to control me, and because he always made me feel so wrong, I began seeing myself as a hypocrite who'd been fooling herself. Now I was being punished. I started reading the Bible, which only reinforced my feelings and made me feel dirty.

I began to feel tired all the time; the least little bit of excitement, and I'd have to sit down. I'd also noticed that my stomach was getting bigger. At first I just figured I was eating too much and sleeping too little. I vowed to take better care of myself.

Earlier in the year we had announced in our fan club's monthly newsletter that we would be appearing at one of Richard Nader's "oldies" shows at New York City's Madison Square Garden on March 4, 1977. Almost immediately we heard from fans who thought this was a terrible idea. The format of the Rock and Roll Spectaculars was old-fashioned, like the shows we used to do at the Apollo or the Brooklyn Fox; a three-and-a-half-hour parade of acts, each doing a handful of numbers. That evening was a typical Nader bill, with Ben E. King, the Duprees, Jay Black and the Americans, Johnny Maestro and the Brooklyn Bridge, and Dion DiMucci (of Dion and the Belmonts) all preceding us, the headliners.

When first offered the date, I seriously considered what our appearing on an oldies-but-goodies show would mean. I respected and admired the performers on the bill, particularly Ben E. King, whom the original Supremes performed with countless times in the early sixties, but there were many good reasons not to play the Garden. The audience generally viewed these events as opportunities to stroll down Memory Lane. The years of trying to put the Supremes back on top taught me a thing or two about what the American public expected from performers. In concert, our seventies hits, like

"Nathan Jones" and "Floy Joy," rarely got the same wild response as the older stuff. I had no problem with that; I was proud of all our records. Yet it hurt to know that in some people's eyes we might never do anything as good. As I once replied when asked about the public's taste, "What they had yesterday, they want today."

Almost anywhere else in the world, a performer is respected for his talent and accomplishments; in America, your past accomplishments can kill you. Here we see no middle ground between superstar and has-been. You're either one or the other, regardless of the artistic merits of what you're doing today. If your face is not on television once a week, if every one of your records is not in heavy rotation on radio and MTV, you simply do not exist.

At that point the Supremes were in a sort of netherworld. We weren't really an oldies act, but the general public had lost track of us. Where many acts on the bill had not been on the charts in several years, the Supremes were still a contemporary presence, if not a strong one. The deciding factor to accept the booking was Madison Square Garden itself, and the lure of its capacity. The average audience for one of Nader's shows was around fifteen thousand to eighteen thousand. It was irresistible.

The afternoon of the show we met with Richard Nader and ran down our set. He became very upset that we were doing too many new songs and not enough of the old hits. But we had a relatively new album out, and I wasn't about to pass up this opportunity to promote it.

"Everything will be just fine," I assured Nader. "We know our fans."

He looked at me like I was crazy, and I left the rehearsal hall furious.

When we got backstage at the Garden that night, we could hear the thousands upstairs screaming as Dion finished his set. We were confident they would love us. One of our more devoted fans whispered in my ear, "Mary, girl, I don't think you should go out there. This isn't a Copacabana audience."

"Don't worry," I answered. "We're going to go out there and sing our wigs off for them. And they're going to love it. We're doing 'Tossin' and Turnin' ' and all sorts of old songs and—"

"You don't understand, girl. These are a bunch of bikers from New Jersey. They hate disco songs like your new hits."

I thanked him for his concern, but my mind was made up. There were more than fifteen thousand people out there expecting the Supremes, and we were going to give them a show. We opened with our current disco hit, "You're My Driving Wheel," teamed with another song from *Mary, Scherrie & Susaye*, "Let Yourself Go." The crowd was on its feet, cheering and hollering. I believed we had won them over.

"Hello, New York!" I shouted.

"Yeahhh!" the crowd cheered back.

"We're the Supremes!"

"Yeahhh!"

"We want you to sit back, relax, and enjoy yourselves. We want you all to know that it ain't nothin' but a party—"

"Yeahhh!"

"And we want you to get on down and party!"

Next I introduced Susaye, and she began singing her slow version of the Hollies' "He Ain't Heavy, He's My Brother," which always elicited a standing ovation. The crowd cheered at first, but by the end some people were booing. It was bizarre. For the next twenty minutes the boos just got louder and meaner. What we didn't know until later was that while half the crowd was booing, the other half was applauding and shouting in support. Fights broke out around the arena between the Supremes fans who loved what we were doing and "old rock and roll" fans who disapproved. We tried to redeem ourselves with the greatest-hits medley, but it was too late. Finally, Susaye, Scherrie, and I looked at one another and realized we had to get off the stage before a riot erupted. A group of security men and a few diehard fans accompanied us back to our dressing rooms.

On the way backstage I started laughing just to keep from crying. Scherrie and Susaye were dumbstruck, and Scherrie was particularly unnerved. Her mother was in the last stages of a terminal illness, and Scherrie was feeling very down. Neither of them had wanted to play the Garden, and they were proved right. Their glares and the fans' looks that said, "I told you so," were more than I could bear. In all the years I'd performed, I had never, ever been booed. A scene like that was every performer's nightmare, but I never imagined that it would cut so deeply. Scherrie and Susaye blamed Pedro; however, the fault was really mine. I should have known better.

Pedro and I went with some friends to Regine's disco. I started drinking champagne and was pretty tipsy before long. I couldn't stop talking about what happened; I was dying inside, but Pedro didn't want to hear about it. Out on the dance floor, I started dancing alone with a drink in my hand. When a waiter asked me to put it down, Pedro angrily told me that I was "acting like a nigger, not a star." I was stunned. I'd never felt so rejected in my life.

A few days later *Variety*'s critic wrote: "The Supremes, unfortunately, provided the low point of the evening. The audience, which had been receptive until then, became rude, with much booing, and many leaving the arena in response to the Supremes' slick act, with their coordinated wardrobes and choreography. Fans who remained applauded the closing medley of their hits."

Two days later it was my thirty-third birthday.

Here I was, three months pregnant with my second baby, unhappily married, and setting out on the biggest challenge of my life. My leaving the group brought me head to head with Motown. Pedro was planning most of my legal strategy and hired Mark Turk, the attorney who just the year before had helped the Temptations get out of their Motown contract with their name and move to Atlantic Records. He was confident he could handle Motown, probably get me back more or maybe all of the name, and persuade the label to give me either a generous settlement, a solo contract, or even both.

I gladly let Pedro take over the legal business too. From then on, most of the information I got about how my legal situation was progressing came to me through my husband. The positive aspect was that Pedro had studied and understood the law; he made the complexities of the business comprehensible to me, and that was a big help. The negative side became clear to me nearly a decade later, when I realized that there might have been different approaches to take. It's impossible to know what might have been done that wasn't— especially since no attorney will criticize the actions of the attorney who preceded him on your case. The wheels that Pedro and this attorney set into motion in the spring of 1977 have created consequences that I am still dealing with today.

Back then, I was cautiously optimistic about the situation at home. Then came the Supremes' last tour of Europe, which was dismal and depressing in almost every way. Many times during this tour I wished that after Pedro announced I was leaving, I'd just left. Scherrie and Susaye were not comfortable with me, and since I was on my way out, they became more critical of Pedro. Scherrie, basically a very warm person, was at her worst; the stress of her mother's recent death wore her down. Despite Scherrie's occasional outbursts, we still remained friendly. I could see that had there not been so much adversity, Scherrie would have proved to be the best person of all the Supremes, in terms of talent and personality, to carry on with.

Susaye, on the other hand, had clearly come into the group with her own agenda. She was an ambitious girl, and it showed. She was increasingly difficult to work with, because she refused to sing the background parts we had rehearsed and often stepped out of the choreography, keeping Scherrie and me guessing where she'd be, in the song and on the stage. Scherrie and I always pulled back vocally so that it wouldn't sound like all of us were trying to sing lead at once. I respected Scherrie for being so professional and gracious; many lead singers would have thrown a fit.

After a gig in Austria the subject of Motown's plans for Scherrie and Susaye came up. Pedro wasn't on this trip, so we were a little more relaxed. I said, "Scherrie, when Diane left, Motown stopped doing anything for the Supremes. With me out of the way, they'll do nothing for you."

"Well, Mary," Scherrie said, "they've promised us a lot. They're even allowing both Susaye and me to write our own songs."

"Believe me, Scherrie, they have no intention of pushing another group of Supremes. If they had, they would have done it by now, and we wouldn't be in this position."

No one listened.


This European tour preceded my final dates with the group. I had known it was approaching as we toured through Austria, Germany, and Sweden—ending up in England. Before I knew it, we had landed in the British Isles, and the big night rapidly grew nearer and nearer.

Our last shows were on June 12 at the Drury Lane Theatre in London, an old-style legitimate theater. With its heavy red-velvet curtains and gold-leaf decor, it had a wonderful, dignified atmosphere. Unlike in the States, where the Supremes were all but forgotten, the English treated this final farewell performance as every bit the event the 1970 farewell had been. We had flowers, champagne, and our closest friends and fans all there to bid the Supremes good-bye. It was heavily covered by the media, and the BBC broadcast the show live.

I felt so many different emotions. I decided to just go with the experience; it was going to happen only once. That afternoon I told Scherrie and Susaye that I would like to sing "The Way We Were," a number we hadn't done for a while.

"Do we *have* to?" Susaye whined, obviously feeling put out.

"Yes. It's my last appearance, and that's my last request of the group. I think I deserve at least that, don't you?"

The two of them more or less agreed that I should get to do the song. We ran down the choreography and our parts, but it wasn't really all together. It wasn't until then that it really dawned on me: *This is it.* More than half my life I'd been a Supreme, and in a few moments, it would be over.

Billy Ocean, not as famous then as he'd become in the eighties, opened our show. I stood in the wings and listened to him; he was soulful all right, but the crowd just wasn't very receptive. They were waiting for us.

During the first show I started my solo, "How Lucky Can You Get," and suddenly started crying. I was so choked up with emotion that when I opened my mouth to sing, nothing came out. I stood there silently through the first verse, afraid that I'd sob all the way through it. I came in on the second verse, and sang my heart out. I got one of the most wonderful ovations ever. When we got offstage, Susaye sequestered herself in her dressing room.

Right before the second and last show, the whole backstage area got as quiet as a funeral. Herb and Mauna Loa

Avery had flown over to wish me luck. Gill and Hazel were crying as they carried in more telegrams, flowers, and bottles of champagne. I tried to cheer everyone up, but inside I was sad too. Then it was time to go on. Hazel helped me into my dress. Five months pregnant, I was radiant.

We opened our last show with a frenetic version of "Everybody Gets to Go to the Moon." English audiences were usually put off by our Vegas-type numbers, and one reviewer called this a "manic" and "improbable" opener. "Stoned Love," "Baby Love," and "Stop! In the Name of Love" followed, then an excellent slow rendition of "My World Is Empty Without You," which was Scherrie's showstopper.

This time I was able to sing "A Song for You" and "How Lucky Can You Get" without crying. Everything seemed perfect. I felt it happen. Suddenly, it was just me. I did all kinds of things on stage I had never dared try before. It was like I was a new person up there. Every number seemed to hit, and after our conductor Teddy Harris made a little speech about me, I felt like I was in a dream. Before I went into my next solo, I called for Turkessa, who toddled onstage in a beautiful white dress Pedro's mother had given her. As I sang, she sat beside me and hugged and kissed me. I felt like there were only the two of us there, in our own world. The big difference was that this wasn't the same old tired Mary Wilson. I was someone else, someone I knew deep down all along I could be.

Next we did several songs from *High Energy* and *Mary, Scherrie & Susaye*, including "I'm Gonna Let My Heart Do the Walking," "You're My Driving Wheel," and "You're What's Missing in My Life." We teased the crowd with a playful performance of "He's My Man," then closed with "Someday We'll Be Together." We did three encores, each to standing ovations, and flowers carpeted the stage as the crowd pressed to the front. Teddy handed me a beautiful bouquet, then made another little speech, calling this "the end of an era." I embraced Scherrie and Susaye, for the last time, I hoped. My bass player kissed me on the cheek, and I could see Teddy had tears in his eyes. It was beautiful and sad too. When it was all over I felt relieved.

It was three months after the Madison Square Garden disaster, and suddenly here I was, the toast of London. Everywhere I went people congratulated me and wished me well on my solo career. I was approached by lords and ladies, barkeeps at Annabol's and Tramps, cashiers at Boots and Harrod's. After the last show, Motown's EMI affiliate threw us a party at the swank London disco Maunkberry's. Pedro, Gill, Turkessa, Hazel, Herb, Mauna Loa, and the guys in the band had a ball. Despite my pregnancy, I partied late into the night. This was really it: my grand farewell was over, the Supremes were gone.

We spent the next few days in London, where Pedro and I bought some antiques for the house in Hancock Park, including a French armoire, some eighteenth-century paintings, a twelve-foot sideboard with matching dining-room chairs, and many other fabulous items. Herb and Mauna Loa came with Turkessa, Pedro's mother, and us as we began a long European vacation. We drove a rented green Mercedes to San Remo, Paris, the French Riviera, and Rome, dining and drinking fine wines everywhere. It was wonderful. There's nothing like stopping in the ancient French vineyards, or visiting small villas and opulent palaces, like Versailles. Taking a trip like this had been my lifelong dream, so I treasured every precious moment.

When we arrived on the French Riviera, we got in touch with Barry Sinco, a friend of Pedro's from Puerto Rico. Barry then managed a hotel in Monte Carlo. We planned to stay in the city a few days before heading for Rome. There we drove the winding roads that make up the Grand Prix race course, looked for nude beaches, and ate fabulous pasta at outdoor cafés. Even at six months pregnant, I looked gorgeous. Being the only black foursome just about everywhere we went, we turned heads. Even Turkessa; she was so cute.

Each night Mauna and I changed into exquisite gowns and emerged looking like two bronze Folies Bergère girls. Stepping out with Herb and Pedro, we headed for the fine restaurants, Regine's original disco, Jimmy's, and the Grand Casino. We stayed out in Monte Carlo's great casinos. Ringo Starr hung around with us, and between his wry sense of humor and Mauna Loa's natural outrageousness, I was laughing every minute.

Barry Sinco arranged for us to be treated to the most sumptuous, decadent meal of our lives at the Hotel de Paris, a classic, old-style European grand hotel. We were served caviars, soufflés, and the finest wines. The rarest china, crystal, and silver were laid out for us. We were dressed in the best clothes, having the time of our lives. Between bites of caviar, Mauna Loa said, "You guys are so great for giving us this fabulous trip."

We strolled out of the Hotel de Paris and stood in the square, right across from the palace where Prince Rainier and Princess Grace resided. Looking up at the clear, star-filled sky, I thought, *Will I ever experience this kind of life again?*

Suddenly several trucks pulled to a screeching halt in the square. Dozens of gendarmes, each armed with a semi-automatic machine gun, jumped out and surrounded us. None of them spoke English, but we gathered that we were under arrest. They took us to the police station, where for almost an hour no one told us why we'd been arrested. Pedro and Herb finally couldn't stand it and reverted to what I call their street ways. "Just because we're black," Herb shouted, "you're harassing us!"

Pedro added, "Wait till we get out of here! I'm calling Prince Rainier!"

"Yeah, me too," a cop replied, laughing. So some of them did speak English after all! They were still pointing their machine guns at us, so none of us was laughing.

Finally, after a couple hours, someone came from one of the hotels to identify us—and our car. It turned out that the police were on the lookout for a famous fugitive who happened to speak Spanish, drive a green Mercedes, and look like Pedro. Apparently, someone in a casino overheard Pedro's accent, saw the car, and figured he was one of Europe's ten most wanted. It was a simple case of mistaken identity, but for a while the situation was pretty tense.

We drove on to Rome and tried to enjoy the rest of the trip, partying at exclusive clubs and savoring the last moments of my grand vacation. Before I knew it, it was over, and I was back in Los Angeles, getting ready for my new baby and my new career.

# CHAPTER 13

July 1977

You won't believe this, but I am rehearsing Cindy Birdsong and Debbie Sharpe to replace Susaye and Scherrie as the Supremes! Actually, the show is called "the Mary Wilson of the Supremes Show." We are to leave for South America in one day. The tour is three weeks long. How is that, you ask? Well, it's a long story.

As far as I knew, Motown was proceeding with Scherrie and Susaye's plan to find a third singer. I wasn't surprised to read the numerous stories on Scherrie and Susaye where they talked about how "their" new Supremes would be different. They boasted about Motown letting them write their own songs and all the plans they had in store.

I don't think they meant anything they said maliciously, but it seemed like the Supremes were being tossed in the trash. "We'll be adding another girl," Susaye told one reporter, "then we shall be setting about forming a totally new concept for the Supremes. . . . Instead of just being singers, we'll have some measure of creative control."

We did not talk about their plans after I officially left the group, although they did keep in touch with Hazel. That entire year represented a major coup for Susaye. She and her mother were so happy; they saw my leaving as their first step toward a great future. I think they really believed they would succeed where I had failed. Because of her mother's death, Scherrie still wasn't herself and, I was told, basically let Susaye and her mother call the shots.

I left the Supremes assured that all the business was taken care of. Tours, which are booked months in advance, were to be handled by Motown and the William Morris Agency. I felt that if Motown wanted the Supremes to fulfill these previously arranged commitments, it should send the "new" Supremes—Scherrie, Susaye, and a third girl—or come up with another solution.

However, when our agent informed Pedro and me that some dates in South America had not been canceled, and the "new" Supremes weren't doing them, we panicked. If we didn't fulfill the contracts, we would be sued, I was told. The Supremes had to do it, but how? We had given our "farewell" performance! Against my wishes, Pedro called Scherrie and asked her to come back; both she and Susaye refused. They were upset by the short notice, but it was short notice for me too. Frankly, we all needed the money from this tour desperately, so I decided to find two background singers and get ready to go. I had two days.

We called Lynda Laurence, but she wanted far too much money. Cindy was happy to go, bringing her son David along. Through Reggie Wiggins, a former employee, we found our third member, Debbie Sharpe. She had sung professionally with the Oral Roberts World Action Singers, so she had concert and television experience. When we called her, she was working a temporary job. She auditioned on her lunch hour, and by the time she got off work that day, she was in.

We were ready—almost. Visas, passports, papers, plans, wardrobe fittings, and musicians still had to be taken care of. While Cindy, Debbie, and I rehearsed all day, Hazel worked out the myriad details. It would take a miracle to put it all together, but good ol' "Red Haze," as we called her, came through. We flew to Caracas, Venezuela, the next morning, dead on our feet, but all during the flight Debbie rehearsed the songs. Cindy, Debbie, and I went over choreography in the airplane's aisles.

We arrived in Caracas to find that our gowns hadn't made it and that the musicians' charts and music sheets had vanished. Fortunately, they all knew the music, and later the gowns showed up, but every moment was nerve-racking.

I was still working on the terms of my new contract with Motown as a soloist. Shortly after we got to South America we were notified that Motown did not approve of my taking out another group of Supremes—even though we were not billed as the *Supremes*. Pedro, who'd stayed home to attend to the contract, warned all the promoters and television people we worked with not to announce us as "the Supremes," but as "Mary Wilson *of* the Supremes," a crucial distinction. The name issue was further complicated by the fact that Scherrie and Susaye planned to continue as the Supremes. They were probably sure that when they refused to come with me to South America, I wouldn't go. I could only imagine their surprise when they learned otherwise.

Obviously, they and Motown didn't want a "competing" group out there, which I understood. At the same time, the debt I had assumed on behalf of the Supremes and Motown through the Supremes, Inc., was now hanging over *my* head, not theirs. Nobody offered to help pay off these bills, but

Motown or the booking agent had approved this short tour and had not bothered to cancel it; letting me "borrow" the name was the least it could do. And there was another technicality: both Cindy and I were still under contract to Motown as the Supremes. Confusing? You bet.

One promoter complained about getting only two out of three "real" Supremes. I was quite proud of my command of Spanish, and without Pedro, it fell to me to handle all the business. Some of the promoters were less than gentlemanly, ranting, raving, and yelling at me. By the time Pedro arrived with Herb and Mauna Loa, my spirits were really low. Cindy and Debbie pretty much kept together, which was fine, but I really needed a friend then. At nearly seven months pregnant, I was getting bigger each day and more tired. I still hadn't fully recovered from the tour of Europe, and before long I contracted a severe case of pneumonia.

July 1977

Small money, small club. It was all so small and cheap. Don't get me wrong: the club was first-rate by today's standards. Everyone who came were of the upper-class population of Caracas. It's just that when we were on top we never would have taken these gigs.

I thought Europe was the end. Here I am in it all over again. One thing made it worth it. It's now very clear that I am a soloist, not a Supreme. I sang lead on all tunes. They were all strange, but when we finished, I felt proud of myself. So as a group it was sloppy, but my future was what I was interested in; my development as a solo artist.

Despite everything that was wrong about this tour—Motown trying to stop it, the small clubs, my first time singing all the lead vocals, and forgetting many of the lyrics to our Supremes songs—one of the shows there proved to be the greatest performance I'd ever given. It's hard to describe the magic when you are onstage and know that every note, every gesture, every nuance is perfect. This particular night in Buenos Aires, Argentina, the theater was full, and the crowd was very receptive. From our travels, the band was irritable; as I noted in my diary, all of us were "ugly, tired people." Still, onstage the magic took over, and, as usual, that made all the problems seem unimportant. I *felt* every song and was beginning to feel truly comfortable in my new role as soloist. No longer was I the shy, sweet background singer of the past.

My baby was very heavy and kicked all the time, especially when I was onstage. Right before the show I had such pain I couldn't even move, but we went out there, and even though I knew everything was going against me, I drew on my sickness, my baby, everything. I was on my own now; I had to make it work. Somehow, it did. For the first time in years I could stand onstage without feeling I was cheating the audience.

"Bravo! Bravo!" the crowd shouted. I smiled graciously, but my exhaustion and pain were so great, Debbie and Cindy had to help me offstage. My body ached, my mind was numb. If I only could have slept for several days. Instead, I had to play a private party at a nearby hotel. The room was small, the lighting and sound awful. I was miserable, but I'd had my first triumphant moment as a soloist, and I would cherish it forever.

We gratefully returned home. The house, though, was a mess; Willie had been "entertaining," and our money problems were looming larger than ever. Because Motown had misinterpreted my intentions for taking the South American tour, I was now in a full-fledged lawsuit with them. I certainly didn't have enough money to continue, so my best bet was a quick settlement. Life is funny: one minute they were giving me a solo contract, and the next they were cutting off my lifeline. To prepare for the possibility that there would be trouble, Pedro and new attorney Mark Turk had gone to work gathering up all of our old contracts, back from the very beginning, and putting together a case against Motown.

The company had sent a barrage of threatening letters and telegrams to all the South American promoters, warning them about using the Supremes name in any form. The only way I could fight back was to report its actions to the California State Labor Commission. Under California law, the Labor Commission offered us the best relief. Because so much of the world's entertainment industry is based there, California has very strict laws regarding contracts for performers. Since we were under contract to Motown in California, Motown had been subject to these laws since the early seventies, and possibly earlier.

In September 1977 I filed my complaint against Motown with the labor commissioner. In it I made a number of allegations against Motown Record Corporation, Multi-Media Management Corporation, International Management Company, and Berry Gordy, Jr. The case fell under the labor commission's jurisdiction in part because in California it is illegal for a single person or entity to function as both manager (an adviser) and agent (someone who finds work and negotiates contracts for work). Motown managed us through its Multi-Media Management Corporation, even when we hired outside managers, and functioned as an agent through its International Management Company as well.

The fact that these were all interrelated subsidiaries of Motown and all under Berry Gordy, Jr.'s control presented a clear conflict of interest. Furthermore, because they had the same address and were controlled by the same people, they were in effect a single entity, which violated California law.

In addition, all managers and agents in California must be registered and licensed, which Motown was not. In fact, these Motown-related companies were not even qualified to do business at all in the state, since they were not corporations organized in California, or in any other state, as we later found. The name the company was doing business under at the time, Motown Record Corporation of California, Inc., was not a corporation. Since it wasn't even listed in the telephone directory, it may have been a fictitious company altogether.

I wasn't surprised to learn that Motown's setup constituted a conflict of interest. The company managed us, booked us, provided us with legal advice, made all our career decisions, and invested our personal money for us. Even when Motown made a show of finding us so-called independent managers, they were all culled from a list that met label approval, and were paid by Motown. Any correspondence between us was also sent to Motown. Having spent so many years in the industry, however, I knew there were few options. Either you played by the record company's rules, or you didn't play. Those were your "choices."

As annoyed as I was with Motown, I was still very reluctant to leave, because it was my family, because it was black-owned. To me, that was extremely important, though the people actually handling contracts and running the business were mostly white. Yes, most of the artists fault Berry, and, yes, he graciously accepts the blame. But he still says, "I don't know anything about the legal aspect. I let the legal department handle that. I'm too busy being creative."

Throughout the years, whites such as Barney Ales, Mike Roshkind, Tom Noonan, George Schiffer, Ralph Seltzer, brothers Harold and Sidney Novack, and others have run Motown, with Berry out front as chairman and a few other blacks in seemingly important positions. I'm surprised that we artists never addressed these issues back in the late sixties and seventies. There were blacks in creative areas, and there had been some black executives back in Detroit, but once we moved to L.A., Motown was white-run.

For all his personal flaws and unpopular business decisions, Berry accomplished what no black man had before him. Though the old "Motown family" had no contemporary relevance to me, it still held a place in my heart. Whenever something went wrong, or some Motown executive treated me disrespectfully, I automatically thought back to when I was one of four girls giggling in Hitsville's lobby, or swooning over Marvin Gaye, or getting a lecture from Berry. What broke my heart was the realization that while Motown had changed immensely over the years, its strength—and the artists' weakness—was our clinging to memories of those old days, those happy, happy times.

The final decision to proceed against Motown and Berry took me a long time to reach, and I resisted it every step of the way. But now I was forced to fight. Berry's accomplishments weren't his alone; they were shared by the other artists, writers, producers, musicians—everyone who worked at Motown—and, symbolically, by black people the world over. Motown was so much more than a record label, a roster of artists, a sound. It was a shining beacon of possibilities realized, talent rewarded, and, yes, dreams come true.

Returning to reality, I asked myself, *What had Motown really done to other artists like Flo? Or the lesser-known but no-less-talented singers and musicians the company unceremoniously abandoned in Detroit?* I often thought, *What will those people do?* There was nothing for them in Detroit. I saw the toll the financial inequities took on my fellow artists. People think artists file these lawsuits just to make a financial killing. They don't realize how little money most artists have. Sure, you wear great clothes and ride around in a fancy car. It's all part of the image. Some of the performers I'd come up with couldn't buy health insurance for their children or keep their modest homes. It was morally wrong, but a very real part of show business.

Now I found myself facing the possibility of losing my own house and having my career imperiled by an overreaching and possibly illegal series of contracts. I didn't set out to get revenge against Berry and Motown, or to spend the next dozen years in exorbitant litigation. All I wanted was to keep them from shattering my life.

As I later learned, Motown conducted business just like every other record company. Large or small, black or white, they all treated their artists as commodities. That is the story of the record business. Today's young artists have the benefit of learning from what happened to their predecessors, people like Little Richard and countless others who lost everything to unscrupulous record companies. But even with special attorneys and advisers far more savvy than the advisers Diane, Flo, and I had when we signed to Motown in January 1961— our parents—there are traps no one escapes. In other words, even if my mother had been a lawyer, I'm pretty sure Motown would have worked its way around her.

For one thing, the record company is always in the most advantageous position. Of course we should have asked the right questions and protected our interests, but at that time our interests were simply to get a record deal. When someone offers you what is probably the chance of a lifetime, is it really human nature to look for all the strings attached? Besides, we were idealistic teenagers, with no experience in the cutthroat world of business. Motown certainly wasn't as shrewd with us in 1961 as it would be later with Flo and me. But it was smart enough to get what it wanted from us for next to nothing. The question I'm asked most often is what advice I'd give up-and-coming artists. My answer is, Understand the nature of the business. It's not you the business loves—it's your money and you as long as you make it. So learn how to handle and control it yourself.

My official complaint against Motown was lengthy and

extremely complicated, boiling down to several crucial points: that Motown had illegally acted as both my manager and agent; that because of various aspects of my contracts, the label could not record another act under the name the *Supremes;* and that, as the sole remaining original group member, I should be granted full ownership of the name.

There was also the question of whether or not my contracts with Motown were even legally valid. Because I was a minor in 1961, my mother signed my contract on my behalf. Motown asked her to sign an addendum to that contract, stating that she had read and understood the agreement and, further, guaranteed my performance under it—despite the fact that everyone knew my mother was functionally illiterate and could not read the papers she was signing! Because all our subsequent Motown contracts were essentially extensions of the original, if the original proved unenforceable for *any* reason, the consequences for Motown would be great.

All through the talks that took place that spring between Motown and my attorney, the issue of who owned the Supremes name was never settled. Back in 1974 Ewart Abner convinced me to sign the deal giving me 50 percent of the name. Now I still was entitled to 50 percent. The catch was that even though I technically owned half the rights to the name, Motown retained all the right *to exploit* the name. What Motown was trying to do—make it impossible for me to build upon my past sixteen years of my career by denying me *any* use of the name—was exactly what it did to Florence.

There was also the fact that regardless of Motown's claim, it did not have another group of Supremes waiting in the wings, a group whose reputation would somehow be compromised by my identifying myself as a Supreme. As of fall 1977, Scherrie and Susaye still had not found a third girl, although the press mentioned several candidates, among them Joyce Wilson of Tony Orlando and Dawn. Technically, Scherrie and Susaye were still under contract to perform for my corporation, Supremes, Inc.

As with most legal matters, there were endless postponements and delays, leaving me in limbo for months. Since Motown knew I wasn't earning a great deal of money, we suspected it was trying to wear me down. Pedro and I had just bought the new house, record sales were very slow, there were no concert dates in sight, and we were paying an attorney nearly $1,000 a day to pursue my case. It's very easy for a large corporation like Motown to just drag things along, knowing that eventually you will be bled to death financially by legal fees. One of the main reasons that artists, or anyone, challenging a major company are destined to lose is that for all the lip service we give the idea of justice and fairness in this country, the cost of getting what is due you is beyond most people's reach.

The stress got to me. I was told in late August, a month before my due date, to stay off my feet, or the baby could be born prematurely. I was bored stiff and worried about so many things. We had to lay off some employees. Hazel volunteered to work without pay, and we had no money to even buy groceries.

In his depression and desperation, Pedro continued spending money, feeling he had failed me and the group. We contemplated selling the house and moving to a small apartment. Neither of us could bear the thought of how far we had fallen. One day my life was working, and I was happy; now that seemed so long ago. And, worse, I knew in my heart that part of it was my fault.

I wanted so badly to hate Motown for everything, but I had to face the facts: I was responsible for where I was. I just hadn't had the right advisers, and I didn't have all the answers. Now I was truly paying the price. It was like the line in the song "Send in the Clowns" that laments, "Isn't it rich, isn't it queer, losing my timing this late in my career." When I was afraid to step out front in the act, I had everything I needed except for the nerve. Today I was ready to take on the world, but without any resources to draw upon. Every now and then I'd start to think that maybe I wasn't meant to have this solo career, but I just wouldn't believe that. So, I dove into the deep end and held on for dear life.

Once the press began covering the complaint I'd filed against Motown, people I hadn't seen or spoken to in months started dropping by. Cindy started coming over often. She told me that she had been going to church and had been saved. I went with her the next Sunday. My life was in such shambles—maybe it was because I had strayed too far from God and from the things that meant so much to me when I was younger. I started attending church regularly and read the Bible.

Everyone was thrilled that I'd taken a stand against the label. Jean Terrell was the biggest surprise, since I hadn't seen or spoken to her since she quit the group. "It's the right thing to do," she said supportively, "and I'm glad you're doing it."

When I phoned Scherrie about it, she was surprised to hear from me. "I just want you to know that there are no hard feelings," I said, "and I hope you have none toward me."

"Mary, it wasn't you that I was angry at, it was Pedro," she responded. "Especially the way that he treated you." Not long after that I learned that she and Susaye were going to release an LP as a duo. I was relieved. There would be no more Supremes. My prayers had been answered. I also knew I had been right about Motown.

Soon after, on September 29, 1977, my second child and first son, Pedro A. Ferrer, was born. Again the delivery was by caesarean; in those years it was believed that once a caesarean, always a caesarean. Complications kept me in the hospital for over two weeks. I was overjoyed to have my little son, and yet very sad. A couple of times I sat in my hospital bed and cried my eyes out.

Once I regained my health, I had to get right to work. While Cindy and Debbie had been great on the South American tour, I needed new girls for my solo act. Many vocalists tried out, including soul singer Merry Clayton, whom you might know from *Dirty Dancing*. Before that she'd worked with such greats as Joe Cocker, the Rolling Stones, and many others. As we sat in my house, she said sweetly, "Mary, I'd be honored to sing with you."

"Girl, *I* am the one honored," I said. "You sing too good to be just a backup singer." And with that, I turned her down. She and I sang and chatted for the rest of the afternoon in between other auditions.

In the end, I found two wonderful ladies. Karen Jackson, who was to be with me for the next eight years, worked as a telephone operator and had sung with a few local bands. Kaaren Ragland was an actress and singer from Virginia. Both were single, attractive, and dedicated. Cindy and I rehearsed them, so that by the time we stepped out, I was a full-fledged soloist, and they were great backups.

Dates for my first tour kept getting moved around, and some were even canceled, as Motown brought its weight to bear on promoters, threatening who knows what if they billed us using the Supremes' name. It wasn't hard to imagine Motown killing my solo career if this kept on much longer. We called our booking agent and got started. As always, my English promoters Barry and Jenny Marshall stood by me every step of the way, and we prepared to leave for a year-end tour of Europe.

---

*Supreme Faith*

It was early December, around six in the morning, and I was asleep in bed when Pedro came home after being out all night. He opened the bedroom door, then stormed through the large room, looking in the bathroom and in the closet, like he expected to find someone there. As I lay there, taken aback by his bizarre behavior, he came to the bed and tore the covers off me.

"Who is here?" he demanded angrily. His eyes were wild. When I didn't say anything, he grabbed me and pushed me into the bathroom, forcing me to look at myself in the mirror.

*"Tell me who was here!"* He slapped me hard across the face, and I felt my eye swell up immediately. Then I saw the gun, which Pedro kept in the house for protection. He pushed it against my face. I kept thinking how insane he looked, and I felt the cold metal graze my forehead. Over and over again he asked me who had been there. I felt that if Pedro truly believed I'd been with a man, he would surely kill me. I'd never been more frightened in my life, yet inside I was strangely calm. It was as if time had stopped, and I remember thinking, *This is my life, and if this is the end, I have to accept it. But no, this can't be the end.* In that split second I thought about how silly I had been all my life to be so afraid of everything else. The things I thought I should fear, I could now laugh at.

After several moments of me insisting that there was no one else, I saw his face change. I had seen this often. I would stare at Pedro, and it would be as if I were watching a dissolve in a movie; his face would change, and he became someone else.

I kept thinking how afraid Pedro would get too when he realized how far he'd gone. He finally put down the gun, then told me to feed little Pedro because he was crying. I said to him, "You will never find another woman like me," and for the first time I believed it. Pedro tried to get me to stay, but I had to get away. After camouflaging my freshly blackened eye with makeup, I went to stay with my mother, now living in Los Angeles. She was sad but asked no questions.

My mind was flooded with ideas of what to do next. Stay with Pedro, because of the children? Get a divorce? Stay but withhold my love? Get revenge somehow? In the end I went home and prepared dinner. Pedro's repeated threats to take away my babies if we split was the most frightening thought I had to deal with. I couldn't see how to get away from him and take my children without him either hurting or killing me, or getting Turkessa and Pedrito.

Why did I go home to my abusive husband? Pedro gave me something I needed: I was learning to be strong in the trenches. No matter that it was gained through such destructive, violent means. I had come full circle, and while I still felt we would eventually divorce, it wasn't something I could deal with just then.

# CHAPTER 14

In early 1978 things were so desperate financially that we couldn't pay our bills. Payroll taxes were due, the musicians were again threatening to quit, and everyone wanted a raise.

But where would the money come from? Pedro had an idea: "If we can just come up with some immediate cash, work will come in, and we can cover everything. Why don't we pawn your heart-shaped diamond ring?"

Of all my possessions, my four-and-a-half-carat heart-shaped diamond ring signified everything that the Supremes meant to me. In 1965 when we had each received one of our first royalty checks—after paying off our debts to Motown—I had bought the heart-shaped diamond ring. Eddie and Brian Holland had told me about a wonderful jeweler in Highland Park where they purchased all their diamonds. Since this was my first diamond, they told me that they would assist me in picking it out. The moment I saw the pure white diamond for $20,000, I gasped. Here it had only been a year since our first hit record had hit the charts, and we were still living in the projects, but to me this ring meant that I had made it. I had accomplished something, and this represented my achievement.

The money Pedro and I needed would come from somewhere, anywhere but my ring. We racked our brains for another solution, but it finally came down to either hocking the ring or filing for bankruptcy.

Someone Pedro met on the nightlife circuit said he would front us a few thousand dollars and hold the ring. When we repaid him the loan plus interest, I'd get my ring back. The man was Ron Levin; he made headlines in the eighties, disappearing without a trace, presumably murdered by members of the so-called Billionaire Boys' Club.

Several weeks later, some money came in, and I asked Pedro to get my ring. "Oh, I meant to tell you," he replied a little sadly, "I already called Ron, and we waited too long. He sold the ring." I was crushed. No one would ever know what that ring meant to me, and now it was gone forever. At that moment, I knew I hated Pedro.

Once again I was back on the road, working just to pay the bills. The only good thing about all this ridiculous touring was that I was gaining more confidence on stage.

Cindy had done a fine job of training Karen and Kaaren, so we were ready for our tour of Germany and Europe, where we performed at officers' clubs and a few swank discos. The trip became awkward, because Motown was still threatening promoters. We were supposed to have gone on to England, but Motown quashed that tour and caused various cancellations in several other countries. Each cancellation dealt another financial blow, but, fortunately, our loyal staff and many of the people we worked with stayed with us.

Pedro was constantly on the phone with our attorney Mark Turk and Motown's in-house counsel, Lee Young, Jr.

In the end, Motown succeeded in getting injunctions against me. At the time I was satisfied with the way Pedro stood up to Motown. Looking back today, I realize I needed a top professional manager to deal with this complex, delicate situation.

Another depressing aspect of this tour was the schedule. We'd do two shows nightly, but usually in two different clubs, so there was a lot of travel. Often these places had no dressing rooms, so we changed in the public bathrooms. It was like going out in the early sixties with the Motown Revue and having to change in high school gyms or on the bus. I had hit rock bottom.

The bright side was singing for the American servicemen, who were always a great audience. One evening a serviceman approached me. It turned out he was one of the boys who'd promised me the moon and the stars one night long ago in the Brewster Projects. We had a laugh.

My nineteen-year-old son Willie was with us. He'd dropped out of school in the eleventh grade. He came along to work the sound and lights for us, having learned from the pros we'd had throughout the seventies. He was great at his job. We were still a traveling family—me, Pedro, the two children, Mom, Willie, the band, Karen, and Kaaren—a situation that would continue well into the eighties.

After Europe, we went to Spain, where an Englishman arrived at our hotel in Madrid with some legal papers. Motown was suing Pedro and me for, among other things, using the name *Supremes*.

The company continued harassing almost everyone we worked with. Promoters again were told not to use us because we weren't really the Supremes and I wouldn't be any good. That was odd, since I had been picking singers ever since 1973 and running the group since 1970. How was it that all those years, Motown had no problem with the quality of the group, yet now it was an issue? We fought, but eventually Motown prevailed, and shows were abruptly canceled. We found out later that Motown's people not only said that we weren't the Supremes, but that I was not the real Mary Wilson! If I had ever wondered how low they might stoop, now I knew.

One night in February 1978 I found myself in a fifteenth-century hotel in Wales called the Royal Oak Inn. It was a magnificent place, with a roaring fireplace, a pub, and very friendly innkeepers. There I started writing my first book. I felt calm and relaxed, and I recall it as a sort of magical place. I had a brief respite from Pedro, which I needed. I feared him more and more. As things went against us, he became increasingly irrational, more intent on hurting me.

While in Wales I decided to ask Pedro for a divorce. I thought back over everything that had happened between us, all the abuse, the insults, the black eyes and bruises, the constant control. It had reached the point where he was so suspicious, I couldn't use the rest room without leaving the door open.

When Pedro called early one morning from London, I told him that I was leaving him. He replied that he was tired; that he'd given me everything, and I'd given him nothing. He called me a "a cold, dull piece of meat." He threatened to take the children, maybe not Pedrito, but definitely Turkessa.

The whole night I lay in bed, tormented. For the first time in my life, I could understand how people committed suicide, though it was never a possibility for me. I prayed to God and hoped that he heard me. I hadn't slept all night, so I was up at eight when a telegram from our lawyer arrived. It contained a strange reference to "a lower price." I asked

Pedro about it, and he broke the bad news: we were selling the Hancock Park house. He, all our accountants, and Hazel saw no other way out unless we filed for bankruptcy. I tried to figure out a plan to save my beloved house, but we simply couldn't afford it anymore. In one day I felt that I'd lost my husband, my daughter, my house, and my career. While still in Wales, conductor Teddy Harris and another musician left. The only thing that distracted me from my problems was playing chess with my bass player, Duke Billingsley. I could only pray that I wouldn't have to endure this emptiness forever.

Within the week Pedro and I were back together again, but as desperately unhappy as ever. On March 8, 1978, just two days after my thirty-fourth birthday, our house was sold. I remember lying on my bed in London and crying and crying. Would I always be fighting a losing battle?

Before this tour started, I'd sent Turkessa to Santo Domingo. The longer I was away from her, the more I thought about how she must feel. Even though I know that my mother gave me to my aunt and uncle because she was doing what was best for me, I never outgrew feeling like an abandoned child. With my own baby thousands of miles away, I began feeling sad and guilty. More than anything I wanted my whole family together. Once the tour was over, we flew to Santo Domingo; I couldn't wait to hold my Turkessa.

While I was in England, Hazel had called to tell us that Motown wanted to settle and offer me a solo contract. We were off on a six-week summer tour of New Zealand, Australia, and the Orient. Pedro stayed behind to finalize some business details. We were fighting all the time, and by now everyone who worked for us knew about the beatings. Meanwhile, in the press writers and fans attacked Pedro for "butchering" my career.

*E*ver since meeting Josephine Baker, I have longed to portray her in a
movie or a theatrical play. This is my tribute to La Baker, fashioned after one
of her famous poses from the 1920s. (Photo: Marc Raboy)

*T*urkessa feeding her
baby brother, Pedro, Jr.
(Photo: Mary Wilson
Collection)

*M*y children and my mother
in 1983. (Photo: Mary Wilson
Collection)

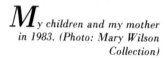

*W*ith Diane's father, Fred
Ross, in Las Vegas in 1984, before joining him and Diane for
dinner at Dionne Warwick's
club. (Photo: Mary Wilson
Collection)

*With* two of my 1980s background singers, Robin Alexander (left) and Karen Jackson (right). (Photo: Mary Wilson Collection)

*The* infamous Mercedes-Benz limousine that I bought from George Harrison, which was once owned by John Lennon. A Supreme and two Beatles . . . Honey, if this car could talk!!! (Photo: Steve Wood)

*With comedian and activist Dick Gregory, who is now famous for his Bahamian Diet. (Photo: Mary Wilson Collection)*

*Duke Fakir and I during the taping of the TV special "Motown 25." (Photo: Jack "The Rapper" Gibson / Mary Wilson Collection)*

*L*isa Figouroia, Eddie Murphy, and I at the opening-night party of the Hard Rock Cafe in New York City, March 12, 1984. (Photo: Robin Platzer)

*W*ith Al Green at the 50th anniversary of the Apollo Theatre in Harlem. (Photo: Robin Platzer)

*S*howing my muscle with Sgt. Slaughter (left) and a whole crew of wrestlers at the club Area in New York City. (Photo: Robin Platzer)

*W*hen fur was still chic, designer Tony Chase (left) draped me in mink. To my right are Mark Bego, Lorna Luft, and Marilyn Michaels, at a party at Panache, in New York City. (Photo: Robin Platzer)

*W*ith Nona Hendryx at the opening of Stringfellows in New York City, March 12, 1986. (Photo: Robin Platzer)

*O*nstage at Hollywood's famed club the Roxy, singing a duet with my youngest son, Rafael. (Photo: Roger Karnbad Michaelson)

*W*ith Florence's three daughters (left to right)—Nicole, me, Lisa, and Michelle. (Photo: Michigan Chronicle/Steve Holsey)

*O*ne of my favorite artists, Ted LeMaster, painted this beautiful Supremes portrait, which now hangs in my living room. (Photo: Mary Wilson Collection)

*W*ith Barry Manilow, Dionne Warwick, Arista Records president Clive Davis, and Senate Black Legislative Caucus member Jackie Parker. (Photo: Robert Earl Marshall / Mary Wilson Collection)

*F*reda Payne and I out on the town. *(Photo: Danny Evans / Jeffrey Wilson's Hot Wax Music Archives)*

*A*rriving at the Rock and Roll Hall of Fame, January 20, 1988, amid the paparazzi. This was an exciting evening of mixed emotions for me. (Photo: Robin Platzer)

*L*ittle Richard, Flo's daughter Lisa, me with my statuette, and Ahmet Ertegun. (Photo: Robin Platzer)

*W*ith my buddy George Harrison after we were both honored that night for our contributions to rock and roll history. (Photo: Robin Platzer)

*A*t the all-star jam session that concluded the Rock and Roll Hall of Fame presentation with (left to right) *Mike Love of the Beach Boys, Mick Jagger, and Bruce Springsteen.* (Photo: Mary Wilson Collection)

*A*t Dionne Warwick's all-star AIDS fund-raiser, held at Lincoln Center, June 10, 1989. Left to right: Cyndi Lauper, me, Leslie Uggams, Dionne Warwick, Patti LaBelle, Gladys Knight, Whitney Houston, Blair Underwood, and Rita Coolidge. (Photo: Robin Platzer)

*T*aking a bow with (left to right) Cyndi Lauper, Leslie Uggams, Lauren Bacall, Patti LaBelle, and Tony Orlando. (Photo: Robin Platzer)

*A*t a party at Regine's in New York City with my dear friend Rita Coolidge. (Photo: Robin Platzer)

*S*tarring in the play Beehive was a big thrill for me. (Photo: Mary Wilson Collection)

*Photo by Sam Emerson*

*Photo by Don Lynn*

*Photo by Marc Raboy*

*Photo by Greg Gorman*

*T*he many looks of
Mary Wilson . . . (All
photos: Mary Wilson
Collection)

*Photo by Marc Raboy*

*Photo by Terry Johnson*

*Photo by Richard Aramas*

*Photo by Elsa Braunstein*

*Photo by Richard Aramas*

*Photo by Elsa Braunstein*

*Photo by Elsa Braunstein*

*This is the real Mary Wilson—always looking forward to the next adventure and ready to pack my bags at a moment's notice! (Photo: Greg Gorman / courtesy of Thomas Smallwood at Rich's)*

Coming home from the tour in Australia and not having a home was one of the biggest downers I've ever felt. Pedro took an apartment in Westwood that cost $900 a month. I hated it. They didn't allow children, but thank God for Mom. She loved having them with her until we found a place. I stayed many nights at Mom's, as Pedro and I started having some terrible fights.

One evening when Pedro had gone to Mexico City I decided to go out with some friends. I don't know what got into me; I just rebelled. I got home very late, and Pedro had been calling all night and not getting an answer. By the time he reached me, he was so furious he flew home. The next thing I knew, at six in the morning he was standing in the room, as mad as I'd ever seen him.

"Where were you?" he demanded.

Feeling like a child, I lied and said I'd been somewhere I hadn't. Why did I lie? Whenever we had these scenes, it was as if I lost control. Pedro beat me as I tried to run from the apartment, then he pulled out the gun again. I was so frightened I could barely move, but I had two children to think about. I had to live.

Before I got too far Pedro caught me and dragged me down the hallway. I screamed as loudly as I could, but, our neighbors just looked at me and did nothing. I felt like I could read their minds: *Oh, they're black.* I couldn't believe it. I managed to break away from Pedro and run outside to the parking-garage attendant, screaming, "Please! Please call the police!"

As if in a nightmare, Pedro grabbed me from behind, and I fell to the ground. He dragged me back upstairs. The police came, but because this was a domestic dispute, they did nothing. "He tried to kill me!" I said. "He should be in jail and charged with attempted murder."

"It's a civil case, ma'am," one of the cops replied. "There's nothing else we can do."

I stood there, half-naked, bruised all over, crying. "What am I supposed to do? Just stay here and be killed?"

The police offered to escort me out of the building, to the street, where I could get a cab. I was so angry at them for not helping me, and I was furious at Pedro for reducing me to some kind of tramp; I knew that was how people saw me that day. I walked up and down Wilshire Boulevard, barely dressed, in a daze. Cabs in Los Angeles are as rare as snowflakes, so it was nearly an hour before I found one to take me to my mother's house. Later I thought maybe I should have said, "Hey, I'm Mary Wilson of the Supremes. Can you do something for me now?" But I wonder if it would have made a difference.

Mom and my sister Cat were so wonderful. They put me in a tub of hot water and cleaned all my cuts and bruises, never once saying anything about my marriage. All they did was care for me. I stayed for a week and again decided, *This is it*. But one evening Pedro came over, and I went home with him.

It was over a year since I'd officially left the Supremes. Scherrie and Susaye had not been able to revive the group and were at work on a duo album, *Partners*, which was released in 1979 to mixed reviews. Scherrie filed a lawsuit against Pedro and me, alleging that we had withheld an accounting of the Supremes' income from her. This case was later settled amicably out of court. Bit by bit we were finally able to negotiate my solo deal with Motown. One condition of the contract was that Motown and I agreed to drop our suits against each other. By dismissing our respective charges "with prejudice," we each legally forfeited our rights to bring up those charges again in the future. In other words, Motown could never contest my using the Supremes name again, and I could never bring them back to court on any of my charges.

All along I'd been told that my Labor Commission case was very strong. I didn't fully understand everything about my case. It was proceeding fine, then suddenly my attorney and my husband were telling me to drop everything. I did, partially because again I needed to be recording, and Motown was offering that. Years later I would learn that I had a stronger case than I knew.

Right then, all I could think about was making my solo career work and strengthening myself emotionally and financially so that I could finally leave Pedro and get on with my life. All this was complicated by the fact that I was pregnant with my third child.

For many women, their abuse is a "well-known secret." Friends and relatives might suspect or even know what's going on, but no one says anything or acknowledges the truth. Too many people find it impossible to understand the battered woman's plight; they can't sympathize with her until she does what they think she should do: leave her abuser.

I was fortunate during this period to be surrounded by several very supportive people. Among those who were really on my side were Hazel, Gill Trodd, and Barry and Jenny Marshall, the promoters who kept me working overseas. The Marshalls have since gone on to well-deserved success in their field, promoting shows for, among others, Lionel Richie, Tina Turner, and, most recently, Paul McCartney. Barry Marshall offered to manage me, but my husband would never allow it.

Ironically, one of the saddest moments in my life was one of my happiest. I was in London, and Barry, Jenny, Hazel, Gill, Karen, and Kaaren gave me a surprise party for my thirty-fifth birthday. They had balloons, champagne, a beautiful cake, and all the trimmings. And there I was, a pound of makeup covering my latest black eye. I remember feeling so touched and happy. These people really did care about me and believed in me. This love and support of fans and friends gave me the extra encouragement that let me know that I was on the right track.

By now Pedro seemed unconcerned about who might know that he was beating me, especially Hazel. He'd beat me up right before a show, and I'd have to go on stage with a pound of makeup to disguise the bruises. He would go for several days or weeks and not touch me—then he'd explode.

The constant fear and worry about when his temper would erupt constantly kept me on pins and needles. Onstage I projected an aura of cool confidence and control. Offstage I was living a nightmare of total degradation.

Finally, in early 1979, Pedro, my lawyers, and Motown came to terms, and I got my solo record contract. The next thing I knew I was back in the Motown studios recording my first solo album with Hal Davis, the staff producer who was responsible for the Jackson 5's "I'll Be There" and "Dancing Machine," Diane's recent Number One hit "Love Hangover," and Thelma Houston's "Don't Leave Me This Way." It felt odd being in the Motown studio—because of my problems with Motown I was being portrayed as a rebel or an outcast.

Hal and his staff of writers worked diligently to come up with the right material to make my album a hit. Although I felt that my strong point was ballads, the majority of the songs I recorded were up-tempo dance numbers, which were the rage at the time. I viewed this album as a beginning to my solo recording career, and planned to develop from there. We finished the LP just two weeks before I gave birth to my youngest son, Rafael.

The album *Mary Wilson* was released in August of 1979,

and I was quite pleased with it. On the cover I was draped in fur and looking every bit the star. Because I had taken the photos only weeks after Rafael was born, the fur concealed the weight I had gained during my pregnancy. I was also thrilled to see the album cover blown up into a huge mural in front of Tower Records on Sunset Boulevard. The record garnered a lot of press, and most of the album reviews were enthusiastic. I was especially happy when the single "Red Hot" became very popular with the fans, especially with disco enthusiasts from Fire Island to Key West. I heard it in clubs wherever I went, from Studio 54 to Studio One. I immediately added the song to my live act, and always got a fabulous response when I performed it. It was recognized around the world as my solo signature song.

On August 28, 1979, I made my true American solo debut at Manhattan's hot nightclub New York New York. The date was very exciting for me personally. The press came out in full force, and the room was packed with celebrities and fans.

There were all kinds of stylists running around backstage helping me. One came in, obviously excited. "Girl, guess who just came in? Miss Ross! And I think she's on her way up here."

Well, everyone went crazy.

"Here, girl, put on some lipstick! Put this in your hair! Hurry!"

Just then, Sammy Davis, Jr.'s wife, Altovise, came in with the guys from the Village People. Andy Warhol stopped in and gave me a good-luck kiss, and Geoffrey Holder and his wife dropped in to tell me to "break a leg." When Diane and her first husband, Bob Ellis, got there, they both made it clear that they were really supportive of my solo debut. The minute she walked in the door she embraced me, and was very warm and expressed genuine happiness over my debut.

She looked great, wearing a pink two-piece silk outfit and a glittering decoration painted on her face. That night she wasn't playing the star. She stood back and allowed me to be the center of attention. I felt that she was content and happy, and it was a pleasure to have her there.

Out front there were klieg lights, and the club bubbled with the excitement of a Hollywood premiere. "The whole town's talking about your opening tonight," Randy Jones, the Village People's cowboy, said enthusiastically. The excitement was mounting, and I was glad to be back, basking in the limelight.

Then it was showtime, and it was off to a brilliant start. The evening's funniest moment occurred a few minutes into the set, when my costume split open down the back. One of my assistants rushed to my dressing room to grab a cape, which was draped over me. I kept right on singing—without missing a single beat. Naturally I had several costume changes, so by the next number I was in a new gown, and the show was flowing along very smoothly.

While I was onstage, Diane held Turkessa on her lap, in the audience. When the spotlight hit Diane, she couldn't stand up, because the tables were crushed in so tightly together. I began the set with a medley of "Everybody Gets to Go to the Moon" and "Corner of the Sky," then jumped into "Midnight Dancer" from my solo album.

"Thank you," I said after the loud round of applause. "It's so wonderful to be in New York. I love it! I'd like to say hello to everybody, and welcome you to my show. Wow! 'My show!' " People cheered, and I thought, *Just two years ago, about twenty blocks from here, I was booed out of Madison Square Garden. Now here I am.*

"Before we go any further, I would like to sing a medley of my greatest hits."

"All right!" someone shouted as the band played the

opening chords to "Come See About Me." I sang only my background parts: "Boo hoo . . . for you . . . to tears . . . the fears . . . hey, hey, hey, hey, hey . . . hey, hey, hey, hey, hey . . . come see about me." Everyone cracked up, then I did the same for "The Happening" and "Reflections."

"Wow, so you guys really did listen to the backgrounds!" I said, laughing. I introduced Diane, "my very, very dear friend for twenty-one years." As I sang the opening lines to "The Way We Were," I thought about all those years when there had been the three of us. Now it was just me. And I felt wonderful.

I sang a medley of Supremes hits that included "You Keep Me Hangin' On," "Where Did Our Love Go," "Baby Love," and "Stop! In the Name of Love," followed by "Stoned Love," "Can't Take My Eyes off of You," "Quiet Nights," "You're What's Missing in My Life," "I've Got What You Need," "Red Hot," and "A Song for You." When I hit the final notes of "How Lucky Can You Get" and heard the audience's applause, I knew they really wanted me to make it.

Naturally, I finished with "Someday We'll Be Together." I was so lost in thought by then, though, that I forgot the lyrics! Laughing, I asked Teddy Harris to start it over again, and this time I really put my heart into it. I asked audience members to sing along with me on the chorus. Then I got to Diane.

"You think that the stars don't do anything," I said, making my way to Diane's table. "They don't wash dishes or whatever. But Diane is out here baby-sitting my daughter tonight. Sure she's asleep—you're a good baby-sitter, honey. With three children, you should be.

"You look so beautiful. Give me some of that glitter you got on you, girl," I said, leaning forward to kiss Diane's cheek. "Diane, would you sing this song with me, please? Now, remember, I'm singing the background. You sing the lead, okay?" We traded off a couple lines of the songs, sharing the microphone, and the crowd went absolutely wild.

"First, I want to say, Mary and I have never left each other," Diane said. "Of course we haven't, darling. We're sisters. Let the world think we fight. It's all right."

With that, the house came down. After the show everyone streamed upstairs for a party that lasted all night. Before I joined them, Diane and I had a few minutes of private girl talk in the club kitchen. This was one of our rare moments together. She was really there for me.

The reviews were positive. The surprising thing was that so many writers expressed surprise that I could sing. *Gee*, I wondered, *what did they think Flo and I were doing all those years? Just moving our mouths?* Other critics were quite rough, saying I had a lot of nerve, with little talent. To me, they missed the point. I perform because I like to perform. I work hard, and I'm getting better all the time. Hit records, Grammy awards—all that stuff is great—but in the end it's the joy of entertaining that keeps me doing it, not the reviews.

After a six-day engagement, we left for England, where we toured through October before leaving for the Middle East. We were in England around Christmastime. My mother was with us, watching the children. Even though Pedro had become crazier, there were still those nice, quiet times. One evening after one of the shows we were just sitting around in our room, talking, mostly about business. We were having a little champagne, and it was very late.

We seemed to be having a great conversation, so I took a chance and started talking about our problems, which we never discussed. I felt that this was the right time to work some of them out because Pedro seemed so open and amenable. However this proved to he a huge mistake on my part. Suddenly a creative conversation turned into a hot verbal confrontation, and he started going off on me. Before I knew what was happening he thrust his champagne glass toward me, intending to smash the glass directly into my face. Instinctively I turned my head in the nick of time, just as the glass shattered against the side of my face. It had happened so fast that I didn't know what had been cut. *Has he destroyed my face?* was my first thought, as I felt the warmth of blood running from my face. When I put my hand up to the wound, part of my severed ear was hanging in my hand, barely attached by a strand of flesh.

Suddenly Pedro was very concerned, running around the apartment, getting a towel to wrap my head in. He quickly gathered me up, and we dashed around the corner to a hospital. The whole time Pedro comforted me, and I remember thinking that he was behaving as if someone else had done this to me. He really had become two people. In the emergency room, no one questioned our story. We simply said that we'd had a fight. Pedro was so attentive and loving that no one suspected that he had really "meant" it. No reports were filed. No one even asked me if something might be wrong.

My mother and Cat, who were upstairs with the kids, came running down as we left for the hospital. My poor mother! Seeing all the blood, she assumed that Pedro had finally killed me. All the years I was with him, she never said anything to me, though she knew full well what was going on. After this Pedro was very attentive, and we both brushed this horrible incident into the background.

Throughout this period I had been touring exclusively in Europe. Overseas I was recognized as a solo star instead of just an ex-Supreme, and I could earn many times more money than I might expect in the United States. I'd need a huge hit record in America to be booked in the kind of venues I played regularly everyplace else in the world. In 1980, after having performed in Asia, Poland, Tunisia, Italy, and the

Middle East—with my husband and three children in tow—I started working on my second solo album.

My contract with Motown called for me to record two LPs per year over five years. Pedro thought it would be good for me to work with someone from outside Motown, and he and Motown's English representative found Gus Dudgeon, the producer responsible for virtually all Elton John's seventies hits. We chose four songs: "Love Talk," "You Dance My Heart Around the Stars," "Save Me," and Creedence Clearwater Revival's "Green River."

I was very excited about these four songs. It wasn't the formula disco of my first album. Two of the songs were big ballads, and the other two were rock and roll in the style of Tina Turner's mid-eighties hits; I was certainly ahead of the time. Motown didn't like any of it, saying that no one was doing ballads then and that it could release only dance music. With that, the company showed me the door, giving me the tapes and dropping me from the label at the end of the year. This was the first time Motown, which has a policy of controlling all its artists' master, or original, recordings, ever gave an artist her masters back. It seemed that the label had given me a solo deal just to get me to drop my lawsuit against it.

Leaving Motown was one of the saddest events in my life. I had long since ceased being a member of the "Motown family." What foolish little girls we must have been to believe that Berry and Motown would always take care of us.

Now I had no record label and, because of all the years I'd spent overseas, no track record in the States. American record companies are interested in you only if you are a success here. That I had sold out the London Palladium, that I had collected piles of great reviews for my performances—all this meant nothing.

In my personal life things were changing too; I was

stronger now. In late 1979 I had given Pedro one year to clean up his act. If he didn't, our marriage would be over. He made some attempts to change, but couldn't. Throughout 1980 the abuse continued, and his violent sexual aggression became unbearable. Pedro always viewed sex as an expression of power, and violence became a big part of that. He was getting rougher and rougher with me. Out of desperate fear, I gave in to wild nights of cocaine and champagne— anything to numb the pain of the inevitable degradation. He then went one step further, humiliating me in front of my own children. That was the last straw.

I knew that if I could just hold on a few more weeks, it would soon be all over. The sheriff was going to serve Pedro with divorce papers on New Year's Day 1981. The week before, Pedro beat me so badly that my face was bruised and swollen beyond recognition. When little Pedrito first saw me, he exclaimed, "Mommy! Do you know who you look like?"

"No, honey," I replied.

"The Incredible Hulk! Mommy, you look like the Incredible Hulk!" Despite everything, I had to laugh. We both looked at my face in the mirror, and my baby was right.

The few days before New Year's, I hid in the house with the children, afraid that someone might come by and see me. New Year's Day I heard a knock at the door. I stood in another room, half relieved, half terrified. Pedro answered the door, and when they handed him the papers, he was totally shocked. He never, ever believed that I would carry out my threat. He had finally learned that while I may not say much, when I do say something, I mean it. Still, the sheriff wouldn't be moving in with us, and anything could go wrong. Again my biggest fear was that my husband would try to keep the children.

Pedro said nothing until the sheriff left. I stood, tense,

waiting. "Get out!" he shouted. I had started to gather up the children when he stopped me. "No, no, you are not taking my children. I'm keeping the children."

I panicked and started crying. Then I thought for a moment: Pedro wasn't the kind of man to change his ways for his children, though he loved them very much. He wouldn't be able to cook, clean, and care for them the way I did, no matter how much he loved them. So I called Cat to come get me. It killed me to see my three babies standing against a sliding glass door, waving good-bye, crying. Pedro stood in the middle of them, like the father-protector. I got into the car, hoping and praying that I was right.

I was with my mother only a few days before Pedro returned the children to me. It was one of the happiest days of my life. He must have realized what a job it was to be a parent. My mother told me how much she had worried about me and that she loved me. Despite everything, I felt like the luckiest person alive. From that point on, I was really on my own.

# CHAPTER 15

January 1981

I am now a free woman: free of my husband, free of Motown, and free of the weight of the Supremes. Now I can *finally* be myself. I'm on my own, my solo career is now a reality, and the only way for me to go is up. This is the beginning of the rest of my life, and so what if I don't have a house of my own. Sitting here in my mother's house, I can truly say that there is no love like a mother's love. You can always come home to Mom when things go wrong.

My mother, who had always been my greatest inspiration, came up with the perfect solution. Now that I had filed for the divorce, I needed a down payment on a house I had found for me and the children. This was a dilemma, because all my cash was tied up in my marriage. I didn't want to stay in my mother's house for the rest of my life, so I tried to come up with a plan.

Mom said, "Why don't you call Diane and ask her to loan you the money?"

As the realization hit me, I thought to myself, *Why not? Who else could come up with that amount?* I was damn lucky to have a friend like Diane, whom I could call at a moment like this.

But still I had too much pride. "I can't do that," I said to Mom.

"Mary, if Diane was in trouble, you know that you would help her. And you know that she will do the same for you."

My timing was perfect. Diane was playing Caesars Palace in Las Vegas. So, I picked up the phone and called her, telling her that I really needed to talk. We made plans for me to come to Vegas and talk one night after her show.

I arrived there and saw the show. She was great as always. I went backstage afterward, and she introduced me to everyone. Then we went back to her private dressing room, where I told her of my plight. She was very sympathetic.

In a completely honest voice she said to me, "I'm so surprised. I really thought that you and Pedro made such a great couple."

We spent over an hour just talking about our lives, the children, and how things had changed—it was a wonderful reunion. Diane had recently surprised everyone by leaving Motown Records, and I told her I was glad.

"Diane, I told you years ago that Berry wasn't doing any more for you as a girlfriend than he was doing for us. If he gave you a fur coat, Flo and I each got one too. When you got a diamond ring, we got diamond rings. Think about it. Frankly, I'm glad you left Motown."

"Really?" she asked, surprised.

Once Diane got to RCA Records, I think she must have realized that after a certain point almost any other label would have taken better care of her financially than Motown. However, it was Berry Gordy who was totally responsible for making Diane the star she is today. She agreed to give me the loan, and later Hazel and Diane's business people drew up the papers. Over the next two years I repaid the loan with interest, as she had requested.

My marriage over, I turned my full attention to my career and my children. Without a record label and with a family to support, I was back working all over the United States and the rest of the world. My backup singers were now Karen Jackson and Gloria Scott. We were billed as the Supremes' Mary Wilson.

We toured such exotic, far-off places as Bahrain, Sharja, Muscat, and Saudi Arabia, where we were guests of nomad families who lived in tents in the desert. We passed our time petting camels and dancing in the clubs, where native women were forbidden. Arab men continually approached us, whispering, "Come to my room, I will pay you well." At buffet tables they tried to touch, pinch, and proposition us shamelessly. One New Year's Eve I committed a real faux pas when I asked, "Where's the champagne?" Alcohol is not allowed in the Arab countries, but that doesn't stop people there from hiding it under tables in Coca-Cola bottles. Several sheikhs even put necklaces around my neck.

Karen Jackson, one of my most faithful background singers, reminded me of myself when I was a young Supreme. Several others came and went, including Robin Alexander and Debbie Crofton. Teddy Harris stayed with me, as did bassist Duke Billingsley and drummer Jerome Spearman. I always appreciated their loyalty. It made my job a lot easier.

In October 1981 a booking agent asked me if I wanted to perform at Studio 54, New York's premier disco. I said yes, of course, and my friend John Christy quickly designed, printed, and covered Manhattan with posters of me, announcing the date. Unfortunately, the deal fell through, but before long people were asking about when I was coming to New York. Randy Jones of the Village People and my friend Mark Bego threw a party in my honor at another New York club, Bolero.

My self-confidence wasn't at its highest, so I was excited when the club rolled out the red carpet for me. The party was packed full of friends, fans, and well-wishers that night at Bolero, including Geoffrey Holder and Grace Jones. The four songs that I sang were a huge hit, and it was extremely gratifying for me to have an endless stream of people coming up to me and telling me how much they loved me and wanted good things to happen in my career. I remember hanging out for hours on the cushions of one of the cubicles talking to everyone.

At one point late in the evening—about 3:00 a.m.—I was sitting down surrounded by friends, and Grace Jones, who was sitting next to me, said, "I'd like to propose a toast to the star of the night," as everyone lifted a champagne glass. "It's long overdue, Mary," Grace said, "and it's only the beginning of good things that are going to happen to you."

I was still figuring out what to do with the Gus Dudgeon-produced masters. The record business had changed in the wake of disco. Before, the label did everything for you when it came to making records. Disco showed the labels that they could save a lot of money if they purchased completed masters from independent producers. Now an artist needed a finished product in hand in order to be signed. I met with various label executives, once even auditioning for Merv Griffin's new record company, but no luck.

In the spring of 1982 I was just days from signing a deal with Casablanca Records and Boardwalk Records founder and chairman Neil Bogart when he died of cancer. In many ways, Neil reminded me of Berry Gordy. In the sixties he was a driving force behind the bubblegum-music trend, and in the seventies he built an empire with such varied acts as Kiss, the Village People, and Donna Summer, and, later, Joan Jett.

After Neil heard my four-song tape, he invited me to his house. Gill Trodd went with me. Neil was in his robe, and he and his wife, Joyce, said they loved my voice. "After the bad experience I had with Donna Summer, I swore I'd never work with a female artist again," Neil said. "But we're not only going to sign you, we're going to turn you into a huge star." He promised to have my contracts ready in a few days.

Gill and I acted very cool, but once we were around the block, we pulled my Rolls-Royce over to the curb and let out a scream. It was too good to be true. I knew that Neil was ill, but I didn't realize he was dying of cancer. Besides being a great personal disappointment for me, Neil's death at age thirty-nine was a tremendous loss to the record industry. By the early eighties megacorporations had taken over the business altogether, devouring independent labels such as Boardwalk.

Even though I was no longer with Motown, the family feelings among the artists endured. We all kept in touch. While a few acts returned to the company, including the Tempts and the Four Tops, more were gone, including Marvin Gaye.

Marvin, who had so often felt that Motown was against him, was living in Belgium then, cut off from his audience. When we were teenagers, Flo, Diane, and I loved Marvin. He was so sweet and *so* sexy.

I shared a delightful evening with him in London. From traveling so much for so many years, I had made little groups of friends in every town. One such friend, Omar, lived in London. Soon after I arrived, I phoned him just to say I was back in town.

"Guess who's here?" he asked me, a trace of mischief in his voice.

"Who?"

"Marvin!"

"What?! I'll be right over."

It was wonderful to see Marvin. We had all heard about his various personal and professional problems. Everyone always felt very protective toward Marvin; there was something about him that made you want to take care of him.

Marvin and I were sitting alone in the living room. "I've got these great tracks I want you to hear," he said. "I want you to listen to this."

He slipped a cassette in the tape player, and the songs that would make up his 1982 comeback album, *Midnight Love*, filled the room. "Marvin," I said, "this is *it*, you know. This is really great." Even though several of the songs were just backing tracks, without the vocals, they were very powerful.

"Which one do you like best?" he asked.

"I like the last one, Marvin. That was really hot."

"Yeah, everybody seems to like that one." The song was "Sexual Healing," which was to be his last Top 10 hit record. "Baby, do you really think they'll make it?"

It pained me to hear the doubt in his voice. Marvin was clearly bracing himself for disappointment. It seemed such a pity that someone so creative and brilliant could feel so insecure, so undeserving. It struck me that a lot of us came out of Motown feeling that way about ourselves.

"Oh, Marvin, of course they'll make it," I said. "These are great. I mean that. You know, everybody's dying for you to come back to the States. Everybody, all the fans everywhere, want to know what you're doing and when you'll have something new out."

"Do they really miss me?" he asked softly.

"Are you kidding, Marvin?" On the one hand, I couldn't believe I was hearing him say these things, but on the other, when I thought about how I felt sometimes, faced with the industry's—the world's—indifference, I understood it. Without current hits, an artist disappears. Marvin knew he had to make the comeback, and this was his big chance. When you're an artist, you have to believe in yourself, even though you know that belief may not be rewarded. It hurts, but you have to go on.

"People love you, Marvin."

"Really?" It was as if he couldn't believe it. He responded as if someone had just told him he could fly. Lying there on the floor, we were like two hopeful teenagers dreaming about our futures.

There has been a lot written and said about where Marvin was in his personal life during these years. The evenings I spent with him, he looked great. He was happy, if cautiously so, and during the next couple of days that we were together, we went out with Omar and Marvin's wife, Jan, and had a grand time.

Once Marvin asked, "Do you really think that people love me, Mary? I mean really love me?"

"Marvin, everybody loves you. The women love you. I've always loved you."

He smiled shyly as I continued. "You know, Marvin, you are the kind of guy that women want to take home and baby. *I'd* take you home and baby you." I laughed. We were always comfortable together, and even though I had a huge crush on him when I was younger, there was never anything romantic between us, despite some writers' allegations. Our relationship was much more than that.

When "Sexual Healing" took off, I was very happy for him. Marvin was one of the few Motown artists to leave the label and succeed someplace else. Sadly, his comeback and a richly creative life were cut short in 1984 when his father shot him to death. I still miss him.

When I saw Michael Bennett's Broadway play *Dreamgirls* in New York, I had no doubt that it was based on the Supremes. I sat motionless as I watched our life story unfold. When the first act ended with Jennifer Holliday (as the Flo character, Effie) singing "And I'm Telling You I'm Not Going," tears streamed down my face. The producers changed many details, but I knew, as they did, that the "Dreams" were the Supremes. Of course, in the play Effie emerges triumphant, which Flo did not.

I went to see it again in Los Angeles and, unknowingly, was seated behind one of the show's chief writers, Tom Eyen. At intermission someone tried to introduce us, but Tom appeared upset and declined. I've never understood why. I only wanted to tell him how much I loved the play, which I've now seen nine times. Diane, however, was so infuriated by *Dreamgirls* that she publicly announced that she refused to see the show and wouldn't let her daughters see it, either. People are entitled to their own opinions—I loved it.

After battling with Motown and Pedro for all those years, I was spending a great deal of time returning to Manhattan to hang out with all my New York friends. All anyone had to do was tell me about an event and I'd fly in. Everyone there made me feel so warm and wanted at a time when I needed it the most.

Marvin's and Diane's leaving Motown and the success of *Dreamgirls* seem like three disparate events, but they worked together on the people at Motown. No matter what you might say about Berry, he has a sentimental streak. He wooed back the Four Tops and the Temptations, and in the spring of 1982 launched a much-publicized reunion of all seven living Tempts. Included were not only the originals—

Melvin Franklin, Eddie Kendricks, Richard Street, and Otis Williams—but David Ruffin, Dennis Edwards, and Glenn Leonard.

Around this time someone at Motown figured that it would be a good idea to get the Supremes back together too. The difference between the Supremes and the Temptations was that the general public seemed to have accepted every edition of the Tempts, despite their having gone through seven different lineups since signing to Motown. It was interesting that even though the Supremes had endured a mere five lineups since Diane left, reporters always referred to the group as a "revolving door," an "employment agency," or something else that suggested we'd become an assemblage of faceless singers.

Suzanne dePasse and I talked about Motown's plans for a possible Supremes reunion. Although I have not always agreed with Suzanne over the years, she is fair. At one point she said that she really liked my voice and that she thought they could "do something with it." That was the first time anyone at Motown had ever complimented me. I found that encouraging, and so I dropped my guard long enough to see what was going on. There was never any plan to ask Diane to join; it was out of the question. If the group re-formed, it would be Cindy, Scherrie, and me.

For years Suzanne would go on and on about what good friends she and Diane were. Diane was even quoted in the press as saying that Suzanne was her best friend. However, Suzanne later told me, "I was thrilled when Diana finally left Motown." She should have been, because with Diane out of the way, she was the top-ranking female at the company.

Suzanne described some very elaborate plans, including an album and a tour, à la the Temptations reunion. It all sounded good enough, but my first priority was my solo career, and I knew that Motown had to do more than make promises. Another condition, which I felt very strongly about, was that I sing leads. Not surprisingly, there was some hedging on that point. Motown wanted Scherrie to do all the leads. No one seemed to care that I had put the Supremes ahead of my life for over twenty years. My request was, I believe, very fair.

We set up a meeting at Berry's house. It was to be Berry, ex-Supremes manager Shelly Berger, and me. Shelly didn't show up, and when I arrived, there was Berry in his bathrobe. "Berry," I said, "here you are, receiving me in your bathrobe. Don't you think you could put something else on?"

We laughed, and the whole meeting was very congenial. Finally I said, "What do you feel about this reunion idea? I'm not going to do anything unless you're involved, Berry, because if you're not in it, it's not going to happen. For me to give up what I've accomplished as a solo just isn't worth it to me."

"Well, Mary, the truth is, somebody else brought the idea to me . . ."

"So, in other words, you really aren't interested, are you, Berry?"

Instead of answering me directly, Berry went off on a long digression, saying, "I'm doing this and that. I'm into the movies. You see what I did with Diane?" It was going to be the same old story I'd heard a hundred times.

"That's fine, Berry, I understand. I don't want to do it anyway."

He seemed a little relieved; then we switched subjects, among them Diane's leaving the label. "I just don't understand why she left," he said, visibly hurt and confused.

"Well, you know you created a monster, Berry, don't you? And the monster turned on you."

"I never thought about it like that," he answered.

The Motown-produced television special "Motown 25: Yesterday, Today, Forever," taped in April 1983, was a once-in-a-lifetime event. As a live show, it was definitely the grandest edition of the Motor City Revue. Martha Reeves, Stevie Wonder, the Temptations, the Four Tops, and the Supremes would all be sharing the stage, just like in the old days at New York's Apollo or Detroit's Fox Theatre.

Billed as "the night everyone came back," it was truly magical. The show's most talked-about and eagerly anticipated event was the promised Supremes reunion. It would be our first appearance together in over thirteen years. This event was a big feather in Suzanne dePasse's cap, because she had done the impossible: coaxed dozens of acts to return to Motown, even those, such as Marvin Gaye, the Jacksons, Mary Wells, the Four Tops, the Temptations, Diane, and me, who at one time or another had left the label. With the exception of Gladys Knight and the Pips, we all came "home," happy to bury the old feuds in the joy of seeing the Motown family back together again.

When Suzanne called, she said, "Mary, Smokey Robinson is getting together with the Miracles, and Michael and Jermaine are going to rejoin the Jackson 5. Mary Wells is going to be there, and so are Marvin and Martha. The event will raise money to fight sickle-cell anemia.

The details were finally settled. I agreed to sing a medley of four Supremes hits with Diane and Cindy. It promised to be a tremendous historical moment, and I was looking forward to it. When I arrived at the Pasadena Civic Center for a brief rehearsal that day, things were already going awry. Diane greeted Cindy and me with a cocktail party hug and quick pecks on the cheeks, as if we were acquaintances she'd just run into on the street. For the rest of the evening, Cindy and I might as well have been invisible, but she and I did have some time alone to go over a few things. For one thing, we decided to sing softly at soundcheck, because our microphones were always turned down to half the volume that Diane's was set at.

Diane claimed she wasn't feeling well, so our rehearsal consisted of about a minute of "Someday We'll Be Together." With that she retired to her dressing room. I was to give a brief speech saluting Motown's musicians and songwriters. The minute I read the self-serving text prepared for me, I knew what I had to do: write my own. There were some things that I felt ought to be said, and I was going to say them.

At the pretaping cocktail party for executives of Motown and other key entertainment corporations, Diane was the only artist. My escort was Jim Lopes, then an MCA executive who was among the invited. He came out of the cocktail party and announced, "Come on, Mary, you're going with me to the 'A' list party."

Before I took a step, the chaperone Motown assigned to keep tabs on me said, "I'm sorry, but Miss Ross is the only celebrity allowed to attend."

"That's too bad," I said, taking Jim's arm and heading toward the party.

"No, you don't understand," the chaperone blurted in fear. "If *you* show up there I'll be fired on the spot."

"Really?" I asked. He nodded, looking very frightened. "Okay, then, I'll stay out here." After all, the cocktail party wasn't the big stakes tonight.

The taping began, and the show was magnificent. Marvin, in the last major television appearance of his life, was inspiring. The Tempts and the Tops were fantastic together, and Michael Jackson brought down the house with "Billie Jean."

For my speech I wore designer Tony Chase's tight black

dress that glittered with long silver beads. Gorgeous—and impossible to sit down in. Ignoring the TelePrompTer, I ad-libbed my own heartfelt message. "I couldn't be here tonight without mentioning some of the people who are not with us," I began, and then named Paul Williams, Berry's parents, "Mom" and "Pops" Gordy, and, of course, Flo.

"She's not here with us tonight, but I know that wherever she is, she's up there—whoo!—doing it!" My speech was directly from the heart, and I received a thunderous round of applause.

Before the last number, our reunion, I took Cindy aside and said, "Remember, this is a reunion, and for once all three of us are going to get equal play. Whenever Diane takes a step forward, we step forward as well."

I'd changed into another Tony Chase number, a fire-red beaded gown that was slit up the back. I was waiting in the wings. Diane sang her solo, "Ain't No Mountain High Enough." She was wearing a short black skirt, a silvery top, and a white foxtail fur. Sashaying across the stage, she dramatically flung the fur downstage. By this time everyone was fed up with her prima-donna attitude.

"Step on that fur, Mary!" Richard Pryor hollered from backstage.

"Kick it!" Martha Reeves said venomously.

I have to admit that I was amazed at the overwhelming feelings of animosity that Diane had brought upon herself. I wanted this show to have the kind of dignity that was befitting the Supremes. I refused to let a fight happen. The music to "Someday We'll Be Together" started.

"Mary? Cindy?" Diane called, as if wondering where we were.

Cindy entered from stage right to a huge round of applause. I let her get to the middle before making my entrance. When Diane announced, "This is Cindy Birdsong, and *that's* Mary Wilson," the crowd went crazy. At last, the Supremes were together on stage again. I was so proud and thrilled. We started singing "Someday We'll Be Together." Then something went wrong.

Diane seemed genuinely confused. Attempting to distance herself from us, she took two steps closer to the audience. As agreed, Cindy and I stepped two paces forward too. Diane again moved forward; we followed.

The third time it happened, Diane turned and forcefully shoved me aside. The audience gasped, appalled. Diane's eyes widened in shock at the realization that I wasn't about to back down, and that all these people had just witnessed her little tantrum. She got so flustered she lost her place in the song, so I sang a line, thinking Diane would compose herself and assume the lead again in a few seconds.

I kept singing lead. The only thing that she could think of doing was to begin to talk while I sang. She proceeded to speak to Berry, out in the audience.

"Berry, come on down," I called while the music continued.

With that comment, Diane grabbed my microphone and pushed it away from my face. "It's been taken care of!" she snapped at me with fire in her eyes.

The audience gasped again. I was told later that Suzanne dePasse panicked and sent out Smokey Robinson to defuse the crisis. In seconds the stage filled with other artists, and the Supremes "reunion" was over.

Diane had given the media the cat fight they were praying for, and they licked their collective chops in delight. I have never been so mad at her in my entire career. Just when I thought that we were at a stage where she was going to bury the hatchet, she went and pulled something like that. I was hurt and stunned.

Naturally, when the television special was edited, all but

about ten seconds of "Someday We'll Be Together" was snipped out of the special. And they billed this debacle as the reunion of the Supremes? What a sad travesty. To further get my goat, they also scissored out my entire speech.

The press had a field day when they wrote about the taping of "Motown 25," and *US* magazine ran photos of Diane pushing and shoving me on stage. If I live to be a hundred I will never figure out what prompts her to act this way. The funny thing is that the next time I ran into her, she pretended like this incident had never happened. I am told that to this day the full finale footage is locked up in a vault and that only Suzanne and Berry have access to it.

Later that year, I got a call from Motown saying that the "Motown 25" special had been such a success it now wanted to distribute it as a videocassette. At first, I was excited. The label wanted me to sign a release with a "favored-nation clause," meaning that all artists would get minimum scale for their appearances, plus a tiny percentage. Immediately, I grew suspicious. It seemed that everyone had signed their releases already—everyone but me. It made me think that while taping "Motown 25" the company had intended this all along. The more I thought, the more I felt that it was trying to take advantage of everyone.

The original performance had been a charity event to raise money for sickle-cell anemia. Doing a TV special was one thing, putting out a video for profit another. I felt the artists should be compensated; after all, it was we who had donated our services. I said I wanted to negotiate my agreement on the video; the label flat out refused. I sued Motown, and it in turn countersued me. This started a lawsuit that continued until 1990.

My separation from Pedro did not always protect me from his jealous rages. As many battered women can attest, court orders of protection are not worth the paper they're written on if somebody really wants to get at you. Even after our divorce, there were confrontations between me and my ex-husband.

One evening my good friend Mark Bego and I were getting ready to go see a show at L.A.'s Roxy when Pedro showed up at my house unannounced. The minute he walked in, I sensed his rage. I had to get Mark out of the house before Pedro blew up.

"Where do you think you're going?" Pedro demanded, staring at Mark and me.

"What do you want?" I asked as coolly as I could. "I don't have time to stand here and argue with you. Mark and I are late for a meeting with a record company. Now, will you please leave?"

Surprised, Pedro turned on his heel and stalked out. I hurried to my bedroom to get my lipstick, thinking, *That ought to leave us just enough time to get out of here before he changes his mind and comes back.*

Mark and I climbed into Grace. Unfortunately for us, my 1959 Rolls was badly in need of a tune-up, her door locks were broken, and one of the windows didn't shut completely. I didn't want to alarm Mark by explaining what might happen. I quickly got behind the wheel and backed out of the drive and onto Ventura Boulevard. I pressed the accelerator to the floor, but we were still going too slow. I glanced in the rearview mirror.

"Darn!"

"Something wrong?" asked Mark.

"Yes. Pedro is following us, and I'll have to lose him. I haven't told you this, but Pedro goes into insanely jealous rages."

I tried zigzagging through traffic to lose Pedro, but Grace was so big and slow, it was hopeless. I shouted, "Mark, find a police car. There's no telling what he'll do if he catches us!"

"Where's a doughnut shop?" Mark screamed. "You can always find a policeman at an all-night doughnut shop. There's one! Quick, turn in!"

We pulled into a Winchell's Donuts, and, sure enough, three police cars were parked there. Mark hopped out and told the cops what was happening. Pedro must have seen this, because he sped off down Santa Monica Boulevard. The policemen promised they would detain Pedro if they saw his car again in the area. We thanked them and left, detouring through a residential neighborhood with winding streets, as a precaution.

Just when we thought we were home free, Pedro's car pulled in front of us and stopped, blocking the narrow street. He jumped out of his car, jerked open my door, and reached across me to grab Mark by the throat. Then he smacked Mark in the forehead, causing him to crack his head against the windshield.

"If I ever see you with my wife again," Pedro growled, "I'll kill you!" He slapped me five times in about five seconds. "And if I ever catch you with another man, you know what I'll do."

Before either of us could react, Pedro was gone. Mark and I looked at each other as if to say, "Did that just happen?" My makeup was smeared all over my face, and Mark was seeing stars. We freshened up at my friend Jim Lopes's nearby apartment and then went on to the party. Pedro was not going to ruin our evening.

Afterward, Mark came to my house for a nightcap. It was four in the morning by the time we'd stopped talking and laughing about the evening's events. Mark had a huge welt on his forehead, so perhaps it wasn't really funny, but finding whatever humor there was in these situations helped me keep it together. We decided it would be better for Mark to stay over, so I prepared the sofa for him.

No sooner had I gotten into my bed than I heard Pedro screaming in the front yard. "Mary, if Mark is in there, I'm going to kill both of you!" He pounded on the front window, and Mark and I called the police. While we waited, Pedro circled the house. Not knowing what he would do, I took out a pistol that I kept in the house for protection. I don't think Mark understood the gravity of the situation until he saw the gun, then he went to get a weapon—a silver-plated champagne bucket.

The police finally came and ran Pedro off the property, but he continued calling and threatening us for hours. Mark and I were in the kitchen making breakfast, waiting for a police officer to come and take our formal complaint. Mark looked at the gun and said, "You'd better unload that pistol, Mary, before someone gets hurt."

"Don't worry," I said, pointing the gun toward the kitchen cupboard, "it isn't loaded." Just then a gunshot went off, and a bullet pierced a hole in the ceiling molding.

In the spring of 1983 I came to New York City to sing a jingle for an ice cream company that was introducing its line of Tuscan Supremes flavors. I enjoyed working with the musical director, Paul Shaffer, from the David Letterman show. During the eighties I came to New York often to work and to audition for shows and plays. Friends in the business introduced me to people they thought I should know; Mark Bego especially did all he could to help me.

One evening I met an up-and-coming club DJ and record producer named John "Jellybean" Benitez. Jellybean had a hot reputation for remixing hit singles and turning them into blockbuster disco hits. We chatted for a few minutes, then Jellybean played me a song he wanted me to sing.

I listened carefully, trying to envision myself singing it. There weren't a lot of lyrics; the words "holiday" and "celebrate" seemed to be repeated over and over. It was cute and catchy, but I didn't think it was right for me. I passed on it, thanked Jellybean for his time and interest, and wished him luck. Mark kept telling me I could sing it, so I changed my mind and called Jellybean back, but it was too late. He'd already given the song to someone else.

Several months later I was listening to the car radio when the disc jockey announced a new song by a new singer called Madonna. It was "Holiday," the very song Jellybean had handed me on a silver platter. I thought I would die. It went on to become Madonna's first Top 10 hit, and . . . well, you know the rest of the story.

I was working constantly: performing, auditioning for Broadway parts, and expanding into other areas. That summer I sang the National Anthem in the Disney film *Tiger Town,* starring Roy Scheider. At the suggestion of my good friend Bill Cosby, whom I opened for in Las Vegas, I auditioned for the part of his wife on *The Cosby Show.*

One of my tours that year took me to Key West, Florida, where my two background singers and I spent a fun-filled five days basking in the sun and performing to hundreds of party-loving people at night—the people who come to Key West *really* love to party. One afternoon, while I was dining with the promoter who had brought us there, he asked, "Would you like to have lunch with Tennessee Williams?"

He said that Tennessee had been at my show the night before and had absolutely loved it. By coincidence, our promoter, Gary, was working with Williams on what was to be his last play. Gary told me that Tennessee had been very down, but listening to my music helped to give him some happiness. Tennessee had said that he would have loved to meet me after the show, but since it had been so hectic, he didn't get the chance.

I told him that I'd be thrilled to meet the famous playwright, and the next afternoon Tennessee joined me and my background singers for a wild luncheon at an oceanside restaurant. What was to be a simple lunch ended up to be a five-hour fete. We were absolutely flying on great wine, raw fish, and Tennessee's wonderful stories. The man was truly fascinating.

Because of the warm tropical air, the outfit that I had chosen that afternoon was a beautiful bright-orange and yellow two-piece sun suit with a wild orange straw hat. At one point in the evening, as the sun began to set, Tennessee looked at me and said, "There is only one other woman who can wear colors like that, and that is Liz Taylor. My dear, you are in her class."

As always, I took part in celebrity charity events. I have always wanted to save the world, and thanks to my friends, particularly Dionne Warwick, I have been able to lend my name and my time to a wide range of causes, including substance abuse, sickle-cell anemia, the homeless, AIDS, and such organizations as the Heart Foundation, the Starlight and Make a Wish programs, the United Negro College Fund, the Bill Cosby Illiteracy Program, and the Dionne Warwick AIDS Foundation.

I've performed at concerts for Dionne's foundation and visited people with AIDS, including little babies, in hospitals and hospices all over the country. While performing recently in Chicago, I went to an AIDS ward. One patient was extremely ill, and I was told that he was an avid Supremes fan but that for medical reasons I could not enter his room. The poor young man had lost most of his sight and was nearly in a coma.

"I'm sorry," I said. "but I *have* to see him." I approached his bed and gently took his hand.

"You're Mary Wilson," he said weakly, smiling. "You're just like I pictured you to be. You're like an angel of mercy."

Through my charity work I made new friends, among them Rita Coolidge. She is truly a beautiful person, both inside and out. We found that we had so much in common, like single-parenthood, and whenever we get together we have a ball. After years of feeling that I didn't have a close girlfriend in the business, she came along. In 1989 I joined her in a march on behalf of the homeless in Washington, D.C.

Today in America tens of thousands have no place to live. These people are not criminals, or strung out on drugs or alcohol. They're just people who ran into hard times or hard luck. Having grown up in the Brewster Projects, I know that even though we didn't consider ourselves poor, my family just got by financially. I also know that if Diane, Flo, and I were growing up today instead of back in the fifties, our families might very well be homeless.

When I heard, in 1984, that Diane was booked at Caesars Palace the same week I was appearing at the Sands, I became so excited. Her name loomed above the Vegas Strip in huge letters on her hotel's marquee, and my name topped the massive marquee at my hotel: "MARY WILSON Now Appearing at the Sands." At last I had made it all the way back to the top—and this time I did it as Mary Wilson. Not as "one of the girls who sang in the background in the Supremes." Not as "one of the girls who sang with Diana Ross." I was Mary Wilson, headliner.

Diane and I had had no contact since the "Motown 25" special; our relationship has run hot and cold over the years, and I never know what to expect. As odd as this might sound to most people, though, there is still a part of her that I love, the person she was when we first met as young girls, a part that I believe is still there.

It's always been my custom to call up any Motown act appearing in the same town just to say hi and catch their show. When I found out Diane would be in Vegas too, I decided to wait and see if she called me. The days passed, and it seemed like everyone in the world was stopping by, including Sister Sledge and some of Diane's band, but still no Diane.

Finally one night I said to my friends John and Tony, "What the hell, why don't we just go to see her at Caesars?" We were walking from my dressing room to the casino when I heard, "Mary! Mary!" It was Diane, on her way to see me.

We embraced, and she said, "My dad and a friend of mine and I are on our way to a club and Italian restaurant Dionne Warwick owns. Would you like to join us?"

John, Tony, and I went to the restaurant, an intimate place on the strip, and joined Diane and her party. Her date for the evening was a car dealer. I was wearing a jumpsuit and a punk-style wig.

"I love your hair, Mary," Diane remarked. "Wait until you see the billboard on Sunset Boulevard for my new album. I have a punk cut as well!"

When I lit up a cigarette, Diane acted surprised. "Are you still smoking, Mary?" she asked.

"Yes, Diane," I answered coolly. "It's my only bad habit. How about you?"

"Well, I'm alone, and sometimes I may drink a little too much."

I laughed to myself, knowing that for Diane more than two drinks was "a little too much." She was never a big drinker. There wasn't much to say to that. The rest of the evening was pleasant enough, but I remember that all through dinner Diane's father kept talking about his other daughter,

Barbara, who is a doctor. When we finished, Diane and her father got into her limousine, while John and I rode back to the Sands with the car dealer. That was the last time Diane and I were together as friends. Never once was her shoving me during the "Motown 25" special ever mentioned. It was as if it hadn't happened. I wasn't going to bring it up, and she wasn't going to apologize, so that was that.

Shortly after this friendly evening, Diane apparently decided—long before my book *Dreamgirl* came out—that I was her rival.

In 1985 Motown produced a television special, "Motown Returns to the Apollo," a tribute to all the Motown and other r&b acts who'd performed there over the years. The Supremes played the Apollo many times, beginning in 1962 when Florence, Diane, and I sang "My Heart Can't Take It No More" as part of the original 1962 Motown Revue.

Smokey Robinson and the Miracles, Martha and the Vandellas, Stevie Wonder, and the Four Tops were also on the bill in 1962, and on this night they and Diane were all invited back by Motown to relive the old days; I, however, was not, because of my "behavior" during the "Motown 25." I attended as the date of Jim Lopes, an invited guest, and, as luck would have it, our seats were in the front row.

When Bill Cosby, the evening's master of ceremonies, spotted me, he said, "What are you doing down there? You should be up here!" I laughed when during breaks in the taping Bill, who's always been a good friend, made pointed but funny comments about the fact that I wasn't on the show. He hinted several times that he would do something to "rectify" the situation.

Late in the show Bill introduced Stevie Wonder, who was performing his new single, "Part-Time Lover," backed by what they called an all-star backup group: the Four Tops, Boy George, and Smokey. Bill looked out over the audience and asked, "Are there any more background singers out there?" Then he pointed at me. "How about you?" He came down and helped me up onstage, where I joined the other six. When it was over, one of the Tops escorted me back to my seat.

Of course, except for a tiny glimpse of my face that couldn't be edited out, none of this appeared in the final show. A friend of mine who works at Motown told me they were going crazy trying to edit me out altogether. During the big finale, I was again invited up, to join other celebrities from the audience in a number. As I approached the stage, Diane looked at me and said, "Want to pick a fight tonight, Mary?"

I ignored her comment and, hugging her, said, "Diane, I love you."

In the summer of 1989, Diane was performing at the Universal Amphitheatre in Studio City; she was on her "Working Overtime" tour. Jay Schwartz, my publicist, had arranged for Turkessa and me to accompany him to the concert. Jay had also made arrangments for us to visit her.

When the show was over, we went backstage and chatted with Bobby Glenn and some members of Diane's band I was friendly with. Diane was still sequestered in her dressing room, and because my Rolls-Royce was parked near the backstage door, I was obviously around. One of Diane's employees came up to Jay and said to him, "You'd better leave, because Diane doesn't want Mary here."

I'd had just about enough of her nonsense and informed Jay, "I'm not leaving until I'm ready to leave."

With that, the Motown executive who had given the tickets and the backstage passes was becoming uncomfortable and implored us to go before an ugly scene ensued. I was a guest of Motown's, and I wasn't about to leave.

Jay then told me that we had best leave. With that I

decided to return to the car, and Turkessa stayed with my friend Ian Lawes, because she wanted to see her godmother, Diane. Turkessa went into a small lounge outside Diane's dressing room and stayed there about ten minutes until Bobby Glenn came by and said to Ian and Turkessa, "I'll do what I can to get you into the dressing room."

A half hour passed, and finally Turkessa told Ian, "Oh, let's just leave."

Jay then escorted Turkessa and Ian to my Rolls. As Turkessa was leaving, someone approached Jay and again mentioned that Diane wouldn't come out until I left. I was quite upset over this display of childish nonsense. I have seen her act like this time and time again, but for a forty-five-year-old woman to act like a spoiled child really affected me emotionally. After this, I knew that we could never be friends again.

Turkessa was crushed by the way her godmother was acting. She had never believed that Diane was anything less than benevolent, but her image of her was shattered.

Jay wanted to go out for a drink to smooth over what had become an upsetting evening. "Let's go to Le Dôme," he suggested. "Or should we just go home?"

"Let's just go home," I said wiping away a tear.

Turkessa was so let down that she conceded, "Let's just go to Carlos's and Charlie's."

With that, I decided that after this slap in the face, we should go to Spago, where Diane was holding an afterconcert party in part of the restaurant. I have been there several times when private affairs are being held in the back, and the front restaurant is still open to the public.

We arrived at Spago, and as Turkessa and I got out of the car and were on the way to the front door, we were surrounded by photographers, reporters, and television camera crews. The manager of the restaurant, who had obviously been instructed to keep the press away, started to yell at them, "Get off my property!" This only encouraged them to want to get a statement from me.

We started walking closer to the door, and the camera crew from *Entertainment Tonight* was a few feet behind us. We went up the two steps to the door, and the woman greeting people said, "I'm sorry, but you can't come in." I never even told her my name. She then said curtly, "You are not on the guest list."

I was stunned by this rude display, which was evidently on orders of Diane. With that, the camera crew from *Entertainment Tonight*, which had witnessed this scene, jumped at the opportunity to film my comments.

That was the last time I saw Diane, or had any desire to. She wanted a feud, and now she has one. I have never been so insulted and hurt by someone I once considered to be a friend.

# EPILOGUE

*O*ne thing that's kept me going is knowing that there are people around the world who love the Supremes. Not the Supremes as an institution, or the Supremes at our mid-sixties height, but each and every Supreme. In terms of fans and friends, I have been truly blessed. I knew they were out there, but the real proof came when my first book, *Dreamgirl: My Life as a Supreme*, was published in 1986. After years of talking about it, and almost as many years writing it, it was finally real. It was a thrill to see the name Mary Wilson and the word Supreme back in the Top 10, only this time on the national best-seller list.

The book's success afforded me the opportunity to do many things, for which I am thankful. I purchased a huge house in Hollywood, sent my children to school in England, and we all took a long-overdue family vacation in Hawaii.

*Dreamgirl* was a real turning point in my life. Writing it and later talking about it forced me to look at both the positive and negative aspects of my life and myself. It also gave me the confidence to try new things. I did some acting on television *(227)* and onstage, in a production of *Beehive,* a tribute to the women of rock and roll, including the Supremes. I even got the chance to audition for songwriter Stephen Sondheim.

So much had occurred in the last couple of years. In 1987 the old Hitsville building in Detroit was officially acknowledged with a state historical marker. The Motown Historical Museum was finally a reality. Berry didn't bother to attend the ceremonies, but legions of fans did.

When I got to visit the museum in the fall of 1989, it was a mixed experience. It was an unusually warm autumn day, and I was starring in *Beehive* in Windsor, Canada, site of the first semiprofessional singing contest Diane, Flo, Betty, and I won, back in 1960. I remembered pleading with Diane's father to let her go. Had it really been thirty years?

I arranged to meet a local reporter, a camera crew, and several fans at the museum. One of the first things I noticed was that the Supremes were conspicuously absent from the front-window display of artists' pictures. There were photos of Diane, the Smokey-less Miracles, the current Temptations, and *Bad*-era Michael Jackson (over fourteen years after he'd left the label), but no Supremes.

As I walked through the rooms and hallways that had been my second home, I felt very hurt and sad. The tour guide referred to the Supremes as "Diana Ross and Her Supremes," and as I looked at the walls, it was obvious that someone had made a very determined effort to erase Flo, as if she had never existed. One displayed photograph of the Supremes, taken on our 1966 tour of the Orient, showed just Diane and me. In the original, the three of us are standing side by side, with Flo in the middle. Visit the museum, and you will see that someone has crudely cut Flo out of the picture!

MARY WILSON

Many of the photos were mislabeled, and there was a makeshift air about everything. Motown's lack of respect for its artists extended even to cutting "troublemakers" out of photographs. I looked around the museum and can honestly say I felt no sense of nostalgia being there.

But not everyone had forgotten Flo. In 1987 Florence's fan club held the first annual Florence Ballard Exhibit, a tribute to Flo in pictures and memorabilia, in Hollywood. Among the people who attended were Flo's youngest daughter, Lisa Chapman, as well as Scherrie Payne, Gladys Horton of the Marvelettes, Mike Warren, Fuller Gordy, Janie Bradford of Entertainment Connection, and fans from all over the world.

In October 1987 it was announced that the Supremes were to be inducted into the Rock and Roll Hall of Fame. I was excited and honored that the group should receive such a dignified and prestigious homage from its peers. This was only the third year of the Hall of Fame's existence, and the Supremes were going to be honored along with the Beatles, Bob Dylan, the Drifters, and the Beach Boys. Since the Supremes had never even won a Grammy, I wasn't about to miss this big event.

It was also a wonderful coincidence that our induction would occur in early 1988 because later that year I had the very special honor of presenting Brian Holland, Lamont Dozier, and Eddie Holland with their induction certification from the Songwriters' Hall of Fame. It was great to give Eddie, Lamont, and Brian an award in return for all those terrific songs they gave the Supremes.

As the date for the ceremonies drew closer, I began thinking about my acceptance speech. Music history and the record business in general still accord the Supremes far less respect than I believe we deserve. I'm sure part of it is because, as women, we were viewed as not being "creative"; that is, we didn't write our own songs. But another part of it was Motown's doing. For years and years Motown had sought to make the Supremes disappear in Diane's shadow, and, I was sorry to admit, it had nearly succeeded.

On January 20, 1988, I flew to New York City and checked into my room at the Waldorf-Astoria on Park Avenue. The whole place was already buzzing with excitement over the fact that the inductees were going to be honored by the Rolling Stones, Little Richard, and Bruce Springsteen.

I checked into my suite—and in classic Supremes fashion laid out several beaded and sequined gowns—so that I could figure out which one, or ones, I would be wearing. I was hardly at a loss for dates that evening. Five minutes after the announcement came about the Supremes being inducted into the Hall of Fame, Mark Bego was on the phone asking if he could be my date. I instantly agreed, but explained that I was also going to be meeting a lawyer friend of mine, Mitchell Ware, and that my publicist, Jay Schwartz, would also be with me. Mark was undaunted.

That evening I dressed in a shoulderless, tight-fitting beaded white gown, designed by my godson.

Just then I heard a knock on the door. It was Jay, and he had a list of press people who wanted to talk to me. I explained to him that Florence's daughter had not yet arrived and I was concerned. He agreed to wait in the room until she checked into the hotel and said that he'd come downstairs to get me when she got there.

At the appointed hour Mark and Mitchell Ware escorted me downstairs to the cocktail party, where I was nearly blinded by the flashbulbs of dozens of paparazzi from every major newspaper and magazine in the country. Since I was the only female inductee to arrive, I was treated like the belle of the ball.

"Is Diana coming this evening?" one reporter asked me, shoving a microphone in front of me.

"I really couldn't say," I answered. "I can only speak for myself and say that I'm thrilled to be accepting this honor tonight." All of a sudden, every photographer ran to greet Yoko Ono as she arrived to accept for John Lennon. Thank God there was another woman besides me.

Also at the ceremonies that night was Berry Gordy, Jr., who was being honored as a "nonperforming inductee" for having formed Motown Records.

The room that the cocktail party was held in was packed so full of people that maneuvering around it was nearly impossible. Just then I spotted Berry, who was being accompanied by the humorless Michael Roshkind.

While we were still at the cocktail party, a publicist who represents Paul McCartney announced that Paul wasn't attending because he was still mad at George Harrison, Ringo Starr, and Yoko Ono, because of a pending lawsuit over royalties from the Beatles' former record company, Apple Records. On Diane's behalf, her publicist showed up and said that she had "a personal family reason" for declining the invitation to attend. For a moment, my heart sank. I was surprised at how much I had really wanted to share that moment with Diane one last time. If only just to say thanks and to acknowledge that dreams do come true.

The cocktail party ended, and we all filed into the ballroom to find our places for the $1,000-a-plate dinner and ceremony. I shared the table, located off to stage right, with another of the evening's inductees, guitar innovator Les Paul. They began to serve dinner—a Liverpudlian specialty in honor of the Beatles, bangers and mash (sausage and mashed potatoes)—but still no Lisa. Jay Schwartz rushed to our table to say that Lisa had arrived, but the airline had lost her luggage. I excused myself and ran to help her. She was standing in the hallway outside the ballroom, very upset.

"Auntie Mary, what am I going to do? I don't have a thing to wear!" I, naturally, was never at a loss for an outfit. "Just come upstairs with me. I have the perfect thing for you," I said as we rushed up to my suite.

She looked wonderful in the simple black dress I gave her. She had Flo's statuesque bearing, long, pointed chin, and steady gaze. As I looked at Lisa, I hoped that her mother could see her.

"All set? Now let's go back downstairs," I said. "You're going to look great onstage. Your mother would be so proud."

"I have to go up there?" Lisa asked nervously.

"Don't worry. Let's get something together for you right now. I'll be onstage with you, so don't worry. You loved your mom very much, didn't you?"

"Yes."

"And you are very proud of her accomplishments, aren't you?"

"Yes."

"Well, let's take those two thoughts, embellish them, and put them down on paper. You're going to be just fine."

We hurried back to the table, and I was just sitting there, looking around, when I spotted Berry making his way across the room. As I watched him move toward us, my first thought was, *Why should I stop him?* It could only be embarrassing for me and for Lisa. Then I thought, *Right is right, and there is no way I can let Berry go the whole evening without acknowledging my existence or paying his respects to Lisa. He's not going to get out of this ballroom without looking me in the eye.*

"Hi, Berry. How are you doing?"

"Oh, hi," he said. "You look beautiful tonight."

"Thank you. Berry, this is Lisa, Florence's daughter."

"Nice to meet you," he said. I wondered if he saw the resemblance. After a few more words, he returned to his table. We did not speak again for the rest of the evening.

The presentations began. Berry was the first inductee, followed by a few more nonperformers. The first of the other five inductees were the Beach Boys. Following the Hall of Fame's standard procedure, they were inducted by someone who had been inspired by their work, Elton John. Elton had always been one of my favorite people, so it was nice seeing him.

As the rest of the group was leaving the stage, Mike Love suddenly began criticizing Paul McCartney and Diane. He just went off on them, proclaiming, "I think it's sad that there are other people who aren't here, and those are the people who passed away [referring to John Lennon, Beach Boy Dennis Wilson, and Flo], but there are also . . . people like Paul McCartney, who couldn't be here because he's in a lawsuit with Yoko and Ringo . . . that's a bummer, because we're talking about harmony . . . in the world. It's also a bummer when *Miss* Ross can't make it."

The audience howled, hissed, laughed, and booed. Mike's tirade obviously struck a nerve. Bandleader Paul Shaffer cut him off by cuing the band to play, ironically, "Good Vibrations."

Next Billy Joel inducted the Drifters. I was so happy for them. In the early years, Diane, Flo, and I had shared many bills with the Drifters, and we considered them our friends. They had inspired us as young teenagers. It was wonderful to see Ben E. King, Johnny Moore, Bill Pinkney, Gerhart Thrasher, and Charlie Thomas acknowledged for their accomplishments. Artists like the Drifters, who meant so much to so many performers who followed them, should never be forgotten. Bruce Springsteen inducted Bob Dylan, who got a standing ovation. Then it was our turn.

Lisa and I stood backstage as Little Richard began making his speech about the Supremes. Since the Hall of Fame ceremony, many people have asked me how I felt about Little Richard's induction statements. Some people thought he was fantastic; others felt that his asides were inappropriate. He had been among the first artists inducted, in 1986, but couldn't attend because of injuries from a car accident. He spent a good deal of his speech thanking the Hall of Fame for his own award, and just being himself.

Little Richard was one of my idols, so it didn't bother me that he went off on tangents and talked over his time. I had to laugh when he said, "I love the Supremes so much, 'cause they remind me of myself. They dress like me. Diana Ross been dressin' like me for years. You all know that! And they also do my holler: *Whoo!*"

He had the crowd laughing, but he also said some very kind things about the group and about us as individuals. "You know, Miss Ballard passed away, but she was a great singer too." The whole room burst into applause. "The first women in rock and roll are the Supremes, to me. There's never been anything like them, and I don't think there ever would be. They are the greatest, and I just love the Supremes.

"I am proud to present to you Miss Mary Wilson of the Supremes." The band struck up "You Keep Me Hangin' On," and I walked across the stage to the podium with Lisa, stopping once to do the "Stop" gesture.

"First of all," I began, "I'd like to talk about the fact that I was really privileged to have sung with two really wonderful people, Diane and Flo. [I'm sorry] that Florence could not live to be here to know that what we as three little girls— three insecure little girls—had dreamt of could possibly come true. It saddens me to know that, but that's life, and there's nothing we can do about it. We're very proud that everyone has given us this honor so that her daughter could be here to see how much we loved her.

"Now I'm gonna read my speech. Since I've written my book I had to get glasses, but I'm not wearing them tonight.

"It was my wish, of course, that Diane be here, but we must all recognize that people have to live their lives. And there comes a time in a star's life when you have to really assess what's important to you. And I would say that perhaps since Diane has received so many, many accolades in life and so much success, she probably has felt that—she's married, she has a child—that this is something that is very, very important. And I respect the fact that maybe she saw fit to stay with something very personal, a personal achievement more than a public achievement.

"This is one of those rare moments in a person's life and in history that we all dream of. And like I wrote in my book, dreams do come true. Sometimes people have to just keep dreaming. We all hope that the world is looking in when we receive our award, and that the world can share in the moments of happiness we each receive. I'm told that in order to be eligible to receive an award from the Rock and Roll Hall of Fame, you had to have recorded some twenty-five years ago. Well, I was six when I started. It's very obvious, I'm sure.

"It was because of one young man, Berry Gordy, who was there for us. We had a place at Motown Records to go. And I'm very happy to say he gave us the opportunity. And we cannot forget Holland, Dozier, and Holland, whose music still lives on today.

"Florence, Diane, and I shared a success that you were all looking in on, throughout the world. And I certainly hope that you . . . were able to see the hopes and desires that we had and that it helped your lives along the way. I'd like to thank the directors of the Rock and Roll Hall of Fame for honoring us at this moment. And we can all remember that rock and roll will never die as long as we, the people, out there make it. I thank you very much."

Before Lisa got up to the podium, "You Keep Me Hangin' On" started, but was cut short. She spoke softly but with such dignity, saying, "I would like to say that I'm very pleased to be here tonight representing my mother. I'd like to thank the Rock and Roll Hall of Fame for inducting my mother. Thank you."

We posed for photographs with Little Richard and Atlantic Records chairman Ahmet Ertegun; then everyone sat down for the final induction, the Beatles.

After that began a large and initially unorganized jam session. Among the dozens of people onstage, in addition to the inductees, were Elton John, Billy Joel, Mick Jagger, Bruce Springsteen, Neil Young, Nile Rodgers, Jeff Beck, Peter Wolf, Dave Edmunds, and Julian Lennon. It seemed so symbolic of the record industry, and rock and roll in general, that the only two women onstage were Yoko Ono, there to accept her late husband John Lennon's award, and me. I noticed her standing a bit off to the side and looking a little left out, so I went up to her and got her to join me. I felt so funny being the only other woman up there, but the jam turned out to be the highlight of the evening for me. I sang "Stop! In the Name of Love" with Ben E. King and Yoko helping on background vocals. I got her to join me in the traffic cop "Stop" choreography, making her a Supreme for the night. Then I did a lot of backup singing with Mick Jagger. It was fun.

While it was a very special evening, it was also one of the saddest in my life. Except for a few friends I'd known for many years, such as Ringo, George Harrison, Elton, Paul Shaffer, and the Drifters, hardly anyone spoke to me that evening. It drove home something I had always known, which was that despite all my efforts and through all those years, the record industry recognized only one Supreme: Diane.

As I stood at the podium giving my speech, I could see that many people in the room, even musicians and singers, probably didn't know who I was, or who Flo was. And didn't care, either. Literally and figuratively, we were history. In many people's minds, we were three people: the big star who made good, the one who died in poverty, and me, the background singer. For so many years I had dreamed and hoped that I might one day change that, but it's probably impossible, and that's probably the only thing I've stopped dreaming about.

Maybe it's because I'm a Pisces that I can have two totally opposing reactions to the same situation. That evening I felt like two different people. One Mary Wilson was hurt and mad because of how she was being treated; the other was happy, thrilled, and honored to be saluted. The Supremes were taught to always behave like proper ladies, with class and breeding. That night I checked my hurt feelings at the door. I could have predicted how the evening would go, but I was determined to enjoy it for what it was. I don't ever want anyone to cry for me, because I don't.

What I felt that night was deeper, and more important to me. It had taken me a lifetime, but I finally knew in my heart that no one could make me feel like less than I was. Did it hurt to be snubbed? To be regarded like somebody's secretary sent to pick up an award in her boss's absence? Of course. It was like being six years old again, looking out my parents' picture window at the other kids playing in the street and not being allowed out to join them. I had to learn to be happy all alone, and I have.

The lesson that came from all I'd been through that night was that it had nothing to do with me, or how I thought about myself. Whatever hurt I felt, I acknowledged and accepted.

The difference between it and so much of my life before was that I didn't let it push me or frighten me. I knew who I was and what I'd done, and, at last, I could honestly say that was all that mattered.

For me the seventies and eighties were a time of growth and learning. In the sixties, with the Supremes, I went from having nothing to having it all. These past two decades taught me that just being the "sexy one" wasn't enough. There were things I had to fight for, like my self-respect.

After the huge success of my book *Dreamgirl* and being inducted into the Rock and Roll Hall of Fame, I decided to start my life over. My ongoing lawsuit over the ownership of the Supremes' name was coming to trial soon. And to be honest, I was tired of fighting a losing battle.

In the first days of 1990, before I turned forty-six, I called Berry Gordy and said, "Look, after nearly sixteen years of arguments and lawsuits, I'm tired of fighting over the Supremes' name."

He agreed that we should talk, and we met several times to discuss the matter. Not once did Berry ever apologize for what he or Motown did; he couldn't even acknowledge that Diane had pushed me during the "Motown 25." *Fine*, I thought. *If this is how it is, that's how it is.*

There was never any question in my mind that I would have won had the case gone to court. But that seemed so far away, and I knew that even if I won, there would be endless appeals. The fight had already cost me more than $1 million and would cost probably hundreds of thousands more before it was all over. Realistically, I had to consider the financial needs of my family before setting off on what might have been another legal wild-goose chase.

It was a hard decision, but I made it. We finally came up with a satisfactory agreement, and I signed away my rights to the name—forever. Yes, I was sad, but I was also relieved.

Motown's action back in the 1970s made it so that I had to work very hard to keep a roof over my children's heads, which is unforgivable. But I go to sleep every night with a clear conscience; I doubt many of those who had a hand in creating this situation can say the same. For the first time in years, I didn't have to fight.

I'm still traveling the world, singing and performing. Of course, we're all raised to believe that there's only one place to be, and that's on top, but I feel so fortunate to be doing what I love. As long as I'm making people happy, I'm proud to be wherever I am. I try new things all the time, but I never tire of singing the great old songs. There's always going to be a place in my heart for the Supremes. I stayed with the group through all the ups and downs, and as much as I often felt hurt and defeated, I've reached heights few of us dare dream of. For that I feel blessed.

With the Hall of Fame induction and the success of *Dreamgirl,* the Supremes finally received the recognition we long deserved. No, it didn't all turn out the way I expected, but that was okay too. My promise to Flo—and myself—had been kept:

I'd taken care of it.

# DISCOGRAPHY

*Mary Wilson, Cindy Birdsong, Jean Terrell*

## 1970

February    "Up the Ladder to the Roof" b/w "Bill, When Are You Coming Back" [Motown 1162]

April       ***Right On*** [Motown MS–705]

April       ***Farewell*** (Diana Ross and the Supremes) [Motown MS2–7088]

July        "Everybody's Got the Right to Love" b/w "But I Love You More" [Motown 1167]

September   ***The Magnificent 7*** (with the Four Tops) [Motown MS–717]

October     "Stoned Love" b/w "Shine on Me" [Motown 1172]
            ***New Ways . . . but Love Stays*** [Motown MS–720]

November    "River Deep—Mountain High" b/w "Together We Can Make Such Sweet Music" (with the Four Tops) [Motown 1173]

## 1971

April
"Nathan Jones" b/w "Happy (Is a Bumpy Road)" [Motown 1182]

May
"You Gotta Have Love in Your Heart" b/w "I'm Glad About It" (with the Four Tops) [Motown 1181]

June
*The Return of the Magnificent Seven* (with the Four Tops) [Motown MS–736]
*Touch* [Motown MS–737]

September
"Touch" b/w "It's So Hard for Me to Say Good-bye" [Motown 1190]

December
"Floy Joy" b/w "This Is the Story" [Motown 1195]
*Dynamite* (with the Four Tops) [Motown M–745L]

## 1972

April
"Automatically Sunshine" b/w "Precious Little Things" [Motown 1200]

May
*Floy Joy* [Motown M–751L]

July
"Your Wonderful, Sweet Sweet Love" b/w "The Wisdom of Time" [Motown 1206]

### *Mary Wilson, Jean Terrell, Lynda Laurence*

October
"I Guess I'll Miss the Man" b/w "Over and Over" [Motown 1213]

November
*The Supremes Produced and Arranged by Jimmy Webb* [Motown M–756L]

## 1973

March
"Bad Weather" b/w "Oh Be My Love" [Motown 1225]

### *Mary Wilson, Cindy Birdsong, Scherrie Payne*

## 1975

June
*The Supremes* [Motown M6–828S1]

| June | "He's My Man" b/w "Give Out, but Don't Give Up" [Motown 1358] |
| October | "Where Do I Go from Here" b/w "Give Out, but Don't Give Up" [Motown 1374] |

## *Mary Wilson, Cindy Birdsong, Scherrie Payne, Susaye Green*

## 1976

| April | **High Energy** [Motown M6–863S1] |
| May | "I'm Gonna Let My Heart Do the Walking" b/w "Early Morning Love" [Motown 1391] |

## *Mary Wilson, Scherrie Payne, Susaye Green*

| October | "You're My Driving Wheel" b/w "You're What's Missing in My Life" [Motown 1407] |
| | **Mary, Scherrie & Susaye** [Motown M6–873S1] |

## 1977

| February | "Let Yourself Go" b/w "You Are the Heart of Me" [Motown 1415] |

## 1978

| July | **At Their Best** [Motown M7–904R1] |

## **Mary Wilson Discography**

## 1979

| August | **Mary Wilson** [Motown M7–927R1] |
| October | "Red Hot" b/w "Midnight Dancer" [Motown 1467] |

| 1980 | "Love Talk," "You Dance My Heart Around the Stars," "Green River," "Save Me" (produced by Gus Dudgeon) [Unreleased; recorded for Motown] |
|---|---|
| 1986 | "My Lovelife Is a Disaster" [Unreleased; demo only] |
| 1987 | "Don't Get Mad, Get Even" [Nightmare Mare 39] |
| 1989 | "Ooh Child" [Nightmare MOT-C7] |

## Album Guest Appearances

With Neil Sedaka

"Come See About Me," from *Come See About Me*

With Paul Jabara

"This Girl's Back," from *Dela Noche Sisters*

With Dionne Warwick

"Heartbreak of Love" (Unreleased)

## Supremes Compact Discs

*Meet the Supremes*
*I Hear a Symphony*
*Supremes A Go-Go*
*Supremes Sing Holland-Dozier-Holland*
*Diana Ross & the Supremes with the Temptations Together*

*Right On*
*Touch*
*Floy Joy*
*Anthology*
*25th Anniversary* (two-disc set)

*Two Albums Per Disc*
*Love Child/Supremes A Go-Go*
*More Hits by the Supremes/The Supremes Sing Holland-*
    *Dozier-Holland*
*A Bit of Liverpool/TCB* (with the Temptations)

*Available on Compact Disc Only*
*Never Before Released Masters*
*The Rodgers & Hart Collection*
*Motown Around the World*
*Love Supreme* (England Only)
*Every Great #1 Hit*

# PEOPLE WHO HAVE WORKED WITH THE SUPREMES OVER THE YEARS

## *Comedians*

Herb Eden
Rodney Dangerfield
Stiller and Meara
Rip Taylor
Skiles and Henderson
George Carlin

## *Back-ups for Mary Wilson*

Debbie Sharpe and Cindy Birdsong
Karen Jackson and Kaaren Ragland
Gloria Scott and Karen Jackson
Debbie Crofton and Karen Jackson
Karen Jackson and Robin Alexander
Silvia Cox

Elizabeth Fields
Anna Beaumont
Rhonda Trodd
Linda Levine
Damia Satterfield
and numerous other ladies

## *Wardrobe Mistresses—Chaperones*

Mrs. Powell
Esther Edwards
Mrs. Morrison
Margie Wooden
Doris Postles
Ardeena Johnson

## *Designers*

Pat Campano
Michael Nicola
Bob Mackie
Mike Travis
Stephen Burrows
Allen Poe
Barnard Johnson

## *Hair Stylists*

Gregory
Winnie Brown
Jan Dochier

## Musicians

Bob Cousar
Teddy Harris
Duke Billingsley
Mel Brown
Phil Upchurch
Gil Askey
Curtis Kick
Napoleon "Snaps" Allen
Jerome Spearman
Lorenzo Brown
Travis Biggs
Darrell Smith
Joe Harris
Louis Spears
and many others

# SEVENTIES SUPREMES FAN CLUBS

There were many Supremes fan clubs, but these lasted the longest:

Jerry Jaco
SUPREMES FAN CLUB
U.S.A./Texas

Russ Bart
SUPREMES FAN CLUB
Scotland

Randy Taraborrelli
Carl Feuerbacher with
    Wayne Brasser assisting
SUPREMES FAN CLUB
U.S.A./Pennsylvania

Mario de Laat
SUPREMES FAN CLUB
Holland

David Barrie
SUPREMES FAN CLUB
Canada

Mark Douglas
SUPREMES PUSH FAN CLUB
U.S.A./New York

Ernie Brasswell
SUPREMES FAN CLUB
U.S.A./Los Angeles

Carl Feuerbacher
MARY WILSON FAN CLUB*
International

*still operating now

302

FLORENCE BALLARD
FAN CLUB*
P.O. Box 36A02
Los Angeles, CA 90036

Danny Williams
Harold Winley, Jr.
FAN CLUB

Dave Godin
TAMLA-MOTOWN
APPRECIATION SOCIETY
London, England

*still operating now

# AFTERWORD

*The 1990s: Dare to Dream*

or me, the 1990s have been a decade of happiness, tragedy, triumph, and ultimately, the decision to move forward and capitalize on the opportunities that lie before me. I have received some wonderful honors, such as induction into the Rock & Roll Hall of Fame, Vocal Group Hall of Fame, the Hollywood Walk of Fame, the New York's Harlem Chamber of Commerce Award, and the Women History Makers Award from the Caribbean American Chamber of Commerce. I have been blessed with some terrific creative opportunities as well, such as acting in two off-Broadway plays, and I have recorded two CDs that were released in Europe. I have even become a D.J. on a NY Classics R & B station, WWRL. In the last decade of the twentieth century I have experienced highs and lows that dwarf the highs and lows of the previous three decades combined. I often have had to fight for things that I felt were right. I have grown as a person and an artist.

Now that we are approaching the millennium, I have decided to tell my side of the truth about my ongoing fights over the ownership of the name of the Supremes. The creativity that made the Supremes famous at Motown had been fulfilling in the '60s and the '70s. I loved the old company, and had much success with them throughout the years. However, they have been the source of all my legal battles i.e. using my trademark application to get ownership of the name Supremes. Though I have given up the fight with Motown over the ownership, I will not give up the fight for the goodwill and the legacy of the Supremes, a legacy that I, Florence, and Diana created and I have spent a lifetime maintaining. As the only original member I still own that legacy—one that no one can take away. Motown of today is not the company I joined as an impressionable young girl and my fight is not with them.

In the 1990s I made a conscious decision to get on with my life, and concentrate on my art, my business, and my children. I wanted to be free of the negative energy, and to recoup the millions of dollars I had spent on litigation in the previous twenty years.

After all the drama of the '70s and '80s, I had decided that enough was enough. I picked up the phone and called Berry Gordy in 1990. He was happy that I wanted to resolve all of our problems. He agreed that it was time to put the past behind us. We set up a meeting for this settlement. This was after Motown was sold to MCA Records. My attorney advised me not to do it, "Mary, you still have a chance to win your lawsuit." But he didn't know how much I loved Motown, or Berry. He did know that I had spent millions in lawsuits trying to get back the name Supremes. The loss was both a spiritual one and a material one, and I was tired.

After learning Motown had been sold to MCA Records, I recalled that I had been given 50 percent of the name Supremes if it were ever sold. So coming to this meeting I expected to get some profits from the sale of the name Supremes. But when I asked Berry about my 50 percent he said, "We just sold it as a package deal, along with everything else in the company. The name was included for the token payment of one dollar. So, you don't get anything." I thought to myself, "I've been screwed again!"

Surely the Supremes name was worth much more than a dollar, everyone knows that. But I had come there to end all

4

of this craziness. Because all of this in-house fighting, I had made so many enemies at the old Motown trying to stand up for my rights. I just wanted to get on with my life.

When I look at my situation with Motown and compare it to Florence's, I begin to understand what must have gone on in her mind when she died. It was the feeling of defeat. The small monetary settlement she'd received for giving up her rights to the name Supremes was $75,000 more than the $100,000 I'd received, but nothing close to the millions I have spent trying to get the name back. Eventually it was about more than money. I just wanted to get on with my life and raise my children. The thought of having to work for another ten years had not been in my plans, but given the outcome it was a hard reality. I could look back with pride on what three little black girls from the projects accomplished, but I couldn't rest on that. Although we had had great success and helped changed the world's perception of black women along with pioneers like Josephine Baker, Dorothy Dandridge and many others. I still needed to work and make a living. So I sat there at this meeting with Berry and all of his lawyers and I took a deep breath, and dared to dream again. I said to Berry, "I want you to promise me that there will never be any other groups of Supremes." He said to me, "You got it." Well, so much for those famous words. I remember in 1967 when Berry had changed the name of the group from the Supremes to Diana Ross and the Supremes. He said, "Mary don't worry about it, trust me. I'll always take care of you."

I didn't want our Supreme legacy to become cheapened. I didn't want it to be like the running joke in the industry where on any day of the week you could go and see several different groups calling themselves the Coasters and the Drifters, and now even the Temptations and the Marvelettes. I walked out of the meeting feeling relieved on one hand, because I had ended the feud with Motown, but on the other

5

hand I had given away a fortune. People often ask me about my opinions about the business.

To my knowledge there are at least six groups claiming to be the Supremes today, and the fight has become a global one. One weapon that has been used against bogus groups is the Truth in Rock Act. The Truth in Rock Act is a legislative attempt to protect the rights of recording artists whose rights are being violated by false groups using their names to cash in on reputations that these ersatz groups had no part in building. Imagine if four contemporary musicians from Liverpool, or Los Angeles for that matter, purchased the name the Beatles and announced a reunion tour, and you get a sense of the absurdity. Everyone knows the Fab Four. But groups like the Coasters are not so individually familiar and it is possible for unscrupulous promoters to take advantage of the music audience and the artists by advertising shows and selling tickets. In their defense those promoters will protest that they own the names, that everything is legal, and that there is nothing deceptive about these practices.

One such promoter has even said that people go to these shows not expecting to see any of the original members in a group like the Coasters. That argument is ridiculous and immoral. Why use the name the Coasters at all? In a statement drafted by Dean Goodman for Reuters Wire Service he pointed out the absurdity: "The Drifters must be one of the hardest-working groups in show business. One night last year 'The 1950's Soul Legends' played three shows, in three different states. The problem is that this magical feat was performed by three different groups, each called the Drifters, and none of them bearing the slightest similarity to the original group." Republicans and Democrats don't concur on much, but they do agree on this matter. Legislators such as Representatives Charles Norwood (Republican, Georgia) and Dennis Kucinich (Democrat, Ohio), recognizing the injustice of these practices, have introduced legislation that would help protect the rights of artists like the Coasters.

Representative Kucinich puts it this way: "Knockoff groups should not be permitted to pass themselves off as the real thing. Those artists who have put their heart and soul into building a career, and making a name, and into stunning achievements in music, ought not to be deprived in later years of the fruits of their labor."

The bill is an amendment to the Trademark Act of 1946 (The Lanham Act) to increase the penalties for infringing the rights pertaining to famous performing groups and to clarify the law pertaining to the rights of individuals who perform services as a group. Supporting these efforts are groups like F.A.M.E. (Friends Against Musical Exploitation) of East Boston, Massachusetts. F.A.M.E., along with Kucinich's office, has been instrumental in arranging press conferences and launching publicity campaigns to protect the rights of groups like the Vogues, Danny and the Juniors, the Casinos, the Classics IV, the Platters, the Coasters and many more groups who are subject to this sort of exploitation, including the Supremes. We lobbied in Washington and gained support from the legislators on Capitol Hill.

These efforts are supported by fans who feel that the misuse of groups' names to cash in on their reputations is unjust and exploits the fans as well as the originating artists by presenting a false product to the audience. The problem is compounded in the case of the younger fan base. A twenty-year-old who has heard his/her parents Coasters records might not know that Carl Gardner is not only a member of the Rock and Roll Hall of Fame, but is also an original member of the Coasters. Yet a group calling itself the Coasters with whom Carl has never worked has made a great deal of money presenting itself to the audiences as the Coasters while Carl is stopped from performing with the name.

Charlie Thomas of the Drifters is put into the ridiculous

and unfair position of having lost any claim to the name. Now in his sixties, he is in the position of having to bill himself as "Charlie Thomas, formerly of the Drifters," while men with whom he never sang make money performing under the name the Drifters. If the Truth in Rock Act is successful he will be able to go on the road as "The Drifters featuring Charlie Thomas." *As this book went to press Truth in Rock bill was tabled because it couldn't accommodate the many different issues of all the '50s and '60s groups. But the fight will go on.*

Today there are several different Motowns, an ironic reflection of the fact that there are several different groups of Supremes. In my mind and heart Motown is no longer the enemy. Their rights too are being violated by the groups that bill themselves as Supremes and sell records with photos of Diane, Florence and me while covering our old hits. And you know who is really hurt by all this? The fans. Those people who are paying money for the Supremes music and getting ersatz groups instead. My final allegiance is to those fans who have stood by me all these years.

My feeling is this: what's past is past. Crying over spilt milk is not only useless, it is a waste of my time and energy. This is not to say I am going to roll over and play dead for the phony groups. I will continue to fight on that issue. I will continue to fight for what is mine from the Supremes legacy. And I will continue to lend my name to the larger issue of the trademark legislation that seeks to restore the rights of original members of legendary groups like the Coasters, the Platters, the Angels, and the Marvelettes. But my days of being victimized are over. In many ways I have been taken advantage of, I know this. Maybe it was because I was just too naïve, too trusting of those around me, not aggressive enough in protecting my rights. But at this stage of my life I take full responsibility for all that has happened. Perhaps education would have alleviated my problems. That is why in 1995 I enrolled in New York University in New York City after 30 years outside the classroom. It was also a wish of my mother that one of her children attend college. I am now in my third year maintaining a B+ average. Another factor in my return to school was my mother's illness. We know now that Alzheimer's Disease can be genetic. Great strides are being made to battle this terrible illness. It has been theorized that one way to forestall the effects of Alzheimer's is to keep the mind active. So my return to college to get my degree is a proactive attempt on my part to make sure I do everything in my power to keep my mind strong and clear.

## The New Supremes: 1970s

After Diane left the group in 1970, I received my one-third of the three way split from the group's earnings from all of our twelve number one million-selling recordings. It totaled just $100,000. I couldn't believe that was all I had left, after all the endorsements, TV shows, and the tours. I was so angry that I immediately took over all of the Supremes' business affairs. I began hiring managers, business accountants, and advisors. Many people think that the Supremes ended when Diane left, but for me the Supremes started to change in 1968 when Florence had to leave the group. Because she was an integral part of the group it was a fundamental change. Flo and I had sung all the legendary hits by our producers Holland, Dozier & Holland. When this great writing team left Motown in the midst of their own legal hassles in 1968, the Supremes were left without writers to pen our hits. So, like the situation with the ill-starred duo Milli Vanilli, Motown recorded without me on numerous unsuccessful records. Cindy, new at the time, was also left out of these recordings. The Supremes era was definitely waning. Before Diane left we were saved with the release of "Love Child" and "Someday We'll Be Together." With Diane's departure in 1970 most people thought that the group would fail, but I was determined that it would not. As it ended up, I had to hire new members as needed. From 1970 to 1977, I brought in four different singers to keep the group going. With Jean Terrell, Cindy Birdsong, and myself we scored four Top Twenty singles, starting with "Up the Ladder to the Roof," "Stoned Love," and continuing with hits "Nathan Jones," and "Floy Joy."

Motown's support of the group began to weaken despite the success of four hit records. I can understand Motown pulling back on us to an extent. In my heart, The Supremes would always be Diane, Florence, and myself. But I was in no mood to give up. I would not let my dream die. I live by the motto "dreams don't die, people just stop dreaming. Others just move on." As girls departed the group I replaced them myself. One by one these replacements left just as I needed them to help me fight the demise of the Supremes. Jean Terrell left, along with Lynda Laurence. Lynda had only been in the group one year. Lynda, by the way, had recorded only one single, "Bad Weather," and although her picture appeared on the *Floy Joy* LP, she did not sing one song on it. What you hear is Cindy's voice. In Lynda's defense she did record background vocals on a few songs on the Jim Webb album. It was at this point in 1974 after Jean and Lynda had quit that I found myself the only Supreme again. I was again left responsible for the obligations of Supremes, Inc., my corporation. It was I who sustained the name and reputation of the group during this time. I called up Cindy Birdsong, who was always there when I needed her. In 1974 I found and hired Scherrie Payne, and I started rehearsing the new Supremes.

## Theft of a Dream

Most of what follows I have written about at length in *Supreme Faith*. What I have described can be found in chapter

10

eight. But the bottom line is, this girl started thinking. Having others control my life, as I had throughout my career, had hurt me artistically and financially. In the early '70s I didn't even know how to balance my checkbook. Motown had been our managers, accountants, and legal representatives; we knew nothing about business matters. For the money men at Motown it was like taking candy from babies. They got the money, we got the fame. I wondered if I could get the name Supremes back, then leave Motown. That is when I asked the question, "what constitutes ownership?" In the case of Motown, could they have owned the name Supremes just because they said so? I had no proof that they weren't telling me the truth, but something told me to investigate it. At the time, I was operating on instinct alone. The only other proof was our first recording contract in 1961, in which Motown had put in the phrase that they owned the name Supremes. Around the time these thoughts were occurring to me I ran into my dear friend Nancy Wilson. She said that she had a new and brilliant black attorney, and suggested I speak with him. I called him and told him my story. I had already spoken with a fan that worked in the trademark office. This fan had done a search for ownership of the name. She had found that on that day in January 1974 there had never been a trademark for the name the Supremes. After relaying all this to the attorney he said he would check into it for me, and I hired him. This was the first time a Supreme had acquired a lawyer outside of Motown.

The attorney came back with the news that his own search at the trademark office had also come up empty. I couldn't believe my luck. Up until then, Motown had been telling us all along that it was they who owned the name Supremes. I told him to do whatever was necessary to take the trademark out in my name, and he agreed to do this. While we waited for my trademark to come through, I rehearsed Scherrie and Cindy. I had new gowns made, old gowns altered, and I was truly excited by the idea that I might control my own destiny. To think Motown had slipped up and I had a chance to right the wrongs of the past!

I asked the attorney how I would know that my trademark had gone through. He said we would have to wait for them to notify us. I never did hear from the trademark office. Everyday I called him to find out if my trademark had been registered. It was while I was planning my wedding that this was going on. I was also rehearsing the ladies for a tour. Just prior to my wedding day in Las Vegas my attorney sold me out. "Mary, we were wrong: Motown *does* own the name." My heart was broken. I never even thought to ask him to show me proof. I threw myself into my wedding plans and the Supremes' big Las Vegas opening to bury my pain.

A wise man once said, "Time wounds all heels." My brilliant attorney was eventually disbarred for ethical transgressions unrelated to what he did to me.

## The 1974 Assignment Paper

While getting ready for my wedding in Las Vegas, it seemed like every big shot from Motown came up for our opening, and the signing of "the new Supremes" to a recording contract. It was sad that I had lost the chance to own the name Supremes. Ewart Abner, the vice-president of Motown at that time, approached me with the recording contract, but he also brought me the infamous 1974 assignment paper, the document that would eventually sink my efforts. At that time my mind was on my wedding the next day, and also on the fact that I would have to get the Supremes into the recording studio soon afterwards. I was about to sign that recording contract and Abner said, "Mary, you have to sign this assignment paper before you sign the recording contract." As I read the paper that stated that I had to give up all my rights, I snapped and said, "If you already own the name Supremes why do I have to sign this paper?" He said, "Oh Mary, don't worry, it's nothing. Our legal department just needs it for their files." My husband-to-be said, "Mary, don't sign that paper." I thought to myself, if they already owned the name Supremes like my attorney said, I didn't have anything to give away. I might as well sign it and get the group back into the recording studio.

From 1974 to 1977, Motown released the final three Supremes albums, and we received even less promotion than we had in the previous four years. By 1977, I felt that it was time to disband the group, but hesitantly I left it to Scherrie and Susaye. Scherrie Payne was such a sweet lady, and had been so cooperative in my battles against Motown, that I didn't want to abandon the group and leave her hanging. I say hesitantly because I felt that once either Diane, Florence or I were no longer in the group, the Supremes era was over. But I am a woman who prides herself on being fair and honest. I am not a taker.

## The 1990s

Now in 1999 I've lost the last hearing in the Superior Court in Los Angeles because of that 1974 assignment paper. The court decided I had no standing as I had given up the rights. After this hearing all of the deposition papers from Motown were sent to me and I stumbled upon the evidence that I had been lied to by that attorney over twenty years ago. I can only guess from reading these papers, which I had never seen back in 1974, that Motown and my attorney got together and agreed my attorney would lie to me. The dates clearly showed that I was the first one to file for the Supremes trademark on January 7, 1974. Motown knew that my trademark had officially gone through, but I never knew. Nor had I ever received the paperwork from the trademark office because it had been sent to Motown, perhaps by my attorney. Someone had actually crossed my address off the legal papers, and stuck a sticker with Motown's corporate address in Detroit over the top of it. All this time I legally owned 100 percent of the rights, but they convinced me that I did not. At this time I have the documents to prove it. Now, after more than $3 million spent in legal fees, I have the legal papers that document how they plotted to steal my rights. This is truly the theft of my dream.

I have recently retained a competent and established law firm from New York to review all of my records.

My new lawyers told me that the 1974 agreement not only bound me, it enabled me to enter into the 1990 agreement with Berry Gordy that ended either side's opportunity to sue the other in these matters. They conceded that in the larger scheme of things the agreement was unfair, but they were binding. I have accepted their assessment, and I knew that it was time to let that go and move on.

There are injustices that grate on me, of course. I am only human. When I think about how Motown had forbidden Florence in her lawsuit to ever use the name publicly, it breaks my heart, but the hard truth is that she signed away her royalty rights for the small sum of $175,000. Motown didn't even own the name, and Florence's children (Lisa, Nicole, and Michelle) do not receive a penny from the sale of records for which Motown continues to receive royalties. In my opinion it is unfair and unjust, but it is legal. Life is not always fair.

In 1998 I had to work with a group of Marvelettes in Las Vegas. The show was billed as "The Legends of Motown," starring the Temptations, Mary Wilson of the Supremes, and the Marvelettes. I know everyone who has ever recorded as a Marvelette in Motown. I didn't know any of those girls. Gladys Horton, who sang lead on "Please Mr. Postman," can't tour as the Marvelettes, just as I can't tour as the Supremes. Because we are so well known in the United States, that kind of situation is not as destructive here. However in Europe there are, at any given moment, four, five, or even six sets of groups touring as the Supremes. In countries like Japan and other points around the globe, people do not always recognize the faces of the original Supremes like people in the United States. Here they know us by name. In other countries any three black girls that can sing can now be Supremes.

The problem of people stealing a group's identify stems from the shortsightedness of all of us back in the beginning. Even a businessman as savvy as Berry Gordy had neglected to trademark our name early on. It is ironic that the trademark laws, originally written to protect artists and their intellectual properties, are being used against us by the sort of people who send groups like the bogus Drifters and Marvelettes out into the world because they have paid a fee for the rights to the name.

False groups like these tour the United Kingdom, Europe, and the world, singing old hits, and representing themselves as the originals. Some of these people were not yet born in the '50s and '60s. Now these people are beginning to infiltrate the United States! As for my old friends Scherrie and Lynda, despite their own admissions in *Ebony* magazine in the '70s, where they conceded that I am the leader, owner of the name, and heart and soul of the Supremes legacy, they are touring as the Former Ladies of the Supremes against my wishes. In the '90s Lynda Laurence and Scherrie Payne are continuing work as Supremes, exploiting my legacy by calling themselves "the legendary Supremes." Thank God Motown is not sending out a group of Supremes. The only way I can see erasing all of these ersatz groups is if I, Diane, and Cindy get back together for a Supremes reunion tour. Then we'd see who has the last laugh.

After the 1990 Motown settlement, it seemed like there had been closure in my life. I was glad that I had been big enough to phone Berry. Even though I have had financial difficulties dealing with Motown, I wouldn't trade my life as a Supreme for anything. I just wish I had had more *"ed-ja-me-cation."*

I loved my life at Motown. The lifelong friendships that I have made with Stevie Wonder, Martha Reeves, the Temptations, the Four Tops, and those whose lives have been shortened like Florence Ballard, Melvin Franklin, Mary Wells, Junior Walker, Marvin Gaye, and Tammi Terrell, are friendships I cherish to this day. And the love of the millions of fans around the world has made my life rich and fulfilling.

In the early '90s I felt that it was time for a change of scenery. Los Angeles no longer seemed to hold the glamour or the excitement it once had. I had witnessed many changes in life there. First there was the demise of the Supremes in the '70s. I had watched disco come and go. Drugs and AIDS had taken many of my friends. Not only had many great creative individuals died, but many of my personal friends as well. Like my godson Allen Poe who not only designed my stage gowns but also ran my office and helped raise my three children. Not long after he passed my bodyguard Kenny Ray also died. I wanted out of Hollywood. Our optimistic visions in the '60s for a better future had been an illusion. I had to find a better life for my children and me.

With this thought in mind, I sold my big Hollywood home, packed up my belongings, and moved to Washington, D.C., in late 1990. After only one year of living in the D.C. area I again packed my bags, and moved my mom and my children (Turkessa, Pedrito, and Rafael) to the outskirts of Las Vegas. My children came from Los Angeles and had no interest in the East Coast. I found that as teenagers they were at an age where it would be unfair to uproot them and move them cross-country. I should have moved while they were still young.

Though at first it seemed like a good situation for me and my family, my little boys and I soon discovered that racism and provincialism were alive and well in Las Vegas. Whenever they went out to play, they were viewed as threatening and someone would call the police. Whenever there was a school-yard fight, it was viewed as a racial incident. When my then 14-year-old son Pedrito broke a boy's nose it was also viewed as racial, when in fact it was just two teenage boys fighting. The court battle that ensued ended up costing me nearly $25,000. Being African American, along with being a celebrity, made me a target. Whether it was my dog biting the mailman or a parking lot fender-bender, everyone was eager to sue me simply because I was famous and assumed to be rich. I decided to pack my bags and leave town. There seemed to be no place safe for me to raise my children.

Since the boys were now teenagers, I decided to let them live with their father. We moved back to Los Angeles. Being a caring mom, I took a small apartment close by. Turkessa, now 18, stayed with Anthony, her fiancee, in Las Vegas. My daughter and Anthony were both in college, so they had no reason to move. This arrangement seemed like the best of all options, and for the first time in years I was living on my own again. Unfortunately, it was a situation that led to the greatest tragedy of my life.

Since my place in Los Angeles was small, I decided to take several things back to Turkessa to help set up her new apartment, things like dishes, comforters, and pots and pans. My beautiful son Rafael stopped by the morning I had planned to make the trip. I was so pleased to see him! When I told him of my plans for the day, his response was immediate: "Mommy, I want to go with you." It was the weekend. It was a beautiful day. I so loved the company of my son. I told him he could come along.

*It was amazing to me how much Rafi had grown since we moved from Las Vegas. All of a sudden he was now nearly six feet tall, and was growing up to be a handsome young man. He had grown from a little baby who would run up to me and*

17

*give me a big kiss as he would run out to play, to a handsome young man who filled my heart just to see him. In Vegas he had taken up music. I was so happy going to his school concerts where he would play tenor saxophone. He spent hours practicing for his band recital, playing to Marvin Gaye and John Coltrane. In our big house in Las Vegas, each of the children had their own room, and his was always filled with music. I was very proud that one of my children was going to follow in my footsteps by choosing a career in music.*

*I remember peeking into his room one day while he was practicing. He was wearing a little cap, and actually looked like a young Marvin Gaye. They say that a parent never has a favorite, but that's not true for me. Though all my children are special to me, Rafi was my favorite. Rafi and I had a special bond. He had also taken up basketball while in school in Las Vegas. His awkward, slender body was always a joy to see as he ran up and down the basketball court. His coach in Las Vegas thought Rafi had the potential to play in the National Basketball Association.*

Rafi and I packed up all of the boxes of housewares, and off we went to Las Vegas. It was a beautiful Saturday morning. Rafael had brought his Walkman and headphones to listen to his own music. My guys had a habit of jumping in our vehicle and changing the radio to their loud music, which drove me crazy. They said my music was for old folks. As he sat there in the car, his long legs and arms were moving to the music that I couldn't hear, thank God. It was so nice to be a mom for the day. My children loved when I was a mom and not the star, and it would break my heart to have to leave them to go on the road. But I was no longer recording as often, so I needed the fees I made touring.

As I drove down the road towards Turkessa's home, nothing foretold what was about to happen. Rafael and I were enjoying each other's company. The sun was brilliant and strong. The road was somewhat rough and unfinished, and at some point the car drifted to the shoulder. When I attempted to steer it back to the middle of the road it responded awkwardly, and tipped. Then it began a roll that seemed to last forever. Over and over it rolled, finally landing on the other side of the highway. Often in movies traumatic events unfold in slow motion, giving time an unreal quality, and it was like that in the accident. In my mind time seemed strange and warped, almost as if it was standing still. I remember the event as occurring in a void of silence. I thought, "This can't be the end, I have so much more to live for." And time stretched out and lasted much longer than the several seconds events took to develop.

*On the wall of my home there are photographs of my friends, my loved ones, and my business friends. On one such wall is a picture of Rafi in his school military uniform looking like an angel. His big, brown-doe, almond shaped eyes were so clear. He was wise even in his baby years. He'd always tell me that he was only on this earth because of his love for me.*

When my vehicle's roll finally ended, I was shocked and badly injured. It took a few moments to realize I had even come through it. Death felt so close at hand. As my mind began to clear and sort itself out I again recognized that there was silence, terrible silence. I looked for Rafael in the tangled wrecked space of the vehicle. I found him caught between the car and the road, half in, half out of the car. My baby made no noise, his form was still, and only his long legs were still in the car. The seat belt had unraveled, instead of holding him in as mine had held me in, allowing the top part of his body to be partially thrown out of the vehicle. He was caught and crushed between the car and road instead of belted to the seat.

I was later to learn that a series of deadly events had unfolded as the vehicle, which was top-heavy in design, had started the fatal roll. As it rolled to Rafael's side the vehicle door was opened by contact with the road (a design flaw since changed by the company). Had the seat belt held him, this mistake might have done no harm, but the belt unraveled. My son was thrown out of the door as the vehicle rolled, and his body suffered terrible and mortal injuries before the vehicle finally came to rest.

*It's strange and sad the thoughts that come back to you when something as devastating as the loss of a child occurs. Rafael used to say to me, "Mom, I would die for you." It was a thought that touched my heart, and when he said that it never occurred to me that he would die so young. On that terrible day, as I struggled with my senses to come to grips with what had happened, and the terrible pain that was flooding my body, my thoughts went to him immediately. And the knowledge that I had lost him was on me, in my heart, before my mind had cleared. My first sense was that perhaps I was dead. But as my head cleared and I came to the realization that I had not died, I knew that he had.*

*And how can I describe a feeling like that? The realization that I had lost my beautiful son? That life would never, ever be the same?*

The next thing that I remember was someone asking me, "Miss, are you alive? Can we get you out of the car?" It was then that I realized that I couldn't move. I realized that I was seriously hurt, but I didn't know how badly, or what my injuries were. To get myself out of the wreckage, I had to climb over my son's body, but now I couldn't breathe and could barely move. "Climb over your son," someone said to me, "we don't want to move him, he is unconscious." The vehicle had been filled to the brim. A dog transport cage was also in the car, with my black cocker spaniel Onyx inside. Our belongings were strewn all over the highway. I was lying there, and Onyx was lying there, and I thought she was dead too. I kept asking, "Is my son alive?" In my heart I knew he was dead. It seemed like forever before the ambulance came. The people who happened upon the scene in other cars were wonderful that day. A couple of the passengers from passing cars stopped at the scene and were praying for me and talking to me. One kind man sat with me and held my hand as we waited. I knew I was badly hurt and I wasn't sure I was going to survive. I asked myself, "Is this how it's going to end?" The song by Peggy Lee echoed in my heart: "Is That All There Is?" Is it going to end here?

All of my ribs on the left-hand side were broken, making it hard to breathe, and I learned later that my collarbone was broken. My left lung was pierced by shards of broken bone, and I was bleeding inside. To drain the blood flowing into my lungs it was necessary to punch a tube through the wall of my left breast, without the benefit of anesthetics, and that was excruciating. I have a scar there now. As the helicopter transported me to the hospital in Barstow, California, I was in unreal pain. But I couldn't even think about the pain. I kept asking about my son. All I could think was, "I lost my baby," although no one told me until we got to the hospital.

Finally, we arrived at the hospital. Those transporting me decided not to tell me that Rafael had passed on until my family arrived, but I knew. I remember my daughter was there, my ex-husband, and my other son Pedro, Jr. In my confusion I kept wishing for Rafi. I recalled at how sometimes when my husband was enraged it was Rafael who would stand up to him. I felt that he would be the one to protect me when I needed him, and his death was devastating.

I spent the next five days in the hospital. The news had gotten all over the world. People were calling me from everywhere expressing their concern. People I hadn't heard from in years. Family, friends from the business, and my wonderful fans all reached out to me through prayers, cards, flowers, and other expressions of love and concern.

*After family, there is probably nobody closer to my heart than my dear friends Rita Coolidge and Brenda Russell. Lying in my hospital bed, trying to come to grips with what happened, among the first by my side was Rita. Her words, so comforting, so much from the heart, spoke directly to my heart about Rafi. "You haven't lost him, Mary. He's still with you. He's right here. He's crying, and he's hoping you hold on, and get through this." She knew him. Rita knew Rafi so well, and she loved him. I remember how Rafi loved Rita's cooking. He used to tell her that she had to teach me this dish or that. Rita knows me well enough. She replied, "If you want this dish again baby, just come on over and I'll make it for you." Rita called Rafi my little angel. She knew him.*

One of the concerned friends who contacted me was Diane. It speaks to the depth of our history, our friendship, and Diane's character that she reached out to me as a friend when I needed friends the most. It saddens me when people don't understand the depth of our friendship. Even Berry and those people at Motown don't understand that it has only been their business that came between us. When the time is right, we will be there for each other. I have never ever had friends that I love more than Florence and Diane.

In the days that followed, my friends and family rallied to my side and took care of me. Even my mom, who by then was very ill with Alzheimer's, and my best friends Rita and Brenda Russell, came and stayed at the hospital. They took turns spending the night. I was surrounded by an outpouring of love and concern. My friends took care of me, while my body began to heal.

*From this difficult time Rita remembers that there was laughter that sometimes stemmed from humor, and at other times was the product of heartbreak. "Johnnie Mae by that time was afflicted with Alzheimer's in a way that was apparent to all of us, but she made a real effort to help with Mary and show her great love. At one point I was spending nights at the hospital with Mary, and the hospital was kind enough to provide me with a bed next to her in the intensive care ward when it became apparent to them that I would be at Mary's side throughout the ordeal. At another point Johnnie Mae decided that she would share the care of Mary's doctor and she got into the bed next to Mary's and demanded that she too be cared for. Mary loved Johnnie Mae so much she had a hard time kicking Johnnie out of it, but she saw the humor. She told me that it hurt so much to laugh, and it was easy to see why. Her body was filled with tubes. Her face was swollen. Her left eye was a bloody mess for weeks afterward. And one of those tubes was the one paramedics had to push into her body at the site of the crash. She was a picture! But she maintained. Mary is a very spiritual person, and her spirituality was deepened by this crisis in her life. A lot of people might have withdrawn, disappeared into grief and vanished. With Mary that wasn't an option. In those days after the accident, she had already begun to show the strength that would carry her through the tragedy. And in the five years that have followed her commitment to that spirituality hasn't wavered."*

I had been accustomed to taking care of my family all my life, but this time my family had to take care of me, and they did a fine job. My daughter, son, and their father, Pedro Ferrer Sr., made all the preparations for Rafael's funeral. It was a beautiful funeral. All of my best friends were there, and all of my family. Mauna Loa and her husband Dr. Herbert Avery who had delivered all my babies. Rafael's godmother Joanne Ewing, my family from Detroit, Los Angeles, Atlanta, and Chicago, and many of my friends from the entertainment business. Among them were Patti LaBelle, Freda Payne, the Jackson family, and Martha Reeves. Even Berry Gordy and members of his family were in attendance.

The person who was really there for me was my very dear friend Duke Fakir of the Four Tops. I will never forget the emotional support that he gave me during that difficult time. I began to accept the fact that Rafael's life was meant to be short, and that I had been blessed to have him in my life for those fourteen years.

They say that it is a mother's greatest fear to lose one of

her children, and I have to agree. Thank God I have two remaining. One of my best friends, Beverly Todd, lost her only child a few years back, and I know how difficult it has been for her, but she is strong and has carried on. I know that I am very fortunate. One of the things I became involved with in the aftermath of Rafi's death was a support group for parents who have lost children. It is a group I have maintained contact with to this day. A special bond forms among people who share a common grief, and the group is important in a special way to each member.

I was very proud of my children at Rafael's funeral. Turkessa was nineteen years old at the time, and Pedrito was sixteen. They handled Rafael's passing so well, they were so strong for me. They saw to it that all the funeral arrangements were made. After the funeral, we all celebrated Rafael's life at the home of his godmother, Joanne. Martha Reeves, Nancy Wilson, and my other friends were there for me too, and I am so grateful for their kindness, as well as all the prayers of people that I don't even know who come up to me to this day and tell me how sorry they are for my loss.

Once I was released from the hospital, Pedro, Sr., Rafael's father, got a hospital bed to put in my apartment. My injuries were all internal, in fact to look at me you'd never know how broken up I was on the inside. For a long time it was difficult to sit, lie down, or do anything but stand, which was exhausting. When I could sleep, it was at an angle. More often than not terrible pain interrupted my sleep, and this was hard for me because I am known to sleep through anything. I convalesced in my Beverly Hills apartment with my friends taking turns staying with me. The first week it was my dear friend Linda Greene from Washington, D.C. The next week Cindy Birdsong came and nursed me. I have always been able to rely on Cindy, no matter what the circumstances. My dear friends Rita and Brenda were both incredibly supportive. The Four Tops invited me to their Los Angeles concert. Concert producer David Gest was also helpful in making sure that I was as comfortable and happy as possible that evening. The next day the press, which had been kind after the accident, jumped on the fact that I was out in public so soon after the funeral. For me it was a part of the healing process. The only way I knew how to get through my tragedy was to go on living my life.

Within a month I was back on the road working again, singing my hour-long concert show on stage. To be able to get through my show while my bruised and broken ribs healed, I sat on a stool on stage. By the time I began to work again, I was far from being healed. There is a part of my heart that will never heal. My son Pedrito might have said it best to me in one of our heart-to-heart conversations, when at some point he looked at me and told me that the loss of Rafael was like having a big hole in his heart, a piece that was missing. It made sense to me, because it was exactly how I felt. Though we all have been devastated losing Rafael, he took the loss of his brother hardest. Maybe it is because they were brothers, and close in age. Maybe because they tended to get into trouble together. I was always telling them, "Boys, go to your room!" or "Boys, knock it off!" They were together most of the time. Losing his brother hurt him so. I think it was the first time he realized how much he loved him. I am proud to say it has made him stronger, with more quiet strength. It also deepened him spiritually. I know that for a time he was very angry that his brother had died. He went through a very bad period, even ending up in prison for six months. Both my ex-husband and my daughter handled the loss quietly, and in their own way. We all have been changed by it. I feel that many times in our lives it is the tragedies that give us the most opportunit to grow.

Perhaps I am just growing up, but losing him has give me, for the first time, the ability to put many things in perspec tive. I've never been one to hold a grudge, but I held on to m hurt and pain from having so much taken from me. Hurt and anger of past wrongs that at one time might have saddened my heart are now easier to let go of.

Rafael's death was my wake up call. In my studies I came upon an old and well-known phrase uttered by the philosopher Nietzsche: "That which does not kill me makes me stronger." In the years following Rafi's death my life has changed in so many dramatic ways. Even the pace of my life was altered by this loss. New energy, new opportunity, new directions in my life have come fast and furious. My business, Mary Wilson Enterprises, is growing in leaps and bounds. Sometimes it seems like there aren't enough hours in the day to get things done, and there is always more to be done, more things to learn and explore.

One of the greatest honors I have received was presented to me only weeks after the accident, when the Supremes were honored with their own star on Hollywood Boulevard on the Hollywood Walk of Fame. The Walk of Fame is the biggest tourist attraction in Hollywood. It honors achievement in the entertainment industry in film, the recording industry, and all the entertainment arts. Joe Bensen, a true fan, was responsible for spearheading this project along with all of our closest fans. It was they who argued for, and won, the star. For that and so many other things I will always be grateful to them. Besides being a great honor, being given a star on the Hollywood Boulevard provided me with an opportunity to reflect on all the strong and positive things being a Supreme has meant to me, and what it has meant to African Americans in general. We joined some pretty impressive company: Lena Horne, Sammy Davis Jr., Nat "King" Cole, Eddie "Rochester" Anderson, and Sidney Poitier, to name a few.

I think the Supremes touched a lot of lives. I think we were about more than music. We were about hope; we were the American Dream. We came along at a time when black people were considered citizens in name only. In 1964 we had our first hit records. We became citizens of the world. We became role models for other black girls.

*For all this, I want to thank Berry Gordy for backing us, Cholly Atkins, who taught us those wonderful moves, and Maxine Powell, who taught us poise and grace. I want to thank all the DJs around the world. They were many other stars who came along before the Supremes. They paved the way for us. But I do think that the Supremes, in 1964, showed the world that black was not only beautiful, but that black women were gorgeous and talented. We were ambitious. We won. We proved the American Dream. We were the American Dream.*

"I'm still changing. I'm still growing. And I wish the same for all of you because if we want to change this world of ours, it does start with each and every one of us." (From the Hollywood Star Dedication Ceremony, March 11, 1994.)

It was a difficult day physically because it was only a month after the accident. It was also a day I wanted to share with my partners Florence and Diane. Diane issued a statement saying that she had deferred to me and felt that it was my event, my day as a Supreme, and didn't want to do anything to detract from it. We did arrange for one of Florence's daughters to fly in from Detroit. It was important to me to have Florence represented, though I knew she was there in spirit. There was media to meet, details to attend. My body was still very sore but it was so heartening to be acknowledged. I think that for any entertainer, to be given a star represents a career of achievement, and because of that it is an opportunity to reflect and appreciate the positive things in life.

Shortly after the star ceremony I was invited to be a guest of the *Sally Jesse Raphael* show. Appearing on that show was, for me, another positive part of the healing process. I had not known Sally prior to the show. I knew that she too had lost a child. She, like all the people who were reaching out to me, was concerned about me. The show itself was a wonderful experience. I remember that backstage I was fairly calm, and

27

I hoped I wouldn't break down on national TV. I wanted to share some of my feelings with Sally and her audience. I was prepared for the flood of emotion that washed over me, but I wanted to control it. No such luck. I am such a crybaby, and always have been, so I was upset that I was messing up my makeup. I am also very vain, and the idea of appearing on TV a liquid mess was upsetting.

Every member of the audience stood and applauded as I walked out to greet Sally. The ovation was sustained for a while, and I was, for a moment, overwhelmed. One thing that perhaps the fans aren't aware of, and one thing that entertainers and athletes and all those supported by fans sometimes lose sight of, is the importance of the support and love of those who are fans. Beyond the trappings and the rewards of fame, beyond the houses, the cars, the bank accounts, everyone needs to be loved. Everyone needs approval. Everyone needs to believe that what they contribute to the world is special and makes a difference. For the most part that sort of validation comes from family, friends, and fellow workers. For people like me, having been a Supreme, having been in the public eye for most of my adult life, having the love and support of the fans is one of the most important parts of my life. That day in the studio, looking out into the audience, I saw the faces of fans I had known for years, as well as new faces. The love came at me in waves, and it moved me. In one of her greatest songs Joni Mitchell sings about the effect the love of her fans has on her when she refers to "those velvet curtain calls."[1] That is such a beautiful way to describe the pure physical effect the love of fans has on an entertainer like myself. Looking into the faces of those fans that day I saw not only love, but concern and care. Looking into those faces I saw fans that had been listening to my music, and the music of the Supremes, for periods ranging from three months to thirty years.

[1] From "For Free," Joni Mitchell.

One of the things that was said that day was uttered by my friend Rita Coolidge, who was also a guest of the show. She pointed out that some people couldn't understand how I dealt with my grief in those days. She said that my grieving process was different than most people, and she was right. She understands that Rafael's death has had a profound effect upon me. She also understands that the spiritual foundations that have sustained me came from my mother. I have always believed in God. I learned from my mother Johnnie Mae at an early age that that is where it all starts and ends. At some point it occurred to me that I had to move on. It is like what Rita said to me in the hospital, and something that I believe as a product of my faith: Rafael is with me. He will always be with me. Rafael's death was the great tragedy of my life, but it has also had the effect of putting things in perspective. Of making me appreciate what I have. I have always felt blessed but now I see how brief life really is.

I celebrated my fiftieth birthday in the same month as the star ceremony. I had a wonderful birthday party at Georges in Los Angeles. I was once again surrounded by friends and loved ones, and although I was still very uncomfortable physically it was a wonderful day. I had originally planned to have a big theme party based upon the fifties with bobby socks and jump skirts. But it was too close to Rafael's death, and I opted instead for a quieter gathering.

Los Angeles had been hit hard by an earthquake just two weeks before the accident, one of the worst ever. The aftershocks would have me jumping up in the middle of the night in a cold sweat; I decided it was time for a big change in my life. I needed to make a change, because it was too painful passing by Beverly Hills High School, where the boys had gone to school. I could still see Rafael in his football uniform looking for me in the bleachers. He loved it when I was off the road and could make his games. This was another factor in my decision to move.

I had always loved London, England, and for a while I considered relocating there. But then New York City had always had an allure for me. I was alone again, my son Pedro was still living with his father, and I felt it was best to stay in the United States. By the fall of 1995, I moved to New York City. I found a beautiful apartment on the Upper West Side. From the windows of my apartment I can see Lincoln Center, where Diane, Florence, and I had one of our biggest triumphs in 1965; the famous Eula painting was commissioned for this gig. Moving to Manhattan was the best move I have ever made in my life. It's a wonderful city, the most interesting in the world, and it has been a new home for me and my career. I have become a member of the community. On a local level I am on the Board of the Figure Skaters of Harlem. I have lectured at the Harlem Public Library. I've received a beautiful award from the Harlem Chamber of Commerce. I am more comfortable in New York than in Los Angeles. New York has more history, and a longer memory for achievements like mine. It seems as if in Los Angeles you are judged by what you have done in the last five minutes. A young actor who has made three appearances in a sitcom is given more respect than an entertainer who has been in the business for thirty years. In New York people remember the big picture. In Los Angeles they don't seem to be able to remember past yesterday.

Though I have not secured and received a major record deal in twenty years, I have recorded throughout the '90s. I recorded my LP titled "Walk the Line" with one single of that same title. It is a funky R & B song. I enjoyed the fact that I was stretching out musically in the studio. Another song on the record was a Jennifer Holiday song from *Dreamgirls* called "I'm Changing." This song reminded me so much of Flo. After seeing *Dreamgirls* and hearing Jennifer sing it, I had to record it. Another song on the same record is the classic "Oooh Child," which I also identified with. It is a beautiful and comforting song about getting through a rough time, something I could relate to. I originally recorded this song in the 1980s for a British record company.

Of all the modern pop composers one of my favorites is Diane Warren, so it was wonderful to have the chance to record her song, "Under the Moon." Diane writes beautiful material that has been recorded by everyone from Cher to LeAnn Rimes, and she is one of the hottest songwriters in the music industry. The minute I heard this song, I longed to record it. Unfortunately, the record company went bankrupt. Later in 1995 I recorded with Mark Skeet and Mark Smilow. This ended up being a good deal for me. Mark Skeet really pushed to record and get the music played, but radio did not play it. B.E.T. (Black Entertainment Television) did play my video for a long while. Mark Smilow's parents had put up the money to finance these two young men, and it's a shame that their company couldn't make it. They took me over to Amsterdam, Holland, and recorded me with their friend, Ray Slinjguarrd of "Two Unlimited" fame, at Ray Vano-Ray MarRecords. There I recorded and released the song "Turn Around."

## Turkessa's Wedding in 1996

I got a call from Turkessa with wonderful news. She and Anthony had decided to get married. They have had a storybook romance. She has known him since she was thirteen. I love him. He is everything a mother wants for her daughter: kind, loving, and protective. I worried about how the wedding would be planned, who I was going to get to cater it, where it would be, how many people I would invite. Of course that is typical of me. As I worried, it hadn't occurred to me that Turkessa is my daughter and an Aries who likes to do things her own way. She was on top of all the planning already, and she knew what she wanted. Isn't that the way children are? One day you are worrying about how they are going to get on in the world, and the next day it seems they don't need any help from you at all! Except when the bills start coming in. Her father and I footed all the bills. (Yes, he and I are getting along these days. I am happy to report that we have both grown up a lot.)

The wedding was held at St. Anthony's Croatian Catholic Church, a small and beautiful church where Anthony's family attends mass, and the reception was held in the Beverly Hills Hilton. It was a special day for a lot of reasons. It was one of the last times I was with my mother before she passed. Johnnie Mae was especially beautiful to me that day because she was so excited about one of her grandchildren getting married. As the mother of our family she took great pride in events like this one.

Turkessa and Anthony danced to Marvin Gaye's beautiful recording, "Sexual Healing." Later Turkessa took a turn on the floor with her dad, who used to think he was a great dancer. Turkessa held on for dear life as Pedro, Sr. whirled her around the dance space. Among the people watching was John Mackey, the former pro football great, there with his beautiful wife Sylvia. (John came in for a lot of teasing that day when we noticed he was wearing blue contacts!) My good friend Freda Payne sang for Turkessa and Anthony, and Anna Marie Horsford and Dr. Herbert Avery and his wife were there too. It was a beautiful wedding and it even made *Ebony* magazine.

I was in a play in Sweden when my mother Johnnie Mae passed, so I am glad that I had the time to spend with her at Turkessa's wedding. At the time I made the decision not to return to the states. I made my decision based upon a couple of considerations that were important to me. One was the fact that I knew my mom was at peace. She struggled in the last few years of her life. Her illness was a terrible, life-robbing affliction. As it progressed it was difficult for her, and it was difficult for her family to see. When she passed, I felt it was because she had decided that it was time to go. Losing my mother was a tragedy, but it was comforting to know that her suffering was in the past, and that she had gone home, which is the way it felt to me. I grieved, and I celebrated her life, but I did so in private, by myself.

## Turkessa's Baby

Of all the life affirming blessings of the past decade, none come close to matching the birth of my daughter Turkessa's baby, Mia Marie Ferrer-Babich. Doesn't time fly? It seems like only yesterday that Turkessa was a toddler, joining me on stage to sing. Now she is the mother of a lovely girl. Mia came into the world on September 7, 1998. I was in New York when Turkessa first called me with the news that she was expecting. It was a hectic time. I was taking courses at N.Y.U., doing a morning radio show, and I was back and forth between Las Vegas and Manhattan during the time before and after the birth.

*Turkessa remembers the time very well, of course. "In the days leading up to the birth Mom was there to make sure Anthony and I got our rest. She sent me out for a manicure and a massage so that I felt relaxed and prepared for the big event, and she made sure the house was clean and that the cooking was taken care of. She was wonderful. Dr. Rebecca Tyre delivered Mia. My mother was with me during the birth. She helped me relax, and took care of me. She sang to Mia Marie even before she was born. Mom is a big Doris Day fan, and the song I remember her singing to my baby is 'Que Sera, Sera.' She even made up her own lyrics, wondering if Mia would be a lawyer or a doctor.*

*"She was also recording the event, and later Mom, Dad, Anthony and I sat and watched the video. Mom and Dad were crying while they watched it. At one point we all had to laugh*

*as we watched because Mom made more noise than I did! Mom
also stayed with me after the birth of my daughter, and she
took such good care of me, pampering me, making sure the
household was taken care of and looking after the baby when I
needed to rest. I remember that she got up at 3:00 a.m. the
morning after the birth to do her radio show, and that she
talked about the birth on that program. She must have been
exhausted!"*

Mia Marie was my first grandchild. In early 2000 our
family will be blessed with Turkessa's second child. She says
she thinks it will be a boy, and mothers usually know about
these things. If it is a boy, the name has been chosen: Marc
Anthony Raphael. Whether the baby is a boy or girl is something only time will tell, but I can't wait!

## Rock & Roll Hall of Fame

I was excited when I heard that the Rock & Roll Hall Of
Fame Museum was scheduled to open in the fall of 1995, and
that they were actively looking for rock & roll memorabilia. I
thought that some of the items I had collected and saved from
the Supremes' history, especially the Supremes' gowns, would
be to their liking. So I called and offered them a set. At first
they seemed reluctant to take them. But now through my persistence a set of Supremes' gowns can be seen there. I see the
exhibit as a tribute to the entire Motown family.

Unfortunately, not all of the members of the Motown family have fared as well as others. In the 1990s we lost six of the
most important figures: Mary Wells, Eddie Kendricks, David
Ruffin, Melvin Franklin, Lawrence Payton, and Junior Walker.
I'll miss all these friends, especially Mary Wells. Mary and I
go way back together. She always supported me in the early
years, and in the later years I had a chance to pay her back in
a small way. Mary took ill with cancer. She had a difficult time

34

with the illness and the costs. When I heard that she was ill it occurred to me that my friends at *Entertainment Tonight* might be able to help her, and they came through in a major way. With my help they did a feature outlining Mary's problems and asking people to contribute to a fund that would help pay for her medical bills. As they so often do in crises, people responded. After the *Entertainment Tonight* piece aired, Bruce Springsteen, Berry Gordy, Diane Ross, and others made substantial contributions to Mary's health care. Since I loved and admired Mary it shook me that a woman who was once the queen of Motown, who in fact put Motown on the map, died nearly destitute. To this day she has not been inducted into the Rock & Roll Hall of Fame, an oversight I hope will one day be corrected. It also makes me appreciate how blessed I have been.

*As I write this the year 2000 is just around the corner. So many good things have happened to me in the 1990s that I find it impossible not to look forward to the new century with a renewed sense of optimism and hope. I have a strong and loyal fan base that never hesitates to show me love and support through the tribulations as well as the triumphs. I have a business enterprise that is thriving. I have loving friends and family around me. And I have my spiritual faith, which has sustained me since the beginning. With all I have going on in my life it is just impossible not to feel that the new century can only bring good things.*

*Many of my fans ask me about the possibility of a Supremes reunion in the future, a time when they might see Diane, Cindy, and me back together, singing the songs we are loved for. To them I say, "I never say never." Since the Supremes split up many earth-changing events have unfolded. The Berlin Wall has tumbled. Apartheid in South Africa has died. Nelson Mandela, a black man, became president. In our own country the battles for civil rights, as well as rights for gays, women, and the disabled, have continued. The world con-*

*tinues to move and change at a quickening pace. A reunion of Diane, Cindy, and me should not be so difficult. It would be foolish and shortsighted of me to say the world will never see a reunion, just as it was shortsighted of all of us years ago not to see that the music we loved would last for so long.*

*If my experiences of the last ten years have taught me anything, it is this: no one knows the future. Another thing I have learned is that there are no limits to what the human heart can endure, no limit to the human heart's capacity to heal, to grow, to love. So to those fans that wonder, I say simply: I wonder too. I don't know what the future holds. I do know that the door is open, but that life moves on. With my children, my schooling, my business, and my careers in the recording arts and acting, I don't have time to sit and think about what might be. My time is devoted to those things which are at hand, and which need my attention. What lies in the future only God knows. I do believe that dreams do come true!*

Touch,
Mary Wilson
New York City, 1999

# MARY WILSON 1990S
# DISCOGRAPHY

## *Mary Wilson Solo Recordings:*

Album: *Walk the Line* (CEO Records / 1992)

—"Walk the Line"
—"The Stare"
—"Keep Me Hanging On"
—"One Night with You"
—"All Over Now"
—"Ooh Child"
—"Under Any Moon"
—"Shelter Me"
—"Bodyguard"
—"I'm Changing"

Singles:

—"One Night with You" (CEO Records / 1991)
—"Walk the Line" (CEO Records / 1992)

—"U" (Contract Records / 1996)
—"Turn Around" (Raymar Records / 1996)

Solo Performance on Compilation Album: *Motown Year-By-Year 1980* (Motown Records / 1995)

—"Pick Up the Pieces"

## *Supremes Albums featuring Mary Wilson:*

*The Supremes ('70s) Greatest Hits and Rare Classics* (Motown Records/ 1991)

Songs with Mary Wilson lead vocals:
    —"Floy Joy"
    —"Automatically Sunshine"
    —"He's My Man"
    —"You Turn Me Around"

*Motown Meets The Beatles* (Motown Records / 1995)

Mary, Diane, & Flo:
    —"A Hard Day's Night"
    —"You Can't Do That"

Mary, Cindy, & Jean:
    —"Come Together"

*The Supremes Anthology* (Motown Records / 1995)
[Two disk, 52-cut greatest hits collection 1961–1977, featuring several rare cuts]

—"Buttered Popcorn" led by Florence Ballard
—"Times Are Changing" produced by Phil Spector
—"Paradise" produced by Jimmy Webb

*The Supremes / The Ultimate Collection* (Motown Records / 1997)
[One disk, 25-cut greatest hits collection 1963–1969]

*The Ultimate Rarities Collection #1: Motown Sings Motown Treasures* (Motown Records / 1998)
[Includes two Supremes songs originally recorded for the *Supremes-A-Go-Go* album]

—"In My Lonely Room" (never-before-released)
—"Can I Get a Witness" (never-before-released)

*Motown Salutes Frank Sinatra* (Motown Records / 1998)

—"The Lady Is a Tramp"
—"Strangers in the Night" (never-before-released)